Lecture Notes in Artificial Intelligence 5032

Edited by R. Goebel, J. Siekmann, and W. Wahlster

Subseries of Lecture Notes in Computer Science

D1390974

Lecture Notes in Artificial Intelligence (LNAI)

Vol. 4790: N. Dershowitz, A. Voronkov (Eds.), Logic for Programming, Artificial Intelligence, and Reasoning. XIII, 562 pages. 2007.

Vol. 4788: D. Borrajo, L. Castillo, J.M. Corchado (Eds.), Current Topics in Artificial Intelligence. XI, 280 pages. 2007.

Vol. 4775: A. Esposito, M. Faundez-Zanuy, E. Keller, M. Marinaro (Eds.), Verbal and Nonverbal Communication Behaviours. XII, 325 pages. 2007.

Vol. 4772: H. Prade, V.S. Subrahmanian (Eds.), Scalable Uncertainty Management. X, 277 pages. 2007.

Vol. 4766: N. Maudet, S. Parsons, I. Rahwan (Eds.), Argumentation in Multi-Agent Systems. XII, 211 pages. 2007.

Vol. 4760: E. Rome, J. Hertzberg, G. Dorffner (Eds.), Towards Affordance-Based Robot Control. IX, 211 pages. 2008.

Vol. 4755: V. Corruble, M. Takeda, E. Suzuki (Eds.), Discovery Science. XI, 298 pages. 2007.

Vol. 4754: M. Hutter, R.A. Servedio, E. Takimoto (Eds.), Algorithmic Learning Theory. XI, 403 pages. 2007.

Vol. 4737: B. Berendt, A. Hotho, D. Mladenic, G. Semeraro (Eds.), From Web to Social Web: Discovering and Deploying User and Content Profiles. XI, 161 pages. 2007.

Vol. 4733: R. Basili, M.T. Pazienza (Eds.), AI*IA 2007: Artificial Intelligence and Human-Oriented Computing. XVII, 858 pages. 2007.

Vol. 4724: K. Mellouli (Ed.), Symbolic and Quantitative Approaches to Reasoning with Uncertainty. XV, 914 pages. 2007.

Vol. 4722: C. Pelachaud, J.-C. Martin, E. André, G. Chollet, K. Karpouzis, D. Pelé (Eds.), Intelligent Virtual Agents. XV, 425 pages. 2007.

Vol. 4720: B. Konev, F. Wolter (Eds.), Frontiers of Combining Systems. X, 283 pages. 2007.

Vol. 4702: J.N. Kok, J. Koronacki, R. Lopez de Mantaras, S. Matwin, D. Mladenič, A. Skowron (Eds.), Knowledge Discovery in Databases: PKDD 2007. XXIV, 640 pages. 2007.

Vol. 4701: J.N. Kok, J. Koronacki, R. Lopez de Mantaras, S. Matwin, D. Mladenič, A. Skowron (Eds.), Machine Learning: ECML 2007. XXII, 809 pages. 2007.

Vol. 4696: H.-D. Burkhard, G. Lindemann, R. Verbrugge, L.Z. Varga (Eds.), Multi-Agent Systems and Applications V. XIII, 350 pages. 2007.

Vol. 4694: B. Apolloni, R.J. Howlett, L. Jain (Eds.), Knowledge-Based Intelligent Information and Engineering Systems, Part III. XXIX, 1126 pages. 2007.

Vol. 4693: B. Apolloni, R.J. Howlett, L. Jain (Eds.), Knowledge-Based Intelligent Information and Engineering Systems, Part II. XXXII, 1380 pages. 2007.

Vol. 4692: B. Apolloni, R.J. Howlett, L. Jain (Eds.), Knowledge-Based Intelligent Information and Engineering Systems, Part I. LV, 882 pages. 2007.

Vol. 4687: P. Petta, J.P. Müller, M. Klusch, M. Georgeff (Eds.), Multiagent System Technologies. X, 207 pages. 2007.

Vol. 4682: D.-S. Huang, L. Heutte, M. Loog (Eds.), Advanced Intelligent Computing Theories and Applications. XXVII, 1373 pages. 2007.

Vol. 4676: M. Klusch, K.V. Hindriks, M.P. Papazoglou, L. Sterling (Eds.), Cooperative Information Agents XI. XI, 361 pages. 2007.

Vol. 4667: J. Hertzberg, M. Beetz, R. Englert (Eds.), KI 2007: Advances in Artificial Intelligence. IX, 516 pages. 2007.

Vol. 4660: S. Džeroski, L. Todorovski (Eds.), Computational Discovery of Scientific Knowledge. X, 327 pages. 2007.

Vol. 4659: V. Mařík, V. Vyatkin, A.W. Colombo (Eds.), Holonic and Multi-Agent Systems for Manufacturing. VIII, 456 pages. 2007.

Vol. 4651: F. Azevedo, P. Barahona, F. Fages, F. Rossi (Eds.), Recent Advances in Constraints. VIII, 185 pages. 2007.

Vol. 4648: F. Almeida e Costa, L.M. Rocha, E. Costa, I. Harvey, A. Coutinho (Eds.), Advances in Artificial Life. XVIII, 1215 pages. 2007.

Vol. 4635: B. Kokinov, D.C. Richardson, T.R. Roth-Berghofer, L. Vieu (Eds.), Modeling and Using Context. XIV, 574 pages. 2007.

Vol. 4632: R. Alhajj, H. Gao, X. Li, J. Li, O.R. Zaïane (Eds.), Advanced Data Mining and Applications. XV, 634 pages. 2007.

Vol. 4629: V. Matoušek, P. Mautner (Eds.), Text, Speech and Dialogue. XVII, 663 pages. 2007.

Vol. 4626: R.O. Weber, M.M. Richter (Eds.), Case-Based Reasoning Research and Development. XIII, 534 pages. 2007.

Vol. 4617: V. Torra, Y. Narukawa, Y. Yoshida (Eds.), Modeling Decisions for Artificial Intelligence. XII, 502 pages. 2007.

Vol. 4612: I. Miguel, W. Ruml (Eds.), Abstraction, Reformulation, and Approximation. XI, 418 pages. 2007.

Vol. 4604: U. Priss, S. Polovina, R. Hill (Eds.), Conceptual Structures: Knowledge Architectures for Smart Applications. XII, 514 pages. 2007.

Vol. 4603: F. Pfenning (Ed.), Automated Deduction – CADE-21. XII, 522 pages. 2007.

Vol. 4597: P. Perner (Ed.), Advances in Data Mining. XI, 353 pages. 2007.

Vol. 4594: R. Bellazzi, A. Abu-Hanna, J. Hunter (Eds.), Artificial Intelligence in Medicine. XVI, 509 pages. 2007.

Vol. 4585: M. Kryszkiewicz, J.F. Peters, H. Rybinski, A. Skowron (Eds.), Rough Sets and Intelligent Systems Paradigms. XIX, 836 pages. 2007.

Vol. 4578: F. Masulli, S. Mitra, G. Pasi (Eds.), Applications of Fuzzy Sets Theory. XVIII, 693 pages. 2007.

Vol. 4573: M. Kauers, M. Kerber, R. Miner, W. Windsteiger (Eds.), Towards Mechanized Mathematical Assistants. XIII, 407 pages. 2007.

Vol. 4571: P. Perner (Ed.), Machine Learning and Data Mining in Pattern Recognition. XIV, 913 pages. 2007.

Sabine Bergler (Ed.)

Advances in Artificial Intelligence

21st Conference of the Canadian Society
for Computational Studies of Intelligence, Canadian AI 2008
Windsor, Canada, May 28-30, 2008
Proceedings

Q
334
.C36
2008

 Springer

Series Editors

Randy Goebel, University of Alberta, Edmonton, Canada
Jörg Siekmann, University of Saarland, Saarbrücken, Germany
Wolfgang Wahlster, DFKI and University of Saarland, Saarbrücken, Germany

Volume Editor

Sabine Bergler
Concordia University
Department of Computer Science and Software Engineering
1455 de Maisonneuve Blvd. West, Montréal, Québec H3G 1M8, Canada
E-mail: bergler@cs.concordia.ca

Library of Congress Control Number: 2008927367

CR Subject Classification (1998): I.2

LNCS Sublibrary: SL 7 – Artificial Intelligence

ISSN   0302-9743
ISBN-10   3-540-68821-8 Springer Berlin Heidelberg New York
ISBN-13   978-3-540-68821-1 Springer Berlin Heidelberg New York

This work is subject to copyright. All rights are reserved, whether the whole or part of the material is
concerned, specifically the rights of translation, reprinting, re-use of illustrations, recitation, broadcasting,
reproduction on microfilms or in any other way, and storage in data banks. Duplication of this publication
or parts thereof is permitted only under the provisions of the German Copyright Law of September 9, 1965,
in its current version, and permission for use must always be obtained from Springer. Violations are liable
to prosecution under the German Copyright Law.

Springer is a part of Springer Science+Business Media

springer.com

© Springer-Verlag Berlin Heidelberg 2008
Printed in Germany

Typesetting: Camera-ready by author, data conversion by Scientific Publishing Services, Chennai, India
Printed on acid-free paper   SPIN: 12277247   06/3180   5 4 3 2 1 0

Preface

This volume contains the papers presented at AI 2008, the 21st conference of the Canadian Society for the Computational Study of Intelligence (CSCSI). AI 2008 attracted 75 paper submissions. Each paper was assigned to four reviewers. One goal for AI 2008 was to reflect a wide range of different research, thus in addition to regular papers, these proceedings also include short papers of research that is still in its early stages. The Program Committee selected 30 regular papers and 5 short papers for publication.

AI 2008 was a collaboration of many people. Most importantly, my thanks go to the members of the Program Committee and the additional reviewers, who provided high-quality reviews, making the task of selecting from a wide variety of papers possible. I also benefited greatly from the patient advice from the previous Program Chairs and current Local Arrangements Chairs Dan Wu and Ziad Kobti, as well as the General Conference Chair, Howard Hamilton. The EasyChair conference management system by Andrei Voronkov once again lived up to its name. Final thanks go to the CSCSI Executive Committee, and especially Danny Silver, for their support and for making AI 2008 a successful conference.

May 2008 Sabine Bergler

Organization

AI 2008 was organized by the Canadian Society for the Computational Study of Intelligence (CSCSI).

Executive Committee

General Chair	Howard Hamilton, University of Regina
Program Chair	Sabine Bergler, Concordia University
Graduate Symposium Chair	Scott Buffett, NRC
Local Arrangements Chairs	Ziad Kobti and Dan Wu, University of Windsor

Program Committee

Esma Aimeur	Grigoris Karakoulas
Massih Amini	Kamran Karimi
Caroline Barrière	Vlado Keselj
Scott Buffett	Iluju Kiringa
Cory Butz	Ziad Kobti
Laurence Capus	Yves Kodratoff
Nick Cercone	Grzegorz Kondrak
Brahim Chaib-draa	Leila Kosseim
Yllias Chali	Adam Krzyzak
Maiga Chang	Philippe Langlais
David Chiu	Guy Lapalme
Robin Cohen	Kate Larson
Lyne Da Sylva	François Laviolette
Mariana Damova	Bernard Lefebvre
Douglas Dankel	Oscar Lin
Jon Dron	Alejandro Lopez-Ortiz
Larbi Esmahi	Joel Martin
Michael Fleming	Stan Matwin
Richard Frost	Gord McCalla
Dragan Gasevic	Jean-Marc Mercantini
Ali Ghorbani	Robert Mercer
Scott Goodwin	Guy Mineau
Volker Haarslev	David Nadeau
Robert Hilderman	Eric Neufeld
Graeme Hirst	Jian-Yun Nie
Diana Inkpen	Roger Nkambou
Nathalie Japkowicz	Gerald Penn

Fred Popowich
Doina Precup
Robert Reynolds
Luis Rueda
Anoop Sarkar
Weiming Shen
Daniel L. Silver
Michel Simard
Bruce Spencer
Eleni Stroulia
Stan Szpakowicz
Ahmed Tawfik
Choh Man Teng
Nicole Tourigny
Thomas Tran

André Trudel
Marcel Turcotte
Peter van Beek
Herna Viktor
Harris Wan
Shaojun Wang
Dunwei Wen
René Witte
Dan Wu
Yang Xiang
Yiyu Yao
Jia-Huai You
Xiaokun Zhang
Harry Zhang
Nur Zincir-Heywood

Reviewers

Ahmed Alasoud
Xiangdong An
Sebastien Gambs
Baohua Gu
Franklin Hanshar
Dan He
Malcolm Heywood
Jiye Li
Mario Marchand
Maxime Morneau
Robert Price
Maxim Roy
Ahmed Sayed
Javier Thaine
Bin Wang

Sponsoring Institutions

The Canadian Society for the Computational Study of Intelligence (CSCSI)

Table of Contents

Local Decision Bagging of Binary Neural Classifiers[*]

Rocío Alaiz-Rodríguez

Dpto. de Ingeniería Eléctrica y de Sistemas y Automática,
Universidad de León, 24071 León, Spain
rocio.alaiz@unileon.es

Abstract. Bagging as well as other classifier ensembles have made possible a performance improvement in many pattern recognition problems for the last decade. A careful analysis of previous work points out, however, that the most significant advance of bagged neural networks is achieved for multiclass problems, whereas the binary classification problems seldom benefit from the classifier combination. Focusing on the binary classification applications, this paper evaluates the standard bagging approach and explores a novel variant, local bagging, that, while keeping the standard individual classifier generation, attempts to improve its decision combination stage by (a) dynamically selecting of a set of individual classifiers and (b) subsequently weighting them by their local accuracy. Experimental results carried out on standard benchmark data sets with Neural Networks, SVMs, Naive Bayes, C4.5 Decision Trees and Decision Stumps as the base classifier, show that local bagging yields significant improvements in these practical applications and is found more stable than Adaboost.

1 Introduction

Many classifier ensembles that successfully improve the predictive accuracy of a single classifier have been developed in the last decade. Bagging and boosting appear as the two most popular ensembles whose effectiveness has already been tested in many experimental studies with decision trees [14,2,5,9] and in fewer works (in comparison) with neural networks [14,7] as well as SVMs [10].

When developing a committee of classifiers two general key steps are faced: (a) generating the individual classifiers and (b) computing the hard final decision from the individual outputs. For this latter step, numerous classifier combination as well as classifier selection techniques have been widely investigated in the literature:they vary from a simple majority vote to specific decision machines that fuse individual classifier outputs. For a comprehensive survey on classifier combination see [12] and references therein.

Surprisingly, however, the bagging approach assessed in many exhaustive comparative works [14,2,5] still employs a simple uniform weight among its members as it was initially proposed. In spite of this simple vote, these studies with

---

[*] This work has been partially supported by the Spanish MEC project DPI2006-02550.

© Springer-Verlag Berlin Heidelberg 2008

decision trees or neural networks as the base learning algorithm find bagging competitive to boosting. Bagging, however, is regarded [14] as a general technique appropriate for most problems since (i) its performance is either similar or significantly better than a single classifier (but it does not hurt performance as boosting may do) and (ii) it allows a parallelized development of its members, while boosting is a necessarily sequential approach. Nonetheless, statics suggest that much more research has been carried out around the boosting approach.

Although not independent assessment has been conducted for binary and multiclass problems, a detailed analysis of the empirical results in [15] reveals that the most significant gains in performance for the bagging approach with neural networks are achieved for data sets with more than two classes. Taking into account that a high percentage of machine learning applications are stated as binary classification problems and neural networks appear as one of the most popular learning algorithms, our aim in this paper is to assess bagged neural networks in the context of two class problems.

We also address the question whether it is possible to improve bagging performance by means of variations in the member decision fusion stage. Up to our knowledge, not much work has been done in order to explore bagging variants except for a couple of proposals in [2] (p-Bagging and Wagging that, when tested together with decision trees, lead only to marginal or no improvements, respectively). We hypothesize here that a more elaborate decision fusion technique that takes into account the performance of individual members in the ensemble could yield an accuracy increase. Specifically, a variant that takes into account local accuracy for small regions of the feature space is explored and evaluated in this work. Local decision bagging (*local bagging*, hereafter) is a dynamically weighted ensemble where its members are generated as in the standard bagging approach but lately, dynamically selected and combined in a way determined by the unseen test sample. It differs from the local learning approach in [11], where decision stumps in the ensemble are induced, for every single test example, from a subset (defined in terms of the example local region) of the whole training set.

The remaining of this paper is organized as follows. In Section 2, the bagging fundamentals are revised and *local bagging* described. Experimental results are presented in Section 3 and finally, Section 4 summarizes the main conclusions.

2   Bagged Classifiers

Consider a supervised classification problem with L classes. Let $S = \{(\mathbf{x}^k, \mathbf{d}^k), k = 1, \ldots, K\}$ denote a labeled data set where $\mathbf{x}^k \in \Re^N$ is an observation feature vector, $\mathbf{d}^k$ is the class label with components $d_i^k \in \{0, 1\}$ that satisfy $\sum_{i=0}^{L-1} d_i^k = 1$.

Without loss of generality we consider a learning process with two steps: first it computes a soft decision and then, makes the hard final decision. We assume a learning process that estimates parameters $\mathbf{w}$ of a non-linear mapping $\mathbf{f_w} : \Re^N \rightarrow \mathcal{P}$ from the input space into probability space $\mathcal{P} = \{p \in [0, 1] | \sum_{i=0}^{L-1} p_i = 1\}$.

Consider, now, an ensemble with M individual classifiers where $\mathbf{f}^{(m)}(\mathbf{x})$ denotes the m-th member of the ensemble. Thus, the *soft* decision of the m-th classifier is given by $\mathbf{y}^{(m)} = (y_0^{(m)}, \ldots, y_{L-1}^{(m)}) = \mathbf{f}^{(m)}(\mathbf{x}) \in \mathcal{P}$ and the hard output is denoted by $\widehat{\mathbf{d}}^{(m)}$. Note that $\mathbf{d}$ and $\widehat{\mathbf{d}}^{(m)}$ will be used to distinguish the actual class from the predicted by the m-th classifier, respectively.

2.1   Standard Bagged Classifiers

Bagging (Bootstrap aggregation), proposed by Breiman [4] and based on bootstrap sampling, consists on learning a group of classifiers from bootstrap replicates of the original training data set (examples drawn randomly with replacement). Let matrix

$$\widehat{\mathbf{D}} = \begin{pmatrix} \widehat{d}_0^{(1)} & \ldots & \widehat{d}_0^{(M)} \\ \ldots & \ldots & \ldots \\ \widehat{d}_{L-1}^{(1)} & \ldots & \widehat{d}_{L-1}^{(M)} \end{pmatrix} \tag{1}$$

denote the hard outputs given by the M trained classifiers for observation vector $\mathbf{x}$ where the m-th column corresponds to column vector $\widehat{\mathbf{d}}^{(m)}$.

The standard bagging approach makes the final decision after computing

$$\widehat{\mathbf{y}}^{\text{BAGGED}} = \widehat{\mathbf{D}}\alpha^T \tag{2}$$

where $\alpha = (\alpha_1, \ldots, \alpha_M)$ is the ensemble weight vector (in this case, $\alpha_i = 1$, what is interpreted as a simple vote from the individual members). Hard output $\widehat{\mathbf{d}}^{\text{BAGGED}}$ from the bagging ensemble is taken in a *winner-takes-all* way from the soft output $\widehat{\mathbf{y}}^{\text{BAGGED}}$ whose components contain the number of votes for each class.

$$\widehat{d}_i^{\text{BAGGED}} = \begin{cases} 1 \text{ if } i = \arg\max_j \widehat{y}_j^{\text{BAGGED}} \\ 0 \text{ Otherwise.} \end{cases} \tag{3}$$

Note that the weight vector α does not depend on the data example $\mathbf{x}$ to be classified and is uniform across the ensemble members. Thus, all the members in the ensemble are considered to make the final decision and all of them have the same weight in that final hard decision. Next, we discuss issues related to ensemble member selection and member weight assignment.

2.2   Local Bagging Approach

In the most popular ensemble approaches, the final decision is either computed as a uniform or as a weighted vote but, in general, no individual classifiers are discarded in the ensemble. However, Hansen and Salamon [8] show that a necessary and sufficient condition for an ensemble to be more accurate than its members is the fact that the classifiers are accurate and diverse. That is, performance better than random guessing and uncorrelated errors. Bootstrap samples in the Bagging approach aim at guaranteeing diversity (as long as the algorithm is an unstable learner such as neural networks or decision trees). However, the majority vote fusion method does not consider the classifier accuracy. In spite of this, and probably because individual members are usually accurate enough in a global sense,improvements over a single classifier is frequently achieved.

The basic idea of *local bagging* stems from the fact that individual members in an ensemble as well as experts in a committee may show different accuracy in different regions of the input space. We consider that their performance in a small region around a new data example to be classified may be relevant to make the final decision. In this sense, the *local bagging* approach dynamically discards those classifiers that are not accurate in that small region around the test example. In this work, a classifier is considered locally accurate when its error rate (in the region analyzed) is lower than 0.5. This matches with the weighting scheme explained next so that weights are higher or equal to zero. Note that classifiers do not have to be retrained for each test example.

A related discussion, although not motivated by local accuracy reasons, also arises in [19,20] where their experiments confirm that ensembling some of the members can be better than considering all. Selection is guided by genetic algorithm principles and it was initially shown effective for neural network ensembles [19] and later, generalized for decision trees base learners [20].

Unlike the standard bagging approach, the *local bagging* variant (based on local accuracy) (a) carries out a dynamic selection of classifiers and (b) dynamically weights each selected member as explained in the following section.

Local regions. When a new sample has to be categorized, individual classifier accuracy for similar feature vectors is taken into account in the *local bagging* approach. These local areas around a new example, denoted by $\phi_k(\mathbf{x})$, are defined by the k-Nearest Neighbors in the training set and similarity is measured as the Euclidean distance between feature vectors.

Accuracy in that region (local accuracy) is defined by how well the classifier performs on that neighborhood area and it is estimated as the fraction of training examples that are correctly classified. The issue of selecting the size of this neighborhood will be discussed later in this section.

Dynamical weight and selection. Given a new test sample $\mathbf{x}$, the local bagging approach assigns a normalized weight for the i-th member of the ensemble α_i given by

$$\alpha_i(\mathbf{x}) = \frac{\beta^{(j)}(\mathbf{x})}{\sum_{j=1}^{M} \beta^{(j)}(\mathbf{x})} \tag{4}$$

with

$$\beta^{(j)}(\mathbf{x}) = u(e^{(j)}_{\phi_k(\mathbf{x})} - 0.5) \log \frac{1 - e^{(j)}_{\phi_k(\mathbf{x})}}{e^{(j)}_{\phi_k(\mathbf{x})}} \tag{5}$$

where $\beta^{(j)}$ stands for the the unnormalized weight assigned to the j-th member as a function of its local accuracy, $e^{(j)}_{\phi_k(\mathbf{x})}$ is the error rate of j-th classifier in the neighboring region $\phi_k(\mathbf{x})$ and the Heaviside step function u (with output equal to one for positive arguments and zero, otherwise) dynamically selects those classifiers with local accuracy higher than 0.5. Note that $0 \leq \alpha_i \leq 1$ and $\sum_{i=1}^{M} \alpha_i = 1$.

Our approach follows a "local" orientation similar to the applied in [13] for the boosting ensemble , but in this case discarding classifiers generated by bootstrap samples that are not locally accurate and weighting their votes with weights $\alpha_i \propto \log \dfrac{1 - e^{(i)}_{\phi_k(\mathbf{x})}}{e^{(i)}_{\phi_k(\mathbf{x})}}$ so that combined decision reaches its maximum accuracy. A demonstration for this weighting expression, but for global accuracy based schemes, can be found in [12]. Moreover, the weighting scheme in (5) is also employed by the popular boosting approach, proposed by Schapire [16] and posteriorly improved in [6], where it is known to work satisfactorily.

The adaptive selection technique proposed in this work differs from previous approaches, such as the work in [19,20] and in [18]. In [19,20], ensemble selection is static since it does not depend on the new example and in [18], the feature space is divided into regions where only the most locally accurate classifier of the ensemble is responsible for classification and so, an individual classifier (but not an ensemble) is dynamically chosen as a function of the observation vector.

Local region size. For each particular problem, the local region size (defined by k) has to be fine-tuned. We propose an exploratory method that chooses among a predefined set of sizes the one that assures the maximum accuracy. The lack of data is a general rule for most problems and here no validate set is required in order to select the k value but it is only based on the available training examples. Nonetheless, as we will see, estimation is not likely to be overfitted to training data.

Given a predefined set of region sizes $k_1, \ldots, k_r$ where $k_i \leq N_{train}$ represents the cardinality of the nearest neighbor set that defines the $\phi_{k_i}(\mathbf{x})$ local region and N_{train} is the size of the training data set, the exploratory procedure selects k_i satisfying

$$E^{\text{BAGGED}}_{\phi_{k_i}} = \min_j E^{\text{BAGGED}}_{\phi_{k_j}} \tag{6}$$

where $E^{\text{BAGGED}}_{\phi_{k_i}}$ stands for the error rate of *local bagging* when it makes a decision based on the accuracy in the local region defined by the k_i nearest neighbors.

$E^{\text{BAGGED}}_{\phi_{k_i}}$ is computed as the average error in the training set as follows. It is known that each individual classifier in the bagging approach is trained with what we call the *bag samples* and the remaining can be referred as the *out of bag samples*. When trying to estimate how well the local bagging approach works for a given training example $\mathbf{x}^i$, it makes no sense considering those individual classifiers that were trained with sample $\mathbf{x}^i$. Only those classifiers where samples $\mathbf{x}^i$ belong to the *out of bag samples* are taken into account. Since these samples have not been seen by the classifier, a good estimation of its generalization capability is expected (actually, a good performance estimation is not required but only a good ranking that allows to choose the optimal region size).

The local bagging learning algorithm (individual generation classifier as well as the dynamical selection and weighting strategy) is summarized as follows,

---

Input:
M: Number of individual classifiers in the ensemble
f: Learning algorithm
$K_r = \{k_1, \ldots, k_r\}$: Local region sizes

---

for $m = 1$ to M **do**
    Extract bootstrap sample S_m from available training set
    Build classifier $\mathbf{f}^{(m)}(\mathbf{x})$
end for
for $i = 1$ to r **do**
    Compute $\widehat{\mathbf{y}}^{\text{BAGGED}}$ for the training dataset according to (2), (4) and region ϕ_{k_i}. Members trained with a given example are discarded when computing the ensemble output for that example.
    Compute Error rate $E_{\phi_{k_i}}^{\text{BAGGED}}$ for the training dataset
end for
Select local region size $k = k_i$ with $i = \arg\min\limits_{i} E_{\phi_{k_i}}^{\text{BAGGED}}$

Output for each new example:
Compute $\widehat{\mathbf{y}}^{\text{BAGGED}}$ according to (2) and (4) where region is defined by ϕ_k
Compute $\widehat{\mathbf{d}}^{\text{BAGGED}}$ according to (3)

---

3   Experimental Results

In this section, *standard bagging*, *local bagging* and a single classifier are compared in terms of error rate. Moreover, another two variants to *standard bagging* are also assessed: *p-Bagging*(this approach, explored in [2] for decision trees, uniformly averages the soft outputs of individual classifiers and predicts the class with highest probability) and *global bagging* (this vote-based technique introduced in this work considers the weight scheme proposed in *local bagging* but with k equal to the size of the training data set, that is, it considers global accuracy).

Twelve binary classification problems were assessed in this work. Most of them come from the UCI repository [3] (Pima-Indians Diabetes, Sonar, Yeast, Phoneme, Breast-w, Wdbc, Credits-g [1], Heart-Statlog, Heart-Cleveland, Arrhythmia [2], and Spambase) and the Mailmark data set from the Department of Mathematics & Statistics at McMaster University [3].

3.1   Base Classifier: Neural Network

The ensemble approach presented in this work can be applied to any learning algorithm classifier architecture and here, we have chosen a neural network based on the softmax non-linearity with soft decisions given by $y_i = \sum_{j=1}^{M_i} y_{ij}$, with

---

[1] Dataset with continuous features produced by Strathclyde University.
[2] The original problem has been converted into a binary classification problem.
[3] This test collection is available at
   http://www.math.mcmaster.ca/peter/sora/case_studies_00

$$y_{ij} = \frac{\exp(\mathbf{w}_{ij}^T \mathbf{x} + w_{ij0})}{\sum_{k=0}^{L-1} \sum_{l=1}^{M_k} \exp(\mathbf{w}_{kl}^T \mathbf{x} + w_{kl0})}$$

where L stands for the number of classes, M_j the number of softmax outputs used to compute y_j and $\mathbf{w}_{ij}$ are weight vectors. We will refer to this network (see Fig. 1) as a *Generalized Softmax Perceptron*(GSP)[4][1]. A simple network with $M_j = 2$ and $L = 2$ is used in the experiments.

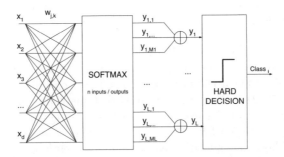

Fig. 1. Individual Classifier: GSP(Generalized Softmax Perceptron) Network

Learning consists of estimating network parameters $\mathbf{w}$ by means of the stochastic gradient minimization of certain objective functions. In the experiments, the *Cross Entropy* objective function given by $CE(\mathbf{y}, \mathbf{d}) = -\sum_{i=1}^{L} d_i \log y_i$ have been considered. Note that, the standard stochastic gradient learning rule for the GSP network is given by

$$\mathbf{w}_{ij}^{n+1} = \mathbf{w}_{ij}^n + \mu^{(r)} \frac{y_{ij}^n}{y_i^n}(d_i^n - y_i^n)\mathbf{x}^n \tag{7}$$

with learning step $\mu^{(r)}$ that decreases according to $\mu^{(r)} = \frac{\mu^{(0)}}{1+r/\eta}$ where r is the iteration number, $\mu^{(0)}$ the initial learning rate and η a decay factor.

This approach is illustrated with a feedforward network, a widely used and well known architecture. On the other hand, the fact that intermediate outputs y_{ij} of the GSP can be interpreted as subclass probabilities may provide quite a natural way to cope later with the unexplored approach of considering accuracy in a subclass (and unsupervised) level. Nonetheless, both architecture and cost function issues are not the goal of this paper, but merely illustrative tools.

Classifier performance is estimated by 10-fold cross validation. Preliminary results for both *local bagging* and bagging with different number of individual classifiers (from 20 to 100) show either no difference or a slight decrease in error rate. In order to conduct a general evaluation, and provided that computational resources are not a serious constraint, ensembles were built with 100 members.

---

[4] Note that the GSP is similar to a two layer MLP with a single layer of weights and with coupled saturation function (softmax), instead of sigmoidal units.

Influence of Local Region Sizes on Local Bagging Performance
The method proposed to tune the value of k (local region size) is assessed and illustrated here with the Sonar, Spam and Heart-s data sets. Table. 1 shows misclassification error rate of *local bagging* for $k = 3, 5, 10, 20, 30$. It can be noticed that the bagging performance depends on the local region size. Thus, for Sonar, error rate varies from 0.155 ($k = 3$) to 0.189 ($k = 30$). For Spam and Heart-s, variations around 12% have been found in the regions evaluated. Thus, the performance can be improved by optimal selecting the local region size. Obviously, no access to test data is available when developing the classifier.

Running the algorithm that estimates the optimal size based on training data leads to an error rate shown in the last column, where $\widehat{k}$ is the averaged (over the 10 folds) region size selected. Results evidence that the algorithm proposed reasonable succeeds in finding the optimal region size (For Sonar, it achieves 0.149 error rate against 0.141 if the test conditions had been known; for Spam 0.219 against the ideal 0.217). Note that, even when $\widehat{k}$ matches other value shown in the Table. 1, the error rates may not. Differences come from the fact that the same uniform k is chosen for every fold in the first case while the estimation approach may choose a slight different k value for each fold.

Table 1. Error rate for the local bagging approach for different region sizes: $k = 3$, $k = 5$, $k = 10$, $k = 20$ and $k = 30$ and the averaged estimated $\widehat{k}$ value

Data set	$k = 3$	$k = 5$	$k = 10$	$k = 20$	$k = 30$	$\widehat{k}$
Sonar	0.155	0.141	0.160	0.184	0.189	0.149 ($\widehat{k} = 3$)
Spam	0.218	0.217	0.228	0.240	0.246	0.219 ($\widehat{k} = 3$)
Heart-s	0.274	0.248	0.241	0.240	0.244	0.244 ($\widehat{k} = 20$)

Number of individual classifiers in the ensemble
Determining to what degree performance of an ensemble approach depends on the number of individual classifiers is an important issue. After assessing the error rate for both local bagging and bagging against a number of individual classifiers that vary between 20 and 100, two behaviors are observed: (i) classification problems where no dependence is observed on that interval (see Figure 2(a) as an illustration) and (ii) those problems where a slight decrease in error rate is achieved when a higher number of classifiers is considered (see Figure 2(b)). For these reasons, and provided that computational resources are not a serious constrain, an ensemble of 100 classifiers is built for the practical applications evaluated in this work.

Evaluation of Local Bagging
The single classifier together with three different bagging approaches are assessed in this section: *standard bagging, local bagging, p-bagging* and *global bagging* (*global* bagging with $k = N_{train}$ where N_{train} is the training set size).

Classifier comparison is carried out in terms of misclassification rate error rate. Table 2 shows a cross validated t-test with 95% confidence interval. Each

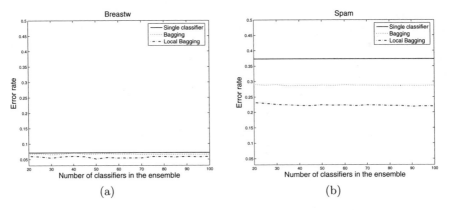

Fig. 2. Expected error rate vs. number of individual Neural Network classifiers in the ensemble for the standard bagging (dotted line) and local bagging (dashed-dotted line). The horizontal line shows the single classifier error rate.(a) Breastw and (b) Spam.

cell in the matrix indicates whether a significant difference is found between the strategy in the row and that in the column for the twelve data sets evaluated [5]. The bullet symbol "•" indicates the approach in the row is significantly better than the one in the column and the symbol "∘" denotes no significant differences. A detailed analysis of this test shows the following facts:

- **Bagging vs. p-bagging vs global bagging**
  An immediate conclusion drawn from the test is that *bagging, p-bagging* and *global bagging* performance is not significantly different in any of the evaluated problems. Thus, considering decision confidence by taking soft decisions (as *p-bagging* does) provides no increase in accuracy in neural bagged classifiers. This also generalizes previous results [2] with decision trees bagged ensembles. Secondly, it shows that the weighting scheme used in global bagging (same as in boosting) does not incorporate by itself any improvements over the simple vote approach in bagging.
- **Bagging vs. a single Neural Network**
  Opitz and Maclin [14] observe that the most significant improvements for the bagging ensemble seem to be achieved for multiclass data sets. Results in this work evidence that neural bagged ensembles for binary classification problems only outperforms the single classifier accuracy occasionally (just for 3 problems (spam, arrythmia and wdbc) out of the 12 datasets. It is worth to highlight that bagging never leads to a drop in performance with respect to a single classifier.
- **Local bagging vs. bagging and a single Neural Network**
  Local bagging, however, achieves an error rate lower than a single classifier in 8 of the evaluated problems (the same where *bagging* does besides another 5).

---

[5] Domains are given in the following order: Diabetes, Sonar, Yeast, Phoneme, Breastw, Wdbc, Credits-g, Heart-s, Heart-c, Arrhythmia, Mailmark and Spam.

Table 2. All pairwise comparisons among classifiers. A 10-fold cross validated t test with 95% confidence interval for the difference in the accuracy has been constructed. The symbol "•" indicates the approach in the row is significantly better than that of the column, the symbol "×" denotes it is significantly worse and the symbol "○" denotes no significant differences.

	Single	Bagging	p-Bagging	Global bagging
Local Bagging	• ○ • • • ○ ○ ○ • •	• ○ • ○ ○ ○ ○ ○ ○ •	• ○ • ○ ○ ○ ○ ○ • •	• ○ • ○ ○ ○ ○ ○ ○ •
Global bagging	○ ○ ○ ○ • ○ ○ ○ • ○ •	○ ○ ○ ○ ○ ○ ○ ○ ○ ○	○ ○ ○ ○ ○ ○ ○ ○ ○ •	
p-Bagging	○ ○ ○ ○ • ○ ○ ○ • ○ •	○ ○ ○ ○ ○ ○ ○ ○ ○ ○		
Bagging	○ ○ ○ ○ • ○ ○ ○ • ○ •			

The error rate reduction carried out by *local bagging* goes up to 41%(in Spam, for instance, the misclassification rate is reduced from 37.3% with the single classifier to 21.9% with *local bagging* while in Phoneme is reduced from 21.1% to 13.4%, whereas in these problems neither *standard bagging* nor other bagging approaches show improvements in these scenarios). On the other hand, it should be noticed that neither the single classifier nor the bagging approach are significant better than *local bagging* in any of the classification problems assessed in this work.

3.2 Local Bagging with Different Base Classifiers

In this section, the bagging ensembles and Adaboost are assessed for different base classifiers. We use WEKA [17] to implement Adaboost (with 100 iterations) and the baseline classifiers (options set as default). Weka is called from Matlab to build the classifier and the error reduction (with respect to the single classifier) is measured in % and reported in Table 3. *Local bagging* yields higher error rate reduction than other bagging variants for SVMs (9.1% against 0.8%), Decision Stumps (22.0% against 9.6%) and Naive Bayes (NB) (11% vs. 1.3%), whereas no significant differences are found for a C4.5 decision tree (22.8% against 21.0%). Besides, it is worth to note that conventional Bagging does not yield significant performance improvements with NB, SVM and NN baseline classifiers for binary problems. On the other hand, Adaboost shows a great variability: worsening the performance for a SVM base classifier or clearly outperforming local bagging with a Decision Stump.

Table 3. Misclassification Error rate for a single classifier and the reduction in % accomplished by different bagging ensembles

	Single Classifier Overall Error Rate	Overall Error reduction in %			
		Bagging	Global Bagging	Local Bagging	Adaboost
Neural Network	0.23	6.9%	7.5%	**17.6%**	6.9%
Decision Stumps	0.26	9.6%	8.8%	22.0%	**35.3%**
C4.5 Decision Tree	0.20	21.0%	21.0%	**22.8%**	14.3%
Naive Bayes	0.21	1.3%	1.4%	**11.0%**	8.6%
SVM	0.18	0.8%	0.6%	**9.1%**	-3.2%

4   Conclusions

In this work, bagging ensembles of neural networks are assessed in the context of binary pattern recognition problems. Moreover, it presents *local bagging*, a simple and novel variant that makes the final decision based on the local accuracy of a dynamically selected set of individual classifiers. Selection of the local region size is conducted straightforwardly by means of cross-validation.

Comprehensive empirical results with neural classifiers show no success of *standard bagging* in binary problems: it does not outperform the single classifier for most data sets, although it is not significantly worse than a single classifier as other ensembles like boosting may be. *Local bagging*, however, yields a performance improvement in terms of error rate both over a single classifier and the standard bagging.

Considering several base classifiers, we can summarize that, in general, *local bagging* improves the *standard bagging* ensemble and is found to be more stable than Adaboost.

Future research lines include assessing *local bagging* in general cost sensitive problems and in an scenario where deployment conditions are uncertain.

References

1. Alaiz-Rodríguez, R., Guerrero-Curieses, A., Cid-Sueiro, J.: Minimax classifiers based on neural networks. Pattern Recognition 38(1), 29–39 (2005)
2. Bauer, E., Kohavi, R.: An empirical comparison of voting classification algorithms: Bagging, boosting, and variants. Machine Learning 36(1-2), 105–139 (1999)
3. Blake, C.L., Merz, C.J.: UCI repository of machine learning databases (1998)
4. Breiman, L.: Bagging predictors. Machine Learning 24(2), 123–140 (1996)
5. Dietterich, T.G.: An experimental comparison of three methods for constructing ensembles of decision trees: Bagging, boosting, and randomization. Machine Learning 40(2), 139–157 (2000)
6. Freund, Y.: Boosting a weak learning algorithm by majority. Inf. Comput. 121(2), 256–285 (1995)
7. Ha, K., Cho, S., MacLachlan, D.: Response models based on bagging neural networks. Journal of Interactive Marketing 19(1), 17–30 (2005)
8. Hansen, L.K., Salamon, P.: Neural network ensembles. IEEE Trans. Pattern Anal. Mach. Intell. 12(10), 993–1001 (1990)
9. Hothorn, T., Lausen, B.: Bagging tree classifiers for laser scanning images: a data- and simulation-based strategy. Artificial Intelligence in Medicine 27(1), 65–79 (2003)
10. Kim, H.C., Pang, S., Je, H.M., Kim, D., Bang, S.Y.: Pattern classification using support vector machine ensemble. In: 16th International Conference on Pattern Recognition, p. 20160. IEEE Computer Society Press, Los Alamitos (2002)
11. Kotsiantis, S.B., Tsekouras, G.E., Pintelas, P.E.: Local bagging of decision stumps. In: Proceedings of the 18th international conference on Innovations in Applied Artificial Intelligence, pp. 406–411. Springer, London (2005)
12. Kuncheva, L.I.: Combining Pattern Classifiers: Methods and Algorithms. Wiley-Interscience, Chichester (2004)
13. Maclin, R.: Boosting classifiers regionally. In: Proceedings of the fifteenth AAAI/ tenth IAAI, pp. 700–705 (1998)
14. Opitz, D., Maclin, R.: Popular ensemble methods: An empirical study. Journal of Artificial Intelligence Research 11, 169–198 (1999)
15. Opitz, D.W., Maclin, R.F.: An empirical evaluation of bagging and boosting for artificial neural networks. In: International Conference on Neural Networks, pp. 1401–1405 (1997)
16. Schapire, R.E.: The strength of weak learnability. Machine Learning 5(2), 197–227 (1990)
17. Witten, I.H., Frank, E.: Data Mining: Practical Machine Learning Tools and Techniques with Java Implementations. Morgan Kaufmann, San Francisco (1999)
18. Woods, K., Kegelmeyer, W.P., Bowyer, K.: Combination of multiple classifiers using local accuracy estimates. IEEE Trans. Pattern Anal. Mach. Intell. 19(4), 405–410 (1997)
19. Zhou, Z.-H., Wu, J., Tang, W.: Ensembling neural networks: many could be better than all. Artif. Intell. 137(1-2), 239–263 (2002)
20. Zhou, Z.H., Tang, W.: Selective ensemble of decision trees. In: Wang, G., Liu, Q., Yao, Y., Skowron, A. (eds.) RSFDGrC 2003. LNCS (LNAI), vol. 2639, pp. 476–483. Springer, Heidelberg (2003)

Assessing the Impact of Changing Environments on Classifier Performance*

Rocío Alaiz-Rodríguez[1] and Nathalie Japkowicz[2]

[1] Dpto. de Ingeniería Eléctrica y de Sistemas y Automática,
Campus de Vegazana, Universidad de León, 24071 León, Spain
rocio.alaiz@unileon.es
[2] SITE. University of Ottawa.
150 Louis Pasteur, P.O. Box 450 Stn. A Ottawa, Ontario, Canada
nat@site.uottawa.ca

Abstract. The purpose of this paper is to test the hypothesis that simple classifiers are more robust to changing environments than complex ones. We propose a strategy for generating artificial, but realistic domains, which allows us to control the changing environment and test a variety of situations. Our results suggest that evaluating classifiers on such tasks is not straightforward since the changed environment can yield a simpler or more complex domain. We propose a metric capable of taking this issue into consideration and evaluate our classifiers using it. We conclude that in mild cases of population drifts simple classifiers deteriorate more than complex ones and that in more severe cases as well as in class definition changes, all classifiers deteriorate to about the same extent. This means that in all cases, complex classifiers remain more accurate than simpler ones, thus challenging the hypothesis that simple classifiers are more robust to changing environments than complex ones.

1 Introduction

A common assumption in supervised learning is that training and future data come from the same, although unknown, distribution. This fundamental assumption, however, does not often hold in practice [3] and this may lead to a significant performance deterioration in the induced classifiers.

Several approaches have been proposed so far in order to deal with different mismatches between training data and data drawn from the real operating conditions. They either follow an adaptive strategy, relying on an unlabeled dataset representative of the new conditions to update the classifier accordingly [10] or they deal with this uncertainty problem by using a particularly robust approach [1]. An important claim made by David Hand in [3] says that, because in real world domains the distributions involved in the training set are often not representative of future data, performance gains reached by more sophisticated

---

* Supported by the Natural Science and Engineering Council of Canada and the Spanish MEC project DPI2006-02550.

S. Bergler (Ed.): Canadian AI 2008, LNAI 5032, pp. 13–24, 2008.
© Springer-Verlag Berlin Heidelberg 2008

classifiers that are able to model small idiosyncrasies found in the underlying distribution of the training set are marginal with respect to the performance of simple standard classifiers.This paper focuses on this hypothesis and analyzes whether complex classifiers keep their advantage at testing time once the distributions have shifted, or as suggested in [3], simpler classifiers that focus on the more general features of the training set distribution—which will persist throughout the distributional shift occurring between training and testing time—will be more robust than (or at least as robust as) the more sophisticated classifiers. In this work, the complexity concept refers to the classifier capability to define arbitrarily complex decision frontiers.

To our knowledge, there has previously been no such comparative studies of the robustness of different classifiers against these mismatches between training and test data. Although Hand's work [3] illustrates the performance of two classifiers (LDA and a tree model) in a bank application over time, no detailed description of the experimental methods is provided and there is no chance to refer to the ideal scenario. We set out to investigate this hypothesis using a simulated medical domain whose distributions we were able to control fully. In particular, we generated a number of variations of our standard domain, relying on common-sense scenarios and distribution changes studied in the literature, and tested four different classifiers on all these domains. The classifiers range from simple models such as 1R rules or simple Neural Networks to more sophisticated models such as Decision Trees and Neural Networks with a more complex architecture.

Experimental results show different trends in the relative performance between simple and more sophisticated classifiers. Although we observed that under some of the assessed changing scenarios, as suggested by Hand [3], the superiority of the complex classifiers over the simple ones is not that significant, we also found that this does not necessarily imply that simple classifiers are less susceptible to performance deterioration. In fact, their apparent robustness may be due to a simplification in the classification task.

The remainder of this article is organized as follows. Sect. 2 summarizes the distribution changes studied in the literature. Sect. 3 describes our hypothesis testing methodology, detailing the domain generator we designed and the variations we applied to it. Sect. 4 shows our experimental results and discusses their implications. Sect. 5 concludes with a summary and suggestions for future work.

2   Changing Environments

Consider a standard supervised classification problem with a labeled data set $S = \{(\mathbf{x}^k, \mathbf{d}^k), k = 1, \ldots, K\}$ and examples independently drawn from an unknown distribution, where $\mathbf{x}^k$ is an observation feature vector and $\mathbf{d}^k$ is the class label.

The fundamental assumption of supervised learning is that the joint probability distribution $p(\mathbf{x}, \mathbf{d})$ will remain unchanged between training and testing. There are, however, some mismatches that are likely to appear in practice and have already been studied in the literature.

One of the most studied mismatches is a situation where the conditional probability $p(\mathbf{d}|\mathbf{x})$ remains unchanged, but the input distribution $p(\mathbf{x})$ differs from training to future data. This has been referred to as *population drift* [7,3], *covariate shift* [11,13] or *sample selection bias* [5,3], although this last term in fact refers to the design data acquisition. Such mismatches can be encountered in practical fields such as banking applications, medical diagnosis or bioinformatics. In this work we will refer to it as *population drift*.

Another kind of distribution change is the *class definition change* where $p(\mathbf{x})$ is not altered but, $p(\mathbf{d}|\mathbf{x})$ varies from training to test [3]. The term *concept drift* is also used to refer to this variation [8] as well as *functional relation change* [13]. In this work, we will use the term *class definition change* to refer to this change.

Another widely studied scenario is the change in class distribution, where the class prior probability $p(\mathbf{d})$ varies from training to test, but $p(\mathbf{x}|\mathbf{d})$ remains unaltered. The problem of changing class distributions has been studied from different perspectives in [10,1,9,2].

In the remainder of the paper will focus on the problems of population drift and class definition change and we will specifically focus on the following two issues: (a) Whether, in case of both, population drifts and class definition changes, an actual drop in performance can generally be observed by all kinds of classifiers, (b)Whether it is correct to assume that the simpler classifiers will maintain their performance more reliably than the more sophisticated ones in such cases.

3   Our Experimental Framework

In order to test the hypotheses put forth in [3], we generated an artificial domain, that we subsequently tested under various regimen of population drifts and class definition changes. We chose a simple domain that anyone could relate to in order to be able to consider rational rather than completely random variations. In order to make the problem interesting, we also introduced some instance of attribute dependency as well as a great deal of uncertainty, in various cases. All the domains were generated completely automatically following the attribute and class rules described in this section.

3.1   General Setting

Our domain is a simulated medical domain that states the prognosis of patients infected with the flu and described by the following attribute vector $\mathbf{x}$ where:

- x_1 is the patient's age (described by a discrete value [Infant, Teenager, YoungAdult, Adult, OldAdult, Elderly]).
- x_2 defines the severity of the flu symptoms (described by a discrete value [Light, Medium, Strong]).
- x_3 represents the patient's general health condition (described by a discrete value [Good, Medium, Poor]).
- x_4 represents the patient's social position (described by a discrete value [Rich, MiddleClass, Poor]).

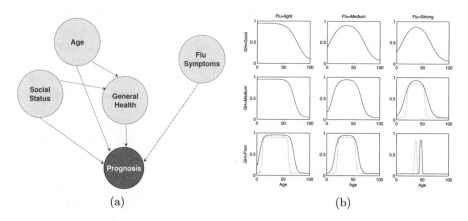

Fig. 1. 1(a) Attribute dependency in our simulated domain. 1(b) Probability of Normal Remission as a function of Age, Flu Symptoms and General Health. When two lines appear, the discontinuous one applies to instances with Social Status equal to Poor.

The patient's classification is the patient's prognosis after a month (described by a nominal value: NormalRemission, Complications).

In order to make the problem interesting for classifiers, we assume that the features are not independent of one another and that certain feature values may be irrelevant. We assume that the dependency relations of the features are as shown in Fig.1(a), where each node represents a feature (or the class) and an arc between two nodes represents the dependency relation.

3.2   Original Setting

We will consider several settings for our domain. In this section, we describe the original one that corresponds to a Negative Growth Population (NGP) with the age distribution shown in Table 1. The next subsections will focus on others.

The original setting reflects the following common-sense rules:

– Infants, old adults and the elderly are more prone to complications than people in other categories.
– Severe flu symptoms cause more complications than mild ones.
– People in poor general health are more prone to complications than generally healthier people.
– People at the bottom of the social ladder are likely to be in poorer general health than wealthier people, and are, thus, also more prone to complications.

We do not have the space necessary to describe the details of our data generator, but Figure 1 (b) illustrates the distribution of the NormalRemission class we obtain as a function of our four attributes.

Having described the original domain, we now turn to the various kinds of modifications that we considered. Three general situations will be studied: *Population drift, Population drift-NR with not Represented cases* and *Class definition change*. We now detail each of these situations.

Table 1. Age group distribution for a Negative Growth Population (NGP)

Age Group	Prior Probability
Infant	0.07
Teenager	0.10
Young	0.36
Adult	0.24
Old Adult	0.17
Elderly	0.06

Table 2. Age group distribution for a Developing Population (DP)

Age Group	Prior Probability
Infant	0.30
Teenager	0.25
Young	0.20
Adult	0.12
Old Adult	0.08
Elderly	0.05

Table 3. Age group distribution for a Zero Growth Population (ZGP)

Age Group	Prior Probability
Infant	0.14
Teenager	0.20
Young	0.20
Adult	0.20
Old Adult	0.14
Elderly	0.12

3.3   Population Drift with Full Representation

The purpose of our experiments in population drifts with full representation is to test whether, indeed, changes in case proportions do not have any effect on classification accuracy. We investigated several scenarios, each plausible.

Developing population (DP). The population where the classifier is deployed corresponds to a developing country region with high birth rates and also high death rates. The age distribution for the Developing Population (DP) is given in Table 2.

Zero Growth Population (ZGP). The population has zero growth with age distribution given in Table 3.

Season changes (NGP/W). Flu symptoms get stronger. In the season change category, we investigated the scenario in which the original data set corresponds to a normal time, and the new data set corresponds to a rougher season (colder winter) during which the flu symptoms get stronger.

Season changes (NGP/SW). Flu symptoms get softer. This situation corresponds to a milder winter.

Season changes (NGP/DW). Drastic Winter-Flu symptoms get stronger and General health declines. In addition to the previous situation with strong winter, we are adding changes in the general health. In general, more cases of complications occur, with a greater markedness in poor people with poor health and elderly and infants.

Population is much poorer (NGP/P). Instead of the Normal distribution that we previously used for social status, we are considering a distribution skewed towards the poor class.

Population is much poorer and the winter is drastic (NGP/P+DW). The changes of situations in DW and P are implemented simultaneously.

3.4 Population Drift-NR (Not Represented Cases)

We consider several situations where an age group is missing in the training population set (No Infant, No Teenager, No Young, etc) or two groups (neither Infant nor Elderly, neither Teenager nor Old Adult, neither Infant nor Teenager, neither Old Adult nor Elderly). The remaining groups are represented proportionally to their original prior probability.

3.5 Class Definition Change

In this case, the population is exactly the same, but the labeling rules change. We assume that the test set was generated later, and there has been either fewer complications or more complications at that time.

Class definition change (MC). More complications. Class definition changes are defined so that the probability of Normal Remission decreases for certain ages, social statuses and flu symptoms.

Class definition change (FC). Fewer complications. Unlike the changes described above, parameters in the labeling rules have been modified in order to widen the age interval for which the probability of Normal remission is high.

4   Experimental Results

The effect of changing conditions between training and test sets was assessed in both simple and sophisticated classifiers. As simple classifiers we used a *1R* classifier [4] and a *Simple NN* (Neural Network with a multilayer perceptron architecture and only 1 node in the hidden layer). As more complex classifiers, a C4.5 *Decision Tree* and *Complex NN* with a higher number of nodes (10, for this experiment) in the hidden layer so that, decision frontiers can be more complex.

Training and test sets with 1000 instances each one were generated and the results are the average over 30 different trials (with different data sets). Classifier training was carried out using Weka [12] with the following parameters selected for the NGP population: 1R with a minimum bucket size of 6 for discretizing numeric attributes, C4.5 decision tree with a 0.40 confidence factor used for pruning, Simple NN and Complex NN with 100 training cycles, learning rate equal to 0.3, momentum to 0.2, normalized attributes and with the mean squared error cost function.

Next, we analyze the experimental results obtained for the case of population drift, population drift with non-represented cases and class definition changes.

For simplicity, we will compare the classifiers' performance using accuracy, despite the weaknesses of this measure (see [6], for example, for a discussion). The same study could be repeated using another performance measure that would focus on different trends in the classifier's behavior.

The drop in performance of a classifier deployed in a test environment will be assessed by means of our new *performance Deterioration* metric (pD), that refers to the proportion of the difference between the trivial classifier and a classifier trained with the same data distribution used for testing. More specifically, pD is defined as

$$pD = \begin{cases} \dfrac{E_{test} - E_{ideal}}{E_0 - E_{ideal}} & \text{if } E_{test} \leq E_0 \\ 1 & \text{otherwise} \end{cases} \qquad (1)$$

where E_0 stands for the frequency of errors of the trivial classifier (which assigns data to the majority class), E_{test} is the frequency of errors on the test set and E_{ideal} is the error frequency of the classifier if it had been trained with the same distribution as the test distribution. This metric is similar to the analysis conducted in [3] to compare the relative performance between two classifiers.

When the classifier performance is no worse than the trivial classifier, it takes values in the interval [0-1]. A value close to zero indicates low deterioration, that is, that classifier performance is close the ideal situation. A value equal to one means that the classifier is no better, and, perhaps, worse than the trivial classifier in that environment.

4.1   Experiment 1: Population Drift

This experiment allows us to see the performance of the classifiers trained on a Negative Growth Population (NGP) and deployed, afterwards, in different environments that may have different proportions of poor/rich, young/old people, flu symptoms, but all of them represented in the training set. Fig. 2 shows the error rate for 8 different test conditions: NGP, DP, ZGP, NGP/W, NGP/SW, NGP/P, NGP/DW, NGP/P+DW.

It can be seen that the relative performance between the classifiers does not hold under changing environments. Complex NN and Decision Trees are affected in almost the same way by changes in the data distribution. 1R shows a worse performance, but follows the same trend as Complex NN and Decision Trees, except for NGP/DW and NGP/P+DW where its performance is relatively much worse. Simple NN shows a different trend (sometimes yielding a decrease while sometimes yielding an increase in relative performance vis-à-vis the complex classifiers). It is worth highlighting, though, that under the seven changing conditions assessed here, the ranking between the classifier remains the same, even though relative differences in performance may become larger or smaller. Next, we will analyze a few cases in more detail.

Looking at the DP case in Fig. 2 may suggest that classifiers are experimenting a relevant decrease in performance with respect to the one observed in the design set NGP: the Complex NN's error rate increases from 18.6% to 24.4%, the Decision tree's from 18.9% to 24.7%, the 1R from 23.7% to 34.2% and the Simple NN from 21.2% to 33.4%. However, we may ask the question of whether this decrease in performance is due to a mismatch between the training and test conditions or whether it is only caused by the fact that the data that comes from a DP environment is more difficult to classify. Taking this eventuality into consideration, how much performance deterioration is indeed taking place?

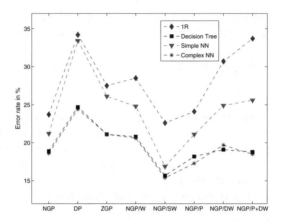

Fig. 2. Error rate (in %) for classifiers trained with data drawn from a Negative Growth Population(NGP) and deployed in different environments with population drift: DP, ZGP, NGP/W, NGP/SW, NGP/P, NGP/DW, NGP/P+DW.

Table 4. Classifier performance under a *Population drift with all the cases represented* in the training set. The error rate of a trivial classifier, an ideal situation (the same training and test set distribution), and a classifier trained with data from a NGP are shown. Performance Deterioration (pD) is shown for each particular case.

| | | Test Sets | | | | | | | | |
		NGP	DP	ZGP	NGP W	NGP SW	NGP P	NGP DW	NGP P+DW	Averaged pD
Trivial Classifier	Error rate	36.0	32.9	40.8	37.2	34.4	39.8	41.4	46.2	
1R	Training: **NGP**	23.7	34.2	27.5	28.5	22.6	24.1	30.7	33.7	
	Ideal situation	23.7	32.8	27.3	27.2	19.0	23.6	28.3	27.4	
	pD		1	0.01	0.13	0.24	0.03	0.19	0.33	0.28
Decision Tree	Training : **NGP**	18.9	24.7	21.1	20.8	15.7	18.2	19.1	18.8	
	Ideal situation	18.9	23.4	20.7	20.2	15.1	16.8	18.7	16.8	
	pD		0.14	0.02	0.04	0.03	0.06	0.02	0.07	0.05
Simple NN	Training: **NGP**	21.2	33.4	26.1	24.8	16.9	21.1	24.9	25.6	
	Ideal situation	21.2	25.9	25.6	23.7	16.4	20.4	23	22.9	
	pD		1	0.03	0.08	0.03	0.04	0.10	0.12	0.20
Complex NN	Training: **NGP**	18.6	24.4	21.1	20.6	15.4	17.3	19.7	18.5	
	Ideal situation	18.6	23.8	20.8	20.2	14.9	16.6	18.6	16.7	
	pD		0.07	0.02	0.02	0.03	0.03	0.05	0.06	0.04

Working with our controlled environment allows us to compute the actual performance deterioration that is taking place and understand that the analysis is not as straightforward as it may have appeared at first. Table 4 shows the error rate obtained by each classifier under different population drift scenarios (training set drawn from NGP) and under ideal conditions (training set drawn from the same distribution as the test set). In column DP of Table 4 we see that the Decision Tree classifier deviates from 23.4% (ideal conditions) to 24.7%, indicating a performance deterioration of 0.14, while the Complex NN's deterioration is 0.07. The 1R and Simple NN performance deterioration, on the other hand, are equal to 1, meaning that they become useless in practice since their performance is worse than or equal to that of the trivial classifier. To sum up, the increase in error rate observed in our experiments is in part due to a performance deterioration and in part due to an increase in the classification problem difficulty.

On the other hand, focusing on the case NGP/SW we may think that the effort put in developing a more complex classifier may be worthless since, eventually, the Simple NN performance is very close to that of a more complex NN. But, does it mean the Simple NN is more robust under this particular change? It can be seen in Table 4 that the performance deterioration experienced by the Decision Tree, the Simple NN and the Complex NN is 0.03 for all of them. In this case, the reason why the Simple NN's error rate is very close to those of the more complex classifiers is just that the NGP/SW environment is easier to classify. Note also that the error rate is even lower than that of the original NGP.

Analyzing the seven environments with a population drift as a whole, the averaged performance deterioration is much higher for the simple models (0.28 for 1R and 0.20 for the Simple NN) than for the more complicated ones (0.05 for the Decision Tree and 0.04 for the Complex NN). To sum up and get back to the questions posed in Sect. 2, we found that: (a) a drop in performance is observed by all the classifiers but to a lesser extent by the complex ones and (b) although differences may increase or decrease when a population drift takes place, the complex classifiers remain either more accurate or as accurate as the simple ones.

4.2 Experiment 2: Population Drift-NR (Not Represented Cases)

In this experiment we assess the classifiers' error rate deterioration in the NGP domain when some groups (clusters) are not represented in the design set. Instances are removed based on the age attribute. As a result, we have different training data sets with: no Infants, no Teenagers, no Young Adults, no Old Adults, no Adults, no Elderly, as well as, data sets where two groups are absent.

Table 5[1] shows more severe performance deterioration for the scenarios in which the missing population has a high representation in the test set (Young Adults, Adults, Old Adults). Both complex and simple classifiers are affected by these population drifts with unrepresented cases with the simple classifiers behaving similarly to one another ($pD = 0.29$ for 1R and $pD = 0.23$ for the Simple NN) and in the complex ones too ($pD = 0.17$ for the Decision Tree and $pD = 0.18$ for the Complex NN). Note, though, that the difference in robustness against unrepresented cases for the complex classifiers when compared with the simple ones (on average pD of 0.26 against 0.175) is not as pronounced as it was in the case where all groups were represented (on average pD of 0.24 vs. 0.045).

---

[1] Due to space limitations, we omit a figure to represent the information in the Table.

Table 5. Classifier performance under a *Population drift with Not Represented cases* in the training set. Error rate of the trivial classifier and a classifier trained with data from a NGP population are shown as well as the performance Deterioration (pD).

	Test Set: NGP							
	1R		Decision Tree		Simple NN		Complex NN	
	Error	pD	Error	pD	Error	pD	Error	pD
Trivial classifier	36.0		36.0		36.0		36.0	
Training =Test conditions	23.7		18.9		21.2		18.6	
No Infant	23.7	0.00	19.0	0.01	22.2	0.07	19.2	0.04
No Teenager	24.0	0.02	19.4	0.03	21.3	0.00	18.6	0.00
No Young	25.0	0.11	18.9	0.00	23.3	0.14	19.8	0.07
No Adult	26.5	0.23	22.2	0.19	23.5	0.16	20.2	0.09
Training No Old Adult	24.6	0.07	19.6	0.04	23.8	0.17	19.8	0.07
set: No Elderly	24.1	0.03	19.5	0.03	22.9	0.11	19.3	0.04
No Old Adult+No Elderly	33.3	0.78	24.5	0.33	32.7	0.77	27.4	0.50
No Infant + No Teenager	24.4	0.06	20.7	0.11	21.4	0.01	20.0	0.08
No Elderly + No Infant	24.2	0.04	20.0	0.06	21.4	0.01	19.2	0.04
No Old Adult+No Teenager	25.0	0.11	20.2	0.08	21.8	0.04	19.2	0.04
Averaged pD		0.29		0.17		0.23		0.18

In summary, (a) all classifiers show a drop in performance when there are unrepresented cases in the training set, with (b) a slightly higher impact on simple classifiers than in complex ones.

4.3 Experiment 3: Class Definition Changes

Error rates for the four classifiers have also been assessed in the presence of changes in class definition: rules that lead to more complications (MC) and rules that lead to fewer complications (FC). A comprehensive evaluation has been carried out assessing all the possible mismatch combinations (see Table 6 for details). It turns out that the Simple NN, the Complex NN and the Decision Trees are affected on average in the same way (pD around 0.24) by these changes in class definition. The 1R classifier, however, shows more sensitivity to these changes, with its pD always higher than that of the other three classifiers, being trivial in one case and with an overall pD equal to 0.36. In [3], Hand suggests that under class definition changes it is possible that models that fit the training data less well will perform better in the new changing environments. Our analysis point out that in this experimental framework the simple 1R rule is affected to a greater extend than the other three classifiers for the class definition change defined here. On the other hand, we have not found significant differences between the simple NN and the other complex classifiers in terms of performance deterioration. Such a result, thus, reflects Hand's suggestion, except for the fact that the complex classifiers, that yielded better results in the original scenario, will also yield better classification rules under the class definition changes evaluated here, and, thus, remain a better choice.

Table 6. Class Definition Changes. Error rate of the trivial classifier is shown together with the error rate for a classifier trained and tested with different sets: original rules (NGP), fewer (FC) and more (MC) complications. Performance Deterioration (pD) is shown (The symbol - is used when no deterioration performance applies).

			Test: NGP		Test : MC		Test: FC		Averaged
			Error	pD	Error	pD	Error	pD	pD
Trivial classifier	**Training conditions**		36.0		28.4		34.4		
1R		**NGP**	23.7	-	27.1	0.33	22.8	0.10	
	Training	**MC**	26.1	0.20	26.5	-	26.1	0.36	
		FC	25.8	0.17	29.5	1	21.5	-	
									0.36
Decision Tree		**NGP**	18.6	-	21.6	0.08	19.0	0.08	
	Training	**MC**	20.6	0.11	21.0	-	24.1	0.38	
		FC	20.4	0.11	25.9	0.67	17.7	-	
									0.24
Simple NN		**NGP**	21.2	-	26.3	0.17	19.4	0.08	
	Training	**MC**	23.1	0.13	25.9	-	23.0	0.30	
		FC	22.0	0.05	25.9	0.73	18.1	-	
									0.24
Complex NN		**NGP**	18.6	-	21.6	0.12	19.0	0.10	
	Training	**MC**	20.8	0.13	20.7	-	23.4	0.36	
		FC	20.5	0.11	25.0	0.56	17.3	-	
									0.23

5   Conclusions and Further Research

In this work we have evaluated the impact of several changing environments on simple classifiers (1R, Simple NN) and more sophisticated ones (Complex NN, C4.5 Decision Tree). Our results show that the trend noticed by David Hand [3] does happen in some cases, while in other cases, differences between simple and sophisticated classifiers become wider under changing conditions.

By analyzing the behavior of two different classes of classifiers in an artificial environment, we have observed that the resultant relative performance between the simple and complex classifiers under changing conditions can be decomposed as the additive effect of the classifier's performance deterioration and the complexity of the new classification scenario. Thus, a decrease in the error rate difference between a complex and a simple classifier may be caused by the fact that (i) the complex classifier (with lower initial error rate) is more vulnerable to changing conditions and/or (ii) the classification problem becomes easier for the simple classifier. The same reasoning applies when the difference increases.

Given our use of a controlled classification framework, we were able to propose a measure of performance deterioration which compares the results obtained in a changed environment to those obtained in an ideal situation with no mismatch. Our experimental results show that the changing conditions evaluated here lead to a drop in performance by all classifiers. In the case of *population drift* it is higher for simple classifiers than for the more sophisticated ones, while in the case of *population drift with non-represented cases* the differences between the two categories of classifiers become less pronounced. Finally, under *class definition changes*, putting aside the simple 1R rule (which was shown to be very sensitive to all the shifts evaluated here), the remaining three classifiers show the same amount of performance deterioration. Results in this experimental framework, thus, show that simple classifiers do not become more accurate than complex ones, although we can not expect the differences in error rates to hold under changing environments. They may increase or decrease depending on the kind of changes that take place in the data.

Our immediate future work will consist of studying the effect of training classifiers on different data sets of various sizes. Longer term studies will include the development of more realistic models for artificial data set generation.

References

1. Alaiz-Rodríguez, R., Guerrero-Curieses, A., Cid-Sueiro, J.: Minimax regret classifier for imprecise class distributions. Journal of Machine Learning Research (2007)
2. Drummond, C., Holte, R.C.: Cost curves: An improved method for visualizing classifier performance. Machine Learning 65(1), 95–130 (2006)
3. Hand, D.J.: Classifier technology and the illusion of progress. Statistical Sciences 21(1), 1–15 (2006)
4. Holte, R.: Elaboration on two points raised in classifier technology and the illusion of progress. Statistical Science 21(1) (2006)
5. Huang, J., Smola, A.J., Gretton, A., Borgwardt, K.M., Schölkopf, B.: Correcting sample selection bias by unlabeled data. In: Schölkopf, B., Platt, J., Hoffman, T. (eds.) Advances in Neural Information Processing Systems 19, pp. 601–608. MIT Press, Cambridge (2007)
6. Japkowicz, N.: Why question machine learning evaluation methods? an illustrative review of the shortcomings of current methods. In: AAAI-2006 Workshop on Evaluation Methods for Machine Learning, Boston, USA (2006)
7. Kelly, M.G., Hand, D.J., Adams, N.M.: The impact of changing populations on classifier performance. In: Proceedings of Fifth International Conference on SIG Knowledge Discovery and Data Mining, San Diego, CA, pp. 367–371 (1999)
8. Lane, T., Brodley, C.E.: Approaches to online learning and concept drift for user identification in computer security. In: Knowledge Discovery and Data Mining, pp. 259–263 (1998)
9. Provost, F., Fawcett, T.: Robust classification systems for imprecise environments. Machine Learning 42(3), 203–231 (2001)
10. Saerens, M., Latinne, P., Decaestecker, C.: Adjusting a classifier for new a priori probabilities: A simple procedure. Neural Computation 14, 21–41 (2002)
11. Shimodaira, H.: Improving predictive inference under convariance shift by weighting the log-likelihood function. Journal of Statistical Planning and Inference (2000)
12. Witten, I.H., Frank, E.: Data Mining: Practical Machine Learning Tools and Techniques with Java Implementations. Morgan Kaufmann, San Francisco (1999)
13. Yamazaki, K., Kawanabe, M., Watanabe, S., Sugiyama, M., Müller, K.: Asymptotic bayesian generalization error when training and test distributions are different. In: ICML 2007, pp. 1079–1086. ACM Press, New York (2007)

A Comparison of Sentiment Analysis Techniques: Polarizing Movie Blogs

Michelle Annett and Grzegorz Kondrak

Department of Computing Science, University of Alberta
{mkannett,kondrak}@cs.ualberta.ca

Abstract. With the ever-growing popularity of online media such as blogs and social networking sites, the Internet is a valuable source of information for product and service reviews. Attempting to classify a subset of these documents using polarity metrics can be a daunting task. After a survey of previous research on sentiment polarity, we propose a novel approach based on Support Vector Machines. We compare our method to previously proposed lexical-based and machine learning (ML) approaches by applying it to a publicly available set of movie reviews. Our algorithm will be integrated within a blog visualization tool.

1 Introduction

Imagine the following scenario: you hear about a movie which opened in theaters last weekend that made $75 million, but you have not heard anything about it. Before trekking to the movie theater and potentially wasting your money, you want to determine if this new movie is worth seeing or not. While this may seem like a trivial problem, it raises an important question: What sources of information do you use to assist you with your decision? Roughly ten years ago, one would poll the opinions of their friends or listen to movie critics such as Siskel and Ebert. Nowadays, most individuals consult websites or blogs such as *Yahoo!Movies* or *RottenTomatoes.com* to obtain this same information. While it is undoubtedly true that useful information can be obtained from these sources, the methods that one uses to gather this information, such as navigating through an endless number of websites or using an unintuitive RSS interface, are time consuming and potentially frustrating.

In order to assist users in managing the overwhelming amount of information present within the movie blog domain, and to increase the navigability between numerous blog sites, Tirapat *et al.* [1] have created *eNulog*, a blog visualization tool. *eNulog* mines and dynamically displays large collections of data, such as movie blogs, in an appealing and intuitive manner. The visualizations are based on a node and cluster structure, with each node representing a specific movie and each cluster containing nodes that are related in some way (either by director, genre, or actor). The application is very interactive: by selecting a node, the user can view each post relating to the selected movie and watch movie clusters form within the visualization (Figure 1).

S. Bergler (Ed.): Canadian AI 2008, LNAI 5032, pp. 25–35, 2008.
© Springer-Verlag Berlin Heidelberg 2008

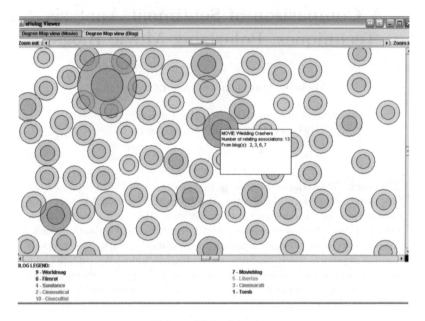

Fig. 1. *eNulog* Interface

Currently, *eNulog* is unable to create polarity generalizations for a collection of movie reviews. In order to find out if a collection's composition is positive or negative, a user has to click on a movie node and read all of its blog posts. The lack of generalization functionality in *eNulog* provided the motivation for our research on sentiment analysis. Sentiment analysis, or statement polarity classification, is concerned with determining the relative positivity or negativity of a document, web page or selection of text. A program that could reliably determine the polarity of a collection of blog postings would allow users to save time and alleviate frustration.

The task of sentiment analysis is difficult due to the variability and complexity of language expressions. One of the biggest challenges of this task is brought about by *thwarted* and *negated* expressions. A thwarted expression contains a number of words that have a polarity which is opposite to the polarity of the expression itself. For example: 'Johnny Depp was alright. The previous two pirate movies were unrealistic and boring. The plot was awful. However, the special effects made the third pirate movie excellent.' In this statement, the number of negative words incorrectly implies that the statement is negative, when in reality it is actually positive and supportive. On the other hand, a negated expression is composed of a negating word (such as 'not' or 'never') followed by a noun, adjective, adverb or verb. It is easy for a human reader to discern the polarity of a statement such as, 'this movie was neither enjoyable nor entertaining', but to an automated entity or program, this is not an easy task. Due to the presence of thwarted and negated expressions, the task of sentiment analysis is non-trivial.

In this paper, we propose a novel approach based on Support Vector Machines. We investigate variations of feature vectors involving different sizes of feature vectors, different feature representations, and different feature types. We compare our approach against previously proposed techniques, within a unified framework, utilizing the same data set.

The paper is structured as follows. In Section 2, we provide the reader with a review of the state of the art of the field. In Section 3, we describe the methods we used in our experiments. The results of the experiments are presented in Section 4. Section 5 describes how our results will be applied to the *eNulog* program. Finally, in Section 6, we leave the reader with some concluding thoughts and future work that could be undertaken.

2   Related Work

Typically, within sentiment analysis classification, there are two main avenues of research. We first review the lexical approaches, which focus on building successful dictionaries, and then review the machine learning approaches, which are primarily concerned with feature vectors. Almost all of the related works presented in this section have been developed and tested on corpora from the movie domain.

A lexical approach typically utilizes a dictionary or lexicon of pre-tagged words. Each word that is present in a text is compared against the dictionary. If a word is present in the dictionary, then its polarity value is added to the 'total polarity score' of the text. For example, if a match has been found with the word 'excellent', which is annotated in the dictionary as positive, then the total polarity score of the blog is increased. If the total polarity score of a text is positive, then that text is classified as positive, otherwise it is classified as negative. Although naive in nature, many variants of this lexical approach have been reported to perform better than chance [2,3,4].

Because the classification of a statement is dependent upon the scoring it receives, there is a large volume of work devoted to discovering which lexical information works best. As a starting point for the field, Hatzivassiloglou and Wiebe [5] demonstrated that the subjectivity of an evaluative sentence could be determined through the use of a hand-tagged lexicon comprised solely of adjectives. They report over 80% accuracy on single phrases. Extending this work, Kennedy and Inkpen [2] utilized the same methodology and hand-tagged adjective lexicon as Hatzivassiloglou and Wiebe, but they tested the paradigm on a dataset composed of movie reviews. They reported a much lower accuracy rate of about 62%. Moving away from the hand-tagged lexicons, Turney utilized an Internet search engine to determine the polarity of words that would be included in the lexicon [3]. Turney performed two AltaVista search engine queries: one with a target word conjoined with the word 'good', and a second with the target word conjoined with the word 'bad'. The polarity of the target word was determined by the search result that returned the most hits. This approach improved accuracy to 65%.

In other research, Kamps *et al.* [4] and Andreevskaia *et al.* [6] chose to use the WordNet database to determine the polarity of words. We compared a target word to two pivot words (usually 'good' and 'bad') to find the minimum path distance between the target word and the pivot words in the WordNet hierarchy. The minimum path distance was converted to an incremental score and this value was stored with the word in the dictionary. The reported accuracy level of this approach was 64% [6]. An alternative to the WordNet metric, proposed by Turney and Littman, was to compute the semantic orientation of a word [7]. By subtracting a word's association strength to a set of negative words from its association strength to a set of positive words, Turney and Littman were able to achieve an accuracy rate of 82% using two different semantic orientation statistic metrics.

The other main avenue of research within this area has utilized supervised machine learning techniques. Within the machine learning approach, a series of feature vectors are chosen and a collection of tagged corpora are provided for training a *classifier*, which can then be applied to an untagged corpus of text. In a machine learning approach, the selection of features is crucial to the success rate of the classification. Most commonly, a variety of unigrams (single words from a document) or n-grams (two or more words from a document in sequential order) are chosen as feature vectors. Other proposed features include the number of positive words, number of negating words, and the length of a document. Support Vector Machines (SVMs) [8,9] and the Naive Bayes algorithm are the most commonly employed classification techniques. The reported classification accuracy ranges between 63% and 82%, but these results are dependent upon the features selected.

3   Methods

In this section we describe the methodology behind the two sets of experiments that we performed.

3.1   Lexical Methods

The basic paradigm of the lexical approach is outlined below:

1. Preprocess each blog post (i.e. remove punctuation, strip HTML tags).
2. Initialize the total blog polarity score: $s \leftarrow 0$.
3. Tokenize each blog post. For each token, check if it is present in a dictionary of General Inquirer [10] (+ Yahoo! [11]) words.
   (a) If token is present in dictionary,
       i. If token is positive, then $s \leftarrow s + w$.
       ii. If token is negative, then $s \leftarrow s - w$.
4. Look at total blog polarity score s,
   (a) If $s >$ threshold, then classify the blog post as positive.
   (b) If $s <$ threshold, then classify the blog post as negative.

We investigated five variants of the lexical approach.

1. In the baseline approach, the dictionary is limited to a fixed number of positively and negatively tagged words.
2. To determine the effects of stemming on the classification accuracy, we applied a stemmer to each of the words in the dictionary (thereby increasing the size of the dictionary), as well as to each token in the blog post.
3. Because the dictionary does not contain 'slang' words, a part-of-speech tagger was applied to the blogs in the development set to search for 'slang' adjectives and adverbs. If a new 'slang' word was found, we used Turney's method in [3] to classify the word and add it to the dictionary.
4. To counter-balance the thwarted expressions, the words in the dictionary were assigned weights using the word's minimum path distance from the pivot words in WordNet.
5. The final variant combined variants two, three and four with the baseline approach.

It should be noted that the value of w in the general lexical method paradigm was dependent upon the paradigm variant that was being used. In the first, second and third variants, the value of w was 1, and in the fourth and fifth variants, the value of w was equivalent to the token's minimum path distance from the pivot words in WordNet.

3.2   Machine Learning Methods

The basic paradigm for the creation of the feature vectors was as follows:

1. Apply a part of speech tagger to each blog post in the development set.
2. Collect all of the adjectives/adverbs which were present in each blog post.
3. Make a popular word set composed of the top N adjectives and adverbs.
4. Traverse all of the blogs in the experimental set to create the following features:
   (a) Number of positive words
   (b) Number of negative words
   (c) Number of negating words
   (d) Presence, absence or frequency of each word in the popular word set (N words)

For the generation of feature vectors, we re-used some of the methods outlined in the previous section. We investigated the following four feature sets:

1. A fixed number of the most frequently occurring popular words (or unigrams), each of which is assigned an integer value representing the frequency of the word in the blog post.
2. Same features as in #1, but with binary representations of the unigrams (instead of integer values), corresponding to the presence or absence of a word in the blog post.
3. Same features as in #1 plus three *aggregate* features: the number of positive, negative, and neutral words present in the blog post.
4. Same features as in #3, but with binary representations of the unigrams as in #2.

4   Evaluation

In this section, we describe the results of our experiments with the lexical and the machine learning approaches.

4.1   Resources

We used the following resources:

1. Cornell Movie Review Dataset of Tagged Blogs (1000 positive and 1000 negative) [12].
2. List of 2000 positive words and 2000 negative words from the General Inquirer lists of adjectives [10].
3. Yahoo! Web Search API [11].
4. Porter Stemmer [13].
5. WordNet Java API [14].
6. Stanford Log Linear POS Tagger built with the Penn Treebank tag set [15].
7. WEKA Machine Learning Java API (only used for machine learning) [16].
8. SVM-Light Machine Learning Implementation [17].

Before both experiments were performed, we randomly divided the Cornell Movie Review Dataset of Tagged Blogs into a 200 member development set and a 1800 member training set (to ensure that our baseline would be evenly distributed, 100 positive and 100 negative blogs were extracted from the Cornell set). As we needed to find the most popular words present in blog posts, the development set was set aside and mined for this purpose. The results reported in Section 4.2 were obtained using the entire set of 1800 blogs and the results reported in Section 4.3 used this same set, but also applied 10-fold cross validation.

4.2   Lexical Results

Table 1 shows the results of applying the five variants of the lexical approach described in Section 3.1 to our test set. Stemming does not help classification much; the increase in accuracy is negligible. It appears that the additional word matches made possible by stemming are counter-balanced by the loss of information represented by morphological endings. On the other hand, the use of WordNet has a positive influence; the addition of the WordNet word weightings increases the accuracy level by 10%.

The addition of new words also improved accuracy, but not as dramatically as the WordNet weight inclusion did (57.7% versus 60.4%). We believe that this occurred because a majority of the words that were classified using Yahoo! ended up as positive, which created an imbalance in the dictionary (originally the dictionary was composed of 50% positive words and 50% negative words). Because the polarity of the experimental set was split at 50-50, any large imbalance in the distribution of the dictionary results in the classification being skewed in one direction (as more words are counted as positive), thereby reducing the number of correct classifications.

Table 1. The Accuracy of Various Lexical Methods (%)

Approach	Accuracy
Baseline	50.0
Baseline + Stemming	50.2
Baseline + Yahoo! Words	57.7
Baseline + WordNet	60.4
Baseline + Stemming + WordNet + Yahoo! Words	55.7

Combining all three ideas lead to a surprising drop in accuracy. By simultaneously increasing the number of words in the dictionary, applying a stemming algorithm, and assigning a weight to each dictionary word, we substantially increased the size of the dictionary. The proportion of positive and negative token matches did not change, and we hypothesize that for each positive match that was found, it was equally likely to find a negative match, thereby creating a neutral net effect.

Given these results, it appears that the selection of words that are included in the dictionary is very important for the lexical approach. If the dictionary is too sparse or exhaustive, one risks the chance of over or under analyzing the results, leading to a decrease in performance. In accordance with previous findings, our results confirm that it is difficult to surpass the 65% accuracy level using a purely lexical approach.

4.3   Machine Learning Results

During the initial experimentation phase of the machine learning approach, we used the WEKA package [16] to obtain a general idea of which ML algorithms and methods would be best suited to classify the dataset we had. Our preliminary experiments indicated that the SVM, Naive Bayes and Alternating Decision Tree (ADTree) algorithms were the most accurate (with the SVM results being superior). We then decided to use the very popular SVM-Light package [17] to further examine the benefits of using an SVM approach. The methodology described in Section 3.2 was used to obtain feature vectors for each of the blogs in the test set and the results were converted into WEKA and SVM-Light formats. A number of popular words, or N, was first tested to determine the optimal number of features to utilize for this classification task.

Table 2 shows the results of testing a varying number of features in SVM-Light. From the results, it is fairly clear to see that the utilization of a small number of features such as 50 is ineffective. While the results for such a small number of features are better than those obtained using a lexical based approach, they pale in comparison to the effects of using 1000 to 2000 features. Due to the nature of the corpora we are dealing with, it makes sense that the utilization of larger feature vectors is beneficial. Classifying an unstructured document, such as an online blog, cannot be done by using a small number of features that have a low probability of being present in the blog to begin with. Within a different domain, this approach might be feasible, but due to the variability

Table 2. SVM-Light Accuracy Results for Varying Numbers of Features (%)

Number of Features	Accuracy
50	66.2
600	68.1
1000	77.1
1600	77.4
2000	77.4

between writing styles and the complexity and size of the English language, this approach is inadequate. The more features one introduces into the equation, the higher the probability of successful classification by an automated ML technique.

Table 3 shows the results of utilizing four different feature representations gathered from our test set, in three different machine learning algorithms. The unigram feature representations were the most effective across all algorithms. We believe that the disappointing performance of the combination of the aggregate and unigram features can be attributed to the fact that they represent two different classes. The information contained in the aggregate features is already present in the unigram features. Instead of helping a ML classifier, the addition of the aggregate features has a confounding effect.

The difference between utilizing a presence/absence or frequency representation for each feature is small (2% to 3%). We hypothesize that the reasons for this difference are the same as the reasons that WordNet weights were more effective than categorical $+/-1$ weights in the lexical approach. The weights eliminate the neutralizing effects of the negating sentences and thwarted expressions. By keeping track of how many times a word was found, some of the errors caused by these types of expressions are eliminated.

In comparing the results obtained from the three different algorithms, it is fairly obvious that even the best decision tree algorithm (ADTree) was the least effective. We believe that this decrease in performance is due to the nature of the decision tree algorithm and the fact that a fairly large tree is needed to handle all of the feature attributes that are present in the datasets. Due to the inherent size of the tree, an unclassified testing instance has to traverse through many prediction nodes until it reaches a leaf node. The longer the path an instance has to travel, the higher the likelihood that an incorrect prediction will be made,

Table 3. Machine Learning Accuracy Results (%)

Approach	SVM-Light	NaiveBayes	ADTree
Unigram Integer	77.4	77.1	69.3
Unigram Binary	77.0	75.5	69.3
Unigram Integer + Aggregate	68.2	77.3	67.4
Unigram Binary + Aggregate	65.4	77.5	67.4

thereby decreasing the classification performance on this task. The Naive Bayes approach performs quite well in all situations (greater than 75%). The unigram results classified by the SVM algorithm are on a similar level.

After initially running the SVM-Light experiments, we observed that the confusion matrix results were heavily skewed to the negative side, for all the feature representation vectors. To correct this imbalance, we tried introducing a threshold variable into the results. This threshold variable was set to -0.2, and whenever a blog was assigned a value greater than -0.2, it was classified as positive. Unfortunately, although this modification did succeed in evening out the confusion matrix, it did not increase the overall accuracy of the results.

The results from Tables 1 and 3 clearly indicate the superiority of machine learning approaches. Even the worst of the ML results is superior to the best of the lexical results. It seems that the lexical approaches rely too heavily on semantic information. As both the lexical and ML approaches demonstrated, the inclusion of any type of 'dictionary' information in an experiment does not automatically increase the method's performance. Even though the ML results are superior, one must not forget that in order for a ML approach to be successful, a large corpus of tagged training data must first be collected and annotated, and this can be a challenging and expensive task.

5   Application

The *eNulog* program is composed of two sections, the visualization program and the dataset. The visualization program reads in XML formatted files, extracts multiple dependencies from these files and then visualizes each of these dependencies. The *eNulog* dataset contains 6000 untagged blog posts that were mined from 10 very popular online movie blogs from June to December of 2006. The original intent of the *eNulog* application was to allow users to navigate and make quick judgments about large collections of data. Although initial conclusions can be obtained from the program (e.g. the distance between nodes indicates the relative similarity between movies in terms of their genres), it is very time consuming to read through a large number of blog posts about a certain movie to gather the gist of what the posters had to say.

As we have demonstrated with our SVM approach, it is quite easy to obtain an acceptable level of accuracy when classifying movie blog posts. By applying our SVM method to the *eNulog* dataset, we 'color classified' all of the blog posts in the *eNulog* data set according to their polarity values relative to the -0.2 threshold that was discovered in the ML results (Figure 2). There are three different node colors which are present in the visualization: the red nodes represent movies that have been classified as negative, the green nodes indicate movies that are considered positive, and a yellow color is used to indicate instances where there were too few blogs to make an accurate polarity judgment or instances where the classification of a movie was neutral because the total blog score was close to

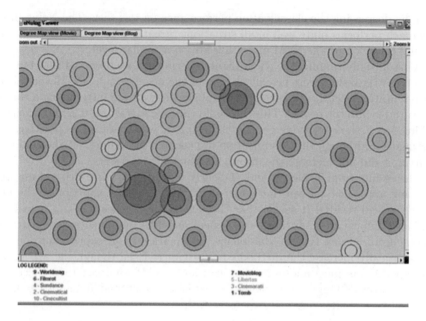

Fig. 2. *eNulog* with Sentiment Polarity Classification

zero. The addition of a 'polarity color coding' node scheme increases the utility of the *eNulog* program.

6   Conclusion

From the two experimental studies that were performed, we can conclude that the application of ML techniques for sentiment classification is quite successful. As expected, the ML results which were obtained supported the conclusion that the types of features which are chosen have a dramatic impact on the classification accuracy of an algorithm. As the lexical approaches have demonstrated, there is an upper bound on the accuracy level that a dictionary based approach can have, and it is currently unknown how this bound can be removed.

We foresee our future research on blog polarity proceeding in two main directions. First, we would like to experiment with classifying blog reviews according to a four or five star rating, as opposed to a simple binary classification scheme. Another, more challenging avenue of research would be to extend our application to take into account the user's attitudes and preferences toward specific genres, actors or actresses. Following Sato, Anse and Tabe [18], we could use *Kansei Engineering* to determine the relationship between one's movie tastes and certain features that are present in movies they have already seen. These relationships can then be exploited and extrapolated onto new, unseen movies, and our visualizations could transform the initial, general classifications into user-specific classifications, and in essence, turn *eNulog* into a recommender system.

References

1. Tirapat, T., Espiritu, C., Stroulia, E.: Taking the Community's Pulse, One Blog at a Time. In: Proceedings of the Sixth International Conference on Web Engineering, Palo Alto, CA, July 2006, pp. 169–176 (2006)
2. Kennedy, A., Inkpen, D.: Sentiment Classification of Movie and Product Reviews Using Contextual Valence Shifters. Computational Intelligence, 110–125 (2006)
3. Turney, P.: Thumbs Up or Thumbs Down? Semantic Orientation Applied to Unsupervised Classification of Reviews. In: Proceedings of ACL, Philadelphia, PA, July 2002, pp. 417–424 (2002)
4. Kamps, J., Marx, M., Mokken, R.J.: Using WordNet to Measure Semantic Orientation of Adjectives. In: LREC 2004, vol. IV, pp. 1115–1118 (2004)
5. Hatzivassiloglou, V., Wiebe, J.: Effects of Adjective Orientation and Gradability on Sentence Subjectivity. In: Proceedings of the 18th International Conference on Computational Linguistics, New Brunswick, NJ (2000)
6. Andreevskaia, A., Bergler, S., Urseanu, M.: All Blogs Are Not Made Equal: Exploring Genre Differences in Sentiment Tagging of Blogs. In: International Conference on Weblogs and Social Media (ICWSM-2007), Boulder, CO (2007)
7. Turney, P.D., Littman, M.L.: Measuring Praise and Criticism: Inference of Semantic Orientation from Association. ACM Transactions on Information Systems, 315–346 (2003)
8. Akshay, J.: A Framework for Modeling Influence, Opinions and Structure in Social Media. In: Proceedings of the Twenty-Second AAAI Conference on Artificial Intelligence, Vancouver, BC, July 2007, pp. 1933–1934 (2007)
9. Durant, K., Smith, M.: Mining Sentiment Classification from Political Web Logs. In: Proceedings of Workshop on Web Mining and Web Usage Analysis of the 12th ACM SIGKDD International Conference on Knowledge Discovery and Data Mining (WebKDD-2006), Philadelphia, PA (August 2006)
10. Stone, P.J., Dunphy, D.C., Smith, M.S.: The General Inquirer: A Computer Approach to Content Analysis. MIT Press, Cambridge (1966)
11. Yahoo! Search Web Services (October 2007),
    Online http://developer.yahoo.com/search/
12. Pang, B., Lee, L., Vaithyanathan, S.: Thumbs Up? Sentiment Classification Using Machine Learning Techniques. In: Proceedings of EMNLP-02, Association for Computational Linguistics, Philadelphia, PA, pp. 79–86 (2002)
13. No Title (October 2007),
    Online http://tartarus.org/~martin/PorterStemmer/java.txt
14. Fellbaum, C.: WordNet: An Electronic Lexical Database. Language, Speech, and Communication Series. MIT Press, Cambridge (1998)
15. Toutanova, K., Manning, C.D.: Enriching the Knowledge Sources Used in a Maximum Entropy Part-of-Speech Tagger. In: Proceedings of EMNLP/VLC-2000, Hong Kong, China, pp. 63–71 (2000)
16. Witten, H., Frank, E.: Data Mining: Practical Machine Learning Tools and Techniques, 2nd edn. Morgan Kaufmann, San Francisco (2005)
17. Joachims, T.: Making Large-Scale SVM Learning Practical. In: Schölkopf, B., Burges, C., Smola, A. (eds.) Advances in Kernel Methods - Support Vector Learning, pp. 169–184. MIT-Press, Cambridge (1999)
18. Sato, N., Anse, M., Tabe, T.: A Method for Constructing a Movie-Selection Support System Based on Kansei Engineering. In: Smith, M.J., Salvendy, G. (eds.) HCII 2007. LNCS, vol. 4557, pp. 526–534. Springer, Heidelberg (2007)

Some Simplified Forms of Reasoning with Distance-Based Entailments

Ofer Arieli[1] and Anna Zamansky[2],[*]

[1] Department of Computer Science, The Academic College of Tel-Aviv, Israel
oarieli@mta.ac.il
[2] Department of Computer Science, Tel-Aviv University, Israel
annaz@post.tau.ac.il

Abstract. Distance semantics is a robust way of handling dynamically evolving and possibly contradictory information. In this paper we show that in many cases distance-based entailments can be computerized in a general and modular way. We consider two different approaches for reasoning with distance semantics, apply them on some common cases, and show their relation to other known problems.

1 Introduction

Distance semantics has a prominent role in reflecting the rationality behind the principle of minimal change. This is a primary motif in different areas, such as belief revision, database integration, and decision making in the context of social choice theory. While there is no consensus about the exact nature of this semantics and the properties that it should satisfy, some particular distance-based approaches have been extensively used in those areas and are more common in practice. As shown in [1,2], many of these distance-based semantics have similar representations in terms of entailment relations, so it is not surprising that similar computational forms may be used for providing reasoning platforms in those cases. The goal of this paper is therefore to consider some of the *computational aspects* behind these approaches, that is: to identify some general principles for distance computations and apply them on some specific, nevertheless common test cases. For this, we consider the following two reasoning paradigms:

- *Deductive systems.* This traditional approach to automated reasoning should be taken with care in our context, as many classically valid rules do not hold when distance semantics is involved. Consider, for instance, an inference system for majority votes, in which ψ follows from Γ if there are more formulas in Γ implying ψ than those implying $\neg\psi$. As it is shown below, this consideration can be used for a distance semantics. Yet, it is evident that this system is neither reflexive nor monotonic (p follows from $\{p\}$ but not from $\{p, \neg p\}$). Moreover, it is not even closed under logical equivalence as, e.g., $\{p, \neg p\}$ and $\{p, p, \neg p\}$ have different conclusions (which also invalidates

[*] Supported by the Israel Science Foundation, grant No. 809–06.

S. Bergler (Ed.): Canadian AI 2008, LNAI 5032, pp. 36–47, 2008.
© Springer-Verlag Berlin Heidelberg 2008

the contraction rule in this case). This example indicates that even sound systems for distance semantics, based on structural rules, are hard to get.

In what follows, we shall define a sound and complete system for one case (minmax reasoning with uniform distances), and consider some useful sound systems for other distance semantics. For the latter, we shall consider situations in which automated solvers for known problems may be incorporated for reaching completeness.

– *Set computations.* The other approach for reasoning with distance semantics is based on computations of a minimal nonempty intersection of sets of interpretations. The elements of each set are equally distant from the formulas that they evaluate, and the minimal nonempty intersection of those sets determines the valuations that are 'closest' to the premises. This idea resembles that of Grove [5], who defines revision in terms of set intersections. We introduce iterative processes for computing those intersections for different distance-based settings, and show the correspondence between this problem and similar problems in the context of constraint programming.

In this paper, we consider a general framework for reasoning with distance semantics and concentrate on three common cases: minmax reasoning, reasoning by voting, and reasoning by summations of distances. Each of these reasoning strategies is augmented with different distances (metrics), and algorithms for computing entailments induced by these settings are provided. It is shown that in some cases distance semantics is reducible to other well-known problems (e.g., a variation of maxSAT), and so off-the-shelf solvers for those problems may be useful for distance-based reasoning as well.

2 Distance-Based Semantics

2.1 Preliminaries

We fix a propositional language $\mathcal{L}$ with a finite set $\mathsf{Atoms} = \{p_1, \ldots, p_m\}$ of atomic formulas. A finite multiset of formulas in $\mathcal{L}$ is called a *theory*. For a theory Γ, we denote by $\mathsf{Atoms}(\Gamma)$ the set of atomic formulas that occur in Γ. The set of valuations for $\mathcal{L}$ is $\Lambda = \{\langle p_1 : a_1, \ldots, p_m : a_m\rangle \mid a_1, \ldots, a_m \in \{t, f\}\}$. The set of models of a formula ψ is a subset of Λ, defined as follows:

$$\mathsf{mod}(p_i) = \{\langle p_1 : a_1, \ldots, p_i : t, \ldots, p_m : a_m\rangle \mid a_1, \ldots, a_{i-1}, a_{i+1}, \ldots, a_m \in \{t, f\}\},$$
$$\mathsf{mod}(\neg\psi) = \Lambda \setminus \mathsf{mod}(\psi),$$
$$\mathsf{mod}(\psi \wedge \varphi) = \mathsf{mod}(\psi) \cap \mathsf{mod}(\varphi),$$
$$\mathsf{mod}(\psi \vee \varphi) = \mathsf{mod}(\psi) \cup \mathsf{mod}(\varphi).$$

For a theory $\Gamma = \{\psi_1, \ldots, \psi_n\}$ we define $\mathsf{mod}(\Gamma) = \mathsf{mod}(\psi_1) \cap \ldots \cap \mathsf{mod}(\psi_n)$.

For defining distance-based entailments we recall the definitions in [1,2].

Definition 1. A *pseudo-distance* on U is a total function $d : U \times U \to \mathbb{N}$ so that for all $\nu, \mu \in U$ $d(\nu, \mu) = d(\mu, \nu)$ (symmetry), and $d(\nu, \mu) = 0$ iff $\nu = \mu$ (identity preservation). A *distance* (metric) d on U is a pseudo-distance that satisfies the triangular inequality: for all $\nu, \mu, \sigma \in U$, $d(\nu, \sigma) \leq d(\nu, \mu) + d(\mu, \sigma)$.

Example 1. It is easy to verify that the following functions are distances on the space Λ of two-valued valuations on Atoms:

- *The drastic distance:* $d_U(\nu, \mu) = 0$ if $\nu = \mu$ and $d_U(\nu, \mu) = 1$ otherwise.
- *The Hamming distance:* $d_H(\nu, \mu) = |\{p \in \text{Atoms} \mid \nu(p) \neq \mu(p)\}|$.

Definition 2. A *numeric aggregation function* is a total function f whose argument is a multiset of real numbers and whose values are real numbers, such that: (i) f is non-decreasing in the value of its argument, (ii) $f(\{x_1, \ldots, x_n\}) = 0$ iff $x_1 = x_2 = \ldots x_n = 0$, and (iii) $f(\{x\}) = x$ for every $x \in \mathbb{R}$.

Aggregation functions are, e.g., summation, average, maximum, and so forth.

Notation 1. Given a finite set S and a (pseudo) distance d, denote: $\text{max}_d S = \max\{d(s_1, s_2) \mid s_1, s_2 \in S\}$.

Definition 3. Given a theory $\Gamma = \{\psi_1, \ldots, \psi_n\}$, a valuation $\nu \in \Lambda$, a pseudo-distance d, and an aggregation function f, define:

$$- d(\nu, \psi_i) = \begin{cases} \min\{d(\nu, \mu) \mid \mu \in \text{mod}(\psi_i)\} & \text{if } \text{mod}(\psi_i) \neq \emptyset, \\ 1 + \text{max}_d \Lambda & \text{otherwise.} \end{cases}$$

$$- \delta_{d,f}(\nu, \Gamma) = f(\{d(\nu, \psi_1), \ldots, d(\nu, \psi_n)\}).$$

Note 1. In the two extreme degenerate cases, when ψ is either a tautology or a contradiction, all the valuations are equally distant from ψ. In the other cases, the valuations that are closest to ψ are its models and their distance to ψ is zero. This also implies that $\delta_{d,f}(\nu, \Gamma) = 0$ iff $\nu \in \text{mod}(\Gamma)$ (see [2]).

The next definition captures the intuition that the relevant interpretations of a theory Γ are those that are $\delta_{d,f}$-closest to Γ (see also [9]).

Definition 4. The *most plausible valuations* of Γ (with respect to a pseudo distance d and an aggregation function f) are defined as follows:

$$\Delta_{d,f}(\Gamma) = \begin{cases} \{\nu \in \Lambda \mid \forall \mu \in \Lambda \ \delta_{d,f}(\nu, \Gamma) \leq \delta_{d,f}(\mu, \Gamma)\} & \text{if } \Gamma \neq \emptyset, \\ \Lambda & \text{otherwise.} \end{cases}$$

Distance-based entailments are now defined as follows:

Definition 5. For a pseudo distance d and an aggregation function f, define $\Gamma \models_{d,f} \psi$ if $\Delta_{d,f}(\Gamma) \subseteq \text{mod}(\psi)$.[1]

Example 2. Let $\Gamma = \{p, \neg p, q\}$. As q is not related to the contradiction in Γ, there is no intuitive justification for concluding $\neg q$ from Γ. This, however, is not possible in classical logic, as Γ is not consistent. In our case, on the other hand, we have that $\Gamma \models_{d_U,\Sigma} q$ while $\Gamma \not\models_{d_U,\Sigma} \neg q$, $\Gamma \not\models_{d_U,\Sigma} p$ and $\Gamma \not\models_{d_U,\Sigma} \neg p$. Similar results are obtained for $\models_{d_H,\Sigma}$.

---

[1] I.e., conclusions should hold in *all* the most plausible valuations of the premises.

2.2   Computing Distance-Based Entailments

Proposition 1. *Denote by $\models$ the classical (two-valued) entailment. For every pseudo distance d and aggregation function f,*
(a) *If Γ is satisfiable, then $\Gamma \models_{d,f} \psi$ iff $\Gamma \models \psi$.*
(b) *For every Γ there is a ψ such that $\Gamma \not\models_{d,f} \psi$.*

Proof (outline). Part (a) follows from the fact that $d(\nu, \psi) = 0$ iff $\nu \in \mathsf{mod}(\psi)$ and $\delta_{d,f}(\nu, \Gamma) = 0$ iff $\nu \in \mathsf{mod}(\Gamma)$. Thus, Γ is satisfiable iff $\Delta_{d,f}(\Gamma) = \mathsf{mod}(\Gamma)$ (see also [2]). Part (b) follows from the fact that for every Γ, $\Delta_{d,f}(\Gamma) \neq \emptyset$ (as Λ is finite, there are always valuations that are minimally $\delta_{d,f}$-distant from Γ). $\square$

Taken together, the two items of Proposition 1 imply that every entailment relation induced by our framework coincides with the classical entailment with respect to consistent premises, while (unlike classical logic) it is not trivial with respect to inconsistent theories. Thus, one cannot hope for better complexity results than those for the classical propositional logic, as for consistent premises the entailment problem is coNP-Complete. On the other hand, it is clear from Definition 5 and the fact that Λ is finite, that for computable distances and aggregation functions, distance-based reasoning for finite propositional languages is in EXP, i.e., it is decidable with (at most) exponential complexity.

The purpose of this work is, therefore, to consider some useful distance-based settings for which there are some *practical* ways of computing entailments. In particular, we consider some cases in which distance-based reasoning is reducible to the question of satisfiability, and so off-the-shelf SAT-solvers may be incorporated for automated computations of distance-based consequences. For this, we first need the following definitions:

Definition 6. Let d be a pseudo distance. Define a function $\mathcal{R}_d : \mathcal{L} \times \mathbb{N} \to 2^{\Lambda}$ by $\mathcal{R}_d(\psi, i) = \{\mu \mid \exists \nu \in \mathsf{mod}(\psi) \; d(\mu, \nu) \leq i\}$. Also, let $\mathcal{R}_d^0(\psi) = \mathcal{R}_d(\psi, 0)$ and $\mathcal{R}_d^i(\psi) = \mathcal{R}_d(\psi, i) \setminus \mathcal{R}_d(\psi, i - 1)$ for any $i \in \mathbb{N}^+$.

Note 2. For any ψ, the sequence $\mathcal{R}_d(\psi, i)$ is non-decreasing in i (with respect to set inclusion). Also, for every satisfiable ψ and $i \in \mathbb{N}$, $\nu \in \mathcal{R}_d^i(\psi)$ iff $d(\nu, \psi) = i$. Thus, for a satisfiable ψ, $\mathcal{R}_d^0(\psi) = \mathsf{mod}(\psi) = \Delta_{d,f}(\psi)$, and $\mathcal{R}_d(\psi, k) = \Lambda$ for $k = \mathsf{max}_d \Lambda$. If ψ is not satisfiable, then $\mathcal{R}_d(\psi, i) = \mathcal{R}_d^i(\psi) = \emptyset$ for every i.

Lemma 1. *If all the formulas in a theory $\Gamma = \{\psi_1, \dots, \psi_n\}$ are satisfiable, then there is some $0 \leq k \leq \mathsf{max}_d \Lambda$, such that $\bigcap_{1 \leq i \leq n} \mathcal{R}_d(\psi_i, k) \neq \emptyset$.*

Proof. By Note 2, for every $1 \leq i \leq n$ there is a $k_i \leq \mathsf{max}_d \Lambda$ such that for every $j \geq k_i$, $\mathcal{R}_d(\psi_i, j) = \Lambda$. Let $k = \mathsf{max}\{k_i \mid 1 \leq i \leq n\}$. Then $\mathcal{R}_d(\psi, k) = \Lambda$ for all $1 \leq i \leq n$, and so $\bigcap_{1 \leq i \leq n} \mathcal{R}_d(\psi_i, j) = \Lambda$. $\square$

Definition 7. A pseudo distance d is called *inductively representable*, if there is a computable function $\mathsf{G} : 2^{\Lambda} \to 2^{\Lambda}$ such that for every formula ψ and every $i \in \mathbb{N}$, $\mathcal{R}_d(\psi, i) = \mathsf{G}(\mathcal{R}_d(\psi, i - 1))$. G is called an *inductive representation* of d.

Example 3. As Propositions 6 and 9 below show, both d_U and d_H are inductively representable.

3   MinMax Reasoning

In this section we study distance-based reasoning by min-max methods, that is: minimization of maximal distances. This kind of reasoning may be viewed as a skeptical approach, since it minimizes worst cases (maximal distances). Distance entailments of this type are induced by the max aggregation function.

3.1   Inductively Representable Distances

Min-max distance-based reasoning is characterized as follows: [2]

Proposition 2. *For any pseudo distance d and theory $\Gamma = \{\psi_1, \ldots, \psi_n\}$,*

a) *If there is a non-satisfiable element in Γ, then $\Delta_{d,\max}(\Gamma) = \Lambda$.*

b) *If all the elements in Γ are satisfiable, then $\Delta_{d,\max}(\Gamma) = \bigcap_{1 \leq i \leq n} \mathcal{R}_d(\psi_i, m)$, where m is the minimal number such that $\bigcap_{1 \leq i \leq n} \mathcal{R}_d(\psi_i, m)$ is not empty.*

Corollary 1. *For every pseudo distance d and a theory Γ of satisfiable formulas, $\Delta_{d,\max}(\Gamma) = \bigcap_{1 \leq i \leq n} \mathcal{R}_d(\psi_i, m)$, where $m = \min\{\delta_{d,\max}(\nu, \Gamma) \mid \nu \in \Lambda\}$.*

In case that d is inductively representable by G, the results above induce the iterative procedure in Figure 1, for computing $\Delta_{d,\max}(\Gamma)$:

MPV$(\mathsf{G}, \{\psi_1, \ldots, \psi_n\})$

    /* Most Plausible Valuations of $\{\psi_1, \ldots, \psi_n\}$ w.r.t. d and max */
    /* G – an inductive representation of d */

    for $i \in \{1, \ldots, n\}$: $X_i \leftarrow \mathsf{mod}(\psi_i)$
    if X_j is empty for some $j \in \{1, \ldots, n\}$, return Λ
    while $(X_1 \cap \ldots \cap X_n)$ is nonempty:
        for $i \in \{1, \ldots, n\}$: $X_i \leftarrow \mathsf{G}(X_i)$
    return $(X_1 \cap \ldots \cap X_n)$

Fig. 1. Computing the most plausible valuations of $\{\psi_1, \ldots, \psi_n\}$ w.r.t. d and max

Proposition 3. *If d is inductively representable by G, then for every theory Γ, **MPV**(G, Γ) terminates after at most $\max_d \Lambda$ iterations and computes $\Delta_{d,\max}(\Gamma)$.*

Proof. It is easy to see that in the i-th iteration it holds that $X_j = \mathcal{R}_d(\psi_j, i)$ for every $1 \leq j \leq n$. Hence, by Lemma 1, the condition in the loop is satisfied after at most $\max_d \Lambda$ iterations, and so the procedure always terminates. Also, by Proposition 2, the procedure returns $\Delta_{d,\max}(\Gamma)$.   □

Note 3. It holds that $\Delta_{d,\max}(\Gamma) = \Delta_{d,\max}(\Gamma \setminus \{\varphi\})$ for every tautology $\varphi \in \Gamma$. Thus, in the computations above, tautological formulas may be disregarded.

---

[2] Due to a lack of space some proofs are omitted.

3.2   Uniform Distances

In this section we consider uniform distances, a generalization of the drastic distance (see Example 1).

Definition 8. A distance d on Λ is called *uniform*, if there is some $k_d > 0$, s.t.:

$$d(\nu, \mu) = \begin{cases} 0 & \text{if } \nu = \mu, \\ k_d & \text{otherwise.} \end{cases}$$

Proposition 4. *Let d be a uniform distance and $\Gamma = \{\psi_1, \ldots, \psi_n\}$. Then:*

$$\Delta_{d,\text{max}}(\Gamma) = \begin{cases} \text{mod}(\Gamma) & \text{if mod}(\Gamma) \neq \emptyset, \\ \Lambda & \text{otherwise.} \end{cases}$$

Proof. If $\text{mod}(\Gamma) \neq \emptyset$, then $\Delta_{d,f}(\Gamma) = \text{mod}(\Gamma)$ for *every* d and f (see [2]). Otherwise, there is at least on element in Γ that is not satisfiable, and so, for every valuation $\mu \in \Lambda$, $\delta_{d,\text{max}}(\mu, \Gamma) = \text{max}\{d(\mu, \psi_1), \ldots, d(\mu, \psi_n)\} = k_d$. It follows, then, that in this case $\Delta_{d,\text{max}}(\Gamma) = \Lambda$. $\square$

Proposition 4 implies that for describing reasoning with uniform distances under the minmax strategy, it is enough to examine the drastic distance (and so henceforth we focus only on d_U):

Corollary 2. *For any uniform distances d_1, d_2 and any theory Γ, $\Delta_{d_1,\text{max}}(\Gamma) = \Delta_{d_2,\text{max}}(\Gamma)$. Thus, for every formula ψ, $\Gamma \models_{d_1,\text{max}} \psi$ iff $\Gamma \models_{d_2,\text{max}} \psi$.*

Another consequence of Proposition 4 is that $\models_{d_U,\text{max}}$ is strongly paraconsistent: only tautological formulas follow from inconsistent theories:

Corollary 3. *If Γ is inconsistent, then $\Gamma \models_{d_U,\text{max}} \psi$ iff ψ is a tautology.*

Proof. Suppose that Γ is not consistent. By Proposition 4, $\Delta_{d_U,\text{max}}(\Gamma) = \Lambda$, and so $\Gamma \models_{d_U,\text{max}} \psi$ iff $\Delta_{d_U,\text{max}}(\Gamma) \subseteq \text{mod}(\psi)$, iff $\text{mod}(\psi) = \Lambda$, iff ψ is a tautology. $\square$

By Proposition 1 and Corollary 3 we conclude that reasoning with uniform distances under the minmax strategy has a somewhat 'crude nature': either the set of premises is classically consistent, in which case the set of conclusions coincides with that of the classical entailment, or, in case of contradictory premises, only tautologies are entailed. It follows that in this case questions of satisfiability and logical entailment are reducible to similar problems in standard propositional logic, and distance considerations do not cause further computational complications. Moreover, standard SAT-solvers and theorem provers may be incorporated for implementing this kind of reasoning.

Next we provide two methods for computerized reasoning in this case. One is based on the procedure **MPV** defined in the previous section, and the other is based on deduction systems.

Proposition 5. *If ψ is satisfiable, then $\mathcal{R}_{d_U}(\psi, 0) = \text{mod}(\psi)$ and $\mathcal{R}_{d_U}(\psi, i) = \Lambda$ for every $i > 0$.*

Proposition 6. *The function* $\mathsf{G}_U : 2^\Lambda \to 2^\Lambda$ *defined by* $\mathsf{G}_U(V) = \Lambda$ *for all* $V \subseteq \Lambda$, *is an inductive representation of* d_U.

Proof. Immediate from Proposition 5. $\qquad\qquad\qquad\qquad\qquad\qquad\square$

Corollary 4. *For every theory* Γ, *the procedure* $\mathbf{MPV}(\mathsf{G}_U, \Gamma)$ *terminates after at most* $\max_{d_U} \Lambda$ *iterations and computes* $\Delta_{d_U,\max}(\Gamma)$.

Proof. By Propositions 3 and 6. $\qquad\qquad\qquad\qquad\qquad\qquad\qquad\qquad\square$

Another way of computing consequences of the entailment relation $\models_{d_U,\max}$ is by the deduction system $\mathbf{S}^{\mathbf{u}}_{\max}$, defined in Figure 2. This system manipulates expressions of the form $\Gamma : V$, where Γ is a theory and $V \subseteq \Lambda$.

- Axioms:

$$\emptyset : \Lambda \qquad\qquad\qquad\qquad (A_0)$$
$$\{\psi\} : \mathsf{mod}(\psi) \quad \text{if } \mathsf{mod}(\psi) \neq \emptyset \ (A_1)$$
$$\{\psi\} : \Lambda \qquad \text{if } \mathsf{mod}(\psi) = \emptyset \ (A_2)$$

- Inference Rules:

$$\frac{\Gamma_1 : V_1 \quad \Gamma_2 : V_2}{\Gamma_1 \cup \Gamma_2 : V_1 \cap V_2} \quad \text{if } \mathsf{mod}(\Gamma_1 \cup \Gamma_2) \neq \emptyset \ (I_1)$$

$$\frac{\Gamma_1 : V_1 \quad \Gamma_2 : V_2}{\Gamma_1 \cup \Gamma_2 : \Lambda} \quad \text{if } \mathsf{mod}(\Gamma_1 \cup \Gamma_2) = \emptyset \ (I_2)$$

Fig. 2. The system $\mathbf{S}^{\mathbf{u}}_{\max}$

Definition 9. For a theory Γ and a set $V \subseteq \Lambda$, denote by $\vdash_{\mathbf{S}^{\mathbf{u}}_{\max}} \Gamma : V$ that $\Gamma : V$ is provable in $\mathbf{S}^{\mathbf{u}}_{\max}$, and by $\Gamma \vdash_{\mathbf{S}^{\mathbf{u}}_{\max}} \psi$ that $\vdash_{\mathbf{S}^{\mathbf{u}}_{\max}} \Gamma : V$ for some $V \subseteq \mathsf{mod}(\psi)$.

Example 4. Let $\Gamma = \{p, q, \neg p \wedge \neg q\}$. We show that $\Gamma \vdash_{\mathbf{S}^{\mathbf{u}}_{\max}} p \vee \neg p$. Indeed,

$$\frac{\dfrac{p : \{\langle p : t, q : t\rangle, \langle p : t, q : f\rangle\} \quad q : \{\langle p : t, q : t\rangle, \langle p : f, q : t\rangle\}}{\neg p \wedge \neg q : \{p : f, q : f\} \quad p, q : \{\langle p : t, q : t\rangle\}} \ (I_1)}{p, q, \neg p \wedge \neg q : \Lambda} \ (I_2)$$

Thus, $\Gamma \vdash_{\mathbf{S}^{\mathbf{u}}_{\max}} \psi$ iff $\mathsf{mod}(\psi) = \Lambda$. In particular, $\Gamma \vdash_{\mathbf{S}^{\mathbf{u}}_{\max}} p \vee \neg p$.

Proposition 7 (soundness and completeness). $\Gamma \models_{d_U,\max} \psi$ iff $\Gamma \vdash_{\mathbf{S}^{\mathbf{u}}_{\max}} \psi$.

Proof (outline). The main observation is that for every theory Γ, $\vdash_{\mathbf{S}^{\mathbf{u}}_{\max}} \Gamma : V$ iff $V = \Delta_{d_U,\max}(\Gamma)$. This immediately implies the proposition, since if $\Gamma \models_{d_U,\max} \psi$ then $\Delta_{d_U,\max}(\Gamma) \subseteq \mathsf{mod}(\psi)$. By the observation above, $\Gamma : \Delta_{d,\max}(\Gamma)$ is provable in $\mathbf{S}^{\mathbf{u}}_{\max}$, and so $\Gamma \vdash_{\mathbf{S}^{\mathbf{u}}_{\max}} \psi$. Conversely, if $\Gamma \vdash_{\mathbf{S}^{\mathbf{u}}_{\max}} \psi$, then there is some $V \subseteq \mathsf{mod}(\psi)$ such that $\Gamma : V$ is provable in $\mathbf{S}^{\mathbf{u}}_{\max}$. By the main observation again, $V = \Delta_{d_U,\max}(\Gamma)$, thus $\Delta_{d_U,\max}(\Gamma) \subseteq \mathsf{mod}(\psi)$, and so $\Gamma \models_{d_U,\max} \psi$. $\qquad\square$

3.3 Hamming Distances

Next, we examine min-max reasoning with the Hamming distance d_H (see Example 1). First, we consider some important cases in which reasoning with Hamming distances coincides with reasoning with uniform distances.

Definition 10. Denote: $\mathbf{K}_i^n = \sum_{j=1}^i \binom{j}{n}$.

Definition 11. A formula ψ is *i-validated* for $i \in \mathbb{N}^+$, if among the $2^{|\mathsf{Atoms}(\psi)|}$ valuations on $\mathsf{Atoms}(\psi)$, at most $\mathbf{K}_i^{|\mathsf{Atoms}(\psi)|}$ valuations do *not* satisfy ψ.

Note 4. An i-validated formula ψ is also j-validated, for $1 \le i \le j \le |\mathsf{Atoms}(\psi)|$.

Example 5. Any tautology is 1-validated (thus it is i-validated for any i). Also, every literal (i.e., an atomic formula or its negation) is 1-validated. Moreover, as a disjunction of literals is either a tautology or is falsified by only one valuation,

Lemma 2. Every clause is 1-validated.

Proposition 8. *If Γ consists of 1-validated formulas, then for every aggregation function f and every formula ψ, $\Gamma \models_{d_H,f} \psi$ iff $\Gamma \models_{d_U,f} \psi$.*

Proof (outline). It is sufficient to show that for any 1-validated formula ψ and any $\mu \in \Lambda$, $d_H(\mu, \psi) = d_U(\mu, \psi)$. Indeed, if $\mu \in mod(\psi)$, $d_H(\mu, \psi) = d_U(\mu, \psi) = 0$. Otherwise, $\mu \notin mod(\psi)$, and so $d_H(\mu, \psi) = d_U(\mu, \psi) = 1$. This follows from the fact that if ψ is i-validated, then for every $\mu \in \Lambda$, $d_H(\mu, \psi) \le i$. $\qquad\square$

Corollary 5. *If Γ is a set of clauses, then*

- $\Gamma \models_{d_H,f} \psi$ iff $\Gamma \models_{d_U,f} \psi$ for every aggregation f and formula ψ,
- $\Gamma \models_{d_H,\max} \psi$ iff $\Gamma \vdash_{\mathsf{S}_{\max}^{\mathsf{u}}} \psi$.

Proof. The first item follows from Lemma 2 and Proposition 8; the second item follows from the first item and Proposition 7. $\qquad\square$

For 1-validated premises we therefore have a sound and complete proof system. The remainder of this section deals with the other cases.

Definition 12. For $\mu \in \Lambda$, denote by $\mathsf{Diff}(\mu, i)$ the set of valuations differing from μ in exactly i atoms.

The next result is an analogue, for Hamming distances, of Proposition 6.

Proposition 9. *The function $\mathsf{G}_H : 2^\Lambda \to 2^\Lambda$, defined for every $V \subseteq \Lambda$ by $\mathsf{G}_H(V) = V \cup \bigcup_{\mu \in V} \mathsf{Diff}(\mu, 1)$, is an inductive representation of d_H.*

Proof. Straightforward from the definition of $\mathcal{R}_{d_H}$. $\qquad\square$

Proposition 10. $\mathbf{MPV}(\mathsf{G}_H, \Gamma)$ *terminates after no more than $\max_{d_H} \Lambda$ iterations and returns $\Delta_{d_H,\max}(\Gamma)$. If Γ consists of i-validated formulas, $\mathbf{MPV}(\mathsf{G}_H, \Gamma)$ terminates after at most i iterations.*

Proof. The first part follows from Propositions 3 and 9. As for every $\mu \in \Lambda$ $d_H(\mu, \psi) \le i$ when ψ is i-validated, we have that $\mathcal{R}_{d_H}(\psi, i) = \Lambda$ for all $\psi \in \Gamma$. In the notations of Figure 1, then, after i iterations $X_1 \cap \ldots \cap X_n = \Lambda$, so $\mathbf{MPV}$ must terminate by the i-th iteration. $\qquad\square$

4   Reasoning by Voting

Definition 13. Given a multiset $D = \{d_1, \ldots, d_n\}$, denote the number of zeros in D by $\mathsf{Zero}(D)$. A $\frac{k}{m}$-*voting function* $\mathsf{vote}_{\frac{k}{m}}$, where $k < m \in \mathbb{N}$, is defined as follows:

$$\mathsf{vote}_{\frac{k}{m}}(D) = \begin{cases} 0 & \text{if } \mathsf{Zero}(D) = n, \\ \frac{1}{2} & \text{if } \lceil \frac{k}{m} n \rceil \leq \mathsf{Zero}(D) < n, \\ 1 & \text{otherwise.} \end{cases}$$

In what follows, we shall assume that the argument of $\mathsf{vote}_{\frac{k}{m}}$ is a multiset of elements in $\{0, 1\}$ (e.g., a multiset of drastic distances). In this case, it is easy to verify that $\mathsf{vote}_{\frac{k}{m}}$ is an aggregation function. Intuitively, $\mathsf{vote}_{\frac{k}{m}}$ simulates a poll and requires a quorum of at least $\lceil \frac{k}{m} \rceil$ of the 'votes' to determine implications of inconsistent theories. Indeed, if Γ is not consistent and there are valuations that satisfy at least $\lceil \frac{k}{m} \rceil$ of the elements of Γ, then $\Delta_{d_U, \mathsf{vote}_{\frac{k}{m}}}(\Gamma)$ contains all such valuations. Otherwise, $\Delta_{d_U, \mathsf{vote}_{\frac{k}{m}}}(\Gamma) = \Lambda$. It follows that for every $\frac{k}{m} \geq \frac{1}{2}$, $\mathsf{vote}_{\frac{k}{m}}$ acts as a *majority-vote function*.

Definition 14. Let $\Gamma = \{\psi_1, \ldots, \psi_n\}$. Let $\mathsf{Sub}_{\frac{k}{m}}(\Gamma)$ be the set of all subsets of Γ of size $\lceil \frac{k}{m} n \rceil$, and denote $\mathsf{mod}_{\frac{k}{m}}(\Gamma) = \bigcup_{H \in \mathsf{Sub}_{\frac{k}{m}}(\Gamma)} \mathsf{mod}(H)$.

Proposition 11. *For every theory* Γ,

$$\Delta_{d_U, \mathsf{vote}_{\frac{k}{m}}}(\Gamma) = \begin{cases} \mathsf{mod}(\Gamma) & \text{if } \mathsf{mod}(\Gamma) \neq \emptyset, \\ \mathsf{mod}_{\frac{k}{m}}(\Gamma) & \text{otherwise, if } \mathsf{mod}_{\frac{k}{m}}(\Gamma) \neq \emptyset, \\ \Lambda & \text{otherwise.} \end{cases}$$

By Proposition 11, $\Delta_{d_U, \mathsf{vote}_{\frac{k}{m}}}(\Gamma)$ is computable as follows:

Vote$_{\frac{k}{m}}(\{\psi_1, \ldots, \psi_n\})$

/* Most plausible valuations of $\{\psi_1, \ldots, \psi_n\}$ w.r.t. d_U and $\mathsf{vote}_{\frac{k}{m}}$ */

for $i \in \{1, \ldots, n\}$: $X_i \leftarrow \mathsf{mod}(\psi_i)$

$Y \leftarrow \emptyset$

if $(X_1 \cap \ldots \cap X_n)$ is nonempty, return $(X_1 \cap \ldots \cap X_n)$

for every subset $\mathbf{I}$ of $\{1, \ldots, n\}$ of size $\lceil \frac{k}{m} n \rceil$: $Y \leftarrow Y \cup \bigcap_{j \in \mathbf{I}} X_j$

if Y is nonempty return Y else return Λ

Fig. 3. Computing the most plausible valuations of $\{\psi_1, \ldots, \psi_n\}$ w.r.t. d_U and $\mathsf{vote}_{\frac{k}{m}}$

Proposition 12. **Vote**$_{\frac{k}{m}}(\Gamma)$ *always terminates and returns* $\Delta_{d_U, \mathsf{vote}_{\frac{k}{m}}}(\Gamma)$.

Proof. Immediately follows from Proposition 11.   □

5   Summation of Distances

Summation of distances is probably the most common approach for distance-based reasoning. In this section we consider this kind of reasoning. Again, we first consider the general case and then concentrate on more specific distances.

5.1   Arbitrary Pseudo Distances

Consider the system $\mathbf{S_\Sigma}$ in Figure 4. Again, $\mathbf{S_\Sigma}$ manipulates expressions of the form $\Gamma : V$, where Γ is a theory and $V \subseteq \Lambda$. We denote by $\Gamma \vdash_{\mathbf{S_\Sigma}} \psi$ that $\Gamma : V$ is provable in $\mathbf{S_\Sigma}$ (i.e., $\vdash_{\mathbf{S_\Sigma}} \Gamma : V$) for some $V \subseteq \mathsf{mod}(\psi)$.

- Axioms:

  $\emptyset : \Lambda$ (A_0)

  $\{\psi\} : \mathsf{mod}(\psi)$ if $\mathsf{mod}(\psi) \neq \emptyset$ (A_1)

  $\{\psi\} : \Lambda$ if $\mathsf{mod}(\psi) = \emptyset$ (A_2)

- Inference Rule:

  $$\frac{\Gamma_1 : V_1 \quad \Gamma_2 : V_2}{\Gamma_1 \cup \Gamma_2 : V_1 \cap V_2} \text{ if } V_1 \cap V_2 \neq \emptyset \quad (J_1)$$

Fig. 4. The system $\mathbf{S_\Sigma}$

Proposition 13 (soundness). *For every d, if $\Gamma \vdash_{\mathbf{S_\Sigma}} \psi$ then $\Gamma \models_{d,\Sigma} \psi$.*

Proof (outline). If $\Gamma \vdash_{\mathbf{S_\Sigma}} \psi$ then $\vdash_{\mathbf{S_\Sigma}} \Gamma : V$ for some $V \subseteq \mathsf{mod}(\psi)$. By induction on the length of the proof of $\Gamma : V$ in $\mathbf{S_\Sigma}$ one shows that this implies that $V = \Delta_{d,\Sigma}(\Gamma)$, and so $\Delta_{d,\Sigma}(\Gamma) \subseteq \mathsf{mod}(\psi)$. Thus, $\Gamma \models_{d,\Sigma} \psi$. $\qquad\square$

For another way of reasoning with summation of distances we note that, as in the case of max and the voting function, it is possible to characterize distance-summation conclusions by a set-theoretical condition.

Definition 15. Let d be an inductively representable pseudo distance. Denote: $\Omega_d^{i_1,\dots,i_n}(\{\psi_1,\dots,\psi_n\}) = \bigcap_{k=1}^n \mathcal{R}_d^{i_k}(\psi_i)$.

Proposition 14. *For an inductively representable pseudo distance d and a theory $\Gamma = \{\psi_1,\dots,\psi_n\}$, let m be the minimal number s.t. $\Omega_d^{i_1,\dots,i_n}(\{\psi_1,\dots,\psi_n\})$ is not empty for some sequence $i_1,\dots,i_n$ in which $\Sigma_{k=1}^n i_k = m$. Then $\Delta_{d,\Sigma}(\Gamma) = \bigcup_{j_1+\dots+j_n=m} \Omega_d^{j_1,\dots,j_n}(\Gamma)$.*

Proposition 14 indicates that reasoning with summation of distances is a constraint programming problem: given a theory $\Gamma = \{\psi_1,\dots,\psi_n\}$, the goal is to minimize the value of $\Sigma_{j=i}^n i_j$ for which the intersection $\mathcal{R}_d^{i_1}(\psi_1) \cap \dots \cap R_d^{i_n}(\psi_n)$ is not empty. Hence, CLP-solvers may be used here for checking entailments.

Note 5. For any pseudo distance d it holds that $\Delta_{d,\Sigma}(\Gamma) = \Delta_{d,\Sigma}(\Gamma \setminus \{\varphi\})$ whenever φ is a tautology or a contradiction. Thus, tautologies and contradictions have a degenerate role in the computations above (cf. Note 3).

5.2   Uniform Distances

As we show below, summation of uniform distances is closely related to the max-SAT problem.[3]

Definition 16. Let $\mathsf{SAT}(\Gamma)$ be the set of all the satisfiable multisets in Γ and $\mathsf{mSAT}(\Gamma)$ the set of the *maximally satisfiable* elements in $\mathsf{SAT}(\Gamma)$ (that is, $\mathsf{mSAT}(\Gamma)$ consists of all $\Upsilon \in \mathsf{SAT}(\Gamma)$ such that $|\Upsilon'| \leq |\Upsilon|$ for every $\Upsilon' \in \mathsf{SAT}(\Gamma)$). Denote: $\mathsf{mod}(\mathsf{mSAT}(\Gamma)) = \{\mu \in \Lambda \mid \mu \in \mathsf{mod}(\Upsilon)$ for some $\Upsilon \in \mathsf{mSAT}(\Gamma)\}$.

Note 6. Clearly, $\mathsf{mSAT}(\Gamma)$ is not empty whenever Γ has a satisfiable element. Also, all the elements in $\mathsf{mSAT}(\Gamma)$ have the same size.

Proposition 15. *Let d be a uniform distance. Then:*

$$\Delta_{d,\Sigma}(\Gamma) = \begin{cases} \mathsf{mod}(\mathsf{mSAT}(\Gamma)) & \text{if } \mathsf{mSAT}(\Gamma) \neq \emptyset, \\ \Lambda & \text{otherwise.} \end{cases}$$

By Proposition 15 we conclude the following:

- Entailments w.r.t. $\models_{d,\Sigma}$ may be computed by max-SAT solving techniques and by incorporating off-the shelf max-SAT solvers (see, e.g., [3,6,7,11]).
- As in the case of max, uniform distances behave similarly w.r.t. summation:

Corollary 6. *For any two uniform distances d_1, d_2 and a theory Γ, $\Delta_{d_1,\Sigma}(\Gamma)$ is the same as $\Delta_{d_2,\Sigma}(\Gamma)$, and so $\Gamma \models_{d_1,\Sigma} \psi$ iff $\Gamma \models_{d_2,\Sigma} \psi$.*

By the second item above, we may concentrate on the drastic distance d_U. Now, the system $\mathbf{S}_\Sigma$ defined in Figure 4 is not complete for $\models_{d_U,\Sigma}$, as its inference rule does not cover all the inter-relations among the premises. By Proposition 15, for a complete system one may add the following rule:

$$\frac{\Gamma_1 : V_1 \quad \Gamma_2 : V_2}{\Gamma_1 \cup \Gamma_2 : \mathsf{mod}(\mathsf{mSAT}(\Gamma_1 \cup \Gamma_2))} \text{ if } V_1 \cap V_2 = \emptyset \quad (J_2)$$

Obviously, (J_2) is not an inference rule in the usual sense, as its conclusion is not affected by V_1 and V_2. As such, this rule is not very useful. Yet, the combination of (J_1) and (J_2) may be helpful, e.g., in the context of belief revision, as:

a) if the condition of (J_1) is satisfied, the most plausible valuations of the revised theory should not be recomputed, and

b) if the condition of (J_1) is not met, (J_2) indicates the auxiliary source of computations, namely: revision can be determined by max-SAT calculations.

Definition 17. Denote by $\mathbf{S}_\Sigma^u$ the system $\mathbf{S}_\Sigma$ together with (J_2).

Proposition 16 (soundness and completeness). $\Gamma \vdash_{\mathbf{S}_\Sigma^u} \psi$ iff $\Gamma \models_{d_U,\Sigma} \psi$.

---

[3] The original formulation of max-SAT is about finding a valuation that satisfies a maximal set of clauses in a set Γ (see, e.g., [10] for some complexity results and [8] for related approximation methods). By the max-SAT problem in our context we mean an extended version of the problem, according to which one has to find *all* the valuations that satisfy a maximal set of *formulas* from a multiset Γ.

5.3   Hamming Distances

Summation of Hamming distances is very common in the context of belief revision and database integration. Yet, the deductive systems developed so far for this semantics are limited to a very narrow fragment of propositional languages. One example is the logic MF, introduced in [4], in which the premises are sets of literals. In this case, reasoning with $\models_{d_H,\Sigma}$ reduces to 'counting' majority votes:

Fact 1. Let Γ be a multiset of literals. Then $\Gamma \models_{d_H,\Sigma} \psi$ iff ψ is in the transitive closure of $\mathsf{Maj}(\Gamma)$, where $\mathsf{Maj}(\Gamma)$ consists of the literals in Γ whose number of appearances in Γ is strictly bigger than the appearances in Γ of their negations.

Based on this fact, the modal logic MF in [4] assumes that the set Γ of premises consists only of literals, and represents the fact that a literal l appears i times in Γ by the modal operator B_Γ^i. Then, l follows from Γ (l is believed; $B_\Gamma l$) if it holds that $B_\Gamma^i l \wedge B_\Gamma^j \neg l$ for some $i > j \geq 0$.

The following result suggests an alternative way for automated reasoning with summation of Hamming distances, in more general contexts:

Proposition 17. *For every theory Γ and a formula ψ we have that $\Gamma \models_{d_H,\Sigma} \psi$ if $\Gamma \vdash_{\mathbf{S}_\Sigma} \psi$. If Γ is a set of clauses, then $\Gamma \models_{d_H,\Sigma} \psi$ iff $\Gamma \vdash_{\mathbf{S}_\Sigma^u} \psi$.*

Proof. The first part of the proposition is a particular case of Proposition 13; The second part follows from Propositions 8 and 16.   □

Proposition 17 provides a first step toward automated reasoning with Hamming distances. More general techniques are a subject for future work.

References

1. Arieli, O.: Commonsense reasoning by distance semantics. In: Proc. TARK 2007, pp. 33–41 (2007)
2. Arieli, O.: Distance-based paraconsistent logics. International Journal of Approximate Reasoning (in press, 2008) doi = 10.1016/j.ijar.2007.07.002
3. Bonet, M.L., Levy, J., Manyá, F.: Resolution for Max-SAT. Artificial Intelligence 171(8–9), 606–618 (2007)
4. Cholvy, L., Garion, C.: A logic to reason on contradictory beliefs with a majority approach. In: IJCAI 2001 Workshop on Inconsistency in Data and Knowledge (2001)
5. Grove, A.: Two modellings for theory change. J. Phil. Logic 17, 157–180 (1988)
6. Heras, F., Larrosa, J.: New inference rules for efficient Max-SAT solving. In: Proc. AAAI 2006, pp. 68–73. AAAI Press, Menlo Park (2006)
7. Joy, S., Mitchell, J., Borchers, B.: A branch-and-cut algorithm for max-sat and weighted max-sat. Satisfiability Problem: Theory and Applications 35 (1997)
8. Karloff, H., Zwick, U.: A 7/8-approximation algorithm for MAX 3SAT? In: Proc. FOCS 1997, IEEE Press, Los Alamitos (1997)
9. Konieczny, S., Pino Pérez, R.: Merging information under constraints: a logical framework. Journal of Logic and Computation 12(5), 773–808 (2002)
10. Papadimitriou, C.: Computational complexity. Addison-Wesley, Reading (1994)
11. Xing, Z., Zhang, W.: axSolver: An efficient exact algorithm for (weighted) maximum satisfiability. Artificial Intelligence 164(1–2), 47–80 (2005)

A Belief-Theoretic Reputation Estimation Model for Multi-context Communities

Ebrahim Bagheri, M. Barouni-Ebrahimi, Reza Zafarani, and Ali A. Ghorbani

Faculty of Computer Science,
University of New Brunswick, Fredericton, Canada
{e.bagheri,m.barouni,r.zafarani,ghorbani}@unb.ca

Abstract. Online communities have grown to be an alternative form of communication for many people. This widespread growth and influence of the members of these communities in shaping the desire, line of thought and behavior of each other requires subtle mechanisms that are often easily attainable in face-to-face communications. In this paper, we address a special case of the trust-making process, where a person needs to make a judgment about the propositions, capabilities, or truthfulness of another community member where none of the community members has had any previous interaction with. Our proposed model estimates the possible reputation of a given identity in a new context by observing his/her behavior in the perspective of the other contexts of the community. This is most important for websites such as amazon.com, ebay.com, epinions.com, etc whose activities encompass multiple domains. Our proposed model employs Dempster-Shafer based valuation networks to represent a global reputation structure and performs a belief propagation technique to infer contextual reputation. The evaluation of the model on a dataset collected from epinions.com shows promising results.

1 Introduction

Reputation is a distributed, socially ascribed, and collective belief of a society towards the stand point of a single person, group, role or even a non-human entity within the context of that given society. Reputation is developed based on the general belief of society actors whether or not a given identity has fully satisfied the expectations of its roles. If an actor fails to comply with social standards and show acceptable performance, it will develop a negative reputation amongst the rest of the community members. Similarly, if the society develops a positive perception of that identity's effectiveness, it will be rewarded with the attribution of a positive reputation. A high degree of reputation directly contributes to the development of stronger social status and influence; however, a weak or even negative reputation discourages society members to develop the required trust for embarking on any social interaction with the reputation holder. It is hence to the participators high interest to optimize their performance to construct a positive social face. The notion of reputation has been employed in various application areas, such as electronic market places, peer to peer systems,

S. Bergler (Ed.): Canadian AI 2008, LNAI 5032, pp. 48–59, 2008.
© Springer-Verlag Berlin Heidelberg 2008

information sharing communities, and recommender systems, to name a few [2]. It is believed that the formalization of reputation is a context-dependent process. This means that the formal definition of reputation structure is reliant on contextual features, societal values, and environmental goals of the target domain where reputation is being defined and deployed.

Even though the assessment and ascription of reputation is fundamentally a process that relies on specific contextual values and norms, it is common practice within human societies, to consider one's reputation in a certain context to infer his/her reputation in other contexts. For instance, people with high reputation values in a particular context will be looked upon as successful and highly reputed members of the society even from the perspective of other contexts. This shows that while the formalization of reputation is to a great extent context-dependent, still the mutual effects of different contexts on each other cannot be overlooked. The independence of reputation formalization in different contexts on the one hand, and the obscure implicit relationship and effect of reputation in conceptually related contexts on the other hand, complicates the development of a global reputation value for each entity in multi-context environments.

Bagheri and Ghorbani [1] have proposed a framework for dynamically updating and inferring the unobserved reputation of environment participants in different contexts. This framework proposes the employment of a reputation structure tree to represent the relationship between the contexts of the environment. Reputation of a given identity in one context can be propagated to other contexts through two mechanisms, namely: *forward update* and *backward adjustment*. In this paper, we propose a framework based on *valuation networks* [7]. Global reputation is modeled as Dempster-Shafer belief functions on a *Markov tree* through which the relationship between various contexts of a unique environment are modeled through hyper-vertices of the Markov tree. Reputation of each identity in a given context is represented using a *belief mass assignment* function. The estimation of reputation in various contexts of the environment is performed by the employment of the message passing-based belief propagation model of the Shenoy-Shafer architecture [6].

The remainder of this paper is organized as follows: in the next section, some preliminaries are introduced. A structured problem definition and the organization of the proposed model is given in Section 3. The application of the proposed model to the epinions.com website is studied in Section 4. The paper is then concluded in Section 5.

2   Preliminaries

We define Θ_x as the state space of the variable x. Each variable x should have a finite state space, that is all the possible values for x are known. Given a set of variables denoted D, we let Θ_D represent the Cartesian product $\Theta_D = \times \{\Theta_x : x \in D\}$. Θ_D is called the state space of D; therefore, the members of Θ_D are configurations of D.

2.1 Basics of Dempster-Shafer Theory of Evidence

Dempster-Shafer (DS) theory of evidence is one of the most widely used models that provides means for approximate and collective reasoning under uncertainty [3]. The employment of the DS theory requires the definition of the set of all possible states in a given setting, referred to as the frame of discernment represented by θ_D. The powerset of θ_D, denoted 2^{θ_D}, incorporates all possible unions of the sets in θ_D that can receive belief mass.

Definition 1. *A belief mass assignment function is a mapping* $[\phi]_m : 2^{\theta_D} \rightarrow [0,1]$ *that assigns* $[\phi(A)]_m$ *to each subset* $A \in 2^{\theta_D}$ *such that:*

$$[\phi(A)]_m \geq 0, \tag{1}$$

$$[\phi(\varnothing)]_m = 0, \tag{2}$$

$$\sum_{A \in 2^{\theta}} [\phi(A)]_m = 1. \tag{3}$$

The belief in A is interpreted as the absolute faith in the truthfulness of A, which not only relies on the belief mass assigned to A but also to belief masses assigned to subsets of A.

Definition 2. *A belief function corresponding with* $[\phi(B)]_m$, *a belief mass assignment on* θ_D, *is a function* $[\phi]_b : 2^{\theta_D} \rightarrow [0,1]$ *defined as:*

$$[\phi(B)]_b = \sum_{A \subseteq B} [\phi(A)]_m, \quad A, B \in 2^{\theta_D}. \tag{4}$$

For any belief functions $[\phi]_b$ defined over D, D is called the domain of $[\phi]_b$. All subsets of Θ_D ($A \subseteq \Theta_D$) that satisfy $[\phi(A)]_m \neq 0$ are known as focal sets of Θ_D.

The fundamental operations of the Dempster-Shafer theory are the *combination* and the *marginalization* functions.

Definition 3. *Let* $[\phi(A)]_m$ *be a mass assignment function on domain* D *and let* $C \subseteq D$. *The marginalization of* $[\phi(A)]_b$ *to* C *produces a belief function over* C:

$$[\phi^{\downarrow C}(B)]_m = \sum_{A:A^{\downarrow C}=B} [\phi(A)]_m. \tag{5}$$

The base combination rule for multiple mass assignment functions within the framework of Dempster-Shafer theory of evidence is Dempster's rule of combination, which is a generalization of Bayes' rule [5]. This combination operator ignores the conflicts between the functions and emphasizes on their agreements.

Definition 4. *Let* $[\phi_1(A)]_m$ *and* $[\phi_2(A)]_m$ *be two mass assignment functions on domain* D_1 *and* D_2, *respectively. The non-normalized combination of these two functions produces a mass assignment function over* $D = D_1 \cup D_2$:

$$[\phi_1(A)]_m \oplus [\phi_2(A)]_m = \sum_{B_1, B2} \{ [\phi_1(B_1)]_m \cdot [\phi_2(B_2)]_m \;\; : \;\; B_1^{\uparrow D} \cap B_2^{\uparrow D} = A \}, \tag{6}$$

where $B^{\uparrow D}$ represents B extended to domain D. The normalized form of the combination operator is defined as:

$$[\phi_1(A)]_m \oplus [\phi_2(A)]_m = \frac{\sum_{B_1, B_2} \{[\phi_1(B_1)]_m \cdot [\phi_2(B_2)]_m : B_1^{\uparrow D} \cap B_2^{\uparrow D} = A\}}{1 - \sum_{B_1, B_2} \{[\phi_1(B_1)]_m \cdot [\phi_2(B_2)]_m : B_1^{\uparrow D} \cap B_2^{\uparrow D} = \varnothing\}}.$$

(7)

2.2 Belief Propagation

The corresponding domains of a set of mass assignment functions $[\phi_1]_m$, $[\phi_2]_m, ..., [\phi_n]_m$ form a hypergraph. From the hypergraph, a covering hypertree can be developed that can be employed to construct a Markov tree.

Definition 5. *Let $(\mathcal{V}, \mathcal{E})$ be a tree where $\mathcal{V}$ is the set of vertices, and $\mathcal{E}$ is the set of its edges. Each $v \in \mathcal{V}$ is itself a non-empty set; therefore, $\forall v \in \mathcal{V}$, v is a hypergraph. We call $(\mathcal{V}, \mathcal{E})$ a hypertree if the following conditions are satisfied:*

(1) $\mathcal{V}$ is a hypertree,
(2) if $(\{v, v'\} \in \mathcal{E})$ then $v \cap v' \neq \varnothing$,
(3) if v and v' are distinct vertices, and X is in both v and v', then X is in every vertex on the path from v to v'.

Each node of the Markov tree consists of a belief mass assignment function $[\phi_i]_m$ that operates over Domain D_i. Belief propagation in the Markov tree in the Shenoy-Shafer architecture is performed through a message passing scheme [6]; hence, each node in the Markov tree will possess the global mass assignment function $[\phi]_m = ([\phi_1]_m \oplus \cdots \oplus [\phi_n]_m)$ marginalized to its own domain D_i. In order to perform message passing, and enable local computation, two base operations: *marginalization* and *combination*, and three simple axioms, namely: *transitivity of marginalization, commutativity and associativity of combination*, and *distributivity of marginalization over combination* are required [4].

Belief propagation over a Markov tree structure (valuation network) can be performed by passing messages between tree nodes using the following two rules:

1) Each node sends a message to its neighbor. Let $\mu^{A \to B}$ be a message from A to B, and $\Phi(A)$ be the set of neighbors of A and the belief mass assignment of A be $[\phi_i(A)]_m$, then the passed message from A to B is defined as a combination of messages from all neighbors of A except B and the belief mass of A:

$$\mu^{A \to B} = \left(\oplus\{\mu^{X \to A} | X \in (\Phi(A) - \{B\}) \oplus [\phi_i(A)]_m\}\right)^{\downarrow A \cap B}$$

(8)

2) When node B receives messages from its neighbors, it combines all the received messages with its own belief mass and employs the result as its own marginal.

3   Model Overview

The model we propose in this paper, will formally address the following two issues: 1) The definition of a structure for permitting global reputation management through local-contextual reputation computations, 2) The development of a theoretical framework for the propagation of local-contextual reputation values as belief masses between different contexts. In Section 1, we informally mentioned that there are two main characteristics for multi-context reputation formalization that complicates the definition of a straightforward reputation estimation model, i.e. independence of reputation formalization in different contexts , and implicit relationship between reputation in conceptually related contexts. Here, we show how the reputation of various contexts of an environment can have implicit relationship and cross-context impact, while preserving their independence by definition. We first define the interpretation of contextual reputation.

Definition 6. *The interpretation of a contextual reputation CR_i for context i represented through a set of social (contextual) norms, denoted $\mathcal{N}$, is a pair (U, I) where U is the domain of interpretation of all contextual reputations CR, and I is a total morphism that maps $\forall \mathcal{N}_i \in \mathcal{N}$ onto a relation R.*

An interpretation of a contextual reputation relates each social (contextual) norm onto its corresponding underlying concept in the contextual domain of discourse; therefore, an interpretation conveys how the contextual reputation is understood with regards to the given domain of discourse based on context foundations.

Definition 7. *Let $\mathcal{N}_{i,k}$ and $\mathcal{N}_{j,l}$ be only two social norms of two different contextual reputation formalizations CR_i, and CR_j, and let $T_i = (U_i, I_i)$, and $T_j = (U_j, I_j)$ be interpretations of CR_i and CR_j, respectively. The implicit impact relationships between CR_i and CR_j can be defined as follows: With $I_i(\mathcal{N}_{i,k}) \neq \varnothing$, $I_j(\mathcal{N}_{j,l}) \neq \varnothing$:*

- *(no impact) $I_i(\mathcal{N}_{i,k}) \cap I_j(\mathcal{N}_{j,l}) = \varnothing$,*
- *(total impact) $I_i(\mathcal{N}_{i,k}) = I_j(\mathcal{N}_{j,l})$,*
- *(inclusive impact) $I_i(\mathcal{N}_{i,k}) \subseteq I_j(\mathcal{N}_{j,l})$,*
- *(partial impact) $I_i(\mathcal{N}_{i,k}) \cap I_j(\mathcal{N}_{j,l}) \neq \varnothing$, $I_i(\mathcal{N}_{i,k}) - I_j(\mathcal{N}_{j,l}) \neq \varnothing$, $I_j(\mathcal{N}_{j,l}) - I_i(\mathcal{N}_{i,k}) \neq \varnothing$.*

Definition 7 shows that two contextual reputations can only have implicit impact on each others behavior if the interpretation of their social norms have some degree of overlap; therefore, contexts with no overlapping social norms have no degree of effect on each other, while contexts with total overlapping social norm interpretations have total impact on each other. The degree of impact, denoted $\mathcal{DI}$, can be easily defined using the interpretation of contextual norms as:

$$\mathcal{DI}(I_i, I_j) = \frac{I_i(\mathcal{N}_i) \cap I_j(\mathcal{N}_j)}{I_i(\mathcal{N}_i) \cup I_j(\mathcal{N}_j)}. \tag{9}$$

Based on Definitions 6 and 7 global reputation for a specific environment comprising multiple contexts can be defined as a hypergraph.

Definition 8. *Let $\mathcal{EN}$ be an environment, and $\mathcal{C}_{\mathcal{EN}}$ be the set of all its contexts. Global reputation $\mathcal{GR}$ for $\mathcal{EN}$ is defined as a hypergraph $(\mathcal{V},\mathcal{E})$ where $\mathcal{V}$ is the set of all its vertices, and $\mathcal{E}$ all of its edges, such that $\mathcal{V} \equiv \mathcal{C}_{\mathcal{EN}}$, and $\forall \mathcal{C}_i, \mathcal{C}_j$ that $\mathcal{DI}(I_i, I_j) > 0$ then $\{\mathcal{C}_i, \mathcal{C}_j\} \in \mathcal{E}$.*

The global reputation hypergraph $\mathcal{GR}$ can then be reduced to a Markov tree to avoid loops while reputation is propagated between its contexts. The reduced hypergraph converted into a Markov tree is the final structure for global reputation representation denoted $\mathcal{GR}^m$.

Each hyperedge of the $\mathcal{GR}^m$ Markov tree contains the global reputation value marginalized to its constituting vertices (contexts), i.e. the reputation of a given entity can be calculated for the contexts in that hyperedge using the belief mass assignments of this hyperedge through marginalization. Suppose that $\mathcal{GR}^m$ only contains two contexts (vertices): $\mathcal{C}_{\mathcal{EN}}^1$, and $\mathcal{C}_{\mathcal{EN}}^2$, and only one hyperedge $\mathcal{E}_1 = \{\mathcal{C}_{\mathcal{EN}}^1, \mathcal{C}_{\mathcal{EN}}^2\}$. The reputation of a given entity can be calculated for any of the two contexts by marginalizing the belief mass assignments of $\mathcal{E}_1$ onto that specific context. For instance, a reputation in $\mathcal{C}_{\mathcal{EN}}^1$ can be calculated through $[\phi_{\mathcal{E}_1}^{\downarrow \mathcal{C}_{\mathcal{EN}}^1}]_m$, where $[\phi_{\mathcal{E}_1}]_m$ represents the belief mass assignment of $\mathcal{E}_1$.

In cases where $\mathcal{EN}$ consists of more than two contexts, and therefore, more than one hyperedge may exist, the process of local reputation computation over $\mathcal{GR}^m$ is more complex. In such a situation, the local belief mass assignments in each hyperedge of $\mathcal{GR}^m$ needs to be propagated to the target hyperedge (the hyperedge that requires the local-contextual reputation calculation) using the belief propagation scheme introduced in Section 2.2. Having received all the messages, the destination hyperedge that needs the computation of the local reputation value should compile all the messages into one belief mass assignment using Dempster's rule of combination. The resulting belief mass assignment can then be marginalized to the context of interest in order to calculate the local-contextual reputation. Figure 1 depicts the steps of this process.

In the following section, our experience in applying the proposed global reputation markov tree structure and the reputation propagation theme to compute and propagate reputation in the data collected from the epinions.com dataset is elaborated.

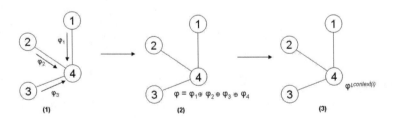

Fig. 1. Reputation Calculation for *Context i* in a Global Reputation Markov Tree

4   Experience with Epinions.com

For experimental purposes, we collected data from a popular online community: epinions.com. Epinions.com is a website that collects consumer experience reports and beliefs about various products. The users are able to participate in epinions.com by writing reviews about the products of different categories, rating the items, and also rating the previously written reviews. We collected information for $33,876$ distinct users from which only $25,541$ users had at least provided one review in the website. For each of the users up to 100 of their submitted reviews were also gathered. These reviews were from 71 different categories. Overall, $463,398$ reviews were accumulated. The dataset was structured as $\langle \mathcal{U}, \mathcal{C}, \mathcal{R} \rangle$, where $\mathcal{U}$, $\mathcal{C}$, and $\mathcal{R}$ represent the username, the category where the review was submitted, and the overall rating that the given review had received from the community, respectively.

The analysis of the collected dataset is complex, since most of the users in the epionions.com dataset suffer from the *cold start problem*, which is the submission of a very low number of reviews. Figure 2 shows that the majority of the users have submitted less than 10 reviews, and that their participation is limited on average to less than 8 categories from the set of 71 possible categories. Furthermore, it can be seen that the average number of reviews written by each user for a given category is less than 7. Comparing these statistics, we can trivially infer that since an average user typically submits around 10 reviews in epinions.com and 7 reviews for a category where he/she frequently participates, that the users of epinions.com are mostly concentrated on a specific category of their interest. For instance, although a user specializing in Music submits several ratings to categories such as Movie, Travel, Sport, and etc., his/her main contribution is towards the Music category. This issue makes the detection of conceptually related categories from the participation behavior of the users difficult.

In the following, assuming that each category of epinions.com is a context within the the online community environment, we will explain how *degree of impact*, $\mathcal{DI}$, for any two categories is calculated. The formalization of $\mathcal{DI}$ would provide the basis for crafting the global reputation markov tree structure for the categories.

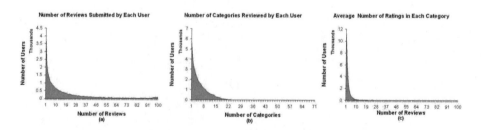

Fig. 2. The Behavior of the epinions.com Dataset

4.1 Formalizing the Degree of Impact ($\mathcal{DI}$)

Let us informally assume that two categories of an online community can be considered to have some shared underlying principles which make them conceptually equally appealing for the community if there are a common group of like-minded users in both of those categories. Based on this assumption, suppose there is a group of users $\mathcal{U}_c = \{u_1, ..., u_m\}$ that have reviewed items in category c, and each user has received $\mathcal{R}_{u,c} = \{r^u_{1,c}, ..., r^u_{n,c}\}$ ratings for his/her reviews in category c, while each user has submitted $\mathcal{N}_{u,c}$ reviews for that specific category. For any given two categories, we would believe them to be conceptually close, if the behavior of their shared users are similar, i.e. the number of ratings that each user submits in these two categories are alike ($\mathcal{N}_{u,c} \sim \mathcal{N}_{u,c'}$) and also the average rating received by that specific user is also similar in both categories ($\bar{r}_{i,c} \sim \bar{r}_{i,c'}$). Simply stated, we are looking for categories that have users with similar participation rate and review quality.

For each category $\mathcal{C}_i$, and the set of users participating in $\mathcal{C}_i$, denoted $\mathcal{U}_{c_i}$, we can form a set of data points $\Theta_{\mathcal{C},i} = \{\theta_{\mathcal{C}_i,1}, ..., \theta_{\mathcal{C}_i,n}\}$, where $\theta_{\mathcal{C}_i,u}$ for a given user $u \in \mathcal{U}_{c_i}$ is defined as follows:

$$\theta_{\mathcal{C}_i,u} = (\theta^x_{\mathcal{C}_i,u}, \theta^y_{\mathcal{C}_i,u}). \tag{10}$$

$$\theta^x_{\mathcal{C}_i,u} = \frac{\mathcal{N}_{u,\mathcal{C}_i}}{\sum_{c \in \mathcal{C}} \mathcal{N}_{u,c_i}}. \tag{11}$$

$$\theta^y_{c_i,u} = \frac{\sum_{j=1}^{\mathcal{N}_{u,c_i}} r^u_{j,c_i}}{\mathcal{N}_{u,c_i}}. \tag{12}$$

where $\theta^x_{\mathcal{C}_i,u}$ represents the fraction of effort that a given user u has spent in category $\mathcal{C}_i$, and $\theta^y_{\mathcal{C}_i,u}$ shows the average quality of the reviews written by user u in category $\mathcal{C}_i$ (ascribed by other community members in the form of ratings).

Figure 3 shows the overlapping distribution of the data points $(\theta_{\mathcal{C}_i,u})$ of categories: (Movie) and (Home and Garden) in (a), and (Electronics) and (Computer Hardware) in (b), respectively. As we observed and is also clear from Figure 3, the overlap of two distributions for any two categories produces a similar non-separable overlap pattern, which is undesirable when high discriminative power is required to distinguish between high impact and low impact categories.

To discriminate between the closely related and poorly associated categories, we perform an iterative normalization process on the data points of each category before comparing them. In each iteration the data points of the previous iteration are normalized and $\tilde{\Theta}^{i+1}_{\mathcal{C}_j} = \{\frac{\tilde{\theta}^i_{\mathcal{C}_j,1} - \mu_{\tilde{\Theta}^i_{\mathcal{C}_j}}}{\sigma_{\tilde{\Theta}^i_{\mathcal{C}_j}}}, ..., \frac{\tilde{\theta}^i_{\mathcal{C}_j,n} - \mu_{\tilde{\Theta}^i_{\mathcal{C}_j}}}{\sigma_{\tilde{\Theta}^i_{\mathcal{C}_j}}}\}$ is developed.

This process is continued until $|\mu_{\tilde{\Theta}^{i+1}_{\mathcal{C}_j}} - \mu_{\tilde{\Theta}^i_{\mathcal{C}_j}}| < \epsilon$ where $\mu_{\tilde{\Theta}^{i+1}_{\mathcal{C}_j}}$ and $\mu_{\tilde{\Theta}^i_{\mathcal{C}_j}}$ represent the average of values in $\tilde{\Theta}^i_{\mathcal{C}_j}$ and $\tilde{\Theta}^i_{\mathcal{C}_j}$, respectively. The result of this process can be seen in Figure 4 where in (a), the data points have been clearly separated (the majority of data points on the right are non-overlapping) while in (b) the

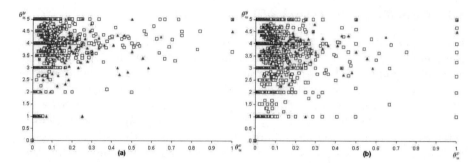

Fig. 3. The Non-normalized Overlapping Distribution for Different Categories: (Movie) and (Home and Garden) in (a), and (Electronics) and (Computer Hardware) in (b)

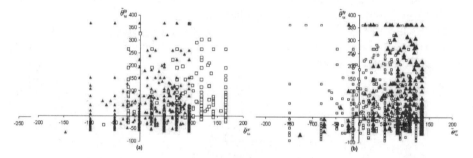

Fig. 4. The Normalized Overlapping Distribution for Different Categories: (Movie) and (Home and Garden) in (a), and (Electronics) and (Computer Hardware) in (b)

data points are totally overlapping, whereas this discrimination could not have been observed in Figure 3. The degree of overlap on these data distributions can show the degree of relative closeness of any two categories; therefore, it can be inferred from Figure 4 that categories (Electronics) and (Computer Hardware) are more closely related as compared to (Movie) and (Home and Garden). Let us now define the *degree of impact* ($\mathcal{DI}$) as the Euclidean distance of the centers of the distributions of each two categories; therefore, let $\wp_i$ and $\wp_j$ be the centers of the data point distributions of categories $\mathcal{C}_i$, and $\mathcal{C}_j$, the degree of impact of these two categories on each other, denoted $\mathcal{DI}_{\mathcal{C}_i,\mathcal{C}_j}$, is defined as:

$$\mathcal{DI}_{\mathcal{C}_i,\mathcal{C}_j} = \left(|\wp_i^x - \wp_j^x|^2 + |\wp_i^y - \wp_j^y|^2 \right)^{1/2}. \tag{13}$$

4.2 Forming the Global Reputation Markov Tree Structure

The degree of impact of two categories can be naïvely interpreted as a distance measure between two categories. With this interpretation, a fully connected weighted graph represented by an $n \times n$ matrix, $G_{\mathcal{EN}}$, where n is the number of categories in $\mathcal{EN}$, can be created such that:

$$G_{\mathcal{EN}}(\mathcal{C}_i, \mathcal{C}_i) = \infty, \tag{14}$$

$$G_{\mathcal{EN}}(\mathcal{C}_i, \mathcal{C}_j) = \mathcal{DI}_{\mathcal{C}_i, \mathcal{C}_j}. \tag{15}$$

Kruskal's algorithm was further applied on the formed matrix $G_{\mathcal{EN}}$, to find the minimum spanning tree $(\tilde{G}_{\mathcal{EN}})$ for the corresponding connected weighted graph. The neighboring nodes of $\tilde{G}_{\mathcal{EN}}$ with equal distances were then cloned into a single node to form a hypertree required for the belief propagation scheme. The final result shown in Figure 5 illustrates the global reputation Markov tree structure developed by only considering the top 19 most active categories in the epinions.com dataset.

4.3 Allocating Initial Reputation Belief Masses

Each node of the global reputation Markov tree contains a joint belief distribution over the categories that form it. For instance, in Figure 5, the belief mass assignment in the node $C - M$ is distributed over the categories: (Media) and (Cars & Motorsports). In order to be able to propagate belief through the reputation tree, the belief mass assignment function of each node should be specified. The simplest way to do this is to initially assign the highest possible belief mass to the superset, and gradually, as new evidence about the performance of a given user in the environment is received, the belief mass assignments of that specific user is updated to reflect the information gained from his/her performance.

It is also possible to assign an initially similar belief mass assignment for all the users based on the information in the epinions.com dataset, and then update

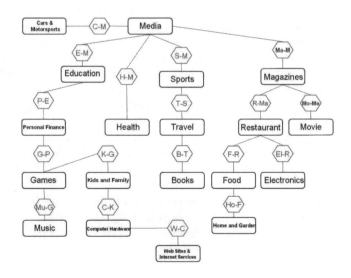

Fig. 5. The Global Reputation Markov Tree Structure

that belief mass assignments for each user separately. The initial belief mass assignment should assign belief masses based on the frequency of observation of the possible states related to the categories of each node. Let's suppose that reputation is described using High, Medium, and Low values. In our experiments, we suppose that the average rating that a user's reviews in a specific category receives represents the user's reputation in that category. We convert the five scale ratings $[1, 5]$ into High, Medium, and Low. Therefore for example, the state space which can receive belief mass for the $C - M$ node would be $\Theta_{C-M} = \{(High, High), (High, Med), (High, Low), (Med, High), (Med, Med), (Med, Low), (Low, High), (Low, Med), (Low, Low)\}$. The belief mass assigned to a state such as (High,High) for a node with two categories: C_i and C_j is calculated as follows:

$$[\phi_{(C_i, C_j)}(High, High)]_m = \frac{\mathcal{N}(High, High)}{\sum_{\mathcal{X}, \mathcal{Y} \in \mathcal{RP}} \mathcal{N}(\mathcal{X}, \mathcal{Y})} \tag{16}$$

where $\mathcal{RP} = \{High, Medium, Low\}$, and $\mathcal{N}(High, High)$ is the number of users that have a High reputation in C_i and also a High reputation in C_j.

4.4 Performance Evaluation

The collected epinions.com dataset was split into two testing and training datasets for evaluation purposes. The training dataset was employed to create the global reputation Markov tree structure and form the initial belief mass assignments of each node of the Markov tree. Based on the structure of the reputation tree we conducted an experiment similar to label prediction in machine learning datasets. In our experiments, for each user in the training dataset, we removed one of his/her known reputation values for a given category (one of the environments contexts), and tried to estimate the hidden reputation value based on the other available reputation values of the user in other categories.

The available reputation values for each user were handled as incoming evidences about the overall performance of the user in the other categories. These evidences were then propagated through the reputation structure towards the node containing the target category using the introduced belief propagation scheme, where the belief masses were combined and marginalized to that category. Finally, the state space (either High, Medium or Low) with the highest belief mass assigned to it was selected to serve as the representative of that user's reputation in the given category. The proposed model's estimation capability showed to be able to correctly predict the missing reputation values in 76.923% of the test cases. In our opinion, this is a significant achievement, since a lucky guess by the other users of the target context to ascribe reputation and trust to a given user is only 33.3% successful. Our model increases the chance of correct reputation ascription in a given context where a user has not had any previous performance to an extent of 2.31 times.

5   Concluding Remarks

In this paper, we have proposed a global reputation representation structure, and a reputation estimation model for multi-context environments. The proposed structure is based on the idea of valuation networks, and employs the belief propagation scheme introduced in the Shenoy-Shafer architecture [6]. The model is most suitable for online communities that constitute multiple contexts. Currently, most such communities have only envisioned a single reputation value for each person. This has the disadvantage that users with a high reputation in an irrelevant issue can enter a new context where they do not possess any expertise and effect the community (possibly in a negative manner by deceiving the members of that context). In a three-scale reputation formalization, a lucky guess by the other members is only successful in 33.3% of the cases. Our model assists the users by estimating reputation values of new users in the contexts where their performance has not yet been observed. The proposed model has shown a 76.923% accuracy rate on a dataset collected from the epinions.com website.

Acknowledgement

This work was funded through grant RGPIN 227441 from the National Science and Engineering Research Council of Canada (NSERC) to Dr. Ali A. Ghorbani.

References

1. Bagheri, E., Ghorbani, A.A.: Behavior analysis through reputation propagation in a multi-context environment. In: International Conference on Privacy, Security and Trust (PST 2006), ACM, New York (2006)
2. Bagheri, E., Ghorbani, A.A.: Exploiting trust and suspicion for real-time attack recognition in recommender applications. In: iTrust/PST (2007)
3. Diaconis, P.: A mathematical theory of evidence (glenn shafer). Journal of the American Statistical Association 73(363), 677–678 (1978)
4. Lehmann, N., Haenni, R.: An alternative to outward propagation for dempster-shafer belief functions. In: Hunter, A., Parsons, S. (eds.) ECSQARU 1999. LNCS (LNAI), vol. 1638, pp. 256–267. Springer, Heidelberg (1999)
5. Pearl, J.: Reasoning with belief functions: An analysis of compatibility. Int. J. Approx. Reasoning 4(5-6), 363–389 (1990)
6. Schmidt, T., Shenoy, P.P.: Some improvements to the shenoy-shafer and hugin architectures for computing marginals. Art. Intel. 102(2), 323–333 (1998)
7. Shenoy, P.P.: Valuation network representation and solution of asymmetric decision problems. Euro. J. Operation. Res. 121(3), 579–608 (2000)

A Frequency Mining-Based Algorithm for Re-ranking Web Search Engine Retrievals

M. Barouni-Ebrahimi, Ebrahim Bagheri, and Ali A. Ghorbani

Faculty of Computer Science,
University of New Brunswick, Fredericton, Canada
{m.barouni,e.bagheri,ghorbani}@unb.ca

Abstract. In this paper, we propose an online page re-rank model which relies on the users' clickthrough feedbacks as well as frequent phrases from the past queries. The method is compared with a similar page re-rank algorithm called I-SPY. The results show the efficiency of the proposed method in ranking the more related pages on top of the retrieved list while monitoring a smaller number of query phrases in a hit-matrix. Employing thirteen months of queries for the University of New Brunswick search engine, the hit-matrix in our algorithm was on average 30 times smaller, while it showed better performance with regards to the re-rank of Web search results. The proposed re-rank method is expandable to support user community-based searches as well as specific domain Web search engines.

1 Introduction

Common Web search engines such as Google and Yahoo employ different types of parameters and consider various issues in order to rank the retrieved pages. Furthermore, some researchers have recently focused on re-ranking the outputs of the conventional Web search engines. In this approach, the algorithms take advantages of an already ranked search result set from a conventional Web search engine and apply a more specific algorithm to re-rank the provided result list.

In this paper, a model is proposed to re-rank the retrieved pages of a conventional Web search engine. The proposed model provides solutions to the following issues: 1) extracting frequent phrases from a query log requires appropriate stream mining techniques since query logs have conceptually evolved into data streams, which are the result of an endless and continuous sequence of queries known as query streams; 2) mining frequent phrases from the query stream while keeping track of user clicks is not a straightforward task; and 3) a query may contain more than one frequent phrase. Each frequent phrase contains a list of related pages (based on user clicks in the hit-matrix). An appropriate method is needed to combine the lists and prepare an ordered list of related pages to the submitted query.

S. Bergler (Ed.): Canadian AI 2008, LNAI 5032, pp. 60–65, 2008.
© Springer-Verlag Berlin Heidelberg 2008

2   The Proposed Page Rank Reviser (P2R) Algorithm

In [4], a Web search method is proposed called I-SPY that uses the past users' selections to re-rank the query results for the needs of the communities of the users. The number of the users in a community selecting each page of the results is stored in a hit-matrix. Therefore, the rows of the hit-matrix are the queries and the columns are the clicked pages. Each query q_i is a submitted query by a user, each page url_j is a retrieved page for q_i and the value of the cell, H_{ij}, is the number of users selecting url_j for q_i. For a new query, the result is re-ordered based on the relevancy of the retrieved pages to the submitted query using the hit-matrix. The relevance value of the page url_j to the query q_i is calculated as follows:

$$Relevance(url_j, q_i) = \frac{H_{ij}}{\sum_{j=1}^{n} H_{ij}}. \tag{1}$$

Smyth et al [4] have reported that only 15% of the queries observed in their experiments were duplicated. This causes two problems. First, the number of queries rapidly increases, which makes the hit-matrix very large that has negative effects on the performance of the system. Second, for some queries, the number of selections may not be large enough to be considered valid by the algorithm. Therefore, a similarity measure between queries is used calculated by Equation 2 to increase the amount of query duplication. Two queries are considered to be the same if they are within a given similarity threshold.

$$Sim(q, q') = \frac{|q \cap q'|}{|q \cup q'|}, \tag{2}$$

where q and q' are two queries, $|q \cap q'|$ is the number of the identical items in q and q' and $|q \cup q'|$ is the number of the distinct items in q and q' . This helps the system to have a smaller hit-matrix as well as more hits for a specific page of a submitted query. However, this has a negative effect on *precision*.

We improve this approach by manipulating the phrases within the queries rather than considering the whole query as a single element. Therefore, the queries q_1 to q_m in the hit-matrix are replaced with the frequent phrases extracted using an online single-pass algorithm called Online Frequent Sequence Discovery (OFSD), which mines the set of all frequent sequences in a data stream whose frequency rates satisfy a minimum frequency rate [1,2]. Informally speaking, search engine query streams are provided to the OFSD algorithm which extracts the most frequently observed phrases in the query stream and inserts them into a set called candidate set. The queries in the previous form of the hit-matrix are replaced with the frequent phrases in the candidate set from OFSD. In this way, the number of queries in the hit-matrix is much smaller, while there are more precise hits. The P2R algorithm re-ranks the output of a conventional Web search engines by employing the frequent clicked pages in the hit-matrix.

As an example, assume that the query "student financial services" has been submitted to a Web search engine and two retrieved pages url_1 and url_2 have been selected. Further, suppose that two phrases P_1 ="student financial services" and P_2 ="financial services" have already been extracted as frequent phrases by the OFSD algorithm. The hit-numbers of url_1 and url_2 are incremented for both P_1 and P_2 in the hit-matrix. To track the frequency rate of each url_j related to a phrase P_i, $F(P_i, url_j)$, which represents the frequency rate of the page url_j for the phrase P_i, is defined as:

$$F(P_i, url_j) = \frac{N_{url_j}}{CN_{P_i} - t_{url_j} + 1},$$ (3)

where N_{url_j} denotes the number of clicks on the url_j for the submitted phrase P_i (H_{ij} in the hit-matrix) and t_{url_j} represents the birth number of the page url_j for the phrase P_i, which shows the first time that url_j has been observed for P_i. In the P2R algorithm, a page url_j is considered as a frequent hit for a phrase P_i, if $F(P_i, url_j)$ is satisfied a minimum threshold, F_{min}.

The P2R algorithm divides the submitted query to a set of the longest frequent phrases called $QFL = \{P_1, ..., P_n\}$. There is no overlap between the divided phrases in QFL. For each phrase P_i in QFL, the related $urls$ from the hit-matrix that their frequency rate satisfy F_{min} are extracted and ordered based on their frequency rates called $list(P_i)$. The position of the url_j in the $list(P_i)$ is the rank of the url_j for the phrase P_i called $Rank(P_i, url_j)$. For example, $Rank(P_i, url_j) = 1$ means that the url_j is the most frequent clicked url for the phrase P_i in the $list(P_i)$ based on Equation 3. For each url_i in the retrieved pages of the conventional Web search engine, a rank list is assigned as follows:

$$rankList(url_i) = \{Rank(P_1, url_i), ..., Rank(P_n, url_i)\}.$$ (4)

If url_i is not in the $list(P_j)$, the maximum rank is assigned to it (which means that the url_i is not related to the phrase P_j).

Definition 1. *Let $Rank(P_i, url_j)$ be the position of url_j in the $list(P_i)$ for the phrase P_i. The priority of url_j, denoted $Rank(url_i)$, is defined as:*

$$Rank(url_i) = \mu(url_i) + \sigma(url_i),$$ (5)

where $\mu(url_i)$ is the arithmetic mean of the $rankList(url_i)$ which is calculated as follows:

$$\mu(url_i) = \frac{\sum_{j=1}^{n} Rank(P_j, url_i)}{n},$$ (6)

and $\sigma(url_i)$ is the standard deviation of the $rankList(url_i)$ which is calculated as follows:

$$\sigma(url_i) = \sqrt{\frac{1}{n} \sum_{j=1}^{n} (Rank(P_j, url_i) - \mu(url_i))^2}.$$ (7)

Higher priority $urls$, which possess a smaller $Rank(url_i)$, represent more important $urls$. The average of the ranks are important since a url that has low ranks for the phrases in QFL should be on top of the list. On the other hand, average is not a sufficient factor. Standard deviation is also added to mean in Equation 5. Assume a scenario in which:

$QFL = \{P_1, P_2\}$, $list(P_1) = \{url_1, url_2, url_3\}$,
$list(P_2) = \{url_4, url_2, url_1\}$, $searchResult = \{url_5, url_6, url_2, url_1\}$,
$\implies \mu(url_1) = \mu(url_2) = 2$, $\sigma(url_1) = 1, \sigma(url_2) = 0$.

Although the average ranks of both url_1 and url_2 are the same, url_2 is a more related page for the submitted query compared to url_1. The reason is that it has the same rank for both phrases P_1 and P_2 of the submitted query. The final output would be: $outputResult = \{url_2, url_1, url_5, url_6\}$,

3 Experiments

The P2R algorithm is compared with I-SPY [4] using the University of New Brunswick (UNB) query log which consists of about 200,000 queries collected from November 2006 to November 2007 (13 months). The I-SPY and P2R performances are comparable on UNB query log since both methods are intended for community oriented search engines; therefore, because the queries directed to UNB Web search engine are domain specific (related to university issues) it can be considered a community search engine and a suitable testbed for both algorithms. Each query in the UNB query log follows by a list of clicked *urls* along with their ranks in the retrieved pages. Since there is no way to realize if a clicked *url* was actually related to the query in the view of the user, we borrow the idea from [4] in which each selected page is assumed to be related to the query. Based on the discussion in [3],counting the clicked pages for a given query can be used as a basic relevancy measure. A simple but effective metric has been employed to evaluate our re-rank method called click satisfaction.

Definition 2. *Let $BR(q)$ be the optimal ranking given in the best case by a Web search engine (the rank of the best url is 1, the rank of the second best is 2, etc), $DR(q)$ be the ranking proposed by a re-rank algorithm, $clicked(q)$ represent the set of clicked pages for a query q in the query log, R_{url} be the optimal rank of the url, N_{url} be the rank of the url after re-rank and $|clicked(q)|$ be the number of clicked pages for q. The click satisfaction rate, denoted as $ClickSatisfaction(q)$, which shows the degree of retrieval rank optimization by a given re-rank algorithm is defines as follows:*

$$BR(q) = BasedRank(q) = \sum_{\forall url \in clicked(q)} R_{url} \qquad (8)$$

$$DR(q) = DerivedRank(q) = \sum_{\forall url \in clicked(q)} N_{url} \qquad (9)$$

$$ClickSatisfaction(q) = \frac{DR(q) - BR(q)}{|clicked(q)|} \qquad (10)$$

Lower click satisfaction values show better performance of the re-ranking algorithm. For example, assume that for a submitted query q_1, three *urls* have been

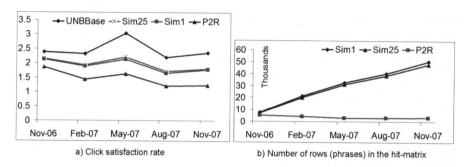

a) Click satisfaction rate   b) Number of rows (phrases) in the hit-matrix

Fig. 1. The shaded areas represent the click satisfaction rate/ number of rows of each algorithm in the UNB query log

clicked: url_1 with the rank value of 2, url_2 with the rank value of 8 and url_3 with the rank value of 10. The *BaseRank* would be 6. The P2R algorithm is applied to the query q_1 and the ranks of the three *urls* are extracted. In this case, assume that it is url_1 with the rank value of 2, url_2 with the rank value of 3 and url_3 with the rank value of 13. The *DerivedRank* is 18. Based on Equation 10, the *ClickSatisfaction* is 4. It is important to note that a clickSatisfaction value equal to zero for a given query shows that the re-rank algorithm has an optimal performance.

The proposed algorithm, P2R, has been compared with the results obtained from the I-SPY algorithm. The I-SPY algorithm has been employed in two different settings Sim1 and Sim25 where the threshold values for similarity are set to 1 and 0.25, respectively. The obtained results from the UNB search engine were also used as the baseline. There are two important issues that need to be considered in the evaluation. First, the algorithms need to show good performance with regards to the click satisfaction metric, i.e. the algorithm that yields the smallest value for this metric has the best performance with regards to the re-rank of the search engine results. Second, the algorithms should not possess a high space complexity which means that the size of the hit-matrix should be small enough for the algorithm to be able to perform required calculations in a timely manner. A small hit-matrix allows faster inference from the data and requires less storage space.

As it can be seen in Figure 1-a, the P2R algorithm has the lowest click satisfaction rate compared with the other models, which is an indicator of its better re-ranking performance. This figure also depicts that the two different cases of the I-SPY algorithm do not have a significant difference with respect to re-rank of the result pages. Furthermore, it can be seen in Figure 1-b that the P2R algorithm requires and stores a significantly smaller hit-matrix compared with the I-SPY algorithm in both settings. This is a major advantage since the P2R algorithm is able to achieve better performance in re-ranking the search engine results by only storing a much smaller hit-matrix in comparison with the I-SPY algorithm. More interestingly, as it can be seen in Figure 1-b, the size of the P2R hit-matrix is bounded and does not grow beyond a certain size because of its internal pruning process. However, the size of the hit-matrix stored in the I-SPY algorithm grows significantly larger as new queries are observed. In the final stage, the size of the P2R hit-matrix is about 30 times smaller than that of the I-SPY algorithm.

4   Conclusions

In this paper, the P2R algorithm is proposed which applies a hit-matrix to the retrieved pages of the conventional Web search engines for refinement of the search results. The hit-matrix keeps track of the frequently clicked pages for each frequent phrase of the queries. The frequent phrases are extracted from a query stream by the OFSD algorithm. The results show the advantage of the P2R compared to the I-SPY model. Employing the queries of the UNB query log, the hit-matrix was much smaller in the proposed model, while the click satisfaction metric showed better performance for the P2R algorithm based on the proposed evaluation method. Since the size of the hit-matrix is considered as the main performance bottleneck of our algorithm as well as for the I-SPY model, our approach significantly increases the performance by reducing the size of the hit-matrix.

Acknowledgments

This work was funded by the Atlantic Canada Opportunity Agency (ACOA) through the Atlantic Innovation Fund (AIF) and through grant RGPIN 227441 from the National Science and Engineering Research Council of Canada (NSERC) to Dr. Ali A. Ghorbani.

References

1. Barouni-Ebrahimi, M., Ghorbani, A.A.: A novel approach for frequent phrase mining in web search engine query streams. In: Communication Networks and Services Research Conference (CNSR 2007), Fredericton, Canada, May 14-17, pp. 125–132 (2007)
2. Barouni-Ebrahimi, M., Ghorbani, A.A.: On query completion in web search engines based on query stream mining. In: International Conference on Web Intelligence (WI 2007), November 2-5, pp. 317–320 (2007)
3. Joachims, T., Granka, L.A., Pan, B., Hembrooke, H., Radlinski, F., Gay, G.: Evaluating the accuracy of implicit feedback from clicks and query reformulations in web search. ACM Transaction on Information Systems 25(2), 7 (2007)
4. Smyth, B., Balfe, E., Freyne, J., Briggs, P., Coyle, M., Boydell, O.: Exploiting query repetition and regularity in an adaptive community-based web search engine. User Modeling and User-Adapted Interaction 14(5), 383–423 (2005)

Multi-agent Framework for a Virtual Enterprise of Demand-Responsive Transportation

Daniel Cabrera and Claudio Cubillos

Pontificia Universidad Católica de Valparaíso, Escuela de Ingeniería Informática,
Av. Brasil 2241, Valparaíso, Chile
daniel.cabrerap@gmail.com, claudio.cubillos@ucv.cl

Abstract. This work presents a multiagent framework design for Demand-Responsive Transportation, considering a virtual enterprise domain. The agent architecture obtained provides a baseline for the integration between end-users of the transport service and multiple transport operators affiliated to a virtual enterprise which provides flexibility in the incorporation and leaving of transport operators. The participation of governmental organizations and active destinations within the system allows the virtual enterprise having additional information on potential opportunities of business and assures transport system users a wider and more complete service search. The PASSI methodology has been used as base software engineering methodology for leveraging the multiagent architecture.

Keywords: Framework, Agents, Virtual Enterprise, Demand-Responsive Transportation, PASSI.

1 Introduction

Passenger transportation in urban areas constitutes an increasingly important problem in our society. Given the quantity and nature of the different actors involved in the passenger transportation scenario, it is required that these systems are able to effectively integrate various heterogeneous systems, and provide criteria to ensure the efficiency and quality of service to passengers. Therefore, the trend is to move from a group of transport operators, partial or totally disconnected among them, towards the conformation of an integrated transport service, sustained by a virtual enterprise (VE) for passenger transportation.

The framework development has been realized on the basis of the use of PASSI (Process for Agent Societies Specification and Implementation) [1], a multiagent-oriented methodology for systems development, which integrates design models and concepts from both, OO software engineering and artificial intelligence approaches using the UML notation. Additionally, we have incorporated some elements offered by a non-standard UML profile called UML-F [7], devoted to the development of object-oriented software frameworks.

The novelty of our work relies on conceptualizing the integration of diverse passenger transportation operators as a Virtual Enterprise and modelling it as a multi-agent

S. Bergler (Ed.): Canadian AI 2008, LNAI 5032, pp. 66–71, 2008.
© Springer-Verlag Berlin Heidelberg 2008

framework. A second issue is the use of PASSI complemented with a general process for framework development plus UML-F for formalizing the variable points in the resulting agent architecture.

2 Related Work

In some european countries, pilots for DRT systems were developed during projects such as SAMPLUS [9], SIPTS [3], and FAMS [5]. Regarding to examples of MAS applied to ITS, only to mention some iniciatives, Roozemond and Danko [2] proposed a UTC model primarily based on several coupled intersection control Intelligent Traffic Signaling Agents (ITSA), some authority agents and Road Segment Agents (RSA). In 2001, an intelligent forecasting system was presented by Shou-Feng et al. [8], in which agents were used to select the best traffic forecast model suited to the current traffic state, evaluating the performance of the models and to update the parameters automatically.

It should be noted that none of the above initiatives used to some extent the agent paradigm as modelling abstraction, nor considered a formal modeling of the software architecture obtained (for example, through the use of UML artifacts). These are two important contributions of the current work. Additionally, this work takes the ideas of the FAMS project regarding an integrated agency for transportation and concretizes it by means of a virtual enterprise devoted to passenger transport services offer.

This work represents the continuity of a past reseach in this transportation domain [6], concerning the development of an agent system for passenger transportation for a single operator under a demand-responsive scenario.

3 Towards a Virtual Enterprise for Passenger Transportation

The Intelligent Transport Systems (ITS) have been attracting interest of the transport professionals, the automotive industry and governments around the world. Regarding the public transport domain, in the last years the Demand Responsive Transport (DRT) services have risen in popularity for several reasons, among them strong incorporation of information and communications technologies, increasing the efficiency and diminishing the operations cost. However, geographical coverage problems among transport operators' services, difference in the volume and quality of handled information and, in general, a fragmentation in the transport service provision, gives origin to problems that range from wrong evaluations coming from state-regulatory entities, up to direct problems with the system final users, which definitively results in a poor quality of service. For these reasons in many cases the solution implies a better integration and coordination of the diverse parties, leveraging the concept of virtual enterprise. In this sense, we may think in a virtual transportation enterprise, with an increased level of adaptability to the offer, considered the variability in the levels of existing demand. With this, and under new business opportunities, the virtual transportation enterprise adapts its structure to meet the existing demand.

4 Multi-agent Framework Design

The first diagram presented corresponds to the Agents Identification Diagram (see Figure 1), which is framed within the first stage of the PASSI methodology, corresponding to the System Requirements Model.

It is possible to indicate that the generation of diagrams is given on the basis of the use of a graphical tool available for PASSI, denominated PASSI Toolkit [4]. This diagram takes as starting point the description of UML use-cases, offering a general view of all the functionality provided by the system and in addition, it incorporates a grouping of use-cases for each agent identified within the system in order to visualize the responsability level that each of the agents has regarding the system.

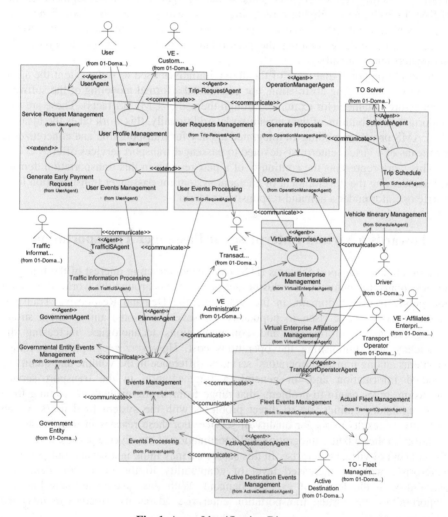

Fig. 1. Agent Identification Diagram

The figure 2 shows the Domain Ontology Description, which corresponds to a class diagram that contains specific domain concepts and its relations. The common knowledge of the domain is described through this diagram. In this sense, the ontology allows the definition of a common vocabulary, necessary for trips programming, transport operators management within the virtual enterprise, as well as the events that can arise and may affect the itineraries planned previously.

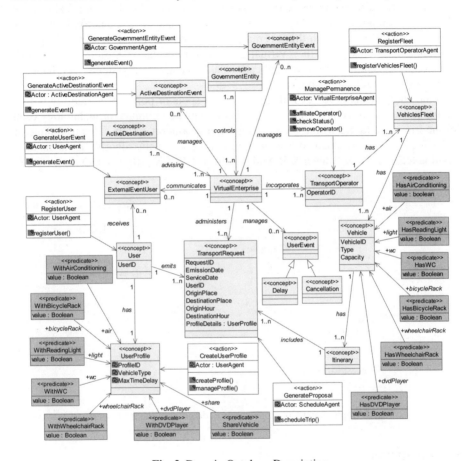

Fig. 2. Domain Ontology Description

According to the defined ontology, the virtual enterprise incorporates one or many transport operators, which on their turn can as well have multiple fleets of vehicles, each one composed with at least one. Each vehicle has associated a trip itinerary, which includes at least one transport request emitted by a transport (end) user. Each transport request defines, among other things, the date of emission and service fulfilment for the required trip, origin and destination points involved, departure and arrival hour to destination and a user identifier. Each transport user has associated a user profile, which contains his service preferences (type of vehicle, need of wheelchair rack, etc.). Also, transport users, governmental entities and active destinations they are all qualified to indicate events that are external to the virtual transportation enterprise and that may alter in some way or another the normal flow of activities.

Finally, a deployment/component hybrid diagram of the general framework architecture is included (see Figure 3). On it, a set of "compute nodes" are identified, each one distinguishable by its representation as a package. Inside each package a set of software components are identified, those of which can correspond to agents (as is the case of the package with the <<Transport Operator Terminal>> stereotype) or to independent systems (as in the "Virtual Enterprise Information System" package) or to a mixture of both, agents with applications and management systems, as it happens in the case of the remaining packages.

Some components have been identified as hot-spots or points of variability within the framework architecture. One example is the type of technique or technology used for the trips scheduling within the passenger transportation system. This technique or technology may correspond to a heuristic algorithm (genetic algorithms, to name a possible technique), or Branch & Bound solvers as CPLEX [10], LINDO [11], etc.

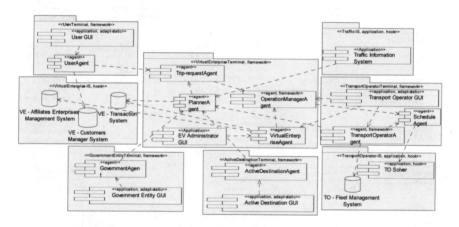

Fig. 3. Deployment/Component hybrid diagram of the framework

5   Conclusion

A multi-agent framework for a virtual enterprise devoted to passengers' transportation has been achieved. The domain context and their involved actors have been defined, which can correspond to information systems or people. Also, the domain ontology allows understanding the most fundamental concepts of the software framework, knowledge base for the obtaining of a flexible architecture. Such architecture includes a set of identified agents which conform a society of agents and that interact with both, the final user of the transport system, and information systems and applications external to it.

Currently, a functional prototype is being developed by extending the multi-agent framework proposed, and is being tested with Solomon's benchmark data sets for VRP and specially adapted for the passenger transportation problem.

Acknowledgements

This work has been partially funded by the Pontifical Catholic University of Valparaíso (www.pucv.cl) through project No. 209.746/2007 entitled "Coordinación en una sociedad multiagente dedicada a la programación y control bajo ambiente dinámico".

References

1. Burrafato, P., Cossentino, M.: Designing a multiagent solution for a bookstore with the passi methodology. In: Fourth International Bi-Conference Workshop on AgentOriented Information Systems (AOIS 2002) (2002)
2. Roozemond, D.: Using Intelligmt Agents for Pro-active Real-time Urban Intersection Control. European Journal of Operational Research 131(2), 293–301 (2001)
3. SIPTS - TEN45607 - Services for Intelligent Public Transport Systems, http://www.novacall.fi/sipts/e_default.htm
4. PASSI Toolkit (PTK), http://sourceforge.net/projects/ptk
5. FAMS - Flexible Agency for Collective Demand Responsive Services. IST-2001-34347, http://www.famsweb.com/
6. Cubillos, C., Guidi-Polanco, F., Demartini, C.: MADARP: Multi-Agent Architecture for Passenger Transportation Systems. In: Proceedings of the 8th IEEE International Conference on Intelligent Transportation Systems (ITSC 2005), Vienna, Austria (September 2005)
7. Fontoura, M., Pree, W., Rumpe, B.: The UML Profile Framework Architectures. Addison Wesley, Reading (2000)
8. Ma, S.-F., He, G.-G., Wang, S.-T.: A traffic flow forecast supported system based multi-agent. In: IEEE Intelligent Transportation Systems Conference Proceedings, pp. 620–624 (2001)
9. SAMPLUS TR 4023 - Systems for the Advanced Management of Public Transport Operations http://www.cordis.lu/telematics/tap_transport/research/projects/samplus.html
10. Ilog Cplex, http://www.ilog.com/products/cplex
11. Lindo Systems, http://www.lindo.com

Use of Fuzzy Histograms to Model the Spatial Distribution of Objects in Case-Based Reasoning

Alan Davoust, Michael W. Floyd, and Babak Esfandiari

Department of Systems and Computer Engineering
Carleton University
1125 Colonel By Drive
Ottawa, Ontario

Abstract. In the context of the RoboCup Simulation League, we describe a new representation of a software agent's visual perception ("scene"), well suited for case-based reasoning.

Most existing representations use either heterogeneous, manually selected features of the scene, or the raw list of visible objects, and use ad hoc similarity measures for CBR. Our representation is based on histograms of objects over a partition of the scene space. This method transforms a list of objects into an image-like representation with customizable granularity, and uses fuzzy logic to smoothen boundary effects of the partition. We also introduce a new similarity metric based on the Jaccard Coefficient, to compare scenes represented by such histograms.

We present our implementation of this approach in a case-based reasoning project, and experimental results showing highly efficient scene comparison.

Keywords: Case Based Reasoning, Fuzzy Histograms, Knowledge Representation, Soccer Simulation.

1 Introduction

The paradigm of case-based reasoning (CBR), where the decision-making process of an agent is based on a database of past situations, has been applied to a variety of artificial intelligence applications. A notable application is the problem of *modeling others from observation.*

An ongoing project at Carleton University is a CBR project in which an imitative software agent is trained to imitate the behavior of another target agent, based on the logs of this target agent's actions ([1], [2]). The agent of interest in this project is a simulated soccer-playing agent in the RoboCup Simulation League [3]. In this League, teams of autonomous agents play a simulated soccer game, interacting only with the game server. The server sends each player his perception of the playing field (the *"scene"*), described as a list of all the visible objects, with their coordinates w.r.t. the player. Objects include the ball, other players, lines, etc. This raw data could be compared to the result of a feature extraction in a real robot.

S. Bergler (Ed.): Canadian AI 2008, LNAI 5032, pp. 72–83, 2008.
© Springer-Verlag Berlin Heidelberg 2008

Each agent (player) replies with its action (which may be *"dash"*, *"kick"*, or *"turn"*, with a parameter), and the server uses all the agents' actions to simulate another time step in the game, and so forth.

Emulating such an agent in a CBR approach requires forming a database of "cases" modeling the scene, and the agent's response action, which can be seen as the known solution to the problem. When presented with a new situation, the imitative agent's playing algorithm involves searching the case base for one or several similar scenes, and using these similar "cases" to decide on an action.

Initiatives to use CBR in the RoboCup context include [4], [5], [6] and [7]. In these other works, the authors selected particular features of the scenes, based on their intuition of what seemed important or not in a soccer game simulation. Features included lists of objects, counts of objects present in particular "strategic zones" of the playing field, and other indicators of the game situation, such as possession of the ball.

In earlier work with our imitative agent, [1] and [2], a scene was represented using a simple data translation of the server message, listing each object with its coordinates. This raw representation avoids the bias inherent in manually selecting domain-specific scene features, but does not support practical similarity metrics, which is a serious handicap for our real-time CBR problem.

We present here a new approach similar to the idea of occupancy grid maps [8] used in robotics. We model the scene by means of a 2-dimensional grid map, onto which we project the objects, using fuzzy logic to smoothly approximate their location in a discrete representation.

We obtain a fuzzy histogram of objects, which is an image-like representation of a scene, showing the spatial distribution of objects with a customizable granularity. We present a similarity metric based on the set-theoretic Jaccard Coefficient. We have implemented this scene representation in our imitative agent framework, and experimental results in this setting show that our approach compares favorably with previously presented approaches in terms of accuracy, while reducing the computational cost of comparisons by a factor of ten.

The rest of the paper is organized as follows: first, in Section 2, we define our approach with respect to related work, then in Section 3, we present our fuzzy histogram scene representation, and some distance and similarity metrics to compare such data structures. In Section 4, we give some practical details on our implementation of this approach in our CBR project, and finally we discuss our experimental results in Section 5, with some directions for future work.

2 Related Work

Our CBR imitation framework for Robocup agents was initially presented in [1], and a number of optimizations were presented in [2]. In this previous work, the scene representation was a simple data translation of the server message, i.e., a list of objects with their position in polar coordinates. Comparing two scenes involved matching the objects in one scene with the objects in the other. It was then possible to compare, for instance, the position of the ball in one scene with the position of the ball in the second scene, if the ball was present in both scenes. The cartesian distance between these two positions could be computed, and then the sum of distances for all pairs of objects across the scenes was used as a "distance" metric measuring the dissimilarity of the scenes.

The first problem with this representation is that is does not form an ordered set of features. At a given time the agent sees only a small fraction of the full list of objects present on the field; furthermore, objects may be interchangeable, e.g., two players of the same team, or two lines, cannot necessarily be recognized[1]. Matching the objects in this case may not be trivial. Lam *et al.* [1], as well as Karol *et al.* [5], who were also faced with the problem of interchangeable players in their own work, note that this object-matching problem accounts for the bulk of the computational cost in comparing two scenes.

As noted in the introduction, most other teams that have used CBR in the RoboCup context have tackled this problem by selecting particular features deemed important for soccer, to suit their particular needs. Our main motivation in this work is to propose a practical scene representation (in terms of comparison cost), while avoiding a biased selection of features by a human expert.

In a non-biased approach, we can draw a parallel with a robot navigating an unknown environment, in that the robot attempts to build a map of its environment. The typical example is a *grid occupancy map* [8], which is a grid in which each cell is assigned a probabilistic indication that an obstacle is found at this location. Such a representation also aims to project all the available information (e.g, from a sonar) on a feature map that represents the entire known environment.

Wendler et al. [4] used a representation of the pitch in the spirit of grid occupancy maps, noting the presence or absence of players in a segmented area around the ball. Other works have considered partitions of the playing field, e.g. [6], where the players in the "offensive zone" and "defensive zone" are counted, and make up two features of the scene representation.

In both cases this is used as only a small part of the representation. Furthermore, as noted in [1], such a segmentation induces boundary issues, artificially separating objects that may, in fact, be very near, or assigning to the same segment two relatively distant objects.

Our approach here is to use this general idea to draw a symbolic grid map, over which we place all the objects in the scene, and avoid the boundary issues by approximating an object's position using fuzzy logic.

3   Methodology

In this Section, we detail the method by which we obtain the data representation of a scene, and compare two scenes thus represented. We describe the method

---

[1] Depending on the context, it may be desirable to recognize them, or else to maintain a level of abstraction where they are interchangeable.

for the context of the RoboCup Simulation League, but it is general enough to be extended to other domains.

3.1   Position of an Object

The basis of our approach is a segmentation of the scene space (the visible part of the playing field), using a two-dimensional grid, as shown in Figure 1. We discuss the specific parameters of the grid in our implementation, in Section 4.1.

```
ball (-20.0, 2.0)
player_opponent (20.0, 7.5)
player_opponent (52.0, 28.0)
player_opponent (-48.0, 37.0)
goal (8.6, 42.0)
```

Fig. 1. An example scene described as a list of objects in polar coordinates, and segmented using a 3 × 5 grid

The position of an object in a segmented area can be smoothly approximated using fuzzy logic.

We consider each cell of the grid as a fuzzy set, rather than a conventional crisp set. This way, an object that is in the center of a cell might fully belong to it, whereas an object near the edge of the cell might have only a small membership in the cell. A logical approach is then to make the fuzzy sets corresponding to neighboring cells overlap, so that an object at the edge of one cell also belongs to the next cell. This way, as we move in the scene space, we smoothly transfer from one cell to the next, using this fuzzy membership function. Being able to smoothly transfer from one cell to the next makes the location of the boundaries much less important than in the crisp case.

Formally, our "grid" is a fuzzy partition of the *universe of discourse* of each coordinate, thus obtaining a two-dimensional fuzzy partition of the scene space. As defined in [9], a collection of fuzzy sets A_i is a fuzzy partition of a universe X if the so-called *orthogonality condition* (1) is satisfied:

$$\forall x \in X \sum_{i=1}^{n} \mu_{A_i}(x) = 1 \tag{1}$$

where μ_{A_i} is the membership function of the fuzzy set A_i.

This condition, which we need to apply when designing the membership functions of each grid cell, is consistent with the crisp approach of assigning each object to exactly one cell, i.e., making the grid a (crisp) partition of the scene. It ensures that all the objects are given equal importance, wherever they are located. Following this approach, the position of each object in the scene is given by the membership value of this object in each cell of the grid.

3.2   Definition of a Histogram

Whether using fuzzy or crisp sets, we can represent the scene by listing the contents of each cell. More specifically, if several objects are interchangeable, then the "contents of a cell" can be reduced to the number of such objects that the cell contains.

Following this approach, we represent a collection of interchangeable objects using a histogram over the grid. In a way, this is an extension of the grid occupancy map defined by [8] to an environment where we identify a number of precisely positioned objects in the grid, rather than a boolean notion of "cell occupancy."

In order to adapt this representation to our context, in which not all objects are interchangeable, we can represent a scene by several histograms, one per object *category*. Categories include *ball*, *teammate_player*, *line*, etc.

Finally, using the fuzzy partition presented in the previous Section, we can extend the concept of a histogram to a fuzzy histogram, by taking the fuzzy cardinality of each cell. We define this fuzzy cardinality as the sum of the membership values of the objects contained in the cell.

According to this definition, if the grid contains a total of $n \times m$ cells, and we have a total of k different object categories, then a scene can be represented by a histogram, which is a matrix of dimension $k \times n \times m$. For practical purposes, we can also use an isomorphic representation, e.g, k vectors of dimension $n \times m$. Formally, let A_{ij} be the fuzzy set representing a cell (i, j) in the grid, and $\mu_{A_{ij}}$ its membership function. We define X_p to be the set of visible objects of type p. Using a matrix notation our full fuzzy histogram is a matrix H of dimension $k \times n \times m$, with elements h_{pij} such that:

$$h_{pij} = \sum_{x \in X_p} \mu_{A_{ij}}(x) \qquad (2)$$

3.3   Similarity Metrics

In case-based reasoning, the agent, when presented with a new problem, needs to compare this problem with his database of reference "cases," and select one or several of the most similar cases in order to compute its solution regarding the new problem.

In our case of interest, this means that the key problem for our imitative agent is to compare two scenes. Our scene representation is isomorphic to a feature vector, and comparisons can be made using standard distance metrics for vectors in a space of dimension $k \times n \times m$ (or $n \times m$).

We propose here a similarity metric based on the set-theoretic Jaccard coefficient (also known as Tanimoto coefficient), which we expose for a histogram represented simply by a vector of length n, without loss of generality.

Swain and Ballard introduced in [10] a similarity metric for comparing histograms, called the histogram intersection, which they defined as follows:
Let $H(h_1, h_2, h_3 \cdots h_n)$ and $G(g_1, g_2 \cdots g_n)$ be two histograms.

The histogram intersection of H and G is:

$$inter(H, G) = \sum_{i=1}^{n} min(h_i, g_i) \tag{3}$$

They also proposed a normalized version, which they called the *normalized histogram intersection*. Here a sample H is compared to a reference G:

$$inter_{norm}(H, G) = \frac{\sum_{i=1}^{n} min(h_i, g_i)}{\sum_{i=1}^{n} g_i} \tag{4}$$

This similarity comparison was introduced to compare color histograms of images, and in that context, the normalizing factor is the number of pixels in the "reference" image. However, it is not symmetrical, which can be a problem.

Adapting this measurement to make it symmetrical has been done in various ways in the image-processing community.

We propose here to normalize the histogram intersection by a factor that can be seen as the histogram *union*. By extending Swain and Ballard's histogram intersection notion to a corresponding[2] union notion, we obtain a histogram union defined as follows:

$$union(H, G) = \sum_{i=1}^{n} max(h_i, g_i) \tag{5}$$

In the case of sets the Jaccard Coefficient is defined as the norm of the intersection of the sets over the norm of their union :

$$j(A, B) = \frac{|A \cap B|}{|A \cup B|} \tag{6}$$

Extending this formula to histograms, we can normalize Swain and Ballard's histogram intersection by the histogram union. We then obtain the following similarity metric, which we will refer to here as the Histogram Jaccard Coefficient[3].

$$j_{hist}(H, G) = \frac{\sum_{i=1}^{n} min(h_i, g_i)}{\sum_{i=1}^{n} max(h_i, g_i)} \tag{7}$$

Note that these definitions have been presented without concern as to whether the histograms and sets were fuzzy or crisp, but here we assume that the fuzzy partition we defined in Section 3.1 allows us to extend the rest of the framework, implicitly defined in a "crisp" context, to the fuzzy case.

---

[2] By analogy with the correspondence between T-norms and S-Norms for intersection and union of fuzzy sets (see [9] for details).

[3] This metric is very similar to various extensions of the Jaccard Coefficient used in market basket data analysis, and in information retrieval (see, e.g. [11], and [12]).

In this work, we choose to compare scenes by comparing each of the k pairs of fuzzy histograms that represent the scenes, and consider the final result to be a weighted sum of those partial results.

The weights, meant to reflect the importance of each object type in the similarity evaluation, are discussed in Section 4.2.

4   Implementation

The scene representation presented in the previous Section is a general definition, which can be customized by selecting particular membership functions, and defining particular categories of objects for a specific application. In this Section we describe our specific implementation of this approach in the CBR framework defined in [1].

4.1   Membership Functions

The main parameters for designing our fuzzy partition of the scene space are the following:

- *Dimension of the grid.* The dimension of the full scene representation will be $k \times n \times m$, where k is the number of object categories, and $n \times m$ is the grid size. These parameters will fully determine the processing time of the case comparison, and the memory occupation of the case base.

    We present here results with the following grid sizes: 3×5, 4×6, and 5×8, and we have $k = 7$ types of objects. These sizes give a total dimension of 105, 168, and 280, respectively, for the full feature vector representing the scene.
- *Boundaries of the cells.* As noted previously, fuzzifying the boundaries of the cells makes their exact location less important, as they do not introduce any "drastic" separation of the data points. The location of objects in the scene is expressed in polar coordinates, and in our implementation we simply spaced the cells equally over the central-nearer area of the visible field. Cells defining the extremities of the visible space (sides and most distant points) are simply defined by their boundaries nearer to the origin (lower distance bound, higher bound of the angle for the extreme-left, lower bound of the angle for the extreme-right).
- *Membership functions.* The membership functions are constrained by the orthogonality condition, and by the boundaries of each cell. In order to avoid boundary effects, we use continuous membership functions. Simple functions allowing straightforward orthogonality include triangular membership functions, and functions based on sin^2 (sinus squared). In our implementation, membership functions for the angle coordinate are based on sin^2, whereas membership functions for the radial coordinate are triangular. In both cases, the membership function for the extremities of the grid are constant, in the region where they do not overlap with the neighboring cell.

Our 1-dimensional membership functions for a 3×5 grid are shown in Fig. 2.

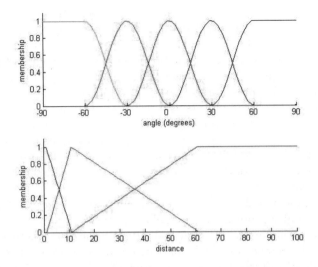

Fig. 2. Fuzzy partition of the polar angle (top) and radius (bottom)

4.2   Case-Based Reasoning Algorithm

We have integrated our scene representation in the framework defined in [1], and in this Section, we briefly describe the CBR algorithms adapted to our scene representation.

- **Setup:** We first set the general parameters of the framework: the size of the grid used to discretize the scene, and the membership functions to be used for the cells of this grid.
- **Preprocessing algorithm:** Using a log file, we compute a data structure that the agent will use as its case base. For each line in the log file, we create a scene using our fuzzy histograms representation, and attach the response action (also recorded in the log). The scene and response action compose a case. The cases are then aggregated as a single case base.
- **Real-time CBR algorithm:** When presented with a new scene, the agent creates the fuzzy histogram representation of this scene, and matches it to its case base. The agent selects the most similar scene, and outputs the action that was associated with that scene.

5   Evaluation

5.1   Evaluation Criteria

In this paper, we have put forward several characteristics of our scene representation, which we consider make it more adequate for real-time case-based reasoning.

First of all, our representation is a simplified representation of the original list of objects, in which we replace exact coordinates by a fuzzy histogram showing the spatial distribution of the objects, so we need to evaluate the new representation to ensure that this loss of information is acceptable. In our imitative agent framework [1], we evaluate this by comparing the imitative performance of the agent using our scene representation with the results of the original studies ([1] and [2]) which use the list of objects as a scene representation.

The main benefit of our representation is to provide a feature vector representation, which allows for much more computationally efficient scene comparisons. Comparisons are a key issue since our agent needs to meet real-time constraints. We report here the processing time of our agent, showing a significant improvement.

Thirdly, keeping in mind the essential assumption of the CBR paradigm, namely that "similar problems have similar solutions," we evaluate the effect of scene segmentation on the distinguishability of scenes, i.e. whether using our scene representation we can still tell apart two scenes that were originally different when originally described as lists of objects. Clearly, if two scenes associated to different actions become indistinguishable, then we have similar problems with *different solutions*, and this will set a theoretical upper bound for our performance in any CBR application.

From a significant number of logs, we counted how many scenes had a representation identical to that of another scene, and compared whether the actions were similar or not. Similar actions meant the same action label and statistically similar parameters, i.e the two parameter values differ by less than the standard deviation of the parameter[4].

Finally, as the Jaccard coefficient is reputed to be more "robust" in the datamining literature, we compared it with the Euclidean distance for our experiments, analyzing how different dimensions for the scene representation impacted the imitative accuracy of the agent.

5.2   Experimental Results

As the absolute performance of the agent depends on many factors, we have simply compared our results with those reported by Floyd *et al.* in [2]. As a target agent for our imitation experiments, we used an existing RoboCup agent called Krislet [13], a stateless agent that exhibits a simple decision-tree type behaviour, looking for the ball, running after it, and kicking it towards the goal.

The imitative performance of an agent was obtained by cross validation, using three independent sets of logs from the same target agent. We used a first set of logs as a training set, i.e., we preprocessed those logs and used them as a case base for the agent, and we used a second set of logs as a validation set. We tested each pair-wise combination of log files and computed the average results.

Many indicators could describe the accuracy of the imitation. However, as this aspect is secondary to our discussion, here we only report the overall accuracy

---

[4] Calculated from all the instances of the action throughout the logs.

Table 1. Accuracy and processing time of the imitative agent using list of objects representation, Histograms, Fuzzy Histograms

Representation	List of objects	Histograms		Fuzzy Histograms	
dimension	N/A	3×5	5×8	3×5	5×8
Accuracy	68.4	67.9	82.1	70.7	80.4
Processing time (ms per scene)	27	2.5	5.4	2.5	5.4

of the imitative agent in discriminating between the three possible actions, i.e *kick*, *dash*, and *turn*, without considering the parameter value. Hence a positive match is a test scene for which the imitative agent selects the same action as the original agent.

Table 1 lists the results of the imitative agent in terms of predictive accuracy and computation time (average time for each scene comparison). The similarity metric used here is the Histograms Jaccard Coefficient, and the case base comprises 3000 scenes, as in the experiments of [1] and [2]. It clearly appears that our histogram-based approach can easily attain the accuracy of the original "list of objects approach," while being computable in significantly less time. Our interpretation of this result is that the loss of information resulting from the fuzzy histogram representation is not a problem, and on the contrary we could conjecture that it actually improves the representation by generalizing the data. In this particular evaluation, the use of fuzzy logic does not make a clear difference. Varying the dimension of the representation causes a near-linear increase in processing time, but the method remains highly efficient.

However, as noted in the previous Section, the scene segmentation causes a loss of information, which places an impassable upper bound on the potential accuracy of the non-fuzzy logic approach. Assuming we optimized some parameters of our CBR agent, as in [2], we still could not surpass a certain level of accuracy.

Table 2. Indistinguishability of scenes, with and without fuzzy logic

Number of indistinguishable[a] scenes (total 9264)

Grid Dimension	3×3	3×5	4×6	5×8
Non-fuzzy	5309	4697	4773	3075
Fuzzy	354	328	221	209

Number of indistinguishable scenes with different actions

Non-fuzzy	2320	1660	1712	578
Fuzzy	34	6	4	4

---

[a] We refer to a scene as indistinguishable if there exists at least one distinct scene that has the same representation

This limitation is shown in Table 2. Here, from our full list of working logs, we counted every scene which is not unique (in terms of histogram representation), and for these non-unique scenes, how many were identical to another scene but associated to a different action, i.e. a "similar problem with a different solution." As expected, the use of fuzzy logic clearly removes this overgeneralisation. The few indistinguishable scenes in the fuzzy case are due to the constant value used for the membership functions of the extremity grid cells (see Fig. 2).

Finally, in order to evaluate the robustness of the similarity metrics, we varied the grid size from 3 × 5 to 5 × 8, i.e. the total dimension of the representation varying from 105 to 280 dimensions. The accuracy of the imitation is plotted against the total dimension of the representation in Fig. 3. The Histograms Jaccard Coefficient clearly scales better than the Euclidean distance measure.

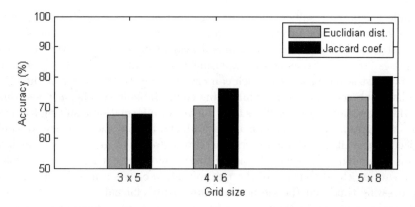

Fig. 3. Accuracy obtained using the Jaccard Coefficient Similarity, and Euclidian distance, for different grid dimensions. (note accuracy range represented 50-100%)

6   Conclusion

We have presented a method to represent the visual perception of an agent, based on a segmentation of the visible space. The distribution of objects is represented using a histogram over the segments, for each object category. Fuzzy logic allows for the smooth spreading of the count of objects over neighbouring segments according to the actual position of the objects, and thus limits boundary effects.

This representation supports practical similarity metrics, including a robust metrics based on the set-theoretic Jaccard Coefficient, and the efficient computation of the similarity metrics make this representation highly suitable for case-based reasoning.

Furthermore, this feature vector representation opens doors for the application of other machine learning techniques while avoiding the need of *a priori* manual feature selection. In our RoboCup imitation framework, we intend to build on this work by exploring automated feature selection methods.

References

1. Lam, K., Esfandiari, B., Tudino, D.: A scene-based imitation framework for Robocup clients. In: MOO Modeling Others from Observation, AAAI workshop (2006)
2. Floyd, M., Esfandiari, B., Lam, K.: A Case-based Reasoning Approach to Imitating RoboCup Players. In: Proceedings of FLAIRS-2008, Florida AI Research Symposium (to appear, 2008)
3. Robocup, http://www.robocup.org
4. Wendler, J., Lenz, M.: CBR for Dynamic Situation Assessment in an Agent-Oriented Setting. In: Aha, D., Daniels, J.J. (eds.) Proc. AAAI 1998 Workshop on Case Based Reasoning Integrations, Madison, USA (1998)
5. Karol, A., Nebel, B., Stanton, C., Williams, M.: Case Based Game Play in the RoboCup Four-Legged League Part I The Theoretical Model. In: Polani, D., Browning, B., Bonarini, A., Yoshida, K. (eds.) RoboCup 2003. LNCS (LNAI), vol. 3020, pp. 739–747. Springer, Heidelberg (2004)
6. Marling, C., Tomko, M., Gillen, M., Alexander, D., Chelberg, D.: Case-based reasoning for planning and world modeling in the robocup small size league. In: IJCAI Workshop on Issues in Designing Physical Agents for Dynamic Real-Time Environments (2003)
7. Ros, R., Veloso, M., López de Mántaras, R., Sierra, C., Arcos, J.L.: Retrieving and Reusing Game Plays for Robot Soccer. In: Roth-Berghofer, T.R., Göker, M.H., Güvenir, H.A. (eds.) ECCBR 2006. LNCS (LNAI), vol. 4106, pp. 47–61. Springer, Heidelberg (2006)
8. Moravec, H.P., Elfes, A.: High resolution maps from wide angle sonar. In: Proc. IEEE Int. Conf. Robotics and Automation, pp. 116–121 (1985)
9. Dubois, D., Prade, H.: Fuzzy Sets and Systems, theory and applications. Academic Press, New York (1980)
10. Swain, M., Ballard, D.: Color indexing. International Journal of Computer Vision 7(1), 11–32 (1991)
11. Strehl, A., Ghosh, J.: Value-based customer grouping from large retail data-sets. In: Proceedings of the SPIE Conference on Data Mining and Knowledge Discovery, Orlando, Florida, April 24-25, vol. 4057, pp. 33–42. SPIE (2000)
12. Haveliwala, T., Gionis, A., Klein, D., Indyk, P.: Similarity Search on the Web: Evaluation and Scalability Considerations, Stanford Technical Report (2000)
13. Langner, K.: The Krislet Java Client (1999), http://www.ida.liu.se/~frehe/RoboCup/Libs/libsv5xx.html

Aspects of Inconsistency Resolution in Modular Ontologies

Faezeh Ensan and Weichang Du

Faculty of Computer Science,
University of New Brunswick, Fredericton, Canada
{faezeh.ensan,wdu}@unb.ca

Abstract. Modularization entails more efficient reasoning and better performance in the ontology manipulation process. Therefore, the development of modular ontologies has recently received much attention. One of the most important issues in modular ontologies is dealing with inconsistencies. An inconsistent module may affect the other modules and cause a modular ontology to become inconsistent. Furthermore, the integration of different consistent modules may also result in inconsistency. In this paper, we investigate various types of inconsistencies in modular ontologies. We mostly focus on an interface-based ontology modularity formalism and propose a strategy and an algorithm for isolating inconsistent modules and resolving inconsistencies arisen from the integration of different ontology modules.

1 Introduction

It is well argued that the development of ontologies in a modular manner results in more efficient reasoning and better performance in comparison with monolithic approaches, specially in the case of large ontologies and distributed systems [17]. In recent years, a considerable number of models have been reported that either introduce mechanisms for extracting modules from a large ontology [8] or define new formalisms for creating modular ontologies (see [9,2] for rather comprehensive surveys). Distributed Description Logic (DDL) [6], Package-Based Description logics (P-DL)[2], $\mathcal{E}$-connections [13] and semantic import [4] are among these formalisms.

In [1], we have introduced a new formalism for modularity of ontologies based on the notion of interfaces and the exploitation of epistemic queries for retrieving the ABox assertions from ontology modules. Through this formalism, the development and configuration times of a modular ontology are distinguishable, such that ontology modules can be developed independently of each others' language and signature at development time and be integrated at configuration time. Furthermore, this formalism supports a reliable mechanism for separating local (private) definitions and axioms of a module from the (public) global ones and hence endows ontology modules with a kind of black-box behavior. Each ontology module considers the others' private section *complete enough* so that it can make assumptions based on their current knowledge.

S. Bergler (Ed.): Canadian AI 2008, LNAI 5032, pp. 84–95, 2008.
© Springer-Verlag Berlin Heidelberg 2008

One of the most important issues in modular ontologies is dealing with inconsistencies. Up until now different proposals have been given for handling inconsistency in knowledge bases [5]. They mostly attempt to either repair inconsistencies or tolerate them and find meaningful answers to queries posed to inconsistent knowledge bases. Since each module in a modular ontology is itself a description logic database, the existing works can be exploited to manage inconsistencies in each module. However, the integration of modules may arise new inconsistency problems that should be taken into account. Analogous to peer-to-peer systems [7] we can recognize two sources which may yield an inconsistent modular ontology. First, when an ontology module is not consistent and affects the consistency of the modular ontology. Second, when all ontology modules are consistent but their integration leads to an inconsistent modular ontology. [16] addresses the first inconsistency problem in the DDL formalism by providing a new semantic for DDL. Nonetheless, the second problem is an open issue in most formalisms.

Our contribution in this paper is to first explain the interface-based modular ontology formalism by means of different examples and definitions and second, to inspect its inconsistency issues. We point out both types of inconsistencies which are caused by either integrating consistent modules or propagating inconsistency from an inconsistent module to the others. Based on the idea of *hole* interpretation for inconsistent modules in [16], we propose a new semantic for the interface-based formalism to isolate the source of inconsistent in the modular ontology. In addition, We investigate the inconsistencies arisen by integrating consistent modules in some of the exiting formalisms and present an algorithm for resolving this type of inconsistency in our proposed formalism.

The rest of the paper is organized as follow: The next section gives some preliminaries of description logics and epistemic queries. The interface-based formalism for modular ontologies is discussed in Section 3. In Section 4 we provide a solution for isolating inconsistent modules in modular ontologies. In Section 5 we explore the inconsistency problems of integrating consistent modules in some exiting formalisms with some examples and propose an algorithm for dealing with inconsistency in the interface-based formalism. In Section 6 we will review the related work and finally, Section 7 concludes the paper.

2 Preliminaries

Having C_N, a set of concept names, R_N a set of role names and I_N, a set of individual names, a *concept expression* is defined as $\rho(e_1, ..., e_k)$, where ρ is a *concept constructor* which is provided by a particular description logic and e_i are either members of C_N, R_N or I_N or concept expressions.

A DL-TBox, $\mathcal{T}$, is a finite set of axioms with the form of $C \sqsubseteq D$ where C and D are concept expression. A DL-ABox, $\mathcal{A}$, is a finite set of assertions in form of $C(a)$ or $r(a, b)$ where $a, b \in I_N$, C is a concept name and r is a role name. A DL-Knowledge base is defined as $\Psi = \langle \mathcal{T}, \mathcal{A} \rangle$ and the signature of a knowledge base is the union of C_N, R_N and I_N. The semantic of a DL is defined by an interpretation $\mathcal{I} = (\Delta^{\mathcal{I}}, \cdot^{\mathcal{I}})$ where $\Delta^{\mathcal{I}}$ is a non empty set of individuals and $\cdot^{\mathcal{I}}$ is a function which maps each $C \in C_N$ to $C^I \subseteq \Delta^{\mathcal{I}}$, each $R \in R_N$ to $R^I \subseteq \Delta^{\mathcal{I}} \times \Delta^{\mathcal{I}}$ and each $a \in I_N$ to an $a^{\mathcal{I}} \in \Delta^{\mathcal{I}}$. An interpretation $\mathcal{I}$ is a model of a TBox $\mathcal{T}$, if for every inclusion axiom like $C \sqsubseteq D$ in $\mathcal{T}$, we have $C^{\mathcal{I}} \subseteq D^{\mathcal{I}}$. A TBox is consistent iff it has a model. A concept C is *satisfiable* if there is a model $\mathcal{I}$ for $\mathcal{T}$ such that $C^{\mathcal{I}} \neq \emptyset$.

Let C be a concept in a description logic DL, KC conveys a set of individuals which are known to belong to C in every model of DL. K is called an epistemic operator for description logic. An *epistemic interpretation* for DL is defined as $\mathfrak{I} = (\mathcal{J}, \mathcal{M})$, where $\mathcal{J}$ is an interpretation of DL with the domain Δ, and $\mathcal{M}$ is a set of interpretations for DL over Δ. The epistemic interpretation of non-epistemic concepts and roles does not differ in $\mathfrak{I}$ rather than $\mathcal{J}$. The epistemic interpretation for simple epistemic concepts and roles are defined as follows:

$$(KC)^{\mathfrak{I}} = \bigcap_{j \in \mathcal{M}} (C)^j$$
$$(KR)^{\mathfrak{I}} = \bigcap_{j \in \mathcal{M}} (R)^j$$

An epistemic model for a DL knowledge base Ψ is a maximal non-empty set $\mathcal{M}$ such that for every $\mathcal{J} \in \mathcal{M}$, $(\mathcal{J}, \mathcal{M})$ satisfies all TBox inclusion axioms and ABox assertions of Ψ. Queries of the form $KC(x)$ and $KR(x,y)$ are called epistemic queries. Consider an epistemic query $KC(x)$ posed to a knowledge base Ψ, $\Psi \models KC(x)$ if for every epistemic model $\mathfrak{I} = (\mathcal{J}, \mathcal{M})$ for Ψ, $x \in C^{\mathfrak{I}}$. Similarly, for a role R, $\Psi \models KR(x,y)$ if for every epistemic model $\mathfrak{I} = (\mathcal{J}, \mathcal{M})$, of Ψ, $(x, y) \in R^{\mathfrak{I}}$.

3   An Interface Based Formalism for the Modularization of Ontologies

In this section, we introduce an interface-based formalism for modular ontologies. The two drivers of the formalism are 1)the exploitation of the notion of interfaces in modular ontologies, 2) the utilization of epistemic queries for creating a mapping between individuals of different modules. An interface is a set of concept and role names and their inclusion axioms. A module is an ontology in any description logic language, which can utilize or realize a set of interfaces. A module utilizes an interface if it uses the concepts and roles of the interface in its local knowledge base, according to the TBox axioms of that interface. A module realizes an interface when it provides definitions and more specialized inclusion axioms as well as appropriate ABox assertions for the interface concepts and roles. Different modules and interfaces can be configured to form a meaningful modular ontology, in the sense that for every module which uses an interface, a realizer module is assigned to it. This formalism provides a black-box behavior so that each module which uses an interface makes the assumption that the current knowledge of the realizer module is *complete enough* for reasoning, hence there is a *closed world assumption* between different modules in a modular ontology. The formalism uses epistemic queries to allow a utilizer module employ the local knowledge base of the others. In the following, we precise the definition of the formalism.

Definition 1. *An interface I is defined as $I = \langle C_N, R_N, \mathcal{T} \rangle$ where $\mathcal{T}$ is the TBox of the interface and C_N and R_N are sets of concept and role names used in $\mathcal{T}$. I has no ABox assertions.*

Definition 2. *An ontology module M is defined as $M = \langle \mathcal{T}, I_r, I_u \rangle$ where I_r is the set of all interfaces which are realized by M, I_u is the set of all interfaces which are utilized by M and $\mathcal{T}$ is a DL TBox comprised of inclusion axioms like $C \sqsubseteq D$, C and D are concept expressions constructed by concepts and roles in the union of the signatures of M, I_r and I_u. M can be in any description logic language but it should support nominals.*

let Ψ be the knowledge base of module M. We define M is consistent regards to its interfaces iff $\Psi \sqcup (\bigcup_{i \in I_r} \mathcal{T}_i) \sqcup \bigcup_{j \in I_u} \mathcal{T}_j)$ is consistent. A module which utilizes or realizes an interface should be consistent regarding to it. A module M realizes an interface I, if $I \in I_r^M$.

A concept or role name P in an interface I is used in a module knowledge base as $I : P$. Based on definitions of interfaces and modules, we can now define a modular ontology as the follows:

Definition 3. *A modular ontology is a triple $O = \langle M, I, F \rangle$ where M is a set of ontology modules which are consistent regarding to their interfaces, I is a set of all interfaces realized or utilized by ontology modules and a configuration function F, which is defined as $F : M \times I \rightarrow M$, such that $F(M, I) = M'$ if:*

(c1) $I \in I_u^M$ and $I \in I_r^{M'}$
(c2) M and M' are consistent regarding to I
(c3) For all $I : C_i, I : R_j \in I$, Let C_i and R_j be the result sets of queries $K\,I : C_i$ and $K\,I : R_j$ posed to M', respectively. $\Psi_M \bigsqcup_i (I : C_i \equiv C_i) \bigsqcup_j (I : R_j \equiv R_j)$ should be consistent.

The third condition in Definition 3 ensures that the integration of a realizer and utilizer module at configuration time be consistent. For example, consider a module $M1 = \{\texttt{I:A} \sqsubseteq \texttt{I:B}\}$ which uses interface I. Moreover, consider there is another module $M2$ which realizes I, but the result set of queries $\texttt{KI:A}$ and $\texttt{KI:B}$ posed to $M2$ is equal to $\{a_1\}$ and $\bot$, respectively. According to condition *(c3)*, $M1$ and $M2$ cannot be connected by F at configuration time.

We name the set of all modules which are connected through the configuration function F in an modular ontology as a *path* and show it by P. $P(M)$ is a path which includes module M. The formalism does not define a global semantic for a modular ontology, instead it defines semantics for a module whose knowledge base is *augmented* by integrating with other modules through its interfaces, hence the symbol $\top$ does not have a global meaning, its interpretation will be changed in different modules.

The example in Figure 1 shows the main issues of the formalism. M is an accommodation module which utilizes interface I which is about cities and un-polluted cities. $M2$ is a module which realizes the interface I. $M2$ defines the term `UnpollutedCity` as a `City` which has at most one `factory`. In addition

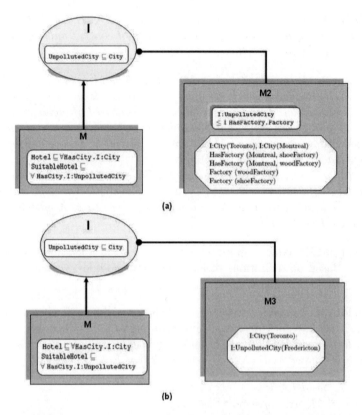

Fig. 1. Two example modular ontologies with different configurations

$M2$ has some ABox assertions about City. Note that the concepts Factory and HasFactory is completely private and can not be seen by other modules, even though they are used for defining interface concepts. $M3$ is another module in Figure 1 which realizes I. There may exist two different configurations for the modular ontology either when $F(M, I) = M2$ (Figure 1.a) or while $F(M, I) = M3$ (Figure 1.b). Note that the different configurations lead to different results for a query such as 'City(x)'. (*Toronto* and *montreal* in the first configuration and *Fredericton* and *Toronto* in the second configuration).

Example 4 shows the closed world assumption feature in the formalism.

Example 4. *(Closed World Assumption)*
In Figure Figure 1.a, the UnpollutedCity *in module $M2$ are defined as those cities that at most have one factory. Let the configuration when $F(M, I) = M2$. The module M in the modular ontology considers that the current knowledge of module $M2$ is complete enough so that it concludes that Toronto is an* UnpollutedCity.

In the following we give the definition of augmented semantic for ontology modules.

Definition 5. *Let M be an ontology module in a modular ontology $O = \langle M, I, F \rangle$, $PTBox(M)$ a set of all axioms in the TBox of all interfaces in the $P(M)$, an augmentation function $Aug : M \to M$ is a function, such that $\Psi^{Aug(M)}$ is equal to the union of the following components:*

(i) $\mathcal{T}^M$
(ii) $PTBox(M)$
(iii) $\{I : c_1\} \cup \ldots \cup \{I : c_n\}$ *where c_i is a member of the result set of the query* $KI : C$ *which is posed to $F(M, I)$ for all concepts in all $I \in I_u^M$*
(iv) $\{I : x_1\} \cup \ldots \cup \{I : x_n\} \cup \{I : y_1\} \cup \ldots \cup \{I : y_m\}$ *where $\langle x_i, y_j \rangle$ is a member of the result set of $KI : R$ which is posed to $F(M, I)$ for all roles in all $I \in I_u^M$*

Definition 6. *An augmented semantics for a module M_j in a modular ontology $O = \langle M, I, F \rangle$, is defined as $\mathcal{I}_j = (\triangle^{\mathcal{I}_j}, \cdot^{\mathcal{I}_j})$, where $\triangle^{\mathcal{I}_j}$ is a non empty domain for $Aug(M_j)$ and a mapping function $\cdot^{\mathcal{I}_j}$ which maps each concept of $Aug(M_j)$ to a subset of $\triangle^{\mathcal{I}_j}$, each role of $Aug(M_j)$ to a subset $\triangle^{\mathcal{I}_j} \times \triangle^{\mathcal{I}_j}$ and each individual name from $Aug(M_j)$ to an element $a^{\mathcal{I}} \in \triangle^{\mathcal{I}_j}$. The $\cdot^{\mathcal{I}_j}$ maps complex roles and concepts of M_j based on the semantic of concept and role constructors of M_j. For concepts and roles in utilizing interfaces, the function maps as below:*

(i) For every interface concept $I : C$, $x \in (I : C)^{\mathcal{I}_j}$ iff $\{x\}^{\mathcal{I}_j} \subseteq \triangle^{\mathcal{I}_j}$ and $\Psi_k \models KC(x)$ where KC is an epistemic query posed to $M_k = F(M_j, I)$.
(ii) For every interface role $I : R$, $\langle x, y \rangle \in (I : R)^{\mathcal{I}_j}$ iff $\{x\}^{\mathcal{I}_j} \subseteq \triangle^{\mathcal{I}_j}$ and $\{y\}^{\mathcal{I}_j} \subseteq \triangle^{\mathcal{I}_j}$ and $\Psi_k \models KR(\langle x, y \rangle)$ where KR is an epistemic query posed to $M_k = F(M_j, I)$.

An ontology module is augmentedly consistent if there is an augmented interpretation, (augmented model) $\mathcal{I}$ which satisfies all axioms and assertions in $\Psi_{Aug(M)}$. $\Psi_{Aug(M)} \models A \sqsubseteq B$ if for every augmented model $\mathcal{I}$, $A^{\mathcal{I}} \subseteq B^{\mathcal{I}}$.

Conditions (i) and (ii) in Definition 6 ensure that the individuals assigned to an interface concept or role in a module should be the same as those which are inserted to the module by querying the realizer module. For example, let M be a module which utilizes I, $C \in I$, $F(M, I) = M2$, and the result set of $K(I : C)$ posed to $M2$ be $\{c_1, c_2\}$. According to Definition 5, two nominal sets $\{c_1\}$ and $\{c_2\}$ will be inserted to $Aug(M)$. Moreover, for every augmented model $\mathcal{I}$ for module M, $(I : C)^{\mathcal{I}} \subseteq \{c_1, c_2\}^{\mathcal{I}}$.

The following lemma shows that the problem of consistency checking for augmented module is decidable. (for more details see [1])

Lemma 7. *Let M be a module in a modular ontology. It is decidable whether M is augmentedly consistent if the problem of consistency checking for M is decidable.*

Analogous to [11], the formalism does not assume a unique name assumption, so different nominals may refer to the same individual. This assumption is useful specially in the case when different nominals which are taken from different realizer modules can be interpreted as equivalent.

4   Isolating Inconsistent Modules in a Modular Ontology

Suppose a module which realizes an interface is inconsistent or it is inconsistent with regards to its interfaces. This situation may happen when in a modular ontology, a realizer module evolves and moves to an inconsistent state. Definition 8 describes the conditions that should hold in order to isolate an inconsistent module.

Definition 8. *Let I be an interface and $M1$ and $M2$ be two modules in a modular ontology such that $F(M1, I) = M2$. $M2$ is isolated from the point of view of $M1$ if for a given axiom α we have*

$$\Psi_{Aug(M1)} \models \alpha \ \text{iff} \ (\Psi_{M1} \sqcup PTBox(M1)) \models \alpha$$

Intuitively, the result sets of queries which are posed to an isolated module should not have influence on reasoning tasks of the other modules in a modular ontology. For instance, if $M1$ in the example of Figure 1.a be inconsistent, I:City is not required to be interpreted as $\{Monteral, Toronto\}$ and can be interpreted as any subset of the domain of M. We use the definition of a *hole* for an knowledge base from [16] and extend it for epistemic queries.

Definition 9. *A hole for a knowledge base Ψ is an interpretation $\mathcal{I}^h = \langle \emptyset, \cdot^{\mathcal{I}^h} \rangle$, where the domain is empty. Furthermore, an epistemic hole for a knowledge base is defined as $\mathfrak{I}^h =(\mathcal{J}, \mathcal{M})$ where the domain of for all $\mathcal{J} \in \mathcal{M}$ be epmpty set. We say $\Psi \models_h KC$ if Ψ is inconsistent and has an epistemic hole.*

Obviously, the result set of any query posed to an inconsistent knowledge base with a hole interpretation will be the empty set. We represent this empty set with the $\perp_h$ symbol and modify the definition of the augmented semantic, Definition 6, as follows:

(i) For every interface concept $I : C$, $x \in (I : C)^{\mathcal{I}_j}$ iff $\{x\}^{\mathcal{I}_j} \subseteq \Delta^{\mathcal{I}_j}$ and $\Psi_k \models KC(x)$ where KC is an epistemic query posed to $M_k = F(M_j, I)$ and it is not equal to $\perp_h$.

(ii) For every interface role $I : R$, $\langle x, y \rangle \in (I : R)^{\mathcal{I}_j}$ iff $\{x\}^{\mathcal{I}_j} \subseteq \Delta^{\mathcal{I}_j}$ and $\{y\}^{\mathcal{I}_j} \subseteq \Delta^{\mathcal{I}_j}$ and $\Psi_k \models KR(\langle x, y \rangle)$ where KR is an epistemic query posed to $M_k = F(M_j, I)$ and it is not equal to $\perp_h$.

(iii) $(I : C)^{\mathcal{I}_j} \subseteq \Delta^{\mathcal{I}_j}$ iff KC posed to $M_k = F(M_j, I)$ be equal to $\perp_h$.

(iv) $(I : R)^{\mathcal{I}_j} \subseteq \Delta^{\mathcal{I}_j} \times \Delta^{\mathcal{I}_j}$ iff KR posed to $M_k = F(M_j, I)$ be equal to $\perp_h$.

Proposition 10. *Let $M1$ be an inconsistent module with an epistemic hole which realizes interface I, $M1$ will be isolated from the point of view of all modules like M which utilize I and $F(M, I) = M1$.*

5   Handling the Inconsistencies Arisen from the Integration of Consistent Modules

In this section, we first investigate the problem of inconsistency in DDL, P-DL and semantic import formalisms through several examples and compare them to inconsistency in the interface-based formalism. Afterwards, we propose a solution for repairing an inconsistent modular ontology in the interface-based formalism.

5.1 Investigating the Inconsistency Problems in Different Formalisms

DDL [6] is a formalism for distributed distributed description logics which defines a modular ontology as a set of local TBoxes which can be semantically connected through a set of '*bridge rules*'. A bridge rule from ontology i to j can be in one of the following forms:

$$i : x \xrightarrow{\sqsubseteq} j : y \text{ an into-bridge rule}$$
$$i : x \xrightarrow{\sqsupseteq} j : y \text{ an onto-bridge rule}$$

Example 11 shows how different bridge rules may conflict with each other and lead to an inconsistent modular ontology even though each local TBox is consistent.

Example 11. *(Inconsistency arisen by integrating consistent TBoxes in DDL)*

Let $T1 = \{$ Penguin $\sqsubseteq$ HaveWings$\}$ *and* $T2 = \{$ Bird $\sqsubseteq$ Fly$\}$ *be two local TBoxes and* B_{12} *a set of two following bridge rules from* $T1$ *to* $T2$:

(1) 1:Penguin $\xrightarrow{\sqsubseteq}$ 2 : ¬Fly
(2) 1:HaveWings $\xrightarrow{\sqsubseteq}$ 2 :Bird

Obviously, the concept Penguin *is not satisfiable in TBox* $T1$. *(For a formal definition of distributed interpretation and satisfiability in DDL see [6]).*

P-DL [2] and semantic import [4] are two formalisms for modular ontologies which rely on importing concepts and roles from other modules rather than setting a linkage between them [3]. Both formalisms imply that a modular ontology is consistent if the union of all compound modules is consistent. ([9] shows that the consistency checking of a P-DL modular ontology comprised of $\mathcal{SHIQ}$ TBoxes can be reduced to checking the consistency of the union of the compound TBoxes). Note that the inconsistency problem of integrating different modules is similar to inconsistency issues in integrating a set of independent ontologies, hence the modularity does not ease the problem of inconsistency in these approaches.

Since the interface-based formalism introduced in Section 3 uses epistemic queries for retrieving ABox assertions, its consistency problem cannot be reduced to the consistency of the union of all modules. Example 12 shows an instance of the inconsistency problem in this formalism which is caused by integrating consistent modules.

Example 12. *Let* M *be a module with the TBox axiom:* $\{$ A $\sqsubseteq$ (¬I1:B $\sqcap$ I2:C) $\sqcap$ $\exists$R.(I1:B $\sqcap$ I2:C) $\}$, *where* $I1, I2 \in I_u^M$. *Furthermore, let* $F(M, I1) = M1$

and $F(M, I2) = M2$ and the result set of the queries KB and KC posed to $M1$ and $M2$ be nominals $\{o_1\}$ and $\{o_2\}$, respectively. The augmented semantic of M leads A to be unsatisfiable. (two distinct nominals cannot have any intersection so $(\text{I1:B} \sqcap \text{I2:C}) = \bot)$ i.e, $\Psi_{Aug(M)} \models A \sqsubseteq \bot$.

An important point in Example 12 is that since this formalism does not assume unique name assumption, $\{o_1\}$ may be interpreted to be equivalent to $\{o_2\}$. Even in this case, A cannot be satisfiable, because $(\neg\text{I1:B} \sqcap \text{I2:C})$ will be an empty set.

5.2   Repairing Inconsistencies in Interface Based Modularity Formalism

The main issue that we concentrate on for repairing inconsistencies in the interface based modularity formalism is to *weaken* the restrictions implied by the realizer modules in order to reach a consistent augmented ontology module. For example in the case of Example 12, a consistent ontology can be obtained by removing either $\text{I1:B} \equiv \{o_1\}$ or $\text{I2:C} \equiv \{o_2\}$ restrictions. Note that we do not remove the inserted nominals from the domain of ontology module. We only remove those restrictions where the interface concept should be equal to this nominal. Having this goal, we add new definitions to those introduced in Section 3. We say a module M is *consistently-augmented* by an interface $I \in I_u^M$, if there is a model $\mathcal{I} = \langle \triangle^{\mathcal{I}}, \cdot^{\mathcal{I}} \rangle$ for $Aug(M)$ such that it satisfies the conditions (i) and (ii) of Definition 6 for all concepts and roles in I.

The decidability of consistency checking problem of a module which is augmented by a set of interfaces can be concluded From Lemma 7, hence we have:

Proposition 13. *Let M be a module in a modular ontology and $I \subseteq I_U^M$. It is decidable whether M is consistently-augmented by I, if the problem of consistency checking for M is decidable.*

For resolving inconsistencies, we try to find the maximum number of interfaces in the utilizing interface set of a module when their realizations do not have conflict with each other. Subsequently, we augment the module with this set of interfaces. Obviously, we prefer to keep as much interface realizations as possible in a module, so the maximality of this set is important for us. Definition 14 presents a formal definition for a maximal consistent interface set for a module.

Definition 14. *A Maximal Consistent Interface set for a module M is defined as $MCI(M) \subseteq I_u^M$ such that M is consistently-augmented by $MCI(M)$ and if $|MCI(M)| = n$, for each set $I \subseteq I_u^M$ that $|I| > n$, M cannot be consistently-augmented by I. $\Psi_{Aug(M)} \models_{MCI} \alpha$ if α holds for every model of M which is consistently-augmented by $MCI(M)$.*

In the following, we present an algorithm (Algorithm 1) for finding maximal consistent interface set and prove that it will always terminate.

Algorithm 1. Maximal Consistent Interface Set (MCI)

Input: An ontology module $M = \langle \mathcal{T}, I_u^M, I_r^M \rangle$ in a modular ontology $O = \langle M, I, F \rangle$.
Output: A set of maximal consistent interfaces for M
$MCI := \emptyset$
$n := |I_u^M|$
repeat
    $MCI = I$ when $I \subseteq I_u^M$ and $|I| = n$
    $n := n - 1$
until M is consistently-augmented by MCI
return MCI

Algorithm 1 selects a subset of utilizing interfaces for a module M, check whether M is consistently-augmented by this set or not. As we have shown in Proposition 13, this is a decidable problem. If so, the algorithm terminates and returns this set as MCI, else it decrease the size of the selected subsets by 1 and repeats the process. In the first iteration the size of the selected subset is equal to the size of I_u^M, so if the algorithm terminates in this step, it implies that there are no conflicts between different interfaces of the module. Lemma 15 shows that the algorithm always terminates.

Lemma 15. *Given a module M in an modular ontology O, Algorithm 1 always terminates.*

Proof. The integration of the knowledge base of M with each of its utilizing interfaces is consistent due to condition *(c3)* of Definition 3. So in the worst case the algorithm will terminate for $n = 1$.

The following example shows the operations of Algorithm1:

Example 16. *Given a modular ontology according to Example 12, in the first iteration, the algorithm selects $MCI = \{I1, I2\}$ and checks the consistency of M which is augmented by the realization of both $I1$ and $I2$. As it is shown in Example 12, M is not consistent in this condition. In the second iteration, Algorithm 1 selects either $MCI = \{I1\}$ or $MCI = \{I2\}$ and checks the consistency of M augmented by MCI. M is consistent in this step since for example for $MCI = \{I1\}$, $I2 : C$ is not required to be equal to $\{o_2\}$ and can be interpreted as any subset of the domain of M.*

6 Related Work

The problem of inconsistency management and resolution in description logics and ontologies has been addressed by several work in the literature [12,10,15,14]. The existing proposals mostly attempt to either tolerate inconsistencies or resolve them and repair the inconsistent ontology. The tolerating approach attempts to apply a kind of non standard reasoning strategy on an inconsistent ontology and obtain meaningful results for queries. [12] introduces a framework for reasoning with inconsistent ontologies. It's idea is that for a given query Q, select a consistent subset of the inconsistent ontology which is *relevant* to Q, and pose the query to it. This idea is also employed in [10] for reasoning with evolving ontologies which have moved to an inconsistent state.

Repairing inconsistencies is comprised of finding the inconsistent part of an ontology and resolving it. [14] presents an algorithm for resolving inconsistencies in *stratified* description logic knowledge bases by weakening the knowledge bases which are found to be responsible for inconsistency. A *stratified* description logic knowledge base is defined as $K = \{S_1, ..., S_n\}$ where S_i is a knowledge base while its axioms and assertions have been assumed to have the same reliability, and for each $S_j, j > i$ S_i is more reliable. The notion of *stratified* DLs, prioritize the knowledge bases hence the less reliable the DL knowledge base is, the more likely to be weakened by the resolving algorithm. [15] introduces a mechanism for resolving inconsistencies arisen by ABox assertions in *stratified* description logic knowledge bases. The mechanism applies a strategy for weakening the conflicting knowledge bases by adding some *exceptions* to general inclusion axioms. For example, if a knowledge base contains $\{C \sqsubseteq D, C(a), \neg D(a)\}$, the weakening strategy changes $C \sqsubseteq D$ to $C \sqcap \neg\{a\} \sqsubseteq D$.

The above proposals investigate the inconsistency issues in monolithic ontologies or a set of DLs without any linkage or mapping between them. There are a few work for investigating the inconsistency issues in exiting modular ontology formalisms [16]. We believe that modularity can ease the process of finding and resolving inconsistencies. For example, in the case of interface-based modular ontology which is investigated in this paper, instead of examining the role of each assertional or inclusional axiom in the inconsistency of the integrated ontology (as is suggested by the above introduced mechanisms), one can only check the utilizer interfaces of a module.

7   Concluding Remarks

In this paper, we have investigated the issue of inconsistency in an interfaced-based modular ontology formalism. We addressed two types of inconsistencies in a modular ontology: when a module is inconsistent and causes the modular ontology to be inconsistent and when all modules are consistent but the integration of them results in inconsistency. For isolating the inconsistent module, we extend the semantics of the interface based formalism such that the inconsistency of a module does not affect to the other modules which utilize it. In addition, we have proposed an algorithm for resolving inconsistencies arisen by integrating consistent modules in a modular ontology.

As future work, we intend to scrutinize the impact of changes in a module on the other modules inconsistencies in the interface based modular ontology formalism. A similar effort has been done in [17] to examine the influences of changes in DDL. However the problem of change consequences vary from one formalism to another. Specially, introducing epistemic queries in the interface-based formalism brings non-monotonic features that should be taken into account during change analysis.

References

1. On the formalization of interface-based modular ontologies under the closed-world assumption. Tech. rep. (2008)
2. Bao, J., Caragea, D., Honavar, V.: Modular ontologies - a formal investigation of semantics and expressivity. In: Mizoguchi, R., Shi, Z.-Z., Giunchiglia, F. (eds.) ASWC 2006. LNCS, vol. 4185, pp. 616–631. Springer, Heidelberg (2006)
3. Bao, J., Caragea, D., Honavar, V.: On the semantics of linking and importing in modular ontologies. In: International Semantic Web Conference, pp. 72–86 (2006)
4. Bao, J., Slutzki, G., Honavar, V.: A semantic importing approach to knowledge reuse from multiple ontologies. In: AAAI, pp. 1304–1309 (2007)
5. Benferhat, S., Dubois, D., Prade, H.: Some syntactic approaches to the handling of inconsistent knowledge bases: A comparative study part 1: The flat case. Studia Logica 58(1), 17–45 (1997)
6. Borgida, A., Serafini, L.: Distributed description logics: Assimilating information from peer sources. J. Data Semantics 1, 153–184 (2003)
7. Calvanese, D., De Giacomo, G., Lembo, D., Lenzerini, M., Rosati, R.: Inconsistency tolerance in P2P data integration: an epistemic logic approach. In: Bierman, G., Koch, C. (eds.) DBPL 2005. LNCS, vol. 3774, pp. 90–105. Springer, Heidelberg (2005)
8. Grau, B.C., Horrocks, I., Kazakov, Y., Sattler, U.: Just the right amount: extracting modules from ontologies. In: WWW 2007: Proceedings of the 16th international conference on World Wide Web, pp. 717–726. ACM, New York (2007)
9. Grau, B.C., Kutz, O.: Modular ontology languages revisited. In: Proceedings of the IJCAI 2007 Workshop on Semantic Web for Collaborative Knowledge Acquisition, Hyderabad, India (January 2007)
10. Haase, P., van Harmelen, F., Huang, Z., Stuckenschmidt, H., Sure, Y.: A framework for handling inconsistency in changing ontologies. In: International Semantic Web Conference, pp. 353–367 (2005)
11. Horrocks, I., Sattler, U.: Ontology reasoning in the shoq(d) description logic. In: IJCAI, pp. 199–204 (2001)
12. Huang, Z., van Harmelen, F., ten Teije, A.: Reasoning with inconsistent ontologies. In: IJCAI, pp. 454–459 (2005)
13. Kutz, O., Lutz, C., Wolter, F., Zakharyaschev, M.: E-connections of abstract description systems. Artif. Intell. 156(1), 1–73 (2004)
14. Meyer, T., Lee, K., Booth, R.: Knowledge integration for description logics. In: AAAI, pp. 645–650 (2005)
15. Qi, G., Liu, W., Bell, D.: A revision-based approach to handling inconsistency in description logics. Artif. Intell. Rev. 26(1-2), 115–128 (2006)
16. Serafini, L., Borgida, A., Tamilin, A.: Aspects of distributed and modular ontology reasoning. In: IJCAI, pp. 570–575 (2005)
17. Stuckenschmidt, H., Klein, M.C.A.: Integrity and change in modular ontologies. In: IJCAI, pp. 900–908 (2003)

Fast Markov Blanket Discovery Algorithm Via Local Learning within Single Pass

Shunkai Fu and Michel C. Desmarais

Ecole Polytechnique de Montreal,
C.P.6079, Succ. Centre-ville, Montreal, Quebec, Canada
{shukai.fu,michel.desmarais}@polymtl.ca

Abstract. Learning of Markov blanket (MB) can be regarded as an optimal solution to the feature selection problem. In this paper, an efficient and effective framework is suggested for learning MB. Firstly, we propose a novel algorithm, called Iterative Parent-Child based search of MB (IPC-MB), to induce MB without having to learn a whole Bayesian network first. It is proved correct, and is demonstrated to be more efficient than the current state of the art, PCMB, by requiring much fewer conditional independence (CI) tests. We show how to construct an AD-tree into the implementation so that computational efficiency is further increased through collecting full statistics within a single data pass. We conclude that IPC-MB plus AD-tree appears a very attractive solution in very large applications.

Keywords: Markov blanket, local learning, feature selection, single pass, AD-tree.

1 Introduction

Classification is a fundamental task in data mining and machine learning that requires learning a classifier through the observation of data. Basically, a classifier is a function that maps instances described by a set of attributes to a class label. How to identify the minimal, or close to minimal, subset of variables that best predicts the target variable of interest is known as feature (or variable) subset selection (FSS). In the past three decades, FSS for classification has been given considerable attention, and it is even more critical today in many applications, like biomedicine, where high dimensionality but few observations are challenging traditional FSS algorithms.

A principle solution to the feature selection problem is to determine a subset of attributes that can render the rest of all attributes independent of the variable of interest [8,9,16]. Koller and Sahami (KS) [9] first recognized that the Markov blanket (see its definition below) of a given target attribute is the theoretically optimal set of attributes to predict the target's value, though the Markov blanket itself is not a new concept and can be traced back to 1988 [11].

A Markov blanket of a target attribute T renders it statistically independent from all the remaining attributes, that is, given the values of the attributes in the Markov

S. Bergler (Ed.): Canadian AI 2008, LNAI 5032, pp. 96–107, 2008.
© Springer-Verlag Berlin Heidelberg 2008

blanket, the probability distribution of T is completely determined and knowledge of any other variable(s) becomes superfluous [11].

Definition 1 (Conditional independent). Variable X and T are conditionally independent given the set of variables Z (bold symbol is used for set), iff. $P(T \mid X, Z) = P(T \mid Z)$, denoted as $T \perp X \mid Z$.

Similarly, $T \not\perp X \mid Z$ is used to denote that X and T are **NOT** conditionally independent given Z.

Definition 2 (Markov blanket, *MB*). Given all attributes U of a problem domain, a Markov blanket of an attribute $T \in U$ is any subset $MB \subseteq U \backslash \{T\}$ for which

$$\forall X \in U \setminus \{T\} \setminus MB, \ T \perp X \mid MB$$

A set is called **Markov boundary** of T if it is a minimal Markov blanket of T.

Definition 3 (Faithfulness). A Bayesian network G and a joint distribution P are faithful to one another, if and only if every conditional independence encoded by the graph of G is also present in P, i.e., $T \perp_G X \mid Z \Leftrightarrow T \perp_P X \mid Z$ [12].

Pearl [11] points out that: if the probability distribution over U can be faithfully represented by a Bayesian network (BN), which is one kind of graphical model that compactly represent a joint probability distribution among U using a directed acyclic graph, then the Markov blanket of an attribute T is unique, composing of the T's parents, children and spouses (sharing common children with T). So, given the faithfulness assumption, learning an attribute's Markov blanket actually corresponds to the discovery of its Markov boundary, and therefore can be viewed as selecting the optimal minimum set of feature to predict a given T. In the remaining text, unless explicitly mentioned, Markov blanket of T will refer to its Markov boundary under the faithfulness assumption, and it is denoted as $MB(T)$.

$MB(T)$ is trivial to obtain if we can learn a BN over the U first, but the BN's structure learning is known as NP-complete, and readily becomes non-tractable in large scale applications where thousands of attributes are involved. Until now, none of existing known BN learning algorithms claims to scale correctly over more than a few hundred variables. For example, the publicly available versions of the PC [12] and the TPDA (also known as PowerConstructor) [2] algorithms accept datasets with only 100 and 255 variables respectively.

The goal of this paper is to develop an efficient algorithm for the discovery of Markov blanket from data without having to learn a BN first.

2 Related Work

A reasonable compromise to learning the full BN is to discover only the local structure around an attribute T of interest. We refer to the conventional BN learning as *global learning* and the latter as *local learning*. Local learning of $MB(T)$ is expected to remain a viable solution in domains with thousands of attributes.

Local learning of *MB* began to attract attention after the work of KS [9]. However, the KS algorithm is heuristic, and provides no theoretical guarantee of success. Grow-Shrink (GS) algorithm [10] is the first provably correct one, and, as indicated by its name, it contains two sequential phases, growing first and shrinking secondly. To improve the speed and reliability, several variants of GS, like IAMB, InterIAMB [15,16] and Fast-IAMB[17], were proposed. They are proved correct given the faithfulness assumption, and indeed make the *MB* discovery more time efficient, but none of them are data efficient. In practice, to ensure reliable independence tests, which is essential for this family of algorithm, IAMB and its variants decide a test is reliable when the number of instances available is at least five times the number of degree of freedom in the test. This means that the number of instances required by IAMB to identify $MB(T)$ is at least exponential in the size of $MB(T)$, because the number of degrees of freedom in a test is exponential with respect to the size of conditioning set, and the test to add a new node in $MB(T)$ will be conditioned on at least the current nodes in $MB(T)$ (Line 4, Table 1 in [8]).

Several trials were made to overcome this limitation, including MMPC/MB[14], HITON-PC/MB[1] and PCMB[8]. All of them have the same two assumptions as IAMB, i.e. faithfulness and correct independence test, but they differ from IAMB by taking into account the graph topology, which helps to improve data efficiency through conditioning over a smaller set instead of the whole $MB(T)$ as done by IAMB. However, MMPC/MB and HITON-PC/MB are shown not always correct by the authors of PCMB since false positives will be wrongly learned due to non-complete conditional independence tests [8]. So, based on our knowledge, PCMB is the only one proved correct, scalable and represents a truly data-efficient means to induce the MB.

In this paper, we propose a novel MB local learning algorithm, called Iterative Parent-Child based search of Markov Blanket (IPC-MB). It is built on the same two assumptions of IAMB and PCMB. IPC-MB algorithm is compared with two of the algorithms discussed above: IAMB and PCMB. IAMB is a well known algorithm and referred to as MB local discovery. PCMB is the most successful break over IAMB to our knowledge and our own work is based on this algorithm.

Akin to PCMB, IPC-MB is designed to execute an efficient search by taking the topology into account to ensure a data efficient algorithm. We believe this approach is an effective means to conquer the data inefficiency problem occurring in GS, IABM and their variants. As its name implies, IPC-MB starts the search of $MB(T)$ from its neighbors first, which actually are the parents and children of T, denoted as $PC(T)$. Then, given each $X \in PC(T)$, it further searches for $PC(X)$ and checks each $Y \in PC(X)$ to determine if it is the spouse of T or not. So, our algorithm is quite similar to PCMB, but it finds the *PC* of an attribute in a much more efficient manner. More detail about the algorithm can be found in Section 3. Considering that the discovery of $PC(X)$ is a common basic operation for PCMB and IPC-MB, its efficiency will directly influence the overall performance of algorithm. Experiment results of algorithms comparison are reported and discussed in Section 5.

3 Local Learning Algorithm of Markov Blanket: IPC-MB

3.1 Overall Design

As discussed in Section 1 and 2, the IPC-MB algorithm is based on two assumptions, faithfulness and correct conditional test, from which the introduction and proof of this algorithm will be given.

Table 1. IPC-MB Algorithm

```
RecognizePC (T: target,                      IPC-MB( D: Dataset, ε:threshold )
  ADJ_T :Adjacency set to search
  D: Dataset,  ε:threshold)                  {
{                                                // Recognize T'parents/children
1  NonPC = ∅ ;                                1  CanADJ_T = U \ {T} ;
2  cutSetSize = 0;                            2  PC =RecognizePC(T ,CanADJ_T ,D , ε );
3  do                                         3  MB = PC ;
4    for(each X ∈ ADJ_T ) do                 4  for(each X ∈ PC ) do
5      for(each S ⊆ ADJ_T \{X}              //Recognize a true positive, and its
                                              //parents/children as spouse candidates.
6        with |S| =cutSetSize) do            5    CanADJ_X = U \ {X} ;
7        if (I_D(X_i,T|S)≤ ε ) then           6    CanSP = RecognizePC( X, CanADJ_X , D , ε );
8          NonPC = NonPC∪{X} ;                7    if( T ∉ CanSP ) then
9          Sepset_T,X = S ;                   8       MB = MB\{ X };
10         break;                            9       continue ;
11       end if                             10   end if
12     end for                                   //Recognize true positives
13   end for                                11   for(each Y ∈ CanSP and Y ∉ MB ) do
14   if (| NonPC |> 0 )then                  12     if ( I_D(T,Y | Sepset_T,Y ∪ X) > ε ) then
15     ADJ_T = ADJ_T \ NonPC                 13       MB = MB∪(Y) ;
16     cutSetSize +=1;                       14     end if
17     NonPC = ∅ ;                           15   end for
18   else                                    16 end for
19     break;                                17 return MB ;
20   end if                                  }
21 while (|ADJ_T |> cutSetSize)
22 return ADJ_T ;
}
```

On a BN over variables U , the $MB(T)$ contains parents and children of T , i.e. those nodes directly connected to T , and its spouses, i.e. parents of T 's children. We denote these two sets as $PC(T)$ and $SP(T)$ respectively. With these considerations in mind, learning $MB(T)$ amounts to deciding which nodes are directly connected to T and which directly connect to those nodes adjacent to T (connect to T with an arc by ignoring the orientation).

As outline above, local learning of $MB(T)$ amounts to (1) which nodes are adjacent to T among $U \setminus \{T\}$, i.e. $PC(T)$ here, and (2) which are adjacent to $PC(T)$ and point to children of T in the remaining attributes $U \setminus \{T\} \setminus PC$, i.e. $SP(T)$. This process is actually a breadth-first search procedure.

We need not care about the relations among $PC(T)$, $SP(T)$ and between $PC(T)$ and $SP(T)$, considering that we are only interested in which attributes belong to $MB(T)$. Therefore, this strategy will allow us to learn $MB(T)$ solely through local learning, reducing the search space greatly.

3.2 Theoretical Basis

In this section, we provide the theoretical background for the correctness of our algorithm.

Theorem 1. If a Bayesian network G is faithful to a probability distribution P, then for each pair of nodes X and Y in G, X and Y are adjacent in G iff. $X \not\perp Y \mid Z$ for all Z such that X and $Y \notin Z$. [12]

Lemma 1. If a Bayesian network G is faithful to a probability distribution P, then for each pair of nodes X and Y in G, if there exists Z such that X and $Y \notin Z$, $X \perp Y \mid Z$, then X and Y are **NOT** adjacent in G.

We get Lemma 1 from Theorem 1, and its proof is trivial. The first phase of IPC-MB, *RecognizePC* (Table 1), relies upon this basis. In fact, the classical structure learning algorithm PC [12, 13] is the first one designed on this basis.

Theorem 2. If a Bayesian network G is faithful to a probability distribution P, then for each triplet of nodes X, Y and W in G such that X and Y are adjacent to W, but X and Y are not adjacent, $X \rightarrow W \leftarrow Y$ is a sub-graph of G iff $X \not\perp Y \mid Z$ for all Z such that X and $Y \notin Z$, and $W \notin Z$. [12]

Theorem 2 combined with Theorem 1 form the basis of IPC-MB's second phase, the discovery of T's spouses (Table 1). Given each $X \in PC(T)$ learned via *RecognizePC*, we can learn $PC(X)$ in a similar way as we learn $PC(T)$. For each $Y \in PC(X)$, if we known $T \not\perp Y \mid Z$ for all Z such that T, $Y \notin Z$ and $X \in Z$, $T \rightarrow X \leftarrow Y$ is a sub-graph of G; therefore Y is a parent of X; since X is the common child between Y and T, Y is known as one spouse of T. This inference brings us Lemma 2.

Lemma 2. In a Bayesian network G faithful to a probability distribution P, given $X \in PC(T)$, and $Y \in PC(X)$, if $T \not\perp Y \mid Z$ for all Z such that T, $Y \notin Z$ and $X \in Z$, then Y is a spouse of T.

3.3 Iterative Parent-Child Based Search of Markov Blanket

Learn parents/children

As the name of this algorithm indicates, the discovery of parent-child is the critical to the locality nature of this algorithm.

RecognizePC procedure (Table 1) is responsible for the search of parent/child candidates. It starts by connecting the current active target T (its first parameter) to all other nodes not visited by *RecognizePC* before, with non-oriented edges. Then, it deletes the edge (T, X_i) if there is any subset of $ADJ_T \setminus \{X_i\}$ conditioning on which T and X_i is independent based on the significance of a conditional independence test, I_D (line 5-12). X_i is removed finally at line 15.

In IPC-MB (discussed in the next section), *RecognizePC* appears at two different locations, line 2 and 6 respectively. This is designed to ensure that for each pair (X, Y), both *RecognizePC(X)* and *RecognizePC(Y)* will be called, and $X - Y$ is true only when $Y \in PC(X)$ and $X \in PC(Y)$, avoiding that any false nodes enter into $MB(T)$. Overall, this is similar to the conventional PC structure learning algorithm, but it limits the search to the neighbors of the target node. This is why local learning, instead of global learning, is possible and considerable time can be saved especially in applications with a large number of variables.

The correctness of our approach to find the parents and children of a specific node T is the basis for the whole algorithm, so the following theorem is defined.

Theorem 3. All parents and children of the node T of interest can be correctly recognized given the faithfulness assumption.

Proof. (i) A potential link between (T, X), where X is a candidate of $PC(T)$, is kept only when there is no set S such that T and $X \notin S$, and $X \not\perp T \mid S$, i.e. T and X is conditional independent given S. This is the direct application of Theorem 1, and this result guarantees that no false parent/child will be added into $PC(T)$ given a sufficiently low ε; (ii) It is trivial to see that algorithm xxx above [provide a name or a reference because "our" is ambiguous] is exhaustive and covers all possible conditioning sets S. (iii) Since algorithm RecognizePC always start by connecting T with all non-scanned nodes, it follows that no true positive that should be included will be missed by the algorithm. Therefore, all parents and children of T can be identified.

Learn spouses

Learning of T's spouses involves two steps. For each candidate parent/child of T (line 4), *RecognizePC* (X) is called to collect X's parents and children, $PC(X)$, as shown in lines 4-6 of *IPC-MB* procedure. If $T \notin PC(X)$, then we just ignore the remaining part of current loop. If $T \in PC(X)$, we know it is a true parent/child of T, and $PC(X)$ contains the spouse candidates of T. Secondly, we begin to discover those true spouse candidates given Theorem 2 (lines 10-12).

Theorem 4. The result induced by *IPC-MB* is the complete Markov blanket of *T* .

*Proof.(i) True parents/children can be returned by RecognizePC(T) if we use it correctly, as supported by Theorem 3 and our discussion above; (ii)Although some false spouses will be returned when we call Recognize(X), only true spouses that can satisfy the test of line 12 in IPC-MB, based on Theorem 2 and the underlying topology. Therefore, only true spouses will enter into **MB** finally.*

4 All Dimension-Tree (AD-Tree)

Being a CI test-based algorithm, IPC-MB depends intensively on the tabulation of a joint frequency distributions, e.g. $C(X_1 = x_1 \wedge X_3 = x_3)$. At one extreme, we can look through the dataset to collect a specific co-occurrence table on demand, and another data pass for another a new query. This can be terribly time consuming considering thousands of CI tests are required (see our experiment example in Section 4), and it becomes worse quickly when the number of attributes increases, or the dataset becomes larger. In the implementation of IPC-MB, we try to cache as much statistics that can be expected given the current cutset size (see Table 1) as possible, aiming at reducing the data passes. It indeed works, but dozens of data passes still are necessary in our testing, which prohibits IPC-MB from being an economic candidate in large applications. An ideal solution we are looking for should be efficient not only in time, allowing all sufficient statistics to be collected in single data pass, but also in memory, at least scaling relative to the complexity of problems (i.e. number of attributes).

All Dimensions tree (AD-tree), proposed by Moore and Lee [18,19], represents such a solution. It is introduced for representing the cached joint frequency counting statistics for a categorical data set, from which we can query any co-occurrence table we need without having to go through the data repeatedly. Fig 1 is an example from [19], where attributes X_1, X_2 and X_3 have 2, 4 and 2 categories respectively. Each rectangular node in the tree stores the value of one conjunctive counting query, and they are called AD-nodes. The children of AD-node are called Vary nodes, displayed as ovals. Each corresponds to an attribute with index greater than that of its parent node.

A tree built in this way would be enormous for non-trivially sized problems, and its complexity increases quickly as the number of attributes and number of categories per attribute increase. However, considering that normally only a small percent of the all possible instances happens given attributes { X_i }, the actual tree will be sparse very often, with many zero counts [18,19]. This characteristic allows a great reduction in memory consumption, and it is implemented in the IPC-MB algorithm. Readers can also consult the original references by the authors of AD-tree for alternative and potentially interesting techniques which we do not investigate here.

In this project, we refer IPC-MB with AD-tree as IPC-MB++, indicating that it is an enhanced version. Its algorithm specification is just same as IPC-MB (see Table 1)

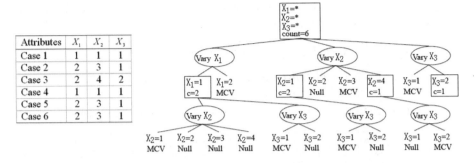

Fig. 1. Sample data with tree attributes and six records (Left), and its corresponding AD-tree (Right)

since we hide the details of tree construction and query, allowing readers focusing on the primary architecture.

5 Experiment and Analysis

5.1 Experiment Design

We only compare our algorithm with PCMB since interested readers can find the comparison of PCMB and IAMB in [8]. In the experiment, we use synthetic data sampled from known Alarm BN [7] which is composed of 37 nodes. The Alarm network is well-known as it has been used in a large number of studies on probabilistic reasoning. The network modeling situations arise from the medicine world. We run PCMB and IPC-MB with each node in the BN as the target variable T iteratively and, then, report the average performance when different size of data is given, including accuracy, data efficiency, time efficiency, scalability, and usefulness of information found.

5.2 Evaluation and Analysis

One of the basic assumptions of these three algorithms is that the independence tests are valid. To make them PCMB and IPC-MB, feasible in practice, we perform a test to check if the conditional test to do is reliable, and skip the result if not. As indicated in [15], IAMB considers a test to be reliable when the number of instances in D is at least five times the number of degrees of freedom in the test. PCMB follows this standard in [8], and so does our algorithm IPC-MB to maintain a comparable experiment result.

Accuracy and data efficiency

We measure the accuracy of induction through the precision and recall over all the nodes for the BN. **Precision** is the number of true positives in the returned output divided by the number of nodes in the output. **Recall** is the number of true positives in the output divided by the number of true positives known in the true BN model. We also combine precision and recall as

$$\text{Distance} = \sqrt{(1 - precision)^2 + (1 - recall)^2}$$

to measure the Euclidean **distance** from precision and recall[8].

Table 2. Accuracy comparison of PCMB and IPC-MB over Alarm network

Instances	Algorithm	Precision	Recall	Distance
1000	PCMB	.76±.04	.83±.07	.30±.06
1000	IPC-MB	.92±.03	.84±.03	.18±.04
2000	PCMB	.79±.04	.91±.04	.23±.05
2000	IPC-MB	.94±.02	.91±.03	.11±.02
5000	PCMB	.80±.05	.95±.01	.21±.04
5000	IPC-MB	.94±.03	.95±.01	.08±.02
10000	PCMB	.81±.03	.95±.01	.20±.03
10000	IPC-MB	.93±.02	.96±.00	.08±.02
20000	PCMB	.81±.02	.96±.00	.20±.01
20000	IPC-MB	.93±.03	.96±.00	.08±.02

Table 2 shows the average precision, recall and distance performance about PCMB and IPC-MB given different size of data sampled from the Alarm network. From which, we notice that PCMB is worse than IPC-MB, which can be explained by its search strategy of minimum conditioning set. It needs to go through conditioning sets with size ranging from small to large, so PCMB has the similar problem like IAMB when conditioned on large set. However, IPC-MB's strategy, always conditioning on smallest conditioning set and removing as many as possible true negative ones first, prevents it from this weakness. Therefore, IPC-MB has higher accuracy rate compared with PCMB given the same size training data, and this also reflects IPC-MB's advantage on data efficiency.

Time efficiency

To measure time efficiency, we refer to the number of data pass and CI test occurring in PCMB, IPC-MB and the enhanced version, IPC-MB++ (IPC-MB plus AD-tree). One data pass corresponds to the scanning of the whole data for one time. In PCMB and IPC-MB, we only collect all the related statistics information (consumed by CI tests) that can be expected currently. However, in IPC-MB++, we collect the full statistics before the learning begins. In Table 3, "# rounds" refers to the total number of data passes we need to finish the MB induction on all the 37 nodes of Alarm BN. "# CI test" is defined similarly. Generally, the larger are these two numbers, the slower is the algorithm.

As Table 3 shows, in this study, IPC-MB requires less than 10% and 60% of the total amount of data passes and CI tests done by PCMB respectively. Compared with IPC-MB, IPC-MB++ needs only one data pass during the whole running procedure, but same CI tests. This is quite an attractive merit if we recognize the time spent in data scanning is quite consuming, especially when we have large observations and it is impossible to store them all in memory.

Table 3. Comparison of time complexity required by different MB induction algorithms, in terms of number of data pass and CI test

Instances	Algorithm	#rounds	#CI test
5000	PCMB	46702±6875	114295±28401
5000	IPC-MB	446±15	34073±1996
5000	IPC-MB++	1±0	34073±1996
10000	PCMB	46891±3123	108622±13182
10000	IPC-MB	452±12	37462±1502
10000	IPC-MB++	1±0	37462±1502
20000	PCMB	48173±2167	111100±9345
20000	IPC-MB	460±9	40374±1803
20000	IPC-MB++	1±0	40374±1803

Scalability

IAMB and its variants are proposed to do feature selection in microarray research [14, 15]. From our study, it is indeed a fast algorithm even when the number of features and number of cases become large. Reliable results are expected when there are enough data. PCMB is also shown scalable by its author in [8], where it is applied to a KDD-Cup'2001 competition problem with 139351 features. Due to the short of such large scale observation, we haven't tried IPC-MB(++) in the similar scenario yet. However, our empirical study, though there are only 37 variables, have shown that IPC-MB(++) runs faster than PCMB in terms of the amount of CI test and data pass. Therefore, we have confidence to do this inference that IPC-MB(++) can also scale to thousands of features as IAMB and PCMB claim. Besides, due to the relative advantage on data efficiency among the three algorithms, IPC-MB(++) is supposed to work with best results in challenging applications where there is large number of features but small amount of samples.

Usefulness of information found

Markov blanket contains the target's parents, children and spouses. IAMB and its variants only recognize that variables of MB render the rest of variables on the BN independent of target, which can be a solution to the feature subset selection. Therefore, IAMB only discovers which variables should fall into the Markov blanket, without further distinguishing among spouse/parents/children. PCMB and IPC-MB(++) goes further by discovering more topology knowledge. They not only learn MB, but also distinguish the parents/children from the spouses of target. Among parents/children, those children shared by found spouses and the target are also separated (the v-structures found).

6   Conclusion

In this paper, we propose a new Markov blanket discovery algorithm, called IPC-MB. It is based on two assumptions, DAG-faithful distribution and correct independence test. Like IAMB and PCMB, IPC-MB belongs to the family of local learning of MB, so it is scalable to applications with thousands of variables but few instances. It is shown correct, and much more data-efficient than IAMB and PCMB, which allows it perform much better in learning accuracy than IAMB given the same amount of instances in practice. Compared with PCMB, IPC-MB(++) provides a more efficient approach for learning, requiring much fewer number of CI tests and data passes than PCMB. Therefore, we can state that IPC-MB(++) shows a high potential as a practical MB discovery algorithm, and is a good tradeoff between IAMB and PCMB.

References

1. Aliferis, C.F., Tsamardinos, I., Statnikov, A.: HITON, a Novel Markov blanket algorithm for optimal variable selection. In: Proceedings of the 2003 American Medical Informatics Association Annual Symposium, pp. 21–25 (2003)
2. Cheng, J., Greiner, R.: Learning Bayesian networks from data: An information-theory based approach. Artificial Intelligence 137, 43–90 (2002)
3. Cheng, J., Greiner, R.: Compared Bayesian Network classifiers. In: Proceedings of the 15th Conference on UAI (1999)
4. Cheng, J., Bell, D.A., Liu, W.: Learning belief networks from data: An information theory based approach. In: Proceedings of the sixth ACM International Conference on Information and Knowledge Management (1997)
5. Cooper, G.F.: The computational complexity of probabilistic inference using Bayesian belief networks. Artificial Intelligence 42, 395–405 (1990)
6. Friedman, N., Geiger, D., Goldszmidt, M.: Bayesian network classifiers. Machine Learning 29, 131–163 (1997)
7. Herskovits, E.H.: Computer-based probabilistic-network construction. Ph.D Thesis, Stanford University (1991)
8. Pena, J.M., Nilsson, R., Bjorkegren, J., Tegner, J.: Towards scalable and data efficient learning of Markov boundaries. International Journal of Approximate Reasoning 45(2), 211–232 (2007)
9. Koller, D., Sahami, M.: Toward optimal feature selection. In: Proceedings of International Conference on Machine Learning, pp. 284–292 (1996)
10. Margaritis, D., Thrun, S.: Bayesian network induction via local neighborhoods. In: Proceedings of NIPS (1999)
11. Pearl, J.: Probabilistic reasoning in intelligent systems: Networks of plausible inference. Morgan Kaufmann, San Francisco (1988)
12. Spirtes, P., Glymour, C., Scheines, R.: Causation, Prediction, and Search. Lecture Notes in Statistics. Springer, Heidelberg (1993)
13. Spirtes, P., Glymour, C.: An algorithm for Fast Recovery of Sparse Casual Graphs. Philosophy Methodology Logic (1990)
14. Tsamardinos, I., Aliferis, C.F., Statnikov, A.: Time and sample efficient discovery of Markov blankets and direct causal relations. In: Proceedings of the 9th ACM SIGKDD International Conference on Knowledge Discovery and Data Mining, pp. 673–678 (2003)
15. Tsamardinos, I., Aliferis, C.F.: Towards principled feature selection: Relevancy, filter and wrappers. In: 9th International Workshop on Artificial Intelligence and Statistics (AI&Stats 2003) (2003)
16. Tsamardinos, I., Aliferis, C.F., Stantnikov, A.: Time and sample efficient discovery of Markov blankets and direct causal relations. In: Proceedings of SIGKDD 2003 (2003)

17. Yaramakala, S., Margaritis, D.: Speculative Markov blanket discovery for optimal feature selection. In: Proceedings of IEEE International Conference on Data Mining (ICDM) (2005)
18. Moore, A., Lee, M.S.: Cached sufficient statistics for efficient machine learning with large datasets. Journal of Artificial Intelligence Research 8, 67–91 (1998)
19. Komarek, P., Moore, A.: A dynamic adaptation of AD-trees for efficient machine learning on large data sets. In: Proceedings of ICML (2000)

Finding Topics in Email Using Formal Concept Analysis and Fuzzy Membership Functions

Liqiang Geng[1], Larry Korba[1], Yunli Wang[1], Xin Wang[2], and Yonghua You[1]

[1] Institute of Information Technology, National Research Council of Canada
Fredericton, New Brunswick, Canada
{liqiang.geng,larry.korba,yunli.wang,yonghua.you}nrc-cnrc.gc.ca
[2] Department of Geomatics Engineering, University of Calgary,
Calgary, Alberta, Canada
xcwang@ucalgary.ca

Abstract. In this paper, we present a method to identify topics in email messages. The formal concept analysis is adopted as a semantic analysis method to group emails containing the same keywords to concepts. The fuzzy membership functions are used to rank the concepts based on the features of the emails, such as the senders, recipients, time span, and frequency of emails in the concepts. The highly ranked concepts are then identified as email topics. Experimental results on the Enron email dataset illustrate the effectiveness of the method.

1 Introduction

Email is one of the most important communication and information exchange tools for modern organizations. It has greatly improved work efficiency. However, with the increasing use of email system, managing emails efficiently becomes an important issue. Identifying activities in emails is a technique to address this issue. At the individual level, identifying topics in emails can facilitate the access to the email messages for users. At the organization level, analyzing the emails in terms of topics can help discover the real workflow within that organization.

Some work has been conducted on identifying activities embodied in emails. The major techniques adopted to tackle this problem are data mining and machine learning methods, such as classification and clustering. Huang et al. proposed to use clustering methods to infer activities from emails based on the subjects and body of the emails [3]. This is one of the first work in this domain. Li et al. incorporated semantic analysis and named entity to email clustering [6]. Khoussainov and Kushmerick combined the relation identification and the speech act classification to improve the performance of email topic identification [4]. Dredze et al. proposed a method to classify emails into activities based on the people involved in the activities and the content of the email messages [1, 2]. Kushmerick and Lau tried to identify a more structured workflow from an email dataset of e-commerce transactions [5].

However, there are some limitations of the above-mentioned classification and clustering based topic identification methods. First, classification method requires that

S. Bergler (Ed.): Canadian AI 2008, LNAI 5032, pp. 108–113, 2008.
© Springer-Verlag Berlin Heidelberg 2008

email messages be labeled before training the classification models, which is a not a trivial task, especially without domain knowledge. Secondly, both clustering and classification methods (except hierarchical clustering) produce a single partition on the data set, i.e., one email message can only belong to one class or cluster. Therefore, an email regarding both "trip" and "meeting" will be either assigned to topic "trip" or topic "meeting". Thirdly, the current work did not distinguish between a topic class and a topic instance. Topic class can be considered as an abstract topic, while a topic instance is a concrete topic. For example, topic class "trip" may contain many instances, one of which could be "Smith's trip to Toronto in May 2007". Classification and clustering methods may achieve good results on identifying different topic classes, but may not be able to distinguish between instances of the same topic class. Lastly, the granularity level of clustering methods, i.e., the number of clusters, is not easy to determine.

In this paper, we use the formal concept analysis (FCA) method to organize the groups of emails in a concept hierarchy. Since FCA groups data based on subsets of features, it has the potential to distinguish between the instances of the same topic class. Also FCA assigns an email message to multiple groups, which allows users to view an email from different perspectives. The groups of emails identified by FCA, which are called concepts, are potential topics. We then use fuzzy membership functions to rank and filter the concepts to find the topic instances. From now on, we will use topic and topic instance interchangeably throughout this paper.

The rest of the paper is organized as follows. In Section 2, we describe the method to identify topics from emails. In Section 3, we present the experimental results on Enron data set. In Section 4, we conclude the paper and discuss some future work.

2 Finding Topics in Emails

We first find concepts in emails using formal concept analysis and then rank them according to the likelihood that they each represent a single topic. We talk about the formal concept analysis in Sections 2.1. Then we present the email topic identification method in Section 2.2.

2.1 Formal Concept Analysis

Formal Concept Analysis (FCA) is a mathematical method for data analysis, knowledge representation, and knowledge visualization [7]. It is similar to clustering in terms of grouping similar objects together, but it generates much more clusters since it views objects from different perspectives, i.e., an object can belong to different clusters rather than belong to only one. For example, an ostrich can be classified as an animal that can not fly. It also can be classified as a bird.

The basic idea of FCA is to extract concepts consisting of similar objects and their common features/attributes from a data table and build a hierarchy according to the generality of the concepts.

The input of the FCA is a two-dimensional table called *formal context*. Each row in the table represents an object. Each column represents an attribute. If an object has an attribute, we put value 1 in the cell in the intersection in the table. Otherwise, we put 0 in the cell. Formally, a formal context is a triplet (O, A, R), where O represents the universe of objects, A represents the universe of attributes, and $R \subseteq O \times A$ is a binary relation between O and A. We define two mappings: $f: 2^O \to 2^A$ and $g: 2^A \to 2^O$ as follows. Given a set of objects $O_1 \subseteq O$, $f(O_1) = \{a \in A \mid \text{for any } o \in O_1, (o, a) \subseteq R\}$. Given a set of attributes $A_1 \subseteq A$, $g(A_1) = \{o \in O \mid \text{for any } a \in A_1, (o, a) \subseteq R\}$. The mapping f finds all the attributes shared by the objects in O_1, while the mapping g finds all the objects that share the attributes in A_1.

With a formal context and the two mappings being defined, FCA can extract formal concepts from the formal context. A *formal concept* is represented as a pair (E, I) such that $E \subseteq O$, $I \subseteq A$, $f(E) = I$, and $g(I) = E$. In other words, (E, I) is a concept if and only if the objects in E only share the attributes in I and the attributes in I are only shared by the objects in E. E and I are called *extent* and *intent* of the concept, respectively. Given a set of concepts, we define a partial order relation $\leq$. For two concepts (E_1, I_1) and (E_2, I_2), we say that $(E_1, I_1) \leq (E_2, I_2)$ if and only if $E_1 \subseteq E_2$ holds. Equivalently, we say $(E_1, I_1) \leq (E_2, I_2)$ if and only if $I_2 \subseteq I_1$ holds. (E_1, I_1) represents a more specific concept than (E_2, I_2), therefore (E_1, I_1) is called a *sub concept* of (E_2, I_2) and (E_2, I_2) a *super concept* of (E_1, I_1).

A complete lattice can be generated based on the relation $\leq$, with each node representing a concept and each arc representing a direct partial relation. This lattice is called *formal concept lattice* or *Galois lattice*.

2.2 Identifying Topics of Emails from Concepts

We first use the FCA to group emails into concepts based on their subjects or content. Preprocessing is needed to transform email corpus into a two dimensional table. Each column in the table represents a keyword and each row represents an email. Then the FCA identifies a set of concepts, which can be considered as potential topics, and generates the concept hierarchy. The user can explore the concept hierarchy to find the concepts which correspond to topics.

One of the advantages of FCA based topic detection is that it can find topics at different levels of granularity. The FCA can also assign an email to different concepts / topics. The disadvantage is that it may produce huge numbers of concepts for a large data set which may overwhelm the users. Also many concepts in a concept hierarchy may not correspond to a topic. For example, a concept regarding *trip* may involve several topics about different cases of trips rather than only one topic. Although some work on visualization has been done to assist the users to explore the concept hierarchy, it is still a burden for the users to find interesting and meaningful topics in the hierarchy. Therefore, besides the navigation functionality intrinsic to the FCA, we need more functionality to facilitate user's explorations and analysis.

In email messages, besides subjects and content, other information can be used as indicators to show how likely a concept really represents a topic. Here we consider three factors: the number of participants (senders and recipients) p, the time span t of the emails in the concept, and the frequency t of the emails in the concept. They are defined as follows.

$$p(C) = \mid \bigcup_{e \in C} (sender\,(e) \cup recipient\,(e)) \mid,$$

$$t(C) = \max_{e \in C}(date(e)) - \min_{e \in C}(date(e)), \text{ and } f(C) = \frac{|C|}{t(C)},$$

where e denotes an email message, C denotes a concept, and $|C|$ denotes the number of emails in concept C.

We use fuzzy membership functions [8] to represent users' domain knowledge. In fuzzy logic, a fuzzy membership function represents how likely an object belongs to a set. The inputs of the function are the values of the attributes of the object. The output is a numeric value between 0 and 1 representing the degree that the object belongs to the set. The value 1 means that the object fully belongs to the fuzzy set. The value 0 means that the object does not belong to the fuzzy set. A value between 0 and 1 means that the object partially belongs to the fuzzy set, with higher value representing higher degree of belongingness.

Intuitively, emails related to a topic should involve a certain group of people and should occur over a short period of time with high frequency, although values for these parameters may differ from application to application. We use these features as the input to the fuzzy membership functions. The output of the functions is the fuzzy values that represent the degree that the group of emails belongs to a topic. Figure 1 shows three examples of the fuzzy membership functions. Figure 1(a) describes the relationship between the degree of a topic and the number of people involved in the group of the emails. We denote the function as f_p. It says that if 2 to 10 people are involved in a group of emails from a concept, the membership degree that they belong

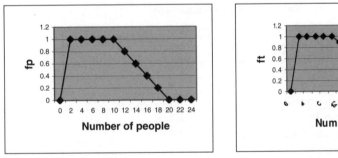
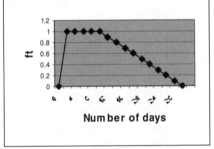

(a) Function f_p (b) Function f_t

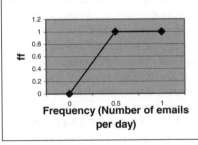

(c) Function f_f

Fig. 1. Fuzzy membership functions for ranking the concepts

to the same topic is 1. If there are 10 to 20 people involved, the degree of membership linearly decreases. If there are more than 20 people involved, the degree becomes 0. Similarly, we define the fuzzy membership functions for the time span (f_t) and frequency of emails (f_f) in Figures 1(b) and 1(c), respectively. In real applications, these functions should be defined by the domain experts.

Finally, we combine these three factors by multiplying the three fuzzy values to get the overall fuzzy value. For example, if a concept includes 2 emails, involves 5 people as senders or recipients, and time span is 6 days, then the final fuzzy value is 0.67 according to Figure 1.

By setting a threshold for the fuzzy values, we can identify the topics in the concepts.

3 Experiments

The experiments are implemented in Java and run on a PC with 3GHz CPU and 2G bytes memory. We chose Enron email data set for our experiments. Enron Email data set is a benchmark for research in fields like link analysis, social network analysis, fraud detection, and textual analysis. We worked on the cleaned version from [9], which contains 252,759 messages from 151 employees distributed in around 3000 user defined folders. We selected emails sent in the year 1999 (4760 emails) for our experiments.

Table 1. Concepts regarding *trip*

Score	Intent	Number of Emails
1.0	london, trip	2
0.91	houston, trip	5
0.0	brazil, trip	9
0.0	trip, canadian	1
0.0	trip, ba	1
0.0	houston, trip, meet, request	1
0.0	trip	26

We extracted the words in the subjects of the emails and cleaned up the data in preprocessing, including removing the stop words and using the Porter algorithm to stem words. After these steps, 935 words were left. Then we set frequency threshold to 5 to prune the words that do not appear frequently enough. Finally we had 402 words left as features. We applied the FCA open source code from [10] and found 782 concepts.

We choose to look into the topics regarding *trip*, which are comprehensible to general readers. Seven concepts concerning *trip* were identified, which are shown in Table 1. We manually checked the concept *london trip* and found that it talks about a schedule for Tana's visit to London, which is a topic. The emails for concept *houston trip* include 5 emails, which involve two topics. The first four emails focus on one topic and the last one belongs to another topic. The concept *brazil trip* contains 9 emails involving three topics. The results show that the higher the fuzzy value is, the more likely the concept corresponds to one topic.

4 Conclusion and Future Work

We proposed a method based on formal concept analysis to find concepts (potential topics) in emails. To deal with the overwhelming number of the concepts produced by formal concept analysis, we used fuzzy membership functions based on the features of email, including timestamps, senders, and recipients, to rank the concepts according to the likelihood that they are topics. Preliminary experiments on Enron email dataset show the promising results.

In the future, we will do more comprehensive experiments on the whole Enron data set and on both subjects and content of emails. We will compare our method with other email classification and clustering methods. We will also improve our method by taking into account the explicit threading information in the emails when ranking the concepts, and looking for more effective method for fuzzy member function aggregation.

References

[1] Cselle, G., Albrecht, K., Wattenhofer, R.: BuzzTrack: topic detection and tracking in email. Intelligent User Interfaces, 190–197 (2007)

[2] Dredze, M., Lau, T.A., Kushmerick, N.: Automatically classifying emails into activities. Intelligent User Interfaces, 70–77 (2006)

[3] Huang, Y., Govindaraju, D., Mitchell, T.M., de Carvalho, V.R., Cohen, W.W.: Inferring ongoing activities of workstation users by clustering email. In: Proceedings of the First Conference on Email and Anti-Spam, Mountain View, California, USA (July 2004)

[4] Khoussainov, R., Kushmerick, N.: Email task management: An iterative relational learning approach. In: Proceedings of the Second Conference on Email and Anti-Spam, Stanford University, California, USA (2005)

[5] Kushmerick, N., Lau, T.A.: Automated email activity management: An unsupervised learning approach. In: Proceedings of the 2005 International Conference on Intelligent User Interfaces, San Diego, California, pp. 67–74 (2005)

[6] Li, H., Shen, D., Zhang, B., Chen, A., Yang, Q.: Adding semantics to email clustering. In: Proceedings of the 6th IEEE International Conference on Data Mining, Hong Kong, China, pp. 938–942 (2006)

[7] Wille, R.: Restructuring lattice theory: an approach based on hierarchies of concepts. In: Rival (ed.) Ordered Sets, pp. 445–470. Reidel, Dordrecht-Boston (1982)

[8] Zadeh, L.: Fuzzy sets. Information and Control 8(3), 338–353 (1965)

[9] http://www.isi.edu/~adibi/Enron/Enron.htm

[10] http://www.iro.umontreal.ca/~galicia/

Recognizing Biomedical Named Entities in Chinese Research Abstracts

Baohua Gu, Fred Popowich, and Veronica Dahl*

School of Computing Science, Simon Fraser University,
Burnaby, B.C., Canada, V5A 1S6
{bgu,popowich,veronica}@cs.sfu.ca

Abstract. Most research on biomedical named entity recognition has focused on English texts, e.g., MEDLINE abstracts. However, recent years have also seen significant growth of biomedical publications in other languages. For example, the Chinese Biomedical Bibliographic Database has collected over 3 million articles published after 1978 from 1600 Chinese biomedical journals. We present here a Conditional Random Field (CRF) based system for recognizing biomedical named entities in Chinese texts. Viewing Chinese sentences as sequences of characters, we trained and tested the CRF model using a manually annotated corpus containing 106 research abstracts (481 sentences in total). The features we used for the CRF model include word segmentation tags provided by a segmenter trained on newswire corpora, and lists of frequent characters gathered from training data and external resources. Randomly selecting 400 sentences for training and the rest for testing, our system obtained an 68.60% F-score on average, significantly outperforming the baseline system (F-score 60.54% using a simple dictionary match). This suggests that statistical approaches such as CRFs based on annotated corpora hold promise for the biomedical NER task in Chinese texts.

1 Introduction

Biomedical named entity recognition is a fundamental task for advanced text mining tasks, e.g., automatic extraction of relations and deeper knowledge from biomedical research publications. By far most research in this area has focused on English texts mostly from the MEDLINE repository[1]. While MEDLINE is currently and will likely remain the largest collection of English biomedical research publications, significant growth has also been seen in other languages. For example, the Chinese Biomedical Bibliographic Database[2] has collected about 3 million articles published in 1600 Chinese biomedical journals after 1978. With the increasingly large volume of these research papers becoming available, we

---

* Currently a visiting professor at Research Group on Mathematical Linguistics, Marie Curie Chair, Universidad de Rovira e Virgili, Tarragona, Spain.

[1] http://www.ncbi.nlm.nih.gov/pubmed/
[2] http://www.imicams.ac.cn/cbm/index.asp

S. Bergler (Ed.): Canadian AI 2008, LNAI 5032, pp. 114–125, 2008.
© Springer-Verlag Berlin Heidelberg 2008

believe that there will soon be strong needs for biomedical NER as well as for mining deeper knowledge in Chinese and other non-English languages.

In this work, we study biomedical NER in Chinese texts. Previous research has shown that for the counterpart task in English texts, the state-of-the-art performance can be achieved by statistical approaches based on annotated corpora. Thus it is natural for us to assume that these approaches would also work for Chinese texts. To validate this hypothesis, however, we face an immediate difficulty: currently there are no annotated Chinese corpora in the biomedicine domain publicly available. Moreover, it is not clear what kinds of features should be used for the task.

We have created a small annotated corpus by ourselves, on which we trained and tested a CRF model. Given that there are no spaces between Chinese words and that doing word segmentation as a preprocessing step might introduce extra errors, we considered the NER task as a character-based sequence labeling problem. We used lists of frequent characters obtained from the training set and some external resources to construct features for the CRF model. We also tried to use word segmentation labels as features. We obtained encouraging results (Precision(P)/Recall(R)/F-Score(F) = 73.27% / 64.65% / 68.60%), which significantly outperforms our dictionary-based baseline system (P/R/F = 69.89% / 52.88% / 60.14%). The results suggest that statistical approaches based on annotated corpora should still be promising for biomedical NER in Chinese texts.

The rest of the paper is organized as follows: Section 2 summarizes the properties of the biomedical NEs in Chinese texts. Section 3 describes how the annotation was done. Section 4 recaps the CRF framework for sequence labeling and explains how it was used for Chinese NER. Section 5 gives evaluation details, Section 6 reviews previous research, and Section 7 concludes the paper.

2   Properties of Biomedical Named Entities in Chinese Texts

Previous studies in the newswire domain have shown that Chinese NER is in general more difficult than English NER. First, while capitalization plays a important role in English names, there is no such information in Chinese text. Second, English words are naturally separated from each other by spaces, however, there is no space between Chinese words. Chinese word segmentation is in itself a difficult task, whose overall performance on newswire texts is still awaiting further improvement.

By reading the Chinese abstracts and consulting domain experts, we observed the following language phenomena that could make Chinese Biomedical NERs more complicated than their English counterparts:

1. mixed use of Chinese words and their English counterparts or synonyms, e.g., 人ACAT1基因P7 (meaning "human ACAT1 gene P7 initiator"), can also be written as: 人酰基辅酶A: 胆固醇酰基转移酶1 (ACAT1) 基因P7 ;

2. One English term may have different Chinese translations, e.g., *Aptamer* has several equivalent translations in use: 寡核苷酸配基, 核酸适体, Aptamer, RNA适体, 核酸适配子;

3. Chinese has its own printing form for punctuation, special symbols, and even English letters. Many times they are mixed with English counterparts, e.g., periods can appear as "." or "。" , dashes can be "-" or "—" , commas can be "," or ", " , English letters GP can be "GP" or "G P" ;

4. One term may have spelling variations, often involved in English and Chinese characters, e.g., ACAT1, A-CAT1, A—CAT1; 人白细胞, 人类白细胞 (meaning: human leukocytes).

3   Annotating a Corpus for Chinese Biomedical NER

Our core annotation was performed by a Chinese Biochemistry PhD student who is familiar with biomedical terms in both English and Chinese. These annotations were then double-checked by the first author, who is also a native Chinese speaker. As most biomedical NER projects are mainly interested in proteins and genes, we decided to only annotate these two types of entities. We issued the query "(enzyme or receptor or antibody) and gene" (in Chinese characters) to the CQVIP portal[3], which returned us 287 abstracts. We downloaded all of them and selected 106 for the annotation, discarding those containing too few protein/gene terms.

Similar to the GENIA corpus, the annotation guideline was to mark all character sequences that are either proteins or genes according to the context. Embedded named entities are also required to be marked. The original annotation was marked by the first annotator using color markers on paper. Double-checking was done by both annotators going through the annotation together. The annotation was then typed into computer using the annotation tool "Callisto" (available from http://callisto.mitre.org/). The annotation was then converted into IOB2 format, where B denotes the beginning character of an NE, I denotes each following character that is inside the NE, and O denotes a character that is not a part of any NE, to agree with the convention of the NER community.

4   Chinese Biomedical NER Using CRF

4.1   The CRF Framework

A conditional random field [8] is a framework to model an undirected graph in which each node represents a random variable whose distribution is to be inferred, and each edge represents a dependency between two random variables. In this framework, there are two assumptions about the distribution of each random variable Y. First, it is globally conditioned on a global random variable X (i.e., each Y has an edge with X). Second, it should obey the Markov property

---

[3] http://www.cqvip.com/

with respect to the graph, which says that the state of the current node only depends on the states of its adjacent neighbors.

In principle, the layout of the graph of random variables Y can be arbitrary. In practice, however, the Y_i are often structured to form a linear chain, with an edge between each Y_{i-1} and Y_i. In such cases, the Y_i can be interpreted as a label for the element X_i in the input sequence. Moreover, this linear layout enables efficient algorithms for model training (i.e., learning the conditional probabilities between the Y_i and the feature functions from some corpus of training data), for inference (i.e., determining the probability of a given label sequence Y given X), and for decoding (i.e., determining the most likely label sequence Y given X).

Let X denote the input token sequence $x_1, x_2, ..., x_n$, and Y denote a possible tag sequence $y_1, y_2, ..., y_n$ that corresponds to X. The conditional dependency of each Y_i on X can be defined through a fixed set of feature functions of the form $f(i, Y_{i-1}, Y_i, X)$, which can informally be thought of as measurements on the input sequence that partially determines the likelihood of each possible value for Y_i. The CRF model assigns each feature a numerical weight and combines them to determine the probability of a certain value for Y_i.

The CRF framework allow us to use an arbitrary number of features. There are usually two kinds of features: the state feature $s(x, i)$ and the transition feature $t(y_{i-1}, y_i, x, i)$, where i is the position in the sequence, y_{i-1} and y_i are tags at positions $i - 1$ and i in the tag sequence, respectively.

An example of the state feature is:

$$s(x, i) = \begin{cases} 1, \text{ if the token } x \text{ at position } i \text{ is "kinase"}, \\ 0, \text{ otherwise} \end{cases} \tag{1}$$

An example of the transition feature is:

$$t(y_{i-1}, y_i, x, i) = \begin{cases} 1, \text{ if } y_{i-1} = \text{ "B-protein"}, \\ \quad \text{and } y_i = \text{ "I-protein"}, \\ 0, \text{ otherwise} \end{cases} \tag{2}$$

A linear chain CRF defines the conditional probability of a state sequence given an input sequence to be:

$$P(s|o) = \frac{1}{Z_o} exp(\sum_{i=1}^{n} \sum_{j=1}^{m} \lambda_j f_j(s_{i-1}, s_i, o, i)) \tag{3}$$

where Z_o is a normalization factor of all state sequences, $f_j(s_{i-1}, s_i, o, i)$ is one of m functions that describes a feature, and λ_j is a learned weight for each such feature function.

Intuitively, the learned feature weight λ_j for each feature f_j should be positive for features that are correlated with the target label, negative for features that are anti-correlated with the label, and near zero for relatively uninformative features. These weights are set to maximize the conditional log-likelihood of labeled sequences in a training set $D = \langle o, l \rangle(1), ..., \langle o, l \rangle(n)$:

$$LL(D) = \sum_{i=1}^{n} log(P(l_{(i)}|o_{(i)})) - \sum_{j=1}^{m} \frac{\lambda_j^2}{2\sigma^2}. \tag{4}$$

When the training state sequences are fully labeled and unambiguous, the objective function is convex, thus the model is guaranteed to find the optimal weight settings in terms of $LL(D)$. Once these settings are found, the labeling for an new, unlabeled sequence can be done using a modified Viterbi algorithm. CRFs are presented in more complete detail in [8].

4.2   Chinese NER as a Sequence Labeling Task

We view each sentence as a sequence of characters, each of which is associated with a tag. The tag indicates whether the character is part of an NE, and the location if it is within the NE. Assume there are k types of entities under consideration, we can reduce the NER problem to the problem of assigning one of $2k+1$ tags to each character. For example, in our small annotated corpus, we label two types of entities: protein and gene. If we are going to recognize each type, the tag set will contain 5 tags: {B-PROTEIN, I-PROTEIN, B-GENE, I-GENE, O}. Thus we need to assign one of the five tags to each character.

Note that in our experiments to be described later, we did not try to distinguish between protein and gene due to the small scale of our annotated corpus. We did not consider embedded entities either. Rather, we considered both of them as an "ENTITY", an imaginary super type of protein and gene. That is, our tag set is {B-ENTITY, I-ENTITY, O}, and we want to assign one of them to each character.

For English NER tasks, a character-based model introduced in [7] proposed the use of substrings within English words. In Chinese NER, the character-based model is more straightforward, since there are no spaces between Chinese words, and each Chinese character is actually meaningful. Besides, using a character-based model can avoid errors made by a Chinese word segmenter. Moreover, there are currently no word segmentation tools available for the biomedicine domain.

5   Evaluation

With the above formulation, we train and test a CRF model on the annotated corpus. In our experiments, we use the CRF++ version 0.42[4] which implements the CRF model and is designed for typical NLP tasks including NER.

5.1   The Annotated Corpus

To better understand the text we are dealing with, we obtained some basic statistics from the corpus. It has 106 abstracts in total, containing 481 sentences or 38645 characters. There are 1199 distinct characters, including Chinese and English ones, and all numbers and special symbols. The top 20 frequent unigram, bi-gram and tri-gram characters are given in Table 1.

---

[4] CRF++: Yet Another CRF Toolkit, http://crfpp.sourceforge.net

Table 1. Top 20 uni-gram, bi-gram, tri-gram characters

1-gram characters	Frequency	2-gram characters	Frequency	3-gram characters	Frequency
的	894	基因	507	RNA	88
，	741	表达	289	DNA	84
基	595	细胞	222	PCR	78
A	577	NA	196	的表达	75
因	543	蛋白	123	mRN	60
。	493	PC	113	ERT	58
T	462	RN	96	TER	57
P	459	方法	96	hTE	57
R	442	RT	91	端粒酶	51
1	420	0.	91	cDN	47
C	399	CR	87	基因型	47
性	389	结果	86	. 05	46
0	377	序列	86	基因的	43
2	356	DN	84	多态性	41
表	352	检测	83	位基因	39
a	340	活性	83	表达，	39
N	303	. 0	79	等位基	39
达	302	hT	76	酶活性	38
e	286	的表	75	基因组	37
D	284	患者	72	P<0	36

In total, there are 1062 mentions of 472 unique named entities, either proteins or genes, annotated in the corpus. Table 2 shows the top 20 frequent entities. The longest entity is spelled as " β-半乳糖苷α1，2-岩藻糖转移酶（α1，2-fucosyltansferase，α1，2-FT）", which is a protein and occurs only once in the corpus.

5.2 Feature Construction

To obtain a good estimation of the conditional probability of the tags given the characters, we should use features that can distinguish the characters. In our experiments, we used two types of features for the CRF model, i.e., character list features and word segmentation features.

We considered four character lists. The first two character lists were made from our corpus. We randomly selected 400 sentences from our corpus to form the training set, and used the remaining 81 sentences to form the testing set. From the training set, we counted character frequencies and selected those appearing in entities more than twice as the first list (called L1), and those appearing outside entities more than twice as the second list (called L2).

The third list was gathered from external resources. We downloaded from the Web a free dictionary[5] (in PDF format) containing Chinese translations of more than 20,000 human gene names from widely-used gene databases such as

---

[5] http://wzhangcnster.googlepages.com/hg608.zip

Table 2. Top 20 Frequent Entities

the Spelling of the Named Entity	the Entity Type	Frequency of Occurrences
端粒酶	PROTEIN	39
hTERT	PROTEIN	36
PEPC	PROTEIN	14
CHS	GENE	13
mRNA	GENE	13
CD147	PROTEIN	11
Survivin	PROTEIN	11
I-PROTEIN	GENE	10
VEGF	PROTEIN	10
survivin	GENE	9
MTHFR	PROTEIN	9
GUS	GENE	9
p53	PROTEIN	8
TS	PROTEIN	8
eNOS	PROTEIN	8
MARs	GENE	8
bax	GENE	7
ST13	GENE	7
MARs序列	GENE	7
SV40	GENE	7

NCBI Gene[6] and GO[7]. We converted it into plain text format, and counted the character frequencies. We used the top 1000 frequent characters as the third list (called L3). We assume this list contains the most frequently seen characters in protein and gene names.

The fourth list was also from external resources. We retrieved the first 1000 abstracts from the CQVIP web site with the disjunction of four Chinese words: "enzyme, antibody, receptor and gene". We used the top 2000 frequent characters as the fourth list (called L4). We assume this list contains the most frequently seen characters in Chinese biomedical texts.

Corresponding to the four character lists, we have four columns of binary features for each character in the corpus. If the character is in any list, then we set the value for the corresponding feature to be 1; otherwise, it is set to 0.

We also considered using word segmentation information. We think this information may be useful in deciding entity boundaries. As we could not find a segmentation tool specifically for Chinese biomedical texts, we used the Stanford Chinese Word Segmenter[8]. Although it is trained for newswire texts, we expect it could still provide some basic word boundary information that would be useful for our CRF model. We used the word segmenter's output to assign a segmentation tag for each character. The segmentation tags are the BMES

---

[6] Entrez Gene, http://www.ncbi.nlm.nih.gov/sites/entrez?db=gene

[7] the Gene Ontology, http://www.geneontology.org

[8] http://nlp.stanford.edu/software/segmenter.shtml

notation, which are commonly used in word segmentation task, where B stands for beginning of a word, M for the middle of the word, E for the end of the word, and S stands for a word with single character.

Using the corpus and the feature construction described above, we prepared the training and testing data in the format of the CRF++ package, part of which is shown in Table 3.

Table 3. Example Data Prepared in CRF++ format

the char	is it in L1?	is it in L2?	is it in L3?	is it in L4?	WS tag	NE tag
初	0	1	0	1	B	O
步	0	1	0	1	E	O
判	0	1	0	1	B	O
定	0	1	1	1	E	O
C	1	1	1	1	B	B-ENTITY
H	1	1	1	1	M	I-ENTITY
S	1	1	1	1	E	I-ENTITY
在	0	1	1	1	S	O
蓝	0	1	1	1	B	O
粒	1	1	1	1	E	O
小	0	1	1	1	B	O
麦	1	1	0	1	E	O
中	0	1	1	1	S	O

5.3   Experimental Results

As mentioned ealier, our annotated corpus contains 481 labeled sentences in total. We randomly selected 400 sentences for training and the rest 81 for testing. Though we have annotated two types of NEs: protein and gene, we combined them into one type "ENTITY" in our experiments, as the size of the corpus may not be sufficient to support fine classification. Thus the NER task became that of assigning one of three tags to each character: {B-Entity, I-Entity, O}.

For comparison purposes, we built a baseline system, which implements a simple dictionary matching strategy to label the testing set with a dictionary consisting of all distinct NEs found in the training set. To see how useful the different types of features are for the CRF performance, we tried different combinations of the features. The averaged results of exact NE boundary matches over 50 random runs (each time the training set, L1 and L2 were rebuilt accordingly) are given in Table 4, where "C+L1" means the character and L1 are used as features and so on. In each cell, the number below is the standard deviation.

Note that the purpose of running the random experiments 50 times is to apply a statistical significance test (e.g., the Welch's t-test[9]) on the sample means, so that we do not assume any knowledge about the distribution of the samples. Probably due to the data sparsity resulted from the small scale of the training

---

[9] http://en.wikipedia.org/wiki/Welch%27s_t_test

Table 4. Performance of CRF vs. Baseline average over 50 runs

Features	Accuracy	Precision	Recall	F-score
Baseline	90.10	68.77	53.79	60.19
	1.71	4.92	6.53	5.15
C	93.44	74.12	57.98	64.98
	1.35	4.15	6.06	5.15
C+L1	93.55	72.69	60.05	65.70
	1.41	5.06	6.43	5.64
C+L2	93.66	73.45	58.34	64.96
	1.27	4.36	5.97	5.17
C+L3	93.56	73.54	58.17	64.88
	1.31	4.28	6.04	5.16
C+L4	93.48	73.81	58.17	64.98
	1.30	4.17	5.91	5.03
C+WS	93.72	74.36	61.22	67.09
	1.29	3.81	5.16	4.35

Table 5. Welch two-sided t-test of two paired sample means for Table 4

Hypothesis	p-value
mean(baseline) $\neq$ mean(C)?	1.014e-05
mean(C) $\neq$ mean(C+L1)?	0.5096
mean(C+L1) $\neq$ mean(C+L2)?	0.4982
mean(C+L2) $\neq$ mean(C+L3)?	0.9395
mean(C+L3) $\neq$ mean(C+L4)?	0.9223
mean(C+L4) $\neq$ mean(C+WS)?	0.0275

data, in some runs of our experiments, the performance of the learned CRF model was a bit worse than that of the baseline. However, it outperforms the baseline in most runs, and our statistical tests, shown in Table 5, confirm that the difference is significant, which suggests that the trained CRF model can do significantly better than the baseline method.

Table 5 shows the results of the Welch two-sided t-test on paired samples of the averaged F-scores for some feature combinations. The calculation was done using **R**[10]. From Table 5, We can see that: (1) the CRF model using the character features alone already outperforms the baseline system; (2) adding any of the four character lists as features does not result in significant increase nor decrease in the F-score of using 'C' alone, while adding word segmentation tags as features can significantly improve the F-score; (3) the two greatest performance improvements over the baseline result from the "C+WS" combination and the "C+L1" combination. This shows that information about word segmentation and frequent entity characters are probably the most important features.

We then used the 'C+WS' combination as the base features and experimented the effects of adding the character list features. The averaged results over 50

---

[10] The R Project for Statistical Computing, http://www.r-project.org/

Table 6. Performance of CRF vs. Baseline averaged over 50 runs

Features	Accuracy	Precision	Recall	F-score
Baseline	90.32	68.44	54.54	60.54
	1.77	6.00	7.28	6.26
C	93.51	74.57	59.45	66.05
	1.42	4.59	6.65	5.58
C+WS	93.61	74.03	61.75	67.24
	1.32	4.49	5.76	4.81
C+WS+L1	93.62	73.90	63.69	68.32
	1.31	4.54	6.31	5.13
C+WS+L1+L2	93.85	73.26	64.40	68.44
	1.27	4.40	6.21	4.91
C+WS+L1+L2+L3	93.89	72.99	64.29	68.27
	1.29	4.55	6.15	5.02
C+WS+L1+L2+L3+L4	93.93	73.27	64.65	68.60
	1.25	4.46	6.07	4.93

independent random runs are given in Table 6, showing that the best performance is obtained by using all the available features, with 68.60% F-score vs 60.54% of the baseline.

6   Previous Work

The NER task was originally set to identify names such as people, locations, and organizations in English newswire texts. Influential approaches make use of either handcrafted rules [13] or machine learning algorithms [1] or their combinations [14]. Most recent works have adopted supervised learning algorithms, e.g., HMM [15], Maximum Entropy [2], SVM [11], and CRF [12]. The state-of-the-art performance (about 94%-96% F-scores) was achieved by supervised learning based systems e.g., [19].

Recent years have also seen some NER works in Chinese newswire texts. The dominant approaches are supervised learning algorithms based on annotated corpora, e.g., HMM [18] and CRFs [3] [4] [5]. As the best performance of Chinese word segmentation is still not very satisfactory (about 85%-90% F-Score on newswire texts), and using it as a preprocessing step of NER would incur errors to the final performance, recent works tend to treat the Chinese NER task as a character-based sequence tagging problem, similar to the segmentation task.

In the biomedicine domain, supervised learning approaches have also been dominant. Representative works include SVM [9], HMM [20], Maximum Entropy [10] and CRF [16]. Two best-known shared tasks held in this area are BioNLP [6] and BioCreAtIvE [17], where most participants used supervised learning techniques. The best performance of the BioNLP 2004 Shared Task was about 73% F-score using a combination of HMM, SVM and hand-craft rules.

Our work is different from all the above works in that we study Chinese NER in the biomedicine domain. To our best knowledge, this is a subarea of NER that has not been explored previously.

7   Conclusion

We have studied the problem of recognizing biomedical named entities in Chinese research abstracts. We adopted the statistical approach based on annotated corpora. The model we used is Conditional Random Fields, which has proven very effective in Chinese NER in newswire texts as well as biomedical NER in English abstracts. As there is no publicly available annotated Chinese corpus, we have created a small one by ourselves, which consists of 106 Chinese biomedicine abstracts. We trained and tested the CRF model on this small corpus, and obtained performance that is significantly better than the baseline system by gaining about 8% in F-score. We also experimented on combinations of different features, and found that among all the features, word segmentation information and frequent characters appearing in targeted entities might be the most useful ones. Our results suggest that the CRF model and perhaps other statistical models such as HMM and the Maximum Entropy model, which are based on annotated corpora, hold good promise on the biomedical NER task in Chinese texts. We hope that this work would elicit more attention to Chinese language processing tasks as well as to other non-English languages.

Acknowledgments

We sincerely thank Mr. Lin Wang of the Department of Molecular Biology and Biochemistry of SFU for manually annotating the corpus and sharing his knowledge and comments with us. Support from the NSERC Discovery Grants of V. Dahl and F. Popowich is gratefully acknowledged.

References

1. Bikel, D.M., Miller, S., Schwartz, R., Weischedel, R.: Nymble: A high-performance learning name finder. In: Proceedings Of The 5th Conference On Applied Natural Language Processing (1997)
2. Borthwick, A.: A Maximum Entropy Approach To Named Entity Recognition. PhD thesis, New York University (1999)
3. Carpenter, B.: Character language models for chinese word segmentation and named entity recognition. In: Proceedings of SIGHAN Bakeoff (2006)
4. Chen, A., Peng, F., Shan, R., Sun, G.: Chinese named entity recognition with conditional probabilistic models. In: Proceedings of the Fifth SIGHAN Workshop on Chinese Language Processing (2006)
5. Feng, Y., Sun, L., Lv, Y.: Chinese word segmentation and named entity recognition based on conditional random fields models. In: Proceedings of the Fifth SIGHAN Workshop on Chinese Language Processing (2006)

6. Kim, J.-D., Ohta, T., Tsuruoka, Y., Tateisi, Y., Collier, N.: Introduction to the bio-entity recognition task at JNLPBA. In: Proceedings of International Joint Work-shop on NLP in Biomedicine and Its Applications (2004)

7. Klein, D., Smarr, J., Nguyen, H., Manning, C.D.: Named entity recognition with character-level models. In: Proceedings of Conference on Computational Natural Language Learning (2003)

8. Lafferty, J., McCallum, A., Pereira, F.: Conditional random fields: Probabilistic models for segmenting and labeling sequence data. In: Proceedings of the Eigh-teenth International Conference on Machine Learning (2001)

9. Lee, K.-J., Hwang, Y.-S., Rim, H.-C.: Two-phase biomedical ne recognition based on SVMs. In: Proceedings of ACL Workshop on NLP in Biomedicine (2003)

10. Lin, Y.-F., Tsai, T.-H., Chou, W.-C., Wu, K.-P., Sung, T.-Y., Hsu, W.-L.: A max-imum entropy approach to biomedical named entity recognition. In: Proceedings of the 4th SIGKDD Workshop on Data Mining in Bioinformatics (2004)

11. Mayfield, J., McNamee, P., Piatko, C.: Named entity recognition using hundreds of thousands of features. In: Proceedings of CoNLL (2003)

12. McCallum, A., Li, W.: Early results for named entity recognition with conditional random fields, feature selection and web-enhanced lexicons. In: Proceedings of CoNLL (2003)

13. Mikheev, A., Grover, C., Moens, M.: Description of the LTG system used for MUC-7. In: Proceedings of 7th Message Understanding Conference (MUC-7) (1998)

14. Mikheev, A., Moens, M., Grover, C.: Named entity recognition without gazeteers. In: Proceedings of Conference of European Chapter of ACL (1999)

15. Miller, S., Crystal, M., Fox, H., Ramshaw, L., Schwartz, R., Stone, R., Weischedel, R.: BBN: Description of the SIFT system as used for MUC-7. In: Proceedings of the Seventh Message Understanding Conference (1998)

16. Settles, B.: Biomedical named entity recognition using conditional random fields and rich feature sets. In: Proceedings of JNLPBA (2004)

17. Yeh, A., Morgan, A., Colosimo, M., Hirschman, L.: BioCreAtIvE task 1A: Gene mention finding evaluation. BMC Bioinformatics (2005)

18. Yu, S., Bai, S., Wu, P.: Description of the kent ridge digital labs system used for MUC-7. In: Proceedings of 7th Message Understanding Conference (1998)

19. Zhou, G., Su, J.: Named entity recognition using an HMM-based chunk tagger. In: Proceedings of 40th Annual Meeting of ACL (2002)

20. Zhou, G., Zhang, J., Su, J., Shen, D., Tan, C.: Recognizing names in biomedical texts: A machine learning approach. Bioinformatics (2004)

Point-Based Planning for Predictive State Representations

Masoumeh T. Izadi and Doina Precup

McGill University

Abstract. Predictive state representations (PSRs) have been proposed recently as an alternative representation for environments with partial observability. The representation is rooted in actions and observations, so it holds the promise of being easier to learn than Partially Observable Markov Decision Processes (POMDPs). However, comparatively little work has explored planning algorithms using PSRs. Exact methods developed to date are no faster than existing exact planning approaches for POMDPs, and only memory-based PSRs have been shown so far to have an advantage in terms of planning speed. In this paper, we present an algorithm for approximate planning in PSRs, based on an approach similar to point-based value iteration in POMDPs. The point-based approach turns out to be a natural match for the PSR state representation. We present empirical results showing that our approach is either comparable or better than POMDP point-based planning.

1 Introduction

Decision making and control of dynamical systems involve taking optimal actions based on a representation of the current *state* of the system. The state must be a sufficient statistic for the observed history that allows accurately predicting future observations. Traditionally, such systems have been modeled using Partially Observable Markov Decision Processes (POMDPs), in which the evolution of the system through time is tracked using belief states, i.e. probability distributions over the hidden state of the system. An alternative, recent model is predictive state representations (PSRs), which use action-conditional predictions of future observations as their representation of the system's state (Littman et al., 2002). Because they only involve actions and observations, and no other latent state variables, PSRs hold the promise of being easier to learn than POMDPs. However, the advantage of this representation for planning methods is less clear.

The work to date has shown that exact planning methods for POMDPs can be easily extended to PSRs, but these algorithms have similar complexity as well as empirical performance with the corresponding POMDP algorithms (James et al., 2004; Izadi & Precup, 2003). A related predictive representation, called memory PSR (mPSR), has been shown to provide faster exact and approximate planning methods (James & Singh, 2005; James et al, 2006). The main difference between PSRs and mPSRs is that the latter incorporate past observations in the representation. This can have big advantages if the "right" past histories are used, but otherwise can produce a bigger representation, which can be more difficult to handle. James et al. (2006) also provided an approximate planning algorithm for PSRs, based on the PERSEUS point-based value iteration

S. Bergler (Ed.): Canadian AI 2008, LNAI 5032, pp. 126–137, 2008.
© Springer-Verlag Berlin Heidelberg 2008

algorithm (Spaan & Vlassis, 2004). But in their experiments, they found that only the memory-based algorithm provided an advantage, and PSR-based planning was comparable in quality and speed to POMDP planning.

In this paper we study further the applicability of the point-based framework to predictive state representations. We focus in particular on the first point-based value iteration method, PBVI, proposed by Pineau, Gordon & Thrun (2003). Our goal is to explore whether PBVI is well-suited for planning using PSRs. In POMDPs, PBVI works by approximating the optimal value function of a POMDP using a finite set of belief points, B. The algorithm alternates between two phases: computing the value function estimates for the current belief set B, and expanding the belief set to get a better approximation. James et al. (2004) showed that the value function for predictive state representation is a piecewise linear and convex function. Therefore, the underlying assumption of the point based value iteration methods that nearby points are likely to have nearby values still holds for PSRs.

Extending the PBVI algorithm to work for predictive state representation requires addressing the two key phases. We modify the value update to work with prediction vectors, in a straightforward way. However, deciding how to expand the set of reachable points is more difficult. In particular, the PBVI heuristics have all been developed for belief points, which are probability vectors; however, PSR prediction vectors do not form a probability space, as they do not sum up to 1. We discuss selection heuristics for PSR prediction vectors, and provide an approximation result similar to that of PBVI in PSRs. Our approach is based on the observation that the canonical mapping from POMDP to PSR is distance preserving (at least for reachable beliefs). This allows us to apply to PSR the alpha vector technology of the point based approach even if the PSR prediction vectors do not form a probability space. Since, moreover the value function is piecewise linear and convex for PSR implies that the POMDP's backup operator straightforwardly apply to PSR. More precisely, each occurrence of the use of the backup operator will give a new policy together with a valid lower bound of its value that is always "better" than the preceding one. We compare the PSR and POMDP planning algorithms on standard POMDP tasks. Our results show that the PSR version of PBVI outperforms the original PBVI when the PSR representation introduces some degree of compression compared to the corresponding POMDP. Otherwise, the results are comparable.

2 Partially Observable Markov Decision Processes

Formally, a POMDP is defined by the following components: a finite set of hidden states S; a finite set of actions A; a finite set of observations Z; a transition function $T :$ $S \times A \times S \rightarrow [0,1]$, such that $T(s,a,s')$ is the probability that the agent will end up in state s' after taking action a in state s; an observation function $O : A \times S \times Z \rightarrow [0,1]$, such that $O(a,s',z)$ gives the probability that the agent receives observation z after taking action a and getting to state s'; a reward function $R : S \times A \times S \rightarrow \Re$, such that $r = R(s,a,s')$ is the immediate reward received when the agent takes action a in hidden state s and ends up in state s'; a discount factor, $\gamma \in (0,1)$; and an initial belief state b_0, which is a probability distribution over the set of hidden states S. Exact solution methods for

POMDPs take advantage of the fact that value functions for belief MDPs are piecewise-linear and convex, and thus can be represented using a finite number of hyperplanes in the space of beliefs (Sondik, 1971). Value iteration updates can be performed directly on these hyperplanes. For any fixed horizon n, the value function can be represented using a set of α-vectors. The value function is the upper bound over all the α-vectors: $V_n(b) = \max_\alpha \sum_s \alpha(s)b(s)$. Given V_{n-1}, V_n can be obtained using the following backup operator:

$$V_n(b) \leftarrow \max_{a \in A} \left[\sum_z P(z|a,b) \left(\sum_s b(s) \sum_{s'} b'(s')R(s,a,s') + \gamma \max_{\alpha_{n-1}} \sum_{s'} b'(s')\alpha_{n-1}(s') \right) \right] \tag{1}$$

where α_{n-1} are the α-vectors used to represent V_{n-1}. Unfortunately, exact value iteration is intractable for most POMDP problems with more than a few states, because the size of the set of hyperplanes defining the value function can grow exponentially with each step. This is why most successful planning algorithms use approximations.

Point-based methods consider only a finite set of belief points and plan for those points only. Plan generalization over the entire simplex is done based on the assumption that nearby points will have similar optimal values and actions. Point-based algorithms rely on the fact that performing many fast approximate updates often results in a more useful value function than performing a few exact updates. PBVI (Pineau et al., 2003), HSVI (Smith & Simmons, 2004), and PERSEUS (Spaan & Vlassis, 2004) are three recent variations of the point based approach. These algorithms consider a starting belief state from which they try to predict the belief states that will be reachable by the agent. The point-based approach updates not only the values of the chosen belief states, but also their gradient. The value function is thus improved for all the belief state space and not only for the chosen belief states. These three methods differ in the approach they use for choosing belief states and the method they use to update the value function at the chosen belief states. The PBVI algorithm (Pineau et al., 2003), which we use in this paper, maintains a set B of belief states reachable from the starting belief state b_0. This is expanded iteratively by adding a new belief state for each belief state already in B, using a one-step stochastic exploration strategy. For each belief state $b \in B$ and for each action $a \in A$, PBVI samples a state s from the distribution b, a resulting state s' from the distribution $T(s,a,s')$ and an observation z from the distribution $O(a,s',z)$. From these samples, it generates a new belief state b' by using the belief update rule. The value-iteration part of the algorithm uses a modified version of the value update operator. The point-based value update operator for the set of beliefs B is defined as:

$$H_B V(b) = \max_a \left[R(b,a) + \gamma \sum_{b'} P(b'|b,a)V(b') \right] \tag{2}$$

Pineau et. al (2003) showed that at any update step, the error introduced by a point-based backup H_B instead of an exact update is bounded above by $\frac{(R_{max}-R_{min})\varepsilon_B}{1-\gamma}$ where R_{max},and R_{min} are the maximum and minimum real values of possible rewards; $\varepsilon_B = \max_{b' \in \bar{\Delta}} \min_{b \in B} ||b - b'||_1$ and $\bar{\Delta}$ is the set of all reachable beliefs. PBVI is an anytime algorithm since it interleaves phases of belief set expansion and value iteration.

3   Predictive State Representation

PSRs are based on testable experiences. The notion of *test*, used in the definition of PSRs, carries the central idea of relating states of the model to verifiable and observable quantities. A test is an ordered sequence of action-observation pairs $q = a_1 z_1 ... a_k z_k$. The *prediction* for a test q, specified as above, is the probability of the sequence of observations $z_1, ..., z_k$ being generated, given that the sequence of actions $a_1, ..., a_k$ was taken. If this observation sequence is generated, we say that the test succeeds. The prediction for a test q given the prior history $h = a_1^h z_1^h ... a_t^h z_t^h$ is denoted by $p(q|h)$. This is the conditional probability of a test q being successful given that the test is performed after history h:

$$P(q|h) = P(z_{t+1} = z_1, ... z_{t+k} = z_k | h, a_{t+1} = a_1, ... a_{t+k} = a_k) \qquad (3)$$

Therefore: $P(q|h) = \frac{P(hq)}{P(h)}$. For any set of tests Q, its prediction is specified by a vector of probabilities, one for each test member $q_i \in Q$:

$$P(Q|h) = [P(q_1|h), ... P(q_{|Q|}|h)] \qquad (4)$$

A set of tests Q is a PSR of a dynamical system if its prediction, which is called the *prediction vector*, $P(Q|h)$, forms a sufficient statistic for the system after any history h, i.e., if a prediction for any test q at any history h can be computed based on $P(Q|h)$. A *linear-PSR* is a PSR in which there exists a projection vector m_q for any test q such that

$$P(q|h) = \rho^T m_q. \qquad (5)$$

The numerical reward for every prediction vector ρ, upon taking action a, is given by:

$$R(\rho, a) = \sum_r r \sum_z \rho^T m_{azr} = \rho^T (\sum_r \sum_z r m_{azr}) \qquad (6)$$

where r and z are the reward and observation, like in the POMDP model. Let:

$$\eta_a = \sum_r \sum_z r m_{azr} \qquad (7)$$

Therefore, we can rewrite the above equation as:

$$R(\rho, a) = \rho^T \eta_a \qquad (8)$$

This is similar to the definition of rewards in POMDPs, with the prediction vector ρ^T playing an analogous role to the belief state.

4   Planning Formulation Using Predictive States

The control problem for PSRs can be defined as follows: given the current prediction for core tests, decide what action should be taken in order to maximize the total return over future time steps. A policy component of a PSR agent must map predictive states to an action given a sequence of action-observation-reward tuples that took place prior to the current time (history). An agent can predict the effects of executing action a for the prediction vector ρ_t at time t as follows. Each observation-reward pair zr can occur after taking action a with a probability $P(zr|a, h_t)$; this is actually the prediction for the test azr at history h_t. The next prediction vector (ρ_{t+1}) is computed based on the resulting extended history, $h_t azr$. Any dynamical system represented by a POMDP can be represented by a PSR model with a number of core tests no larger than the number of states in the POMDP model (Littman et al., 2002). Considering this fact, planning in the space of reachable prediction vectors should intuitively be less complex than planning in the space of reachable POMDP belief states. To verify this we have a closer look at the planning space in a PSR model.

As the dynamical system evolves over time, the prediction vector changes in a space of dimension $|Q|$. But not every point in this space is a valid prediction vector (i.e. not every point corresponds to the prediction of core tests for a given history). By the definition of a prediction vector, the predictive state space (convex hull of prediction vectors) is somewhat different from the belief space of a POMDP. This is due to the fact that a belief state is a probability vector whose elements sum up to 1. Therefore, for a belief vector of size n, we can write $b(s_n) = 1 - \sum_{i=1...n-1} b(s_i)$. This linear combination projects the beliefs into an $(n-1)$-dimensional space. The same projection is not applicable to prediction vectors.

If the linear PSR has the same dimensionality as the corresponding POMDP, then there is a one-to-one mapping between the space of the PSR's prediction vectors and the POMDP's space of reachable beliefs. Let U^Q be the outcome matrix of the PSR core tests. The mapping from belief states to prediction vectors after history h is defined as: $f(b_h) = b_h^T U^Q = \rho$. This transformation is not invertible in general, since U^Q has only $|Q|$ linearly independent columns. However, in the special case in which the PSR model has the same dimensionality as the POMDP model (i.e. $|S| = |Q|$), the matrix U^Q is invertible, and therefore the belief state b_h can be uniquely retrieved from the prediction vector as:

$$b_h = (\rho(U^Q)^{-1})^T \tag{9}$$

The number of distinct prediction vectors that can be experienced by the agent is at most the number of reachable belief states of the corresponding POMDP, given a fixed initial belief, although the space of prediction vectors looks different than the belief space. It must be noted that we considered above only the space of attainable points in both models, i.e. points for which there exists a history, from a common initial state, from which the point can be reached.

4.1 PSR Value Function

We can consider a policy tree at a given prediction vector, similarly to the case of policy trees for POMDP belief states. Such a tree defines an initial action taken under that policy and a one-step shorter policy tree for each observation. A POMDP policy tree for a deterministic π can reach only $|Z|^l$ decision states in the next l time steps because it makes its decisions based solely on the observations made at each time step.

Therefore, with the same analogy, a PSR policy tree contains at most $(|Z||R|)^l$ paths of length l, where $|R|$ is the number of possible rewards. Of course, the possibility of each branch in the tree depends on the prediction probability of the test it represents, given the prediction vector from which it starts. More precisely, given that the initial action a of policy π is taken at the initial prediction vector $\rho_0 = P(Q|h_0)$, policy tree $\pi^z r$, that is shorter by one step has probability $p(zr|a, \rho_0) = \rho_0^T m_{azr}$. The agent must select the best policy tree rooted at each decision point at each time step. The value of a fixed policy tree π with a given initial action a, with respect to its initial decision node, ρ, is:

$$V^\pi(\rho) = R(\rho, a) + \gamma \sum_{z,r} \rho^T m_{azr} V^{\pi^{zr}}(\rho') = \rho^T \left(\eta_a + \gamma \sum_{zr} m_{zr} V^{\pi^{zr}}(\rho') \right) \quad (10)$$

where η_a is defined in (6) and ρ' is the prediction vector obtained from ρ after test azr. Policy trees can be used to search directly in the space of policies, similarly to policy iteration methods for POMDPs. James et al. (2006) showed that the finite horizon value function over the space of prediction vectors is piecewise linear and convex.

5 Why Point-Based Planning for PSRs?

Current exact planning for POMDPs can be extended to work with PSRs. For example, Izadi & Precup (2003) provided a policy improvement planning algorithm based on policy trees, while James et al. (2004) provided a value iteration algorithm with incremental pruning. However, ensuring the validity of the prediction vectors obtained during methods like value iteration is tricky. Recall that each linear segment of the POMDP value function represents the optimal value of at least one belief state, and linear programming is used to find such a belief state. The validity of a solution to this linear programming problem in POMDPs is ensured by the simple constraint $\sum_{i=1}^n b(s_i) = 1$. However, there is no clear constraint to check the validity of a prediction vector corresponding to a linear segment of a PSR value function because prediction vectors are not probability distributions. Several constraints have been proposed in (James et al., 2004): each element of the prediction vector must be a probability, $0 \le p_i \le 1$; the components of the prediction vector corresponding to the same action sequence $a_1...a_n$ should sum to 1; and each component of the prediction vector must correctly predict a core test. However, these constraints are a necessary but not sufficient condition for a valid prediction vector, occasionally causing problems in some domains (James et al., 2004).

Point-based methods avoid this problem in a very natural way. They work by providing a discretization of the continuous space of prediction vectors based on reachable points. No unreachable points are ever included in the value function. Hence, a point-based approach should provide a better representation of the PSR value function than exact approaches. There are other reasons that make predictive state representations a more attractive choice for approximate planning. The generalization property (Rafols et al., 2005), and state space compression (Izadi & Precup, 2005a) are among them. The number of core tests in a linear PSR can be smaller than the number of states in a POMDP, which means that the space of PSR prediction vectors can be lower-dimensional than the belief space of the original POMDP. Hence, PSRs can be viewed as a potential answer to the curse of dimensionality. At the same time, point-based methods have been designed to address the curse of history. Therefore, this combination is very appealing. Here we illustrate some examples to show the state space compression provided by linear PSRs. These examples are very likely in practice and the PSR model can take advantage of their structure.

Figure 1 depicts two domains in which PSRs have a representation advantage over POMDPs. The left panel presents the robot-intersection problem, which we introduced in prior work (Izadi & Precup, 2005a). In this domain, the orientation of the agent together with its physical position defines the state. Therefore, the POMDP representation of this domain consists of a 20-dimensional belief space. The actions are turning left, right and moving forward. The agent receives a reward of +1 for passing through the intersection and 0 otherwise. The agent observes whether the square in front of it is blocked or unblocked, with some noise. The linear PSR representation uses only 5 core tests. Of course, core tests are not unique. The figure shows a set of 5 states corresponding to one set of core tests: turnrightNowall; turnleftNowall; moveforwardNowall; turnrightNowall-turnleftNowall; turnleftWall-turnleftNowall. Another example is the navigation problem depicted in the right side of the figure. The agent has two observations (*black* and *white*) and three actions (*turn left; turn right; forward*). This environment has 576 underlying states (states are position-orientation pairs). Therefore, if the agent could consider only one-step experiences in the environment, it would recognize only two states. But if we do not limit the length of the experiences, experiences there are 288 recognizable states (shown in the triangle). The two arrows shown in the grid indicate a pair of states that produce the same observation sequence distribution given any sequence of actions. Capturing this type of structure in the state representation can be advantageous specially in large domains. However, the inefficiency of current PSR learning algorithms limits the use of this model for large domains.

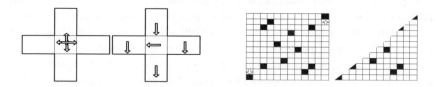

Fig. 1. Left: Robot-Intersection Problem; Right: grid navigation task

6   Approximate Planning with PSRs

We now present an example of point-based planning in PSRs, by adapting the PBVI algorithm (Pineau et al., 2003) to work with prediction vectors. Recall that PBVI alternates between two phases: the value update for a current belief set B and the expansion of the belief set to get a better approximation. Extending the algorithm to work for predictive state representations requires addressing these two key parts. For the first part, we modify the value update to work with prediction vectors in a straightforward way. However, deciding how to expand the set of reachable points is less clear. In particular, the PBVI heuristics for belief point selection have all been developed based on specific criteria which rely on the fact that belief points are probability distributions. PSR prediction vectors do not obey this constraint. We discuss different selection heuristics for PSR prediction vectors and we develop a PBVI algorithm for PSRs.

6.1   Metrics in the Space of Prediction Vectors

The L^1 distance between belief states can give a good idea of how different the values of the points are. We investigate whether the L^1 norm can be applied to prediction vectors as well. Recall that belief points can be mapped to PSR prediction vectors as follows:

$$\rho = b_h^T U^Q \tag{11}$$

We use this mapping to relate pairwise distance between prediction vectors to the distance between reachable belief points.

Theorem 1. *For any dynamical system, the POMDP-to-PSR mapping preserves the pairwise distance between points in the space of reachable beliefs, within a constant factor.*

Proof: Let b_0 be the initial belief of the POMDP and b, b' be two beliefs reachable from b_0 such that their distance is at most ε: $\sum_i |b_i - b'_i| \le \varepsilon$. Since b, and b' are reachable from b_0, there exist histories h and h' that can reach these points respectively. Using the mapping from belief states to prediction vectors, for the two corresponding prediction vectors ρ and ρ' we have:

$$
\begin{aligned}
d(\rho, \rho') &= \|\rho - \rho'\|_1 \\
&= \|(b_h^T U^Q - b_{h'}^T U^Q\|_1 = \|(b_h^T - b_{h'}^T)U^Q\|_1 \\
&\le \|b_h^T - b_{h'}^T\|_1 \|U\|_\infty \text{ (using Holder's inequality)} \\
&\le \varepsilon n \text{ (because the elements of } U \text{ are probabilities)}
\end{aligned}
$$

The last inequality holds according to the definition of the infinity norm of a matrix A: $\|A\|_\infty = \max_i \sum_{j=1}^n |a_{ij}|$, and the fact that there are at most $n = |S|$ columns in U^Q.   □

This theorem suggests that we can use the L^1 distance between PSR prediction vectors as a heuristic in the expansion phase of PBVI. More specifically, we will try to add to the set of prediction vectors new points that are reachable and that are as far away as possible from the current points.

6.2   Extending PBVI to PSRs

The fact that the value function for PSR prediction vectors is piecewise linear and convex allows a good approximation with a finite set of hyperplanes (α-vectors). The computation of the Bellman update equation can be performed on a set of prediction vectors $D = \{P(Q|h_1), P(Q|h_2), ..., P(Q|h_m)\}$ analogously to using a set of beliefs in the case of POMDPs. Hence, the approximation of the values function can be represented by a set of α-vectors $\Gamma = \{\alpha_1, ... \alpha_k\}$, such that each α_i corresponds to the best policy tree

Algorithm 1. PSR point-based value backup(Γ_{t-1})

---

for all $a \in A$ **do**
    for all $z \in Z$ **do**
        for all $r \in R$ **do**
            $\Gamma_t^{a,zr} \leftarrow \{\gamma M_{azr}\alpha | \alpha \in \Gamma_{t-1}\}$
        end for
    end for
end for
for all $\rho \in D$ **do**
    $\alpha^\rho \leftarrow \arg\max_{a \in A}(\eta_a + \sum_{zr}\max_{\alpha \in \Gamma_t^{azr}}\rho^T\alpha)$
end for
if $\alpha^\rho \notin \Gamma_t$
$\Gamma_t \leftarrow \Gamma_t \cup \alpha^\rho$
Return Γ_t

---

for at least one prediction vector $P(Q|h_i) \in D$. The backup operator is only performed on points in D based on the current value function, as follows:

$$V_{t+1}(\rho) = \arg\max_{a \in A} R(\rho, a) + \gamma(\sum_{\rho'} P(\rho'|\rho, a)V_t(\rho')) \tag{12}$$

where $R(\rho, a)$ is the immediate reward for taking action a at predictive state ρ, given by the Equation (7), and $P(\rho'|\rho, a) = P(Q|hao)$ is the next prediction vector. Algorithm 1 details this approach. The set of vectors $\Gamma_t^{a,zr}$ is used to find the estimates of values at the next prediction vector. The number of candidate points to backup can be exponential if we intend to consider all reachable prediction vectors. Planning for horizon h can reach $O(|E|^h)$ points where E is the number of one-step extensions in the PSR model. This is $O((|A||Z|)^h)$ for the PBVI algorithm in POMDPs. In PSRs, the number of extensions can be estimated as $E = |A||Z||R|$, which exceeds $|A||Z|$. However, in practice not every observation-reward pair is possible for every action, and not every observation can generate all the possible rewards. This will be demonstrated in the experiments section. We can derive an approximation bound for PSR-PBVI similar to POMDP-PBVI.

Corollary 1. *The error bounds for PBVI (Pineau et al., 2003) hold for the PSR-PBVI algorithm within a constant factor.*

Proof: The proof is based on the same ida as Theorem 1 of (Pineau et al., 2003) for POMDPs. Suppose the PSR-PBVI worst error is δ_D at a point $\rho' \notin D$. Suppose that instead of the correct optimal prediction vector α' at this point, the algorithm estimates the value using vector α which is the optimal α-vector for prediction vector $\rho \in D$. Then we have:

$$\delta_D = |(\alpha' - \alpha)(\rho - \rho')|$$
$$\leq \max_{\rho'} \min_{\rho \in D} \|\rho - \rho'\|_1$$
$$\leq \varepsilon n \qquad \square$$

The error bound for PBVI is a loose bound; our bound is similarly loose. The running time of the PSR-PBVI algorithm is $O(|Q||A||Z||R|)$ as opposed to the $O(|S||A||Z|)$

for the POMDP representation. Therefore, if the PSR provides a more compact representation, PSR-PBVI could be more efficient than the original POMDP-PBVI.

7   Experimental Results

To evaluate the performance of the PBVI-PSR algorithm we compare the results of this algorithm with the ones from PBVI versions of two other models: the original POMDP version, and the one from an additional model called RPOMDP, proposed in (Izadi & Precup, 2005b). In RPOMDPs, the reward is used in the belief state update. This helps disambiguate the hidden state in some cases, and provides a POMDP setup which is closer to the way in which rewards are treated in PSRs. However, when rewards and observations provide the same information about hidden states, this only increases the size of the problem. Although the RPOMDP model uses the same observation-reward pairs as the PSR model, it does not provide any compression in the dimensionality of the state representation used for planning. Therefore, it might increase the size of the observation space without providing more information.

In the point set expansion phase of all algorithms we used forward simulation with explorative actions (SSEA) (Pineau et al., 2003) and the L^1 metric for measuring distance between points in both belief space and prediction vector space. A set of 250 trajectories starting from a fixed given initial belief and following the policy generated by each method is used to evaluate the algorithms. The performance is measured by averaging the discounted sum of the rewards obtained on this set of trajectories. In all cases, we performed 6 iterative expansions of the point set. The results in Table 1 shows averages over 10 independent runs of the performance measure, the size of the set of points used in the representations and the number of α-vectors representing the final

Table 1. Experimental results of PBVI for PSRs

Domain	Points	α-vectors	Reward	Time
Intersection				
POMDP	115	91	2.04 ± 0.05	6.6
RPOMDP	85	41	2.18 ± 0.02	3.3
PSR	85	27	2.18 ± 0.03	1.4
Coffee				
POMDP	78	18	-3.07 ± 0.84	3.4
RPOMDP	61	3	-2.26 ± 1.49	4.5
PSR	60	3	-2.16 ± 0.84	0.5
4x4-Grid				
POMDP	100	33	3.56 ± 0.06	3.8
RPOMDP	106	22	3.58 ± 0.1	5.8
PSR	103	17	3.63 ± 0.1	1.1
Shuttle				
POMDP	35	13	32.77 ± 0.1	1.1
RPOMDP	30	14	32.89 ± 0.1	2.6
PSR	30	12	32.87 ± 0.1	0.6

estimated value function. The robot-intersection and the coffee domains are difficult to solve by POMDP exact methods and we could not get an optimal solution for these problems within a reasonable time.

All models provide similar quality solutions for all the problems except for the coffee problem. In this domain, since rewards are very informative, the planning space of PSR and RPOMDP is better, which explains the difference in results. It must be noted that the computation time is much lower for PSRs than RPOMDP because the PSR planning space is more compact. The PSR planning algorithm is significantly faster, though, and provides much more compact representations than the other methods, both in terms of the number of points used, and in terms of the number of α-vectors.

Our experimental results in all cases show PSR-PBVI as the wining approach. This confirms our expectation that predictive state representations should provide better time efficiency and speed up the progression of PBVI. The difference between the performance of these methods increases as the algorithms run for more expansions of their point sets.

8   Discussion

The difficulties in solving POMDPs can be attributed to two distinct sources. The curse of dimensionality indicates the increase in complexity because of the number of hidden states. The curse of history refers to the potentially exponential complexity of the policy as a function of the horizon length. Applying point-based techniques to PSRs can be viewed as a step in addressing both the curse of dimensionality and the curse of history simultaneously. Attempts to achieve similar effects also exist in the POMDP literature. Poupart and Boutilier (2004) combine the value directed compression model (Poupart & Boutilier, 2003) with bounded policy iteration to achieve a similar effect in a model called VDCBPI. Another related approach to predictive representations in approximate planning is the recent work on planning through multiplicity automata by Even-Dar et al. (2005). The authors convert the POMDP belief space of dimension n to an MDP of dimension $k \leq n$.

9   Conclusions and Future Work

In this paper we showed how to used point-based planning with predictive state representations. We provided the theoretical background for using PSRs with the PBVI algorithm and empirical evidence that PSRs are particularly well-suited for approximate planning using point-based algorithms. The existing work on exact methods demonstrates that the intractability of finding an exact solution for POMDPs remains almost the same for the case of PSRs. However, using approximate planning, in particular the point-based approach, seems to have a definite advantage in PSRs. Our empirical evaluation shows considerable speed-up compared to point-based planning in POMDPs, while converging a solution that is at least as good, and which is represented more compactly. Other point-based algorithms, such as HSVI2, whose running time is orders of magnitude lower than PBVI-POMDP, can be adapted to PSRs in a similar fashion. We are currently pursuing this idea. The impact of point-based PSR methods is more pronounced for problems in which the PSR representation provides more compression. The predictive representation does not rely on a specific unobservable layout of the environment, so it has the potential of being useful for fast adaptation to new, similar environments. We plan to investigate the use of PSRs for knowledge transfer between tasks in the future.

References

1. Bonet, B.: An epsilon-optimal grid-based algorithm for partially observable Markov decision processes. In: Proceedings of ICML, pp. 51–58 (2002)
2. Cassandra, A.R., Littman, M.L., Kaelbling, L.P.: A simple, fast, exact methods for partially observable Markov decision processes. In: Proceedings of UAI, pp. 54–61 (1997)
3. Even-Dar, E., Kakade, S.M., Mansour, Y.: Planning in POMDPS using Multiplicity Automata. In: Proceedings of UAI (2005)
4. Izadi, M.T., Precup, D.: A planning algorithm for predictive state representation. In: Proceedings of IJCAI, pp. 1520–1521 (2003)
5. Izadi, M.T., Precup, D.: Model minimization by linear PSR. In: Proceedings of IJCAI, pp. 1749–1750 (2005a)
6. Izadi, M.T., Precup, D.: Using rewards in POMDP belief update. In: ECML 2005 (2005b)
7. James, M., Singh, S., Littman, M.: Planning with predictive state representation. In: Proceedings of International Conference on Machine Learning and Applications (ICMLA) (2004)
8. James, M.R.: Using Predictions for Planning and Modeling in Stochastic Environments. PhD thesis, The University of Michigan (2005)
9. James, M.R., Singh, S.: Planning in models that combine memory with predictive representations of state. In: Proceedings of AAAI (2005)
10. James, M.R., Wessling, T., Vlassis, N.: Improving approximate value iteration using memories and predictive state representations. In: Proceedings of AAAI (2006)
11. Littman, M., Sutton, R., Singh, S.: Predictive representations of state. In: Proceedings of NIPS 2001 (2002)
12. Pineau, J., Gordon, G., Thrun, S.: Point-based value iteration: An anytime algorithms for POMDPs. In: Proceedings of IJCAI, pp. 1025–1032 (2003)
13. Pineau, J., Gordon, G.: POMDP Planning for Robust Robot Control. In: Proceedings of International Symposium on Robotics Research (ISRR)
14. Poupart, P., Boutilier, C.: Value-directed Compression of POMDPs. In: Proceedings of NIPS 2002, pp. 1547–1554 (2003)
15. Poupart, P., Boutilier, C.: VDCBPI: an Approximate Scalable Algorithm for Large Scale POMDPs. In: Proceedings of NIPS 2003, pp. 1081–1088 (2004)
16. Singh, S., James, M.R., Rudary, M.R.: Predictive state representations: a new theory for modeling dynamical systems. In: Proceedings of UAI, pp. 512–519 (2004)
17. Smith, T., Simmons, R.: Heuristic search value iteration for POMDPs. In: Proceedings of UAI, pp. 520–527 (2004)
18. Spaan, M.T.J., Vlassis, N.A.: PERSEUS: Randomized point-base value iteration for POMDPs. Journal of Artificial Intelligence Research, 195–220 (2005)
19. Rafols, E., Ring, M., Sutton, R.S., Tanner, B.: Using Predictive Representations to Improve Generalization in Reinforcement Learning. In: Proceedings of IJCAI (2005)

Comparison of Pleomorphic and Structural Features Used for Breast Cancer Malignancy Classification

Łukasz Jeleń, Adam Krzyżak, and Thomas Fevens

Department of Computer Science and Software Engineering
Concordia University
1455 de Maisonneuve Blvd. West
Montreal, Quebec, Canada
{l_jelen,krzyzak,fevens}@cse.concordia.ca

Abstract. Malignancy of a cancer is one of the most important factors that are taken into consideration during breast cancer. Depending on the malignancy grade the appropriate treatment is suggested. In this paper we make use of the Bloom-Richardson grading system, which is widely used by pathologists when grading breast cancer malignancy. Here we discuss the use of two categories of cells features for malignancy classification. The features are divided into polymorphic features that describe nuclei shapes, and structural features that describe cells ability to form groups. Results presented in this work, show that calculated features present a valuable information about cancer malignancy and they can be used for computerized malignancy grading. To support that argument classification error rates are presented that show the influence of the features on classification. In this paper we compared the performance of Support Vector Machines (SVMs) with three other classifiers. The SVMs presented here are able to assign a malignancy grade based on pre–extracted features with accuracy up to 94.24% for pleomorphic features and with an accuracy 91.33% when structural features were used.

Keywords: malignancy grading, FNA grading, breast cancer grading, Bloom–Richardson, features.

1 Introduction

According to statistics breast cancer is one of the most deadly cancers among middle-aged women. Based on the data provided by the Breast Cancer Society of Canada [1] about 415 women will be diagnosed with breast cancer each week in Canada. Most of the diagnosed cases can be fully recovered when diagnosed at an early stage. Cancers in their early stages are vulnerable to treatment while cancers in their most advanced stages are usually almost impossible to treat. During the diagnosis process, the cancer is assigned a grade that is used to determine the appropriate treatment. Successful treatment is a key to reduce the high death rate. The most common diagnostic tools are a mammography and

S. Bergler (Ed.): Canadian AI 2008, LNAI 5032, pp. 138–149, 2008.
© Springer-Verlag Berlin Heidelberg 2008

a fine needle aspiration biopsy (FNA). Mammography, which is a non-invasive method, is most often used for screening purposes rather than for precise diagnosis. It allows a physician to find possible locations of microcalcifications and other indicators in the breast tissue. When a suspicious region is found, the patient is sent to a pathologist for a more precise diagnosis. This is when the FNA is taken. A fine needle aspiration biopsy is an invasive method to extract a small sample of the questionable breast tissue that allows the pathologist to describe the type of the cancer in detail. Using this method pathologists can very adequately describe not only the type of the cancer but also its genealogy and malignancy. The stage of the cancer depends on the malignancy factor that is assigned during an FNA examination. The determination of the malignancy is essential when predicting the progression of cancer.

The grading system originally proposed by Bloom and Richardson [2], later modified by Scarff and known as modified Scarff-Bloom-Richardson system, for grading breast cancer malignancy is one of the best known prognostic factors for this type of cancer [3]. These systems are based on grading of cells' polymorphy, ability to reform histoformative structures, and mitotic index. All of these features are described by the Bloom-Richardson scheme as three factors that use a point based scale for assessing each feature according to the following description:

1. **Degree of structural differentiation (SD)** - In histopathological slides this is also described as tubule formation, which reflects cell tendency to form tubules. Since in cytological smears tubules are not preserved, the scoring given below for this factor is based on the classification of cell groupings within a smear, see Fig. 1a for example. On the right image of the Fig. 1a only one group is visible, which indicates lower malignancy that the case on the left image where dispersed cells are visible.
   - One point - cells in the image are grouped regularly.
   - Two points - both grouped and single cells found within the image.
   - Three points - cells are spread irregularly.

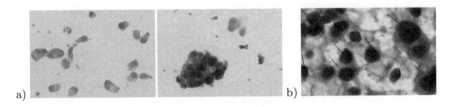

a)   b)

Fig. 1. FNA smears. a) Structural differentiation. b) Pleomorphism.

2. **Pleomorphism (P)** - This factor takes into consideration differences in size, shape and staining of the nuclei. This scoring is fairly straightforward because with the growth of irregularity of the nuclei the prognosis becomes worse. Fig. 1b shows an example of these variations. Arrows in the image indicate cells with visible variations in shape and color.

- One point - nuclei with uniform size, shape and staining.
- Two points - moderate variations are found.
- Three points - very significant variations.

3. **Frequency of hyperchromatic and mitotic figures (HMF)** - Mitosis is a process in the cell life cycle in which a mother cell divides into two identical cells. Main objective of this factor is to assess the number of mitosis in the field of view. Several fields of view on the same slide are taken into account because this step is done in a large magnification. The more cases of mitosis found, the worse the prognosis is. During the staining process, mitotic cells stain the most intensively providing the darkest areas in the nucleus.
   - One point - occasional figures per field are found.
   - Two points - smears with two or three figures in most fields.
   - Three points - more than three figures per fields are found

According to the BR scheme, the malignancy of the tumor is assigned a grade that depends on the quantitative values of the above factors and is determined by the following equation:

$$G = SD + P + HMF. \tag{1}$$

The final grade is obtained by the summation of all the awarded points for each factor described earlier. Depending on the value of G, the tumor is assigned one of three grades according to the chart shown in Fig. 2.

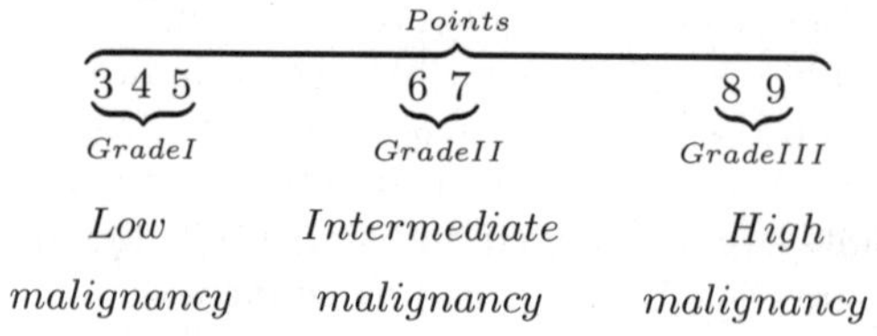

Fig. 2. Grade determination for the Bloom – Richardson scheme, taken from [2]

Based on the evaluation of the malignancy of the tumor an appropriate treatment is suggested. Assigning a diagnosis to a case is a very difficult task and is dependent on the experience of the pathologist. More experienced pathologists that have seen more cases are more reliable in their diagnosis. On the other hand, due to overwork and fatigue, seeing more similar cases may lead to misclassification of the malignancy. To address this problem we present an automated grading approach that is able to evaluate and assign a grade to Fine Needle Aspiration biopsy (FNA) tissue. To achieve this we convert the Bloom – Richardson [2] grading scheme into a classification problem. In our method the input FNA slides are first segmented according to the algorithm described in section 2. Based on the segmentation results, features taken into consideration are calculated (see sections 2.1 and 2.2) and used to train the classifier.

2   Feature Extraction

Classification is a task of assigning an item to a certain category, called a class, based on the characteristic features of that item. This task in any classification system is performed by a classifier that takes a feature vector as an input and responds with a category to which the object belongs.A feature vector is a set of features extracted from the input data. Before we can extract features used for classification our input data needs to be preprocessed and segmented. Preprocessing is a task of removing not important information from the data. Segmentation is an operation during which we isolate the boundaries of the important parts of the data that are then used for feature extraction and classification. For breast cancer malignancy classification two kinds of images are used. One subset consist of images recorded in low magnification, which allows for extracting structural features, the second subset of images is built from high magnification images which are used for polymorphic feature extraction.

2.1   Structural Features

Structural features are extracted from images recorded with 100x magnification. The information collected from these images allows us to extract three features based on cells ability to form groups or to be loosely spread around the image. Here, we segment those areas of the image where cells grouping are visible. For this purpose we make use of an iterative clustering approach for automatic image thresholding. This method was proposed by Riddler and Calvard [4]. In principle, their method seeks a threshold T, represented by a curve, within an image, that is restricted to have a bimodal histogram and the final threshold level is calculated according to the following equation:

$$T = \frac{\mu_1 + \mu_2}{2},\qquad(2)$$

where μ_1 and μ_2 are the means of the components separated by T.

Due to the staining process of FNA images, the red channel provides best information about nuclear structures out of the three RGB channels. During the staining process, nuclei stain with shades purple and when red channel is extracted all the nuclear features are preserved while the background in-formation is lost. This observation allows us to extract and threshold the image red channel and then to use it for further feature extraction.

For the purpose of this study we calculated three structural features. These features are defined, based on the number of groups and their area. Single cells, that are present in the images of high malignancy, are also represented as a group that consists of only one cell. Final decision is based on the relation between the features. If we take into consideration the description of Bloom and Richardson [2] of the dispersion measure and the nature of the images taken during the FNA examination (see Fig. 1) we can see that groups with larger area are less malignant that those with smaller areas. Analogically, we can say that images with larger number of groups are more malignant that those that contain only one or few groups. Taking that into consideration we propose the following three features as a measure of cancer malignancy:

- **Average area** (A_s) – is calculated as the average number of nuclei pixels. This feature represents the tendency of cells to form groups. If A_s is large then there is one or few large groups in the image.
- **Number of groups** (NG) – To measure this feature we calculate the number of groups in the image that weren't removed during segmentation process. Here, if NG is large then there are numerous groups in the image, which suggests high malignancy case.
- **Dispersion** (D) – We define the dispersion as a variation of cluster areas (A_i) which is determined by the following equation:

$$D = \frac{1}{n-1} \sum_{i=1}^{n} (A_i - A_s)^2, \tag{3}$$

where n is a number of cell clusters in the image and A_s is a mean area of clusters.

Large values of this feature represent less disperse cells and therefore lower malignancy of the caner.

According to the above description, we calculated features for all of the images in the database.

2.2 Polymorphic Features

To extract polymorphic features, high magnification images of breast cancer FNA slides were used. These features need more sophisticated segmentation method than structural features due to the fact that shape and staining information of nuclei is needed. To be able to extract shape–based features we make use of the automated segmentation procedure that involves the level set method proposed by Li et al. [5]. Compared to other methods, such as the Hough transform [6], level sets seem to be a better choice for segmentation because of its better time performance. In the literature we can find approaches based on the Generalized Hough transform [7,8] that showed good segmentation results due to the use of an elliptical shape to identify the location and size of nuclei. These approaches are computationally intensive and therefore are time consuming [9]. On the other hand, level set methods, which also proved to be a powerful tool for medical image segmentation [5,10,11,12,13], involve fewer computations than the Hough transform approaches and achieve faster computational times. Depending on the number of iterations used for segmentation, level set are able to segment breast cancer nuclei roughly 10x faster than the Hough transform.

Level sets were first described in 1988 by Osher and Sethian [14] as a method for capturing moving fronts. In the level set formulation, the segmentation problem is equivalent to the computation of a surface $\Gamma(t)$ that propagates in time along its normal direction. The Γ surface is also called a propagating front, which according to Osher and Sethian [14] is embedded as a zero level of a time–varying higher dimensional function $\phi(x,t)$:

$$\Gamma(t) = \{x \in \mathcal{R}^3/\phi(x,t) = 0\} \tag{4}$$

An evolution equation for an interface Γ, where Γ is a closed curve in R^2, can be written in a general form [15] as:

$$\frac{\partial \phi}{\partial t} + F|\nabla\phi| = 0, \tag{5}$$

The function ϕ describes a surface defined by $\phi(x,t) = d$, where d is a signed distance between x and the surface Γ. If x is inside (outside) of Γ then d is negative (positive). Function F is a scalar speed function that depends on image data and the function ϕ. The main drawback of this procedure is that during the evolution, ϕ can assume sharp or flat shapes. To overcome this problem ϕ is initialized as a signed distance function before evolution. Later, during evolution, it is periodically reshaped to be a signed distance function [5]. In our framework, we make use of variational level sets, introduced by Li *et al.* [5], that are more robust than those originally proposed by Osher and Sethian because they incorporate shape and region information into the level set energy functions.

In 2005, Li *et al.* [5] proposed a modification of traditional variational level sets to overcome the problem of reshaping of function ϕ to be a distance function within the evolution cycle. They proposed an evolution equation of the form:

$$\frac{\partial \phi}{\partial t} = -\frac{\partial \mathcal{E}}{\partial \phi} \tag{6}$$

where $\frac{\partial \mathcal{E}}{\partial \phi}$ is a Gateaux derivative of the energy function $\mathcal{E}$ and is represented by the equation 7:

$$\frac{\partial \mathcal{E}}{\partial \phi} = -\mu[\Delta\phi - div(\frac{\nabla\phi}{|\nabla\phi|})] - \lambda\delta(\phi)div(g\frac{\nabla\phi}{|\nabla\phi|}) - \nu g\delta(\phi), \tag{7}$$

where Δ is the Laplacian operator, div is the divergence operator and $\mu > 0$ is a parameter controlling the effect of penalizing the deviation of ϕ from a signed distance function.

All level set methods start with an initial level set function. The closer the initial level set function is to the final segmentation, typically, the more likely the level set method will quickly converge to the segmentation. Therefore, to automate the segmentation process and start with a good initial level set function, we make use of an iterative clustering approach for automatic image thresholding described in section 2.1. Based on the segmentation results four shape–based features were chosen. These features correspond to the indicators used for the Bloom–Richardson scheme. To precisely estimate the necessary features only the nuclear features, rather than cellular features, are taken into consideration because only these features are the most discriminant and these are the features graded by pathologists. Taking this into consideration, as well, we use four shape–based features and one textural feature. Values obtained for these features yield a good differentiation between cancerous and healthy cells [16]. In this study the following features were extracted:

- **Area** – calculated as the sum of all pixels (x) of the segmented nucleus(N).
- **Perimeter** – is the length of the nuclear envelope. Calculated as length of the polygonal approximation of the boundary (B).
- **Convexity** – is calculated as the ratio of nucleus area and its convex hull [17], which is the minimal area of the convex polygon that can contain the nucleus(see Eq. 8).

$$C(N) = \frac{A}{Area(CH(N))}. \qquad (8)$$

where $CH(N)$ is a convex hull of the nucleus.
　　Convex shapes will yield a value of 1, while concave shapes will have a value less than 1.
- **Eccentricity** – allows us to track how much segmented nucleus differs from a healthy nucleus. Healthy nuclei will assume circular shapes while cancerous nuclei can assume arbitrary shapes. We calculate eccentricity as the ratio of the distance between the foci of an ellipse, that has the same second–moments as the extracted nuclei, and its major axis length. Values of this feature vary between 0 and 1. These are degenerate cases because a shape whose eccentricity is 0 is actually a circle, while a shape whose eccentricity is 1 is a line segment.
- **Texture Measure** – represents nuclear intensity changes in the image. We calculate this feature as an average red channel value of a nucleus.

The first four features describe changes in size and shape of the cancer nuclei. The texture measure describes changes in staining of the nuclei and is also used as a feature for the third BR factor – Frequency of hyperchromatic and mitotic figures.

3　Malignancy Classification

Here we make use of the Support Vector Machines for classification purposes. Classification process is based on transforming a feature vector into a higher dimensional space where a separating hyperplane is constructed. During the training process only those vectors that are closest to the separating plane are used because they carry the most valuable information about classification. SVMs used in this study use the idea of large margin classifiers for training that provides good generalization of the problem. Large margin classifiers use a kernel–based methods for data separation.

　　The learning process uses the Adatron algorithm [18] which guarantees the convergence to the solution assuming that the solution exists. According to the authors this method is able to learn nonlinear decision boundaries. This algorithm was extended by substitution of the inner product of patterns in the input space by the kernel function (see eq. 9) which allows for maximization of the following function

$$J(\alpha) = \sum_{i=1}^{N} \alpha_i - \frac{1}{2} \sum_{i=1}^{N} \sum_{j=1}^{N} \alpha_i \alpha_j d_i d_j G_{2\sigma^2}(x_i - x_j) \qquad (9)$$

with constrains: $\sum_{i=1}^{N} d_i \alpha_i = 0$, $\alpha_i \geq 0, \forall i \in 1, ... N$ and where x_i, x_j are feature vectors, $d_i, d_j \in \{2, 3\}$ are malignancy grades, α_i are multipliers and G is a Gaussian kernel with variance σ.

$$g(x) = d_i(\sum_{j=1}^{N} d_j \alpha_j G_{2\sigma^2}(x - x_j) + b) \tag{10}$$

where g is a decision boundary.

$$\begin{cases} \alpha_i(n+1) = \alpha_i(n) + \Delta\alpha_i(n), & if \quad \alpha_i(n) + \Delta\alpha_i > 0 \\ \alpha_i(n+1) = \alpha_i(n) & if \quad \alpha_i(n) + \Delta\alpha_i \leq 0 \end{cases} \tag{11}$$

$$M = min_i g(f_i) \tag{12}$$

where α_j is nonzero if and only if x_j is a support vector.

Training starts with a starting multiplier $\alpha_i = 0.1$ and a terminating threshold $t = 0.01$. We calculate $\Delta\alpha_i = \eta[1 - M]$ and perform an update according to eq.11 as long as $M > t$, η is a predefined learning rate. For testing purposes three feature vectors were used. The first set of features consist of structural features and the second set uses polymorphic features. The third feature vector consists of both structural and pleomorphic features. To classify the FNA cytological tissue we use classifiers that take a three, five and eight–element feature vectors respectively as an input and responds with two element output vector $(1, 0)^T$ for intermediate malignancy and $(0, 1)^T$ for high malignancy.

To compare the performance of the SVM classifier we make use of three additional classifiers, Multilayer Perceptron (MLP), Self–Organizing Maps (SOM), Principal Components based Neural Network (PCA). MLP are simple feedforward neural networks trained with backpropagation method in a supervised manner [19]. SOMs networks reduce the input space into representative features according to self–organizing process [20]. SOMs are trained in an unsupervised manner to produce a map of similarities of the input data by grouping the similar data items together. PCA are a combination of supervised and unsupervised trained neural networks. At first principal components are found from input data with an unsupervised single layer neural network and then supervised MLP is used for classification of the components [21].

4   Results

In this section the performance of features described in section 2 that were used to train and test classifiers are described. Feature extraction was based on images from our database of FNA slides. All of the images stained with the Haematoxylin and Eosin technique (HE) which yielded purple and black stain for nuclei, shades of pink for cytoplasm and orange/red for red blood cells. All the images were obtained by Olympus BX 50 microscope with mounted CCD–IRIS camera connected to a PC computer with MultiScan Base 08.98 software.

Our database consists of 110 fine needle aspiration biopsy images with known malignancy grades collected at Department of Pathology at Medical University

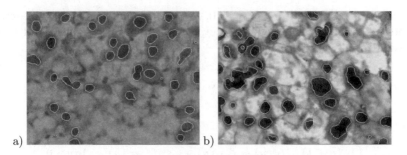

a)   b)

Fig. 3. Segmentation results: a) Intermediate malignancy, b) High malignancy

Table 1. Some of the calculated features along with pathologist grading

Feature	Case 1	Case 2	Case 3	Case 4	Case 5	Case 6
Area	591	434	617	184	218	320
Perimeter	80.5	70.0	105.0	40.8	48.0	56.2
Convexity	0.9420	0.9454	0.9045	0.9420	0.9561	0.9640
Eccentricity	0.7180	0.6761	0.6547	0.6920	0.6036	0.6000
Texture	116.7	124.7	120.3	98.0	123.8	108.2
Av. Area	173.9	122.5	266.1	149	4038.9	2216
No. of Groups	37	4	59	1	7	52
Dispersion $(\frac{1}{D})$	55.56	62.5	7.87	0	0.009	0.031
BR Grade	G3	G3	G3	G2	G2	G2

of Wrocław, Poland. There are 44 images with high malignancy (G3) and 66 images with intermediate malignancy (G2). Also, each malignancy case consist of two types of FNA images recorded with two different magnifications. Benchmark grades of the images were assigned by a pathologist and are used for verification purposes during tests. Since 2004 none of the performed biopsies were assigned with a low malignancy grade, therefore all cases included in the database are graded as intermediate or high malignancy. Fig. 3 shows an example of segmentation that was used for feature extraction and Table 1 shows some of the extracted features along with malignancy grades assigned by an expert pathologist. From the table we can see that features extracted by our framework reflect the tendency of malignant cancer cells, where more malignant cases have larger nuclei and their border is more deformed than those of a healthy nuclei. Using such feature vectors we performed six different tests on our database with different training and testing sets.

Low malignancy cases are very rare and therefore the classification task is reduced to the two–class problem. Training sets were chosen using random sampling to contain different numbers of high and intermediate malignancy cases. The remaining cases were used to form test sets. Using these sets we trained and tested the performance of four different classifiers. We took into consideration four classifiers, Multilayer Perceptron (MLP), Self–Organizing Maps (SOM), Principal Components based Neural Network (PCA) and Support Vector

Table 2. Error rates of tested classifiers

	Structural			Pleomorphic			Both		
	(Average)	(Best)	(Worst)	(Average)	(Best)	(Worst)	(Average)	(Best)	(Worst)
SOM	10.56%	7.8%	16.21%	19.53%	6.32%	23.75%	11.53%	5.22%	17.27%
MLP	10.67%	8.75 %	12.36 %	17.30 %	6.73 %	24.71 %	9.81%	4.36%	15.77%
SVM	13.44 %	8.67 %	17.16 %	19.39 %	5.76 %	24.71 %	13.3%	6.76%	16.73%
PCA	11.30 %	7.79 %	16.61 %	18.82 %	7.22 %	23.66 %	10.92%	7.65%	10.01%

Machines (SVM)(see sec. 3), and compared their performance on our database. Out of the four classifiers the Multilayer Perceptron Neural Network showed the best average performance with an average error rate of 17.3 % for pleomorphic features and 9.81% when all of the features were used for classification. In this case SVMs performed worse achieving 13.3% error for all of the features. When we compare the performance of only pleomorphic and structural features we can see that structural features perform better achieving the lowest average error rate for SOM and MLP while pleomorphic features achieve significantly higher errors. The summary of all achieved error rates is presented in table 2.

In pattern recognition and machine learning, Receiver Operating Characteristics (ROC) is widely used for performance analysis and provides tools to select possibly optimal classification model. ROC shows that SVMs performed better that any other tested classifier. When comparing area under the ROC curve (AUC) one can notice that for SVMs the area is larger that for any other classifier taken into consideration in this study. According to ROC analysis principals we choose the classifier with the largest AUC [22]. This is reflected in Fig. 4 that shows a comparative performance of all tested classifiers.

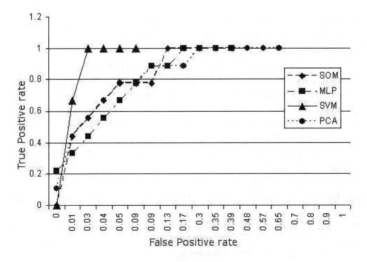

Fig. 4. ROC curves for all classifiers

5 Conclusions

In section 2 we have presented a set of features that were used for breast cancer malignancy grading. In this work we compared a classification performance of four different classifiers using described features. This section also indicates the performance of level sets for nuclei segmentation. Fig. 3 presents example of nuclear segmentation obtained with level sets. From the figure we can see that nuclear boundary is well represented and we can conclude that this method is suitable for segmentation of these kind of images. The performance analysis of our system given in section 4 shows that MLP provides us with the smallest average error rate of 9.81% when all of the features were used for classification. We can also conclude that structural features are able to classify malignancy grade more accurate that pleomorphic features. Since Bloom–Richardson scheme is based on both types of features we can assume that the use of all extracted features will yield better results. This can be confirmed with the results obtained during this study, where usage of both types of features yielded the lowest average error of 9.81%. Presented error rates are very promising and allows us to further investigate this problem on feature extraction and preprocessing levels to achieve better classification rates. Another possibility to lower the error would be to increase the database to include more malignancy cases, which we are currently investigating.

From medical point of view, the application of a computer aided cancer malignancy system is a step forward towards repeatability of the grading procedure. Such a system could allow doctors to make the decisions more objective and would allow to minimize the uncertainty region between the malignancy cases.

References

1. Breast Cancer Society of Canada, www.bcsc.ca
2. Bloom, H., Richardson, W.: Histological Grading and Prognosis in Breast Cancer. Br. J. Cancer 11, 359–377 (1957)
3. Le Doussal, V., Tubiana-Hulin, M., Friedman, S., Hacene, K., Spyratos, F., Brunet, M.: Prognostic value of histologic grade nuclear components of scarff–bloom–richardson (sbr). an improved score modification based on a multivariate analysis of 1262 invasive ductal breast carcinomas. Cancer 64(9) (1914)
4. Ridler, T., Calvard, S.: Picture thresholding using an iterative selection. IEEE Trans. System, Man and Cybernetics 8, 630–632 (1978)
5. Li, C., Xu, C., Gui, C., Fox, M.: Level Set Evolution Without Re-initialization: A New Variational Formulation. In: Proc. IEEE Conference on Computer Vision and Pattern Recognition 2005, pp. 430–436 (2005)
6. Ballard, H.: Generalizing the Hough Transform to Detect Arbitrary Shapes. Pattern Recognition 13(2), 111–122 (1981)
7. Street, W.N., Wolberg, W.H., Mangasarian, O.L.: Nuclear Feature Extraction for Breast Tumor Diagnosis. In: IS&T/SPIE 1993 Int. Symp. Elec. Img., San Jose, California, vol. 1905, pp. 861–870 (1993)
8. Lee, K., Street, W.: Generalized Hough Transforms with Flexible Templates. In: Proc. ICAI, Las Vegas, NV, vol. 3, pp. 1133–1139 (2000)

9. Jeleń, Ł., Krzyżak, A., Fevens, T.: Automated Feature Extraction for Breast Cancer Grading with Bloom-Richardson Scheme. Int. J. CARS 1(1), 468–469 (2006)
10. Droske, M., Meyer, B., Rumpf, M., Schaller, K.: An adaptive Level Set Method for Medical Image Segmentation. In: Insana, M.F., Leahy, R.M. (eds.) IPMI 2001. LNCS, vol. 2082, pp. 416–422. Springer, Heidelberg (2001)
11. Deng, J., Tsui, H.: A fast level set method for segmentation of low contrast noisy biomedical images. Pattern Recognition Letters 23(1-3), 161–169 (2002)
12. Tsai, A., Yezzi, A., Wells III, W., Tempany, C., Tucker, D., Fan, A., Grimson, W., Willsky, A.: A shape-based approach to the segmentation of medical imagery using level sets. Medical Imaging 22(2), 137–154 (2003)
13. Li, S., Fevens, T., Krzyżak, A., Jin, C., Li, S.: Fast and robust clinical triple-region image segmentation using one level set function. In: Larsen, R., Nielsen, M., Sporring, J. (eds.) MICCAI 2006. LNCS, vol. 4191, pp. 766–773. Springer, Heidelberg (2006)
14. Osher, S., Sethian, J.: Fronts Propagating with Curvature-dependent speed: algorithms based on Hamilton-Jacobi formulations. J. Comp. Phys. 79, 12–49 (1988)
15. Sethian, J., Adalsteinsson, D.: An Overview of Level Set Methods for Etching, Deposition, and Lithography Development. IEEE Trans. Semiconductor Manufacturing 10(1), 167–184 (1997)
16. Jeleń, Ł., Fevens, T., Krzyżak, A.: Classification of Breast Cancer Malignancy using Cytological Images of Fine Needle Aspiration Biopsies. J. AMCS 18(1) (in press, 2008)
17. Zunic, J., Rosin, P.: A Convexity Measurement for Polygons. British Machine Vision Conference 24, 173–182 (2002)
18. Friess, T., Cristianini, N., Campbell, C.: The kernel adatron algorithm: a fast and simple learning procedure for support vector machines. In: 15th International Conference on Machine Learning, Morgan Kaufman Publishers, San Francisco (1998)
19. Duda, R., Hart, P., Stork, D.: Pattern Classification, 2nd edn. Wiley Interscience Publishers, New York (2000)
20. Kohonen, T.: The self–organizing map. Proc IEEE 78, 1464–1480 (1990)
21. Oja, E.: A simplified neuron modeled as a principal component analyzer. J. Math. Biol. 15, 267–273 (1982)
22. Bradley, A.: The use of the area under the ROC curve in the evaluation of machine learning algorithms. Pattern Recognition 30(7), 1145–1159 (1997)

Towards a Faster Inference Algorithm in Multiply Sectioned Bayesian Networks

Karen H. Jin and Dan Wu

School of Computer Science
University of Windsor
Windsor Ontario Canada N9B 3P4

Abstract. Multiply sectioned Bayesian network(MSBN) is an extension of Bayesian network(BN) model for the support of flexible modelling in large and complex problem domains. However, current MSBN inference methods involve extensive intra-subnet(internal) and inter-subnet (external) message passings. In this paper, we present a new MSBN message passing scheme which substantially reduces the total number of message passings. By saving on both internal and external messages, our method improves the overall efficiency of MSBN inference compared with existing methods.

1 Introduction

The *Multiply Sectioned Bayesian Network*(MSBN) model [9] successfully extends the traditional BN model for large and complex problem domains. An MSBN is composed of a set of BN subnets organized into a hypertree. An MSBN is usually transformed into a secondary structure named *linked junction tree forest*(LJF) for probabilistic inference. The well established BN global propagation(GP) method is extended for inference in MSBN. However, it calls for two rounds of global external message passings among all MSBN subnets, and repeated application of GP propagation in each BN subnet. The large number of internal and external messages thus generated has a direct impact on the efficiency of MSBN inference.

This paper presents a method that extends the results in [6] to the context of MSBN inference. The method utilizes LJF hyperlink analysis performed at compilation time in order to obtain information about external message flow before the actual message passings take place. External messages are passed as needed between two adjacent subnets. Furthermore, repeated local propagation in each subnet is avoided, thus reducing the number of internal messages generated in each subnet. Preliminary experiments have confirmed the substantial reduction of both internal and external messages using the new method.

The rest of the paper is organized as follows. Section 2 presents the background. Section 3 describes the proposed MSBN inference method. The experiments are presented in Section 4. We conclude this paper and discuss future work in Section 5.

S. Bergler (Ed.): Canadian AI 2008, LNAI 5032, pp. 150–162, 2008.
© Springer-Verlag Berlin Heidelberg 2008

2   Background

A traditional *Bayesian network* (BN) is a probabilistic graphical model [4] for inference with uncertain knowledge. Denoted as a tuple $B = (G, P_V)$, a BN consists of a *directed acyclic graph* (DAG) G and a set $P_V = \{p(x|\pi(x))\}$ of *conditional probability distributions* (CPDs), where x is a random variable that corresponds to a node in G and $\pi(x)$ is the parent(s) of x in G. For example, the DAG shown in Fig. 1(a) together with the CPDs attached to each node defines a BN.

For efficient probabilistic inference, a BN is normally transformed into a secondary structure called *junction tree*(JT). Each JT node is a *cluster* and the intersection of two adjacent clusters is a *separator*. The *global propagation*(GP) method [2,5,1,3] is a well established BN inference algorithm for JT. The potential of each cluster is transformed into marginal after a coordinated sequence of message passes. A single message M_{ij} sent from cluster C_i to C_j over their separator S_{ij} is calculated by marginalizing C_i's current potential $\Phi(C_i)$ as $M_{ij} = \sum_{C_i \backslash S_{ij}} \Phi(C_i)$, where $\backslash$ denotes a set difference operator. The GP method consists of two rounds of message passings, inward and outward, namely *Collect-Evidence* and *Distribute-Evidence*, given an arbitrarily chosen root cluster. Two messages are passed over each JT separator using the GP method. Thus, a total of $2(n-1)$ message passings are required in a JT with n clusters.

The *Multiply Sectioned Bayesian Network* (MSBN) consists of a set of interrelated BNs (called BN subnets thereinafter) that each represents the knowledge of a subdomain within a large problem domain [12,7]. The union of random variables in each BN subnet denoted V, is called the *total universe*. The union of the DAGs of these BN subnets, denoted $\mathcal{G}$, must also be a DAG. These subnets are organized following certain constraints into a tree structure called *hypertree*, denoted $\mathcal{H}$. Each hypertree node, known as *hypernode*, corresponds to a subnet. Each hypertree link, known as *hyperlink*, corresponds to a *d-sepset* that connects two adjacent subnets and renders two sides of the network conditionally independent. Each local BN subnet represents a partial view of the problem domain over the total universe V. For example, the three BN subnets, namely G_0, G_1, and G_2 in Fig. 1(b), together with the hypertree in Fig. 1(c), comprise an MSBN. The box attached to each hyperlink encloses the corresponding d-sepset.

Existing inference methods in MSBN are extensions of BN inference methods. In [12,7,9], Xiang extends the standard GP method with a derived dependence

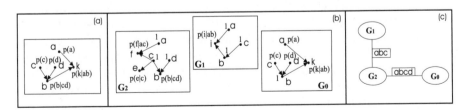

Fig. 1. (a) A BN. (b) An MSBN with three subnets. (c) The corresponding hypertree.

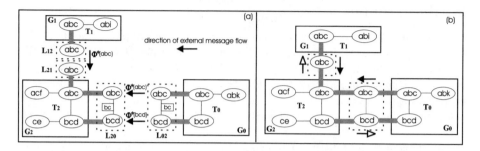

Fig. 2. An MSBN linked junction tree forest. (a) Two external messages: G_1 to G_2 and G_0 to G_2. (b) Two rounds of external message passing among all subnets.

structure called *linked junction tree forest*(LJF). This method has the advantage of localized inference support which is not available in other existing alternatives, such as extended MSBN loop cut-set conditioning and forward sampling [10]. We name this method the *MSBN GP* method in this paper.

An LJF is constructed through a process of cooperative moralization and triangulation among all MSBN subnets. In a hypertree $\mathcal{H}$, each hypernode, which corresponds to a local BN subnet, is transformed into a *local JT* and each hyperlink into a *linkage tree* [8]. A linkage tree is essentially a JT constructed from d-sepset. Each cluster in a linkage tree is called a *linkage*, and each separator called a *linkage separator*. The cluster in the local JT that contains a linkage is called the *linkage host*. Although two adjacent subnets may each maintain a different linkage tree, the two corresponding linkage trees span over the same d-sepset and they have identical set of clusters and separators. They differ only in their topologies. It has been proven that the communication between two subnets is not affected by this difference in their linkage trees [9]. Between two adjacent subnets N_i and N_j, we use L_{ij} and L_{ji} to refer to the linkage tree maintained in N_i and N_j respectively, and the same linkages in each linkage tree are the corresponding linkages.

During initialization of an LJF, exactly one of all occurrences of a variable x(in a subnet containing $\{x\} \cup \pi(x)$), is assigned the CPD $p(x|\pi(x))$. All other occurrences are assigned a uniform potential of 1. Also, a uniform potential 1 is assigned to each separator in each local JT and each linkage in each linkage tree. Thus, the initial potential of a local JT cluster is either the product of all of its assigned CPDs, or 1 if no CPD is assigned. The potential of each subnet P_{G_i} is the product of all cluster potentials in its local JT. The product of $P_{G_i}, i = 0, 1, 2...$, yields $p(V)$ which is the JPD over the total universe of MSBN.

Fig. 2 (a) shows an LJF constructed from the MSBN in Fig. 1(b) and Fig. 1(c). Local JTs, T_0, T_1 and T_2 constructed from BN subnet G_0, G_1 and G_2 respectively, are enclosed by boxes with solid edges. Linkage trees, converted from d-sepsets, are enclosed by boxes with dotted edges. Note that in this example, each pair of adjacent subnets maintain the same linkage trees. The linkage tree L_{02} contains two linkages abc and bcd and their linkage hosts in T_0 are the clusters $\{abc\}$ and $\{bcd\}$. An initial assignment of all CPDs is shown in Fig. 4(a).

Note that only one occurrence of the variable b, which is in G_2, is assigned the CPD $p(b|cd)$.

The MSBN GP inference method brings an MSBN LJF into consistency at two levels: *global consistency* at the inter-subnet level and *local consistency* at the local BN subnet level. *Local consistency* is achieved by passing *internal message* among clusters in the local JT the same way as in the BN GP. This process is called *local propagation* in this context because it occurs locally in each local JT. Inter-subset messages, also called *external messages*, are passed between adjacent subnets over their corresponding linkage trees to achieve *global consistency*. Each external message pass with the MSBN GP method requires local propagation in the sender and the receiver BN subnets. A BN subnet needs to be locally consistent in order to deliver outgoing external messages to its neighbors [9].

For a subnet N_i to deliver a message to N_j over N_i's linkage tree L_{ij}, each linkage Q_i in L_{ij} is assigned a linkage potential $\Phi(Q_i) = \sum_{C_i \setminus Q_i} \Phi(C_i)$ where C_i is Q_i's linkage host in T_i. For example, in Fig. 2(a) the message from G_0 to G_2 consists of the potentials over two linkages abc and bcd. The linkage tree construction enables a more compact representation of d-sepset, but also introduces redundancy over linkage separators. For example, both linkages abc and bcd carry information over bc. The notion of *peer separator* is introduced to solve this problem. By randomly selecting a root linkage and directing all linkage separators away from the root, we associate each linkage separator with one of its two neighboring linkages as the peer separator. Next, for each linkage Q with peer separator R, the notion of *extended linkage potential* is defined as $\Phi^*(Q) = \Phi(Q)/\Phi(R)$ and thus removing the redundancy by division [9]. For example, in linkage tree L_{02} in Fig. 2(a), the separator bc is associated with the linkage bcd as the peer separator and abc has no peer assigned. The extended linkage potential on each linkage are $\Phi^*(abc) = \Phi(abc)$ and $\Phi^*(bcd) = \Phi(bcd)/\Phi(bc)$. The extended linkage potential is actually used to calculate the external messages in the MSBN GP. The steps of an external message pass between two adjacent subnets is described in the algorithm *GPMessagePass* adapted from [9].

Algorithm 1 *(GPMessagePass). Let N_i and N_j be the adjacent subnets associated with the local JTs T_i and T_j, and the linkage trees L_{ij} and L_{ji} respectively. An external message passed from N_i to N_j is performed as follows:*

- *Step 1. For each linkage Q_i in L_{ij} with host C_i in T_i, calculate the linkage potential $\Phi(Q_i)$*
- *Step 2. For each linkage Q_i, calculate the extended linkage potential $\Phi^*(Q_i)$.*
- *Step 3. For each linkage Q_i in L_{ij}, N_j receives $\Phi^*(Q_i)$ through each corresponding linkage Q_j in L_{ji} with host C_j. $\Phi'(C_j) = \Phi(C_j) * \Phi^*(Q_i)/\Phi^*(Q_j)$ and update linkage potential $\Phi^{*'}(Q_j) = \Phi^*(Q_i)$*

Once an external message is delivered, the local GP propagation needs to be performed in the receiving subnet to absorb the incoming message and to maintain its local consistency.

Similar to the BN GP method, the MSBN GP method consists of two rounds of system wide message passings, namely, *CollectBelief* and *DistributeBelief*, over the whole MSBN network given an arbitrarily chosen root subnet. For example, in Fig. 2(b), given G_2 as a root, solid arrows indicate the direction of external messages flow in *CollectBelief*, and empty arrows for those in *DistributeBelief*. During *CollectBelief*, local propagation using the BN GP method is performed in G_0 and G_1 to ensure local consistency before message calculation. Then two external messages are passed to G_2 as illustrated in Fig. 2(a) following the algorithm *GPMessagePass*. In G_2, the local propagation needs to be performed twice to absorb the two incoming messages. During *DistributeBelief*, external messages are passed from G_2 to G_1 and G_0 respectively. G_0 and G_1 both perform the local propagation again to absorb their incoming messages. Overall, there are 4 external messages generated, and the local propagation is performed for a total of 6 times in this example using the BN GP method.

The MSBN GP method is computational costly due to its extensive external and internal message passing. Since two external messages will be passed over each linkage tree in the MSBN GP method, a total of $2(n-1)$ external messages are necessary in an MSBN with n subnets. Although improvements of the MSBN GP method, such as lazy inference [11], have been proposed, all existing LJF based MSBN GP methods consist of two similar rounds of external message passings. For each external message passing, local consistency must be achieved through local propagation in both the sender subnet for accurate message calculation, and in the receiver subnet for absorbing the message. If a subnet N has k neighbors, the local propagation needs to be performed in the subnet N after each external message's arrival, thus for a total of k times. Since the local propagation is performed using the BN GP method, each of its invocation calls for two rounds of internal message passing among local JT clusters. Therefore, this large amount of external and internal messages need to be reduced in order to improve the efficiency of MSBN inference.

3   Improving Message Passing in MSBN

In this section, we present a new message passing scheme for MSBN inference. This method reduces the number of both external and internal messages that are required with the MSBN GP method. This new method is motivated by our previous result in [6].

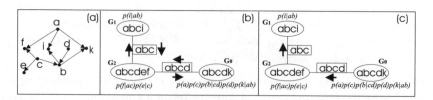

Fig. 3. (a) A BN. (b) A JT constructed from the BN in (a) with potential initialization. The arrows show the messages passed during GP. (c) The arrows show the messages passed using the method in [6].

3.1   Passing Much Less Messages in BN GP

We first briefly review the pertinent result in [6]. The idea is best explained with an example. Consider the BN shown in Fig.3(a) and the JT in Fig.3(b). Applying the BN GP on this JT requires passing two messages over each separator, as illustrated in Fig.3(b). However, an analysis of the factorization of the JPD provides a more informed and efficient passing scheme.

Let V represent all variables in Fig.3(a). The JPD $p(V)$ can be factorized according to the structure and initialization of the JT in Fig.3(b) as follows:

$$p(V) = \overbrace{[p(i|ab)]}^{\phi(G_1)} \cdot \overbrace{[p(f|ac) \cdot p(e|c)]}^{\phi(G_2)} \cdot \overbrace{[p(a) \cdot p(b|cd) \cdot p(c) \cdot p(d) \cdot p(k|ab)]}^{\phi(G_0)}. \quad (1)$$

Each square bracket in Eq. (1) details the composition of a potential for the clusters in the JT. Furthermore, $p(V)$ can also be factorized as:

$$p(V) = \frac{p(abci) \cdot p(abcdef) \cdot p(abcdk)}{p(abc) \cdot p(abcd)}. \quad (2)$$

It is worth pointing out that the BN GP method can be seen as an algorithmic procedure to transform Eq.(1) into Eq.(2). In [6], we took an algebraic perspective to explain the transformation, which resulted in a method that reduces message passings compared to the standard BN GP method.

In order to transform Eq. (1) into Eq. (2) algebraically, one simply needs to multiply $\frac{p(abc) \cdot p(abcd)}{p(abc) \cdot p(abcd)}$ to the right hand side of Eq. (1). By doing so, we get

$$\overbrace{[p(i|ab)]}^{\phi(G_1)} \cdot \overbrace{[p(f|ac) \cdot p(e|c)]}^{\phi(G_2)} \cdot \overbrace{[p(a) \cdot p(b|cd) \cdot p(c) \cdot p(d) \cdot p(k|ab)]}^{\phi(G_0)} \cdot \frac{p(abc) \cdot p(abcd)}{p(abc) \cdot p(abcd)}. \quad (3)$$

Obviously, Eq. (3) is almost identical to Eq. (2), except that it has a different numerator. Therefore, we try to mingle the terms $p(abc)$ and $p(abcd)$ with other terms of the numerator in Eq. (3), in order to reach Eq. (2). A careful examination reveals that in Eq. (1) the potential $\phi(G_0) = p(abcdk)$ already. Next, once the term $p(abcd)$ in Eq. (3) is assigned to $\phi(G_2)$, we have $\phi(G_2) \cdot p(abcd) = p(abcdef)$. Finally, the term $p(abc)$ in Eq. (3) is assigned to $\phi(G_1)$, which results in $\phi(G_1) \cdot p(abc) = p(abcdi)$. These assignments are shown below, where the newly assigned terms are underlined:

$$\frac{\overbrace{[p(i|ab) \cdot \underline{p(abc)}]}^{\phi(G_1)=p(abci)} \cdot \overbrace{[p(f|ac) \cdot p(e|c) \cdot \underline{p(abcd)}]}^{\phi(G_2)=p(abcdef)} \cdot \overbrace{[p(a) \cdot p(b|cd) \cdot p(c) \cdot p(d) \cdot p(k|ab)]}^{\phi(G_0)=p(abcdk)}}{p(abc) \cdot p(abcd)}. \quad (4)$$

The above Eqs.(3) and (4) clearly demonstrate the algebraic transformation from Eq.(1) to Eq.(2), which corresponds to the situations before and after the BN GP is applied. From a message passing or an algorithmic perspective, this algebraic transformation amounts to two message passings, one from G_0

to G_2 and the other one from G_2 to G_1, as indicated in Fig.3(c). The actual message calculation is done in two steps. (1) Since $\phi(G_0)$ is already equal to $p(abcdk)$, the message that G_0 passes to G_2, i.e., $p(abcd)$, can be computed from $\phi(G_0) = p(abcdk)$ as $p(abcd) = \sum_k \phi(G_0)$. (2) Once G_2 receives the message $p(abcd)$, it absorbs this message and the potential $\phi(G_2)$ becomes $p(abcdef)$, from which the message that G_2 passes to G_1, namely $p(abc)$, can be computed by marginalization as well. Once G_1 receives this message of $p(abc)$, the potential $\phi(G_1)$ becomes the marginal $p(abci)$. Overall, we need to pass only two messages, comparing to the four messages required when using the standard BN GP method.

In [6], a procedure was designed to determine the total number of messages and the direction of each based on the initial CPD assignment. This process is known as the *separator marginal analysis* and can be performed at compilation time. Also, a simple criterion was developed to determine if a cluster potential, such as $\phi(G_0)$ in the above example, has become a marginal. Message passings are performed once the result of separator analysis is available. Essentially, a cluster delivers all outgoing messages if its potential has been transformed into marginal. Or, a cluster may send an outgoing message to an adjacent cluster if it is missing only one incoming message generated from that neighbor. For example, a leaf cluster may deliver its outgoing message immediately regardless of its initial CPD assignment and the number of messages it has received.

Experiment results show that the new message passing scheme saves up to 50% messages compared with the standard BN GP method. In this paper, we call this method the *SA-GP* method.

3.2   Extending SA-GP to MSBN

Just as a JT is a secondary structure for performing BN inference using the BN GP method, an LJF is a secondary structure for performing MSBN inference using the MSBN GP method. When ignoring the internal structure of each local JT and linkage tree of an LJF, we obtain the original MSBN hypertree, where the local JTs can be viewed as clusters and linkage trees as hypertree separators(hyperlinks). Therefore, we are motivated to extend the SA-GP method for inference in BN to the domain of MSBN.

A closer examination of the SA-GP example in section 3.1 reveals the similarity between the JT shown in Fig. 3(b) and the MSBN hypertree shown in Fig. 1(c). In fact, the BN in Fig. 3(a) is the union of the three BN subnets in Fig. 1(b). The JT used in Fig. 3(b) is exactly the hypertree on which the MSBN LJF, shown in Fig. 2(a), is constructed. Thus, the message savings of the BN inference, demonstrated in section 3.1, can be intuitively interpreted as the external message savings for inference in an MSBN. However, in order to successfully extend the SA-GP method to inference in MSBN(named *MSBN SA-GP* thereafter), we need to address two essential issues: message analysis at compilation time(similar to SA-GP separator analysis) and actual external message calculation. The latter requires more careful treatment due to the following reasons: (1) External messages are passed between two adjacent MSBN

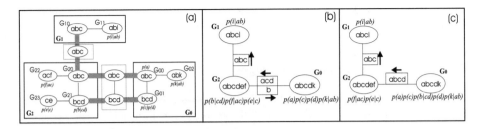

Fig. 4. (a) An MSBN LJF with CPD assignment. (b) Hyperlink analysis. (c) Hyperlink analysis result of a different initial CPD assignment.

subnets over their corresponding linkage trees and the tree structure complicates the calculations. (2) With the MSBN GP method, local consistency is always maintained in an MSBN subnet before the delivery of outgoing messages, which is not applicable to our MSBN SA-GP version. These issues are discussed next.

3.3   Hyperlink Analysis

The goal of hyperlink analysis is to provide us information about external message flow at compilation time and to guide actual message passings. Hyperlink analysis in an LJF is performed similar to the SA-GP separator analysis by treating hyperlinks as separators in an MSBN hypertree. Hyperlink analysis may be initiated by an MSBN system coordinator, who first selects candidate nodes in each subnet that are assigned CPD and contained in at least one hyperlink connecting to an adjacent subnet. For each of these nodes, the system coordinator marks the direction of the node over the hyperlink towards the adjacent subnet, and repeat the process in the adjacent subnet until the node is no longer on any hyperlink connecting to other neighboring subnets. All nodes over each hyperlink will be marked with a direction. The final result is obtained by simply combining all nodes of the same direction over each hyperlink. It provides the total number of external messages required and the direction of each of them.

For example, let's consider the MSBN network with the corresponding LJF and initial CPD assignment shown in Fig 4(a) and hypertree in Fig 4(b). The CPD $p(b|cd)$ is assigned to the variable b in the subnet G_2, therefore we direct the variable b away from G_2 towards its two adjacent subnets G_0 and G_1. The CPDs $p(a)$ and $p(c)$ are assigned to the variables a and c in G_0 and exist on the hyperlink connecting G_0 - G_2 and G_2 - G_1. Thus, we direct the variables a and c away from G_0 to G_1. The final result of linkage analysis is shown with arrows in Fig 4(b), which indicates that two external messages are required between G_0 and G_2 during inference, but only one external message is needed from G_2 to G_1.

The result of hyperlink analysis may vary given different LJF initializations. For example, if the CPD $p(b|cd)$ is assigned to the cluster $\{bcd\}$ in G_0 instead of G_2, we will have a different result of hyperlink analysis between G_0 and G_2, as shown in Fig 4(c). In this case, only one external message is required between G_0 and G_2.

3.4 Computing External Messages

The message passing in the MSBN SA-GP follows a similar schema as the BN SA-GP method. In an MSBN subnet N_i, an outgoing message to the adjacent subnet N_j is delivered when one of the following two situations arises. (1) N_i has received all needed CPDs/external messages, or (2) N_i needs to receive an external message only from N_j. That is, either N_i will not receive any other external message, or it has received all other messages except the one from N_j. In case (1), Since no incoming messages are required, local propagation can then be performed immediately to achieve local consistency and bring each cluster of the local JT to marginal. The subnet is ready to calculate all outgoing external messages, as under the scenario of the MSBN GP method. In case (2), the calculation of a single external message is needed before local consistency is achieved. Thus, we need to ensure that the message consists of information from all clusters in its local JT. We solve this problem by letting linkage hosts absorb messages from all non-host clusters. The steps are described in the algorithm (SAMessagePass) below.

Algorithm 2 (SAMessagePass). *Let N_i and N_j be two adjacent subnets associated with the local JTs T_i and T_j, and the linkage trees L_{ij} and L_{ji} respectively. C is the set of clusters in T_i. H is the set of linkage host of L_{ij} in T_i. An external message passed from N_i to N_j is performed as follows.*

- *Step 1. Randomly select a linkage host $H_i \in H$ as the root and direct all links away from it in T_i. H_i calls recursively its child clusters that are non-host $C_i \in C \backslash H$, to send a GP message, until a leaf cluster is called.*
- *Step 2. For each linkage Q_i in L_{ij} with host H_i, assign linkage potential $\phi(Q_i) = \sum_{H_i \backslash N} \phi(H_i)$, where $N \subset Q_i$ is the set of node directed from N_i toward N_j during hyperlink analysis.*
- *Step 3. For each linkage Q_i in L_{ij}, N_j receives linkage potential through linkage Q_j in L_{ji} with host C_j, such that $\phi'(C_j) = \phi(C_j) * \phi(Q_i)/\phi(Q_j)$ and update linkage potential $\phi^*(Q_j) = \phi^*(Q_i)$.*

For example, given the situation in Fig. 4(b), we can calculate the external message from G_0 to G_2 before G_0 is locally consistent. The message consists of potential over $\{a, c, d\}$ based on the hyperlink analysis result described in the previous section. G_0 has one linkage tree and two linkage host clusters $\{abc\}$ and $\{bcd\}$. In step 1 of the Algorithm *SAMessagePass*, we select cluster $\{abc\}$ as the root. Note that the same result holds regardless of which linkage host is selected as the root. As the only non-host cluster is $\{abk\}$, the potential sent from $\{abk\}$ to $\{abc\}$ is calculated as $\sum_{\{abk\} \backslash \{ab\}} p(k|ab) = 1$. The external message from G_0 to G_2 consists of one potential over each linkage, that is, $\phi(Q_{abc}) = \sum_{abc \backslash acd} \phi(abc)$ and $\phi(Q_{bcd}) = \sum_{bcd \backslash acd} \phi(bcd)$.

3.5   The MSBN SA-GP Method

Once the problem of external message calculation is solved, extending the SA-GP method to the domain of MSBN becomes straightforward. Unlike the standard MSBN GP method, which is carried out in two rounds with an arbitrary subnet selected as the root, the MSBN SA-GP is performed in semi-parallel among all subnets without having a root subnet. The algorithm is described below.

Algorithm 3 (*MSBN SA-GP*). Let $N_i(i = 1, ..., n)$ be the subnets and $\mathcal{H}$ the corresponding hypertree of MSBN. When called, the system coordinator does the following:

1 *In each subnet $C \in \{N_i\}$ that has received all CPDs;*
2   *Perform SA local propagation in C;*
3   *Send all messages with the algorithm GPMessagePass;*
4   *Set $\{N_i\} = \{N_i\}\backslash\{C\}$;*
5 *While($\{N_i\} \neq \emptyset$)*
6   *In each leaf subset N of $\mathcal{H}$*
7   *If $N \in \{N_i\}$ and N has outgoing messages;*
8   *Send each message with the algorithm SAMessagePass;*
9   *Remove N from $\mathcal{H}$;*
10   *In each subnet $C \in \{N_i\}$ that has received all CPDs;*
11   *Perform local propagation in C;*
12   *Send all remaining outgoing messages with algorithm GPMessagePass;*
13   *Set $\{N_i\} = \{N_i\}\backslash\{C\}$*

With the algorithm *MSBN SA-GP*, the system coordinator first identifies all subnets in $\{N_i\}$ that have received all necessary CPDs during LJF initialization. Local propagation is performed immediately in these subnets and all their outgoing messages are delivered(lines 2 and 3). Once the subnet is locally consistent, we use the algorithm *GPMessagePass* to calculate all outgoing external messages. Then, these subnets are removed from the set $\{N_i\}$(line 4).

Next, message passings start with the current leaf nodes of the MSBN hypertree. The algorithm *SAMessagePass* is called for the message calculation since these subnets are not locally consistent(lines 6, 7 and 8). After this round of message passings, the system coordinator again identifies in the set $\{N_i\}$ the subnets that have received all necessary messages. For these subnets, local propagation is carried out and all outgoing messages are delivered. We mark off these leaf nodes from the hypertree, so that the next iteration starts with a new set of subnets for message passings. Several iterations may be required to bring all subnets to local consistency and the whole network to global consistency. The algorithm will terminate as the current leaf nodes are marked off the hypertree during each iteration.

Consider applying the algorithm *MSBN SA-GP* to the MSBN with the initial CPD assignment shown in Fig 4(a) and the hyperlink analysis result shown in Fig 4(b). Initially, no subnet has received all necessary CPDs. Thus, we have hypertree leaf subnets G_0 and G_1 selected to start external message passing during the first iteration. G_1 only receives from G_2, and no message originates from G_1. For G_0, it delivers a message to G_2 with the algorithm *SDMessagePass* as previously described. Once G_2 receives the message, it completes all its required CPD's, and local propagation is performed. Two external messages have originated from G_2 to its adjacent subnets G_0 and G_1. These messages will complete all required information in G_0 and G_1. Local propagation can be performed in them for local consistency. Overall, a total of three external messages are generated, and local propagation is performed once in each subnet.

Additional savings on external messages is available when the same MSBN is initialized as shown in Fig 4(c). When the algorithm *MSBN SA-GP* is called, G_0 performs local propagation immediately since it has received all needed CPDs. The message sent from G_0 to G_2 provides all information required in G_2. Once G_2 is locally consistent, it sends the last required message to G_1. Overall, the total number of external messages are now reduced to two. This example indicates that the efficiency of inference with the MSBN SA-GP method can be optimized by an MSBN initialization at compilation time.

4   Preliminary Experiment

The computational efficiency of different propagation algorithms may be compared by the actual number of arithmetic operations. In [3], the number of additions, multiplications and divisions are used as a measure for the comparison of different BN propagation algorithms. We apply a similar approach and use the number of internal and external messages as a crude measurement to the real calculation. In particular, we count the number of external message generated over the whole network and the number of local propagation required. We have conducted preliminary experiments on 4 available small MSBN networks to compare the MSBN GP method and the MSBN SA-GP method.

Table 1. shows the counting of external messages and local propagation. Given an MSBN network with n subnets, the number of external messages is $2(n-1)$ in the MSBN GP method. With our MSBN SA-GP method, this number is reduced by 50% in all 4 networks. Considering the number of local propagations, our method requires local propagations to be performed once only in each subnet. However, since the algorithm *SAMessagePass* involves internal message passings,

Table 1. Comparison of the MSBN GP and the MSBN SA-GP methods on various MSBN networks

			No. of External Messages		No. of Local Propagation	
MSBNs			GP	SA-GP	GP	SA-GP
Subnets	Variables	Method		Method	Method	Method
(a)	3	5	4	2	6	3
(b)	3	15	4	2	5	3
(c)	4	16	6	3	9	4
(d)	5	12	8	4	11	5

we roughly count each of its invocation as 0.5 local propagation for the purpose of fair comparison. The result shows that the total number of local propagations has also been reduced by an average of 50% in our SA-GP method compared to the GP method with a randomly selected root. These preliminary tests on small networks have shown substantial savings of external and internal message using the MSBN SA-GP method.

5   Conclusion

In this paper, we have presented an MSBN propagation algorithm based on the analysis of LJF hyperlink at compilation time. The hyperlink analysis provides us with information of external messages, such as the total number and orientation of each message, *before* propagation takes place. The main advantages of our proposed new method are: (a) Reduced number of local propagation at it is performed only once in each subnet after all external messages are received. (b) Reduced number of external messages in inter-subnet communication. External messages are passed as needed and no two rounds of message pass among all subnets. We have conducted preliminary experiments on several small MSBNs. The obtained results have confirmed the savings of the total number of internal and external messages, which is a good indication of the actual runtime savings. We expect our result to be scalable to larger networks.

In our future work, we will conduct additional tests on large scale MSBNs and we will extend our method from MSBNs with available centralized control, to distributed MSBNs under multi-agent paradigm.

Acknowledgements

We would like to thank the anonymous reviewers for their valuable comments. This work has been partly supported by a grant from the National Science and Engineering Research Council of Canada.

References

1. Jensen, F.V., Lauritzen, S.L., Olesen, K.G.: Bayesian updating in causal probabilistic networks by local computation. Computational Statistics Quarterly 4, 269–282 (1990)
2. Lauritzen, S.L., Spiegelhalter, D.J.: Local computation with probabilities on graphical structures and their application to expert systems. Journal of the Royal Statistical Society 50, 157–244 (1988)
3. Lepar, V., Shenoy, P.P.: A comparison of Lauritzen-Spiegelhalter, Hugin, and Shenoy-Shafer architectures for computing marginals of probability distributions. In: Proceedings of the 14th Conference on Uncertainty in Artificial Intelligence (UAI 1998), pp. 328–337. Morgan Kaufmann, San Francisco (1998)
4. Pearl, J.: Probabilistic Reasoning in Intelligent Systems: Networks of Plausible Inference. Morgan Kaufmann Publishers, San Francisco, California (1988)

5. Shafer, G.: An axiomatic study of computation in hypertrees. School of Business Working Papers 232, University of Kansas (1991)
6. Wu, D., Jin, K.: Demystify the messages in the hugin architecture for probabilistic inference and its application. In: FLAIRS Conference, pp. 55–61 (2006)
7. Xiang, Y.: A probabilistic framework for cooperative multi-agent distributed inter-pretation and optimization of communication. Artificial Intelligence 87, 295–342 (1996)
8. Xiang, Y.: Cooperative triangulation in msbns without revealing subnet structures. Networks 23, 1–21 (2001)
9. Xiang, Y.: Probabilistic Reasoning in Multuagent Systems: A Graphical Models Approach, Cambridge (2002)
10. Xiang, Y.: Comparison of multiagent inference methods in multiply sectioned bayesian networks (2003)
11. Xiang, Y., Jensen, F.V., Chen, X.: Inference in multiply sectioned bayesian net-works: Methods and performance comparison. IEEE Transaction on Systems, Man, and Cybernetics 36, 546–558 (2006)
12. Xiang, Y., Poole, D., Beddoes, M.P.: Multiply sectioned bayesian networks and junction forests for large knowledge based systems. Computational Intelligence 9, 171–220 (1993)

Using Dependence Diagrams to Summarize Decision Rule Sets

Kamran Karimi[1] and Howard J. Hamilton[2]

[1] Department of Software Engineering
Lakehead University
Thunder Bay, Ontario
Canada, P7B 5E1
kkarimi@lakeheadu.ca
[2] Department of Computer Science
University of Regina
Regina, Saskatchewan
Canada, S4S 0A2
hamilton@cs.uregina.ca

Abstract. Generating decision rule sets from observational data is an established branch of machine learning. Although such rules may be well-suited to machine execution, a human being may have problems interpreting them. Making inferences about the dependencies of a number of attributes on each other by looking at the rules is hard, hence the need to summarize and visualize a rule set. In this paper we propose using dependence diagrams as a means of illustrating the amount of influence each attribute has on others. Such information is useful in both causal and non-causal contexts. We provide examples of dependence diagrams using rules extracted from two datasets.

1 Introduction

In a system exposed as a number of variables that change value over time, exploring the possible influence of some variables on others is important. Dependence of one variable on a second variable may denote an association or a causal relation. In the case of an association, we can expect a change in the value of the first variable when we observe a change in the second one, though we cannot control this process. In the causal case, we can possibly control the value of the first variable by changing the value of the second variable.

Much work has been done in extracting sets of rules that apply to the exposed variables of a system. The rules in such rule sets may be numerous and complicated, making it hard for a human to understand the dependencies represented by these rules. In this paper we introduce dependence diagrams as a way to help a user visually summarize a rule set by displaying the variables' influence on each other.

In a rule, such as {if $x\_1 = 5$ and $a_1 = $ Move_Right, then $x\_2 = 6$} (Rule 1), the variables x_1 and a_1 are called the *condition attributes*, while the variable x_2, whose value is being determined, is called the *decision attribute*. In this rule, x_1 and

S. Bergler (Ed.): Canadian AI 2008, LNAI 5032, pp. 163–172, 2008.
© Springer-Verlag Berlin Heidelberg 2008

a_1 are used to predict the value of x_2. The *accuracy* of such a rule denotes how often the prediction is correct when applied to test data. Such a rule specifies a classification, and this format is widely used to represent decision rules in software such as C4.5 [9].

Existing representations and tools used for analyzing rule sets are inadequate to give a user a quick sense of the dependencies among variables. Decision tables [6] represent a decision space in textual form, but they do not provide visualization or support for summarizing multiple rules or rule sets. Decision trees [9] can be displayed in a visual form helpful to understanding the influences of the condition attributes on a single decision attribute, but they do not show the complex interdependencies among variables when several can be treated as decision attributes. Decision trees can also be very big, making it hard to assess the importance of a given attribute in the decision making process.

Software tools such as MineSet [2] and CART [1] enable the user to see decision rules in a variety of formats, but the summarization property is lacking. The General Logic Diagram (GLD) [7] uses a two-dimensional grid to represent a multi-dimensional decision space. It is similar to a Karnaugh map, but it can represent multi-valued discrete attributes. Although this representation is effective for visualizing all the rules, it is not well suited to representing the amount of influence of the attributes. A new representation is required that allows us to see the inter-relation and influence among the different attributes, and at the same time is independent of the number of generated rules. Focusing on summarization, such a representation should not depend on individual rules. Its complexity and size should depend on the number of variables rather than the number of the rules.

Informally, in the context of a given number of attributes and a set of decision rules generated based on those attributes, a *dependence diagram* is a graphic representation that shows the amount of influence of the condition attributes on the decision attribute. When we change the decision attribute and generate a new set of decision rules, the same dependence diagram can be used to show the results. So a dependence diagram can describe multiple rule sets, each with a different decision attribute, as long the same attributes are involved. To provide examples of dependence diagrams, in this paper we use a synthesized database and a real weather database. For both these datasets, we show how dependence diagrams can be used to summarize the role of the condition attributes in determining the decision attributes' value.

Normally, in a given rule set, the decision attribute and the condition attributes are assumed to have been observed at the same time, so there is no notion of the passage of time between observing the attributes. Dependence diagrams can show such *atemporal* (or *instantaneous*) relationships. However, they can also be of particular interest in understanding potentially causal rules, a concept that is explained next.

Temporal and atemporal rules can be discovered from sequential data using the TimeSleuth software [3]. Assuming that time may have passed between the observations of variables allows interesting possibilities in analysing the data, and can lead to the generation of *temporal* decision rules Temporal decision rules that allow prediction of the future events using only past events are potential candidates for causal rules and are called *p-causal rules*. Such rules can be further evaluated by a domain expert to determine whether they represent actual causal rules. Crucially, dependence diagrams can aid in visualizing dependencies among attributes to aid the domain expert in evaluating the potential causality of these dependencies.

TimeSleuth can combine a number of sequential input records into one merged record. To uncover potentially causal rules, TimeSleuth examines the effects of a condition attribute, from previous time steps, on the decision attribute. Similarly, to identify *acausal* (i.e., not causal, but still temporal) rules, it examines the effects of condition attributes on a decision attribute in a previous time step. If previous values can be *retrodicted* (predicted in reverse), the relationship is assumed to be acausal. The number of consecutive records merged together is determined by a *window size*. Suppose at each time step we register the current position of an object along the x-axis, and also the direction of the movement that will be attempted during the next time step (left or right). So the effect of the attempted movement can be discovered in the next time step. Rule 1, for example, has been produced by merging two consecutive records in such an environment. x_1 and a_1 can be read as the previous position and movement directions, while x_2 can be read as the current location.

We can compare a dependence diagram to a causal Bayesian network [8] for the task of displaying causal rule sets. Both display causal influences, but they employ different methods to derive their corresponding graphs, and their interpretations are different. In a Bayesian network, one can traverse the graph transitively from a grandparent to a parent and then a child node, and so on, while one cannot traverse a dependence diagram. The rest of the paper is organized as follows. Section 2 introduces dependence diagrams first via an example and then formally. Section 3 discusses pruning dependence diagrams. In Section 4 we present examples of dependence diagrams from two data sets. Section 5 concludes the paper.

2 Dependence Diagrams

As previously mentioned, a dependence diagram summarizes multiple sets of decision rules in a compact manner and shows the amount of influence that each condition attribute has on the decision attributes' values. The diagram is not equivalent to a set of decision rules, as the original rule sets cannot be extracted from a dependence diagram. Each attribute in a dependence diagram can be a decision attribute as well as a condition attribute.

In a dependence diagram, attributes are denoted as nodes in a graph and connected together. The strength of the connection (the weight of the edge) depends on how often they are used in predicting each other's values. By definition, a decision attribute d *depends on* another (condition) attribute c_i if attribute c_i appears in rules that are used to predict attribute d. A dependence diagram can summarize instantaneous, acausal, or possibly causal rule sets, as defined in [4, 5].

Before presenting a formal definition, we first provide an example of a dependence diagram. In Figure 1, a dependence diagram for temporal data from a simulated robot is shown. The data comes from a simulated robot doing a random walk in a two-dimensional space, where x and y denote the position, a is the random action taken (the direction of movement), and f shows the presence or absence of food at the robot's location. The data represent repeated observations of the robot's state, consecutively ordered by time.

Figure 1 shows that we can determine the value of x reliably (accuracy of 100% as indicated in the node corresponding to x) from the values of x and a. In particular, the previous values of x and a, namely x_{t-1} (read: x at time t-1, or the previous time step) and a_{t-1}, are used in all the rules that predict the current value of x, namely x_t, (read: x at time step t, or the current time). This is shown by links from nodes x and a to node x having a weight of 100%. The times of occurrence for the attributes are not shown in a dependence diagram. Figure 1 also shows that the value of a can be determined with an accuracy of 47% by using the values of a, x, y, and f attributes. The value of a depends mostly on x and y (x appears in 80% of the rules, while y appears in 76% of the rules), somewhat on a, (which appears in 64% of the rules), and to a lesser extend on f (40% of the rules). A low accuracy value or link weight can suggest that a relationship does not exist or that insufficient evidence is available. For example, several links have 0% weight. Such relationships can be pruned from the diagram.

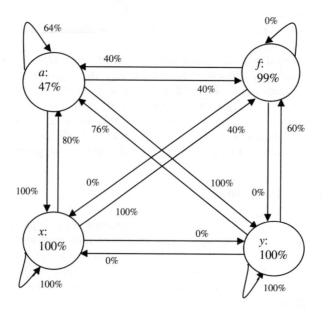

Fig. 1. A dependence diagram for the robot data

We now formally define a dependence diagram. For any rule set R that predicts the value of attribute d, if condition attribute c_i appears in at least one rule in R, then d depends on c_i. This type of dependence is called *static dependence*, because it is determined by the static form of the rule set, as opposed to the run-time or dynamic behaviour of the rule set.

Definition 1. If $r \in R$ and $c_i \in$ CONDITIONS(r), then $d =$ DECISION(r) *depends on* c_i.

Ignoring the time indexes, the percentage of rules in a rule set R in which attribute c_i appears determines the strength of dependence of d on c_i.

Definition 2. Static Dependence Strength: d statically depends on c_i with *strength* $s\%$ with respect to a rule set R, written as $D_d(c_i) = s\%$, if c_i appears in $s\%$ of the rules in R.

In rule r, d statically depends on c_i with strength $s\%$ at time step t if c_i appears in $s\%$ of the rules at time step t, written as $D_{d,t}(c_i)$.

For a temporal rule computed using a window size of $w > 0$, we calculate $D_d(c_i)$ as follows:

$$D_d(c_i) = D_{d,1}(c_i), \qquad\qquad \text{if } w = 1 \text{ or } w = 2$$
$$D_d(c_i) = \max(D_{d,1}(c_i), \dots D_{d,w-1}(c_i)), \qquad \text{otherwise.}$$

Example. Let the set of condition attributes be $\{a, b, c\}$ and the decision attribute be d. Suppose the window size is 3 and the rule set R contains 2 rules: $\{$[If at Time 1: $(a = 1)$ And at Time 2: $(a = 1)$ and $(b = 2)$, Then at Time 3: $(d = \text{true})$], [If at Time1: $(a = 3)$ Then at Time 3: $(d = \text{false}>)$]$\}$. Here, $D_d(a) = 100\%$ (a appears in both rules) and $D_d(b) = 50\%$ (b appears in half of the rules).

From the previous example, we have $D_{d,1}(a) = 100\%$, $D_{d,2}(a) = 50\%$, $D_{d,1}(b) = 0\%$, $D_{d,2}(b) = 50\%$.

Dynamic dependence is similar to static dependence, except the strength of the dependence is determined according to the rules that actually get used for determining the value of the decision attribute. In other words, only the rules that get fired by the test dataset are considered for determining the strength of the edges in the dependence diagram.

Definiton 3. Dynamic Dependence Strength: d dynamically depends on c_i with *strength* $s\%$ with respect to rule set R and data set T, written as $DD_d(c_i) = s\%$, if c_i appears in $s\%$ of the rules that are fired when rule set R is applied to data set T.

In the previous example, suppose only the first rule is fired. In this case we have: $DD_d(a) = 100\%$, $DD_d(b) = 100\%$, $DD_{d,1}(a) = 100\%$, $DD_{d,2}(a) = 0\%$, $DD_{d,1}(b) = 0\%$, and $DD_{d,2}(b) = 100\%$.

We use a threshold value to prune weak and accidental dependencies.

Definition 4. Threshold Dependence and Independence: d is *dependent* on c_i if $D_d(c_i) > \varepsilon$, where ε is a user-specified threshold. Otherwise, d is *independent* of c_i.

Definition 5. Dependence Diagram: A *dependence diagram* is a possibly cyclic, directed, weighted graph $<N, L>$, where N is a set of nodes, each representing an attribute, and L is a set of directed links, each representing the dependence strength of a decision attribute on a condition attribute. The direction of the link is from the condition attribute to the decision attribute. A node represents a decision attribute with respect to the links pointing to it, and a condition attribute with respect to the links pointing away from it.

In a static dependence diagram, weights are assigned to the links but not the nodes. No weights are assigned to nodes because the rules are not run on any data set and so no accuracy values are available. In a dynamic dependence diagram, weights are assigned to both the nodes and the links. The weight of a node is the training or testing accuracy of the rules created for predicting the decision attribute that is represented by the node.

To create a dependence diagram, the rule sets for predicting the values of one or more decision attributes are first generated from a training data set. A static dependence diagram can be drawn directly from the rule sets, but for a dynamic dependence diagram, each rule set must be evaluated on a selected dataset. For a given rule set, only one static dependence diagram can be derived, but multiple dynamic dependence diagrams can be derived by changing the test data set.

If all rules in a rule set get executed, then the static and dynamic link strengths will be the same. This case holds in Figure 1, where the weights on the links show the static (and dynamic) strengths, while the weights of the nodes show the results from a particular run.

Transitivity does not apply to dependence diagram graphs, because by definition only the immediate links to and from a node are meaningful. Thus, dependence diagrams cannot be traversed. This characteristic sets the dependence diagram apart from many other types of graph.

3   Pruning Dependence Diagrams

If the user of a dependence diagram is not interested in nodes or links that have low weight, the diagram can be pruned. Pruning can be performed at two levels, using a link pruning threshold and a node pruning threshold. At the link level, a link is pruned if it does not have enough strength, or in other words, enough importance, in determining the value of a decision attribute. At the node level, a node is pruned if its weight is too low, or in other words if it cannot be predicted accurately enough. Node-level pruning is only possible with dynamic dependence diagrams.

Each link in the dependence diagram has an associated weight that represents the static or dynamic dependence strength of a decision attribute on a condition attribute, as determined by the number of times the attribute has appeared in the rules predicting the decision attribute. In *link oriented pruning*, links that have a weight below the link pruning threshold are removed.

In *node oriented pruning*, the nodes are examined one by one. Each node represents an attribute. Associated with each node is a weight representing the training or testing accuracy for that attribute when it was used as the decision attribute. Any node with a weight below the node pruning threshold is pruned unless there are links that point away from that node to other nodes. In other words, a node that is used is classifying another attribute is not removed. All links that point to a pruned node are also pruned, regardless of their strength.

It is important to note that link-level pruning must be performed before node-level pruning. A node with a low accuracy denotes a decision attribute with low predictability, but the same attribute may be important in predicting the value of another decision attribute. The examples provided later in the text will make this point clear.

Link- and node-level pruning allow the user to choose the amount of detail in a dependence diagram. The user can thus concentrate on more influential attributes. This ability is important because the attributes in a data set may not all have equal importance, and when selecting the attributes to record in the data set, one may have chosen irrelevant attributes because of a lack of a priori knowledge.

4   Examples of Dependence Diagrams

In this section, we show dependence diagrams for two temporal datasets. The first dataset is from a discrete event simulator called URAL [11], where known atemporal and temporal rules govern an artificial environment. The second dataset is from a weather station in Louisiana AgriClimatic Information System [10]. We used TimeSleuth to generate rules from the datasets and then constructed a variety of dependence diagrams.

4.1   Data Domains

The URAL dataset is a synthetic dataset derived from consecutive observations of a artificial robot moving in a simulated world. The world is a rectangular, 8×8 board. The robot performs a random walk in the domain: at each time-step, it randomly decides on one of the following actions a: left (L), right (R), up (U), or down (D). Left and right correspond to moving along the x-axis and up and down to moving along the y-axis. We used 2500 records for training, and 500 for testing the rules (predictive accuracy). When predicting the attribute x, we expect that a rule set derived using a window size of 1 will not contain highly accurate rules. The reason is that, based on our understanding of the domain, the current value of x depends on the previous value of x, and the previous direction of movement. The same holds for y. So we expect that a rule set derived from a window size of 2, called the p-causal rule set, will contain highly accurate rules.

The second example, the Louisiana weather dataset, is a real-world dataset from weather observations in Louisiana. It contains observations of 8 environmental attributes gathered hourly from 22/7/2001 to 6/8/2001. There are 343 training records, each with the air temperature, the soil temperature, humidity, wind speed and direction and solar radiation, gathered hourly. 38 other records were used for testing the rules and generating predictive accuracy values. Since this dataset describes real phenomena, interpreting the dependencies and relationships in it is harder than for the robot dataset.

It should be emphasized that although both these data sets are from temporal domains, a dependence diagram can be generated from any given data set. For a non-temporal dataset, we refrain from mentioning causality or acausality, but we can interpret the links in a dependence diagram as associations.

4.2   The Dependence Diagrams

Suppose a user wants a dynamic dependence diagram for the domain of the artificial robot. To generate such a dependence diagram, the user first creates a data set containing observations of the values of the four attributes. The user then generates four p-causal rule sets with a window size of 2, each with one of the available attributes set as the decision attribute. The results can be used to generate the dependence diagram shown in Figure 1.

The user may decide to prune any link with strength below 80% and any unneeded node with accuracy below 50%. In this case, 12 out of 16 links are removed, but none of the four nodes are removed. The results are shown in Figure 2. Notice that the node corresponding to *a* is not pruned (even though its accuracy is below the threshold), because it is an important participant in determining the values of *x* and *y*.

From the diagram, we can see that the value of *x* can be predicted with 100% accuracy using previous values of *a* and *x*, and the value of *y* can be predicted with 100% accuracy from the previous values of *a* and *y*. The values of *a* and *f* cannot be predicted with sufficient accuracy to meet the constraints.

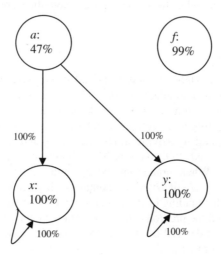

Fig. 2. The pruned dependence diagram for the robot data

The choice of appropriate threshold values depends on the domain and is left to the domain expert. A domain expert can observe the relative strengths and choose to allow only certain links to remain. Various threshold values can be tried to obtain different pruned dependence diagrams.

We can observe the influence of the attributes on each other in the dependence diagram shown in Figure 2. If a link exists from a node to itself, then the value of the corresponding attribute at a different time (preceding or succeeding) is used for predicting the present value. A node can only point to itself if the window size is bigger than 1.

If a rule set is derived from a p-causal investigation with TimeSleuth, the links in either static or dynamic dependence diagrams for the rule set may be examined by a domain expert to see if the dependencies they represent could be causal. These links are based on potentially causal relationships. However, if the rule set is derived from an instantaneous or acausal investigation, the presence of a link in a dependence diagram is unrelated to the existence of causality. In this case, none of the dependencies are suggested as p-causal.

Considering the second dataset, suppose the user is interested in a dynamic dependence diagram for the weather dataset, where the strength of every link is at least 40% and the strength of every node (unless otherwise needed) is at least 50% for a p-causal investigation with window size 2. As with the robot data, the user first constructs the diagram with all nodes and links. Figure 3 shows the diagram after pruning the links by removing any link with strength less than 40%.

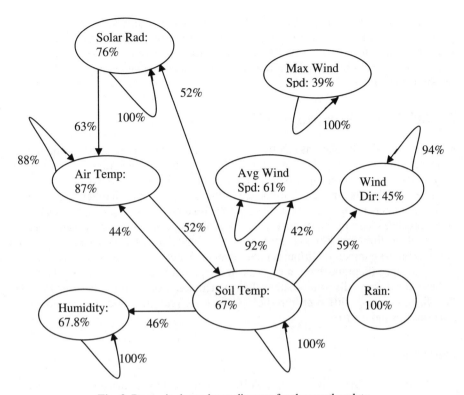

Fig. 3. Dynamic dependence diagram for the weather data

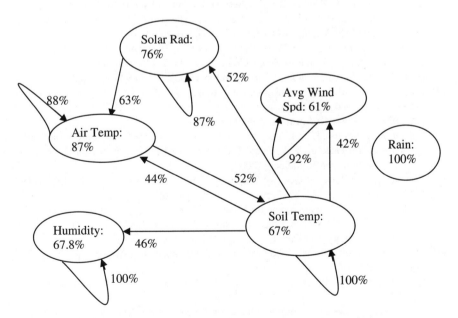

Fig. 4. The pruned dynamic dependence diagram for the weather data

Finally, we prune unneeded nodes with accuracies less than 50%. The results are given in Figure 4. The dynamic dependence diagram in Figure 4 displays how the values of the attribute are related to each other. For example, the value of Soil Temperature is highly dependent on its own previous value and somewhat dependent on Air Temperature.

5 Concluding Remarks and Future Work

Making sense of the relations implied in a rule set is not easy because of the textual representation of such rules. We introduced dependence diagrams as a way of summarizing the relationships among a number of variables. They provide a visual aid for understanding the amount of influence of the attributes on each other. We provided examples of dependence diagrams that describe relations in synthetic and real datasets. A dependence diagram can summarize many rule sets generated from the same dataset, each with a different decision attribute. The complexity of a dependence diagram depends on the number of attributes rather than the number of generated rules.

Dependence diagrams have not yet been integrated into TimeSleuth, so they have to be derived manually. Automating their generation would allow the user to prune the diagram using different threshold values in real-time and notice important relationships more easily.

References

[1] Breiman, L., Friedman, J.H., Olshen, R.A., Stone, C.J.: Classification and Regression Trees. Wadsworth Inc. (1984)
[2] Brunk, C., Kelly, J., Kohavi, R.: MineSet: An Integrated System for Data Access, Visual Data Mining, and Analytical Data Mining. In: The Third Conference on Knowledge Discovery and Data Mining (KDD 1997), Newport Beach, USA (August 1997)
[3] Karimi, K., Hamilton, H.J.: TimeSleuth: A Tool for Discovering Causal and Temporal Rules. In: 14th IEEE International Conference On Tools with Artificial Intelligence (ICTAI 2002), Washington DC, USA, November 2002, pp. 375–380 (2002)
[4] Karimi, K., Hamilton, H.J.: Distinguishing Causal and Acausal Temporal Relations. In: Whang, K.-Y., Jeon, J., Shim, K., Srivastava, J. (eds.) PAKDD 2003. LNCS (LNAI), vol. 2637, pp. 234–240. Springer, Heidelberg (2003)
[5] Karimi, K., Hamilton, H.J.: Using TimeSleuth for Discovering Temporal/Causal Rules: A Comparison. In: Gedeon, T.D., Fung, L.C.C. (eds.) AI 2003. LNCS (LNAI), vol. 2903, pp. 175–189. Springer, Heidelberg (2003)
[6] Kohavi, R.: The Power of Decision Tables. In: Lavrač, N., Wrobel, S. (eds.) ECML 1995. LNCS, vol. 912, pp. 174–189. Springer, Heidelberg (1995)
[7] Michalski, R.S.: A Planar Geometric Model for Representing Multidimensional Discrete Spaces and Multiple-valued Logic Functions, Technical Report UIUCDCS-R-78-897, University of Illinois at Urbana-Champaign, USA (1978)
[8] Pearl, J.: Causality: Models, Reasoning, and Inference. Cambridge University Press, Cambridge (2000)
[9] Quinlan, J.R.: C4.5: Programs for Machine Learning. Morgan Kaufmann, San Francisco (1993)
[10] Contents change with time, http://typhoon.bae.lsu.edu/datatabl/current/sugcurrh.html
[11] http://www.cs.uregina.ca/~karimi/downloads.html/URAL.java

A Fast Computation of Inter-class Overlap Measures Using Prototype Reduction Schemes*

Sang-Woon Kim[1] and B. John Oommen[2]

[1] Dept. of Computer Science and Engineering, Myongji University,
Yongin, 449-728, South Korea
kimsw@mju.ac.kr
[2] School of Computer Science, Carleton University, Ottawa, Canada
oommen@scs.carleton.ca

Abstract. In most Pattern Recognition (PR) applications, it is advantageous if the accuracy (or error rate) of the classifier can be evaluated or bounded prior to testing it in a real-life setting. It is also well known that if the two class-conditional distributions have a large overlapping volume[1], the classification accuracy is poor. This is because, if we intend to use the classification accuracy as a criterion for evaluating a PR system, the points within the overlapping volume tend to have less significance in determining the prototypes. Unfortunately, the computation of the indices which quantify the overlapping volume is expensive. In this vein, we propose a strategy of using a Prototype Reduction Scheme (PRS) to approximately compute the latter. In this paper, we show that by completely discarding[2] the points not included by the PRS, we can obtain a reduced set of sample points, using which, in turn, the measures for the overlapping volume can be computed. The value of the corresponding figures is comparable to those obtained with the original training set (i.e., the one which considers all the data points) even though the computations required to obtain the prototypes and the corresponding measures are significantly less. The proposed method has been rigorously tested on artificial and real-life data sets, and the results obtained are, in our opinion, quite impressive - sometimes faster by *two orders* of magnitude.

Keywords: Prototype Reduction Schemes (PRS), k-Nearest Neighbor ($k-$NN) Classifier, Data Complexity, Class-Overlapping.

1 Introduction

Once a Pattern Recognition (PR) practitioner has designed a PR system, he can effectively put it to use only after guaranteeing its recognition capabilities. The latter are

---

* The second author was partially supported by NSERC, the Natural Sciences and Engineering Research Council of Canada. This work was generously supported by the Korea Research Foundation Grant funded by the Korea Government(MOEHRD-KRF-2007-313-D00714).

[1] Almost all the available work on "Overlapping of Classes" deals with the case when there are only two classes.

[2] We are not aware of any reported scheme which *discards* "irrelevant" sample (training) points, and which simultaneously attains to an almost-comparable accuracy.

S. Bergler (Ed.): Canadian AI 2008, LNAI 5032, pp. 173–184, 2008.
© Springer-Verlag Berlin Heidelberg 2008

usually quantified in terms of accuracy metrics, typically evaluated on benchmark data sets. Sometimes, however, it is advantageous if the classifier's error rates can be stated using well-defined mathematical norms. Some of the established norms for *parametric* classifiers are the Bhattacharyya and the Chernoff bound [8]. Obtaining similar bounds for *non-parametric* classifiers is a very challenging problem because its definition and computation depend on the peculiarities of the method used, and of the data sets, such as their cardinalities, sparseness, outliers etc.

The k-Nearest Neighbor (NN) classifier is one of the most popular supervised classification methods [1]. It is both simple to implement and effective in purpose – its error being closely related to the Bayes' minimum error. However, it is well known that its behavior is strongly dependent on the complexity of the data. While this is a subjective term, researchers have tried to quantify it in numerous ways [11], [18], [22], [23]. The investigated measures can be summarized into three categories (see Table 1 of [11]) as[3]:

1. Measures of Overlap of Individual Feature Values, such as the *Fisher's Discriminant Ratio* (which has been referred to as $F1$), the *Volume of Overlap Region* ($F2$), and the *Feature Efficiency* ($F3$). Some authors also report the applicability of the *Volume of the Local Neighborhood* ($D1, D2$) as pertinent measures.
2. Measures of Separability of the Classes, such as the *Linear Separability* ($L1, L2$) and the *Mixture Identifiability* ($N1, N2, N3$).
3. Measures of Geometry, Topology, and Density of Manifolds, such as the *Nonlinearity* ($L2, N4$), *Space Covering by $\epsilon-Neighborhoods$* ($T1$), and Others ($T2$).

This paper concerns the first of the above classes of measures and their applicability for NN-like PR. Indeed, it is well known (and also intuitively observable) that an excessive overlap of the classes negatively affects the performance of k-NN classifiers [24]. Additionally, it has been identified that the degradation of the performance is not solely caused by class imbalances, but that it is also related to the degree of their respective overlap [2]. The aim of this paper is quite simple: We intend to investigate the possibility of computing these measures *quickly* without invoking expensive strategies which require the entire training sets.

Brief Survey: To present our results in the right perspective, a brief [4] survey of the field is not out of place. It is clear that a natural measure of the effectiveness of a classifier is its associated error rate. However, by employing alternate measures, one could use these as a guide to select a particular classifier for a given problem. In [24], Sotoca and his co-authors reviewed a number of data measures proposed in the literature, and discussed how they could be utilized to devise meta-learning methods for pattern classification. The authors of [24] concentrated on learning from data complexity measures, and claimed that one could estimate the utility of a classifier for a particular problem by

---

[3] Throughout this paper, in the interest of compactness, we shall refer to the following measures symbolically as $F1$, $F2$, $\cdots$ etc. Beside these, measures ($L1, L2$) of the linear separability of classes, and a measure for the nonlinearity of a classifier with regard to a given data set, have also been investigated. The details of these are omitted here as they are not relevant to our present study. They can be found in [11], [24].

[4] This survey is necessarily brief. A more detailed survey can be included if requested by the Referees.

simply computing a number of such complexity measures on the training data, *instead of experimenting with it.*

On the other hand, Hoekstra and Duin [12] proposed a measure for the nonlinearity of a classifier with regard to a *given* data set. Given a training set, they first created a test set by invoking a linear interpolation (with random coefficients) between randomly drawn pairs of points from the same class. Thereafter, they recommended evaluating the error rate of the classifier, trained on the same training set, on *this* newly-created test set.

Recently, Mollineda *et al* [20] attempted to predict how effectively a prototype selection algorithm will perform when applied to a particular problem. They did this by characterizing the training data set with a set of complexity measures. More specifically, they investigated the utility of a set of complexity measures as a tool to predict whether or not the application of a specific prototype selection scheme is suitable for a particular problem. After testing different data complexity measures, they claimed that the measure $F1$ can become especially useful to distinguish the situations in which a prototype selection technique is clearly advantageous. Consequently, for a particular problem, they claimed that based on the value of $F1$, one could decide whether to invoke a selection algorithm to the original training set or to directly invoke the NN classifier.

Rationale for the paper: We start with the premise that it is advantageous to compute some of the above mentioned measure. However, we seek a strategy by which the computational burden can be reduced. Thus, in this paper, we propose a technique[5] for the fast computation of these complexity measures, and in particular, the various class-overlapping measures. We advocate that rather than measure the data complexity (class-overlapping) for the entire data set, the data be first reduced into a smaller representative subset using a Prototype Reduction Scheme (PRS) [3], [6], and that the data distribution be investigated by invoking the corresponding method on *this* reduced set.

The results that we have obtained are both of a positive and negative nature, and somewhat counter-intuitive. Since it is well-known that a PRS has the capability of extracting points in the original feature space that satisfactorily represent the global distribution, at the outset of this research we had hoped that data points which are ineffective in the dimension reduction and classification would be eliminated so as to quickly and effectively compute the complexity without degrading the performance. Unfortunately, this is not always the case. Rather, it turns out that while PRS methods are generally effective in achieving fast approximate computations for *certain* measures - sometimes yielding results faster by *two orders* of magnitude - they are not applicable *at all* for others. This invites further research.

The paper is organized as follows. In Section 2, we briefly summarize several measures of data complexity. Thereafter, we provide a brief introduction to the families of PRS. This leads us (in Section 3) to our proposed strategy to efficiently measure the class overlap by using the PRSs. Experimental results for artificial and real-life benchmark data sets are provided in Section 4. Section 5 concludes the paper.

---

[5] As mentioned earlier, in this paper, we only consider the two-class problem. In some cases, even the effective definition and computation of the measures for the multi-class problem are open.

2   Overlap Measures and Prototype Reduction Schemes

2.1   Data Complexity Measures

Based on the itemized list of class overlapping measures given above, we explain the most pertinent families that we have used in our experiments in a subsequent section.

Fisher's Discriminant Ratio ($F1$): This measure [11], [24] mainly focuses on the effectiveness of a single feature dimension in separating the classes. It examines the range and spread of the values in the data set with respect to each feature, and investigates for overlaps between the different classes. Formally, this ratio is given as:

$$F1 = \frac{(\mu_1 - \mu_2)^2}{\sigma_1^2 + \sigma_2^2},$$ (1)

where μ_1, μ_2, σ_1^2, and σ_2^2 are the means of the two classes and their variances for the specific feature, respectively. A possible generalization for C classes, which also considers all the feature dimensions, is found in [24] – it is irrelevant here.

Volume of Overlap Region ($F2$): The $F2$ measure [11], [24] quantifies the overlap of the tails of the two class-conditional distributions. For a d-dimensional problem, the volume of the overlap region for two classes is obtained as the product of the normalized lengths of the overlapping ranges for all the features, and this quantity has the form:

$$F2 = \prod_{h=1}^{d} \frac{MinMax[f_h] - MaxMin[f_h]}{MaxMax[f_h] - MinMin[f_h]},$$ (2)

where $MinMax[f_h] = Min\{Max(f_h, c_i)|i = 1, 2\}$,
$\quad MaxMin[f_h] = Max\{Min(f_h, c_i)|i = 1, 2\}$,
$\quad MaxMax[f_h] = Max\{Max(f_h, c_i)|i = 1, 2\}$, and
$\quad MinMin[f_h] = Min\{Min(f_h, c_i)|i = 1, 2\}$,

and where $Max(f_h, c_i)$ and $Min(f_h, c_i)$ are the maximum and minimum values of feature f_h in class c_i, respectively. The generalization of $F2$ for the general C-class problem is also found in [24], and omitted here.

Non-Parametric Separability of Classes ($N2$): The measure $N2$ is the ratio of the average distance to the intra-class NN, and the average distance to the inter-class NN. This quantity provides an "estimate" as to what extent the two classes are separable by examining the existence and shape of the class boundary, and has the form:

$$N2 = \frac{\sum_{i=1}^{n} \delta(x_i, N_1(x_i))}{\sum_{i=1}^{n} \delta(x_i, \bar{N}_1(x_i))},$$ (3)

where $N_1(x_i)$ and $\bar{N}_1(x_i)$ are the intra-class and inter-class NNs of a given example x_i, (whose associated class is ω_i) respectively, and δ is the appropriate distance function used in the computation - for example, the Euclidean distance.

Volume of Local Neighborhood ($D2$): The measure $D2$ represents the average volume occupied by the k nearest neighbors of each training instance. Specifically, let $N_k(x_i)$

be the set of the k NNs of a given example x_i, (whose associated class is ω_i). Then, the volume associated with this set can be defined as follows :

$$\nu_i = \prod_{h=1}^{d}(Max(f_h, N_k(x_i)) - Min(f_h, N_k(x_i))), \tag{4}$$

where $Max(f_h, N_k(x_i))$ and $Min(f_h, N_k(x_i))$ represent the maximum and minimum values of features f_h among the k NNs of the sample x_i. From this, the average value of ν_i for the n training samples, $D2$, can be expressed as:

$$D2 = \frac{1}{n}\sum_{i=1}^{n}\nu_i. \tag{5}$$

We study the issue of using PRSs to minimize the computation of the above measures.

2.2   Prototype Reduction Schemes: State-of-the-Art

In non-parametric pattern classification which use the NN or the $k-$NN rule, each class is described using a set of sample prototypes, and the class of an unknown vector is decided based on the identity of the closest neighbour(s) which are found among all the prototypes [1]. To reduce the number of training vectors, various PRSs have been reported in the literature - two excellent surveys are found in [3], [6]. Bezdek *et al* [3], who composed the second and more recent survey of the field, reported that there are "zillions!" of methods for finding prototypes (see page 1459 of [3]). Rather than embark on yet another survey of the field, we mention here a *few* representative methods of the "zillions" that have been reported. One of the first of its kind is the Condensed Nearest Neighbour (CNN) rule [10]. The reduced set produced by the CNN, however, customarily includes "interior" samples, which can be completely eliminated, without altering the performance of the resultant classifier. Accordingly, other methods have been proposed successively, such as the Reduced Nearest Neighbour (RNN) rule [25], the Prototypes for Nearest Neighbour (PNN) classifiers [5], the Selective Nearest Neighbour (SNN) rule, [21], two modifications of the CNN [26], the Edited Nearest Neighbour (ENN) rule [7], and the non-parametric data reduction method [9]. Besides these, in [27], the Vector Quantization (VQ) and the Bootstrap techniques have also been reported as being extremely effective approaches to data reduction. Recently, Support Vector Machines (SVM) [4] have proven to possess the capability of extracting vectors that support the boundary between any two classes. Thus, they have been used satisfactorily to represent the global distribution structure.

In selecting prototypes, vectors near the boundaries between the classes have to be considered to be more significant, and the created prototypes need to be adjusted towards the classification boundaries so as to yield a higher performance. Based on this philosophy, we recently proposed a new hybrid approach that involved two distinct phases, namely, selecting and adjusting [13], [14]. To overcome the computational burden for "large" datasets, we also proposed a recursive PRS mechanism in [15]. In [15], the data set is sub-divided recursively into smaller subsets to filter out the "useless" internal points. Subsequently, a conventional PRS processes the smaller subsets of data points that effectively sample the entire space to yield *subsets* of prototypes – one set of prototypes for each subset. The prototypes, which result from each subset, are then coalesced, and processed again by the PRS to yield more refined prototypes. In this manner, prototypes which are in the interior of the Voronoi boundaries, and are thus ineffective in the classification, are eliminated at the subsequent invocations of the PRS. Thus, the processing time of the PRS is *significantly* reduced.

Changing now the emphasis, we observe that with regard to designing classifiers, PRSs can be employed as a pre-processing module to reduce the data set into a smaller representative subset, and they have thus been reported to optimize the design of KNS classifiers in [16], [17]. The details of these are omitted here as they are irrelevant.

This overview of the state-of-the-art of PRSs should be sufficient to help us proceed in formulating our solution to the problem at hand.

3   Schema for the Proposed Solution

All of the measures that we are interested in investigating have a fundamental common characteristic: They all attempt to determine how the data sets can be most effectively classified *without* actually resorting to a rigorous testing phase. Thus, for example, they extract information about how distant the various elements are from their respective means. From this perspective, consider the motivation for introducing a PRS. Effectively, every PRS attempts to extract the *extremely crucial* and *relevant* information from the respective data sets. This information is symbolized by those prototypes which effectively reduce the cardinality of the data set while simultaneously preserving the PR capabilities.

Put in a nutshell, our goal is to "quickly" evaluate how effective a class-overlapping measure is for a given problem. Thus, rather than measure the data complexity for the entire training set, we advocate that the data be first reduced into a smaller representative subset using a PRS, and that the data distribution be investigated by invoking a computational scheme on *this* reduced data set. Thereafter, the classification accuracy of the NN-like classifier is compared.

The proposed scheme is algorithmically formalized below.

Algorithm 1. PRS_Overlap

Input: The original Training Set, T.

Output: A fast evaluation of a class overlapping measure, γ, which is one of the measures $F1$, $F2$, $F3$, $N1$, $N2$, $D1$ or $D2$, using a reduced data set rather than the entire training set.

   Assumption 1: The algorithm has access to a PRS such as the CNN, PNN or HYB.

   Assumption 2: The algorithm has access to packages which permit the computation of γ.

Method:

   Step 1: Select the representative set, Y, from the training set T by resorting to a PRS.

   Step 2: Compute the measure, γ, being investigated, using Y and T.

   Step 3: Compare the time used and the quality of the approximations obtained by computing γ from Y, rather than from T.

End Algorithm PRS_Overlap

---

4 Experimental Set-Up, Results and Evaluation

Experimental Data: The proposed scheme has been tested and compared with the conventional method. This was done by performing experiments on both "artificial" and "real-life" data sets.

The data sets described as "Rand(i)", (for $i = 1, \cdots, 11$) consisted of eleven synthetic data sets generated with different levels of overlap. Each set was described by two classes, randomly generated by 2-dimensional Gaussian distributions $p_1(x) = N(\mu_1, \Sigma)$ and $p_2(x) = N(\mu_2, \Sigma)$ respectively, where although the covariances were identical, the means were increasingly separate as the indices of the set increased, so as to permit smaller overlaps. More specifically, whereas the Y-coordinates of the means were the same, the X-coordinates of the means, $\mu_{1,x}$ and $\mu_{2,x}$ were:

- For Rand(1): $\mu_{1,x} = 50$, $\mu_{2,x} = 50$ - which represents the case when the classes overlap completely,
- For Rand(2): $\mu_{1,x} = 49$, $\mu_{2,x} = 51$,
- For Rand(3): $\mu_{1,x} = 48$, $\mu_{2,x} = 52$,

  $\vdots$

- For Rand(11): $\mu_{1,x} = 40$, $\mu_{2,x} = 60$, - which represents the case when the classes are almost completely non-overlapping.

The covariance matrix for all these datasets had the components $\sigma_{11} = 6.0$, $\sigma_{12} = \sigma_{21} = 20.0$, $\sigma_{22} = 36.0$. Besides, each data set consisted of $4,000$ instances, half of which would be typically used for training and the other half for test purposes. The computation was done on each subset and subsequently averaged.

The "Iris2", "Ionosphere", "Sonar", "Arrhythmia", and "Adult4", are *Real-life* benchmark data sets, and are cited from the UCI Machine Learning Repository [19]. Their details can be found in the latter site and also in [28], and omitted here in the interest of compactness. In the above data sets, all of the vectors were normalized (i.e, scaled and translated to give particular minimum and maximum values) to be within the range $[-1, 1]$, and the data set for class ω_j was randomly split into two subsets, $T_{j,t}$ and $T_{j,V}$, of equal size. One of them was used for choosing the initial prototypes and training the classifiers, and the other one was used in the validation (or testing). In our setting, the computation was done using each subset, and subsequently averaged.

Experimental Parameters: Choosing the parameters of the PRSs play an important role in determining the quality of the solution. The parameters[6] for the PRSs[7] were:

---

[6] These parameters are included here for the sake of researchers who would like to duplicate the results.

[7] The reader should observe that, as mentioned previously, any PRS can be employed to obtain the reduced set, Y. In the present paper, only three methods, namely the CNN, PNN, and HYB have been used in the testing. The main reason for choosing these is as follow: First of all, the prototype vectors obtained with the CNN and PNN methods are *selected* and *created*, respectively. On the other hand, for the HYB, the prototypes are initially *selected*, after which they are adjusted. Finally, for all the methods, the final number of prototypes is not a quantity that is controlled or determined automatically.

1. For the CNN: Since the number of prototypes depends on the characteristics of the data set, the number of iterations is predetermined by the size of T. Hence, the CNN had no parameters.
2. For the PNN: For the same reason as in the case of the CNN, the PNN had no parameters.
3. For the HYB: In this case, we invoked a hybridized version of the SVM and an LVQ3-type algorithm, both of which are available on publicly distributed packages. The SVM was employed to determine the initial code book vectors for the LVQ3. The parameters for the LVQ3 learning are specified in [13]. For instance, the parameters for the data set "Adult4" were $\alpha = 0.05$, $\epsilon = 0.06$, $w = 0.35$, $\eta = 5,600$.

Experimental Results: We now present the run-time characteristics of the proposed scheme for the artificial data sets, and the five benchmark data sets. To get a better feel for what we have hypothesized, we first graphically illustrate the performance of the scheme for the artificial data sets. Following this, we present the numerical comparison between the measures computed using the entire data sets and the reduced sets as obtained by the respective PRSs.

To examine the rationale for employing a PRS technique in the computation of the class-overlapping measures, we now present the results of obtaining the measures for these data sets. The experimental results obtained for the entire sets for the data sets "Rand(1)" to "Rand(11)" are shown in Fig. 1(a),(b). In these figures, the graphs on the left depict the $F1$, $F2$, $N2$, and $D2$ measures[8], and the graphs on the right depict their respective processing CPU-times. In all the figures, the horizontal axes represent the indexes of the training data sets (which, as explained earlier, correspond to the distances between their means $\mu_{1,x}$ and $\mu_{2,x}$), and the vertical axes represent the values of the class-overlapping measures for the figure on the left, and the processing CPU-times for the figure on the right. In an analogous manner, the measures $F1$, $F2$, $N2$, and $D2$ were computed using the prototypes for the various Rand data sets as extracted using the CNN, PNN, and HYB methods. The corresponding experimental results obtained for the CNN prototypes are shown[9] in Fig. 2(a),(b). The results of the PNN and HYB methods are omitted here in the interest of brevity, but can be found in [28].

Based on these experiments, we report the following interesting conclusions:

1. From Fig.1(a), we observe that the values of the $F1$ and $D2$ measures increase, while the values of $F2$ and $N2$ decrease. This is quite counter-intuitive and seems to imply that the former cannot be used as an appropriate measure for the overlap.
2. From Fig.1(b), we note that the processing CPU-times of all measures are almost the same, and that the processing CPU-times of $N2$ and $D2$ are higher than those required for $F1$ and $F2$.
3. From Fig.2(a) and (b), we see that, generally speaking, the class-overlapping measures possess the same characteristics as those obtained from the whole dataset.

---

[8] To display the figures on the same graph, in the interest of simplicity, the corresponding class-overlapping values are normalized by their respective maximum values.

[9] As in the previous cases, each of the measures were correspondingly normalized.

4. Finally and most importantly, the corresponding processing CPU-times of $N2$ and $D2$ decrease sharply with the index of the Rand(i) set – i.e., according to the distances of the means. This is quite an amazing observation.

5. From these consideration, we can almost unequivocally state that our hypothesis is accurate for these Rand(i) data sets. The advantages are more profound for the $N2$ and $D2$ measures.

We now turn our attention to the real-life data sets and present the pertinent statistics in Table 1. With regard to notation, in the table, the abbreviations *WHL*, *CNN*, *PNN*, and *HYB* correspond to the experimental methods employed for the *WHoLe* data set, and the prototypes extracted with the CNN, PNN, and HYB methods, respectively.

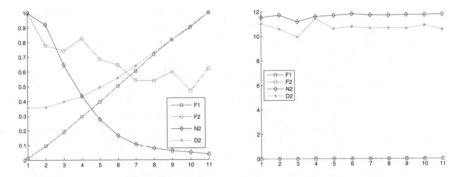

Fig. 1. A comparison of the $F1, F2, N2,$ and $D2$ measures and their respective computation CPU-times for the "Rand" data sets: (a) left and (b) right. (a) and (b) are for the complexity measures and the corresponding CPU-times for the *entire* data set, respectively. Numbers of the X-axis represent the serial numbers of the data sets. The details of the pictures are explained in the text.

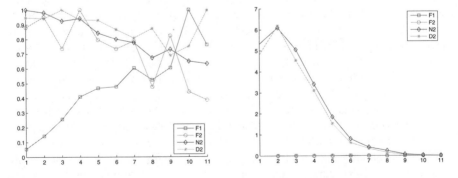

Fig. 2. A comparison of the $F1, F2, N2,$ and $D2$ measures and their respective computation CPU-times for the "Rand" data sets: (a) left and (b) right. (a) and (b) are for the complexity measures and the corresponding CPU-times for the prototypes extracted with the CNN method, respectively. Numbers of the X-axis represent the serial numbers of the data sets. The details of the pictures are explained in the text.

Table 1. A comparison of overlap volumes and processing CPU-times measured with the original data sets and their prototypes. For the five real-life data sets and their prototypes extracted with CNN, PNN, and HYB, the table reports the $F1$, $F2$, $N2$, and $D2$ measures, and their respective processing times within parenthesis.

Datasets	PRS	F1	F2	N2	D2
Iris2	WHL	0.7670(0.0156)	0.0191(0.0000)	0.4075(0.0313)	0.5383(0.0156)
	CNN	0.4747(0.0000)	0.0251(0.0000)	0.8608(0.0000)	0.5190(0.0000)
	PNN	0.4302(0.0000)	0.0076(0.0000)	0.7398(0.0000)	0.5277(0.0000)
	HYB	0.8269(0.0000)	0.0054(0.0000)	0.4817(0.0000)	0.5539(0.0000)
Iono	WHL	0.2399(0.0000)	NaN(0.0000)	0.6336(0.4219)	1.4177(0.3281)
	CNN	0.1118(0.0156)	NaN(0.0156)	0.9600(0.0313)	1.4598(0.0156)
	PNN	0.1175(0.0000)	NaN(0.0000)	0.9338(0.0469)	1.3729(0.0156)
	HYB	0.1357(0.0000)	NaN(0.0156)	0.8850(0.0313)	1.3804(0.0156)
Sonar	WHL	0.1752(0.0000)	0.0000(0.0000)	0.6889(0.2188)	0.9652(0.2031)
	CNN	0.1239(0.0000)	0.0000(0.0000)	0.8939(0.0469)	0.9507(0.0469)
	PNN	0.1302(0.0000)	0.0000(0.0000)	0.8468(0.0156)	0.9128(0.0313)
	HYB	0.1200(0.0000)	0.0000(0.0156)	0.7600(0.0625)	0.9300(0.0469)
Arrhy	WHL	0.3336(0.0469)	NaN(0.0469)	0.7929(7.5625)	1.5440(7.6719)
	CNN	0.2664(0.0000)	NaN(0.0156)	0.9133(0.0781)	1.5816(0.0938)
	PNN	0.3949(0.0000)	NaN(0.0000)	0.7162(0.0313)	1.3837(0.0156)
	HYB	0.3446(0.0000)	NaN(0.0156)	0.7616(0.5469)	1.3889(0.4844)
Adult4	WHL	0.0629(0.0313)	NaN(0.0313)	0.3135(146.0625)	0.9588(143.2188)
	CNN	0.0952(0.0000)	NaN(0.0156)	1.0123(4.1563)	0.9120(3.5156)
	PNN	0.0948(0.0000)	NaN(0.0000)	0.9524(3.2344)	0.9129(2.6719)
	HYB	0.0983(0.0000)	NaN(0.0000)	0.6970(1.1563)	0.8959(1.1875)

Analogously, in the case of *WHL*, the data complexities and the corresponding times were measured for the whole data set, and for the CNN, PNN, and HYB, the measures were computed for the corresponding extracted prototypes.

By examining the results in Table 1, it is clear that the class-overlapping measures, for the benchmark databases can be measured quite efficiently and fairly accurately by first invoking the corresponding PRS techniques. To clarify this, consider, for example, the measures obtained for $D2$ as computed for "Sonar". The complexity measures of WHL, CNN, PNN, and HYB methods are 0.9652, 0.9507, 0.9128, and 0.9300, respectively. But with regard to computation, the processing times of these methods are 0.2031, 0.0469, 0.0313, and 0.0469 seconds, respectively. The effect is more marked in the case of large data sets. For example, in the case of the "Adult4" dataset, the complexity measures of WHL, CNN, PNN, and HYB methods are 0.9588, 0.9120, 0.9129, and 0.8959, respectively, while the processing times involved by using the PRSs are two orders of magnitude smaller – namely 3.5156, 2.6719, and 1.1875 seconds respectively, instead of 143.2188 seconds required for the whole data set. Similar observations can be made for all the data sets, except that the accuracy of the estimate of the $F1$ measure using the reduced prototypes seems to be poor[10]. In other words, we believe that an

---

[10] It is also worth mentioning that based on the accuracy of the NN classifier, the $F1$ measure may actually *not* be an appropriate measure to quantify the overlap.

overall concluding assertion is that a PRS can be effectively invoked for computing all the measures of overlap except the $F1$ measure.

5 Conclusions

In this paper, we have considered the problem of efficiently measuring the class-overlap between two classes. This is pertinent to PR because it is well known that if the two class-conditional distributions have a large overlapping volume, the classification accuracy is poor. Unfortunately, the computation of the indices which quantify the overlapping volume is expensive if the entire training set is taken into consideration. Indeed, we have demonstrated that by completely discarding the points not included by a PRS, we can obtain a reduced set of sample points, using which, in turn, the measures for the overlapping volume can be computed both quickly and efficiently. The method has been rigorously tested on artificial and real-life data sets, and the results obtained are, in our opinion, quite impressive - sometimes faster by *two orders* of magnitude.

References

1. Jain, A.K., Duin, R.P.W., Mao, J.: Statistical pattern recognition: A review. IEEE Trans. Pattern Anal. and Machine Intell. PAMI-22(1), 4–37 (2000)
2. Batista, G.E., Prati, R.C., Monard, M.C.: Balancing Strategies and Class Overlapping. In: Famili, A.F., Kok, J.N., Peña, J.M., Siebes, A., Feelders, A. (eds.) IDA 2005. LNCS, vol. 3646, pp. 24–35. Springer, Heidelberg (2005)
3. Bezdek, J.C., Kuncheva, L.I.: Nearest prototype classifier designs: An experimental study. International Journal of Intelligent Systems 16(12), 1445–1473 (2001)
4. Burges, C.J.C.: A tutorial on support vector machines for pattern recognition. Data Mining and Knowledge Discovery 2(2), 121–167 (1998)
5. Chang, C.L.: Finding prototypes for nearest neighbor classifiers. IEEE Trans. Computers C-23(11), 1179–1184 (1974)
6. Dasarathy, B.V.: Nearest Neighbor (NN) Norms: NN Pattern Classification Techniques. IEEE Computer Society Press, Los Alamitos (1991)
7. Devijver, P.A., Kittler, J.: On the edited nearest neighbor rule. In: Proc. 5th Int. Conf. on Pattern Recognition, December 1980, pp. 72–80 (1980)
8. Fukunaga, K.: Introduction to Statistical Pattern Recognition, 2nd edn. Academic Press, San Diego (1990)
9. Fukunaga, K., Mantock, J.M.: Nonparametric data reduction. IEEE Trans. Pattern Anal. and Machine Intell. PAMI-6(1), 115–118 (1984)
10. Hart, P.E.: The condensed nearest neighbor rule. IEEE Trans. Inform. Theory IT-14, 515–516 (1968)
11. Ho, T.K., Basu, M.: Complexity Measures of Supervised Classification Problems. IEEE Trans. Pattern Anal. and Machine Intell. PAMI-24(3), 289–300 (2002)
12. Hoekstra, A., Duin, R.P.W.: On the nonlinearity of pattern classifiers. In: 13th International Conference on Pattern Recognition (ICPR 1996), pp. 271–275 (1996)
13. Kim, S.-W., Oommen, B.J.: Enhancing prototype reduction schemes with LVQ3-type algorithms. Pattern Recognition 36(5), 1083–1093 (2003)
14. Kim, S.-W., Oommen, B.J.: A Brief Taxonomy and Ranking of Creative Prototype Reduction Schemes. Pattern Analysis and Applications Journal 6(3), 232–244 (2003)

15. Kim, S.-W., Oommen, B.J.: Enhancing Prototype Reduction Schemes with Recursion: A Method Applicable for "Large" Data Sets. IEEE Trans. Systems, Man, and Cybernetics - Part B SMC-34(3), 1384–1397 (2004)
16. Kim, S.-W., Oommen, B.J.: On using prototype reduction schemes to optimize kernel-based nonlinear subspace methods. Pattern Recognition 37(2), 227–239 (2004)
17. Kim, S.-W., Oommen, B.J.: On using prototype reduction schemes and classifier fusion strategies to optimize kernel-based nonlinear subspace methods. IEEE Transactions on Pattern Analysis and Machine Intelligence 27(3), 455–460 (2005)
18. Mansilla, E.B., Ho, T.K.: On classifier domains of competence. In: 17th International Conference on Pattern Recognition (ICPR 2004), pp. 136–139 (2004)
19. http://www.ics.uci.edu/mlearn/MLRepository.html
20. Mollineda, R.A., Sanchez, J.S., Sotoca, J.M.: Data Characterization for Effective Prototype Selection. In: Marques, J.S., Pérez de la Blanca, N., Pina, P. (eds.) IbPRIA 2005. LNCS, vol. 3523, pp. 27–34. Springer, Heidelberg (2005)
21. Ritter, G.L., Woodruff, H.B., Lowry, S.R., Isenhour, T.L.: An algorithm for a selective nearest neighbor rule. IEEE Trans. Inform. Theory IT-21, 665–669 (1975)
22. Singh, S.: PRISM: A novel framework for pattern recognition. Pattern Analysis and Applications 6, 134–149 (2003)
23. Sohn, S.-Y.: Meta analysis of classification algorithms for pattern recognition. IEEE Trans. Pattern Anal. and Machine Intell. PAMI-21(11), 1137–1144 (1999)
24. Sotoca, J.M., Mollineda, R.A., Sanchez, J.S.: A meta-learning framework for pattern classification by means of data complexity measures. Revista Iberoamericana de Inteligencia Artificial 10(29), 31–38 (2006)
25. Gates, G.W.: The reduced nearest neighbor rule. IEEE Trans. Inform. Theory IT-18, 431–433 (1972)
26. Tomek, I.: Two modifcations of CNN. IEEE Trans. Syst. Man and Cybern. SMC-6(6), 769–772 (1976)
27. Xie, Q., Laszlo, C.A., Ward, R.K.: Vector quantization techniques for nonparametric classifier design. IEEE Trans. Pattern Anal. and Machine Intell. PAMI-15(12), 1326–1330 (1993)
28. Kim, S.-W., Oommen, B.J.: On using prototype reduction schemes to enhance the computation of volume-based inter-class overlap measures (unabridged version of this paper)

A Reputation Model Framework for Artificial Societies: A Case Study in Child Vehicle Safety Simulation

Ziad Kobti[1], Shamual Rahaman[1], Anne W. Snowdon[2], and Robert D. Kent[1]

[1] School of Computer Science
[2] Odette School of Business, University of Windsor
401 Sunset Avenue, Windsor, Ontario, Canada
{kobti,rahaman,snowdon,rkent}@uwindsor.ca

Abstract. Formalizing reputation into a complex social model poses significant challenges, mainly due to its distinct social nature. In this paper we introduce the notion of reputation into the child vehicle safety simulation. From a health and safety perspective, the aim of the model is to reduce injury in children by minimizing incorrect usage of child vehicle constraints by influencing driver behaviour. A cultural framework was previously established to enable external injection of knowledge, or intervention, into the artificial society. A dynamic social network allowed the acquisition, and subsequent exchange and evolution of knowledge. We hypothesize that selective intervention criteria would achieve better system convergence. We consequently introduce reputation to be a viable selection criterion. We establish a generic reputation framework that would allow us to test alternate formalizations of reputation models. We report on the generic framework design and three initial reputation models with their respective comparative performance and potential to improve the intervention outcome.

Keywords: Reputation, social networks, vehicle safety, cultural algorithms.

1 Introduction

The concept of reputation in multi-agent based modeling is gaining popularity. In the research literature, reputation mostly refers to trustworthiness of an agent in the artificial society. The use of reputation in multi-agent models was thoroughly investigated in many practical fields like e-commerce [1], [2], distributed computation [3] and distributed artificial intelligence [4]. In previous work [5] we presented a multi-agent based model built around the hierarchical social network and cultural algorithm [6] to model population evolution. We built a framework that allows external injection of knowledge, or intervention in health sciences, of new strategy into the artificial society. The model links the agents in a dynamic social network that allows the exchange of information. Earlier work suggested that proper usage of intervention and capitalization of the social network may lead to better system convergence. Previous implementation carried out the process of intervention on

S. Bergler (Ed.): Canadian AI 2008, LNAI 5032, pp. 185–190, 2008.
© Springer-Verlag Berlin Heidelberg 2008

randomly selected agents. In this paper we propose the hypothesis that a relatively better performance can be achieved if agents could be carefully selected under some social criteria that would allow efficient knowledge propagation in the society through the network. With this objective in mind we introduce the concept of reputation into the model to be a viable selection criterion. Unlike e-commerce and network related modeling problems, formalizing reputation into this model poses significant challenges. Because of the highly complex social nature of the model it is difficult to identify what exactly constitutes reputation. Therefore a trial and error based iterative process is necessary before we could reach any definitive formalization and consequently we further extend the cultural framework to include a reputation framework that would create a test bed for alternate formalization of reputation into the model. Consequently this paper presents the framework for reputation within the cultural framework and different sample formalizations of reputation models in the context of the child vehicle safety research.

2 Reputation in Artificial Societies

Relevant literature reveals many diverse usage of the term reputation in multi-agent based models. The terminology mostly refers trustworthiness or credibility of an agent. It is also referred and measured as an agent's perception of others. But most of the literatures more or less interpret the term from its very intuitive perspective, which is of course trustworthiness of an agent [2,3,4,7,8]. The theoretical framework was experimented with a simulation and evidence toward this scheme was established. Josang in [1] provides a pure statistical approach towards reputation management in e-commerce systems. The system is based on feedback provided by agents in the system and employs the Beta probability function to process the feedback to measure the reputation ratings. Josang outlines various building blocks of the scheme in terms of collecting and providing feedback, rating the feedbacks and measuring the performance. We define reputation not only as a measure of trustworthiness of an agent but also as an influential parameter that can be capitalized to better influence the population to global optima. From the child vehicle safety model's perspective, reputation is a social concept and it is understood that it is primarily dependent on the agent's social characteristics. In this way the nature of the concept of reputation is somewhat similar to [3]. But unlike the problems in [3] it is very difficult to formalize a qualitative or quantitative definition of reputation in the child vehicle safety model because the number and nature of the influencing issues are not clearly known; even the correlations among known issues are also vague. In order to overcome this challenge, in a trial and error based incremental development approach, we begin with a simple formulation and its validation and then proceed towards relatively more complex formulations.

3 A Case Study in Child Vehicle Safety Constraints

The detailed description of the child vehicle safety model can be found in [5], [9] and [10]. In this section we highlight the important definitions relevant to this study. Child

Seat Knowledge is the knowledge an agent's, or driver, perspective on child seat usage. Each driver is equipped with a set of knowledge which they can apply to assign a seat to a child in a specific location in the car. An accurate formulation mechanism for knowledge can be found in [5], [10] and [11]. Standard Knowledge (*K*) is an instance of a knowledge structure which is considered to be the accurate one by many authoritative agencies like Transport Canada or The National Highway Traffic Safety Administration (NHTSA) of the USA. Quality of Knowledge (QK) is a measurement of an agent's knowledge quality against the *K*. This is a bitwise comparison between an agent's knowledge against *K* and can assume a value in the range [1, 10]. Rahaman in [10] provides a detailed description of this process. Correctness Index (CI) and Average Correctness Index (ACI) refer to the level of accuracy at which a child is assigned to a seat in a vehicle by that driver. It can assume a value between [0, 10]. Each driver applies his or her knowledge to assign a seat to a child and depending on the selection and its accuracy's correctness index is evaluated. On the other hand ACI is the average of CI for all agents at any given time. ACI is one of the most important parameters used to measure the performance of the system and optimization of ACI is one of the major objectives of this modeling problem.

The agents form a complex social network which can be represented as a graph where each agent is a node and its association with another agent is an edge. The Node Degree (ND) of an agent in artificial society is the degree of the node in the graph that represents the agent. The ND of an agent therefore provides a measure on its connectedness in the graph or society. Education Level (EL) & Income Level (IL) are two indices to measure the quality of an agent's personal qualification on the respective fields. These indices can assume a value in the range [1, 10] with higher values reflecting a more superior level. A detailed account on these and other related indices can be found in [9]. The Reputation Index (RI) is a quantitative measure of the reputation of an agent. An accurate formal definition for this measure is hard to devise. The primary objective of this study is to establish some preliminary formulation of this index.

3.1 Generic Reputation Framework

The step function of the child vehicle safety model is responsible for simulating one time step of the model, defined as one day. In order to include the concept of reputation and exploit it effectively the step function was altered. At each time step the reputation model is updated to reflect the changed reputation of the agent. Another algorithm which is responsible to drive the logic of agent collaboration, Propagate Knowledge, is also altered. In previous versions, the odds of a knowledge exchange were determined by a random probability function. In this algorithm agents take advantage of the concept of reputation to decide on the transfer and level of acceptance of the transferred knowledge.

The inclusion of the concept of reputation into the model was done with minimal changes to the existing model. Since the exact configuration or formulation of a reputation model is still vague and should be altered frequently in the future, it was implemented as an independent pluggable module. Consequently, a generic framework was built that allows the usage of alternative reputation models.

3.2 Reputation Models

To test the framework we have coined three implementations of increased complexity. The first reputation model is a simplified one with the formulation assuming that the reputation of an agent depends only on its connectedness to the social network. The measure of connectedness is the degree of the agent, or node, in the hypothetical graph representing the social network. The second model extends the hypothesis of the previous model in that the reputation of an agent should also depend on the quality of the knowledge (QK) of the agent. This model allows the reputation of an agent with higher connectivity and more accurate knowledge.

The previous two models assume that being highly connected with the social network could only be a positive factor. Now let's assume that an agent with high connectivity has very poor knowledge and if this agent is allowed to influence others with higher degree of credibility it will end up negatively impacting its associated agents. Eventually, the performance of the system will decrease. This scenario coins the idea that the degree of an agent could act in either direction. It implies an agent could become defective or co-operative depending on the quality of its knowledge (QK). Therefore we can assume that there exists a partition value (x) on QK and if QK > x the agent will be co-operative, otherwise defective. We can outline the hypotheses as follows:

$$RI \; \alpha \; ND \qquad\qquad if \; QK > x$$
$$RI \; \alpha \; 1\,/\,ND \qquad otherwise \tag{1}$$

We can equate the above as follows:

$$RI = K * ND^{P} + C \tag{2}$$

Here p is a function of QK such that it is positive for QK > x, or negative otherwise. In this model, C, instead of being random, it is a default component of RI for an agent which doesn't depend on the social network but rather on the agent itself, its environment, and is unique for each agent. The influencing parameters for C could be Income Level (IL) and Education Level (EL) of the agent. We can express these:

$$C = W2 * f\,(IL, EL) \tag{3}$$

where W2 is a constant factor. Replacing the value of C we can deduce the following model, where W1=K

$$RI = W1 * ND^{P} + W2 * f\,(IL, EL) \tag{4}$$

The above expression describes the Reputation Index (RI) of an agent as a summation of two components. The first one is the component derived from the social network and the second one from the agent's own properties. The constant factors W1 and W2 could be considered as the weight for each component towards the RI. The model in (4) still requires a definition for f(IL, EL). At this time we are approximating this function as a linear combination of IL and EL of the agents.

$$RI = ND^{P} + (IL + EL) \tag{5}$$

The above model assumes equal weight on both components of RI and hence uses W1=W2=1. Also p = 1, if QK > 5.0, or -1 otherwise. It is worth noting that the value of p at this point is limited only between 1 and -1, but in future models a fraction values of p or even higher values of p could be used if we need a quadratic of polynomial formulation of RI in terms of ND.

4 Experiments and Results

If we conduct intervention in the social population space of agents by selecting agents with higher reputation we should be able to achieve quicker convergence of the system. In other words, a more accurate reputation model should allow the child vehicle safety model to achieve higher average correctness. With this hypothesis in mind we devise a validation method for the reputation models described in the previous section. For each model plugged into the system we simulate it 3 times with the following settings respectively: Case 1: Bottom 2% agents in terms of reputation were intervened. Case 2: Randomly chosen 2% agents were intervened. Case 3: Top 2% agents in terms of reputation were intervened. The following settings were fixed for this set of experiments: The total family count in the artificial society was 2000. The total run time of the simulation was 900 days. The intervention was performed right at the end of 300th day to allow the system sufficient time to initialize. For each run we plot the average correctness achieved over time. For brevity, we only report the results of the third model here.

RepuationModel3 was an improvement over RepuationModel2. The hypothesis behind its formulation was that the node degree of an agent could have a positive or negative impact on the system depending on its quality of knowledge (QK). The test results reveal that this model provides a better formulation than that of all the previous models.

5 Conclusions and Future Work

In this paper we exploit reputation to identify significant, or reputable, agents in an artificial society and applied intervention selectively to motivate the whole population towards the global optima. The child vehicle safety simulation model presents a case study for an artificial society based on a subset of realistic factors. Based on the premise that socio-cultural factors play a significant role in driver behaviour which in turn dictates the way they correctly strap a child in the appropriate vehicle safety system, a quantitative formulation of reputation becomes challenging. We devise a qualitative definition of reputation motivating the design and implementation of a generic framework for reputation to function and at the same time enabling us to test various reputation formulations. We proposed three quantitative reputation models to test the framework, each with its own set of hypotheses and formulation. Then we compared their applicability revealing that, from a network perspective, high degree nodes in a social network are not sufficient to be considered along in a reputation model, but rather a model rich with domain knowledge and agent characteristics would be more favourable. In future work we would like to include more complex formulation. Incorporating a feedback or performance rating mechanism from the environment should also be explored.

Acknowledgements

This work was partially supported by grants from NSERC Discovery and Auto21.

References

1. Josang, A., Ismail, R.: The Beta Reputation System. In: 15th Bled Electronic Commerce Conference, e-Reality: Constructing the e-Economy. Bled (2002)
2. Yu, B., Singh, M.P.: Distributed Reputation Management for Electronic Commerce. J. Computational Intelligence 18(4), 535–549 (2002)
3. Sabater, J., Sierra, C.: Reputation and social network analysis in multi-agent systems. In: The proceedings of the first international joint conference on Autonomous agents and multi-agent systems, pp. 475–482. ACM Digital Library, Bologna (2002)
4. Bamasak, O., Zhang, N.: A distributed reputation management scheme for mobile agent based e-commerce applications. In: The 2005 IEEE Int. Conference on e-Technology, e-Commerce and e-Service, EEE 2005, Hong Kong, vol. 29, pp. 270–275 (2005)
5. Kobti, Z., Snowdon, A.W., Rahaman, S., Dunlop, T., Kent, R.D.: A Cultural Algorithm to Guide Driver Learning in Applying Child Vehicle Safety Restraint. In: IEEE Congress on Evolutionary Computation, pp. 1111–1118. IEEE Press, Vancouver (2006)
6. Reynolds, R.G.: Cultural Algorithm: A tutorial, available at http://ai.cs.wayne.edu/
7. Mui, L., Mohtashemi, M., Halberstadt, A.: Notions of reputation in multi-agents systems: a review. In: Alonso, E., Kudenko, D., Kazakov, D. (eds.) AAMAS 2000 and AAMAS 2002. LNCS (LNAI), vol. 2636, pp. 280–287. Springer, Heidelberg (2003)
8. Mahmood, S., ul Asar, A., Mahmood, F., Ahmad, N.: Swarm Intelligence Based Reputation Model for Open Multi Agent Systems. In: IEEE Multitopic Conference, INMIC 2006, Islamabad, pp. 178–181 (2006)
9. Kobti, Z., Snowdon, A.W., Rahaman, S., Dunlop, T., Kent, R.D.: A multi-agent model prototype for child vehicle safety injury prevention. In: Agent 2005 Conference on Generative Social Processes, Models and Mechanisms, Chicago (2005)
10. Rahaman, S.: Intervention in the social population space of cultural algorithm: an application in child seat vehicle safety. In: A thesis submitted to the Faculty of Graduate Studies, University of Windsor, Windsor (2007)
11. Kobti, Z., Reynolds, R.G.: Modeling protein exchange across the social network in the village multi-agent simulation. In: IEEE International Conference on Systems, Man and Cybernetics, vol. 4, pp. 3197–3203. IEEE Press, Los Alamitos (2005)

Selective Sampling for Classification

François Laviolette, Mario Marchand, and Sara Shanian

IFT-GLO, Université Laval, Québec (QC) Canada, G1V-0A6
{first_name.last_name}@ift.ulaval.ca

Abstract. Supervised learning is concerned with the task of building accurate classifiers from a set of labelled examples. However, the task of gathering a large set of labelled examples can be costly and time-consuming. Active learning algorithms try to reduce this labelling cost by performing a small number of label-queries from a large set of unlabelled examples during the process of building a classifier. However, the level of performance achieved by active learning algorithms is not always up to our expectations and no rigorous performance guarantee, in the form of a risk bound, exists for non-trivial active learning algorithms. In this paper, we propose a novel (and easy to implement) active learning algorithm having a rigorous performance guarantee (*i.e.*, a valid risk bound) and that performs very well in comparison with some widely-used active learning algorithms.

1 Introduction

Gathering experimental data is essential for any learning task. In classification, we usually gather an amount of training data and then we infer a classifier from it. This methodology is called passive learning. However, in order to build an accurate classifier, it is generally necessary to gather a large number of labelled examples for training set, which, itself, is an expensive and time consuming task. One way to overcome this problem is to use another methodology called *active learning*. Active learning includes any form of learning in which the learning program has some control over the examples it trains on. Instead of randomly selecting the examples to be labelled, the learning algorithm can more carefully choose or query them from a finite set of examples (*pool based model*) or can choose them from a sequence of examples (*stream-based model*). In this way, we expect to reduce substantially the amount of examples to be labelled in order to achieve a given accuracy. A common example is the World-Wide Web, which provides a profusion of training pages for text categorization problems. Thus, the major goal of any active learning algorithm is to obtain a good classifier within a reasonable number of labelling queries. In order to make a query, the active learner goes through the entire pool or stream of unlabelled examples and selects the example to be labelled next (*selective sampling*).

Active learning methods fall under two main categories based on the criterion used to select the next queries: *Uncertainty Sampling* and *Query by Committee*. For uncertainty sampling [7,9], the learner selects the examples to be labelled

S. Bergler (Ed.): Canadian AI 2008, LNAI 5032, pp. 191–202, 2008.
© Springer-Verlag Berlin Heidelberg 2008

among those for which the predicted label is mostly uncertain. Hence, this approach can only be used with classifiers that also provide a level of confidence with the predicted label (confidence-rated prediction). Considering that many learning algorithms are producing classifiers without any confidence-rated prediction, [2] has proposed to use a committee of classifiers (instead of a single classifier) and measure the uncertainty in the predictions by the degree of disagreement among the classifiers. This idea has later been used for the Query by Committed approach [3] where several hypothesis are uniformly sampled from the *version space*[1] and the learner selects the examples to be labelled among those for which the disagreement among the sampled hypothesis is largest. For binary classification, this means that we choose the examples to be labelled among those which most closely bisect our finite-sample estimation of the version space.

The basic problem with the Query by Committee approach is that the version space is generally empty for noisy data. In this case, we should sample the hypothesis according to the so-called Gibbs distribution where the probability weight assigned to each classifier decreases exponentially rapidly with the amount of training error. But sampling according to this distribution is notoriously difficult. Indeed, finding a single classifier making the smallest number of training error is NP-hard even for simple hypothesis classes such as linear classifiers. One practical way to get around this problem is called the *simple margin method* [12]. The idea is to train a soft-margin support vector machine on the labelled data, and then select the examples to be labelled among those that are closest to the separating hyperplane.

In this paper, we present a new, and easy to implement, active learning algorithm for classification that uses an uncertainty sampling query strategy. However, in contrast with other uncertainty sampling strategies, the query selection is made with respect to a *static* classifier (*i.e.*, a classifier built only from the initial set of labelled examples) that we call the *teacher*. The main motivation of using a static teacher to guide the queries is the fact that, in that case (only), we can establish a valid generalization error (or risk) bound for a dynamic learner that uses the labels provided by these queries. Furthermore, the proposed risk bound provides a clear strategy for the dynamic learner that our proposed algorithm uses: query the unlabelled examples for which the disagreement between the dynamic learner and the static teacher is maximal. We provide experimental evidence that this learning strategy is, in fact, very competitive with state-of-the-art active learners such as the simple margin [12]. Moreover, our experimental results clearly show the advantage for the static teacher to have confidence-rated predictions[2].

---

[1] The version space is the set of all hypothesis which are consistent with the data that has been seen so far.

[2] More precisely, our numerical results show that a perfect classifier (that knows the label of every example to be queried) is a substantially worst teacher than an approximate confidence-rated predictor learned from a small set of labelled examples.

The organization of this paper is as follows. Section 2 presents some basic definitions used throughout the paper. Section 3 presents the proposed active learning algorithm along with its motivation. We then present, in Section 4, a generalization error bound for the proposed learning algorithm. In Section 5, we present some empirical results of the proposed algorithm in comparison with other active learning algorithms. We finally conclude in Section 6.

2   Basic Definitions

In this basic setting of active learning for binary classification, the learner is given a small labelled data set, $Z_l = \{z_i\}_{i=1}^m$, with $z_i = (\mathbf{x}_i, y_i)$, where each input example $\mathbf{x}_i$ belongs to the instance (or input) space $\mathcal{X} = \mathbb{R}^n$ and each label y_i belongs to the output space $\mathcal{Y} = \{-1, +1\}$. We consider a pool-based setting where we also have a set $X_{\mathcal{U}}$ (called the pool) of unlabelled examples.

We suppose that each pair $(\mathbf{x}, y) \in Z_l$ is drawn i.i.d. with respect to a fixed but unknown distribution D and we denote the marginal distribution over $\mathcal{X}$ by $D_{\mathcal{X}}$. The learner is allowed to query an oracle for the labels of a small number of unlabelled examples of his choice to add to the labelled set. The risk $R(f)$ of any classifier f is defined as the probability of misclassifying an example which is drawn according to D. Hence

$$R(f) \overset{\text{def}}{=} \mathbf{P}_{(x,y)\sim D}(f(x) \neq y) \overset{\text{def}}{=} \mathbf{E}_{(x,y)\sim D} I(f(x) \neq y),$$

where $I(a) = 1$ if $a = true$ and $I(a) = 0$ if $a = false$. The empirical risk $R_S(f)$ of any classifier f on training set S of m examples is defined by

$$R_S(f) \overset{\text{def}}{=} \frac{1}{m} \sum_{i=1}^m I(f(x_i) \neq y_i).$$

In this paper, we also consider a stochastic classifier, called the *Gibbs classifier*. Given an input example $\mathbf{x}$, the label assigned to $\mathbf{x}$ by the Gibbs classifier G_Q is defined by the following process. We first choose randomly a classifier h according to a distribution Q over a set $\mathcal{H}$ of classifiers. Then we use h to assign the label to $\mathbf{x}$. The risk $R(G_Q)$ of the the Gibbs classifier G_Q is defined as the expected risk of classifiers drawn according to Q. The empirical risk $R_S(G_Q)$ of G_Q, on training set S of examples is the empirical estimate of $R(G_Q)$ on S. Hence

$$R(G_Q) \overset{\text{def}}{=} \mathbf{E}_{h\sim Q} R(h) \quad ; \quad R_S(G_Q) \overset{\text{def}}{=} \mathbf{E}_{h\sim Q} R_S(h).$$

3   The New Query Selection Strategy and Its Motivation

The starting point of active learning based on uncertainty sampling is the construction a confidence-rated classifier from the set Z_l of labelled examples. The Gibbs classifier G_Q, defined in the previous section, is a classifier where the confidence in its prediction is naturally expressed in terms of the probability associated with the predicted label. Indeed, since G_Q chooses randomly according to Q a classifier h to predict the label of any example $\mathbf{x}$, this assigns a probability $p_{\mathbf{x}}$ of predicting label $+1$ to each $\mathbf{x} \in \mathcal{X}$. A value of $p_{\mathbf{x}}$ near one (or zero) means a very high confidence that the true label is $+1$ (or -1) whereas a value of $p_{\mathbf{x}}$ near $1/2$ means almost no confidence in its predicted label.

AdaBoost [4] is a particularly effective learning algorithm for producing a weighted majority-vote of basis classifiers. The weight associated to each basis classifier defines a distribution Q and, consequently, a Gibbs classifier G_Q. It is easy verify that the region of $\mathcal{X}$, where the weighted majority-vote (produced by AdaBoost) errs most often, consists of the examples for which the predicted label made by the associated Gibbs classifier is mostly uncertain, $i.e.$, those examples $\mathbf{x}$ having a probability $p_{\mathbf{x}}$ closest to $1/2$ of being assign to label $+1$ by G_Q. This property is a consequence of the learning strategy used by AdaBoost, which consists of minimizing the empirical exponential loss. Indeed, by searching for a set of weights that minimizes the empirical exponential loss, AdaBoost will not tolerate any classification error for training examples located far from the separating hyperplane. Consequently, it is very unlikely that testing errors will be located very far from the region where the prediction of G_Q is mostly uncertain.

These observations suggest that the Gibbs classifier, associated with the weighted majority-vote produced by AdaBoost, should provide a good guide (hence a *teacher*) for an active learner (called *student*) that has to select the unlabelled examples for which he is going to query an oracle for their labels. Moreover, the above observations also suggest that a good selection strategy, for the student, should be to choose the unlabelled examples for which the *disagreement* with the teacher is maximum. Indeed, since the teacher errs (almost) only on examples whose predicted labels are mostly uncertain, the unlabelled examples giving the highest possible disagreement are those for which: (1) the teacher is very confident (and thus correct with very high probability) and (2) the label predicted by the student is incorrect. Since the teacher is a Gibbs classifier defined by a distribution Q over some space $\mathcal{H}$ of classifiers, we propose the following measure of disagreement.

Definition 1 (The disagreement function). *Given a student classifier h_{Stud} and a stochastic teacher H_{Teach} (defined by a distribution Q over a space $\mathcal{H}$ of classifiers), the disagreement function on $\mathbf{x} \in \mathcal{X}$ is the probability that the student and teacher disagree on $\mathbf{x}$ with respect to a classifier randomly drawn according to Q. Hence,*

$$d_{\mathbf{x}}(h_{Stud}, H_{Teach}) \stackrel{\text{def}}{=} E_{h \sim Q} I(h_{Stud}(\mathbf{x}) \neq h(\mathbf{x})).$$

Considering the above definitions, we present our active learning algorithm, called *Stud-Teach*. In this algorithm, given the whole set (or pool) $X_{\mathcal{U}} \subseteq \mathcal{X}$ of unlabelled examples, h_{Stud} considers a subset of $X_{\mathcal{U}}^{(\eta)}$ of η elements of $X_{\mathcal{U}}$ for which the value of $d_{\mathbf{x}}(h_{Stud}, H_{Teach})$ is maximal. Then, it asks for the labels of $\mathbf{x} \in X_{\mathcal{U}}^{(\eta)}$ and learns on $Z_l \cup Z_{\mathcal{U}}^{(\eta)}$, where $Z_{\mathcal{U}}^{(\eta)}$ denotes the set of examples of

$X_{\mathcal{U}}^{(\eta)}$ that have been queried. The learning algorithm used for the production of h_{Stud} is arbitrary. To obtain a fair comparison with the simple margin active learner [12], we have used a soft-margin SVM.

Algorithm 1. *Stud-Teach*: an active learning algorithm for classification

---

1: **Input:** A set Z_l of labelled and a set $X_{\mathcal{U}}$ of unlabelled examples ;
2: **Input:** The number η of examples to be activated at each round;
3: **Input:** The maximum number T_A of rounds;
4: **Input:** The teacher classifier H_{Teach} (computed from Z_l by using AdaBoost);
5: **Initialize:** $Z_{\mathcal{U}}^{(\eta)} \leftarrow \emptyset$, $t_A \leftarrow 1$;
6: **repeat**
7:     Learn h_{Stud} on $Z_l \cup Z_{\mathcal{U}}^{(\eta)}$
8:     Select a subset $X_{\mathcal{U}}^{(\eta)}$ from $X_{\mathcal{U}}$ such that for $\mathbf{x} \in X_{\mathcal{U}}$ the value $\mathbf{d_x}(h_{Stud}, H_{Teach})$
        is maximal
9:     Ask for the label y of $\mathbf{x}$ for each $\mathbf{x} \in X_{\mathcal{U}}^{(\eta)}$
10:     $Z_{\mathcal{U}}^{(\eta)} \leftarrow Z_{\mathcal{U}}^{(\eta)} \cup \left\{ (\mathbf{x}, y) \mid \mathbf{x} \in X_{\mathcal{U}}^{(\eta)}, and\ y\ is\ the\ queried\ label \right\}$
11:     $t_A \leftarrow t_A + 1$
12: **until** $t_A > T_A$
13: **output:** h_{Stud} ;

As we explain in the next section, an important motivation for the above definition of disagreement and for using a confidence-rated teacher that learns only from the labelled data, is the fact that these choices enable us to find a valid risk bound for the proposed active learning algorithm.

4   Generalization Error Bound for the Active Learner

Theoretical guarantees on the performance of active learners are hard to obtain because the sequence of examples on which the algorithm is learning (original training set plus queried examples) is not i.i.d.-generated anymore. Based on the idea of Kääriäinen [5], we can circumvent this difficulty by relating the risk of the learner to the risk of the teacher and the expected disagreement between the student and the teacher. More precisely, we have the following result.

Lemma 2. *For any teacher H_{Teach} and student h_{Stud}, we have:*

$$R(h_{Stud}) \leq R(H_{Teach}) + \mathbf{E}_{\mathbf{x} \sim D_{\mathcal{X}}} \mathbf{d_x}(h_{Stud}, H_{Teach})$$

Proof. First observe that for all $h_1, h_2 \in \mathcal{H}$ and for all $(\mathbf{x}, y) \in \mathcal{X} \times \mathcal{Y}$, we have :

$$I(h_1(\mathbf{x}) \neq y) \leq I(h_2(\mathbf{x}) \neq y) + I(h_1(\mathbf{x}) \neq h_2(\mathbf{x})) .$$

To see this, recall that the values of $I(\cdot)$ must be in $\{0, 1\}$. Thus, the case $h_1(\mathbf{x}) = y$ is trivial. For the case where $h_1(\mathbf{x}) \neq y$, we either have $h_2(\mathbf{x}) \neq y$

(which implies the result), or $h_2(\mathbf{x}) = y$ (which also implies the result since then $h_1(\mathbf{x}) \neq h_2(\mathbf{x})$).

It then follows, from Definition 1 and the additive property of $\mathbf{E}_{(\mathbf{x},y)\sim D}$, that

$$
\begin{aligned}
R(h_{Stud}) &= \mathbf{E}_{(\mathbf{x},y)\sim D} I(h_{Stud}(\mathbf{x}) \neq y) \\
&= \mathbf{E}_{(\mathbf{x},y)\sim D} \mathbf{E}_{h\sim Q} I(h_{Stud}(\mathbf{x}) \neq y) \\
&\leq \mathbf{E}_{(\mathbf{x},y)\sim D} \mathbf{E}_{h\sim Q} \Big(I(h(\mathbf{x}) \neq y) + I(h_{Stud}(\mathbf{x}) \neq h(\mathbf{x})) \Big) \\
&= R(H_{Teach}) + \mathbf{E}_{(\mathbf{x},y)\sim D}\, \mathbf{d}_{\mathbf{x}}(h_{Stud}, H_{Teach}) \\
&= R(H_{Teach}) + \mathbf{E}_{\mathbf{x}\sim D_{\mathcal{X}}}\mathbf{d}_{\mathbf{x}}(h_{Stud}, H_{Teach}).
\end{aligned}
$$

The last equality comes from the fact that the value of $\mathbf{d}_{\mathbf{x}}(h_{stud}, H_{Teach})$ is the same for both $(\mathbf{x}, -1)$ and $(\mathbf{x}, +1)$. $\qquad\square$

Therefore, we will obtain an upper bound on $R(h_{Stud})$ if we have an upper bound on $R(H_{Teach})$ and on the expected disagreement between h_{Stud} and H_{Teach}. Considering that H_{Teach} is a Gibbs classifier, we can simply use the following PAC-Bayes Bound for the training set $Z_l = \{z_i\}_{i=1}^m$ of m labelled examples.

Theorem 3. *[6,11] (PAC-Bayes bound) For any set $\mathcal{H}$ of binary classifiers, any prior distribution P on $\mathcal{H}$, for any data-generating distribution D, and any $\delta \in (0,1]$, we have*

$$
\Pr_{S\sim D^m} \left(\forall Q : kl(R_S(G_Q)\|R(G_Q)) \leq \frac{1}{m}\left[KL(Q\|P) + \ln\frac{m+1}{\delta} \right] \right) \geq 1 - \delta,
$$

where $KL(Q\|P) = \mathbf{E}_{h\sim Q} \ln\frac{Q(h)}{P(h)}$ is the Kullback-Leibler divergence between the distribution Q and P, and where $kl(p\|q) = q\ln\frac{q}{p} + (1-q)\ln\frac{1-q}{1-p}$.

For the problem of upper bounding the average disagreement between h_{Stud} and H_{Teach}, we limit ourselves to (deterministic) learning algorithms (like the soft-margin SVM) that always produce the same h_{Stud} when given the same training set of labelled examples. In this case, given the initial set Z_l of labelled examples, each possible classifier h_{Stud} is identified by the subset of unlabelled examples that the student will use to construct h_{Stud}. Since, from Algorithm 1, the number of activated queries is always $\eta \cdot T_A$, the total number of possible classifiers h_{Stud} considered by the student is always at most $\binom{|X_{\mathcal{U}}|}{\eta \cdot T_A}$. This situation is then very similar to the sample-compression setting [10] where each classifier is identified by a subset of the training sample. By using the union bound over the above set of possible classifiers, we can thus obtain a uniform risk bound for classifiers as a function of the disagreement between h_{Stud} and H_{Teach} measured on the subset on $X_{\mathcal{U}}\backslash X_{\mathcal{U}}^{(\eta T_A)}$ where $X_{\mathcal{U}}^{(\eta T_A)}$ is the subset $X_{\mathcal{U}}$ used for the activated queries. Hence we have the following theorem.

Theorem 4. *Given all of the previous definitions, for any $D_{\mathcal{X}}$, any fixed classifier H_{Teach}, and any $\delta \in (0,1]$, we have*

$$\Pr_{X_\mathcal{U} \sim D_\mathcal{X}^n} \left(\forall h_{Stud}: \underset{x \sim D_\mathcal{X}}{\mathbf{E}} \, \mathbf{d_x} \left(h_{Stud}, H_{Teach} \right) \leq \hat{d} \left(h_{Stud}, H_{Teach} \right) + \right.$$

$$\left. \sqrt{\frac{\ln \binom{n}{\eta T_A} + \ln \frac{1}{\delta}}{2(n - \eta T_A)}} \right) \geq 1 - \delta \,,$$

where

$$\hat{d} \left(h_{Stud}, H_{Teach} \right) \overset{\text{def}}{=} \frac{1}{n - \eta T_A} \sum_{x \in X_\mathcal{U} \backslash X_\mathcal{U}^{(\eta T_A)}} \mathbf{d_x} \left(h_{Stud}, H_{Teach} \right) \,.$$

Proof. Given a set $X_\mathcal{U}$ of n unlabelled examples, let $h_\mathbf{i}$ denote the classifier obtained by the student after querying the examples pointed by the k-tuple $\mathbf{i} = (i_1, \ldots, i_k)$ of indices where $i_1 < i_2 < \ldots < i_k$ and each $i_j \in \{1, \ldots, n\}$. Let $\mathcal{I}(k, n)$ be the set of all $\binom{n}{k}$ possible k-tuples $\mathbf{i}$. For any classifier H_T, let

$$P' \overset{\text{def}}{=} \Pr_{X_\mathcal{U} \sim D_\mathcal{X}^n} \left(\exists \mathbf{i} \in \mathcal{I}(k, n): \underset{x \sim D_\mathcal{X}}{\mathbf{E}} \, \mathbf{d_x} \left(h_\mathbf{i}, H_T \right) > \hat{d} \left(h_\mathbf{i}, H_T \right) + \sqrt{\frac{\ln \binom{n}{k} + \ln \frac{1}{\delta}}{2(n - k)}} \right).$$

To prove the theorem, we now show that $P' \leq \delta$. Indeed, by the union bound over the different choices of $\mathbf{i}$ and by using Hoeffding's inequality for each choice of $\mathbf{i}$, we have

$$P' \leq \sum_{\mathbf{i} \in \mathcal{I}(k, n)} \Pr_{X_\mathcal{U} \sim D_\mathcal{X}^n} \left(\underset{x \sim D_\mathcal{X}}{\mathbf{E}} \, \mathbf{d_x} \left(h_\mathbf{i}, H_T \right) > \hat{d} \left(h_\mathbf{i}, H_T \right) + \sqrt{\frac{\ln \binom{n}{k} + \ln \frac{1}{\delta}}{2(n - k)}} \right)$$

$$\leq \sum_{\mathbf{i} \in \mathcal{I}(k, n)} \frac{\delta}{\binom{n}{k}} = \delta \,. \qquad \square$$

Note that Theorem 4 uniformly holds for all h_{Stud} but is valid only for (any) fixed H_{Teach}. This is the motivation for using a static teacher in *Stud-Teach*.

To obtain an upper bound on $R(h_{Stud})$ based on Lemma 2, we simply have to combine Theorem 3 and Theorem 4 with δ replaced by $\delta/2$.

5   Empirical Results

To test the performance of active learning algorithms, we have used the data sets listed in Table 1 (all taken from the UCI repository). In this table, $|Z_l|$ denotes the initial number of labelled training examples, $|X_\mathcal{U}|$ denotes the number of unlabelled examples in the pool set used by active learners, and $|T|$ denotes the number of (labelled) examples used for testing the final classifiers produced by active learners. Each data set was mixed and split at random. The 10-classes Pendigit data set was grouped in the following two classes: $+1$ for $(6, 8, 9)$ and -1 for $(0, 1, 2, 3, 4, 5, 7)$ (the other data sets have only two classes). We have

Table 1. Data sets used for the experiments

Data set name	$|Z_l|$	$|X_{\mathcal{U}}|$	$|T|$
Mushroom	100	8000	1800
Pendigit	100	8000	1821
Splice	100	1805	1270
Image	100	1286	924

chosen $|Z_l|$ to be much smaller than $|X_{\mathcal{U}}|$ to clearly show the advantage of using a set of unlabelled examples when we have very few labelled training examples—which is the case of interest for active learning. The accuracy of all classifiers (returned by active learners) will be computed on the testing set T as one minus the frequency of classification errors measured on T. The advantage of this method over re-sampling methods such as cross-validation is that the frequency of training error is an unbiased estimate of the true risk and, consequently, valid confidence intervals exist for the true risk that can be computed (only) from the number of testing errors, the number of testing examples, and the value $1 - \delta$ of the confidence parameter. Indeed, one can build very tight two-sided confidence intervals from one-sided testing risk bounds expressed with the binomial tail inversion proposed by Langford [6]. Applying this method, on the numerical results presented below, indicates that the 90% confidence interval around the measured frequency of errors on T never exceeds 3%.

The proposed active learning algorithm, *Stud-Teach*, was applied on each data set with $T_A = 200$ (maximum number of rounds) and $\eta = 5$ (the number of activated query in each round). On each round, when new examples were added, the h_{Stud} classifier was retrained and tested on T. Smaller values of η did not change significantly the results (but needed more computing time) and higher values of η produced results that changed more abruptly.

As explained in Section 3, the teacher was always constructed with AdaBoost, equipped with Decision Stumps as basis classifiers (since this is probably the most frequent choice). The student was always a soft-margin SVM (with a linear kernel for Mushroom and Pendigit, and an RBF kernel for the other data sets). We have made this choice in order to make a valid comparison with the Simple Margin [12] active learning algorithm who also produces an SVM as its final classifier. The Simple Margin algorithm uses, however, a completely different query strategy then Stud-Teach: it simply chooses the unlabelled example which is mostly orthogonal to the current weight vector (and uses no teacher). Of course, the kernel used for Stud-Teach and Simple Margin was always the same.

The testing accuracy as function of the number of rounds (of five queries each) for the Stud-Teach and Simple Margin algorithms is presented on Figures 1, 2, 3, and 4 for the data sets described in Table 1. We have also included the results with the *random sampling* query strategy which simply consists of choosing an unlabelled example uniformly at random in the pool set. The random sampling query strategy is often used as a baseline for comparing with different active learning algorithms. We did not compared with active learning algorithms that

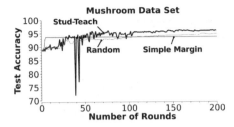

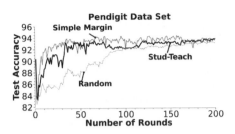

Fig. 1. Comparison of active learning algorithms on Mushroom

Fig. 2. Comparison of active learning algorithms on Pendigit

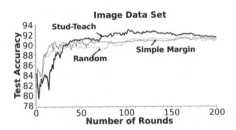

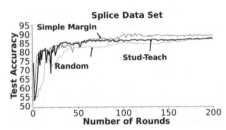

Fig. 3. Comparison of active learning algorithms on Image

Fig. 4. Comparison of active learning algorithms on Splice

rely on the existence of a non-empty version space, like the Query by Committee algorithm, since the version space is generally empty in practice.

As one can see from these figures, Simple Margin and Stud-Teach are "competitive" query strategies (with no clear winner). Stud-Teach appears to be slightly better than Simple Margin on Mushroom and Image whereas the converse seems to be true on Pendigit and Splice. However, both of these active learning algorithms are clearly better than random sampling.

For the next set of experiments, our goal was to investigate if the Stud-Teach algorithm could be improved by making use of a better teacher (than the stochastic Gibbs classifier created by AdaBoost). After all, one might think that if the teacher knew the labels of every examples in the pool set, he would then provide a better guide to the student since the examples giving the maximum disagreement would be only those for which the student is predicting the wrong label. The fact that all the examples of the data sets of Table 1 have labels (which have been ignored up to now for those in the pool set), makes it possible for us to run the Stud-Teach algorithm with a perfect teacher. Hence, we have compared this new algorithm, that we now call *Perfect Sampling*, with the original Stud-Teach algorithm (equipped with a Gibbs teacher). As can been seen in Figures 5 and 6, Perfect Sampling is a very poor algorithm. Indeed, an active learning algorithm whose accuracy changes so rapidly from one query to the next is unusable in practice since the active learner has high probability of stopping at a point achieving very low accuracy.

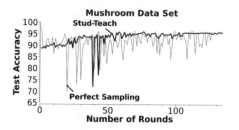

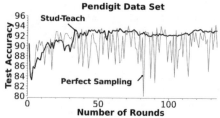

Fig. 5. Comparison of Stud-Teach and Perfect Sampling on Mushroom

Fig. 6. Comparison of Stud-Teach and Perfect Sampling on Pendigit

A reason that could explain why Perfect Sampling is so unstable from one query to the next is the fact that a perfect teacher that indicates to the student the examples on which it errs, will produce a sequence of training examples that deviates substantially from the sequence of testing examples that are i.i.d. generated from the true distribution.[3] In short, the perfect teacher will force the learner to perform well with respect to a distribution that deviates too much from the testing distribution. Active learning is thus confronted with a non-trivial trade-off between the need of selecting examples that provide enough information for the learner to improve and the need of selecting examples in a way which does not differ too much from a sequence of examples that could be generated from the true distribution.[4] In our experiments, we can see that Simple Margin and Stud-Teach lie somewhat in between random sampling (that guides the learner, non-informatively, through a sequence of examples generated according to true distribution—since each example is chosen independently) and perfect sampling (that guides the learner, informatively, through a sequence of examples that deviates from a sequence that could be generated by the true distribution).

6   Conclusion and Future Work

In this paper, we proposed a new active learning algorithm called Stud-Teach. The two main ingredients of this algorithm consist of a static teacher that learns only from the initial set of labelled examples and a (dynamic) student that chooses, from a pool of unlabelled examples, those that will be used to query an oracle for their labels. The selection strategy used by the student consists of choosing the example for which the disagreement with the teacher is maximum. The proposed function of disagreement, in Definition 1, has enabled us to find a valid generalization error bound when the teacher is static. To our knowledge,

---

[3] This is so because each chosen example depends on the student's accuracy and, consequently, on the examples that were previously chosen.

[4] Consequently, active learning is also concerned with *domain adaptation* [1], which is the problem of quantifying the loss of accuracy of a classifier that has been trained on a data set that differs in its nature from the test set.

this is the first valid risk bound that has been proposed for a non-trivial active learning algorithm.[5]

On the practical side, the Stud-Teach algorithm does not assume the existence of a perfect target function (and an non-empty version space) as is the case for the Query by Committee [3] approach. In addition, our empirical results show that Stud-Teach is competitive to one of the most well-known active learning strategies: the Simple Margin [12]. Thus Stud-Teach is competitively accurate, easy to implement, and not computationally expensive.

Our attempt to improve Stud-Teach by increasing the predictive power of the teacher has completely failed. However, this has also directed us to a very important trade-off that active learners have to deal with: their selection strategy should enable the learner to improve its accuracy but with respect to a distribution which should not deviate substantially from the one that generates the testing examples. The random sampling strategy has the advantage of learning with respect to the true distribution but, in comparison with other active learners, this increases the labelling cost (more labelled examples are needed). On the other end, the perfect sampling strategy try to improve the accuracy of the learner as much as possible by always choosing the examples on which the learner errs. But this also forces the learner to perform with respect to a distribution which deviates substantially from the testing distribution. We have observed that the testing accuracy of the perfect sampler changed abruptly from one query to the next (an unstable learning rate). Our results indicates that Stud-Teach and Simple Margin, presenting relatively stable learning rates, lie somewhat in between these two extremes (of random and perfect sampling) and seem to achieve the desired trade-off.

It would be interesting to have some theoretical explanation of the stability of Stud-Teach and Simple Margin. As we have discussed, it is likely that the stability of active learners is related to the mismatch between the training and testing distributions and, consequently, related to the problem of domain adaptation (see [1]). On the practical side, we tried to increase the stability of Stud-Teach by adding a *soft max* query selection method. More precisely, instead of always choosing examples that maximize the disagreement between the student and the teacher, this choice is performed stochastically with respect to a distribution P over the set $X_{\mathcal{U}} \backslash Z_{\mathcal{U}}^{(\eta)}$: the set of pool examples that has not been queried yet. The distribution P is given by

$$P(\mathbf{x}) = \frac{e^{\mathbf{d_x}(h_{Stud}, H_{Teach})/\tau}}{\sum_{\mathbf{x'} \in X_{\mathcal{U}} \backslash Z_{\mathcal{U}}^{(\eta)}} e^{\mathbf{d_{x'}}(h_{Stud}, H_{Teach})/\tau}} ,$$

---

[5] Indeed, the only active learning algorithm known to have a valid risk bound is random sampling since, in that case, the sequence of training examples, each chosen randomly, is still i.i.d. generated according to the true distribution. Consequently, any standard risk bound for classifiers, that learn with respect to the true distribution, is valid for random sampling.

where τ is some tunable parameter called *temperature*. Our encouraging preliminary results indicate that the addition of the *soft max* query selection increases the stability of the learning rate without sacrificing the testing accuracy.

Acknowledgments. Work supported by NSERC Discovery grants 262067 and 122405.

References

1. Ben-David, S., Blitze, J., Crammer, K., Pereira, F.: Analysis of Representations for Domain Adaptation. Advances in Neural Information Processing System 19, 137–144 (2007)
2. Cohn, D.A., Atlas, L., Ladner, R.E.: Improving generalization with active learning. Machine Learning 15(2), 201–221 (1994)
3. Freund, Y., Seung, H.S., Shamir, E., Tishby, N.: Selective sampling using the query by committee algorithm. Machine Learning 28, 133–168 (1997)
4. Freund, Y., Schapire, R.E.: A decision-theoretic generalization of on-line learning and an application to boosting. Journal of Computer and System Sciences 55(1), 119–139 (1997)
5. Kääriäinen, M.: Generalization error bounds using unlabelled data. In: Proceedings of the 18th Annual Conference on Learning Theory, pp. 127–142 (2005)
6. Langford, J.: Tutorial on practical prediction theory for classification. Journal of Machine Learning Research 6, 273–306 (2005)
7. Lewis, D.D., Catlett, J.: Heterogeneous uncertainty sampling for supervised learning. In: Proceedings of the 11th International Conference on Machine Learning (ML 1994), pp. 148–156 (1994)
8. Lewis, D.D., Gale, W.A.: A sequential algorithm for training text classifiers. In: Proceedings of SIGIR 1994, 17th ACM International Conference on Research and Development in Information Retrieval, pp. 3–12 (1994)
9. Lewis, D.D., Gale, W.A.: Training text classifiers by uncertainty sampling. In: Proceedings of the 17th Annual International ACM SIGIR Conference on Research and Development in Information Retrieval (SIGIR 1994), pp. 3–12 (1994)
10. Marchand, M., Sokolova, M.: Learning with Decision Lists of Data- Dependent Features. Journal of Machine Learning Research 6, 427–451 (2005)
11. Seeger, M.: PAC-Bayesian generalization bounds for guassian process. Journal of machine learning research 3, 233–269 (2002)
12. Tong, S., Koller, D.: Support vector machine active learning with applications to text classification. Journal of machine learning research 2, 45–66 (2002)

Full Border Identification for Reduction of Training Sets

Guichong Li[1], Nathalie Japkowicz[1], Trevor J. Stocki[2], and R. Kurt Ungar[2]

[1] Computer Science of University of Ottawa
{jli136,nat}@site.uottawa.ca
[2] Radiation Protection Bureau, Health Canada, Ottawa, ON, Canada
{trevor_stocki,kurt_ungar}@hc-sc.gc.ca

Abstract. Border identification (BI) was previously proposed to help learning systems focus on the most relevant portion of the training set so as to improve learning accuracy. This paper argues that the traditional BI implementation suffers from a serious limitation: it is only able to identify partial borders. This paper proposes a new BI method called Progressive Border Sampling (PBS), which addresses this limitation by borrowing ideas from recent research on Progressive Sampling. PBS progressively learns optimal borders from the entire training sets by, first, identifying a full border, thus, avoiding the limitation of the traditional BI method, and, second, by incrementing the size of that border until it converges to an optimal sample, which is smaller than the original training set. Since PBS identifies the full border, it is expected to discover more optimal samples than traditional BI. Our experimental results on the selected 30 benchmark datasets from the UCI repository show that, indeed, in the context of classification, PBS is more successful than traditional BI at reducing the size of the training sets and optimizing the accuracy results.

Keywords: Border Identification. Progressive Sampling, Convergence Detection, Learning Curve.

1 Introduction

The role of the training patterns located on the border lying close to the boundary separating samples of various classes has been studied in previous research [3][5]. The results show that a neural network trained with border patterns performs worse on the training set, but significantly better on the test set than one trained on the class cores [5]. In this paper, we re-investigate the role of training patterns on the border for reduction of training set size with respect to other common induction algorithms.

There is a demand for this research area in many practical applications. Indeed, learning on massive amounts of data can exhaust computational resources and, thus, hinder learners from building good classifiers [6][9][15]. The work reported in this paper can help find an efficient and effective solution to meet this demand of reduction of training sets.

We propose a new technique called Progressive Border Sampling (PBS). It uses Progressive Sampling (PS) techniques to progressively learn optimal borders by

S. Bergler (Ed.): Canadian AI 2008, LNAI 5032, pp. 203–215, 2008.
© Springer-Verlag Berlin Heidelberg 2008

avoiding the limitation of the traditional Border Identification (BI) methods proposed in previous research. The new method consists of the following two main aspects.

First, PBS can identify the latent full border specified by the entire set of labeled cases and extract the data points from the border lying close to the boundary. The full border identified by PBS is different from the one identified by traditional methods.

Second, an optimal border can be progressively learned by PBS. Therefore, a set of data points from the optimal border that are considered particularly informative can be used as a new training set.

We conducted experiments on a number of selected small benchmark datasets from the UCI repository [1]. The empirical results show that PBS tends to produce optimal samples from the original training sets such that classifiers trained on the resulting samples tend to be more accurate than the ones trained on BI. Therefore, we emphasize the potential of PBS for large datasets by any optimized heuristics.

The remainder of this paper is organized as follows. In Section 2, we introduce the traditional BI method for border identification. In Section 3, we develop the notion of a border by showing the limitation of the traditional BI technique which often results in the computation of an incomplete border. Our new approach, PBS, is proposed in Section 4. In Section 5, we describe our experimental design and results. We conclude and suggest future work in Section 6.

2 Border Identification

A *border* does not concretely exist in a training set. A *latent border*, called a border for short, is specified in a labeled training set by the set of data points lying close to the boundary [3][5][7].

2.1 Previous Methods

The state-of-the-art methods for identifying borders consists of two categories: similarity distance methods [3][5] and active learning [2].

The similarity distance method for Border Identification, denoted as BI, can be described as follows [3][5]. For each data point, the k-nearest neighbors from other classes are identified as data points on the border. As a result, a border can be created by scanning the whole training set. The Nearest-neighbor editing algorithm [4] pertaining to this category can be used to find a border by constructing the full Voronoi diagram in which all adjacent data points are connected with each other. The main drawbacks are that one cannot add training data later because the pruning step requires knowledge of all the training data ahead of time, and its complexity of $O(d^3 n^{\lfloor d/2 \rfloor} \ln(n))$ [4] is still intractable for many practical applications.

Active learning [2] as an indirect method has been applied to the problem of border identification by reducing the region of uncertainty [2]. The method depends on the selection of learners used, e.g., feedforward neural networks and mixtures of Gaussians, etc [2].

In this paper, we embrace the first category of work that uses a similarity distance method and develop a new approach in that category that avoids some of the limitations of traditional BI as follows.

2.2 Definition of a Border in the BI Context

Informative data points are defined for delineating a border as follows.

Definition 1. Given a data point p in a training set, the *informative data points* of p are its nearest neighbors from the other class. A set of informative data points is a *border*.

Basically, this definition follows either Duch's definition of border [3] or Foody's definition of border [5].

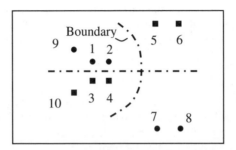

Fig. 1. Identification of border in a synthesized training set

Example 1. Given a labeled (circles and squares) synthesized binary training set with 10 data points, as shown in Figure 1, we use the BI method to identify its border. For each circle point, we find its informative data points. As a result, all informative data points of the circle class is $B_c = \{3, 4\}$. Similarly, all informative data points of the square class is $B_s = \{1, 2\}$. The border $B = B_c \cup B_s = \{1, 2, 3, 4\}$.

However, as shown in Figure 1, a learned classifier built on B might have low performance for predicting data points 5, 6, 7, and 8. We observe that the resulting border does not contain the data points 5 and 7. No boundary between 2 and 5 or 4 and 7 can be easily learned. The data at 5 and 6 or 7 and 8 are far from the others.

3 Full Border Identification

We avoid the limitations of the current BI method by introducing the concept of a *full border*, which reflects our observation as follows.

3.1 Full Border

In Figure 1, we consider how 9 and 10 are close to the border. The data point at 1 on the border is the nearest point to 9. They are both in the circle class. Similarly, 3 on the border is the nearest point to 10. They are both in the square class.

Definition 2. A data point is *redundant* iff it is not on the identified border and is nearest to an informative data point with the same class label from the border.

As we can see, in Figure 1, the points 9 and 10 are two redundant data points while the points 5, 6, 7, 8 are neither informative data points nor redundant ones. For the points 5, 6, 7, and 8, we need to define a new border among these data points for learning the hyperplane. We formalize this case by the following definitions.

Definition 3. A border identified by the BI method is defined as a *near* border. The border which cannot be directly identified by the BI method is called a *far* border.

The simple definition of far border may allow developing a proper method to identify far borders. In practice, far borders in this paper can be defined by Example 2.

Example 2. Given the synthesized training set as shown in Figure 1, redundant data points 9 and 10 can be removed according to the near border $B_n = \{1, 2, 3, 4\}$. The remaining data points are neither the part of a border nor redundant data points. They are 5, 6, 7, and 8. As a result, the *far border* consisting of 5 and 7 can be effectively identified as informative data points of the border from the remaining data points. As a result $B = B_n \cup B_f = \{1, 2, 3, 4\} \cup \{5, 7\} = \{1, 2, 3, 4, 5, 7\}$.

3.1.1 Farther Border
A far border can be a farther border to another already extended one. The farther border can be identified as informative data points of the previously extended border by removing its corresponding redundant data points. This is a recursive process. Simply stated, farther borders are also far borders.

For example, as discussed before, suppose we obtain the extended border $B = \{1, 2, 3, 4, 5, 7\}$. After removing its redundant data points 6 and 8, the remainder is empty. It shows that we cannot find anymore farther borders in this case.

3.1.2 Multi-classes
In Example 2, we describe a method for identifying a full border on a binary domain. For multi-domains, a full border can be found in a pairwise way which is similar to the 1-1 strategy used in learning algorithm for multiclass applications [14].

Suppose we have a training set with c classes. B_{ij} is a border between the class i and the class j. We have $B = \bigcup_{i \neq j} B_{ij}, i, j = 0, \ldots, c$, where those B_{ij} are not necessarily exclusive from each other, i.e., sampling without replacement.

3.1.3 Optimal Border and Bias
A full border should be adequate for training and helps a learner build an optimal classifier. An optimal border is biased towards more informative data points than a narrow full border for building an optimal classifier.

Instead of Definition 1, the semantics of a border can be given as follows.

Definition 4. The semantic border is defined as an optimal border consisting of all the near and far borders.

3.2 Illustrations

On the first synthesized data set, as shown in the leftmost graph of Figure 2, BI with Radial kernel distance function [8], i.e., $e^{-d^2/2}$, where $d^2 = \sum \left(\dfrac{x_{ai} - x_{bi}}{\sigma_i} \right)^2$ for a

Mahalanobis distance by assuming the independences among variables, only identifies an incomplete border, as shown in the second graph, while a full border is identified by our new method BI_2 (see Section 4.1) in the third graph, i.e., those informative data points covered by ovals were not identified by BI. The rightmost graph also shows the result of BI_2 with Cosine, which is believed not to be optimal due to the sensitivity of translation for Cosine similarity [13]. However, on the second synthesized data for a complicated XOR problem, as shown in the leftmost graph of Figure 3, the BI algorithm with Cosine similarity can only find an incomplete border, as shown in the second graph, while BI_2 with Cosine shows its complete capability to identify a full border in the third graph. The rightmost graph also shows the result by BI_2 with Radial Kernel similarity.

Cosine has the natural normalization to the unit sphere [13] and more informative points obtained in class core [5]. Cosine metric is used in this paper for experimental verification of BI_2 although the case in the rightmost graph of Figure 2 is not ideal.

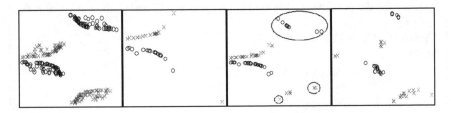

Fig. 2. BI and Radial Kernel. A synthesized data corresponding to Example 1.

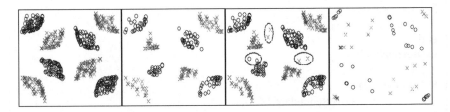

Fig. 3. BI and Cosine. A complicate XOR problem.

4 PBS Algorithm

We propose a new method called Border Identification in Two Stages, denoted as BI_2, for identifying a full border. Based on this BI_2 method, Progressive Border Sampling (PBS), described thereafter, progressively mines an optimal border.

4.1 BI₂

Figure 4 presents the BI_2 algorithm, which assumes two stages to identify a full border for a binary domain. It has three inputs: two categories C_i and C_j; their previously identified border B_{ij} between the class label i and the class label j. At the very beginning, B_{ij} is empty.

At the first stage, BI_2 generates the near border between classes C_i and C_j from Step 1 to Step 4 by generating the informative data points of either C_i from C_j or C_j from C_i. 1stNN(p, C_x) with x: i or j at Steps 1 and 2 searches for all the 1-nearest neighbors of p from C_x in terms of similarity metrics. At Steps 3 and 4, B_{ij}, C_i, and C_j will be updated. At the second stage from Step 5 to Step 6, BI_2 will identify far borders in the two classes, C_i and C_j, with the remaining data points, separately, by farBorder(). As a result, BI_2 simply assumes the *inertial* way without heuristics.

From Step 7 to Step 13, farBorder() in BI_2 initializes D' with the set of the remaining data points D and the identified far border B_f with empty. B_k is one of its inputs, which is denoted as the resulting border in the kth iteration between C_i and C_j at this point, and corresponds to B_{ij} from Step 5 or Step 6.

BI_2 algorithm
Input C_i, C_j: two classes
            B_{ij}: the previously identified border between C_i and C_j; $B_{ij} \cap C_i = \varnothing \wedge B_k$
$\cap C_j = \varnothing$
Update C_i, C_j, and B_{ij}
begin
1    $P_i = \bigcup_{p \in C_j} 1stNN(p, C_i)$

2    $P_j = \bigcup_{p \in C_i} 1stNN(p, C_j)$

3    $B_{ij} = B_{ij} \cup P_i$, $C_j = C_j - P_i$
4    $B_{ij} = B_{ij} \cup P_j$, $C_i = C_i - P_j$
5   farBorder(C_i, B_{ij})
6   farBorder(C_j, B_{ij}))
end
farBorder(D, B_k)
7    $D' = D; B_f = \varnothing;$
8   **while**(true)
9        $D' = removeRedundant(D', B_k)$
10   **if**($D' = \varnothing$) **break**
11       $B'_f = \bigcup_{p \in B_k} 1stNN(p, D')$

12       $B_k = B_k \cup B'_f; B_f = B_f \cup B'_f; D' = D' - B'_f$
13   $D = D - B_f$

Fig. 4. BI_2 algorithm

The while loop between Step 8 and Step 12 first removes all the redundant data points in the remaining database using removeRedundant() at Step 9 according to Theorem 1, i.e., $D' = \{x \mid \forall x \exists y, x \in D' \wedge y \in B_k \wedge y \in 1stNN(x, B_k) \wedge l(x) \neq l(y))$, where the $l(x)$ function returns the class label of x. As a result, those *tied* points are also informative data points, i.e., $l(x) = l(y')$. Step 10 is the only exit point of the while loop. It is activated on condition that D' is empty. A far border B'_f is identified at Step 11 by generating the informative data points of B_k from D'. At Step 13 after the exit at Step 11, the identified far borders B_f must be removed from the original D.

The main procedures in BI_2 are several iterations of the 1stNN() and removeRedundant() procedures in the while loop of farBorder(). The time complexity of BI_2 can be analyzed as follows.

Suppose $n = |D|$ and $n_i = |C_i|$, $n = \sum n_i$. The time complexity of 1stNN() for two classes C_i and C_j is always $O(fn_in_j)$ for its informative data points, where f is the number of features in a training set.

The time complexity of removeRedundant() has an upper bound of $O(fn_in_j)$. The time complexity of the second stage from Step 5 to Step 6 can be computed by $O(frn_in_j)$, where r is the depth of the iteration in the while loop of farBorder().

Therefore, BI_2 has a time complexity of $O(frn_in_j)$ for the binary case. Empirically, r is bounded by a small number ($\ll n$). For example, r in Anneal of UCI is 4.

Theorem 1. If p is identified by BI_2 as a redundant point with respect to any border B extended from the near border, then p is still redundant with respect to the full border.

Proof: Suppose p' is the nearest neighbor of p from B. We can prove that $\forall q$ from a class different from p's, we have $dist(p', p) < dist(p, q)$, where $dist()$ is the selected distance metric. Hence, p cannot be identified as an informative point later on.

4.2 PBS

Technically, Progressive Sampling (PS) [9] can maximize the accuracy of a model by learning on a small sample from the original large population. The standard PS [9] starts with a small sample and generates progressively larger ones until the model's accuracy no longer improves. The convergence detection is related to a learning curve, denoted as acc(n), created by a base learning algorithm, and represented by a curve plotting accuracy versus sample size.

The PBS algorithm is proposed to learn an optimal sample for building a model, which identifies a proper border. It utilizes the progressive learning technique [9], as mentioned above, to iteratively learn a small sample by identifying a full border until it converges to an optimal border.

As shown in Figure 5, at Step 1, getClassset(D) performs a scan on D to partition the data and put data points into exclusive classes. From Step 2 to Step 11, PBS learns an optimal sample by identifying local optimal borders between two classes in a binary way. B_{ij} at Step 3 is denoted as the local optimal border between C_i and C_j, and initialized with empty. C'_i and C'_j are the copies of C_i and C_j, respectively, and C_{ij} is their union used in the test at Step 7. At Step 6, PBS invokes BI_2 to identify a local full border in two stages given C_i and C_j, and the previously generated B_{ij}.

ValidateNBModel() in Step 7 validates B_{ij} by training a NB classifier on B_{ij} and testing it on C_{ij}. Acc describes a learning curve by recording the results of validation with accuracy.

At Step 8, IsConvergence() is used for convergence detection given the current point k and the history of validation in Acc. Its analysis and design are described in Section 4.3. The local optimal border is defined with the previously generated B_{ij} at Step 9 if convergence occurs. Otherwise, the current B_{ij} is kept at Step 10. At Step 11, we obtain an optimal sample B by performing the union of all the local optimal borders B_{ij}.

Because the time complexity of BI_2 is $O(frn_in_j)$ (see Section 4.1), the time complexity of PBS can be obtained in a straightforward manner by sum of all $O(frn_in_j)$, i.e., $\sum_{i \neq j}(frtn_in_j) = frt(\sum n_in_j - (n_1^2+...+n_c^2)) \leq frt(n^2 - n) = O(frtn^2)$, $(n_1^2+...+n_c^2 \geq n)$, where r is the maximum depth of iteration in the second stage of BI_2 and t is the maximum number of tries in the loop of Step 5 for all local optimal borders in PBS.

The value of t depends on the convergence detection. According to the method defined for convergence at Step 8, empirically, PBS always converges to an optimal border with a small number of tries. The average number of tries in the given benchmarks datasets from UCI is 4 while the maximum number of tries in PBS is never more than 6 by assuming the inertial way of BI_2 for the resulting sample.

```
PBS algorithm
Input    D: a sample for training with c classes
Output B
begin
1    B = ∅; C = getClassset(D), C = {Cᵢ | i = 0, ..., c}
2    for ∀i, j, where i < j, Cᵢ ≠ ∅, and Cⱼ ≠ ∅
3        Bᵢⱼ = ∅, C'ᵢ = Cᵢ, C'ⱼ = Cⱼ; Cᵢⱼ = Cᵢ ∪ Cⱼ
4        Acc[k] = 0, k = 0, 1, ..., K, K = 100
5        while(true)
6            BI₂(C'ᵢ, C'ⱼ, Bᵢⱼ)
7            Acc[k]=ValidateNBModel(Bᵢⱼ, Cᵢⱼ)
8            if(IsConvergence(k, Acc))
9                Bᵢⱼ = old; break;
10           old = Bᵢⱼ, k++
11       B = B ∪ Bᵢⱼ
12   return B
end
```

Fig. 5. PBS algorithm

4.3 Convergence Detection

A base learning algorithm is needed for building a learning curve in Step 8 as shown in Figure 5. Naïve Bayes (NB) has a number of advantages and has been used for sampling [6]. We use NB with Gaussian estimator (GNB) instead of NB with Maximum Likelihood estimator (MNB) [8] because GNB is more efficient than MNB.

PBS intends to effectively manipulate the progress of the learning curve of Naïve Bayes, which is a linear machine [4][8]. Furthermore, this adaptive learning curve has been observed as shown for PBS on the Letter dataset in the right graph of Figure 6,

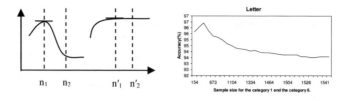

Fig. 6. The rule for convergence detection

and shown for two general fashions in the left graph of Figure 6, and it is different from the traditional learning curve obtained with the power law [6][9].

In IsConvergence() at Step 8 of Figure 5, we define a rule with two points in a learning curve for convergence detection. That is, $Acc[n_2] - Acc[n_1] \leq 0$. For example, in Figure 6, n_2 and n'_2 are two convergent points corresponding to two learning curves.

5 Experiments

We conducted experiments on 30 benchmark datasets from UCI [1]. The characteristics of these datasets are described in Table 1, where the columns are the names of the datasets, the number of attributes and classes(#attr/cl), the number of instances (#ins), the maximum number of tries (t) for border identification between two classes and the maximum depth (r) of iteration of far borders, the number of data points selected by PBS (#PBS), and the percent (%) of data selected by PBS over the overall number of instances (the ratio of #PBS over #ins). A small fraction of #PBS

Table 1. The characteristics of 30 benchmark datasets from UCI

Datasets	#attr/cl	#ins	t/r	#PBS	%	Datasets	#attr/cl	#ins	t/r	#PBS	%
Anneal	39/5	898	3/4	418	46.55	Labor	17/2	57	3/1	33	57.89
Audiology	70/24	226	2/2	211	93.36	Letter	17/26	20000	5/2	18540	92.70
Autos	26/6	205	3/3	187	91.22	Lymph	19/4	148	3/2	121	81.76
Balance-s	5/3	625	3/1	215	34.40	Mushroom	23/2	8124	3/1	1220	15.02
Breast-w	10/2	699	3/2	257	36.77	P-tumor	18/21	339	3/3	326	96.17
Colic	23/2	368	3/2	257	69.84	Segment	20/7	2310	3/2	1343	58.14
Credit-a	16/2	690	3/2	452	65.51	Sick	30/2	3772	3/3	766	20.31
Diabetes	9/2	768	6/2	574	74.74	Sonar	61/2	208	4/2	174	83.65
Glass	10/6	214	3/3	177	82.71	Soybean	36/18	683	2/2	593	86.82
Heart-s	14/2	270	3/3	200	74.07	Splice	62/3	3190	4/2	2847	89.25
Hepatitis	20/2	155	3/2	79	50.97	Vehicle	19/4	846	4/2	707	83.57
Hypothyroid	30/4	3772	4/4	548	14.53	Vote	17/2	435	4/1	181	41.61
Ionosphere	35/2	351	6/3	275	78.35	Vowel	14/11	990	3/2	970	97.98
Iris	5/3	150	3/2	40	26.67	Waveform	41/3	5000	4/3	4283	85.66
Kr-vs-kp	37/2	3196	4/2	2440	76.35	Zoo	18/7	101	21	58	57.43
Avg.									3/2		65.47

over #ins is preferable. For instance, Mushroom is reduced to 15.02%. As a result, PBS reaches convergence in the 30 benchmarks of UCI with a maximal value of t = 6 for Diabetes dataset and a minimal value of t = 2 for Audiology dataset. The depth of iteration for far borders reaches a maximum of 4 in the Anneal dataset and a minimum of 1 in the Mushroom dataset, etc. The averages are shown at the bottom.

We compared the performance of Naïve Bayes (NB), Support Vector Machine (SVM)[10], and Decision Tree (C4.5)[11], built on optimal borders produced by PBS (PBS), on full training sets (Full), and on simple traditional borders produced by traditional BI (BI), which is set with cosine metric and width 1 without loss of its generality while other metrics for BI do not show their merits. We use Weka's implementation [16] with default settings, e.g., NB with Gaussian estimator, SVM with polynomial of 1 for kernel function and constant C of 1 for soft margins, and C4.5 with no reduced error pruning and no C4.5 pruning and no Laplace smoothing.

In Figure 7, we summarize the results obtained for the analysis of time complexity (a) with respect to PBS and BI, and sample sizes (b) with respect to PBS, Full, BI, and the size of far borders (Far) by PBS, in each fold of 10CV. It is shown that PBS is never 5 times slower than BI on average. The sample size of PBS never is 3 times larger than that of BI, where 30 percent of the border points by PBS are far borders on average. For instance, in Mushroom, only 1143 points with 5 far border points are identified by PBS in 168 seconds for modeling as compared with 7311 points by Full.

The paired t-test with 95% confidence level by resampling in 10CV is applied between PBS and Full, and BI. In Table 2, in a small column in front of each result, 'w' and 'l' denote that PBS wins and loses, respectively, against Full and BI while an empty space represents a draw.

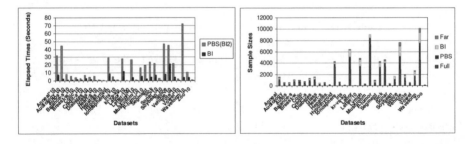

Fig. 7. (a) The scaled elapsed times and (b) sample sizes of PBS, Full and BI

In Hypothyroid, PBS produces a low accuracy for NB while PBS is more successful for nonlinear classifiers, e.g., C4.5. It can be explained that the optimal boundary of NB by PBS leads to a lower accuracy than that built on full datasets because NB learner simply ignores the minor class for high accuracy on datasets with high imbalanced classes. The accuracy metric might not be a proper measure for evaluation on imbalanced datasets while the F-measure, G-Mean, or AUC [7] have been used for evaluation of models on imbalanced domains. We calculate the AUC values for the three learned classifiers corresponding to PBS and Full on Hypothyroid, respectively: 0.9225/(l)0.9387(NB); 0.8241/(w)0.7036(SVM); 0.9618/0.9513(C4.5). According to the AUC values, PBS improves SVM and resembles Full for C4.5 while it only slightly degrades the performance of NB. On the other hand, in Hypothyroid, the size of the optimal border by PBS is 462 with 164 informative data points identified on far borders as compared with 3394 points in the full training set while the size of border by BI is only 291. However, the performance of the classifiers built by BI is much poorer than that built by PBS.

Table 2. The performance (acc) of NB, SVM, and C4.5 built by PBS, Full, BI

datasets	NB			SVM			C4.5		
	PBS	Full	BI	PBS	Full	BI	PBS	Full	BI
Anneal	86.81	86.42 |w|	82.51	95.66 |1	96.94 |w|	87.30	98.33	98.55 |w|	95.32
Audiology	72.35	71.90	73.69	80.71	80.72	80.28	75.39	76.08	74.96
Autos	53.00	54.90	51.49	69.55	69.60	68.31	81.65	83.14 |w|	75.79
Balance-s	89.28	90.63	87.93	87.92 |w|	86.56	87.43	77.69 |1	79.61 |w|	74.66
Breast-w	96.28	96.07	96.36	96.71	96.71	96.50	93.49	94.06	93.06
Colic	79.73	78.76	79.33	81.54	82.20 |w|	77.32	80.30	82.06	79.50
Credit-a	80.29 |w|	77.61 |1	81.67	85.14	84.64 |w|	84.13	80.87	82.46	78.77
Diabetes	74.29	75.26	72.27	76.11	76.70 |w|	73.77	71.56	73.84 |w|	65.24
Glass	54.23 |w|	46.99	51.93	55.35	58.32 |w|	50.89	68.68	69.58	65.63
Heart-s	85.00 |w|	83.33	83.70	82.78	83.89	81.30	74.63	75.37	74.63
Hepatitis	85.08	83.19	85.40	83.15	84.54 |w|	78.27	77.33	78.54	70.65
Hypothyroid	70.76 |1	95.32 |w|	45.27	84.40 |1	93.64 |w|	47.77	94.96 |1	99.54 |w|	92.14
Ionosphere	83.50	82.63	84.21	88.03	88.18 |w|	83.76	90.48	89.90 |w|	87.46
Iris	94.33	95.00	94.33	92.33 |1	96.67	89.67	93.33	95.00	93.00
Kr-vs-kp	93.13 |w|	87.81 |w|	92.68	96.07	95.90	96.23	99.34	99.41	99.30
Labor	91.17	93.83	89.50	89.67	93.83 |w|	83.33	79.67	81.50	77.33
Letter	64.46 |w|	64.02	64.60	82.25	82.29	82.26	87.84	88.05	87.96
Lymph	82.43	82.79	83.10	87.17	86.86	88.21	79.45 |w|	74.12 |w|	73.33
Mushroom	98.18 |w|	95.78	97.94	99.56 |1	100.0 |w|	98.72	99.97	100.0 |w|	99.78
P-tumor	49.71	50.00	49.71	47.50	48.24 |w|	46.17	42.05	43.37	42.49
Segment	79.48 |1	80.24 |1	81.93	92.49	92.86 |w|	91.88	95.24 |1	96.73	95.48
Sick	94.55 |w|	92.74 |w|	90.26	95.77 |w|	93.88 |w|	87.08	95.68 |1	98.79 |w|	90.51
Sonar	69.01	68.81	74.49	81.01	78.15 |w|	76.39	75.02	76.95	73.52
Soybean	92.97	92.90	92.89	93.41	93.41	93.41	90.92	90.63	90.84
Splice	95.61 |w|	95.44 |1	95.99	93.34	93.40	93.12	92.49	92.57	92.32
Vehicle	46.40	45.32 |1	49.17	73.35 |1	74.59	72.11	72.64	71.87	70.50
Vote	93.57 |w|	90.23	94.25	95.74	95.74 |w|	94.59	95.74	95.85 |w|	94.14
Vowel	63.48	63.59	63.54	70.25	69.85	69.90	80.15 |1	82.22	80.35
Waveform	79.75 |1	79.97	79.77	86.37	86.48	86.42	74.84	75.12	74.71
Zoo	95.50	95.05	95.50	96.00	96.00	95.00	93.00	93.50	92.50
Average	79.81	79.88	78.85	84.64	85.36	81.38	83.76	84.61	81.86
t-test		9\18\3	4\22\4		2\23\5	15\15\0		1\24\5	10\20\0

In summary, PBS improves NB in most cases, e.g., non-class imbalanced domains, while PBS with the inertial way of BI_2 degrades SVM, somewhat, and C4.5 for accuracy in some cases as compared to the modeling on the full training sets in 10CV. Furthermore, PBS improves the traditional BI methods overall, although PBS generally produces somewhat larger samples than BI (1.5 times on average). The results for the t-test on the 30 datasets are shown at the bottom of Table 2, where w\ \l denote win\draw\lose for PBS in each case. These results confirm our analysis.

6 Conclusion and Future Work

In practice, all labeled training sets contain a latent border. The semantic border can be defined as an optimal border consisting of all near and far borders. Our proposed algorithm, the Progressive Border Sampling technique can progressively learn optimal samples by avoiding the limitation of the traditional Border Identification (BI) method. One of the main advantages of PBS is shown that it can reduce training sets more effectively with an acceptable learning cost and no loss of performance than the traditional BI can. Our experimental results on 30 benchmarks from the UCI repository show that PBS helps classifiers build models similar to those built on full training sets in most cases (87 for win or draw versus 13 for lose) and overwhelmingly outperforms the traditional BI technique for the reduction of training sets.

Future work will focus on any improvement of the potential scalability of this quadratic PBS for sample selection on large datasets by using Monte Carlo integration [12], and evaluation of strength of Radial kernel function or other metrics for PBS.

References

[1] Bay, S.D.: The UCI KDD archive (1999), http://kdd.ics.-uci.edu
[2] Cohn, D., Ghahramani, Z., Jordan, M.: Active learning with statistical models. Journal of Artificial Intelligence Research 4, 129–145 (1996)
[3] Duch, W.: Similarity based methods: a general framework for classification, approximation and association. Control and Cybernetics 29(4), 937–968 (2000)
[4] Duda, R.O., Hart, P.E.: Pattern Classification and Scene Analysis. Wiley Intersience, Chichester (2000)
[5] Foody, G.M.: Issues in Training Set Selection and Refinement for Classification by a Feedforward Neural Network. In: Proceedings of IEEE International Geoscience and Remote Sensing Symposium. IGARSS 1998, Seattle, WA, USA, vol. 1, pp. 409–411 (1998)
[6] John, G., Langley, P.: Static versus dynamic sampling for data mining. In: Proceedings of the Second International Conference on Knowledge Discovery and Data Mining, pp. 367–370. AAAI Press, Menlo Park (1996)
[7] Kubat, M., Matwin, S.: Addressing the Curse of Imbalanced Training Sets: One-Sided Selection. In: Proc. 14th International Conference on Machine Learning (1997)
[8] Mitchell, T.: Machine Learning. McGraw-Hill Companies, Inc., New York (1997)
[9] Provost, F., Jensen, D., Oates, T.: Efficient Progressive Sampling. In: KDD 1999 (1999)
[10] Platt, J.: Fast training of support vector machines using sequential minimal optimization. In: Scholkopf, B., Burges, C., Smola, A. (eds.) Advances in kernel methods - support vector learning, MIT Press, Cambridge (1998)

[11] Quinlan, J.R.: C4.5: Programs for Machine Learning. Morgan Kaufmann, San Mateo (1993)

[12] Press, W.H., Farrar, G.R.: Recursive Stratified Sampling for Multidimensional Monte Carlo Integration. Computers in Physics 4, 190–195 (1990)

[13] Strehl, A., Ghosh, J.: Value-based customer grouping from large retail data-sets. In: Proc. SPIE Conference on Data Mining and Knowledge Discovery, Orlando, April 2000, vol. 4057, pp. 33–42 (2000)

[14] Sulzmann, J., Fürnkranz, J., Hüllermeier, E.: On Pairwise Naive Bayes Classifiers. In: Kok, J.N., Koronacki, J., Lopez de Mantaras, R., Matwin, S., Mladenič, D., Skowron, A. (eds.) ECML 2007. LNCS (LNAI), vol. 4701, pp. 658–665. Springer, Heidelberg (2007)

[15] Weiss, G.M., Provost, F.: Learning when training data are costly: the effect of class distribution on tree induction. Journal of Artificial Intelligence Research 19, 315–354 (2003)

[16] WEKA Software, v3.5.2. University of Waikato, http://www.cs.waikato.ac.nz/ml/-weka/index/datasets.html

Choosing Best Algorithm Combinations for Speech Processing Tasks in Machine Learning Using MARF

Serguei A. Mokhov

SGW, EV7.139-2
Department of Computer Science and Software Engineering
Faculty of Engineering and Computer Science
Concordia University, Montréal, Québec, Canada
mokhov@cse.concordia.ca

Abstract. This work reports experimental results in various speech processing tasks using an application based on the Modular Audio Recognition Framework (MARF) in terms of the best of the available algorithm configurations for each particular task. This study focuses on the tasks of identification of speakers' as of their gender and accent vs. who they are through machine learning. This work significantly complements a preceding statistical study undertaken only for the text-independent speaker identification.

1 Introduction

Problem Statement. The statistics of the recognition accuracy for the text-independent speaker identification task have been reasonably covered in [1,2,3] in order to select the best combination of the preprocessing, feature extraction, and classification algorithms in the MARF's testbed application, `SpeakerIdentApp`. Those studies focus on the identification *who* the speakers are and provide the best configuration of the implemented algorithms for that purpose. Some further experiments show that the best combination of available algorithms in the pattern recognition pipeline for speaker identification is not necessarily the best when tasked to focus on the gender, spoken accent, or other attributes.

Proposed Solution. We adapt `SpeakerIdentApp` of MARF to treat its speakers' voice utterances database and retrain and test on it for each mentioned task and gather statistics for analysis in a consistent manner using the same training and testing voice sample set data as for the speaker identification task. We adapt the database metadata to suit each particular task as we go with no changes to the MARF's or `SpeakerIdentApp`'s code base.

Organization. The article is organized as follows: we briefly introduce MARF and `SpeakerIdentApp` for the unaware reader, their configuration options, capabilities, the pattern recognition pipeline, and some of the implemented algorithms used in the experimentation and testing. Then, we go over the methodology of the experiments and summarize the results, which are followed by the discussion and some concluding remarks as well as future work on the project.

S. Bergler (Ed.): Canadian AI 2008, LNAI 5032, pp. 216–221, 2008.
© Springer-Verlag Berlin Heidelberg 2008

2 Background

MARF is an open-source collection of pattern recognition APIs and their implementation for (un)supervised machine learning and classification written in Java [1,2,3,4] by the author and collaborators. It acts as a testbed to verify common algorithms found in literature as well as novel ones for the sample loading, preprocessing, feature extraction, training and classification stages. One of the goals and design approaches of MARF is to provide scientists with a tool for comparison of the algorithms in a homogeneous environment and allow for the dynamic module selection based on the configuration options supplied by applications. Over the course of years MARF accumulated a fair number of implementations for each of the pipeline stages allowing reasonably comprehensive comparative studies of *algorithm combinations*, studying their behavior and other properties when used for pattern recognition tasks. MARF is also designed to be very configurable while keeping the generality and some sane default settings to run "off-the-shelf" well. MARF, its derivatives, and applications were also used beyond audio processing tasks due to the generality of the design and implementation in [5,6,7] and several other unpublished or in-progress works.

Pattern Recognition Pipeline. The complete design and implementation of the pattern recognition pipeline in MARF has been specified at length in [2,4]. Its discussion here is trimmed due to the shortage of the alloted space; please refer to the referenced resources for the complete description. Generally, the whole pattern recognition process starts by loading a sample (e.g. an audio recording in a wave form or a text file), preprocessing it (e.g. normalization and filtering out noisy and "silent" data), then extracting the most prominent features, and, finally either training the system such that it learns a new set of features of a given subject or actually classifies what/who the subject is. The outcome of training is either a collection of some form of feature vectors or their mean or median clusters, which are stored per every learned subject. The outcome of classification is a 32-bit unique integer indicating who/what the subject the system believes is.

Algorithms. MARF has an actual implementation of the framework's API in a number of algorithms to demonstrate its abilities in various pipeline stages and modules. There are a number of modules that are under the process of implementation or porting from other project for comparative studies that did not make it to this work at the time of its writing. The below is an incomplete summary of implemented algorithms with a very brief description: 1. Fast Fourier transform (FFT), used in FFT-based filtering as well as feature extraction [8]. 2. Linear predictive coding (LPC) used in feature extraction. 3. Various distance classifiers (Chebyshev, Euclidean, Minkowski [9], Mahalanobis [10], Diff (internally developed), and Hamming [11]). 4. Cosine similarity measure [12,13], which was thoroughly discussed in [14] and often produces the best accuracy in this work in many configurations (see further). 5. A number of math-related tools, for matrix and vector processing, including complex numbers matrix and vector operations, and statistical estimators used in smoothing of sparse matrices (e.g. in probabilistic matrices or Mahalanobis distance's covariance matrix). All these are needed for MARF to be self-contained.

`SpeakerIdentApp`'s **Options.** The list of application's options is quite comprehensive. The majority of them are usually used in the "all-out" exhaustive testing using the `testing.sh` script that comes with the application (it can be customized to the needed setup). Due to the lack of space, the options are not described completely; please refer to the cited resources [2,4,3] for more complete description. Here we list some of the options to better understand the subsequent results (with irrelevant options suppressed): Preprocessing: 1. -silence – remove silence (can be combined with many others); 2. -noise – remove noise (can be combined with many others); 3. -raw – no preprocessing; 4. -norm – just normalization, no filtering; 5. -low – low-pass FFT filter; 6. -high – high-pass FFT filter; 7. -boost – high-frequency-boost FFT preprocessor; 8. -band – band-pass FFT filter; 9. -bandstop – band-stop FFT filter; 10. -endp – endpointing. Feature Extraction: 1. -lpc – LPC; 2. -fft – FFT; 3. -minmax – Min/Max Amplitudes; 4. -randfe – random feature extraction; 5. -aggr – aggregated FFT+LPC feature extraction. Classification: 1. -cheb – Chebyshev Distance; 2. -eucl – Euclidean Distance; 3. -mink – Minkowski Distance; 4. -diff – Diff-Distance; 5. -randcl – random classification; 6. -hamming – Hamming Distance; 7. -cos – Cosine Similarity Measure.

Module Parameters. All modules were tested at their default parameters (that can also be varied by the application if desired, but due to the large number of such variations, there is no statistics on this provided here). The defaults were picked mostly empirically and/or based on the related literature. Below is a brief the summary of the default parameters used for each concrete module (we do not list random number generator-based modules as those are there as a baseline[1] and are not very exciting otherwise; we also do not list some of the modules that did not participate in the study): 1. the default quality of the recorded wave files used in the experiments is 8000 Hz, mono, 2 bytes per frequency sample, PCM-encoded. This sampling rate resembles phone conversations where one domain of the applications of this work is used; 2. LPC – has 20 poles producing a vector of 20 features while using a 128-element window; 3. FFT – does 1024-based FFT analysis (512 features); 4. `MinMaxAmplitudes` – extracts 50 smallest and 50 largest amplitudes (100 features); 5. `MinkowskiDistance` – has a default of Minkowski factor $r = 4$; 6. `FeatureExtractionAggregator` – concatenates the default processing of FFT and LPC (532 features); 7. `DiffDistance` – has a default allowed error of 0.0001 and a distance factor of 1.0; 8. `HammingDistance` – has a default allowed error of 0.01 and a lenient double comparison mode.

3   Experiments, Results, and Analysis

The `SpeakerIdentApp` application collects statistics on the amount of successful vs. unsuccessful guesses. While testing can be done exhaustively through a script for all possible available configurations when analyzing wave forms of the voice sample set, we select a subset of the configurations for this work that are most stable and fast. The classification results are produced after the system models were trained on 319 voice samples of 28 adult speakers and tested on the "unseen" 32 testing samples. Each

---

[1] The baseline is set by the random preprocessing, feature extraction, and classification combination, which results in $0.5 \cdot 3 = 12.5\%$ probability, but we usually look at 60% and higher.

Table 1. Speaker Identification   **Table 2.** Gender Identification   **Table 3.** Accent Identification

Configuration	Good	Bad	%
-silence -bandstop -aggr -cos	29	3	90.62
-silence -bandstop -fft -cos	29	3	90.62
-bandstop -fft -cos	28	4	87.50
-silence -noise -bandstop -fft -cos	28	4	87.50
-silence -low -aggr -cos	28	4	87.50
-silence -noise -norm -aggr -cos	28	4	87.50
-silence -low -fft -cos	28	4	87.50
-silence -noise -norm -fft -cos	28	4	87.50
-silence -noise -low -aggr -cos	28	4	87.50
-silence -noise -low -fft -cos	28	4	87.50
-bandstop -aggr -cos	28	4	87.50
-norm -fft -cos	28	4	87.50
-silence -raw -aggr -cos	28	4	87.50
-silence -noise -raw -aggr -cos	28	4	87.50
-norm -aggr -cos	28	4	87.50
-silence -noise -bandstop -aggr -cos	28	4	87.50
-silence -norm -fft -cos	27	5	84.38
-silence -norm -aggr -cos	27	5	84.38
-low -fft -cos	27	5	84.38
-noise -bandstop -aggr -cos	27	5	84.38

Configuration	Good	Bad	%
-noise -high -aggr -mink	26	6	81.25
-silence -noise -band -aggr -cheb	26	6	81.25
-silence -noise -band -lpc -cos	26	6	81.25
-silence -noise -band -fft -cheb	26	6	81.25
-noise -bandstop -fft -diff	26	6	81.25
-noise -bandstop -fft -cheb	26	6	81.25
-silence -band -lpc -cos	25	7	78.12
-silence -noise -bandstop -fft -diff	25	7	78.12
-noise -endp -lpc -eucl	25	7	78.12
-silence -noise -endp -lpc -cheb	25	7	78.12
-noise -endp -lpc -diff	25	7	78.12
-silence -noise -band -fft -eucl	25	7	78.12
-silence -noise -band -aggr -diff	25	7	78.12
-silence -noise -bandstop -fft -cheb	25	7	78.12
-silence -noise -band -fft -diff	25	7	78.12
-noise -bandstop -aggr -cheb	25	7	78.12
-noise -band -aggr -cheb	24	8	75
-noise -high -fft -eucl	24	8	75
-noise -high -lpc -cos	24	8	75

Configuration	Good	Bad	%
-silence -endp -lpc -cheb	24	8	75
-bandstop -fft -cos	23	9	71.88
-low -aggr -cos	23	9	71.88
-noise -norm -aggr -cos	23	9	71.88
-noise -low -aggr -cos	23	9	71.88
-noise -bandstop -aggr -cos	22	10	68.75
-noise -low -fft -cos	22	10	68.75
-noise -bandstop -fft -cos	22	10	68.75
-norm -aggr -cos	22	10	68.75
-endp -lpc -cheb	21	11	65.62
-silence -noise -low -aggr -cos	21	11	65.62
-low -fft -cos	21	11	65.62
-noise -norm -fft -cos	21	11	65.62
-silence -bandstop -aggr -cos	20	12	62.5
-silence -low -aggr -cos	20	12	62.5
-silence -noise -norm -aggr -cos	20	12	62.5
-silence -bandstop -fft -cos	20	12	62.5
-silence -low -fft -cos	20	12	62.5
-silence -noise -norm -fft -cos	20	12	62.5
-silence -noise -low -fft -cos	20	12	62.5

option constitutes a parameter to the application that selects appropriate algorithms at run-time. The resulting tables are sorted by the accuracy of recognition (descending). We rely on the same setup of MARF and SpeakerIdentApp as for the classical speaker identification task [1,2,3]. What we do differently is changing the meaning of the entries in the database. The usual format of the database entry is a tuple $(ID, name, trainingsamples, testingsamples)$, where $ID, name$ correspond to individual speakers followed by disjoint sets of the training and testing files attributed to the speakers. ID is what the system learns when trained and produces as a classification output.

Speaker Identification. In Table 1 are excerpts of the results for speaker identification from [3] for comparative reference. Those experiments show that most accurate configurations involved the cosine similarity measure classifier. It's been shown that the silence gap removal generally also helps to extract more distinct features of individual speakers, and 512 features of FFT contributed most to the top results by capturing the largest spectrum of voice frequencies ideal for cosine similarity. Band-stop filter, as opposed to just the low-pass filter contributed to better accuracy by preserving low and high frequencies, which, depending on the gender, provide more discriminative power.

Gender Identification. For this task we change the meaning of the ID and $name$ fields to be the gender. We merge the training set filenames of each speaker of the particular gender under one training set. Similarly we do for the testing samples. Having the new database entries made as described, we use the same training and testing set files, but grouped differently while the rest of the system's setup remains the same. We define several gender categories: female, male, group (when more than one speaker is in a voice sample at the same time). In Table 2 are the top results for gender identification. We see that Minkowski, Chebyshev, and Diff distance classifiers, along with the cosine similarity measure (less prominent than in speaker identification), followed by other distance classifiers perform better than others. They are mostly combined with either FFT-based band-pass, band-stop, or high-pass filters for the preprocessing. The latter signifies the high frequencies (retained by the high-pass or band-stop filters) as well as mid-range frequencies keep distinguishing features for gender identification. The high frequencies generally cover the female speakers, and the mid-range and low (low frequencies are retained by the band-stop filter) cover the male speakers. The noise and silence removal contribute to the accuracy, as expected. The aggregator feature extractor concatenates the FFT and LPC features in one feature vector, so it generally influences the accuracy of the result to be at least as good as one of the two or better. Since gender identification is also frequency-bound, the corresponding feature extraction modules contributed to the top results. There is a near-top unique configuration of algorithms where noise removed (using the low-pass FFT filter) with endpointing, LPC, and Euclidean distance among the top contenders.

Accent Identification. To identify speakers' likely accent (when people speak English with an accent one can sometimes determine their place of origin due to typicality of accents of people from the same region) we perform similar alteration to the database entries as done for the gender identification, but grouped differently: *ID* and *name* now mean the accent, and the grouping of the training and testing samples is a union of all training samples of the people with a similar accent and union of all testing samples respectively. In the present experiment we do not distinguish between genders of the speakers of the same accent. We defined several broad accent categories from the available data set: English (native), Arabic, Chinese, Slavic, and Indian without finer regional subdivision. Accent identification top 20 accurate configurations are in Table 3. One can see the configurations yet again are not the same as for the speaker and gender identification tasks. The unique top contender configuration contains silence removal, endpointing, LPC, and Chebyshev distance. Similarly to the other tasks, frequency analysis algorithms for feature extraction, such as FFT and LPC (and their combination through the aggregator) contribute to the best results in top configurations. In general, the cosine similarity measure here was a more prominent classifier than others analogous to the speaker identification task and unlike gender identification. The overall accuracy for accent identification is fairly lower than for the previous two tasks, which may be due to the fact the group and individual speakers were put in the same accent category as well as there is no gender distinction. The low-pass and band-stop FFT filters seem to have contributed to the top results as well.

4   Conclusion

This study is pertinent because identification of various speaker attributes has applications of safety and national security, as well as conference assistance applications. The statistics tables presented here are incomplete in their coverage of all implemented algorithms as of this writing due to space limitations. Interested parties may contact the author for the complete data set of the resulting statistics (of about 1200+ runs) for each task. The source code is available on the web site. The framework and the application present a quick and cheap way for evaluation of algorithm implementations for accuracy, memory usage, and run-time performance in Java. It is a University research system; thus, it does not offer a commercial-grade quality results on the 8000 Hz mono samples (second to lowest vs. 44000 Hz CD quality), yet it can hint the researchers in the field where to concentrate their efforts more depending on the need.

Future Work. There is a vast TODO list found in the MARF's CVS repository [2], but more on the topic, the future work will focus on: 1. Specifying run-time and memory consumption statistics per module and per combination (these data is available, but are not produced in the usable form yet). 2. Emotion detection. 3. Analysis of the customized module parameters other than the presented defaults. 4. Who-vs-what identification. 5. Compilation of the measurements of the "second-best" [3] extracted from this work due to the space constraints. 6. Testing on a larger sample base of 15-20 minute 400 recordings from an online conference that provides the data in the proceedings [4].

References

1. Mokhov, S., Clement, I., Sinclair, S., Nicolacopoulos, D.: Modular Audio Recognition Framework. Department of Computer Science and Software Engineering, Concordia University, Montreal, Canada (2002-2003), http://marf.sf.net
2. The MARF Research and Development Group: Modular Audio Recognition Framework and Applications. SourceForge.net (2002-2008), http://marf.sf.net
3. Mokhov, S.A.: Experimental Results and Statistics in the Implementation of the Modular Audio Recognition Framework's API for Text-Independent Speaker Identification. In: Pending Acceptance at CCCT 2008 (2008), http://www.infocybereng.org/ccct2008i
4. Mokhov, S.A.: Introducing MARF: a Modular Audio Recognition Framework and its Applications for Scientific and Software Engineering Research. In: Proceedings of SCSS 2007/CISSE 2007, Springer, Heidelberg, Accepted for publication at CISSE 2007 (2007-2008), http://cisse2007.org
5. Mokhov, S.: On Design and Implementation of Distributed Modular Audio Recognition Framework: Requirements and Specification Design Document. Department of Computer Science and Software Engineering, Concordia University, Montreal, Canada (2006), http://marf.sf.net
6. Mokhov, S.A., Huynh, L.W., Li, J.: Managing Distributed MARF with SNMP. Concordia Institute for Information Systems Engineering, Concordia University, Montreal, Canada (2007), http://marf.sf.net
7. Mokhov, S.A.: Hardening Security in Scientific Distributed Demand-Driven and Pipelined Computing Systems. In: Pending Acceptance at SEC 2008 (2008)
8. Bernsee, S.M.: The DFT "à pied": Mastering The Fourier Transform in One Day. DSPdimension.com (1999-2005), http://www.dspdimension.com/data/html/dftapied.html
9. Abdi, H.: Distance. In: Salkind, N.J. (ed.) Encyclopedia of Measurement and Statistics, Sage, Thousand Oaks (CA) (2007)
10. Mahalanobis, P.: On the generalised distance in statistics. Proceedings of the National Institute of Science of India 12, 49–55 (1936), http://en.wikipedia.org/wiki/Mahalanobis_distance
11. Hamming, R.W.: Error Detecting and Error Correcting Codes. Bell System Technical Journal 26(2), 147–160 (1950), http://en.wikipedia.org/wiki/Hamming_distance
12. Garcia, E.: Cosine similarity and term weight tutorial (2006), http://www.miislita.com/information-retrieval-tutorial/cosine-similarity-tutorial.html
13. Kishore, A.: Similarity measure: Cosine similarity or euclidean distance or both (February 2007), http://semanticvoid.com/blog/2007/02/23/similarity-measure-cosine-similarity-or-euclidean-distance-or-both/
14. Khalifé, M.: Examining orthogonal concepts-based micro-classifiers and their correlations with noun-phrase coreference chains. Master's thesis, Concordia University, Montréal, Canada (2004)

Predicting User Preferences Via Similarity-Based Clustering

Mian Qin[1], Scott Buffett[2], and Michael W. Fleming[1]

[1] University of New Brunswick, Fredericton, NB, E3B 5A3
{l0i5r,mwf}@unb.ca
[2] National Research Council Canada, Fredericton, NB, E3B 9W4
Scott.Buffett@nrc.gc.ca

Abstract. This paper explores the idea of clustering partial preference relations as a means for agent prediction of users' preferences. Due to the high number of possible outcomes in a typical scenario, such as an automated negotiation session, elicitation techniques can provide only a sparse specification of a user's preferences. By clustering similar users together, we exploit the notion that people with common preferences over a given set of outcomes will likely have common interests over other outcomes. New preferences for a user can thus be predicted with a high degree of confidence by examining preferences of other users in the same cluster. Experiments on the MovieLens dataset show that preferences can be predicted independently with 70-80% accuracy. We also show how an error-correcting procedure can boost accuracy to as high as 98%.

1 Introduction

Before an agent can autonomously perform a task on behalf of a user, such as locating potential trading partners, searching for potential purchases, or negotiating the terms of a deal, a sufficient model of the user's preferences is needed. Since preference models for individual users are not usually available, preference elicitation techniques are used to extract information from the user. Typically this is done by querying the user about preferences for various possible outcomes, different attribute values, utilities or risk attitudes. While it would be ideal to query the user repeatedly until all preference information is known, this is typically infeasible or, at the very least, bothersome to the user, since the number of possible outcomes in most typical scenarios is too high. It is thus desirable to obtain sufficient information through a small number of queries, and to infer or predict new information based on this small amount of elicited information.

It has been shown by existing electronic commerce websites, such as amazon.com for example, that tracking and analyzing actions and choices of previous customers can be extremely effective in determining what may appeal to new customers, allowing a business to target consumers with particular items or products that have a high chance of piquing their interest. Similarly, we attempt to predict new preferences for a specific user by considering the preferences of previous users with similar preference models.

S. Bergler (Ed.): Canadian AI 2008, LNAI 5032, pp. 222–233, 2008.
© Springer-Verlag Berlin Heidelberg 2008

Technologies for doing this analysis and prediction are often based on collaborative filtering. Here, products to recommend to a user are typically determined by examining Likert scale ratings given by previous users. Products that are highly preferred by users with ratings similar to the new user are chosen for recommendation. Rather than only allowing ratings, we consider a richer model where users can specify binary preferences over the set of outcomes. This is useful for a number of reasons. First, ratings offer a limited amount of preference information. Typically a scale including only the integers from 1 to 5 is used, leaving just five levels of preference. As a result there will be "ties" for several pairs of outcomes, for which the user may often actually have a preference. Second, it can be very difficult for a user to rate objects when the domain of objects is constantly changing. For example, a user might rate a product as a "5" only to discover later that a more desirable product exists. Allowing users to specify that "item X is preferred over item Y" solves the issue of scale, and allows the user to always specify a preference where one exists, rather than requiring the user to give both the same rating when the utility for each is close. People also just find it more natural to choose which of two items is preferred, rather than attempt to place an item somewhere on a scale. Using this information, we then attempt to predict new preferences for a user.

To accomplish this, we construct partial preference relations for each user in the database, and explore the notion of clustering such partial preference relations as a means to identify groups of people with similar tastes. When a new user is encountered, he or she is classified into one of these clusters and new preferences are predicted based on preferences of those in the same cluster. We use conditional outcome preference networks (COP-networks) [6] as the representation for users' partial preference relations. These networks allow for a number of different preference specifications over varying types of domains, including single- or multi-attribute outcomes, and can be specified over single attribute values, sets of attribute values, complete objects or even sets of objects.

Clustering is done dynamically, to provide optimal information at any given time regarding the currently desired preference information. That is, if the agent needs to know which of A and B is most likely preferred by the user, it would be most useful to construct clusters in such a way that users within each cluster have a strong agreement on A and B. Finding that the new user belongs to one of these clusters will help give the agent a high degree of confidence in its prediction. To do this clustering quickly, a fast method of computing the distance between two partial preference relations is developed. Three different techniques for doing this dynamic clustering and preference prediction are developed and tested. Once the clustering techniques are used to generate a number of independent preference predictions, an error correction procedure is used to identify and eliminate cycles in the preference network.

The paper is organized as follows. Section 2 discusses the preference elicitation relation model that we consider, and formalizes the current problem being solved. The crux of the paper lies in Section 3 where we present our method for distance calculation, and outline the three techniques for clustering and preference prediction. Our procedure for considering all predicted preferences together to correct prediction errors is then outlined in Section 4. Section 5 gives details on experiments and results, while Section 6 discusses conclusions and related work and Section 7 outlines plans for future work.

2   Preference Elicitation and Prediction

Preference elicitation involves the process of extracting and determining preferences of a human user over a set of possible outcomes in a decision problem. Such processes are commonly executed by an autonomous agent with the intention of performing one or more tasks on behalf of the user, such as negotiation of purchases or service usage. Preference elicitation involves any or all of direct querying, observing activity/choices and inferring or predicting preferential information based on evidence obtained. The goal of preference elicitation is to determine a user's preference information in such a way as to optimize utility of the optimal strategy for solving the decision problem.

Such utility can be optimized if the agent can define the user's complete utility function over the domain of outcomes. This is typically not possible due to two major reasons: 1) people have difficulty specifying utilities for outcomes, even when queries are posed as standard gamble questions, and 2) a user can only be queried a small number of times before becoming overwhelmed and frustrated with the querying process. Therefore, only a small number of cognitively simple queries can typically be posed. The problem then is to determine a high number of preferences from the limited information obtained from the small number of queries. In this paper, we consider simple queries $q = (o_1, o_2)$, where (o_1, o_2) is a pair of outcomes, over which the user responds with the more preferred (or that neither is preferred). If the response is o_1, the fact that o_1 is preferred over o_2 is added to the preference set. Over time, this process will reveal a partial preference relation over the set of outcomes. A utility function can then be estimated to fit this partial relation. Once this utility function is deemed sufficient, the elicitation process can be terminated. Since it is difficult to determine a sufficient utility function based on a partial relation constructed solely from information directly gained from querying, it can be quite useful to attempt to predict other user preferences and add to the partial relation when there is sufficient evidence to do so. This is where our clustering technology comes in.

We consider the problem as follows. Let O be a set of outcomes, over which a number of users each have preferences and utility functions. In particular, user i has utility function $u_i : O \rightarrow \Re$, which induces a preference relation $\succeq_i$ such that $u_i(o) \geq u_i(o') \Leftrightarrow o \succeq_i o'$. Each user reveals a subset $\succeq_i^r$ of their preference relation, perhaps via utility elicitation or other means. Given a user i and outcomes o and o', where i has a preference over o and o' that has not been revealed, the goal is to determine whether $o \succeq_i o'$ or $o' \succeq_i o$ by examining other users j with preferences $\succeq_j^r$ similar to $\succeq_i^r$, and observing which of these two possibilities is typically the case. Such users are determined via the clustering and prediction methods presented in this paper.

3   Clustering of Partial Preferences

3.1   Utility Estimation

In order to model a user's preferences during the elicitation stage, we utilize a structure referred to as a *Conditional Outcome Preference Network (COP-network)*. The structure is a directed graph that represents preferences over the set of outcomes, where every outcome is represented by a vertex. For vertices v and v' in the graph representing outcomes o and o', respectively, if v is a proper ancestor of v' then o is preferred over o'. See Chen [5] for more details.

An example COP-network is shown in Figure 1. Each possible outcome o_i in the decision problem is represented by the vertex v_i in the graph. It is evident from this graph that outcome o_0 is preferred over outcome o_1 since v_0 is the parent of v_1. Outcome o_1 is preferred over outcome o_7 since v_1 is a proper ancestor of v_7. Neither of outcomes o_3 and o_6 is known to be preferred over the other since v_3 is neither an ancestor nor a descendant of v_6.

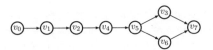

Fig. 1. An example COP-network

In addition to modeling the user's network of preferences, the COP-network can also be used to estimate a utility function over the set of outcomes. Given an initial partial utility assignment, including at least the most preferred outcome (utility 1) and the least preferred (utility 0), and the preferences defined in the COP-network, a utility function $\hat{u}$ over the entire set of outcomes is produced. This is done in such a way as to preserve the preference ordering specified by the COP-network. Specifically, let v and v' represent outcomes o and o'. If v is a proper ancestor of v', then $\hat{u}(o) > \hat{u}(o')$.

The method iteratively selects paths in the graphs containing outcomes for which a utility has not yet been assigned. Formally, let p be a path in the network with endpoints representing outcomes o_1 and o_n. This path is a candidate for selection if it is a longest path such that 1) $\hat{u}$ is known for o_1 and o_n, 2) $\hat{u}$ is unknown for all other outcomes represented by vertices on p, and 3) the assignment of utilities to such outcomes will not cause an inconsistency in the graph[1]. Once a suitable path p has been selected, the utility $\hat{u}$ is assigned for each outcome $o_1, o_2, \ldots o_n$ represented on p, decreasing from o_1 to o_n, by

$$\hat{u}(o_i) = \hat{u}(o_n) + \frac{(n - i)(\hat{u}(o_1) - \hat{u}(o_n))}{n - 1} \tag{1}$$

For example if p represented four outcomes with $\hat{u}(o_1) = 0.8$ and $\hat{u}(o_4) = 0.2$, then $\hat{u}(o_2)$ and $\hat{u}(o_3)$ would be assigned utilities of 0.6 and 0.4, respectively. The

---

[1] Refer to Chen [5] for more on ensuring consistency in path selection.

process of selecting paths and assigning utilities in this way continues until all outcomes are considered.

As the number of outcomes in a decision problem grows exponentially with the number of outcome attributes, COP-networks that consider all outcomes can become unmanageably large in practice. We therefore propose a factored utility approach. Here the set of attributes are partitioned in such a way that dependent attributes are considered together and independent attributes are considered separately. Several considerably smaller COP-networks can then be built, one for each dependent attribute group, giving the partial preference structure over attribute values, rather than over entire outcomes. If ever one wanted to determine which of two outcomes is preferred, then the approach for determining utility functions can applied to the COP-networks, giving utilities for attribute values. Weights for attribute utilities could then be determined by eliciting utilities for a small number of outcomes, yielding a utility function for complete outcomes.

3.2   Distance Computation

Since the clustering described in this paper is performed dynamically, a fast technique is needed for calculating the distance between two partial preference relations. For each preference relation, we use the COP-network-based utility estimation to produce a vector of estimated utilities over the set of outcomes. These vectors will be used to denote the co-ordinates of the preference relations in n-dimensional space, allowing for the Euclidean distance between any two to be computed. For a set of n items, this can be done using $O(n)$ computations, which is significantly faster than the $O(n^3)$ computations required by the probabilistic distance method [7] from the literature.

3.3   Clustering Techniques

Given partial preference relations for a set of users, distances between any two partial preference relations can be calculated as described above. Once distances between all pairs of relations are computed, Y-means clustering is performed. Y-means clustering is similar to the K-means algorithm, with a major difference. One drawback of the K-means algorithm is that the number k of clusters must be specified in advance, and the performance of the K-means algorithm greatly depends on the choice of the value of k. However, it is hard to find an optimal value for k. If the distribution of the data set is unknown, the best k is especially hard to obtain. The Y-means clustering method overcomes the problem by allowing the number of clusters to be adjusted during the clustering.

Clustering is used in this paper to help in the elicitation of users' preferences. Initially, all previously encountered users' preference relations are partitioned into clusters. When a new user is encountered, she will be classified into one of these existing clusters. Based on investigating the users' preferences in this particular cluster, general conclusions can be drawn. For example, consider a user for whom it is not known whether red or blue is preferred. Assume that she is assigned to cluster C_1, and in cluster C_1, 80% of users prefer red over blue. Thus, since the user agrees on many preferences shared by members of this group, the conclusion that she has a much higher probability of preferring red over blue can be drawn. This is only a simple example, but it gives a basic idea of how users' preferences can be estimated by performing clustering.

Different clustering methods can cause different results over the same data points. Various strategies for clustering partial preference relations and for inferring new preferences based on the set of clusters obtained have been tested. This section describes three different applications of the Y-means algorithm for clustering partial preference relations, and demonstrates the technique used for estimating preferences for each application.

Direct Prediction. The Direct Prediction method is the simplest of the three described in this paper. It consists of only one clustering process, where all partial preference relations are partitioned by the Y-means clustering method. Assume that the partial relations are grouped into n clusters. In order to determine which of outcomes o_i and o_j is preferred by a user u, the first step is to determine to which cluster u belongs. Based on u's known partial preferences, a COP-network can be constructed. As mentioned in Section 3.1, u's utility estimates for all outcomes are calculated by the COP-network, and these utilities compose a vector. In order to classify u into one of the clusters, the distances between u and the centroids of the n clusters are computed as the Euclidean distance. The user u belongs to the cluster for which the distance between u and the cluster's centroid is the smallest.

The second step is to predict preferences. Assume u is assigned to the mth cluster. For outcomes o_i and o_j, the average utility estimates are computed, by considering the estimates from all partial preference relations in this cluster. The confidence interval[2] for the average utility of outcome o_i (denoted by $ciu(o_i)$) is compared with the confidence interval for the average utility of outcome o_j (denoted by $ciu(o_j)$). If there is no overlap between $ciu(o_i)$ and $ciu(o_j)$, then the outcome with the higher average utility estimate is predicted to be preferred ($o_i \succ o_j$ or $o_j \succ o_i$). Otherwise, if there is an overlap between the confidence intervals, the preference between o_i and o_j is deemed to be unknown.

Pre-processing Prediction. The Pre-processing Prediction method is more complicated than the Direct Prediction method, and is composed of two clustering phases: cursory clustering and the Y-means clustering. At first, all partial preference relations are cursorily grouped into three large clusters according to whether (1) $o_i \succ o_j$, (2) $o_j \succ o_i$, or (3) neither $o_i \succ o_j$ nor $o_j \succ o_i$ in that particular relation. Each of these three clusters is then partitioned by the Y-means clustering method into sub-clusters. Once the sub-clusters are formed, the user u is classified in one of the sub-clusters. If she is classified in a sub-cluster that belongs to the first or second super-cluster, the relation between o_i and o_j is

---

[2] Confidence interval gives an estimated range of values which is likely to include an unknown population parameter, the estimated range being calculated from a given set of sample data.

predicted to be $o_i \succ o_j$ or $o_j \succ o_i$, respectively. However, if she is classified in a sub-cluster that belongs to the third super-cluster, we concede that the preference between o_i and o_j cannot be determined.

Post-processing Prediction. The Post-processing Prediction method is similar to the Pre-processing Prediction method; however, it works in a reverse fashion. It includes three clustering phases: the Y-means clustering method, cursory clustering, and the Y-means clustering method again. In the first step, all preference relations are partitioned into n clusters by the Y-means clustering method. A new user u is encountered, and, as before, we assume that u's unknown relation between two outcomes o_i and o_j is needed by an agent. The user is classified in one of the clusters formed in the previous stage by comparing the distances between u and each cluster's centroid. Assume that the user u belongs to the mth cluster. At the second step, partial preference relations in the mth cluster are cursorily clustered into three sub-clusters based on whether (1) $o_i \succ o_j$, (2) $o_j \succ o_i$, or (3) neither $o_i \succ o_j$ nor $o_j \succ o_i$. Once the three sub-clusters are built, each sub-cluster is partitioned again by the Y-means clustering method into k small sub-clusters, and u is classified again. Depending on the results of clustering, a conclusion on the relation between o_i and o_j is made. If u is classified in a small cluster that belongs to the first or second sub-cluster, the relation between o_i and o_j is predicted to be $o_i \succ o_j$ or $o_j \succ o_i$, respectively. However, if u is classified in a small cluster that belongs to the third sub-cluster, we concede that the preference between o_i and o_j cannot be determined.

4   Error Correction

When performing this type of clustering and preference prediction, there is bound to be a high number of errors. First of all, the clustering procedures may not work perfectly, due to the sparseness in known preferences. There is no guarantee that we will group a particular user with the n most similar users if we actually know very little about these users. Secondly, even when people are quite similar, they will not necessarily agree on everything, and may even deviate from the entire group on one item while agreeing on most others.

By considering all predicted preferences together, it is possible to correct many of these errors if a sufficient level of accuracy has been achieved. This is done by analyzing the preference network built based on these predicted preferences and identifying cycles in the graph. For every cycle found, there must be at least one error in the direction of the arcs that make up the cycle, as preferences are assumed to be transitive and thus acyclic. Consider the partial preference network in Figure 2. There are two cycles: ABCA and ADCA. At least one arc in each of these cycles (and thus the corresponding preference) runs in the incorrect direction. If we have confidence that a reasonably high number of preferences are correct, then it may be more likely that the one arc that the two cycles have in common, CA, is the culprit, than it would be for two distinct arcs (one from each cycle) to be the cause. If there are several other vertices v such that AvCA

Fig. 2. A partial preference network with two cycles

is a cycle, then it becomes less and less likely that every one of these arc pairs (Av, vC) contain an error, when the alternative is that CA is solely responsible. So the correction here would be to reverse CA.

The problem of identifying whether a graph has a cycle of a particular size is NP-complete, so identifying all cycles in a graph in general is computationally intractable. This is not the case, however, for what is needed in this particular graph. Consider the following theorem:

Theorem 1. *Let G be a directed graph where there exists one arc between every pair of vertices. For every cycle C in G greater than size 3, there exists a cycle C' such that the vertices in C' are a proper subset of the vertices in C.*

Proof: Let u and v be any non-adjacent vertices in C. Let p_{uv} be the arcs on the path from u to v in C, and let p_{vu} be the arcs on the path from v to u in C. If (u, v) is an arc in G, then $p_{vu} \cup \{(u, v)\}$ makes up a cycle, otherwise $p_{uv} \cup \{(v, u)\}$ makes up a cycle.

Thus to eliminate all cycles in a network where the preference has been predicted for any pair of outcomes, only the 3-cycles need to be analyzed and corrected. Once these are gone, no cycles can exist. Identifying 3-cycles is much more reasonable, and can be done easily in $O(mn)$ time, where m is the number of arcs and n is the number of vertices in the graph. Note that errors can still exist when the graph is acyclic. However, by cleverly choosing arcs to reverse and eliminate cycles, we can correct a great deal of these errors.

Once the cycles are identified, candidates for correction are chosen as follows. For every 3-cycle, either 1 or 2 of the 3 arcs must be incorrect. If a majority of the arcs is correct, then it is more likely that only 1 of the 3 should be corrected. To determine which one, recall the discussion above regarding the increased likelihood that arcs that are part of many cycles are more likely to be incorrect. In each iteration then of the correction process, the number of 3-cycles to which each arc belongs is computed. The arc belonging to the most cycles is reversed, and the next iteration commences. The procedure continues until either 1) there are no cycles left, or 2) no arc can be reversed without creating a new cycle.

5   Results

5.1   Independent Preference Prediction

Several experiments were run to determine how accurately each of the three techniques could predict which of two outcomes is preferred for a particular test

Table 1. Performance of each of the three techniques. Percentage of preferences for which a prediction is made (pred. rate) and accuracy of those predictions (success rate) are indicated.

Number Known Prefs	Direct Prediction		Pre-processing Prediction		Post-processing Prediction	
	Success Rate	Pred. Rate	Success Rate	Pred. Rate	Success Rate	Pred. Rate
10	75.3%	42.9%	67.8%	28.3%	72.4%	25.7%
30	70.9%	61.6%	75.8%	40.9%	76.9%	39.4%
50	70.2%	67.1%	76.6%	28.6%	82.3%	44.1%

user. Since our technology relies on the fact that users with similar tastes for particular outcomes should often have similar tastes for other outcomes, testing on computer-generated data would be problematic, due to the difficulty in fairly simulating this dependency in the preferences. Simulating too little dependency would detract from our performance, while simulating too much would unduly stack the deck in our favour. We chose then to instead utilize the MovieLens dataset, which is commonly used to test collaborative filtering technology. While this dataset does not explicitly provide preferences over outcomes for the individual subjects, but rather ratings for particular outcomes (i.e. movies) in the form of integers between 1 and 5, a small number of preferences can be extracted by considering outcomes that are rated differently. That is, if movie A is rated a 4 and movie B is rated a 2, then A is preferred over B.

To test our techniques, a set of users in the database were randomly chosen to be the cluster users, leaving the remainder as the test users. To prevent the preference data from being too sparse, two pre-processing actions were carried out on the cluster data: 1) only the 512 most frequently rated movies were considered, and 2) collaborative filtering was used to predict ratings for unrated data. This meant we had a rating for every outcome. The point was not to have complete preference information for the cluster users; this would be an unrealistic assumption that would unfairly improve our results. Rather, it allowed us to control how many preferences were actually revealed, allowing us to assess performance for preference specifications with various degrees of completeness.

For each user, a predetermined number of preferences were chosen to be revealed, simulating the effect of the system learning a small number of these. COP-networks were built to cluster the partial preference relations, and a test user was classified among them according to the above-described techniques. For each trial, two outcomes were chosen randomly such that 1) the test user had a specified preference over the two outcomes in the original database (to allow us to assess performance), and 2) this preference was not one of those revealed in the initial stage. The goal of the experiments was then to determine how accurately each method could predict the preference over these two outcomes.

For each technique, 1000 trials were performed on the set of 200 test users in each of the cases where 10, 30 and 50 preferences were known for each user. Results are shown in Table 1. From these data one can see that, when the number of known preferences is very small, the Direct Prediction method is the best

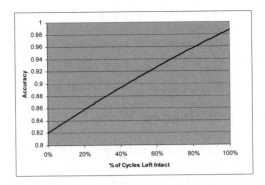

Fig. 3. Prediction accuracy after applying the error correction technique, for a COP-network with varying numbers of cycles

method among the three techniques. When the number of known preferences is relatively high, the Post-processing Prediction method is the best method among three techniques, with its accuracy increasing with the number of known preferences. The Post-processing Prediction method is always better than the Pre-processing Prediction method in the cases tested.

5.2   Error Correction

To give an indication of the performance of the error correction technique, tests were run on simulated data generated from a particular scenario. Simulated data were used here for two reasons. First of all, it would not be possible to test using the data obtained (i.e. the MovieLens dataset), since only sparse information on preferences is actually known. So there would be no way to verify the correctness of our technique for most cases. Second, "real" data that capture preference interdependence among similar users are not needed anyway, since we only focus on a preference network for one particular user. Based on three parameters, the number of outcomes, the percentage of preferences that were predicted, and the accuracy of those predictions, a preference network can be generated accordingly to allow us to determine how many errors would be corrected, on average, for any given scenario.

Data were simulated for the case of the Post-processing technique with 50 known preferences, which had the highest accuracy of all tests discussed in the previous section. For all pairs of outcomes a preference was chosen as the user's true preference (i.e. the 512 outcomes were ordered), and a COP-network was artificially generated such that preferences were predicted for 44.1% of the pairs with 82.3% accuracy. Preferences were chosen in such a way as to reflect the fact that there may often be fewer cycles in a COP-network built based on clustering than there would be if preferences were selected randomly with equal probability. This is because a user may typically be clustered with the same general group of people each time a preference needs to be learned. Since these people will not have cycles in their own preferences, it will be less likely that we would have cycles in preferences that are predicted based on these people. To reflect this possibilty, results are shown for cases with different percentages of cycles removed. Results show that, depending on the likelihood of obtaining cycles in predicted preferences, the error-correcting technique can increase accuracy from 82.3% to as high as 98%.

6   Conclusions and Related Work

This paper examines the idea of clustering partial preference relations for a group of users. In order to negotiate autonomously on behalf of a user, an intelligent agent must obtain as much information as possible about the user's preferences over possible outcomes, but without asking the user an unreasonable number of questions. By clustering similar users together, we can predict new preferences for a user with a high degree of confidence by examining preferences of other users in the same cluster. Three techniques for clustering, and predicting preferences based on these clusters, are developed and evaluated experimentally. We also propose an error-correction procedure, which analyzes the set of predicted preferences as a whole, and determines which of these predictions do not likely fit with the rest of the set. Preliminary results show that this procedure can be considerably effective, boosting accuracy of the best technique to as much as 98% for a particular simulated scenario.

There is a great body of work on preference elicitation in general, and specifically on predicting preferences or estimating utilities. Preference elicitation is becoming an increasingly popular topic in the areas of agents and electronic commerce, and the problem of predicting or estimating preferences and utility functions based on a small sample of directly elicited information is viewed with great importance. Boutilier et al. [1] propose a minimax regret-based approach to preference elicitation. Given a decision problem and a small set of elicited preferences, a total ordering of the user's preferences is chosen so as to minimize potential regret should an adversary choose a utility function for the user consistent with the elicited preferences. Several elicitation strategies for reducing this regret are proposed. Chajewska et al. [4], on the other hand, take a more direct approach by computing the expected utility of the decision strategy based on probability distributions for outcome utilities. Here, the user's utility for an outcome is estimated by a prior probability distribution over the user's utility function, computed based on utilities learned from other people. Questions are then posed about the user's utilities using a standard gamble approach [8], and the distributions are narrowed or modified accordingly. Several works examine techniques for predicting preferences in more specific domains, including preferences of opponents in automated negotiation [2,3,9]. Our work differs from these in that we attempt to identify other users with preferences similar to those directly elicited from the current user. We then predict new preferences for this user using techniques for building and analyzing clusters and correcting errors.

7 Future Work

One direction for future work is to address the fact that we are only attempting to predict preferences for which we have a certain level of confidence. Two items need to be investigated further. First of all, the error correction technique must be studied further to determine where the balance lies in the quality-versus-quantity trade-off. While accuracy would likely decrease if more predictions were attempted, the error correction technique may remedy this, possibly providing even better results due to more predictions being made. Second, it may be possible to infer a large number of preferences for which no prediction is made by considering other known preferences. By computing the transitive closure of the preference network, one should be able to infer several new preferences. We did not investigate this, as the error correcting procedure is currently incomplete, and cycles will often remain in the network. Thus the transitive closure will result in pairs of vertices with arcs between them in each direction. Work needs to be done on selecting good candidate edges to remove from these remaining cycles. Since locating all cycles in a graph is intractable, this is non-trivial.

References

1. Boutilier, C., Patrascu, R., Poupart, P., Schuurmans, D.: Regret-based utility elicitation in constraint-based decision problems. In: Proceedings of IJCAI 2005, Edinburgh, Scotland, pp. 929–934 (2005)
2. Buffett, S., Comeau, L., Spencer, B., Fleming, M.W.: Detecting opponent concessions in multi-issue automated negotiation. In: Proc. of ICEC 2006, Fredericton, Canada, pp. 11–18 (2006)
3. Buffett, S., Spencer, B.: A bayesian classifier for learning opponents preferences in multi-object automated negotiation. Electronic Commerce Research and Applications (2007)
4. Chajewska, U., Koller, D., Parr, R.: Making rational decisions using adaptive utility elicitation. In: AAAI 2000, Austin, Texas, USA, pp. 363–369 (2000)
5. Chen, S.: Reasoning with conditional preferences across attributes. Master's thesis, University of New Brunswick (2006)
6. Chen, S., Buffett, S., Fleming, M.W.: Reasoning with conditional preferences across attributes. In: Proc. of AI 2007, Montreal, Canada, pp. 369–380 (2007)
7. Ha, V., Haddawy, P.: Similarity of personal preferences: Theoretical foundations and empirical analysis. Artificial Intelligence 146(2), 149–173 (2003)
8. Keeney, R.L., Raiffa, H.: Decisions with Multiple Objectives: Preferences and Value Tradeoffs. John Wiley and Sons, Inc., Chichester (1976)
9. Restificar, A., Haddawy, P.: Inferring implicit preferences from negotiation actions. In: Proc. Int'l Symposium on Artificial Intelligence and Mathematics, Fort Lauderdale, USA (2004)

Mathematically Clinching a Playoff Spot in the NHL and the Effect of Scoring Systems

Tyrel Russell and Peter van Beek

Cheriton School of Computer Science
University of Waterloo

Abstract. A problem of intense interest to many sports fans as a season progresses is whether their favorite team has mathematically clinched a playoff spot; i.e., whether there is no possible scenario under which their team will not qualify. In this paper, we consider the problem of determining when a National Hockey League (NHL) team has clinched a playoff spot. The problem is known to be NP-Complete and current approaches are either heuristic, and therefore not always announced as early as possible, or are exact but do not scale up. In contrast, we present an approach based on constraint programming which is fast and exact. The keys to our approach are the introduction of dominance constraints and special-purpose propagation algorithms. We experimentally evaluated our approach on the past two seasons of the NHL. Our method could show qualification before the results posted in the Globe and Mail, a widely read newspaper which uses a heuristic approach, and each instance was solved within seconds. Finally, we used our solver to examine the effect of scoring models on elimination dates. We found that the scoring model can affect the date of clinching on average by as much as two days and can result in different teams qualifying for the playoffs.

1 Introduction

As a season progresses, sports fans become intensely focused on the playoff race and the position of their team in the standings. Sports sections of major newspapers publish the results of the games and announce when teams have qualified for the playoffs and when they have been eliminated (e.g. the Globe and Mail [6]). However, the newspapers use a heuristic measure for determining when teams have qualified for or been eliminated from the playoffs and announcements are sometimes not made until several days after the team has clinched or been eliminated. Using optimization techniques like constraint programming, it is possible to determine exactly when teams have qualified for the playoffs.

In this paper, we present the first complete solution to the problem of determining when a National Hockey League (NHL) team has qualified for the playoffs. The problem of determining when a sports team has mathematically clinched a playoff spot has been well studied for several sports, including baseball [14,12,16,1] and soccer [11]. Schwartz [14] first looked at this problem algorithmically for the historical baseball problem. He showed that this simple model can

S. Bergler (Ed.): Canadian AI 2008, LNAI 5032, pp. 234–245, 2008.
© Springer-Verlag Berlin Heidelberg 2008

be solved with a polynomial algorithm. More recently, research has shown that a wide variety of qualification problems are NP-Complete, including the NHL problem [8]. Cheng and Steffy [4] looked at the problem of determining qualification for the NHL using an integer programming (IP) model but they found that they could not solve the model when secondary and tertiary tie breaking rules were applied. We model the problem as a constraint satisfaction problem and solve the problem using a constraint programming solver based on backtracking search and constraint propagation. By introducing dominance constraints and special-purpose propagation algorithms, our model can handle both secondary and tertiary tie-breaking constraints. Our approach is efficient and can solve all of the instances from the past two seasons within seconds.

The NHL is composed of thirty teams that are broken into two conferences, East and West, of fifteen teams. Each of these conferences is composed of three divisions with five teams in each division. Teams play eighty-two games spread unevenly between division, conference and inter-conference opponents. Each game in the NHL is formed from 3 periods, called regulation time, and, if the game is tied at the end of regulation time, a shorter overtime period and a shootout. The shootout continues until one team has won the game. A team makes the playoffs if they are a division leader or one of the top five teams that are not division leaders in their conference.

In the NHL, teams are placed in the standings by the number of points, for both divisional and overall standings. However, it is possible to have two teams with the same number of points. The NHL has introduced three different tie breaking measures. The first tie breaking measure is to compare the number of wins by each team. If the teams are still tied, the number of points earned against only those teams that are tied are compared. The third measure compares the number of wins earned against teams that are still tied.

The NHL qualification problem is defined with respect to a set of completed games, the number of games left between the teams, the scoring model used, the points accrued so far by each team and the number of wins. Given these factors, the NHL qualification problem is the problem of determining if a team k has qualified for the playoffs. We can find a solution to this problem, known as a wild-card qualification problem, by determining if there is a possible scenario for the remaining games that, according to the scoring model, awards sufficient points to teams other than k to ensure that k cannot be one of the division leaders or have enough points to earn one of the five wild card spots. If there is no scenario then k has qualified for the playoffs.

The calculation of the points for a team is dependent on the scoring model that is used. The NHL has used several different scoring models over the years. A scoring model is defined as a set of tuples defining the possible outcomes, and subsequent reward, of the games. Each of the NHL scoring models can be viewed in Table 1. Referring to Table 1, the current or Shootout model allows for two pairs of outcomes. Either one team wins in regulation time and earns two points while the other receives none or one team wins in overtime and earns two points while the other receives one point.

Table 1. The scoring models that have been used by the NHL. The possible outcomes of an NHL game between two teams (i, j) are A) j wins in regulation time, B) j wins in overtime, C) tied game, D) i wins in overtime and E) i wins in regulation time.

Scoring Model	A	B	C	D	E
Historic Era	{ $(0,2)$		$(1,1)$		$(2,0)$ }
Overtime	{ $(0,2)$	$(0,2)$	$(1,1)$	$(2,0)$	$(2,0)$ }
Extra Point	{ $(0,2)$	$(1,2)$	$(1,1)$	$(2,1)$	$(2,0)$ }
Shootout	{ $(0,2)$	$(1,2)$		$(2,1)$	$(2,0)$ }
Proposed	{ $(0,3)$	$(1,2)$		$(2,1)$	$(3,0)$ }

We experimentally evaluated our constraint programming approach on instances from the 2005-06 and 2006-07 seasons. For these seasons, we can show qualification of teams up to five days earlier than the Globe and Mail [6]. As well, we studied all of the different scoring models that have been used by the NHL as well as a model recently proposed at the 2006 meeting of general managers of the NHL. The NHL has tried various scoring models to increase the competitiveness of the league though there exists no data on how these changes affected the clinching dates. We show that adjusting the scoring model can change the average qualification date by more than two days. Interestingly, the Toronto Maple Leafs would have qualified for the playoffs under any other model than that used by the NHL in 2006-07 season. Another example where the scoring matters is the Edmonton Oilers in 2005-06 who were Western conference champions but would not have made the playoffs if the proposed scoring model had been used.

The remainder of the paper breaks down the various parts of the research. Section 2 introduces the constraint programming model for solving the NHL elimination problem. Also in this section, the specific dominance constraints and custom propagation algorithms are introduced. Section 3 presents the experimental results from our study. Section 4 discusses some concluding remarks.

2   The Model

In this section, we describe the constraint programming model that we used to solve the NHL qualification problem. We also introduce the techniques that we used to make the model solvable for realistic problem sizes.

Constraint programming is a technique for solving combinatorial problems. A problem is defined as a set of variables with a given domain of values and constraints on the values that those variables can take. The goal of constraint programming is to find an assignment of values to those variables such that each of the constraints is satisfied. Typically, these problems are solved with backtracking search or other search techniques that explore the possible set of solutions. A more detailed explanation of constraint programming can be found in either Rossi, van Beek and Walsh [13] or Marriott and Stuckey [10].

A constraint programming approach can often be dramatically improved by adding dominance constraints and special purpose constraint propagation algorithms. Dominance constraints are constraints that remove feasible solutions that can be shown to be equal to or worse than another feasible solution [15]. One application of these constraints is in online scheduling for photo-copiers [5]. Constraint propagation is the process of inference by which domains of a variable is updated due to the constraints on that variable and the values of other variables referenced by the constraints [3]. Laborie [9] presents one example where a special purpose propagation algorithm is used in scheduling.

2.1   Basic Notation

To present our constraint programming approach, we first define some notation. We define a set of teams T with $|T| = n$. For any team $i \in T$, we define the number of points to be p_i and the number of wins to be w_i. We define the initial points—that is, the points earned before a given moment in the season—as p_i^0 and initial wins as w_i^0. We define the number of wins by a team i against a team j as a w_{ij}. The number of games remaining for a team i is denoted g_i and between two teams i and j is denoted g_{ij}.

We define C_i to be the set of teams in the conference that includes i and $C_i = C_j$ if and only if i is in the same conference as j. We define D_m to be the set of teams in division m, where m is one of the six divisions.

2.2   The Basic Model

To specify a constraint programming model, one must specify the variables and their associated domains along with the constraints on the values those variables may take. The variables used in our constraint model, their domains and a short description are shown in Table 2. More complete descriptions of the variables are presented as necessary through the remainder of this section. The following model is described with respect to the current or Shootout scoring model. Small modifications are made to make this constraint model work for the other scoring models. For the remainder of this section, we will refer to the team being tested for qualification as k.

The most basic variable in our model is x_{ij} with domain equal to $[0 \ldots g_{ij}]$ to represent the number of wins by a team i over a team j. Cheng and Steffy [4] observe that if elimination is possible then it always occurs when the worst possible outcome happens to k. Under the current scoring model and with the notion that an elimination solution is found in the worst case for k, we know that a team will always win games against k earning at least one point and, when playing other teams, the worst case situation is for both teams to earn at least one point [4]. Using this observation, we note that it is sufficient under this model to keep track of the number of wins to calculate the number of points earned.

Given that there is a symmetric variable for wins by j over i with the same domain, we define the following constraint on the x variables,

$$x_{ij} + x_{ji} \leq g_{ij} \ . \tag{1}$$

Table 2. Variables within the constraint model

Variable	Domain	Description
x_{ij}	$[0 \ldots g_{ij}]$	The number of wins by i over j
b_i	$[0, 1]$	1 if i is better than k else 0
d_m	D_m	The division leader for division m
div_m	$[0, 1]$	1 if the leader of division m is not better than k else 0

Note that constraint 1 is an inequality. The reason for this is to simplify the addition of dominance constraints.

We must represent the quantities used in the elimination problem in terms of our decision variables. We define the number of wins by a team i against j as,

$$w_{ij} = w_{ij}^0 + x_{ij} \ , \tag{2}$$

and the total number wins for a team i as,

$$w_i = \sum_{j \in T} w_{ij} \ . \tag{3}$$

We can also represent the number of points earned by a team i in a similar manner. One exception is team k, which must not win any games. Therefore, team k does not earn any more points. The number of points earned by a team i against j is denoted as,

$$p_{ij} = \begin{cases} p_{ij}^0 + x_{ij} + g_{ij} & i \neq k \\ p_{ij}^0 & i = k \end{cases} \ , \tag{4}$$

and the number of points earned by a team i as,

$$p_i = \begin{cases} p_i^0 + \sum_{j \in C_i}(x_{ij} + g_{ij}) + 2\sum_{j \notin C_i} g_{ij} & i \neq k \\ p_i^0 & i = k \end{cases} \ . \tag{5}$$

Now that we have defined the wins and points in terms of x_{ij}, we can look at the constraints on the variable in terms of the qualification problem. The first constraint that can be derived is that k should win no games in the worst case solution. This can be denoted as,

$$\forall i \ w_{ki} = 0 \ . \tag{6}$$

The objective function that we are using in this case is the wild card objective, so in order to determine if a team can be eliminated we must keep track of the number of teams better than k. We define a binary variable b_i to be true if and only if team i is better than k. A team is better than k if the team has more points than k or better tie breakers than k. Before we show this constraint, we have to define two sets that are used in the tie-breaking procedure. The secondary tie-breaking set is the set of teams that have identical numbers of points and wins and is denoted as,

$$TB_i^2 = \{j \mid j \in C_i \wedge p_i = p_j \wedge w_i = w_j\} \ .$$

The tertiary tie-breaking set is the set of teams that are in the secondary tie-breaking set and have identical number of points earned between teams in the secondary set. The tertiary tie-breaking set is defined as,

$$TB_i^3 = \{j \mid j \in TB_i^2 \wedge \sum_{y \in TB_i^2} p_{iy} = \sum_{y \in TB_i^2} p_{jy}\} \ .$$

Once we have the tie-breaking sets defined, we can define the constraint between b_i and x_{ij} as,

$$\forall i \quad p_i > p_k$$
$$\vee \ (p_i = p_k \wedge w_i > w_k)$$
$$\vee \ (p_i = p_k \wedge w_i = w_k \wedge \sum_{j \in TB_k^2} p_{ij} > \sum_{j \in TB_k^2} p_{kj})$$
$$\vee \ (p_i = p_k \wedge w_i = w_k \wedge \sum_{j \in TB_k^2} p_{ij} = \sum_{j \in TB_k^2} p_{kj} \wedge$$
$$\sum_{j \in TB_k^3} w_{ij} > \sum_{j \in TB_k^3} w_{kj})$$
$$\Leftrightarrow b_i = 1 \ . \tag{7}$$

A division leader is a team that has the most points in its division and beats any other division member with sufficient points on tie-breakers. We define a variable d_m with domain D_m to be the division leader for division m. We define the maximum number of points in a division m to be $maxp_m$. For conciseness, the secondary and tertiary tie-breakers are omitted for Constraints 8, 10, 13 and 14. We define the constraint between x_{ij} and d_m as,

$$\forall m \ [p_i = maxp_m \wedge \nexists j(j \neq i \wedge p_j = maxp_m \wedge w_j > w_i) \Leftrightarrow d_m = i] \ . \tag{8}$$

We need to ensure that the team that must be eliminated does not become a division leader as this guarantees a playoff spot even if there are many teams with more points. Therefore, we add the following constraint,

$$\forall m \ d_m \neq k \ . \tag{9}$$

Once we have division leaders and none of them are k, we need to determine if we need to count that team in elimination, by setting $div_m = 1$, as a division leader always makes the playoffs. The division constraints ensure that a div_m variable is true only if the division leader is not better than k. There are two situations where div_m is true. The first is when the division leader has less points than k and the constraint is denoted as,

$$\forall m \ maxp_m < p_k \Rightarrow div_m = 1 \ . \tag{10}$$

The second situation is when the division leader has the same number of points as k but is placed lower on tie-breakers. The constraint ensuring this situation is defined as,

$$\forall m \ maxp_m = p_k \wedge w_{d_m} < w_k \Rightarrow div_m = 1 \ . \tag{11}$$

The last constraint on the model ensures that the team is eliminated under the wild card objective. There must be eight teams in front of k either by placing better than k or by being a division leader. The following constraint captures this relationship,

$$\sum_{i \in C_k} b_i + \sum_{m=1}^{\ell} div_m \geq 8 \ , \tag{12}$$

where ℓ is the number of divisions.

The basic model is a complete and correct model for the NHL qualification problem. If there does not exist a solution to the CSP then k has qualified for the playoffs. However, the model as it stands is inefficient and could not solve realistic instances within a time bound of fifteen hours. Once we improved the model using dominance constraints and special purpose constraint propagation algorithms, we could solve all of the instances within seconds.

2.3 Dominance Constraints

It can be observed that if a team has earned more points than k then it is unnecessary for that team to win any more games because under the worst case assumption k will not win any more games and thus earn no more points. This means that once a team has passed k either by points or tie-breakers, that team could lose the remainder of their games to other opponents and still be better than k. This leads to the following dominance constraint,

$$\forall i \ p_i > p_k \lor (p_i = p_k \land w_i > w_k) \Rightarrow$$
$$\forall j [(\neg bound(x_{ij}) \Rightarrow x_{ij} = 0) \land (x_{ji} = g_{ij} - x_{ij})] \ . \tag{13}$$

By a similar token, if a team can no longer earn more points than k then there is no need for that team to win any more games against opponents that could earn more points than k. Therefore, we can introduce another constraint that deals with this situation. But first, we introduce notation for maximum number of points and wins possible for a team i. We denote the maximum number of possible points and possible wins as mp_i and mw_i, respectively. The dominance constraint is given by,

$$\forall i \ mp_i < p_k \lor (mp_i = p_k \land mw_i < w_k) \Rightarrow$$
$$\forall j [(\neg bound(x_{ij}) \Rightarrow x_{ij} = 0) \land (x_{ji} = g_{ij} - x_{ij})] \ . \tag{14}$$

2.4 Calculating Tie-Breakers and Division Leaders

To calculate the sets needed for both the tie-breakers and division leaders requires the values for x_{ij} to be set for all teams. However, it is often possible to determine the result of the calculation earlier and avoid calculating the sets. This means that special purpose propagation algorithms must be used to ensure constraints are propagated as early as possible.

Observe in Constraint 7, secondary and tertiary tie-breakers need the sets of teams tied after primary and secondary tie-breaking, respectively. However, it is not always impossible to calculate these quantities during search and thus these tie-breakers can not be fully resolved during search. When either the points or wins changes for a team i, instead of waiting for all x variables to be completely set to propagate values, the solver uses only the first two disjunctive clauses to determine if b_i values should be set. In many cases, this negates the need to calculate the sets explicitly. Any decisions on teams still tied are delayed until all of the x variables have been assigned values, if necessary. If there are still teams tied, the secondary and, if needed, the tertiary tie-breakers are applied.

Observing Constraints 9, 10 and 11, it can be seen that it is only necessary to know which team is a division leader if the elimination team is possibly a division leader or it is possible for a division leader to have an equivalent or lesser number of points. That means that in all other situations we can avoid calculating which team is actually a division leader. This also means that anytime a team in a given division acquires more points than the elimination team, the division leader will not be a factor. This relationship can be described as the following constraint,

$$\exists i \ \ i \in D_m \wedge i \in C_k \wedge (p_i > p_k \vee (p_i = p_k \wedge w_i > w_k)) \Rightarrow div_m = 0 \ . \quad (15)$$

While Constraint 10 uses the maximum number of points earned by any team in a given division, it is also possible to look at a more relaxed version of this constraint. Instead of determining the maximum number of points once all of the games have been assigned, it is also possible to determine the maximum possible number of points earned by any team in that division at any time. We denote this quantity mp_m. Using this new quantity, we can reformulate a relaxed version of constraint 10 that can be used at any point during search and is defined as,

$$\forall m \ \ mp_m < p_k \Rightarrow div_m = 1 \ . \quad (16)$$

2.5   Different Scoring Models

The previous section described the constraint model for the NHL's current scoring model. Only minor changes must be made to adapt the other models that have been used by the NHL. Two new variables must be introduced to deal with ties for the historic and overtime models and with overtime wins for the proposed model. Also, the calculation of the wins and points must be modified to deal with the new variables when appropriate.

3   Experimental Results

3.1   Overview

We implemented our model using the constraint programming solver built by ILOG [7]. To test the model and to ensure that it can solve practical instances, we tested the solver on all possible elimination instances from the 2005-06 and

Table 3. The results of qualification compared against the published Globe and Mail results. Only results that differ are shown.

	2005-06			2006-07	
Team	Optimal	Globe and Mail	Team	Optimal	Globe and Mail
Ottawa	Mar 22	Mar 27	Buffalo	Mar 18	Mar 22
Montreal	Apr 14	Apr 18	Atlanta	Apr 2	Apr 4
Buffalo	Apr 4	Apr 5	Detroit	Mar 24	Mar 25 or 26
New Jersey	Apr 12	Apr 14	Nashville	Mar 23	Mar 24
Calgary	Apr 8	Apr 9 or 10			
Colorado	Apr 13	Apr 15			
San Jose	Apr 13	Apr 14			
Dallas	Mar 31	Apr 1, 2 or 3			
Nashville	Apr 9	Apr 10			

Table 4. Average days remaining by scoring system for the 05-06 and 06-07 seasons

	Average Days Remaining	
Scoring Model	2005-06	2006-07
Historic	12.75	11.75
Overtime	11.56	12.81
Extra Point	11.75	10.63
Current	11.94	10.75
Proposed	13.13	10.13

2006-07 seasons. We compared our calculated results against those shown in the Globe and Mail [6]. Finally, we modified the constraint model to handle all of the scoring models that have been used by the NHL and compared the results.

3.2   Problem Instances

To generate the qualification problem instances, we took the results from the 2005-06 and 2006-07 seasons and broke down the results into separate days. To create instances from the results for each day of the season, we calculated the number of points and wins earned up to that point in the season. Given the win-loss records, the points accrued so far and the remaining games, we created instances for each day of the season.

3.3   Comparison Against the Globe and Mail

We ran each of the problem instances for the 2005-06 and 2006-07 seasons and determined the date of qualification for each of the teams. We could determine for every team whether they had qualified for the playoffs at every point in the season in just under two and half minutes. For most instances, the time it took was a fraction of a second. We found that, when comparing the results to the results posted in the Globe and Mail, we were able to show qualification earlier

Table 5. Date of clinching under different scoring models in the Eastern conference of the NHL in 2006-07

Team	Historic	Overtime	Extra Point	Current	Proposed
East					
Toronto	Apr 8	Apr 8	Apr 8	—	Apr 9
Ottawa	Mar 19	Mar 18	Mar 21	Mar 25	Mar 21
Montreal	—	Apr 8	—	—	Apr 7
Buffalo	Mar 24	Mar 21	Mar 23	Mar 18	Mar 22
Boston	—	—	—	—	—
NY Islanders	Apr 8	—	—	Apr 9	—
NY Rangers	—	—	Apr 9	Apr 6	Apr 7
...	...	...	...	...	...
Tampa Bay	—	—	—	Apr 6	—
Florida	Apr 6	—	—	—	—
Atlanta	Apr 7	Apr 1	Apr 2	Apr 2	Apr 7
Carolina	—	Apr 2	Apr 6	—	—

Table 6. Date of clinching under different scoring models in the Western conference of the NHL in 2005-06

Team	Historic	Overtime	Extra Point	Current	Proposed
Vancouver	—	—	—	—	Apr 14
Edmonton	Apr 14	Apr 14	Apr 18	Apr 14	—
Calgary	Apr 6	Apr 6	Apr 6	Apr 8	Apr 6
...	...	...	...	...	...

for nine teams during the 2005-06 season and for four teams during the 2006-07 season while never, of course, being later than the Globe and Mail. The results of this experiment are shown in Table 3. In Table 3, entries with multiple dates are due to Sunday editions or unreported results in which it was unclear on which day the result would have been reported.

We show qualification earlier than the Globe and Mail by as much five and four days for the 2005-06 and 2006-07 seasons, respectively. Note that the largest discrepancy between our results and their results is found for the first team to qualify in both seasons. It is possible that this is due to the paper not realizing that teams had clinched playoff spots. Even disregarding these results, we still found discrepancies as large as four days and two days for the 2005-06 and 2006-07 seasons, respectively.

3.4   Comparisons of Scoring Models

Once the solver has been designed for one scoring model, it is relatively straightforward to translate the model to other scoring systems. The instance generator was modified to calculate the points correctly for each of the different scoring models and we ran the instances for all of the scoring models used by the NHL as well as the recently proposed model. The results of this experiment can be found in Table 4. We found that the average number of days remaining in a given season can vary by more than two days in a given season depending on the scoring model used.

The most interesting effect of changing the scoring model was to observe which teams qualified for the playoffs. In the case of the 2006-07 season, we can note that the Toronto Maple Leafs would have qualified for the playoffs under any other scoring model then the one used that season all other things being equal (see Table 5). Another interesting note is that Edmonton, who were the Western Conference Champions in 2005-06, would not have made the playoffs if the proposed scoring model had been imposed and their spot would have gone to divisional rivals Vancouver (see Table 6). It should be noted that these results assume that the games would end in the same way regardless of the scoring system. However, research in economics has shown that teams will modify the way they play depending on the scoring model [2]. Even given this fact, it is interesting to note that some team strategies would have been good enough to secure a playoff spot under any scoring model while other teams strategies only ensure qualification under the current scoring model, for example, Tampa Bay in 2006-07.

4   Conclusion and Future Work

This paper looks at the problem of determining qualification in the NHL. We present the first complete and efficient solution to the NHL qualification problem. The key to scaling up our constraint programming approach was a combination of dominance constraints and special purpose algorithms for dealing with tie-breakers and division leaders. By introducing the dominance constraints to the model, we significantly reduced the amount of search necessary to find a solution or to confirm that no solution was possible. As well, we avoided costly work associated with tie-breakers and division leaders by strategically delaying the calculation of secondary and tertiary tie-breakers and by avoiding the calculation of the actual division leaders as much as possible.

We implemented the proposed model using a constraint programming package developed by ILOG [7]. Using the 2005-06 and 2006-07 seasons, we developed a set of problem instances to verify that our solver could solve realistic problems. We found that solving an individual instance only took a fraction of a second and that all instances of the 2005-06 and 2006-07 seasons could be solved in a several minutes while respecting all tie-breaking rules.

Using the data from the problem instances, we found that we could announce results as much as five and four days earlier than the Globe and Mail [6] for the 2005-06 and 2006-07 seasons, respectively. We also extended our work to look at the effect of scoring model on playoff qualification for the first time. We found that qualification under scoring models could vary by by more than two days. We also found that changing the scoring model caused different teams to qualify for the playoffs.

In the future, we will extend this work to look at not just the decision problem of deciding qualification but also the optimization problem of determining the number of games that must be won to earn a playoff spot. This idea was first proposed by Ribeiro and Urrutia [11] for the Brazilian Soccer championship, which uses a different scoring model and playoff objective.

References

1. Adler, I., Erera, A.L., Hochbaum, D.S., Olinick, E.V.: Baseball, optimization and the world wide web. Interfaces 32, 12–22 (2002)
2. Banerjee, A.N., Swinnen, J.F.M., Weersink, A.: Skating on thin ice: rule changes and team strategies in the NHL. Can. J. of Economics 40, 493–514 (2007)
3. Bessiere, C.: Constraint propagation. In: The Handbook of Constraint Programming, ch. 3, Elsevier, Amsterdam (2006)
4. Cheng, E., Steffy, D.: Clinching and elimination of playoff berth in the NHL. International Journal of Operations Research (to appear)
5. Getoor, L., Ottosson, G., Fromherz, M., Carlson, B.: Effective redundant constraints for online scheduling. In: Proceedings of the Fourteenth National Conference on Artificial Intelligence (AAAI), pp. 302–307 (1997)
6. Globe and Mail. Hockey scoreboard. Metro ed. (2006-2007)
7. ILOG S.A. ILOG Solver 4.2 user's manual (1998)
8. Kern, W., Paulusma, D.: The computational complexity of the elimination problem in generalized sports competitions. Discrete Optimization 1, 205–214 (2004)
9. Laborie, P.: Algorithms for propagating resource constraints in AI planning and scheduling: Existing approaches and new results. Artificial Intelligence 143, 151–188 (2003)
10. Marriott, K., Stuckey, P.: Programming with Constraints: An Introduction. MIT Press, Cambridge (1998)
11. Ribeiro, C.C., Urrutia, S.: An application of integer programming to playoff elimination in football championships. International Transactions in Operational Research 12, 375–386 (2005)
12. Robinson, L.W.: Baseball playoff eliminations: an application of linear programming. Operations Research Letters 10, 67–74 (1991)
13. Rossi, F., van Beek, P., Walsh, T. (eds.): Handbook of Constraint Programming. Elsevier, Amsterdam (2006)
14. Schwartz, B.: Possible winners in partially completed tournaments. SIAM Review 8, 302–308 (1966)
15. Smith, B.M.: Modelling. In: Handbook of Constraint Programming, ch. 11, Elsevier, Amsterdam (2006)
16. Wayne, K.D.: A new property and a faster algorithm for baseball elimination. SIAM Journal on Discrete Mathematics 14, 223–229 (2001)

An Intelligent Automatic Face Contour Prediction System

Seref Sagiroglu[1] and Necla Ozkaya[2]

[1] Gazi University, Engineering and Architecture Faculty, Computer Engineering Department,
06570 Ankara, Turkey
ss@gazi.edu.tr
[2] Erciyes University, Engineering Faculty, Computer Engineering Department,
38039, Kayseri, Turkey
neclaozkaya@erciyes.edu.tr

Abstract. Even if biometric features have been deeply studied, tested and successfully applied to many applications, there is no study in achieving a biometric feature one from another. This study presents a novel intelligent approach analysing the existence of any relationship among fingerprints and faces. The approach is based on artificial neural networks to generate face contour of a person from only his/her fingerprint. Experimental results have shown that there are close relationships among the features of fingerprints and faces. It is possible to generate face contours from fingerprint images without knowing any information about faces. Although the proposed system is initial study and it is still under development, the performance of the system is very encouraging and promising for the future developments and applications.

Keywords: Biometrics, fingerprint verification, face recognition, artificial neural network, intelligent system, biometric prediction system.

1 Introduction

Biometric features such as fingerprint, face, iris, voice, or hand geometry are very important to support security applications including information security, law enforcement, surveillance, forensics, smart cards, access control in university campuses, dorms, building entrances, time/place control points and computer networks [1]-[4]. These applications continue to be developed rapidly to support industrial and government needs with the help of biometric methods, algorithms, architectures and sensors developed. In spite of all these developments in biometrics, there is no study on investigating relationships among the biometric features or obtaining features one from another. It should be emphasized that most of the works in biometrics have been focused on how to improve the accuracy and processing time of the biometric systems, to design the more intelligent systems, and to develop more effective and robust techniques and algorithms [1]-[2].

The aim of this study is to analyse face contour of a person from his or her fingerprint without having any priori knowledge about his or her face. In order to

S. Bergler (Ed.): Canadian AI 2008, LNAI 5032, pp. 246–258, 2008.
© Springer-Verlag Berlin Heidelberg 2008

achieve the analysis, an automatic intelligent system based on artificial neural network was developed. The results achieved from the proposed fingerprint to face contour (F2FC) system was also presented.

The paper is organized as follows. Section 2 mentions the previous works on biometrics, automatic fingerprint identification and verification systems (AFIVSs), face recognition systems (FRSs), respectively. Section 3 briefly introduces artificial neural networks (ANNs). Section 4 presents the novelty of the proposed system including basic notation, definitions, performance metrics related to the F2FC and explains the various steps of the new approach. The experimental results including numerical and graphical results of the F2FC are given in Section 4. Finally, the proposed work is concluded and discussed in Section 5.

2 Previous Works

In many biometric authentication systems, a biometric data from a person is acquired during an enrolment phase; a feature set is extracted from the acquired data and is stored in the system, either in a central database or in smartcards. Later, when the user wants to authenticate him self or her self to the system, a fresh measurement of the same biometrics is taken, the same feature extraction algorithm is applied, and the extracted feature set is compared against the template. If they are sufficiently similar according to some similarity measure, the user is considered as authentic [3], [5]. A biometric system works in four modes depending on the application status [4]: the enrolment, the verification, the identification and the screening. *The enrolment* is responsible for scanning, categorization and registration of the biometric characteristics. All other modes use the biometric data that were acquired to the system by the enrolment mode. *The verification:* A person desired to be identified by submitting to the system a claim to an identity, usually via a magnetic card, login name, smart card etc., and the system either rejects or accepts the submitted claim of the identity at the end [6]. Commercial applications, such as physical access control, computer network logon, electronic data security, ATMs, credit-card purchases, cellular phones, personal digital assistants, medical records management, and distance learning are samples of the verification applications [2], [4]. *The identification:* The system identifies a person's identity without having to claim an identity or fails if the person is not enrolled in the system database. The input and the outputs of the system are just a biometric feature and a combination of a list of identities and the scores indicating the similarity among two biometric features, respectively [6]. Welfare-disbursement, national ID cards, border control, voter ID cards, driver's license, criminal investigation, corpse identification, parenthood determination, missing children identification are from typical identification applications [2], [4]. *The screening:* The results of determination whether a person belongs to a watch list of identities or not is displayed. Security at airports, public events and other surveillance applications are some of the screening examples [4], [7]. It is expected that a biometric system always takes the correct decision when a biometric feature is presented to the system. However, in practice it does not make perfect match decisions and it can make two basic types of errors: false match rate (FMR) and false non-match rate (FNMR) [1]. These errors generally use to show the accuracy and

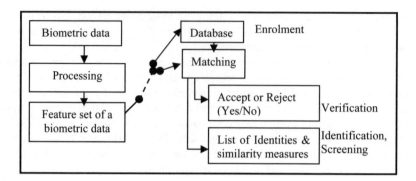

Fig. 1. A generic biometric system

performance of the system in the literature. Nevertheless, it is more informative to report the system accuracy in terms of a Receiver Operating Characteristic (ROC) curve that shows the system performance at all operating points [7]. A generic biometric system is given in Fig. 1.

A fingerprint is a universal, permanent and unique pattern for each person. It has a ridge-valley structure, core and delta points called singular points, end points and bifurcations called minutiaes. These structures are given in Fig. 2. Fingerprint is the most widely used biometric feature due to its uniqueness, immutability and reliability [8]. Many approaches to AFIVSs have been presented in the literature [1], [2], [6], [8]-[21]. Yet, it is still an actively researched area. The AFIVSs might be broadly classified as being *minutiae-based, correlation-based* and *image-based* systems [9]. A good survey about these techniques was given in [1]. *The minutiae-based approaches* rely on the comparisons for similarities and differences of the local ridge attributes and their relationships to make a personal identification [10]-[12]. They attempt to align two sets of minutiaes from two fingerprints and count the total number of matched minutiaes [4]. If minutaes and their parameters are computed relative to the singular points which are highly stable, rotation, translation and scale invariant, then these minutiaes will also become rotation, translation and scale invariant [6], [13]-[15]. Core points are the points where the innermost ridge loops are at their steepest. Delta points are the points from which three patterns deviate [14], [16], [17]. The general methods to detect the singular points are poincare-based methods [18], intersection-based methods [14] or filter-based methods [19].

Main steps of the operations in the minutiae-based AFIVSs are summarized as follows: selecting the image area, detecting the singular points, enhancing, improving and thinning the fingerprint image, extracting the minutiae points and calculating their parameters, eliminating the false minutiaes, properly representing the fingerprint images with their feature sets, recording the feature sets into a database, matching the feature sets, testing and evaluating the system [20]. The results of these processes are given in Fig. 3. The performance of the minutiae-based techniques relies on the accuracy of all these processes. Especially the feature extraction and the use of sophisticated matching techniques to compare two minutiae sets often more affect the performance.

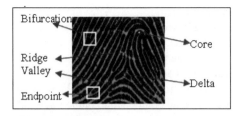

Fig. 2. Ridge-valley structure and features of a fingerprint

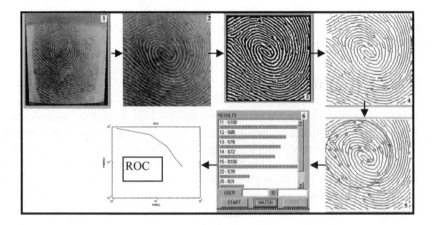

Fig. 3. Main operation steps of a minutiae-based AFIVS [20]

In the correlation-based AFIVSs, global patterns of the ridges and valleys are compared to determine if the two fingerprints align. The template and query fingerprint images are spatially correlated to estimate the degree of the similarity between them. The performance of the correlation-based techniques is affected by non-linear distortions and noise present in the image. In general, it has been observed that minutiae-based techniques perform better than correlation-based ones [21]. *In the image-based approaches,* the decision is made using the features that are extracted directly from the raw image that might be the only viable choice when image quality is too low to allow reliable minutiae extraction [9].

Faces are probably the most highly accepted and user-friendly biometric characteristics. Also they are used by humans to make personal recognition. Face recognition is an active area of research with several applications ranging from static to dynamic [10]. So, face recognition technology is well advanced. In general, a FRS consists of three main steps. These steps cover detection of the faces in a complicated background, localization of the faces followed by extraction of the features from the face regions and finally identification or verification tasks [22]. Face detection and recognition process is really complex and difficult due to numerous factors affecting the appearance of an individual's facial features such as 3D pose, facial expression, hair style, make-up, etc. [23]. In addition to these varying factors, lighting, background, scale, noise and face occlusion and many other possible factors make these tasks even more challenging [22]. The most popular approaches to face detection and recognition are based on each location and shape of the facial attributes, such as the eyes, eyebrows, nose, lips and chin and their spatial relationships or the overall analysis of the face image that a face is represented as a weighted combination of a number of canonical faces [4], [24]. Also many effective and robust methods for the face recognition have been proposed [2], [10], [22]-[26]. They are categorized as follows: knowledge-based methods that encode human knowledge of what constitutes a typical face. Feature invariant methods aim to find structural features that exist even when the pose, viewpoint or lighting conditions vary to locate faces. Template matching based methods whichin several standard patterns of a face are used to describe the face as a whole or the facial features separately. Appearance-based methods operate directly on images or appearances of the face objects and process the images as two-dimensional holistic patterns [24].

3   Artificial Neural Networks

ANNs have been applied to solve many problems [27]-[31]. Learning, generalization, less data requirement, fast computation, ease of implementation and software and hardware availability features have made the ANNs very attractive for many applications [27], [28]. These fascinating features have also made them popular in biometrics as well [25], [26], [29]-[31]. Multilayered perceptron (MLP) is one of the most popular ANN architectures. Because of the MLP structure can be trained by many learning algorithms, it has been applied to a variety of problems successfully in the literature. The MLP structure consists of three layers: input, output and hidden layers. One or more hidden layers might be used. The neurons in the input layer can be treated as buffers and distribute x_i input signal to the neurons in the hidden layer. The output of the each neuron y_j in the hidden layer is obtained from sum of the multiplication of all input signals x_i and weights w_{ji} that follow all these input signals. The sum can be calculated as a function of y_j. This function can be a simple threshold function, a hyperbolic tangent or a sigmoid function. The outputs of the neurons in other layers are calculated in the same way. The weights are adapted with the help of a learning algorithm according to the error occurring in the calculation. The error can be calculated by subtracting the ANN output from the desired output value. ANNs might be trained with many different learning algorithms [27].

4   Proposed Approach

Fingerprint verification and face recognition are two of the few biometric methods that possess the merits of their reliability, performance and high accuracy. So they are topics received significantly increased attention. The proposed ANN based intelligent F2FC system generates the face contour including face border with ears of a person from only one fingerprint of the same person without having any information about his or her face. It is expected that this study will find a considerable attention in scientific arena in biometrics as well as industry. F2FC system has a very simple structure. It consists of a data enrolment module, a feature extraction module, an ANN module, an test & evaluation module and a face contour reconstruction module. These modules are explained below.

4.1   Data Enrolment Module

The data enrolment module helps store biometric data of individuals into the biometric system database. During this process, fingerprints and faces (Fs&Fs) of an individual have been captured to produce a digital representation of the characteristics. Two types of data are used in this study. A real multimodal database that includes Fs&Fs belonging to 120 persons was established by using Biometrica FX2000 for fingerprints and Canon digital camera for faces. A sample for the biometric feature set from the established multimodal database is given in Fig. 4. Only a frontal face image and a fingerprint that was index finger of the right hand (labelled as R-I in Fig. 4) were used in this study.

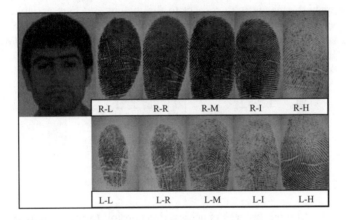

Fig. 4. A sample for the biometric feature set from the established database (R: right hand, L: left hand, L: little finger, R: ring finger, M: middle finger, I: index finger and H: head finger)

4.2   Feature Extraction Module

The feature extraction module extracts discriminative feature sets from the acquired data. Extracting local and global feature sets of the fingerprints including singularities, minutiae points and their parameters are achieved. Fingerprint feature sets were computed using VeriFinger 4.1 SDK developed by Neurotechnologija. The reason of this preference is to establish an objective assessment for the F2FC prediction. This SDK is known as an effective, robust and reliable AFIVS in the field of biometrics and uses a minutiae-based algorithm. Detailed explanation of algorithms, detailed information of fingerprint feature sets and their storage format are given in [32]. Face feature sets were obtained from the faces. 36 reference points were used for representing a face contour in this work. To get the feature sets of the face contours a feature-based face feature extraction algorithm was borrowed from Cox et al. [33] and fundamentally modified and adapted to this application. Increasing the number of the reference points to 36 points helped to represent the faces more accurately and sensitively. Face feature sets were shaped from x-y coordinates of the face contour reference points, not distances or average measures as in [33]. It was also observed that feature sets contain enough information about faces for getting them again with high sensitivity.

4.3   ANN Module

The ANN module is used to analyze the existence of any relationship among Fs&Fs. This part of the system has been implemented with the help of 3-layered MLP structure that is trained with the scaled conjugate gradient algorithm (SCG) to find out and establish a relationship among Fs&Fs. SCG is a network training function that updates weight and bias values according to the scaled conjugate gradient method. SCG is based on conjugate directions, but this algorithm does not perform a line search at each iteration. SCG can train any network as long as its weight, net input, and transfer functions have derivative functions. Back propagation is used to calculate derivatives of performance with respect to the weight and bias variables. The more detailed discussions on the SCG can be found in [34] and [35]. Sigmoid transfer function was used in the proposed study for calculating the output of a layer from its net input. The structure of the ANN is given in Fig. 5.

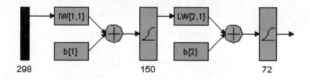

Fig. 5. The structure of the ANN module

In this study, training process is achieved according to the training parameters of the SCG with the following values: maximum number of epochs/achieved epochs, minimum performance gradient/reached gradient, maximum validation failures, sigma that determines change in weights for the second derivative approximation, lambda that is a parameter for regulating the indefiniteness of the Hessian were 20000/4571, 1e-006/0, 9.83923e-007, 5, 5.0000e-005 and 5.0000e-007, respectively. In general, if any of the following conditions is achieved or the maximum number of epochs is reached, the training processed is stopped. The performance has been minimized to the goal. The performance gradient falls below the minimum performance gradient parameter. The validation performance has increased or decreased according to the failures [34]. In the proposed study, training has stopped because of being reached the minimum performance gradient. The training sets included pairs of Fs&Fs while the test sets included only fingerprints. Face feature sets of the test persons were used in the evaluation process as the desired outputs. Randomly selected 80 of 120 data set was used to train the ANN. Remaining 40 of 120 test set was used to test the system. The block diagram of the ANN Module is given in Fig. 6. The ANN module is the most critical and important module of the system. Because, all modules of the system except the ANN module are on duty, either in pre-processing or post-processing of the main process. The ANN structure and the training parameters were determined for achieving the training stage accurately. The training process is started with applying the fingerprint feature set of a person to the system as an input and face contour feature set of the same person as the desired output. The sizes of the input and the output vectors are 298 and 72, respectively. The system achieves the training process with these feature sets according to the learning algorithm and the ANN parameters. Even if the feature sets of the Fs&Fs are required in the training, only fingerprint feature sets are used in the test. These fingerprints are unknown biometric data for the F2FC system. The outputs of the system for unknown test data indicate the success and reliability of the system. This success and reliability of the system must be shown clearly by evaluating the ANN outputs against to the proper metrics in proper way.

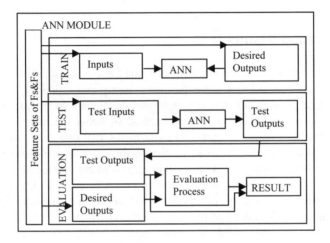

Fig. 6. The block diagram of the ANN module

4.4 Test and Evaluation Module

The traditional metrics of an ordinary biometric system are no longer appropriate to characterize the performance of the F2FC system. So, we have decided to use appropriate performance metrics in this study. In addition to the FMR-FNMR representation and the ROC curve, the results of the system may be evaluated by considering the following metrics: mean squared error (MSE), sum squared error (SSE), average correlation, absolute percent error (APE) and mean APE [36]. In addition to these numerical evaluations a visual evaluation platform is created by drawing the ANN outputs and the desired outputs in the same form. Also another visual evaluation platform is presented by drawing the ANN outputs on the involved real face images of the test people. Consequently, for a more objective comparison, the performance and accuracy of the system have been evaluated and presented on the basis of the combination of these metrics for illustrating the qualitative properties of the proposed methods as well as a quantitative evaluation of their performance.

4.5 Face Contour Reconstruction Module

In order to evaluate the system results comprehensively, a visual evaluation platform software was developed. Face contour reconstruction module is flexible software to convert the ANN outputs and desired outputs to visual face contours with no post-processing. Indeed, it basically transforms the reference points of the face contours to the lines. It is capable of drawing the results of actual and calculated values on the same face as shown in Fig. 8. It also illustrates the ANN results on the real face images as given in Fig. 9. It helps to achieve the processes easily, efficiently and automatically with the support of a graphical interface. Briefly, although its simple structure and functionality, face contour reconstruction module achieves an important task by creating some different visual evaluation platfoms.

5 Experimental Results

Concept of generating face contours from only one fingerprint is a challenging idea to biometrics. In order to achieve the experiments easily and efficiently, the proposed ANN based face contour generation system was developed. In the experiments, the index finger of the right hand was used because of being the most used finger in AFIVSs. Producing the face contours as close to the real one as possible is critical task for this study. In order to evaluate the performance of the developed system effectively, we have benchmarked our system against to the metrics MSE, SSE, APE, average APE, average correlation and human visual evaluation in addition to the traditional evaluation metrics of biometric systems that include FMR-FNMR representation and ROC curve of the test results. The metrics MSE and SSE were computed before rescaling, while the other metrics MSE, SSE, average APE and average correlation were calculated after rescaling as 0.0013, 3.7825, 193.5793, 5.5751e+005, 9.273373 and 0.993556, respectively. FMR-FNMR representation and ROC curve of the test results are given in Fig. 7.

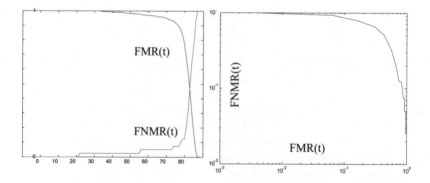

Fig. 7. FMR-FNMR representation and ROC curve of the test results

Fig. 7 indicates that the proposed system performs the tasks with high similarity measures to the desired values. However, for more realistic and compherensive evaluation, all of 40 desired and achieved test results have been drawn on the same platform as shown in Fig. 8. Dark and light lines in Fig. 8 represent the desired and the generated face contours. Because of the page limitation, only 10 of 40 test results have been drawn on the real face images in Fig. 9. However it is possible to show the overall system performance graphically for the all test results. The APE values belonging to each test result was demonsrated in Fig. 10.

Besides the numerical results indicate the system success clearly, graphical results also confirm this success as well. As it can be seen from Figures 7-10, the proposed system is very successful in achieving face contours from fingerprints. The face contours were evaluated according to the metrics both the standart metrics which were defined in the literature and extra metrics which were determined by us. Based on the observations, the fundamental novelty and diversity of the proposed approach was illustrated. This investigation has shown the existence of the relationships among fingerprints and faces.

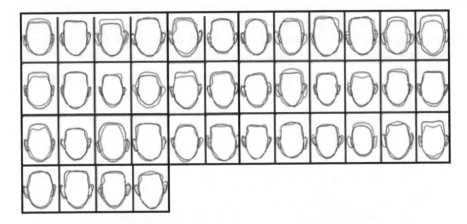

Fig. 8. Test results achieved from the F2FC system

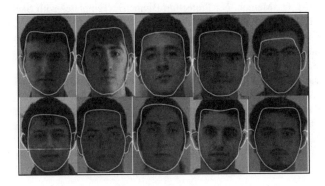

Fig. 9. Test face contours drawn on the real face images

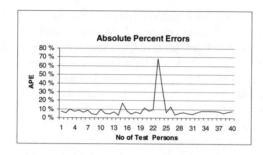

Fig. 10. APE values for all test results

6 Conclusion and Future Work

In this study an F2FC system is designed, implemented and introduced for generating the face contours from only one fingerprint without any need for face information. The relationships among biometrics are experimentally shown. In addition it is demonstrated that it is possible to achieve an unknown biometric feature from a known biometric feature, successfully. It is hoped that this approach would lead to create new concepts, research areas, and especially new applications in the field of biometrics.

References

1. Maio, D., Maltoni, D., Jain, A.K., Prabhakar, S.: Handbook of fingerprint recognition. Springer, New York (2003)
2. Jain, L.C., Halici, U., Hayashi, I., Lee, S.B., Tsutsui, S.: Intelligent biometric techniques in fingerprint and face recognition. CRC press, New York (1999)
3. Jain, A.K., Ross, A., Prabhakar, S.: An introduction to biometric recognition. IEEE Trans. on Circuits and Systems for Video Technology 14(1), 4–19 (2004)
4. Jain, A.K., Ross, A., Pankanti, S.: Biometrics: a tool for information security. IEEE Trans. on Information Forensics and Security 1(2), 125–143 (2006)
5. Sutcu, Y., Li, Q., Memon, N.: Protecting Biometric Templates with Sketch: Theory and Practice. IEEE Trans. on Information Forensics and Security 2(3), 503–512 (2007)
6. Jain, A.K., Hong, L., Pankanti, S., Bolle, R.: An identity authentication system using fingerprints. Proceedings of the IEEE 85(9), 1365–1388 (1997)
7. Jain, A.K., Pankanti, S., Prabhakar, S., Hong, L., Ross, A., Wayman, J.L.: Biometrics: A Grand Challenge. In: Proceedings of the Int. Conf. on Pattern Recognition, Cambridge, UK, August 2004, vol. II, pp. 935–942 (2004)
8. Kovács-Vajna, Z.M.: A fingerprint verification system based on triangular matching and dynamic time warping. IEEE Trans. on Pattern Analysis and Machine Intelligent (PAMI) 22(11), 1266–1276 (2000)
9. Lumini, A., Nanni, L.: Two-class Fingerprint matcher. Pattern Recognition 39(4), 714–716 (2006)

10. Hong, L., Jain, A.: Integrating faces and fingerprints for personal identification. IEEE Trans. on PAMI 20(12), 1295–1307 (1998)
11. Jain, A.K., Hong, L., Bolle, R.: On-line fingerprint verification. IEEE Trans. on PAMI 19(4), 302–314 (1997)
12. Zhou, J., Gu, J.: Modeling orientation fields of fingerprints with rational complex functions. Pattern Recognition 37(2), 389–391 (2004)
13. Hsieh, C.T., Lu, Z.Y., Li, T.C., Mei, K.C.: An Effective Method To Extract Fingerprint Singular Point. In: The Fourth Int. Conf. Exhibition on High Performance Computing in the Asia-Pacific Region, pp. 696–699 (2000)
14. Rämö, P., Tico, M., Onnia, V., Saarinen, J.: Optimized singular point detection algorithm for fingerprint images. In: Int. Conf. on Image Processing, pp. 242–245 (2001)
15. Zhang, Q., Yan, H.: Fingerprint classification based on extraction and analysis of singularities and pseudo ridges. Pattern Recognition 11, 2233–2243 (2004)
16. Wang, X., Li, J., Niu, Y.: Definition and extraction of stable points from fingerprint images. Pattern Recognition 40(6), 1804–1815 (2007)
17. Li, J., Yau, W.Y., Wang, H.: Combining singular points and orientation image information for fingerprint classification. Pattern Rec. 41(1), 353–366 (2008)
18. Kawagoe, M., Tojo, A.: Fingerprint pattern classification. Pattern Rec. 17(3), 295–303 (1984)
19. Nilsson, K., Bigun, J.: Localization of corresponding points in fingerprints by complex filtering. Pattern Recognition Lett. 24, 2135–2144 (2003)
20. Ozkaya, N., Sagiroglu, S., Wani, A.: An intelligent automatic fingerprint recognition system design. In: 5th Int. Conf. on Machine Learning and App., pp. 231–238 (2006)
21. Ross, A., Jain, A.K., Reisman, J.: A Hybrid Fingerprint Matcher. Pattern Recognition 36(7), 1661–1673 (2003)
22. Cevikalp, H., Neamtu, M., Wilkes, M., Barkana, A.: Discriminative common vectors for face recognition. IEEE Trans. on PAMI 27(1), 4–13 (2005)
23. Bouchaffra, D., Amira, A.: Structural Hidden Markov Models for Biometrics: Fusion of Face and Fingerprint. Special Issue of Pattern Recognition Journal, Feature Extraction and Machine Learning for Robust Multimodal Biometrics, available online (in press, 2007)
24. Li, S.Z., Jain, A.K.: Handbook of Face Recognition. Springer, New York (2004)
25. Yang, M.H., Kriegman, D.J., Ahuja, N.: Detecting faces in images: a survey. IEEE Trans. on PAMI 24(1), 34–58 (2002)
26. Zhao, W., Chellappa, R., Phillips, P.J., Rosenfeld, A.: Face recognition: a literature survey. ACM Computing Surveys 35, 399–459 (2003)
27. Haykin, S.: Neural Networks: A Comprehensive Foundation. Macmillan College Publishing Company, New York (1994)
28. Sagiroglu, S., Beşdok, E., Erler, M.: Artificial Intelligence Applications in Engineering I: Artificial Neural Networks (in Turkish), Ufuk Publishing, Kayseri, Turkey (2003)
29. Sagar, V.K., Beng, K.J.A.: Hybrid Fuzzy Logic And Neural Network Model For Fingerprint Minutiae Extraction. In: Int. Conf. on Neural Netw., pp. 3255–3259 (1999)
30. Nagaty, K.A.: Fingerprints classification using artificial neural networks: a combined. structural and statistical approach. Neural Networks 14, 1293–1305 (2001)
31. Maio, D., Maltoni, D.: Neural network based minutiae filtering in fingerprints. In: 14th Int. Conf. on Pattern Recognition, pp. 1654–1658 (1998)
32. Biometrical & Art. Int. Tech. (2008), http://www.neurotechnologija.com/vf_sdk.html
33. Cox, I.J., Ghosn, J., Yianilos, P.N.: Feature-Based Face Recognition Using Mixture Distance. Computer Vision and Pattern Recognition, 209–216 (1996)

34. The Mathworks, Accelerating the Pace of Engineering and Science (2008), http://
    www.mathworks.com/access/helpdesk/help/toolbox/nnet/nnet.html?/access/helpdesk/help/
    toolbox
35. Moller, M.F.: A Scaled Conjugate Gradient Algorithm for Fast Supervised Learning.
    Neural Networks 6, 525–533 (1993)
36. Novobilski, A., Kamangar, F.A.: Absolute percent error based fitness functions for
    evolving forecast models. In: FLAIRS Conf., pp. 591–595 (2001)

Word Clustering with Validity Indices

Ahmad El Sayed, Julien Velcin, and Djamel Zighed

ERIC Laboratory - University of Lyon 2
{asayed,jvelcin,dzighed}@eric.univ-lyon2.fr

Abstract. The goal of any clustering algorithm producing flat partitions of data is to find the optimal clustering solution and the optimal number of clusters. One natural way to reach this goal without the need for parameters, is to involve a validity index in the clustering process, which can lead to an objective selection of the optimal number of clusters. In this paper, we provide two main contributions. Firstly, since validity indices have been mostly studied in small dimensional datasets, we have chosen to evaluate them in a real-world task: agglomerative clustering of words. Secondly, we propose a new context-aware method that aims at enhancing the validity indices usage as stopping criteria in agglomerative algorithms. Experimental results show that the method is a step-forward in using, with more reliability, validity indices as stopping criteria.

1 Introduction

Word clustering has become of great interest in many applications, such as knowledge acquisition [1], information retrieval [2], and word sense disambiguation [3]. It consists of grouping semantically similar words into clusters, such as {*apple, banana*}, {*apple, microsoft*}. Seeking flat partitions of words with clustering methods, the user is often required to input some parameters, such as the desired number of clusters k. This actually violates one of the inherent requirements for clustering methods, namely *minimal input parameters* [4].

The goal of any clustering algorithm producing flat partitions of data is to find the optimal clustering solution and the optimal k. One natural way to reach this goal more objectively, is to evaluate the quality of different solutions along different k values, in order to pick the solution with the best results. In cluster analysis, the procedure of evaluating solutions is known as *cluster validation* [5], and the indices that aim at comparing different solutions with different parameters are known as *relative validity indices* [6]. In this paper, we provide two main contributions:

Contribution I: It is an answer to the following key question: *which relative index, if involved in a clustering process, will most likely guide the algorithm to the optimal partition?*. Since their high computational cost, relative indices were most often studied in small dimensional datasets including small numbers of clusters [6,7,8,9,10]. This surely allows a better visualization of results, but does not reflect the reality of their performance in real-world applications where data is often multi-dimensional. Therefore, we have chosen to study their performance in a widely used task: agglomerative clustering of words.

S. Bergler (Ed.): Canadian AI 2008, LNAI 5032, pp. 259–270, 2008.
© Springer-Verlag Berlin Heidelberg 2008

Contribution II: In literature, the determination of the optimal solution is performed *a posteriori*, after evaluating the different solutions obtained with the different k values [11,6,7,10]. Our second contribution tackles the following question: *How reliable can be the usage of relative indices as stopping criteria in agglomerative clustering?* We propose a new context-aware method that aims to enhance validity indices usage as stopping criteria. Experimental results show that the proposed method is a step-forward in using, with more reliability, validity indices as stopping criteria.

The remainder of the paper is organized as follows. After an overview on validity indices in the next Section, we describe in Section 3 our context-aware method. Experiments performed on the SemCor corpus are presented in Section 4. We conclude in Section 5 by summarizing and drawing some future works.

2   Cluster Validity Indices

There exist three kinds of cluster validity indices VI, namely internal, external, and relative indices [5]: (1) External indices evaluate a clustering solution by comparing it to an *a-priori* specified structure that reflects the desired result over the dataset (e.g., *FScore measure, entropy*). (2) Internal indices assess the intrinsic adequacy between the data structure and the imposed solution basing on quantities and features extracted from the dataset itself (e.g., *CPCC, Hubert τ statistic*). (3) Relative indices compare a clustering solution to another one obtained with different parameters. This can help choosing the parameters that best fit the dataset. Relative indices tend to maximize the intra-cluster compactness and the inter-cluster separation (e.g., *DB, Dunn indices, S_Dbw*). In this paper, we focus on relative indices. According to their behavior, we can distinguish two categories of them [6]:

Relative Indices Scaling with k. With these indices, the optimal k is usually chosen by inspecting the more significant local change (jump or drop) in the values of VI, appearing like a "knee" on the plot. However, given the difficulty of such techniques, two approaches are commonly used, namely the gap statistics approach [10] and the stability approach [12]. Among indices in this category, we can find: *CH, MSE, KL statistic, Diff, modified τ statistic*, etc.

Relative Indices Not Scaling with k. With these indices, the optimal k is more easily chosen as the point on the graph maximizing/minimizing VI. Among indices in this category, we can find: *Dunn* [8], *modified Dunn (m-dunn)* [13], *Davies-Bouldin (DB)* [9], *S_Dbw* [6], and *C1, C2, C3, C4* [11]. Due to their facility of interpretation, we choose to focus on indices in this category[1]. The other reason is related to our aim to enable the usage of relative indices as stopping criteria. This is definitely a hard task that will get much harder if the optimal k must be selected using sophisticated techniques like the gap statistics.

---

[1] To check indices' formula, readers can follow the provided references.

A known drawback when involving indices in clustering is the computational cost that quickly becomes prohibitive as soon as we scale to large and high-dimensional datasets. The main reason is that pairwise similarities between the dataset elements/clusters have to be calculated. As a preliminary attempt to reduce complexity, we propose a new validity index, $H3$, that we define below.

$$H3 = \frac{\sum_{i=1}^{k} n_i \cdot \sum_{j=1}^{n_i} sim(e_j, S_i)}{(\sum_{i=1}^{k} sim(S_i, S))/k}$$

where sim denotes the similarity between two objects, S_i denotes the centroid of cluster C_i containing n_i elements, e_j denotes a data element, and S denotes the collection's centroid which is the average vector of all clusters' centroids.

$H3$ is significantly less expensive than other indices. The reason is that $H3$ deals with centroids to calculate the inter-cluster separation and the intra-cluster compactness. $H3$ is inspired from the $H1$ and $H2$ indices proposed by Zhao [14]. The difference is that $H3$ does not follow the trend of k. As a matter of fact, the intra-cluster similarity decreases as k decreases, thus the quality of clustering continuously deteriorates from an intra-cluster point of view. We consider that an optimal partition is reached, when the average of inter-cluster similarities, that tends to improve while grouping similar objects, is no more able to overwhelm the intra-cluster deterioration.

3   Enhacing Validity Indices Usage as Stopping Criteria

3.1   Problem Definition

Consider in Fig. 1 VI (*index* curve) along the different k values. Using agglomerative algorithms, once reaching the optimal partition at $k = a$, all the remaining actions (until $k = 1$) are obviously a time waste. Hence, finding a relevant stopping criterion is primordial. In probabilistic clustering algorithms (mixture models), many stopping criteria are defined quantifying the degree to which a model fits a dataset; among the most known criteria, we can find Bayesian Information Criterion (BIC) [15], and Minimum Description Length (MDL) [16]. Such criteria have been used in algorithms like X-means [17] and CLIQUE [18]. In non-probabilistic algorithms - which are our concern in this paper - stopping criteria rely in most cases on input user parameters. This has serious limitations since users often ignore the parameters that best fit the datasets [4].

A challenging approach to address this issue is to make use of relative indices in order to develop an incremental agglomerative algorithm [19] able to stop once reaching the "right" optimal solution in terms of a VI at $k = a$. Thus, an intuitive approach is to let the clustering process go on while improving VI in a stepwise fashion, and to stop once reaching a point $k = b$ where no further (significant) improvement can be made [20]. However, such an ad-hoc approach suffers from ignoring, at a specific level b, whether it has truly reached the optimal solution (i.e., $a = b$) or a better solution will come afterward (which is the case in Fig. 1). The major problem is that validity indices are using too much local information to take a global decision, e.g., stopping the process.

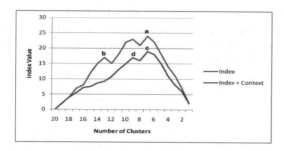

Fig. 1. A validity index values obtained along different k values. The two curves represent the same index involved in a clustering process with or without context-awareness.

3.2   Our Context-Aware Method

Context-Aware Clustering. We developed a method that aims at enhancing the clustering process with context-aware decisions, in order to enhance the indices ability to be used as stopping criteria. Reconsider Figure 1; the goal is to enhance the classic *index* curve with context-awareness, in order to obtain another temperate curve (*index + context* curve) where the first drop FD (at d) approaches as much as possible the optimal solution (at c).

As we are seeking the hierarchical agglomerative algorithms, the method applies the following procedure at each level j of the process: *Consider the M closest pairs of clusters; estimate VI after trying to merge each of the M pairs; among the mergings that improve VI (over the previous VI at $j-1$), assess the merging with the lowest Context Risk (CR); if no merging improves VI, merge the pair that optimizes (maximizes/minimizes) VI.*

At a given level of the agglomerative process, suppose that we have two merging choices: (1) merging C_i and C_j into a new cluster C_p, and (2) merging C_m and C_n into a new cluster C_q. Suppose that C_p optimizes a validity index VI, while C_q simply improves it. Before taking any definitive decision, the method examines the context of C_p and C_q in terms of their K Nearest Neighbors K-NN (i.e., surrounding clusters)[2]. If the context of C_p tells that merging C_i and C_j could lead to a global quality degradation in terms of VI in next iterations, the method chooses to create rather C_q improving VI at a minimal context risk.

Applying this method surely implies a more temperate and a slower improvement in VI (as shown at the curve *index + context* in Figure 1), but has the advantage of continuously pushing, as much as possible, risky merging actions entailing possible future degradations for later processing. We argue that taking the "safest" action at each level leads an expected degradation to occur as late as possible during the process. Thus, a first drop (FD) is likely to occur closer to the optimal solution, which will offer the possibility to the algorithm to consider more relevantly FD at $(d+1)$ as a stopping criteria, and the solution provided at d as the optimal clustering solution.

---

[2] We set $K = 10$ in our experiments.

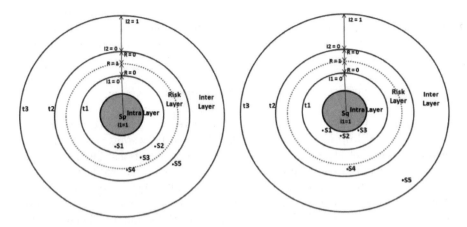

Fig. 2. The three-layer context space of the risky cluster candidate C_p

Fig. 3. The three-layer context space of the non-risky cluster candidate C_q

Note that calculating VI for all the possible mergings between k clusters will lead to a high complexity of $O(k^2)$ at *each level* of the process. We overcome this by considering, at a given level, only the M closest pairs of clusters[3], since they form the most potential candidates to improve VI.

3.3 Context Space Composition

For each new cluster candidate C_p, a Context Risk CR expresses how risky can be assessing C_p for the overall clustering quality in the expected upcoming mergings given the context of C_p. Consider the two new clusters candidates C_p and C_q depicted by their centroids respectively in Figures 2 and 3 with five context clusters each ($C_1...C_5$). We assume that C_p, with its K-NN ($K = 5$) neither too close nor too distant from its centroid, is more risky than C_q, with its K-NN either too close or too distant from its centroid. Therefore, we define a *context space* as the space including the K-NN of a new cluster candidate C_p. Then, as shown in Figure 2, we decompose the context space of C_p into three layers that we define below.

Intra layer. Clusters within this layer reduce CR as they should not lead to a quick drop in VI. For this, they have to be *close* enough to C_p, therefore, likely to be merged with C_p in next iterations without causing a significant degradation (comparing to the previous mergings) in the global intra-cluster compactness. As a matter of fact, the clusters are getting larger over mergings, and thus the intra-cluster is continuously deteriorating. At a level k where FD did not occurred yet, we suppose that all the previous mergings that caused degradations in the intra-cluster are acceptable. This layer is delimited by the thresholds $t0 = 0$

---

[3] We set $M = 10$ in our experiments.

and $t1 = \delta(C_p)$. We define $\delta(C_p)$ as the radius of the new cluster candidate C_p augmented by the standard deviation of radius values obtained following the previous mergings. A radius is the maximum distance between the centroid of C_p and an element within C_p.

$$\delta(C_p) = radius(C_p) + Std(radius(C_n...C_{k-1}))$$

Inter layer. Clusters within this layer also reduce CR as they should not lead to a quick drop in VI. For this, they have to be *distant* enough from C_p, therefore, not likely to be merged with C_p in next iterations. Further, keeping them outside would contribute to improve (or at least not to deteriorate) the global inter-cluster separation. This layer is delimited by a first threshold $t2 = \Delta(\text{K}-NN(C_p))$. We define $\Delta(\text{K}-NN(C_p))$ as the average pairwise inter-cluster distance between the K-NN of C_p, reduced by the standard deviation of its homologous values obtained following the previous mergings. Getting the average separation between clusters surrounding C_p, will give a hint on the minimum required inter-distance to improve the local inter-cluster separation around C_p, which will most likely improve the global inter-cluster separation.

$$\Delta(K - NN(C_p)) = AvgInter(C_p) - Std(AvgInter(C_n..C_{k-1}))$$

$$AvgInter(C_p) = \frac{\sum_{i=1}^{K} \sum_{j=1}^{K} dist(C_i, C_j)}{K.(K-1)/2} \quad i \neq j$$

We decided to set the same margin for the intra and inter layers in order to have balanced scores in both layers. Subsequently, we define the other inter-layer threshold $t3 = t2 + t1$.

Risk layer. Clusters within this layer increase CR because we consider that they could lead to a fast drop in the global clustering quality, whether on the inter- or intra-cluster level. Actually, these clusters, if merged with C_p in next iterations, would contribute to a significant degradation in the intra-cluster compactness since they are not enough close to C_p. Further, clusters within this layer, if not merged with C_p in next iterations, would not contribute to any significant amelioration in the inter-cluster separation since they are not enough distant from C_p. This layer is delimited by the thresholds $t1$ and $t2$ previously defined.

3.4   Context Risk Calculation

In order to calculate CR for a candidate cluster C_p, we use the following formula:

$$CR(C_p) = \frac{1}{K}(\sum_{i=1}^{n1} R(C_i, C_p) - \sum_{j=1}^{n2} I1(C_j, C_p) - \sum_{h=1}^{n3} I2(C_h, C_p))$$

where $R(C_i, C_p)$, $I1(C_j, C_p)$, $I2(C_h, C_p)$ denote the score given for a cluster C_p situated in the risk, intra, and inter layers respectively. All the scores are distributed along a [0,1] range according to their distances with the centroid of C_p (See Figures 2 and 3). $n1$, $n2$, $n3$ denote the number of clusters situated respectively in the risk, intra and inter layers. Consequently, CR varies between -1 (for a minimal risk) and 1 (for a maximal risk).

In terms of complexity, CR does not require heavy computations. In fact, given p clusters at a specific iteration, we compute CR for M candidate clusters resulted from the merging of the M closest pairs of clusters. Therefore, at a given iteration, the added complexity is $O(M(p-1+K+K(K-1)/2))$. Furthermore, we argue that the parameters M and K have "second order" effect on the results in the sense that their choices depend solely on the extent to which we are able to augment the complexity of the algorithm.

4   Experimental Study

4.1   The Benchmark

The benchmark selected for our experiments is composed of two distinct datasets of words (see Table 1). Words are extracted from the SemCor corpus [21], which is a collection of 352 texts where each term is categorized manually in one or multiple senses from WordNet[4].

Table 1. Summary of datasets used for our study on word clustering

Dataset	# of words	# of senses
DS1	500	52
DS2	1000	78

Words are represented following the Distributional Hypothesis [22]. Hence, each word is a vector in a multi-dimensionnal space, where each dimension is a local context expressed by its PMI score [23]. A 2-words window size is considered for contexts. We turned to language-independent practices representing a context by its plain word concatenated with its relative position to the target word (e.g., *Before-tea*). Finally, a semantic similarity is calculated between a pair of words by means of the *cosines coefficient* between their feature vectors.

4.2   Evaluating Validity Indices in Agglomerative Clustering

Our first experimental study aims to answer the following key question: *"Which relative validity index, if involved in the agglomerative clustering as a criterion function, will most likely lead the algorithm to the optimal partition?"* Having words categorized into senses by an expert, one can define such artificial structure as the ideal "Gold Standard" output for a clustering method. Indeed, a predefined structure reflects only a certain level of granularity that could be too

---

[4] http://wordnet.princeton.edu/

specific or too generic for the application at hand. Thus, we cannot claim that it is the *only* correct partition, but it is indeed a correct one that we could reliably consider as a "Gold Standard".

Our experiments include 12 algorithms after having run the agglomerative algorithm separately along with 12 criterion functions: 8 criteria stand for validity indices (i.e., *C1, C2, C3, C4, H3, DB, Dunn, Dunn-like*), and the remaining 4 criteria stand for the classic linkages (i.e., *single, complete, average, mean*). At each level of the clustering process, the quality of the resulted partition is thus assessed by the target VI (predicted quality) and also by an $FScore$ measure (real quality). Following this procedure, we study the ability of each criterion to lead the algorithm towards the predefined structure, in terms of identifying the optimal clustering solution, and the optimal number of clusters.

On Identifying the Optimal Clustering Solution. Firstly, we test the indices ability for evaluating a given solution in order to identify the optimal one. The optimal solution is defined as the solution that maximizes the $FScore$. We present in Fig. 4, the indices results evaluated from three different angles:

- Their correlation with the $FScore$: By studying correlation between the predicted values and the real values, we can figure out to which extent a relative index can behave similarly to an external index. Correlation represents also how "good" are relative indices at (externally) evaluating solutions, independently of the clustering method.
- The optimal $FScore$ reached across the different k values: It represents the optimal clustering quality that a VI can reach if it shares the same optimal k with $FScore$. Values express also to which extent, (merging) actions based on a given index can lead to correct/incorrect partitions among clusters.
- The $FScore$ reached at the optimal value of VI: This is a good indicator of the overall solution quality that a VI can reach. By comparing these values to the previous values (i.e., optimal $FScore$), one can check to which extent the predicted optimal solution detected by a VI can approach the real optimal solution.

On Identifying the Optimal Number of Clusters. Secondly, we test the VI' ability for identifying the optimal k which we define as the number of distinct classes (i.e., senses) in a dataset. We present in Fig. 5 the indices results evaluated from two different angles:

- k at the optimal value of VI, which represents to which extend a VI, with its actual trend for determining the optimal k, is able to approach the real optimal k value,
- k at the optimal value of the $FScore$, which represents to which extend a VI, if it had the trend of $FScore$ for determining the optimal k, is able to approach the real optimal k value.

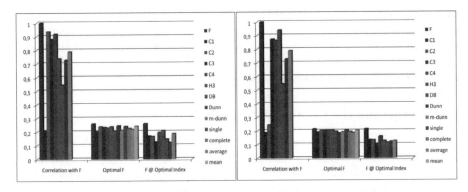

Fig. 4. Indices ability to identify the optimal clustering solution on DS1 and DS2 (left to right)

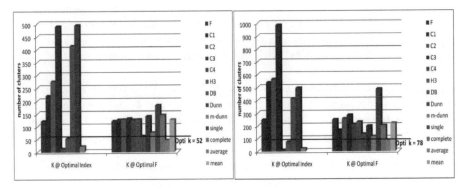

Fig. 5. Indices ability to identify the optimal number of clusters on DS1 and DS2 (left to right)

Discussion. A first observation is that most indices perform generally "well" at evaluating solutions. By looking at Fig. 4, we can notice the high correlations that most indices have with the *FScore*, which means that they have comparable behaviors to an external index. Although "enough accurate" at evaluating partitions, relative validity indices did not lead to significant improvements in the partitions' qualities in comparison to the classic criterion functions (e.g., mean-linkage) (See colomn *"Optimal F"*). Yet, involving relative indices has the inherent advantage of selecting *objectively* the optimal solution on the plot.

By considering the top-ranked solutions in terms of a *VI*, relatively poor solutions are provided in most cases, comparing to the optimal solutions that could have been reached. This can be clearly noticed by the gaps in the *FScore* values between the two colomns *"Optimal F"*, and *"F @ Optimal Index"* in Fig. 4. In our opinion, the gaps are due to the rigid trends of *VI* to the optimal k over different datasets (See Fig. 5). Even if these indices are supposed to be completely insensitive to k, depending uniquely on the dataset, they still depend more or less on k. The only exception is the $H3$ index. In fact, its high ability for reaching the optimal k is surely behind its high ability for reaching high-quality partitions. Although not giving the best correlations with $FScore$, we argue that, in our specific application, the $H3$ index seems to be the most reliable index to involve as a criterion function in the agglomerative algorithm.

4.3   Evaluating the Context-Aware Method

Our second experimental study is an attempt to answer the following question: *How reliable can we make the usage of relative indices as stopping criteria in agglomerative clustering?"* We explore thus the added-value of enhancing a clustering process with context-awareness. Recall that the purpose is to approach, as much as possible, FD from the optimal solution in terms of a VI.

We excluded from the following experiments some indices that showed to be inappropriate for the context-aware method because they provide too unstable curves to be stabilized (e.g., *Dunn*, *m-Dunn*). At last, our experiments will be carried out on 5 indices, namely *DB , C1, C2, C4, and H3*. Therefore, the experiments include 10 algorithms after having run the agglomerative algorithm 2 times for each of the 5 indices (with and without context-awareness).

Approaching the Optimal Clustering Solution. We study to which extend the context-aware method allows FD to approach the k yielding the optimal solution in tems of a VI. Therefore, we demonstrate in Fig. 6 the complete agglomerative clustering process $(k = n \rightarrow 1)$ divided into three parts:

- **P1:** This part goes from the initial set $(k = n)$ to the last point before FD. Thus, using a VI as a stopping criterion will lead the process to the last point of P1.
- **P2:** This part goes from FD to the optimal clustering solution. It represents the part that must be processed but would not if VI is used as a stopping criterion.
- **P3:** This part goes from the optimal solution until the root cluster $(k = 1)$, which form the unnecessary part that would be performed in vain if a VI is not used as a stopping criterion.

By observing Fig. 6, we can quickly notice the added-value of the context-aware method. On the first hand, it avoids a clustering algorithm from processing all the P3 parts which is a time waste. On the other hand, it contributes to reduce P2, since in most cases, FD occurs remarkably closer to the optimal solution. This will surely enable us to consider more relevantly a solution before FD as the optimal solution.

Quality of the Optimal Solutions. Since a context-aware algorithm is no more taking the merging decisions that optimizes VI, one could think that the method, although approaching the optimal solution, can deteriorate the quality of this solution. However, results show the opposite; actually, the $FScores$

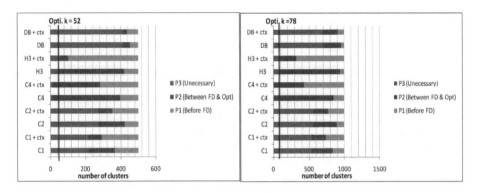

Fig. 6. The added-value of the context-aware method in approaching the optimal k on DS1 and DS2 (left to right)

reached at the optimal solution in terms of each index, assess that with the context-aware method, we can still have a comparable and sometimes better clustering quality than the basic method. In average, using our method led the top-ranked solutions in terms of VI to an $FScore$ improvement of 0.16% in DS1, and to a deterioration of 0.14% in DS2.

Quality of the Final Solutions. More informative than the quality of the optimal solutions, is the quality of the finally provided solutions for the user when stopping before FD. In average, using the context-aware method contributed to an $FScore$ improvement of 10.04 % and 19.53% in DS1 and DS2 respectively.

5   Conclusion and Future Works

To wrap up, our experiments showed that most relative validity indices, although behaving closely to an external index, i.e., $FScore$, have rigid trends for detecting the optimal k, which lead them to provide relatively poor partitions. The only exception was the $H3$ index which showed high ability to detect the optimal k. Following that, we introduced a new method that enhances validity indices with context-awareness, which allowed a more reliable usage of validity indices as stopping criteria. As for future works, we seek similar experimental studies involving larger datasets and more clustering methods, especially k-means and bisective k-means. Finally, we believe that a more flexible and theoretical definition of the context space in our method can lead to better results.

References

1. Cimiano, P., Hotho, A., Staab, S.: Comparing conceptual, divise and agglomerative clustering for learning taxonomies from text. In: ECAI, pp. 435–439 (2004)
2. Qiu, Y., Frei, H.-P.: Concept based query expansion. In: SIGIR 1993: Proc. of the 16th annual Int. ACM SIGIR Conf. on Research and development in information retrieval, pp. 160–169. ACM Press, New York (1993)

3. Stokoe, C., Oakes, M.P., Tait, J.: Word sense disambiguation in information retrieval revisited. In: SIGIR, pp. 159–166 (2003)
4. Han, J., Kamber, M.: Data Mining: Concepts and Techniques. Morgan Kaufmann, San Francisco (2006)
5. Jain, A.K., Dubes, R.C.: Algorithms for Clustering Data. Prentice-Hall, Englewood Cliffs (1988)
6. Halkidi, M., Batistakis, Y., Vazirgiannis, M.: Clustering validity checking methods: Part ii. SIGMOD Record 31(3), 19–27 (2002)
7. Milligan, G.W., Cooper, M.C.: An examination of procedures for determining the number of clusters in a data set. Psychometrika 50(2), 159–179 (1985), http://dx.doi.org/10.1007/BF02294245
8. Dunn, J.C.: Well separated clusters and optimal fuzzy paritions. Journal Cybern. 4, 95–104 (1974)
9. Davies, D.L., Bouldin, D.W.: A cluster separation measure. IEEE Transactions on Pattern Analysis and Machine Intelligence 1(2) (1979)
10. Tibshirani, R., Walther, G., Hastie, T.: Estimating the number of clusters in a dataset via the gap statistic. Dept. of Statistics, Stanford University., Tech. Rep. (2000)
11. Raskutti, B., Leckie, C.: An evaluation of criteria for measuring the quality of clusters. In: IJCAI, pp. 905–910 (1999)
12. Ben-Hur, A., Elisseeff, A., Guyon, I.: A stability based method for discovering structure in clustered data. In: Pacific Symposium on Biocomputing, pp. 6–17 (2002)
13. Bezdek, J.C., Li, W., Attikiouzel, Y., Windham, M.P.: A geometric approach to cluster validity for normal mixtures. Soft Comput. 1(4), 166–179 (1997)
14. Zhao, Y., Karypis, G.: Empirical and theoretical comparisons of selected criterion functions for document clustering. Machine Learning 55(3), 311–331 (2004)
15. Fraley, C., Raftery, A.E.: How many clusters? which clustering method? answers via model-based cluster analysis. Comput. J. 41(8), 578–588 (1998)
16. Rissanen, J.: Stochastic complexity in statistical inquiry. World Scientific Publishing Co., Singapore (1989)
17. Pelleg, D., Moore, A.W.: X-means: Extending k-means with efficient estimation of the number of clusters. In: ICML, pp. 727–734 (2000)
18. Agrawal, R., Gehrke, J., Gunopulos, D., Raghavan, P.: Automatic subspace clustering of high dimensional data for data mining applications. In: SIGMOD Conf., pp. 94–105 (1998)
19. Duda, R.O., Hart, P.E., Stork, D.G.: Pattern classification. John Wiley & Sons, Chichester (2001)
20. Pedersen, T., Kulkarni, A.: Selecting the "right" number of senses based on clustering criterion functions. In: EACL (2006)
21. Landes, S., Leacock, C., Tengi, R.I.: Building semantic concordances. M. Press, pp. 199–216 (1998)
22. Harris, Z.S.: Distributional structure. Oxford University Press, Oxford (1985)
23. Turney, P.D.: Mining the web for synonyms: Pmi-ir versus lsa on toefl. In: EMCL 2001: Proc. of the 12th European Conf. on Machine Learning, pp. 491–502. Springer, London (2001)

The Role of Nominalizations
in Prepositional Phrase Attachment in GENIA

Jonathan Schuman and Sabine Bergler

Department of Computer Science and Software Engineering
Concordia University
1455 de Maisonneuve Blvd West
Montreal, Quebec, H3G 1M8

Abstract. We demonstrate the importance of nominalizations for prepositional phrase attachment for biomedical journal articles. We outline several significant features of the GENIA corpus data and compare them to Wall Street Journal Data. We evaluate a heuristics-based approach to PP attachment based on shallow chunking and domain dependent resources. We conclude that the heuristics based approach performs well, is appropriate for shallow levels of text analysis, and can easily be adapted to or used with other techniques, such as a filter after a statistical parse, or as features in a more complex machine learning environment.

1   Introduction

BioNLP is a field of growing importance that uses general natural language processing techniques to retrieve, extract, and mine for information [1]. Many novel applications choose shallow text preprocessing techniques, such as chunking: Saurí et al. [2], for instance, base event annotation for question answering on chunked input. Chunkers in general return base noun phrases, that is noun phrases without attachments such as prepositional phrases. We present here a set of heuristics for PP attachment that works from chunked input and shows surprising stability across domains. The main feature underlying the heuristics is a distinct treatment of nominalizations, which are more pervasive in biomedical text than for instance in the newspaper domain, as we illustrate through corpus analysis.

Recent work related to prepositional phrases (PPs) largely builds on existing resources, such as treebanks or parsers and attempts to further develop the semantic contribution of the PP. Large repositories for sense inventories for prepositions have been developed for English [3] and French [4]. Annotated resources such as FrameNet [5], PropBank [6], and VerbNet [7] have been developed. PP attachment work focuses mainly on finding the attachment site of PPs when there is the classical ambiguity between NP and VP attachment illustrated in

(1) *I saw the man with a telescope.*

where the ambiguity stems from the lack of context that would determine who had the telescope.

S. Bergler (Ed.): Canadian AI 2008, LNAI 5032, pp. 271–282, 2008.
© Springer-Verlag Berlin Heidelberg 2008

Considering domain specific data from microbiology, the question of ambiguity takes on a different shape. The scientific literature in microbiology, like many genres for specialists, is characterized by heavy NPs. We assume here that NP-heavy styles in literature for experts serves the purpose of reducing redundancy and allowing to convey information more compactly. Redundancy is reduced by allowing to refer to an event via the event nominal only, without specifying any arguments, when the reader can be assumed to know or not need to know the specific details of the event. Information is compacted using chains of prepositional phrases. Thus in the GENIA Treebank [8], a more typical example of attachment ambiguity would be between several postnominal nouns, as in Example (2):

(2) *The effect of hydrolysis of the hemicelluloses in the milled wood lignin on the molecular mass distribution was then examined...*

Hahn et al. [9] point out that PPs are crucial for semantic interpretation of biomedical texts due to the wide variety of conceptual relations they introduce. They note that this is reflected in their training and test data, extracted from findings reports in histopathology, where prepositions account for about 10% of all words and more than 25% of the text is contained in PPs. The coverage of PPs in our development and test data, comprised of varied texts in proteomics, is even higher with 26% of the text occurring in postnominal PPs alone.

The BioNLP community has worked over many different subdomain corpora, driven by application needs. A lack of shared, annotated corpora to develop and test many statistical techniques has been noted in [10]. Tateisi and coauthors have taken on the challenge of annotating predicate-argument structure for the GENIA Treebank, including predicate-argument behavior for nominalizations, noting their importance. In the work reported here, we give a comparative corpus analysis of PP attachment behavior for multiple, postnominal NPs considering nominalizations[1] and entities. Presenting a system that robustly attaches PPs with over 80% accuracy, we propose PP attachment as a first step in semantic role labeling and ultimately predicate-argument structure determination, and offer the robustness, versatility, and modularity of a symbolic, heuristics based approach.

In order to assess the properties of the corpus vs the performance of the heuristics we conducted two comparisons. Our core system attaches postnominal PPs using NP chunker input on GENIA abstracts. It achieves 84% accuracy. In order to evaluate how specialized the language of the GENIA corpus is, we ran the same heuristics on the Wall Street Journal corpus. Performance drops by 10%; corpus analysis shows that this is largely due to a number of prepositions that are not considered in the heuristics. In a second experiment, we extended the heuristics to attach all PPs in a text, including the ones that are not postnominal. Here, the chunker input had to include VP chunks to which to attach PPs. VP chunker input is less reliable than NP chunker input, and together they do not always cover the full sentence. The resulting degradation in PP attachment performance suggests that PPs that do not attach to NPs or VPs require additional attention.

---

[1] In our experiments, we refer to nominalizations as defined in Section 4.

2   Data and Procedures

This work is motivated by the need to process full-text articles from scientific journal articles using shallow techniques. We employ an in-house NP chunker and the verb group chunker distributed with the GATE distribution [11].

The initial problem was that of constructing complete NPs using only the NP chunker, gazetteer lists, and other available resources. For a pilot study[12], we annotated a small proteomics corpus of full-text journal articles for postnominal PP attachment and developed heuristics that achieved 88% accuracy on this corpus, and 85% accuracy on a second, manually annotated test corpus.

Here, we report on the validation and further development of the heuristics on a subset of the GENIA Treebank (GTB) corpus[2]. When applied to the GENIA data, a slightly improved set of heuristics proved surprisingly stable with an accuracy of 84%. The GENIA Treebank has a different subdomain (based on MEDLINE query using MESH terms "Human, Blood Cells and Transcription Factors" as opposed to proteomics, the domain of our development and test corpora) and consists of abstracts only, while the original development data consisted of full-text articles. This experiment suggested that the PP attachment heuristics are specific neither to the proteomics domain nor to full-text articles.

Table 1. PPs in GENIA and Wall Street Journal

	GENIA	Wall Street Journal
Word count	41427	1173766
Words in PPs	21914	478724
	52.9%	40.79%
# of postnominal PPs	3951	73545
# of PPs	6194	117822
NPattachment/VPattachment	2.02	1.15

Running the same heuristics over the Penn Treebank corpus of Wall Street Journal articles[3] incurs a 10% drop in performance. Corpus analysis indicates that this drop is in part due to the Zipfian distribution of prepositions. The 10 most frequent prepositions account for over 83% of the occurrences, yet in total WSJ has over 200 prepositions[4]. We exploit this behavior, since our targeted heuristics cover only the most frequent prepositions, accruing a larger error in WSJ due to wider use of the default rule for lower frequency prepositions. A certain class of prepositions, mainly denoting spatial relationships, such as *next* or *through* are underrepresented in GTB.

Table 1 shows that despite the difference in size and domain, the importance of PPs is similar in both corpora: 53% of the words in GTB are part of a PP, as compared to

---

[2] We use the first 200 abstracts of the first release, see http://www-tsujii.is.s.u-tokyo.ac.jp/~ genia/topics/Corpus/. Treebank annotations are used for testing the accuracy of the heuristics only.

[3] http://www.ldc.upenn.edu/

[4] In contrast, our subset of GENIA has 105 unique prepositions.

41% for WSJ. The difference of 10% accounts for what we perceive as NP heavy style typical of specialist domains.

We also observe a change in attachment patterns: the ratio of NP attachment to VP attachment (the classical case of ambiguity) differs significantly in GTB and WSJ. The NP heavy style is evident in the ratio of NP attachment to VP attachment in GTB being nearly twice that of WSJ. Given these strong differences in style as well as coverage, the difference in performance is lower than expected and suggests that the heuristics form a stable core. Most importantly, they cover the domain of event nominals in both domains.

3   Non-postnominal PPs

In our next experiment we extended the heuristics to cover all PPs, postnominal and otherwise, and all attachment points. This first required extending preprocessing to provide exact attachment points for non-NP-attaching PPs. (Previously, the attachment site for non-NP-attaching postnominal PPs was stipulated to be some verb outside the NP, but its location was not actually determined.) To this end, a verb group (VG) chunker was added to the system to identify verbs as possible attachment sites.

The basic assumption, namely that these heuristics are used with shallow partial chunkers, makes the extension to all PPs and all attachment points more difficult, because the different attachment points have to be part of some chunks. We can provide VGs, NPs, and sentences (from the sentence splitter) for scoring, but our system is currently not able to access attachment points in adjective phrases as annotated in GTB. An example is given in Example 3, where the PP *to the protein synthesis inhibitor anisomycin* is annotated as attaching to the adjective phrase *peculiarly sensitive*.

(3) *After appropriate stimulation, both NF-AT and AP-1 are peculiarly sensitive to the protein synthesis inhibitor anisomycin.*

4   Using Lexical Resources

Input to the previous system was tagged and chunked raw text and the UMLS Specialist lexicon[5] was used for nominalization lookup. The UMLS lexicon is a general English lexicon that includes many biomedical terms, as well as syntactic, morphological, and orthographic information. Its coverage is extensive, but gaps do exist, particularly when running over text from other domains. In an experiment we compared the performance of dictionary lookup in UMLS with simple suffix matching. The suffixes used to flag nominalizations are given in Table 2. Relying only on suffix matching led to a small decrease in system performance (about 1%). However, using both dictionary lookup and suffix matching resulted in slightly better accuracy than when using lookup alone (about 0.5%). While the effect is a small improvement in addition with UMLS, suffix-based matching by itself provides domain independent nominalization recognition at comparable performance.

---

[5] http://www.nlm.nih.gov/pubs/factsheets/umlslex.html

Table 2. Nominal endings that indicate deverbal derivation—from [13], p12

-ANT	inhabitant, contestant, informant, participant, lubricant
-EE	appointee, payee, nominee, absentee, refugee
-ER, -OR	singer, writer, driver, employer, accelerator, incubator, supervisor
-AGE	breakage, coverage, drainage, leverage, shrinkage, wastage
-AL	refusal, revival, dismissal
-ION	exploration, starvation, ratification, victimization, foundation
-SION	invasion, evasion
-ING	building, opening, filling, earnings, savings, shavings, wedding
-MENT	arrangement, amazement, puzzlement, embodiment, equipment

Table 3. Multiword prepositions from the GENIA Treebank

in accordance with	in contrast to	in the presence of	because of
in agreement with	in addition to	in the absence of	in spite of
in parallel with	in proportion to	in the context of	prior to
in conjunction with	in response to	on the basis of	due to
in comparison with	with respect to	by virtue of	relative to
in concert with	in light of	by means of	

The extended heuristics also have access to lists of collocations that were annotated in GTB as prepositions, shown here as Table 3. These 23 complex prepositions account for 0.68% of all annotated prepositions in GTB.

5   Attachment Heuristics

The postnominal attachment heuristics were built on two main principles, *right association* and *nominalization affinity*.

The first principle, right association (RA), accounts for a large portion of the attachment behavior observed in our development corpus. It describes a preference for parses that maximize right branches in the parse tree [14]. In the context of postnominal PPs, right associative attachment results in each PP attaching to the NP that immediately precedes it.

We formulated the second principle, nominalization affinity (NA), based on the observation that PPs in our development corpus regularly deviate from right associative attachment in the presence of nominalizations. Nominalization affinity describes the frequent usage of PPs as arguments and adjuncts that modify nominalizations. Given a postnominal PP, heuristics based on nominalization affinity traverse all possible attachment points (starting at the immediately preceding NP and proceeding from right to left) and attach the PP to the first NP with a nominalized head noun.

The core heuristics apply these two principles in various ways depending on the preposition in case.

Right Association is the sole heuristic for *of* and serves as default for *for* and *from*. Right association is also the default for prepositions that have no heuristic associated.

Strong NA is defined for the prepositions *by, at, to, during, after, as, into, <complex prepositions>* (see Table 3). Attachment point for StrongNA is the closest nominalization that is not the complement of a further nominalization within the postnominal PP chain. If no nominalization is present, the heuristic tries to select the closest preceding verb group. If there is no preceding verb group, the heuristic defaults to RA.

Weak NA is defined for *in, with*. Weak NA attempts to attach to the closest nominalization. If none is present in the postnominal cluster, the PP attaches to the closest NP that is not the object of an *of* PP and does not specify a temperature measurement. If this fails, the heuristic tries to select the closest preceding verb group. If there is no preceding verb group, the heuristic defaults to RA.

"effect on" is defined for *on*. This heuristic encodes the frequent collocation of the nouns *effect, impact, influence* with the preposition *on*. The heuristic attaches to *effect, impact, influence* if they occur as heads of preceding NPs in a postnominal PP chain only if there is no available verb group attachment point or the "effect" NP has a causal *of* PP. If none of *effect, impact*, or *influence* are found, this heuristic defaults to RA.

Non-postnominal PPs This heuristic is applied to PPs that do not occur postnominally, regardless of preposition or object type. Non-postnominal PPs attach to the closest preceding verb group. If there is none, attachment is to the closest sentence tag.

6 Overrides

The core heuristics are very general and associate a single heuristic with each preposition, not distinguishing between arguments, adjuncts, or type of PP. Some complement types, however, systematically select for a different attachment strategy. We use dictionary lookup in UMLS to detect a few types of PP complements and apply override rules in those cases. Overrides also handle a few frequent collocations that select for different attachment points from the general heuristics.

All of the prepositions to which these rules apply are handled by the three core heuristics. Considering the complement type permits to tailor the heuristics to a particular sense of the preposition. For instance, if the complement is a nominalization, procedure, or time expression in a PP headed by *in*, Strong NA applies. Overrides also allow to define more domain dependent rules, such as the observation that in PPs headed by *at*, if the complement is a concentration measurement, it should attach to a chemical in the GENIA Treebank.[6] When applicable, override rules take precedence. Some overrides have no default, and are applied in a cascading order. If all overrides in a cascade fail, attachment defaults to the appropriate core heuristic, as specified above. The

---

[6] Through overrides, the system could be tailored to the domain. Our interest lies in a system that can be used for a different domain with minimal adjustments, and so all overrides hold across domains.

override heuristics are described below, referred to by the prepositions and object types (enclosed in angle brackets) of the PPs to which they apply.

"Same as" *(as)* Attach to the closest NP with *same* occurring as a prenominal modifier.

"Role in/as" *(in, as)* This heuristic only applies, if the head of a preceding NP is *role*. In this case, if attachment to a verb group is possible, then check whether it is a phrasal verb (e.g. *play a role in*). In this case, attach to the verb, else attach to the NP headed by *role.*

after <**any except time**> Attach to the closest NP specifying a time measurement. Default to Strong NA if none is found.

at <**concentration measurement**> Attach to the closest NP with a chemical entity as the head noun. If none is found, default to RA attachment if the PP is part of the first NP in a sentence, and default to VP attachment otherwise.

with <**disorder**> Attach to the closest NP with a "living being" as the head noun.

in <**nominalization|procedure|time**> Override to Strong NA (instead of Weak NA).

for <**measurement**> Override to Strong NA (instead of RA).

7   Results

Of the two experiments to put our postnominal PP attachment heuristics into perspective, testing the postnominal heuristics on the Wall Street Journal illustrated the difference in style between the two genres. The intuitive difference in style seems larger than the drop in performance and this experiment served mainly to confirm the importance and generality of the core heuristics, right attachment and nominalization preference, as well as to illustrate interesting genre differences.

The second experiment, extending the coverage of the system beyond postnominal PPs in the GENIA corpus, illustrated the potential of scalability of the heuristic, chunker based approach from NP chunks only to NP and VP chunks. This extension introduced more attachment ambiguity. Specifically, while the majority of non-postnominal PPs attach to the closest preceding VP, a significant portion of these, 27.3% in GTB, attach to other constituents (e.g. S, ADJP, ADVP, etc). Most sentence-attached PPs can be readily distinguished by their position in the sentence: if no NPs or VPs occur between the start of a sentence and the PP in question, the PP is almost certain to attach to the sentence. However, attachment heuristics for other constituents require additional phrase chunking to handle ADJPs and other less frequent phrases. Currently, all PPs with such attachments are erroneously attached by the system to a preceding VP.

Nonetheless, even with a significant subset of non-postnominal PPs being systematically assigned incorrect attachment, broadening the scope of consideration to all PPs resulted in little loss in accuracy. The overall accuracy for all PPs is 76%, as compared to 84% on postnominal PPs alone. About half of this 8% discrepancy is attributed to ADJP attachment error. A considerable portion of the remaining difference is the result of verb-group chunker errors. The small drop in performance is particularly interesting when considering the scale of the increase in coverage and the simplicity of the rules by which this was achieved. The addition of non-postnominal PPs represents a 50% increase in the number of PPs considered by the attachment module. All of these additional PPs are processed using only two rules: attachment to the closest preceding VP or, in the case of fronted PPs, attachment to the sentence.

Table 4. Performance of extended heuristics over all PPs in GTB by heuristic (%)

Heuristic	Coverage	Accuracy	Heuristic	Coverage	Accuracy
RightAssoc	38.43	96.49	EffectOn	1.67	65.06
Non-Postnom	25.37	79.29	With-Disorders	0.85	100.00
WeakNA	12.72	64.24	Role in/as	0.74	94.59
StrongNA	12.04	56.35	After-NotTime	0.44	45.45
Default (RA)	2.56	48.03	SameAs	0.06	100.00
			Total		76.28

Table 5. Performance of extended heuristics over postnominal PPs in GTB by heuristic (%)

Heuristic	Coverage	Accuracy	Heuristic	Coverage	Accuracy
RightAssoc	57.19	97.03	With-Disorders	1.25	100.00
WeakNA	17.77	67.62	Role in/as	1.07	94.44
StrongNA	15.89	63.04	After-NotTime	0.57	52.63
Default (RA)	3.73	49.60	SameAs	0.09	100.00
EffectOn	2.36	67.09	Total		83.60

We compare the performance of the extended heuristics for all PPs to the performance on postnominal PPs only in Tables 4 and 5. The performance drop for the extended system running over all PPs stems in large part from the ambiguity in attachment points outside the NP and from non-postnominal PPs. It is apparent from these tables that accuracy of the postnominal heuristics were also indirectly affected by the addition of non-postnominal attachment to the system. While no non-postnominal PPs are handled by the core heuristics, changes in the chunkers, which were needed to support the additional PPs, resulted in a performance drop in some of the postnominal heuristics.

Our evaluation mechanisms were designed to isolate measurement of the performance of the attachment module from errors in its input from the rest of the system. Thus, the evaluation module does not consider spurious PPs attached by the system that do not occur in the corpus. Previously, when the system was limited to postnominal PPs, this included discarding PPs found by the system that were not actually postnominal. For example, in

(4) *the expression of the BSAP gene shifts to the fetal liver*

where *shifts* is mistagged as a noun and consequently chunked into the preceding NP, the previous system would discard the PP *to the fetal liver*. With the expansion of coverage to non-postnominal PPs, such errors must now be included in the accuracy evaluation. Though errors as with Example 4 are, strictly speaking, errors in attachment of non-postnominal PPs, they are counted against the heuristic that assigns the attachment; in this case, StrongNA. Accordingly, the postnominal heuristics show some loss in performance with the addition of non-postnominal PPs.

In particular, a significant drop in performance was observed for the StrongNA heuristic. More than half of this decrease is from errors as in Example 4. StrongNA is particularly susceptible to such errors because the prepositions it handles also frequently occur as non-postnominals attaching to VPs. The remaining performance loss for StrongNA results from the added requirement of matching the exact location of VP attachment. The effect is most pronounced for the StrongNA heuristic, as it handles almost all postnominal VP-attachment.

8 Discussion

The performance of the extended PPattach system is limited by a lack of adjective or adverb phrase constituents in its input, this accounts for almost 4% of the overall accuracy. But the NP and verb group chunkers have other limitations that impact performance.

- Coordination is a problem for the NP chunker
- The verb grouper misses certain main verbs in participle form, such as *down-regulated* in Example 5.

  (5) *the number of GR in MNL could be down-regulated by their cognate ligands*

- The NP chunker doesn't recognize certain deverbal nouns, such as *cloning* in Example 6

  (6) *Identification and cloning of TCF-1*

In general, the chunker errors with the most effect on attachment accuracy stem from tagger errors on gerundive and participle forms.

Since the chunkers cannot recognize all PPs, chunker recall—the number of valid PPs recognized by the chunkers divided by the actual number of PPs present in the corpus—should be noted. Chunker recall was 86.8% for the GENIA Treebank.

9 Preposition Senses

Our approach is focused entirely on the preposition. The solid performance of the extended PPattach at 76% is surprising, given the attention that has been paid in the literature to the different senses a preposition can have. The Preposition Project[7] [15] is a developing resource as a complete sense directory for prepositions and a good example of the lexicographic approach to preposition senses. Along with senses, prepositions are described with the different *frames* they participate in, for both verb frames and event nominal frames. While this is an invaluable resource for humans, automatic systems have to be very sophisticated to be able to use the data appropriately.

Assuming that different senses of a preposition differ in attachment behavior, *of* proves to be a puzzling preposition. It is highly ambiguous between three uses, one supplying the subject, one the direct object of an event nominal, and a third corresponding to a genitive, performing an attribution or a causal link, as illustrated in Example 7.

---

[7] http://www.clres.com/cgi-bin/onlineTPP/find_prep.cgi

(7) (a) Inhibition of protein phosphatases by okadaic acid
     (b) a negative reaction of the primary tumor
     (c) the primary site of cancer

It is surprising that right association, the heuristic triggered by *of*, has the high accuracy shown in Table 6 under these conditions. It simply shows that *of* PPs immediately follow their attachment points, disregarding their sense contribution.

Table 6. Performance of extended heuristics over all PPs in GTB by preposition (%)

Prep	Frequency	Accuracy	Prep	Frequency	Accuracy
of	35.01	95.86	at	1.37	64.71
in	19.99	73.31	between	1.01	80.00
by	6.91	74.93	after	0.85	64.29
with	6.78	73.59	during	0.72	66.67
to	5.88	57.88	through	0.66	21.21
for	4.17	85.99	into	0.50	64.00
from	3.34	75.90	within	0.42	71.43
on	2.19	69.72	upon	0.34	64.71
as	1.41	67.14			

Table 7. Performance of extended heuristics over postnominal PPs in GTB by preposition (%)

Prep	Frequency	Accuracy	Prep	Frequency	Accuracy
of	49.85	99.46	as	0.95	59.38
in	17.68	66.78	between	0.83	85.71
with	5.75	81.87	during	0.78	69.23
for	4.29	82.64	after	0.63	52.38
by	4.23	70.42	through	0.54	16.67
to	3.91	54.96	into	0.45	73.33
from	3.25	76.15	within	0.33	45.45
on	2.36	67.09	in response to	0.30	70.00
at	1.16	48.72			

10   Conclusion

This is to our knowledge the first in-depth genre based study of PPs from the point of view of a shallow application system. Statistical approaches do not give the same insight into the corpus linguistic aspects. The most important outcome of the study is the clear illustration that nominalizations can be detected with knowledge-poor means and that their arguments as supplied by PPs can be properly attached using shallow, heuristic techniques. This makes an important part of biomedical text accessible to shallow techniques and thus available to more semantic analysis.

Linguistic studies of prepositions, their sense and attachment behavior have focused largely on simpler problems of disambiguating NP vs VP attachment and paid attention more to distinguishing argument from adjuncts and determining the semantic role of the PP in its larger constituent. Nominalizations have not been given the same attention, but [13] consider PP attachment including attachment to nominalizations with particular emphasis on distinguishing arguments from adjuncts based on corpus-based evidence. They employ a classification task using some linguistic principles based on a constructed and annotated corpus. Here, instead, we use raw and complex data and employ a shallow technique to assess and partly quantify the occurrence of different phenomena in the data. The use of simple, general heuristics makes the technique ready to use on text of other genres and domains, which has been demonstrated by our feasibility study porting the postnominal PP attachment system to the Wall Street Journal without adaptation. The difference in performance informs on genre or domain specific differences, which can in turn be exploited for stochastic techniques. We consider it a feature that the heuristic-based approach presented here consists of a general core system, that can be incrementally tuned to cover specific observations on a particular corpus or domain.

Our focus on postnominal PPs stems from the importance these have in the microbiology domain. We demonstrated that postnominal heuristics can be extended to shallow attachment of all PPs occurring in microbiology texts. A drop in performance of 8% is largely due to preprocessing errors and again underscores that the heuristics are stable.

The understudied phenomenon of postnominal PP chains is of greater importance in domain specific texts geared towards expert readers. Our study provides mechanisms to decide on postnominal PP attachment with shallow means, allowing shallow processing of texts that gives complete NPs, not only bare NPs or named entities. Complete NPs not only contain all PP modifiers for entities, but also the optional arguments for deverbal nominalizations, opening the door for more precise shallow information extraction and event annotation.

References

1. Shatkay, H., Feldman, R.: Mining the biomedical literature in the genomic era: An overview. Journal of Computational Biology (JCB) 10(6), 821–856 (2003)
2. Saurí, R., Knippen, R., Verhagen, M., Pustejovsky, J.: Evita: A robust event recognizer for QA systems. In: Proceedings of HLT/EMNLP 2005, Vancouver, B.C. (2005)
3. Litkowski, K., Hargraves, O.: Coverage and inheritance in The Preposition Project. In: Proceedings of the Third ACL-SIGSEM Workshop on Prepositionsat EACL 2006, Trento, Italy (April 2006)
4. Saint-Dizier, P.: An Overview of PrepNet: abstract notions, frames and inferential patterns. In: Villavicencio, A. (ed.) 2nd Workshop on the syntax and semantics of prepositions, Univ. of Colchester, Colchester, pp. 155–169 (2005)
5. Baker, C., Filmore, C., Lowe, J.: The Berkeley FrameNet project. In: Proceedings of COLING/ACL, Montreal, Canada (1998)
6. Palmer, M., Gildea, D., Kingsbury, P.: The Proposition Bank: An annotated corpus of semantic roles. Computational Linguistics 31(1) (2005)

7. Kipper, K., Dang, H., Palmer, M.: Class-based construction of a verb lexicon. In: Proceedings of the Seventeenth National Conference on Artificial Intelligence (AAAI 2000), Austin, TX (2000)

8. Kim, J.D., Ohta, T., Tateisi, Y., Tsujii, J.: GENIA corpus - a semantically annotated corpus for bio-textmining. Bioinformatics 19(suppl. 1), i180–i182 (2003)

9. Hahn, U., Romacker, M., Schulz, S.: Creating knowledge repositories from biomedical reports: the MEDSYNDIKATE text mining system. In: Proceedings of the 7th Pacific Symposium on Biocomputing, Hawaii, USA (2002)

10. Tateisi, Y., Ohta, T., Tsujii, J.: Annotation of predicate-argument structure of molecular biology text. In: Proceedings of the IJCNLP 2004 workshop Beyond Shallow Analyses (2004)

11. Cunningham, H.: Gate, a general architecture for text engineering. Computers and the Humanities 36, 223–254 (2002), http://gate.ac.uk

12. Schuman, J., Bergler, S.: Postnominal prepositional phrase attachment in proteomics. In: Proceedings of BioNLP 2006, a workshop associated with HLT-NAACL 2006, Brooklyn, NY (June 2006)

13. Merlo, P., Ferrer, E.: The notion of argument in PP attachment. Computational Linguistics 32(2) (2006)

14. Kimball, J.: Seven principles of surface structure parsing in natural language. Cognition 2, 15–47 (1973)

15. Litkowski, K.C.: The preposition project. In: Proceedings of the Second ACL-SIGSEM Workshop on The Linguistic Dimensions of Prepositions and their Use in Computational Linguistics Formalisms and Applications, Colchester, England (2005)

A Statistical Model for Topic Segmentation and Clustering

M. Mahdi Shafiei and Evangelos E. Milios

Faculty of Computer Science, Dalhousie University
shafiei@cs.dal.ca, eem@cs.dal.ca
http://www.cs.dal.ca/~shafiei

Abstract. This paper presents a statistical model for discovering topical clusters of words in unstructured text. The model uses a hierarchical Bayesian structure and it is also able to identify segments of text which are topically coherent. The model is able to assign each segment to a particular topic and thus categorizes the corresponding document to potentially multiple topics. We present some initial results indicating that the word topics discovered by the proposed model are more consistent compared to other models. Our early experiments show that our model clustering performance compares well with other clustering models on a real text corpus, which do not provide topic segmentation. Segmentation performance of our model is also comparable to a recently proposed segmentation model which does not provide document clustering.

1 Introduction

Using statistical models for modeling text corpora has received a lot of attention in recent years. These models can provide a compact description of documents in a corpus, which has been one of the main goals of the research community. Availability of such descriptions will make processing of increasingly large collections of text more efficient while preserving the essential statistical properties of the collection. The output will then be useful for basic tasks such as classification, novelty detection, summarization, and similarity and relevance judgements.

Statistical topic models are generative models for text. The basic idea behind all proposed topic models [4] is that a document is a mixture of several topics where each topic is some distribution over words. Each topic model is a generative model which specifies a simple probabilistic process by which the words in a document are being generated on the basis of a small number of latent variables.

Using standard statistical techniques, one can invert the process and infer the set of latent variables responsible for generating a given set of documents [16]. Assuming a model for generating the data, the goal of fitting this generative model is to find the optimal set of latent variables that can explain the observed data (i.e., observed words in documents). These latent variables capture the correlations between words and are referred to as topics. The direct output of these models, from an application point of view, is a set of overlapping clusters of words. Each of these clusters can be visualized by the the most probable words from their corresponding probability distribution. Clustering documents can be viewed only as a byproduct of the model fitting process and not as a direct output of topic models.

S. Bergler (Ed.): Canadian AI 2008, LNAI 5032, pp. 283–295, 2008.
© Springer-Verlag Berlin Heidelberg 2008

Latent Dirichlet Allocation (LDA) [4] is one of the highly cited works in topic modeling. In LDA, documents are assumed to be sampled from a random mixture over latent topics, where each topic is characterized by a distribution over words. Furthermore, the mixture coefficients are also assumed to be random and by assuming a prior probability on them, LDA provides a complete generative model for the documents [4].

The LDA model has been criticized for its inability to capture correlations between word topics which are common in natural text. A document about environment is more likely to be also about health than religion. In the LDA model, the topic proportions are derived from a Dirichlet distribution and hence are nearly independent. Several models have been proposed to capture the correlation between topics [3,8,14]. In the latter two models [8,14], the concept of topics is extended to include not only the distributions over words, but also distributions over topics. By assuming this, we allow some topics to be mixtures of other topics, thereby capturing the correlation between them. Using this idea, in our previous work [14], we proposed a hierarchical Bayesian model capable of clustering words and documents simultaneously and capturing correlation between word topics.

Splitting a text stream into coherent and meaningful segments is referred to as topic segmentation. In text segmentation, we are looking for the points in text at which focus shifts from one topic to another. For example, a news broadcast usually covers several stories or articles and therefore can be divided naturally into several pieces, each topically different. Topic segmentation is a preprocessing step for several other problems, such as topic detection and tracking in unstructured text. Information produced by a topic segmentation system can be used in summarization, browsing and facilitating the process of retrieving information buried in text data. The results can also be used to provide more informative responses for a search query by using the segmentation output for better navigation and scanning of the results by the user.

In this paper, we propose a statistical model for topic modeling and segmentation. The main contributions of the paper can be summarized as follows:

1. We propose a generative model which is able to segment text data into topically coherent segments while discovering the topic distributions over words.
2. The proposed model, built on our previous work [14] and using a hierarchical structure is able to capture correlations between word topics. The proposed model also provides overlapping clustering of the documents.

The rest of this paper is organized as follows. In section 2, we briefly discuss the previous approaches to topic segmentation and modeling problems. We present our proposed model in section 3 and explain inference and parameter estimation algorithms for the model. In section 4, a set of experiments are provided to show the performance of the proposed model and compare it to related approaches. Finally, we conclude the paper with a review of the paper and discussion on future works.

2   Topic Segmentation and Identification

"Topic models" and "topic segmentation" are two closely related problems. Nevertheless, they have been often approached independently. In this section, we examine the possibility for treating these two problems in a single framework.

LDA is heavily dependent on the "bag-of-words" assumption. In models based on this assumption, the order of words and therefore the information implicit in that ordering is ignored for the sake of simplifying the model and avoiding computational complexity. Several recent works have tried to overcome this limitation [18,17]. This assumption is on the very finest level of a document structure, namely words. Two consecutive words are assumed to be topically independent whereas in reality the contrary is true. The topical dependency is also true for higher levels of text structure such as sentences and paragraphs. Actually, the dependencies in the higher levels originate from the dependencies in the word level. Therefore, one way of going beyond the "bag-of-words" assumption without complicating our model is to model these higher level structural dependencies.

This means that one can assume that a text document is composed of some topically correlated segments where each of these segments is a sequence of words. The "bag-of-words" assumption is still considered valid for the words in each of these segments but one hopes that, by capturing the higher level correlations (among segments), some of the finer level correlations (among words) are also captured. This idea makes topic segmentation a closely related and relevant problem. It suggests that tackling topic modeling and topic segmentation in a single framework provides a solution for going beyond the "bag-of-words" assumption.

Many of the existing topic segmentation algorithms are based on the idea that topic segments tend to be lexically cohesive. In lexical cohesion models, it is assumed that a shift in term distribution indicates a shift in topic. The most notable algorithm based on this assumption [7] uses a sliding window over text and uses a vector space representation of the text under the window. At each step, the term distribution for the text under the window is compared to the left and right regions of the window. The algorithm assigns a score to each topic boundary candidate based on a similarity measure between chunks of words appearing to the left and right of the candidate. Topic boundaries are then represented by the local minima points in the curve formed by these scores. These points are then adjusted to coincide with known paragraph boundaries.

3   Hierarchical Topic Segmentation and Detection Model

The driving idea for the proposed model is that human generated text seems to be composed of topically coherent segments put together. Each of the segments specifically is concerned with a more or less general topic. This topic can be modeled using statistical topic modeling approaches. One usually expects consecutive segments to be topically correlated. It means that considering a topically coherent segment, the next segment should convey a closely related topic as its predecessor. This is an observation similar to the one for words which questions the validity of "bag-of-words" assumption. Although a principal assumption for many statistical models of language, it is not a realistic one. Instead, we assume that the "bag-of words" assumption within each segment is fairly realistic, unlike for the whole document.

In this work, a model is proposed which is able to detect the boundaries of these segments. Each segment is assigned to a topic from a predefined number of topics which are referred to as "document-topics" or "supertopics" hereafter. Then, each segment is modeled based on its word content similar to most probabilistic topic models. These learnt topics on words which are referred to as "word-topics" or simply topics are used to represent document topics. Each document-topic is assumed to be a mixture of word-topics where the mixture coefficients uniquely specify the document-topic.

Our work follows our previous work [14] on clustering documents and words simultaneously. To model the relation between topics of consecutive sentences or paragraphs, we assume a Markov structure on the distribution over document-topics. We assume that it is very likely for a sentence (or a paragraph) to have the same distribution over document-topics as its previous sentence. Otherwise, we sample a new distribution for the document-topic of this sentence. Our model also reduces to the model proposed in [13] if the text segments considered to be speech discourse. Moreover, our model is able to capture the correlations between higher level topics which is not seen in the model proposed in [13].

3.1 The Proposed Hierarchical Bayesian Model

Each document consists of different structural components or units like words, sentences and paragraphs. The proposed model can work with any of these structural components. For this section, we assume that this component is chosen to be sentences of the document. We order sentences of each document and assume a Markov structure on the topic distributions of sentences: with high probability, the topic for sentence i is the same as for sentence $i - 1$; otherwise we sample a new topic for it. We call the topics assigned to sentences "document-topics" or "super-topics". We consider a switching binary variable for the topic of each sentence, indicating whether the topic for the current sentence is the same as the one for its predecessor. If we consider the states for all these switching variables, they will define a segmentation for the given document. We can achieve different levels of granularity for segmentation by choosing different types of structural units (i.e. words, sentences or paragraphs).

The proposed generative probabilistic model is shown as a graphical model in Fig. 1.a. Plate notation [5] is a standard and convenient way of illustrating probabilistic models with repeated sampling steps. In this graphical notation, shaded and unshaded variables indicate observed and latent (i.e., unobserved) variables respectively.

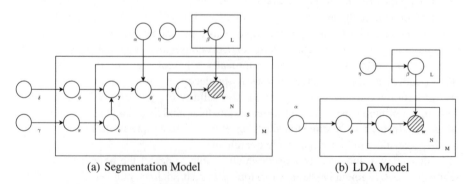

(a) Segmentation Model   (b) LDA Model

Fig. 1. Segmentation Model compared to the LDA Model

The segmentation model assumes the following generative process for each document d in a corpus D(intuitive explanations of model parameters are given in the text following the overview of the generative process.):

1. Choose $S \sim Poisson(\mu)$: number of sentences in the document
2. Choose $\phi \sim Dir(\delta)$
3. For each of the S sentences s
   (a) Choose the same supertopic y_s for s as its previous sentence y_{s-1} with probability $p(c_s = 1) = \pi$
   (b) Otherwise, choose a supertopic for the sentence $y_s \sim Multinomial(\phi)$
   (c) Choose $N_s \sim Poisson(\varepsilon)$: number of words in the sentence
   (d) Choose $\theta_s \sim Dir(\alpha, y_s)$
   (e) For each of the N_s words w_{sn}
      i. Choose a topic $z_{sn} \sim Multinomial(\theta_s)$: we call these topics "word-topics"
      ii. Choose a word w_{sn} from $P(w_{sn}|z_{sn}, \beta)$, a Multinomial probability conditioned on the topic z_{sn}

Because we are interested in changes of topics, c_s indicates whether a change in topic occurs for sentence s. If $c_s = 0$, then $y_s = y_{s-1}$. Otherwise, y_s is drawn from a Multinomial distribution with parameter ϕ. The distribution is given in Eq. 1:

$$p(y_s|c_s, \phi, y_{s-1}) = \begin{cases} \delta(y_s, y_{s-1}) & c_s = 0 \\ Multinomial(\phi) & c_s = 1 \end{cases} \tag{1}$$

This distribution is not well-defined for the first sentence. Therefore, like in [13], we set $c_1 = 1$ and draw the first sentence topic from $Multinomial(\phi)$.

The word probabilities are modeled conditioned on the topics with a $L \times V$ matrix β where $\beta_{ij} = p(w^j = 1|z^i = 1)$. We assume a Dirichlet prior for drawing the parameters of word distribution. ϕ represents the mixing proportion of document-topics in a document. It specifies the parameters of the K-dimensional Multinomial distribution from which the model draws samples for document topics. θ_s is a sample from the Dirichlet distribution and specifies the mixing proportion of word-topics in the text segment s. Note that this mixing proportion depends on the supertopic that the current text segment is generated from. The model assumes that each document-topic is a mixture of several word-topics and this fact is modeled through the matrix of hyperparameters α that will be estimated in the learning phase.

3.2 Inference and Parameter Estimation

The inference problem is to compute the posterior probability of hidden variables given the input parameters $\alpha, \eta, \delta, \gamma$ and observations $\mathbf{w}$:

$$p(\pi, \mathbf{c}, \phi, \mathbf{y}, \theta, \mathbf{z}|\mathbf{w}, \alpha, \eta, \delta, \gamma) = \frac{p(\pi, \mathbf{c}, \phi, \mathbf{y}, \theta, \mathbf{z}, \mathbf{w}|\alpha, \eta, \delta, \gamma)}{p(\mathbf{w}|\alpha, \eta, \delta, \gamma)} \tag{2}$$

For the models in the LDA family, exact inference is intractable. Therefore, approximation methods have been proposed to do the inference. Model parameters can be theoretically estimated using EM based algorithms but these algorithms often face local optima problems for models in this family. Therefore, by adopting a Bayesian approach, we use methods in which some of the hidden parameters are integrated out instead of being explicitly estimated. By using conjugate priors on the model parameters, this task becomes much more mechanical and straightforward. Integrating out some parameters also simplifies the sampling process, explained next. In our model, we need to integrate out the parameters β, ϕ and δ.

Gibbs sampling like other members of the Markov chain Monte Carlo (MCMC) algorithms family is an iterative method used to draw samples from complex and usually high dimensional distributions. Each iteration of the algorithm gives a sample from the target distribution in the long run. In each iteration of the Gibbs sampling method, variables are divided into blocks and each block is sampled from its conditional distribution conditioned on the current values of all other random variables of the target distribution. This process is performed sequentially and continues until the sampled values approximate the target distribution.

For our model, the target distribution is the posterior distribution of word-topics, document-topics and topic-switching variables given the collection of documents. This is an intractable distribution and sampling from it is difficult. By using Gibbs sampling, in each iteration, we sample from the conditional distribution of a single word-topic in a document conditioned on the topic assignment for all other words and sentences in all documents except the current word. We also sample from the conditional distribution of a single document-topic for a text segment and its corresponding switching variable given that the topic assignments of all other words not in the current sentence, topic assignments of all other sentences and all other switching variables values are known.

We order the documents in the corpus randomly and each document is given an index according to its position in this list. We represent the corpus with three lists of indices: word indices wl, sentence indices pl and document indices dl (As mentioned earlier, one can use paragraphs or any other well-defined structural unit of text instead). wl_i denotes the index of the ith word in the sequence of words (if we assume the whole corpus as a sequence of words fed to the algorithm). dl_i is the document index and pl_i represent the sentence index of the corresponding word respectively. Note that the purpose of the model is putting together these structural segments of the text (chosen by user preference) and forming sequences of topically coherent segments. These lists will then be fed to the Gibbs Sampling algorithm. For each word token, the Gibbs sampling algorithm estimates the probability of assigning the current word to word-topics given assignment of all other words to word-topics from the corresponding conditional distribution that we will derive shortly. Then the current word would be assigned to a word-topic and this assignment will be stored for reference when the Gibbs sampling algorithm works on other words.

While scanning the list of words, we watch for new sentences (or the structural unit chosen by the user) as they start. For each such new structural segment, the Gibbs sampling algorithm decides whether this segment should have the same topic as the preceding topic or it should be assigned to a new topic. In the latter case, the Gibbs sampler estimates the probability of assigning this sentence to document-topics given assignments of all other sentences to document-topics. These probabilities are computed from the corresponding conditional distribution for a sentence given all other topic assignments to every other sentence and all words not in this sentence. Then the new sentence would be assigned to a document-topic.

In our case we need to compute the two conditional distributions $p(z_{dsn}|z_{-dsn}, c, y, w)$ and $p(y_{ds}, c_{ds}|z, y_{-ds}, c_{-ds}, w)$, where z_{dsn} represents the word-topic assignment for word w_{dsn} (word n in document d and sentence s) and z_{-dsn} denotes the word-topic assignments for all other words except the current word w_{dsn}. y_{ds} denotes the document-topic assignment for sentence s in document d and y_{-ds} represents the document-topic assignments for all sentences except this current sentence. Beginning with the joint probability of a dataset, and using the chain rule, we can obtain the conditional probabilities conveniently. For our model, we obtain equations 3 and 4.

$$p(z_{dsn}|z_{-dsn}, c, y, w) = \frac{(\alpha_{y_{ds}z_{dsn}} + n_{z_{dsn}}^{(ds)})}{\sum_{l=1}^{L}(\alpha_{y_{ds}l} + n_l^{(ds)})} \times \frac{n_{z_{dsn}w_{dsn}} + \eta_{w_{dsn}} - 1}{\sum_{v=1}^{V} n_{z_{dsn}v} + \eta_v - 1} \quad (3)$$

$$p(y_{ds}, c_{ds}|z, y_{-ds}, c_{-ds}, w) =$$

$$\begin{cases} \frac{n_{d_0}+\gamma}{N_d+2\gamma} \times \frac{\Gamma(\sum_{l=1}^{L}\alpha_{y_{ds}l})}{\prod_{l=1}^{L}\Gamma(\alpha_{y_{ds}l})} \times \frac{\prod_{l=1}^{L}\Gamma(\alpha_{y_{ds}l}+n_l^{(ds)})}{\Gamma(\sum_{l=1}^{L}\alpha_{y_{ds}l}+n_l^{(ds)})} & c_{ds}=0 \ \& \ s>1 \ \& \ y_{ds}=y_{d(s-1)} \\ \frac{n_{d_1}+\gamma}{N+2\gamma} \frac{\delta_k+n_{y_{ds}}^d}{\sum_{k=1}^{K}(\delta_k+n_k^d)} \times \frac{\Gamma(\sum_{l=1}^{L}\alpha_{y_{ds}l})}{\prod_{l=1}^{L}\Gamma(\alpha_{y_{ds}l})} \times \frac{\prod_{l=1}^{L}\Gamma(\alpha_{y_{ds}l}+n_l^{(ds)})}{\Gamma(\sum_{l=1}^{L}\alpha_{y_{ds}l}+n_l^{(ds)})} & \text{if } c_{ds}=1 \\ 0 & \text{otherwise} \end{cases} \quad (4)$$

where $n_l^{(ds)}$ represents how many times a word in sentence s of document d has been assigned to topic l. $n_{lw_{dsn}}$ represents the total number of times that the word w_{dsn} has been assigned to topic l. n_k^d is the number of times a sentence in document d has been assigned to document-topic k. n_{d_0} and n_{d_1} are the number of times that the switching variable c is set to be 0 and 1 in document d respectively.

In most of the statistical topic models inspired by the LDA model, the Dirichlet parameters α are assumed to be given and fixed, which still gives reasonable results. But for the proposed model, as in [14,8], these parameters are a very important part of the model. These parameters determine how the correlations between different word topics through their participation in document topics are captured by the model. For estimating parameters of a Dirichlet distribution, a family of approaches based on maximum likelihood or maximum a posteriori estimation of parameters has been proposed in the literature [11]. There is no closed-form solution for these methods and one should use iterative methods to learn the parameters. But these iterative methods are often computationally expensive and other methods like moment matching [11] are used to approximate the parameters of the Dirichlet prior α. We will also use this approach for our model. This means that in each iteration of Gibbs sampling, we update

$$var_{kl} = \frac{1}{N_k} \sum_{s \in S_k} (\frac{n_l^{(s)}}{n^{(s)}} - mean_{kl})^2, \quad mean_{kl} = \frac{1}{N_k} \sum_{s \in S_k} \frac{n_l^{(s)}}{n^{(s)}}, \quad \alpha_{kl} \propto mean_{kl}$$

$$m_{kl} = \frac{mean_{kl}(1 - mean_{kl})}{var_{kl}} - 1, \quad \sum_{l=1}^{L} \alpha_{kl} = \exp(\frac{\sum_{l=1}^{L}\log(m_{kl})}{L-1}) \quad (5)$$

where S_k represents the set of sentences assigned to document-topic k and N_k is the number of sentences assigned to document-topic k. $n_l^{(s)}$ represents the number of times a word in sentence s has been assigned to word-topic l. $n^{(s)}$ is the number of words in sentence s. Note that for $mean_{kl}$ and var_{kl}, we only consider the sentences assigned to document-topic k. For each document-topic k, we first compute sample mean $mean_{kl}$ and sample variance var_{kl}. They are computed over all sentences assigned to document-topic k.

Algorithm 1 shows the pseudocode for the Gibbs sampling process for our model.

Algorithm 1. LDSEG Segmentation Gibbs Sampling

Input: γ, δ, α, η, L, K,Corpus, $MaxIteration$
Output: topic assignments for all words and sentences in the Corpus
1　Initialization: Randomly, initialize the word-topic assignments for all word tokens and document topic assignments and topic switch variables for all sentences
2　Compute n_k^d for all values of $k \in \{1..K\}$ and all documents
3　Compute n_{lv} for all values of $l \in \{1..L\}$ and all word tokens
4　Compute $n_l^{(ds)}$ for all values of $l \in \{1..L\}$ and all documents and their sentences
5　**if** *doing parameter estimation* **then**
6　$\quad$ Initialize *alpha* parameters using Eq. 5

7　Randomize the order of documents in the corpus, the order of sentences in each document, and the order of words in each sentence. This is not necessary but recommended if multiple chains of Gibbs sampling are used
8　**for** $iter \leftarrow 1$ **to** $MaxIteration$ **do**
9　$\quad$ **foreach** *word i according to the order* **do**
10　$\qquad$ Exclude word i and its assigned topic l from variables $n_l^{(ds)}$ and n_{li}
11　$\qquad$ $newl$ = sample new word-topic for word i using Eq. 3
12　$\qquad$ Update variables $n_l^{(ds)}$ and n_{li} using the new word-topic $newl$ for word i
13　$\qquad$ **if** *entered a new sentence j* **then**
14　$\qquad\quad$ Exclude sentence j and its assigned topic k from variable n_k^d
15　$\qquad\quad$ $(newk, newc)$ = sample new document-topic and the switching variable for sentence j using Eq. 4
16　$\qquad\quad$ **if** $newc == 1$ **then**
17　$\qquad\qquad$ Assign $newk$ as the new document-topic for sentence j;
18　$\qquad\quad$ Update variable n_k^d using the new document-topic $newk$ for sentence j
19　$\qquad\quad$ **if** *doing parameter estimation* **then**
20　$\qquad\qquad$ Update *alpha* parameters using Eqs. 5

4　Experimental Results

In the following sections, we present early results, indicating that our model is able to discover topics that are more coherent compared to the LDA model for two different datasets. We also show that the proposed model outperforms our previous model which does not have the ability to detect segments in the text. We finally compare the segmentation performance of our model with a recently proposed model that has comparable performance compared to some of the well-known topic segmentation algorithms.

4.1 Datasets

We use two real-world datasets in our experiments. Our first dataset is a subset of the Wikipedia XML corpus [1] [6]. This subset contains 261 articles categorized in 5 overlapping classes, namely "Music", "Art", "Archaeology", "Christianity" and "Spirituality". Each document belongs to 2.09 classes on average. The biggest class corresponds to "Art" with 179 documents. The smallest class, "Archaeology" has 63 documents. We removed all the words which occurred in less than 5 documents from the list of final word tokens. We also used a list of standard "stopwords" and deleted all numbers, words with length less than 3 and having non-ASCII characters. We do not consider paragraphs with less than 5 words and do not include documents with less than 3 paragraphs. We do not have the tags for separating words, therefore we used all delimiting characters to separate words. There are 65978 word tokens, 2740 paragraphs and 2311 unique words after preprocessing. The pruning steps are taken to get a cleaner dataset.

Our second dataset has been used in previous studies [9,10] for evaluating the segmentation results. It consists of spoken lecture transcripts from an undergraduate physics class and a graduate artificial intelligence class. A typical 90 minutes lecture has 500 to 700 sentences and over 8500 words. The segmentation of the lecture transcripts are done manually to facilitate access to lecture recordings available on the class website for students. It is aimed to convey the high-level topical structure of the lectures. Each lecture is annotated with six segments on average. The second part of the dataset corresponding to the AI class has on average 12 segments for each lecture.

4.2 Word-Topic Examples

In this section, we show 10 and 9 word-topics derived from the Wikipedia dataset using our model which we call "LDSEG" hereafter, and the LDA model, respectively. The topics are represented each with their 10 most indicative words and are presented in Figs 2 and 3. The topics were derived by assuming the number of document-topics equal to 4 and the number of word-topics equal to 50. Among the 50 word-topics discovered by each model, we are able to match 32 topics. Topics 1 and 2 in Figs 2 and 3 are two examples. The early inspection of the results for the examined models shows that the topics discovered by our model are more coherent. As an example, topic 1 discovered by the LDA model has some words that do not fit in the topic while for the corresponding topic by our model, all the top indicative words compose a more coherent topic. We are able to observe this in most of the topics.

Our model also seems to be able to discover some topics that the LDA model does not detect. Examples of such topics can be seen in the topics 6 and 7 of our model. Topic 3 of our model is especially interesting. It is a topic about "bigfoot" and all the indicative words are the names related to this topic. For the LDA model, we have the word "bigfoot" mixed in the topic 2 which does not make sense. Instead of these topics, the LDA model has some other words put together as a topic that do not strongly indicate a topic. One can see examples of this topic in the topics 4 and 8 discovered by the LDA model. Our model is also able to split some of the more general topics into

---

[1] It is available for download at http://www-connex.lip6.fr/~denoyer/wikipediaXML by registration.

topic 1	topic 2	topic 3	topic 4	topic 5	topic 6	topic 7	topic 8	topic 9	topic 10
alexander	women	nietzsche	church	god	radio	economic	league	computer	house
greek	sexual	bigfoot	catholic	church	day	million	football	game	parliament
ancient	family	dragon	orthodox	christ	television	government	team	system	commons
apollo	men	sasquatch	christian	jesus	year	economy	game	games	lords
gods	male	evidence	churches	baptism	abc	company	club	apple	members
hecate	female	campbell	saint	life	show	world	season	atari	act
mythology	children	verne	roman	christian	advertising	international	home	software	bill
earth	members	krantz	council	heaven	broadcast	trade	won	data	kingdom
archaeology	people	wallace	century	holy	bbc	growth	cup	commodore	ireland
hermes	gay	friedrich	religious	faith	time	development	world	disc	england

Fig. 2. Example word-topics for the Wikipedia dataset discovered by our model

topic 1	topic 2	topic 3	topic 4	topic 5	topic 6	topic 7	topic 8	topic 9
greek	women	church	lennon	league	computer	house	des	russell
alexander	sexual	god	xavier	football	game	parliament	disk	theory
graffiti	family	jesus	voting	team	games	commons	linear	nietzsche
apollo	children	christ	peel	game	system	lords	data	human
khazar	female	orthodox	john	club	atari	members	group	philosophy
gods	male	christian	godzilla	season	commodore	act	lie	work
mythology	gay	baptism	contest	cup	design	khmer	audio	life
hecate	men	catholic	costas	world	software	bill	vector	social
khazars	feminism	churches	borda	boxing	design	government	omega	rousseau
ancient	bigfoot	saint	candidate	teams	video	rouge	space	political

Fig. 3. Example word-topics for the Wikipedia dataset discovered by the LDA model

more specific ones. For example, topic 3 discovered by the LDA is about Christianity and Jesus whereas in our model, the same topic is split into two more specific topics 4 and 5.

4.3 Document Clustering Performance

The Latent Dirichlet Co-Clustering (LDCC) model proposed in our previous work [14], has been shown to have better clustering results compared to several other models including Model-based Overlapping Co-Clustering [15], Model-based Overlapping Clustering [1] and K-Means algorithm in terms of precision, recall and F-measure. We are interested to see if the proposed model in this paper can deliver as our previous work [14] in terms of clustering performance, considering the fact that it is not given any information about the segmentation.

We use the Wikipedia dataset for measuring the clustering performance. In order to compare clustering results, we use precision, recall, and F-measure calculated over pairs of points, as defined in [1]. For each pair of points that share at least one cluster in the overlapping clustering results, these measures try to estimate whether the prediction of this pair as being in the same cluster was correct with respect to the underlying true categories in the data. Precision is calculated as the fraction of pairs correctly put in the same cluster, recall is the fraction of actual pairs that were identified, and F-measure is the harmonic mean of precision and recall.

Table 1 presents the results of LDSEG versus LDCC algorithm in terms of precision, recall and F-Measure for the Wikipedia Corpus. Each reported result is an average

Table 1. Clustering results of LDCC and LDSEG algorithms on Wikipedia dataset

		LDSEG			LDCC		
K	L	Precision	Recall	F-Measure	Precision	Recall	F-Measure
4	10-80	0.734	0.488	0.585	0.727	0.508	0.594
6	10-80	0.718	0.435	0.538	0.717	0.423	0.526

over 50 samples. We take the average results for the number of word-topics varying between 10 and 80. Table 1 contains the results for two different values for the number of super-topics, 4 and 6. The results show that although no information about segmentation is given to the LDSEG model, it is still comparable to the LDCC model in terms of precision, recall and F-Measure.

4.4 Segmentation Results

We use two standard error rate metrics for comparing the segmentation results of our model and the model proposed in [13]. Pk [2] is the probability that two segments drawn randomly from a document are incorrectly identified as belonging to the same topic. WinDiff [12] moves a sliding window across the text and counts the number of times the hypothesized and reference segment boundaries are different within the window. For both these measures, lower values indicate better agreement with a gold standard segmentation.

Segmentation performance of the model introduced in [13] is comparable with previous segmentation algorithms. Thus we compare our model with this model. We use our second dataset which has human-annotated segmentation for evaluation. Table 2 shows that our model is comparable with the model in [13] for different numbers of word-topics. We use the points where the super-topic changes as segment boundaries.

Table 2. Segmentation results of LDSEG and Purver's [13] algorithms

Model	LDSEG		Purver et. al.	
L	Pk	WinDiff	Pk	Windiff
20	0.405	0.431	0.413	0.420
30	0.407	0.432	0.416	0.421
40	0.419	0.450	0.416	0.421

4.5 Conclusions and Future Work

We have proposed a hierarchical Bayesian model that combines topic identification and segmentation in text document collections. The proposed model is able to cluster the documents in the dataset into overlapping clusters. Extracted word-topics seem to be more coherent compared to LDA. Segmentation and clustering performance of the model is comparable to some recently introduced models, although those models are simpler and lack some of the features of our model.

We plan to do experiments using other datasets to compare our model with other topic segmentation and clustering algorithms. We also like to try our model as a preprocessing step towards text summarization and alignment of parallel corpora for machine translation. For learning parameter α in our model, we currently use moment-matching method. We plan to take a fuller Bayesian approach by assuming α is a random variable. Defining a prior on α allows the model to automatically select values for it.

Acknowledgements

We are grateful to the following institutions for their financial support: the Natural Sciences and Engineering Research Council of Canada, IT Interactive Services Inc., and MITACS NCE.

References

1. Banerjee, A., Krumpelman, C., Basu, S., Mooney, R., Ghosh, J.: Model based overlapping clustering. In: International Conference on Knowledge Discovery and Data Mining (KDD) (August 2005)
2. Beeferman, D., Berger, A., Lafferty, J.: Statistical models for text segmentation. Machine Learning 34(1-3), 177–210 (1999)
3. Blei, D., Lafferty, J.: Correlated topic models. In: Advances in Neural Information Processing Systems, vol. 18, pp. 147–154 (2006)
4. Blei, D.M., Ng, A.Y., Jordan, M.I.: Latent Dirichlet allocation. Journal of Machine Learning Research 3, 993–1022 (2003)
5. Buntine, W.L.: Operations for learning with graphical models. Journal of Artificial Intelligence Research (JAIR) 2, 159–225 (1994)
6. Denoyer, L., Gallinari, P.: The Wikipedia XML Corpus. SIGIR Forum (2006)
7. Hearst, M.A.: Texttiling: segmenting text into multi-paragraph subtopic passages. Comput. Linguist. 23(1), 33–64 (1997)
8. Li, W., Mccallum, A.: Pachinko allocation: Dag-structured mixture models of topic correlations. In: 23rd International Conference on Machine Learning, Pittsburgh, USA (June 2006)
9. Malioutov, I., Barzilay, R.: Minimum cut model for spoken lecture segmentation. In: Proceedings of the 21st International Conference on Computational Linguistics and the 44th annual meeting of the ACL, July 2006, pp. 25–32 (2006)
10. Malioutov, I., Park, A., Barzilay, R., Glass, J.: Making sense of sound: Unsupervised topic segmentation over acoustic input. In: Proceedings of the 45th Annual Meeting of the Association of Computational Linguistics, June 2007, pp. 504–511 (2007)
11. Minka, T.P.: Estimating a Dirichlet distribution. Technical report, MIT (2000)
12. Pevzner, L., Hearst, M.A.: A critique and improvement of an evaluation metric for text segmentation. Comput. Linguist. 28(1), 19–36 (2002)
13. Purver, M., Kording, K., Griffiths, T., Tenenbaum, J.: Unsupervised topic modelling for multi-party spoken discourse. In: Proceedings of the 21st International Conference on Computational Linguistics and 44th Annual Meeting of the Association for Computational Linguistics, July 2006, pp. 17–24 (2006)
14. Shafiei, M.M., Milios, E.E.: Latent dirichlet co-clustering. In: Perner, P. (ed.) ICDM 2006. LNCS (LNAI), vol. 4065, pp. 542–551. Springer, Heidelberg (2006)

15. Shafiei, M., Milios, E.: Model-based overlapping co-clustering. In: Proceedings of the Fourth Workshop on Text Mining, Sixth SIAM International Conference on Data Mining, Bethesda, Maryland, April 22 (2006)
16. Steyvers, M., Griffiths, T.: Probabilistic topic models. In: Landauer, T., Mcnamara, D., Dennis, S., Kintsch, W. (eds.) Latent Semantic Analysis: A Road to Meaning, Lawrence Erlbaum, Mahwah (2005)
17. Wallach, H.M.: Topic modeling: beyond bag-of-words. In: ICML 2006: Proceedings of the 23rd international conference on Machine learning, pp. 977–984 (2006)
18. Wang, X., McCallum, A.: A note on topical n-grams. Technical Report UM-CS-2005-071, University of Massachusetts Amherst (December 2005)

Image Transformation: Inductive Transfer between Multiple Tasks Having Multiple Outputs

Daniel L. Silver and Liangliang Tu

Jodrey School of Computer Science
Acadia University
Wolfville, NS, Canada B4P 2R6
danny.silver@acadiau.ca

Abstract. Previous research has investigated inductive transfer for single output modeling problems such as classification or prediction of a scalar. Little research has been done in the area of inductive transfer applied to tasks with multiple outputs. We report the results of using Multiple Task Learning (MTL) neural networks and *Context-sensitive* Multiple Task Learning (*cs*MTL) on a domain of image transformation tasks. Models are developed to transform synthetic images of neutral (passport) faces to that of corresponding images of angry, happy and sad faces. The results are inconclusive for MTL, however they demonstrate that inductive transfer with *cs*MTL is beneficial. When the secondary tasks have sufficient numbers of training examples from which to provide transfer, *cs*MTL models are able to transform images more accurately than standard single task learning models.

1   Introduction

Inductive transfer learning involves the use of knowledge of one or more related secondary tasks while learning a primary task [15,10,14]. The intention is to develop more effective models, having higher generalization accuracy, by using prior knowledge of the task domain. Work in inductive transfer learning has also investigated more efficient learning (short training times) through knowledge transfer [9]. However, prior work in Inductive transfer learning has focussed on single output modeling problems such as classification or prediction of a scalar [3,4,5,6]. Little research has been done in the area of inductive transfer applied to tasks with multiple outputs. This is mostly because of the added complexity that multiple outputs bring to any machine learning problem. More specifically, they complicate the challenge of determining the relatedness between tasks so as to ensure beneficial transfer of knowledge.

In this paper we report the results of using Multiple Task Learning (MTL) neural networks and *Context-sensitive* Multiple Task Learning (*cs*MTL) networks on a domain of image transformation tasks. Models are developed to transform synthetic images of neutral faces to corresponding images of happy, sad or angry faces. The novelty and contribution of the paper is to show that

S. Bergler (Ed.): Canadian AI 2008, LNAI 5032, pp. 296–307, 2008.
© Springer-Verlag Berlin Heidelberg 2008

inductive transfer between tasks with multiple outputs can be beneficial. In particular, csMTL models developed with transfer from related tasks are able to transform images more accurately than standard single task learning models.

2   Learning Image Transformation Functions with Neural Networks

Consider the problem of training a neural network to learn a transformation function f that maps a source image $\mathbf{x}$ with n grey-level pixels to a transformed target image $\mathbf{y}$ with n pixels. More formerly, let $\mathbf{x} \in X$ and $\mathbf{y} \in Y$ where X and Y are sets of integer values on $(0, 255)^n$. For standard single task learning (STL), the target task is a function f that maps the set X to the set Y, $f : X \rightarrow Y$, with some probability distribution P over $X \times Y$. An example for STL is of the form $(\mathbf{x}, \mathbf{y})$, where $\mathbf{x}$ is a vector containing the input values $x_1, x_2, \ldots, x_n$ and $\mathbf{y} = f(\mathbf{x})$ is the target output vector containing the values $y_1, y_2, \ldots, y_n$. A training set S_{STL} consists of all available examples, $S_{STL} = \{(\mathbf{x}, f(\mathbf{x}))\}$. The objective of the STL algorithm is to find a hypothesis h within its hypothesis space H_{STL} that minimizes the objective function, $\sum_{\mathbf{x} \in S_{STL}} error\,[f(\mathbf{x}), h(\mathbf{x})]$; where $error$ is a function that measures the difference between an expected $\mathbf{y}$ and the output of a network hypothesis $h(\mathbf{x})$. The assumption is that $H_{STL} \subset \{f | f : X \rightarrow Y\}$ contains a sufficiently accurate h.

Figure 1 shows some preliminary results of training an STL network to transform real images of peoples faces. Specifically, the challenge was to learn a model that could transform a neutral (passport) image of a person's face to the image of a happy face or sad face for that same person. The images shown are of real faces and are 39 by 55 pixels in size. The neural network models were trained on 30 examples of neutral and happy face images obtained over the web from [7]. A validation set of 12 examples was used to prevent over-fitting. Figure 1 shows two examples from an independent test set. The generated happy and sad face images have a large amount of error, suggesting the complexity of the mapping function. We concluded from this preliminary work that much larger training sets and lengthy training times would be required to develop accurate models for real images.

Based on the above, we decided to scale down the problem domain to a more constrained set of synthetic images with fewer pixels and less variability between images for the same person and between images of the same class (neutral, angry, happy and sad). Figure 2 shows examples of images for one person from this new synthetic domain. Each image contains 4 x 3 pixels with each pixel having a grayscale integer value within the 0-255 range; where 255 is the lightest shade. The grey-scale values represent the features of a cartoon person and remain constant for each image of that person but vary within fixed ranges between persons. The left-most neural image has each of the pixels numbered. Pixels 0 and 2 consistently represent the eyes and have a value range of 0-84, as does pixel 4 for the nose which has a value range of 170-254. Each pixel for the mouth will vary for different expressions but will have a value in the range 85-169. In the

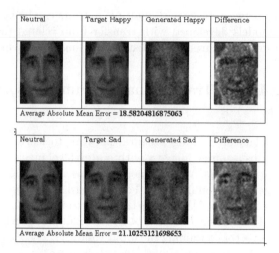

Fig. 1. Examples of image transformation of real face images using neural network models

Neutral Image	Angry Image	Happy Image	Sad Image

Fig. 2. Examples of the synthetic face images for one person

STL Neutral-to-Angry, 20 Hidden Nodes, 100 Training Examples			
Source Neutral	Target Angry	Generated Angry	Reversed Diff
Average Absolute Mean Error = 1.453697479			

Fig. 3. Examples of image transformation of synthetic face images using neural network models

neutral image shown, pixels 9, 10 and 11 represent the mouth. All other pixels are facial background with a pixel value of 255.

Figure 3 shows the results of training a STL network to transform a synthetic neutral face image into a happy face image. Similar results indicate that this would be a better domain for an initial investigation into inductive transfer for tasks with multiple outputs. The level of error is acceptable and the size of the training sets and the time to train the networks are more practical. We will use this synthetic domain of images for the experiments reported in Section 5.

3   Multiple Task Learning and It's Limitations

Multiple task learning (MTL) neural networks are one of the better documented methods of inductive transfer of task knowledge [3,10] when there is a single output value per task. An MTL network is a feed-forward multi-layer network with a separate output for each task that is to be learned and a hidden layer of nodes that are common to all tasks. The standard back-propagation of error learning algorithm is used to train all tasks in parallel. Consequently, MTL training examples are composed of a set of input attributes and a target output for each task. The sharing of internal representation is the method by which inductive bias occurs within an MTL network [1]. The more that tasks are related, the more they will share representation and create positive inductive bias. Typically, relatedness is based on some measure of the similarity between training examples for the primary task and that of the secondary transfer tasks; for example, the correlation of matching output values can be used.

3.1   MTL with Multiple Outputs

Theoretically, MTL networks can be extended to have more than one output per task without loss of generality. Such a network is shown in Figure 4. Formally, MTL with one or more outputs per task can be defined as learning a set of target tasks $\mathbf{f} = \{f_1, f_2, \dots f_k\}$ such that each $f_i : X \rightarrow Y$ with a probability distribution P_i over $X \times Y$. We assume that the environment delivers each f_i based on a probability distribution Q over all P_i. Q is meant to capture some regularity in the environment that constrains the number of tasks that the learning algorithm will encounter. Q therefore characterizes the domain of tasks to be learned. An example for MTL is of the form $(\mathbf{x}, \mathbf{f}(\mathbf{x}))$, where $\mathbf{x}$ is as defined for STL and $\mathbf{f}(\mathbf{x}) = \{f_i(\mathbf{x})\}$, a set of target outputs. A training set S_{MTL} consists of all available examples, $S_{MTL} = \{(\mathbf{x}, \mathbf{f}(\mathbf{x}))\}$. The objective of the MTL algorithm is to find a set of hypotheses $\mathbf{h} = \{h_1, h_2, \dots, h_k\}$ within its hypothesis space H_{MTL} that minimizes the objective function $\sum_{\mathbf{x} \in S_{MTL}} \sum_{i=1}^{k} error\,[f_i(\mathbf{x}), h_i(\mathbf{x})]$ over all n outputs per task. The assumption is that H_{MTL} contains sufficiently accurate h_i for each f_i being learned. Typically $|H_{MTL}| > |H_{STL}|$ in order to represent the multiple hypotheses.

3.2   Limitations of MTL for Machine Lifelong Learning

Machine lifelong learning, or ML3, a relatively new area of research, is concerned with the persistent and cumulative nature of learning [14]. Lifelong learning considers situations in which a learner faces a series of different tasks and develops methods of retaining and using prior knowledge to improve the effectiveness (more accurate hypotheses) and efficiency (shorter training times) of learning. Previously, we have investigated the use of MTL networks as a basis for developing an ML3 system and have found them to have several limitations related to the multiple outputs of the network [11,12,8]. First, the MTL approach requires that training examples contain corresponding target values for each task; this is

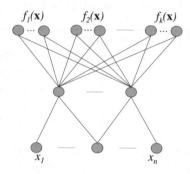

Fig. 4. A multiple task learning (MTL) network with multiple output nodes for each task being learned

impractical for lifelong learning systems as examples of each tasks are acquired at different times and with unique combinations of input values. Second, it has been observed that inductive transfer in MTL networks is most beneficial when it comes from related tasks [1,3,10]. Thus a measure of task relatedness is required in order for it to work optimally. This has remained an open question for almost 15 years [2]. Finally, there is the practical problem of how an MTL based lifelong learning system would know to associate an example with a particular task. Clearly, the learning environment should provide the contextual cues; however, this suggests additional inputs and not outputs. A related problem is managing redundant output representations that can develop for the same task in an MTL network. Over time, a lifelong learning system should be capable of practising a task using new sets of training examples, thereby improving its model for that task. With MTL networks this requires a method of house keeping that eliminates redundant outputs. We have not been able to find a scalable solution for this with single output tasks. Tasks with multiple outputs acerbate the problem.

4   *cs*MTL with Multiple Outputs Per Task

With the above MTL limitations in mind, we have considered alternative methods of inductive transfer in the presence of multiple tasks from the same domain. In [13] we introduced *context-sensitive* MTL, or *cs*MTL, as a method of inductive transfer for tasks with a single output. *cs*MTL is based on standard MTL with two major differences; only one output is used for all tasks and additional inputs are used to indicate the example *context*, such as the task to which it is associated.

Our original definition of a *cs*MTL network can be extended to learn tasks that have multiple outputs such as tasks that transform source images to target images. Figure 5 presents such a *cs*MTL network. It is a feed-forward network architecture of input, hidden and output nodes that uses the back-propagation of error training algorithm. The *cs*MTL network requires only one set of output nodes for learning multiple concept tasks. Similar to standard MTL neural

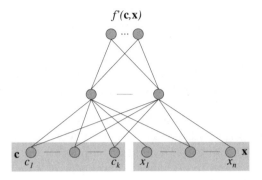

Fig. 5. Proposed system: csMTL with multiple outputs

networks, there are one or more layers of hidden nodes that act as feature detectors. The input layer can be divided into two parts: a set of *primary* input variables for the tasks and a set of inputs that provide the network with the *context* of each training example. The context inputs can simply be a set of task identifiers that associate each training example to a particular task. Alternatively, the context attributes can offer more grounded environmental information, such as the learning agents location, so as to index over a continuous domain of tasks.

Formally, let C be a set on $\{0,1\}^n$ representing the context of the primary inputs from X as described for MTL. Let $\mathbf{c}$ be a particular instance of this set where $\mathbf{c}$ is a vector containing the values $c_1, c_2, \ldots, c_k$; where $c_i = 1$ indicates that the example is associated with function f_i. csMTL can be defined as learning a target concept $f' : C \times X \to Y$; with a probability distribution P' on $C \times X \times Y$ where P' is constrained by the probability distributions P and Q discussed in the previous section for MTL. An example for csMTL takes the form $(\mathbf{c}, \mathbf{x}, f'(\mathbf{c}, \mathbf{x}))$, where $f'(\mathbf{c}, \mathbf{x}) = f_i(\mathbf{x})$ when $c_i = 1$ and $f_i(\mathbf{x})$ is the target output for task f_i. A training set S_{csMTL} consists of all available examples for all tasks and includes the additional context inputs, $S_{csMTL} = \{(\mathbf{c}, \mathbf{x}, f'(\mathbf{c}, \mathbf{x}))\}$. The objective of the csMTL algorithm is to find a hypothesis h' within its hypothesis space H_{csMTL} that minimizes the objective function, $\sum_{x \in S_{csMTL}} error\,[f'(\mathbf{c}, \mathbf{x}), h'(\mathbf{c}, \mathbf{x})]$. The assumption is that $H_{csMTL} \subset \{f' | f' : C \times X \to Y\}$ contains a sufficiently accurate h'. Typically, $|H_{csMTL}| < |H_{MTL}|$ for the same set of tasks because the number of additional context inputs under csMTL is less than the number of additional task outputs under MTL, particularly when the number of outputs per task is large.

With csMTL, the entire representation of the network is used to develop hypotheses for all tasks, $f'(\mathbf{c}, \mathbf{x})$, following the examples drawn according to P' [13]. The focus shifts from learning a subset of shared representation for multiple tasks to learning a completely shared representation for the same tasks. This presents a more continuous sense of domain knowledge and the objective becomes that of learning internal representations that are helpful to producing the output for similar combinations of the primary and context input values.

During learning, **c** selects an inductive bias over H_{csMTL} relative to the examples of secondary tasks being learned in the network. Once f' is learned, if **x** is held constant, then **c** indexes over the hypothesis base H_{csMTL}. Hence, **c** differentiates between otherwise conflicting examples and selects internal representation used by related tasks. If **c** is a vector of real-valued inputs and from the environment, it provides a "grounded" sense of task relatedness. If **c** is a set of task identifiers, it differentiates between otherwise conflicting examples and selects internal representation used by related tasks.

csMTL overcomes the limitations of standard MTL for construction of a ML3 system. First, csMTL eliminates redundant outputs for the same task making it easier for an ML3 system to accumulate knowledge of a task through practice. Secondly, csMTL examples are associated directly with a task via the context inputs, **c**. Finally, we conjecture that relatedness between tasks can be measured by the similarity of the context **c**, if **c** is environmentally grounded [13].

The csMTL approach suffers from the scaling problems of all back-propa-gation neural networks. The computational complexity of the standard back- propagation algorithm is $O(W^3)$, where W is the number of weights in the network. Training of a csMTL network will be computationally as expensive as standard MTL. The number of weights in an equivalent csMTL network will be much smaller because there is only one context input weight added per task as compared to n output weights per task for MTL. However, this decrease in network size is offset by the growth of the csMTL training set to $m \cdot k$ examples, where m is the number of training examples per task and k is the number of tasks.

5   Experimentation

This section reports on a set of experiments that compare the accuracy of image transform models developed under STL neural networks with models developed with inductive transfer using MTL and csMTL neural networks.

5.1   Objective

The synthetic domain of face images described in Section 2 is used. The challenge is to develop a model for the primary task that transforms a neutral face image to an angry face image. The standard STL method will be used as the baseline. This will be followed by the MTL and the csMTL methods that use inductive transfer from secondary tasks: specifically, a task that transforms a neutral face to a happy face image and a second task that transforms a neutral face to a sad face image. The methods are compared in terms of how well their resulting models perform on a set of 500 independent test images as a function of the number of hidden nodes and number of training examples provided.

5.2   Method

STL, MTL and csMTL networks were configured for the study. All have three layers of nodes: input, hidden and output. The number of hidden nodes varies for each from 10 to 100 in steps of 10 nodes. The STL network contains 12 input nodes and 12 output nodes; where the outputs represent the pixels of the output image. The MTL network contains 12 input nodes and 24 output nodes, 12 for each of two tasks. The csMTL network contains 15 input nodes, made up of 12 image pixel inputs, 3 context inputs, and 12 output nodes. The 3 context inputs are used to associate an example with a particular task. For the purpose of brevity, these tasks will be identified as NA for neutral to angry face transformation, NH for neutral to happy face transformation, and NS for neutral to sad face transformation. For each network, the learning rate is set to be 0.001, the momentum is 0.9, and the initial weights are set to be on (-0.1,0.1).

For all runs, three sets of examples are employed: training set, tuning set, and test set. The training sets are either of size 20 or 100. The tuning sets are either of size 10 or 50, respectfully, and are used to prevent over-fitting through early stopping, whereby the network weights are saved at the point of lowest tuning set error. An independent test set of 500 examples is used to evaluate the model's performance for each task. The study will compare the mean absolute error (MAE) over all pixels of an image from five repeated runs; where each run uses a different mix of training and tuning examples and initial network weights.

For STL, the objective is to observe how the primary task model performance decreases as the number of training examples (100 training and 50 tuning) is reduced (to 20 training and 10 tuning). For the MTL and csMTL, the objective is to compare the effect of inductive transfer on the primary task when only 20 training and 10 tuning examples are provided. For MTL, a matching set of examples for the primary and secondary tasks must be provided; if there are 20 training examples for the primary task, there can be only 20 for the secondary task. This is because MTL requires matching target values for all examples. However, this is not the case with csMTL. With csMTL, the number of examples for the primary and secondary tasks can differ. In fact, they do not have to match at all. This makes it possible to train with a larger set of examples (100 training and 50 tuning examples) for the secondary tasks, providing a more accurate source of inductive bias. It is important to note that, under csMTL, the number of training examples for all tasks must be the same. This is to ensure that each task plays an equal role in the update of the network weights. This requires that the primary task training examples to be duplicated until their number equals that of each secondary task.

5.3   Results

Figure 6 shows the mean performance by all STL, MTL and csMTL models (for all network architectures) on the 500 example test set for the NA task. Figure 7 shows a few of the test set images generated (transformed) by various models and the differences between the generated images and their target images. For the most part, it is difficult to visually distinguish the generated images from the target images. csMTL NA(20)<-NS(100) indicates a csMTL model developed with 20 primary task training examples and 100 secondary task training examples.

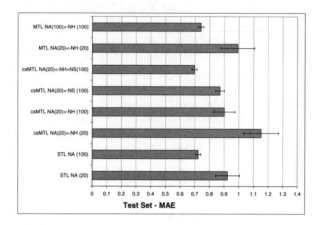

Fig. 6. Comparison of STL, MTL and csMTL model performance over all runs

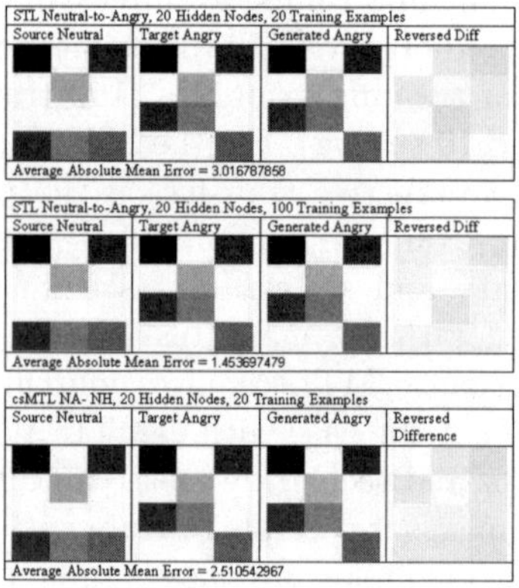

Fig. 7. Examples of actual and generate synthetic face images

Figure 8 compares the STL baseline models to the MTL models developed with either 20 or 100 training examples per task as the number of hidden nodes increases. In both cases, the models benefit from the greater number of training examples and hidden nodes. Surprisingly, under MTL, the NA models do not perform as well with inductive transfer when there are only 20 training examples for the NH task. This is because of the low accuracy of NH models transferred to the primary task. There is no significant difference between the STL and MTL models when 100 training examples are used for both tasks. The results are statistically equivalent and are two of the best sets of models produced.

Figure 9 compares the STL models to the *cs*MTL models developed with 20 training examples for the primary task NA, and either 20 or 100 training

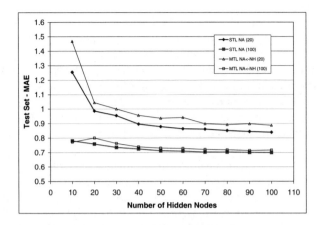

Fig. 8. Comparison of STL and MTL model performance as a function of the number of hidden nodes

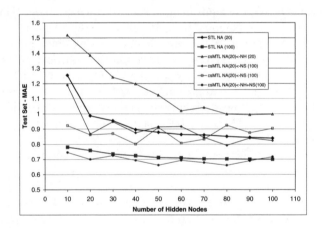

Fig. 9. Comparison of STL and csMTL model performance as a function of the number of hidden nodes

examples for the secondary tasks NH and NS. Similar to the MTL results, transferring from the secondary NH task to the primary task is not beneficial when only 20 training examples for the NH task are used. However, with 100 training examples per secondary task there is a noticeable improvement in the models. The very best model is developed when transfer occurs simultaneously from both the NH and NS tasks using 100 training examples per secondary task, marked csMTL NA(20)<-NH+NS(100). The bar graph of Figure 6 shows that it is possible to develop a primary task *cs*MTL model from only 20 training examples that is as accurate as STL model developed from 100 training examples.

6   Conclusion

This paper investigates inductive transfer learning applied to a domain of tasks where each task has multiple outputs. To the best of our knowledge, this is one of the first studies to consider the use of inductive transfer beyond single output modeling problems such as classification or prediction of a scalar. The paper focuses on the development of more effective models, having higher generalization accuracy, by using prior knowledge of the task domain. We report the results of using Multiple Task Learning (MTL) neural networks and *Context-sensitive* Multiple Task Learning (*cs*MTL) on a domain of image transformation tasks. Models are developed to transform synthetic images of neutral (passport) faces to that of corresponding images of angry, happy and sad faces.

The results are inconclusive for MTL, because our current back-propagation neural network system requires matching output target values for all tasks being learned. Ideally, the number of training examples for the secondary tasks can be much greater than for the primary task, allowing the transfer of accurate secondary task knowledge to the primary task. The results indicate that models developed under MTL with 100 training examples for both the primary and secondary tasks are statistically equivalent to those developed under STL with 100 training examples for the primary task. In future work, we plan to develop an MTL neural network system that is capable of accepting different sized training sets for primary and secondary tasks to have multiple outputs. We plan to develop this on a sufficiently powerful computing platform such that we can model transformation functions for real face images such as shown in Figure 1.

The *cs*MTL results are more conclusive. The experimental results show that inductive transfer with *cs*MTL can be beneficial for a primary task which has only a small number of training examples. When secondary tasks have a sufficient number of training examples, *cs*MTL is able to transfer accurate knowledge from the secondary tasks to the primary task models. This results in primary task models that can transform images more accurately than STL models developed from the same primary task examples. The best image transform models were developed in this way. Further research is needed to determine the best mix of primary and secondary tasks examples to ensure optimal transfer.

Acknowledgments. This research has been funded in part by the Government of Canada through NSERC.

References

1. Baxter, J.: Learning model bias. In: Touretzky, D.S., Mozer, M.C., Hasselmo, M.E. (eds.) Advances in Neural Information Processing Systems, vol. 8, pp. 169–175. MIT Press, Cambridge (1996)
2. Caruana, R.A.: Multitask learning: A knowledge-based source of inductive bias. In: Proceedings of the tenth international conference on machine learning, June 1993, pp. 41–48 (1993)
3. Caruana, R.A.: Multitask learning. Machine Learning 28, 41–75 (1997)

4. Heskes, T.: Empirical bayes for learning to learn. In: Proceedings of the Int. Conference on Machine Learning (ICML 2000), pp. 367–374 (2000)
5. Jebara, T.: Multi-task feature and kernel selection for svms. In: Proceedings of the Int. Conference on Machine Learning (ICML 2004), pp. 185–192 (2004)
6. Micchelli, C.A., Pontil, M.: Kernels for multi-task learning. In: Proceedings of the 18th Conferences on Neural Information Processing Systems (NIPS 2005) (2005)
7. Mitchell, T.: Neural Networks for Face Recognition. Carnegie Mellon University (2007), http://www.cs.cmu.edu/~tom/faces.html
8. O'Quinn, R., Silver, D.L., Poirier, R.: Continued practice and consolidation of a learning task. In: Proceedings of the Meta-Learning Workshop, 22nd Int. Conference on Machine Learning (ICML 2005), Bonn, Germany (2005)
9. Pratt, L.Y.: Discriminability-based transfer between neural networks. In: Giles, C.L., Hanson, S.J., Cowan, J.D. (eds.) Advances in Neural Information Processing Systems, vol. 5, pp. 204–211 (1993)
10. Silver, D.L., Mercer, R.E.: The parallel transfer of task knowledge using dynamic learning rates based on a measure of relatedness. In: Learning to Learn, pp. 213–233 (1997)
11. Silver, D.L., Mercer, R.E.: The task rehearsal method of life-long learning: Overcoming impoverished data. In: Advances in Artificial Intelligence, 15th Conference of the Canadian Society for Computational Studies of Intelligence (AI 2002), pp. 90–101 (2002)
12. Silver, D.L., Poirier, R.: Sequential consolidation of learned task knowledge. In: Webb, G.I., Yu, X. (eds.) AI 2004. LNCS (LNAI), vol. 3339, pp. 217–232. Springer, Heidelberg (2004)
13. Silver, D.L., Poirier, R.: Context-sensitive mtl networks for machine lifelong learning. In: Proceedings of the 20th Florida Artificial Intelligence Research Society Conference (FLAIRS 2007) (May 2007)
14. Thrun, S.: Lifelong learning algorithms. In: Learning to Learn, pp. 181–209. Kluwer Academic Publishers, Dordrecht (1997)
15. Utgoff, P.E.: Machine Learning of Inductive Bias. Kluwer Academc Publisher, Boston (1986)

Using Unsupervised Learning for Network Alert Correlation

Reuben Smith[1], Nathalie Japkowicz[1], Maxwell Dondo[2], and Peter Mason[2]

[1] School of Information Technology and Engineering (SITE), University of Ottawa ON Canada
[2] Defence Research and Development Canada (DRDC) Ottawa ON Canada

Abstract. Alert correlation systems are post-processing modules that enable intrusion analysts to find important alerts and filter false positives efficiently from the output of Intrusion Detection Systems. Typically, however, these modules require high levels of human involvement in creating the system and/or maintaining it, as patterns of attacks change as often as from month to month. We present an alert correlation system based on unsupervised machine learning algorithms that is accurate and low maintenance. The system is implemented in two stages of correlation. At the first stage, alerts are grouped together such that each group forms one step of an attack. At the second stage, the groups created at the first stage are combined such that each combination of groups contains the alerts of precisely one full attack. We tested various implementations of the system. The most successful one relies in the first stage on a new unsupervised algorithm inspired by an existing novelty detection system, and the EM algorithm in the second stage. Our experimental results show that, with our model, the number of alerts that an analyst has to deal with is significantly reduced.

1 Introduction

Intrusion detection systems (IDSs) are computer programs or hardware that attempt to detect attacks against a computer network. IDSs are deployed to inform administrators of the threats against their network services and data. Attacks against networks are common and firewalls are suitable for stopping only certain types of attacks, so IDSs are important in protecting networks.

The output of IDSs, however, is considered low level since a single attack can be represented by several alerts. This makes the work of intrusion analysts quite difficult, if not, virtually, impossible since they have to try to reconstruct the entire pattern of potential attacks from the alerts they received, many of which, incidentally, correspond to false alarms.

Tools that could be of great help to analysts are alert correlation systems, that would automatically find correlations between IDS alerts that represent the same attack. More specifically, such tools would find relationships between alerts that indicate the motives and methods of a particular attack attempt against the network. Previously designed alert correlation systems are either based on machine learning techniques or non-machine learning techniques, including statistical methods, logical rules and graph theory algorithms. In both cases, these methods require a high level of human involvement in creating the system and/or maintaining it, as patterns of attacks change as often as from month to month.

S. Bergler (Ed.): Canadian AI 2008, LNAI 5032, pp. 308–319, 2008.
© Springer-Verlag Berlin Heidelberg 2008

This paper introduces an unsupervised machine learning approach for network alert correlation which does not require any kind of human involvement once the system is installed. The system we present takes as input the output of an IDS which it processes in two stages of correlation. After the first stage of correlation, individual steps of the attacks in the dataset will be clustered. This means that, for example, all similar reconnaissance probes for each of the attacks in the dataset of alerts will be clustered. After the second stage of correlation, different steps of the attacks in the dataset will be clustered. So after the second stage of the correlation system each cluster will represent one specific attack in the dataset.

This work makes three contributions. The first is of an applied nature: our work introduces an alert correlation system that is easy to deploy and maintain on a computer system, and that is more effective than the simple rule-based systems which are commonly used by analysts because of their availability and low costs. The next two contributions are of a more theoretical nature. First, we demonstrate that pure unsupervised learning can be an effective approach for this difficult but practical task and second, we introduce a new clustering algorithm and demonstrates its competitiveness with EM, and SOMs, on a subset of our task. One of our more minor contributions, briefly discussed in the text, consists of extending the two attribute sets previously proposed for this type of task.

The remainder of the paper is divided into four sections. Section 2 presents background research in the area of network event correlation and situates our research within this work. Section 3 introduces our model in greater detail, discussing each correlation stage carefully. The new clustering algorithm we proposed is introduced in this section. Section 4 presents the experimental set up we used to select an optimal implementation for our model and to test it effectively on new data. It also presents and discusses the results we obtained. Section 5 concludes the paper and proposes future extensions of this work.

2 Background Research

The majority of the existing correlation tools use elementary approaches to correlate attacks. For example, Shadow [1] and ACID [2], use the IP addresses to correlate attacks. However, IP addresses may be spoofed, therefore using them alone may not provide a sufficient measure to classify the threat posed by an alert.

Recent work reported by Haines et al. [3], details some of the common correlation tools and approaches. The majority of these approaches use one alert metric at a time to correlate with other possible attacks. More sophisticated approaches use statistical methods on multiple alert metrics [4]. Hatala et al. [5] also analyses various alert correlation efforts by different groups. They give the details of a number of correlation systems, most of which are not based on machine learning techniques. Other approaches that do not involve machine learning are reported in [6,7].

Machine-learning techniques in this area include the work by Julisch et al. [8], Dain and Cunningham [9], Zanero and Savaresi [10], and Laskov et al [11]. The method by Julisch et al. relies on clustering algorithms rather than classification algorithms, and requires an administrator's input to reflect network changes. Dain et al. use machine learning algorithms such as neural networks and decision trees to recognise attacks based on a list of features. Hatala et al. notes that this work uses a simplistic dataset which does not cover a wide range of attack scenarios. The Dain et al. research was tested with a defence conference (DEFCON) dataset. The use of this dataset simplified the problem of alert correlation because attackers were motivated by points in the competition and no points were awarded for stealthy attacks.

Our approach is related to that of Valdes and Skinner [4] who also proceeds by discovering attack step correlations, once lower level correlations have been established. However, their work uses statistical methods, and, thus, depends on the underlying attribute behavioural distributions (such as Gaussian distribution) of deviations from what is expected; by using a machine learning approach, our work was able to avoid the restrictions imposed by such parametric models. Our work is also related to that of Julisch et al. [8] in that it uses unsupervised learning and to that of Dain and Cunninghan [9] in its choice of a data representation, as will be discussed in the next section.

3   The Proposed System

The system is based on the idea that attacks can be decomposed into attack steps, which correspond to one action in the attackers greater plan, and, further, that single attack steps are made up of large numbers of IDS alerts. For instance, one step by an attacker might be running the security scanning tool *nmap*, once, against a network to discover what services are available. This step would likely generate many IDS alerts. With no correlation tool, a systems operator is faced with thousands of IDS alerts and has no way of knowing, easily, which alerts represent the same attack step nor which attack steps should be considered together as parts of the same attack.

We recall that the system we propose is not an IDS, itself, but rather a post-processing module for the output of an IDS. It takes as input a set of uncorrelated IP packets that have been flagged as alerts by an IDS, specifically the Snort IDS in our experiments, and passes the alerts to the First Stage of Correlation module that outputs clusters of similar IP packets supposed to represent the same attack step. These clusters are subsequently input into the Second Stage of Correlation module which outputs *super-clusters* (clusters of clusters) representing a specific attack.

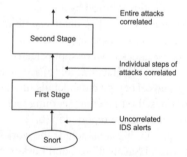

Fig. 1. Architecture of our alert correlation system

Table 1. First stage features

Feature	Feature	Feature	Feature
portSrc	portDest	ipIsIcmpProtocol	ipIsIgmpProtocol
ipIsTcpProtocol	ipIsUdpProtocol	ipLen	ipDgmLen
ipId	ipTos	ipTtl	ipOptLsrr
ipPacketDefrag	ipReserveBit	ipMiniFrag	ipFragOffset
ipFragSize	icmpCode	icmpId	icmpSeq
icmpType	tcpFlag1	tcpFlag2	tcpFlagUrg
tcpFlagAck	tcpFlagPsh	tcpFlagRst	tcpFlagSyn
tcpFlagFin	tcpLen	tcpWinNum	tcpUrgPtr
tcpOptMss	tcpOptNopCount	tcpOptSackOk	tcpOptTs1
tcpOptTs2	tcpOptWs	tcpHeaderTrunc	udpLen

At the first stage of correlation, we cluster the dataset of alerts by constructing features that differentiate Snort alerts at the IP packet level. We are interested in clustering alert IP packets that are numerically similar in their protocol attributes, so we construct our set of attributes to use for clustering in such a way that numerically similar Snort alerts are clustered together. At the second stage of correlation we are interested in the trends between groups of similar Snort alerts. For example, if two separate sets of Snort alerts are comprised of alerts with the same identical IP source address, this might be an indicator that the sets of alerts are related. Our second set of features were constructed to reflect this goal. The next two subsections describe the kind of features that were used in our system while the following one describes the clustering algorithms used in both stages of correlation: AA, a new clustering approach based on a particular feedforword neural network architecture called an autoassociator and the EM algorithm.

Both the final choice of features and clustering algorithm were determined experimentally. This paper will describe a subset of the experiments that lead to our final choices in Section 4. The remainder of the experiments are described in [6,7].

3.1   Features Used in the First Stage of Correlation

The set of features extracted from Snort for the first stage of Correlation are listed in Table 1.[1] This set of features was created to fully represent an IP packet flagged as an alert by an IDS sensor. In this representation, however, we tried to ensure that only protocol features were used. This means that no information specific to Snort was used and that, therefore, our approach is portable to other IDS systems. Another observation of interest is that we did not include the IP source address or IP destination address protocol fields in the list of features. This is because these features tended to impede correct clustering. We also reasoned that if we wish to cluster a number of packets together that make up a distributed denial of service or similar attack, the IP address fields could impede correct clustering since source IP address is easily forged for certain types of attacks, and the destination IP address can be masked by attacking many computers at once even if only one computer is the target.

---

[1] We used Snort's acronyms and shorthands to name our features.

3.2   Features Used in the Second Stage of Correlation

For the second correlation stage, we take the output clusters of the first stage and represent them, each, as new data items, encoded using a new set of features. Feature construction for the data ultimately determines what is learned, therefore, we intentionally constructed our features such that a cluster of alerts representing a single step of an attack will be similar to another cluster of alerts from the same attack.

The set of features constructed for the second stage of correlation are listed in Table 2. This list was inspired from the feature list of Dain et al [9]. Our list includes some of their features as well as some that they did not consider. All the features were meant to capture the type of reasoning an attacker may go through or the kind of behaviour that can be observed when considering groups of alerts. We illustrate this kind of reasoning on a few of our features. Further explanation appear in [6,7].

Table 2. A cluster encoded for the second stage

Feature	Feature
numAlerts	ipSrcAddrCommonPart
ipSrcAddrCommonBits	ipDestAddrCommonPart
ipDestAddrCommonBits	modePortSrc
modePortDest	avgIpHdrLen
avgPayloadLen	avgReconsErr
avgSeqNumDiff	avgTimeSig
varTimeSig	avgTcpFlagsSet

ipSrcAddrCommonPart: Attackers often perpetrate an attack from a single host, or from a single IP subnet. Dain and Cunningham included a feature to indicate similarity between the source IP addresses of two alerts. In our system, we included a feature to indicate the shared part of the most-significant bits of a group of IP addresses from a cluster

modePortSrc and modePortDest: We found that using the TCP source and destination ports was sometimes valuable in determining the grouping of a set of alerts. We also found that when the ports were useful, there was almost always a particular source or destination port that was more common than the rest. Accordingly, we created two features: one feature to encode the most common TCP source port in a cluster of alerts and a feature to encode the most common destination port.

Please note that while the IP source and destination addresses were not used during the first stage of correlation, they are used during the second stage, since they were shown to bring about performance gains. This is because such features are valuable in detecting an attack source for many types of attacks. For those attacks in which IP spoofing (i.e., forging a source IP address) can be used, we found that allowing alerts with dissimilar IP addresses to be clustered together at the first stage of correlation adequately solved the problem without any need to repeat this approach at the second stage.

3.3   Clustering Algorithms Used in Both Stages of Correlation

Along with the selection of features for each stage of correlation, clustering algorithms and their parameters also needed to be chosen. We experimented with three clustering systems: the EM algorithm, self-organizing maps and AA, a new algorithm based on the autoassociator, a particular feedforward neural network architecture. In the early stages of our research, we also experimented with k-means, but it was quickly dismissed given its low performance levels. This section begins by describing AA and then discusses the choices that were made in our final implementation. The EM algorithm [12] and self-organizing maps [13] will not be described here because of lack of space.

An autoassociator (AA) is a fully-connected three-layer, feedforward neural network whose objective is to reproduce an input vector x_i made up of alert attributes, at the output through weights w_i. However, the reproduction is not perfect and a reconstruction error, RE, is a measure of this imperfection. Similar attack scenarios have very similar attributes, and we expect their REs to be very close. Similar alerts are thus expected to be clustered together based on their RE. This idea is an extension of the work by [6,7] on novelty detection. In that work, it was shown that the AA was good at clustering previously seen events, differentiating them from new events. This kind of clustering, however, was coarse-grained as the AA was only trained on the positive class and was only required to recognize data from that class and reject any other. Our purpose, here, is to use the AA in a similar capacity, but as a finer-grained clustering system. Specifically, we will train the AA with all the data available (not simply positive data, but rather, data that may belong to some indeterminate number of clusters) and cluster it according to their RE.

We will now describe this algorithm in more detail. A three-layer fully connected feedforward neural network with N input nodes, N output nodes and $J(< N)$ hidden nodes (unoptimised) was used. Although such feedforward architectures are usually used in a supervised fashion, in this work, we use it strictly in an unsupervised fashion: no instance labels are used. In place of the labels usually indicated at the output layer, the attribute vector used at the input layer is repeated at the output layer for each example. The neural network is, thus, expected to learn the identity function. In other words, the output at node i of each layer is given by:

$$o_i = f(\sum_{k=1}^{K_i} w_{ik} y_k) \tag{1}$$

where y_i is the output of neuron i after receiving K_i signals from the neurons of the preceding layer, and $y_i = x_i$ for the input layer.

The AA was trained using the error-backpropagation algorithm with the objective of reconstructing the input space at the output. The training objective is to minimise the square errors E, as given by:

$$E = \sum_{i=1}^{N} ||x_i - y_i||^2 \tag{2}$$

The neural network's weights were iteratively updated until convergence was achieved. Once training was completed, cluster barriers were created to separate adjacent clusters.

This was achieved by comparing a predetermined threshold value to the resultant RE e_i produced by the difference between the alert vector $\mathbf{x}_i$ and the "new" alert vector $\mathbf{y}_i$. This difference is given by:

$$e_i = ||\mathbf{x}_i - \mathbf{y}_i|| \tag{3}$$

for each input vector $\mathbf{x}_i$. The predetermined threshold value was set experimentally. By varying the cluster barrier and recording the errors, we concluded that the best cluster barrier to use would be 0.0017. Equation 3 essentially reduced a 42-dimensional vector into a 1-dimensional threshold metric e used for clustering. The result of the clustering was multiple alert groups that have similar or closely similar attributes.

Note that an important difference between this algorithm and other more traditional ones is its reliance on imperfection. Indeed, we are exploiting the fact that the autoassociator is not able to fully reconstruct the input layer at the output level, to cluster the data, and that it will make different kinds of reconstruction "errors" on different categories of data, thus, allowing us to cluster them accurately. This kind of reasoning worked well in the case of novelty detection and we wanted to test whether this result would extend to the case of clustering.

There were three other reasons underlying our decision to explore the performance of the AA rather than content ourselves exclusively with off-the shelf algorithms. First, unlike other clustering algorithms like the *EM algorithm* or SOMs, the AA does not require knowledge of the number of output clusters in advance. It determines it through a self-optimisation process in the training algorithm. Second, unlike SOMs and traditional uses of the EM algorithm, the AA naturally performs soft-clustering that is then interpreted by the simple cluster barrier setting algorithm just discussed into hard clusters. More specifically, the AA can assign a number to each data point—the RE—such that data points corresponding to the same alert are roughly assigned similar numbers. This feature corresponds loosely to the notion of a ranking classifier in the supervised case. We believed that such flexibility could enhance clustering performance. Last but not least, we noticed that the RE of an alert was quite stable in that it is mostly independent of the data set that contains it. This is particularly important in our application given that we separated the first correlation stage data into windows in order to make the results more manageable for the clustering algorithm as well as to include a rough form of correlation based on alert generation time. This means that the same alert appears surrounded by different alerts in various training scenarios and that its outcome should remain the same from one scenario to the next. Through its RE, initial experiments revealed that AA appears to obtain similar REs for the same alert in different context, a feature that the other algorithms do not provide.

4 Experiments Set-Up and Results

As previously mentioned, a large experimental study was performed prior to settling on the model presented in the previous section. It will be impossible for us to discuss the entire study in this paper. Therefore, we had to focus on a subset of our experiments. We chose to present the experiments which allowed us to select an optimal clustering approach for the first stage of correlation since these experiments highlight the usefulness of our new clustering algorithm, at least on one type of practical problem. Our other experiments were designed to select an optimal clustering approach for the second stage of correlation, to select the best parameters for all clustering algorithms (beyond the few results that are presented here), to choose an optimal cluster barrier setting approach for the AA (the one described above is the best one we identified), to select the best attribute sets for both stages of correlation, and to select an optimal method for scaling our attribute values in both stages (the optimal scale we settled on was $[-1, 1]$). These experiments are all detailed in [6,7].

In order to validate our system's overall utility, we conclude this section by presenting the results obtained by our final model and by comparing them to a simple rule-based algorithm similar to those usually employed in real-world settings. The section starts with a presentation of the data sets used in both the development and testing parts of our study.

4.1 Data Sources

The system was tested using two alert data sets. We tested our system with Snort [14] alerts from incidents.org. We also used labelled alerts from the 1999 DARPA [15] IDS evaluation data. Since the labelled DARPA data was in packet form, we ran the data through Snort using commonly used configuration filters. We developed some Perl scripts to read the text-based Snort alerts into numeric data for use with our system.

In the incidents.org data set, we selected a training set of 10,000 alerts and a validation set of 500 alerts. In the DARPA data set, we selected a training set of 10,000 alerts, a validation set of 100 alerts and a testing set of 500 alerts. The incidents.org data set did not require a testing set since it was only used during the development of our system. We chose to develop our system using the incidents.org data set because it contains real and complex sets of attacks in contrast with the DARPA data which is simulated and, thus, of lesser value for the development stage. The DARPA data was set aside for formal testing of the completed system.

The data in the validation and testing sets of both domains were manually labeled for our task: based on our knowledge and experience, we placed alerts into clusters, each representing an attack step and super-clusters, each representing an attack attempt. This was a tedious and time consuming process, which is why the size of our labeled data sets is quite small.

4.2 Clustering Algorithm Selection Experiments

We examined three algorithms: the autoassociator introduced in the previous section, self-organization maps and the EM algorithm. All the experiments reported in this section were conducted on the incidents.org data set since they are part of the design of our system. The results obtained by each clustering method were compared against the benchmark clusters to determine performance. As mentioned above, we only report on the selection process in the first stage of correlation because of lack of space in the paper. The selection of a clustering system for the second stage of correlation was conducted in a similar fashion (see [6,7]).

For the first stage of correlation, rather than training SOMs and the autoassociator with 10,000 training examples, we trained the two algorithms with only 1,017. This is

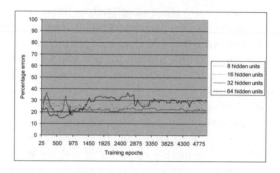

Fig. 2. First stage performance with the autoassociator

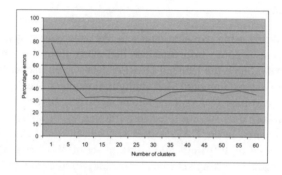

Fig. 3. First stage performance with the EM algorithm

because there were difficulties in training SOMS on the 10,000 alert set and we wanted the two algorithms to be trained on the same data for fair comparison purposes. EM was not trained at all, since it is not designed to be trained with unlabelled data. Rather, it builds clusters directly on the testing data. 1,017 training alerts comprises roughly the first 10% of each type of alert available from the 10,000 alert training set. We tested the system on the 500 alerts from the validation set.

The results of these experiments are presented in Figures 2, 3 and 4. In Figure 2, we tested the AA by simultaneously varying the number of hidden units and the number of epochs. The learning rate was fixed and set at 0.4. From the graph, it is clear that the autoassociator attains the best performance if constructed with 64 hidden units and if trained for between 500 and 1000 epochs. Its error rate, in this region, falls below the 20% mark. For the performance graph of the EM algorithm in Figure 3, we varied the number of clusters. We can see that if the number of clusters chosen is 10 or more, the performance results are consistently in the range of 30% to 40% errors. The best performance for the EM algorithm is reached at 30 clusters where it obtains a 30% error rate, or a 10% worse error rate than the AA. In Figure 4, we present the results of the self-organizing maps for which we varied the lattice configuration and epochs

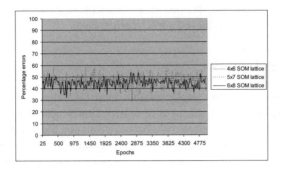

Fig. 4. First stage performance with the SOM algorithm

simultaneously. The results for the SOM algorithm are noticeably worse than the results with the autoassociator and the EM algorithm. The results for all three lattice configurations vary significantly with no discernable range of best performance. From this we see that the performance of SOMs is universally poor on our problem, especially if compared with the autoassociator, which does not generate an error percentage greater than 40% in this evaluation.

We, thus, conclude that the autoassociator performs better than the EM algorithm and SOMs for this dataset against the incidents.org benchmark evaluation dataset.

4.3   Testing the Overall System

We conducted our final tests on the fresh data set provided by DARPA. It is important to note, though, that although we did not use the DARPA data to design the system, we still needed to tune and train the autoassociator on the 10,000 training and 100 validation alerts, respectively, prior to testing the overall system on the 500 testing alerts.

The system clustered the DARPA data set into 21 clusters, i.e., 21 attacks. From the benchmark labels, however, only 13 attacks were expected. This suggests that our system produced a number of "separation errors", in which alerts of the same kind were clustered into different groups. Indeed, we found that 54 out of 500 alerts were separated from the cluster they should have been in, but were nonetheless clustered along with similar alerts. Conversely, we found that very few "clustering errors" took place since we found that only 4 out of 500 alerts were clustered along with unrelated alerts. This is quite encouraging since separation errors are much less serious than clustering errors which may cause and IDS analyst to miss important events. Please see [6,7] for tables and more complete descriptions of our results.

If considering both kinds of errors together, we can conclude that our system obtained an accuracy of 88.4%. On its own, this figure is not terribly meaningful, so we compared the results to those obtained using a simple rule-based correlation system based on the correlation descriptions of Northcutt [16] and the web-based ACID alert console [2]. Such a correlation algorithm is quite often used in practice. Using the

Simple Correlator system, we obtained an accuracy of 79.4% on the DARPA data set. This means that our system achieved a 9% improvement.[2]

5 Concluding Remarks

In this work, we designed and implemented a two-stage alert correlation model and demonstrated how this model was able to cluster similar alerts with better accuracy than what we achieved with a simple rule-based correlation algorithm of the type often used in practice. The model we created is of a purely unsupervised nature and does not require any maintenance, once all the initial parameters are determined. This should provide intrusion analysts with a simple and effective solution to their alert flooding problem.

The paper also introduced a new clustering algorithm based on a neural network architecture called an autoassociator (AA). The main advantages of this algorithm is that it does not require knowledge of the number of output clusters in advance, that it performs soft-clustering and that its output remains stable in various contexts. Of particular interest here, the AA was also shown to be quite accurate on the first of our two clustering tasks.

Many avenues for future work stem from this study. First, we would like our results to be examined by a seasoned IDS analyst who could give us feedback on how to improve the system. Second, we recognize that our system still requires a lot of tuning, both in terms of algorithm and feature selection. In particular, we would like to experiment with other clustering algorithms and new features. Finally, we would like to examine the AA more carefully to establish its strengths and weaknesses.

References

1. Northcutt, S., et al.: SHADOW: Second heuristic analysis for defensive online warfare
2. Danyliw, R.: ACID: Analysis console for intrusion detections
3. Haines, J., Ryder, D.K., Tinnel, L., Taylor, S.: Validation of sensor alert correlators. IEEE Security and Privacy, 46–56 (2003)
4. Valdes, A., Skinner, K.: Probabilistic alert correlation. In: Lee, W., Mé, L., Wespi, A. (eds.) RAID 2001. LNCS, vol. 2212, pp. 54–68. Springer, Heidelberg (2001)
5. Hätälä, A., Särs, C., Addams-Moring, R., Virtanen, T.: Event data exchange and intrusion alert correlation in heterogeneous networks. In: Proceedings of the 8th Colloquium for Information Systems Security Education (CISSE), Westpoint, NY, CISSE, June 2004, pp. 84–92 (2004)
6. Smith, R., Japkowicz, N., Dondo, M.: Clustering using an autoassociator: A case study in network event correlation. In: Proceedings of the 17th IASTED International Conference on Parallel and Distributed Computing and Systems, Phoenix, AZ, November 2005, pp. 613–618. ACTA Press (2005)

---

[2] Out of curiosity, we compared the two systems on the incidents.org domain. Our approach obtained an accuracy of 67.4% while the simple Correlator only reached an accuracy of 41.6%. This result, however, is optimistically biased given its reliance on the validation data set as well as the fact that it is based on internal, rather than external validation (i.e., testing within the same data set rather than on a separate one).

7. Japkowicz, N., Smith, R.: Autocorrel ii: Unsupervised network event correlation using neural networks. Contractor Report CR 2005-155, DRDC Ottawa, Ottawa, ON (October 2005)
8. Julisch, K., Dacier, M.: Mining intrusion detection alarms for actionable knowledge. In: Proceedings of SIGKDD 2002, the 8th International Conference on Knowledge Discovery and Data Mining, Edmonton, Alberta, Canada, July 2002, pp. 366–375. ACM Press, New York (2002)
9. Dain, O., Cunningham, R.K.: Fusing a heterogeneous alert stream into scenarios. In: Proceedings of the 2001 ACM Workshop on Data Mining for Security Applications, Philadelphia, PA, November 2001, pp. 1–13. ACM Press, New York (2001)
10. Zanero, S., Savaresi, S.M.: Unsupervised learning techniques for an intrusion detection system. In: Proceedings of the 2004 ACM Symposium on Applied Computing, Nicosia, Cyprus, pp. 412–419. ACM, New York (2004)
11. Laskov, P., Dussel, P., Rieck, C.S.: Learning intrusion detection: Supervised or unsupervised? In: Roli, F., Vitulano, S. (eds.) ICIAP 2005. LNCS, vol. 3617, pp. 50–57. Springer, Heidelberg (2005)
12. Dempster, A., Laird, N., Rubin, D.: Maximum likelihood from incoming data via the EM algorithm. J. Royal Stat. Soc., Series B 39(1), 1–36 (1977)
13. Kohonen, T.: Self-Organizing Maps. Springer Series in Information Sciences, vol. 30. Springer, Berlin (1995); (Second Extended Edition 1997)
14. Roesch, M.: Snort—lightweight intrusion detection for networks. In: Proceedings of LISA 1999: 13th Systems Administration Conference, Seattle, Washington, November 7–12, 1999, pp. 229–238. The USENIX Association (1999)
15. Lippmann, R., Haines, J.W., Fried, D.J., Korba, J., Das, K.: The 1999 darpa off-line intrusion detection evaluation. Computer Networks 34(4), 579–595 (2000)
16. Northcutt, S.: Network Intrusion Detection: An Analyst's Handbook. New Riders Publishing, Indianapolis (1999)

Verbs Speak Loud: Verb Categories in Learning Polarity and Strength of Opinions

Marina Sokolova and Guy Lapalme

Département d'informatique et de recherche opérationnelle
Université de Montréal
sokolovm@iro.umontreal.ca,
lapalme@iro.umontreal.ca

Abstract. We show that verbs reliably represent texts when machine learning algorithms are used to learn opinions. We identify semantic verb categories that capture essential properties of human communication. Lexical patterns are applied to construct verb-based features that represent texts in machine learning experiments. Our empirical results show that expressed actions provide a reliable accuracy in learning opinions.

1 Introduction

The English saying *Actions speak louder than words* states that we learn more from people's actions than from their words. This statement may express human wisdom and be true for human learning, but could it be also true for machine learning as well? We show that, under certain conditions, people's expressed actions, i.e. verbs that they use, provide for more accurate machine learning of opinions than all words, even when the latter are re-enforced with the history of speakers' opinions. We consider verbs that indicate stronger personal physical actions (speak, write), mental and sensual actions (think, feel), and intentions (could, should, can, will). We apply ideas from communication theory to build semantic verb categories, we then formalize their use by language patterns from which we construct text features.

We apply machine learning techniques (regression and classification) to texts represented by the verb-based features. These texts are debates from the US Congress and consumer-written forum messages. Regression problems for opinion learning have not been studied before. Previous opinion studies mainly focused on binary classification [1], while sometimes solving a three-class classification problem [2]. Our combination of regression and classification learning provides a more detailed opinion analysis and relies only on the data. Other methods achieve a similar accuracy by adding personal information about speakers, e.g. history of previous comments [3]. However, additional information is not often available. Our method's accuracy is close to human-human agreement on positive and negative sentiments, when it is based on verbs [4]. Our results complement opinion and sentiment mining, a research area whose results are in an increasing demand from government, media and business practitioners.

S. Bergler (Ed.): Canadian AI 2008, LNAI 5032, pp. 320–331, 2008.
© Springer-Verlag Berlin Heidelberg 2008

2   Semantic Verb Categories

Sentiment and opinion analysis are more subjective and difficult to solve than traditional text classification and mining tasks [5]. We propose a method that uses interpersonal aspects of communication and views language as a resource of accomplishing goals within context of social interactions. This approach is reminiscent of the Systemic Functional Linguistics developed by Halliday [6].

We consider that opinion can be emotional or rational. Emotional opinion may be expressed by attitude (enjoy, hate) and, partially, by the perception of the situation (smell, feel). Rational opinion may require the person to list facts such as events (meet, send), the state of affairs (depend, have). Possibility, necessity, politeness or irony can be directly shown by the use of primary modals (can, will) or more conditional secondary modals (could, should) [7].

We also consider that an informal, loosely structured, spoken-like language differs from a formal, structured, written-like one. Verbs denoting activity (play, write, send) and cognition verbs (think,believe) are the two most frequent categories when opinions are expressed in spoken-like language. Activity, the largest among verb categories, is the most frequent in all types of texts. The high frequency of mental verbs is specific for spoken language [8,9]; thus, we separate mental verbs into three categories: perception, attitude and cognition. Verbs denoting process (live, look, stay) often appear in written language, sometimes as often as activity verbs [10]. Table 1 shows the semantic categories we built from the seed verbs given in Leech[7] to which we added synonyms from Roget's Interactive Thesaurus [11].

Table 1. The list of non-modal verb categories and examples of corresponding verbs

Category	Refers to	Examples
cognition	mental state	consider, hope, think, know
perception	activity of the senses	see,feel,hear
attitude	volition and feeling	enjoy,hate,love
activity	a continuing action	read, work, explain
event	happening or transition to another state	become,reply,pay,lose
process	continuing or eventual change of state	change,increase,grow

We generalize the use of the verb categories by means of patterns defined by grammar rules in Figure 1. The semantic categories make up the lower level. The intermediate level forms four groups. Physical action verbs are considered to be more direct in expressing opinions, whereas mental verbs correspond to more hesitation and condition [12], e.g. We played well expresses more confidence than I think we played well. At the highest level, we consider whether the person involves herself in evaluation (*firstPerson*) or projects it on interlocutors (*you*).

The rules at the top of Figure 1 define the expression of an author's involvement, either in the form of closeness or distancing.

closeness	→ *firstPerson* (*logic* | *physicalAction* | *mentalAction* | *state*)
distancing	→ you (*logic* | *physicalAction* | *mentalAction* | *state*)
logic	→ *primaryModal* | *secondaryModal*
physicalAction	→ [*modifier*] (*activity* | *event* | *process*)
mentalAction	→ [*modifier*] (*cognition* | *perception* | *attitude*)
state	→ [*modifier*] *havingBeing*
firstPerson	→ I | we
primaryModal	→ can | may | will | shall | have to | must
secondaryModal	→ could | might | should | would
activity	→ read | work | explain | ...
event	→ become | reply | pay | send | ...
process	→ change | increase | stay | ...
cognition	→ believe | consider | hope | ...
perception	→ feel | hear | see | smell | taste
attitude	→ enjoy | fear | like | love | hate
havingBeing	→ have | be | depend | consist | ...
modifier	→ *negation* | *adverb*

Fig. 1. Grammar rules generalizing the use of verb categories. | separate alternatives, [] indicate optional parts and parentheses are used for grouping.

We now outline some involvement implications for each rule:

closeness uses I or we to indicate a direct involvement of the author. Its sub-rules indicate different degrees of the author's involvement:

    logic expresses permission, possibility, and necessity as the representation of logic, and superiority, politeness, tact, and irony as the representation of practice:

        primaryModals such as can and may express direct possibility, permission or necessity of an action.

        secondaryModals use a more polite, indirect and conditional pattern than a primary modal and indicate more hypothetically and tentatively the author's intentions.

    physicalAction denotes an author's goal-oriented actions (*activity*), actions that have a beginning and an end (*event*) and a series of steps towards a defined end (*process*). The pattern corresponds to a direct and active involvement of the author.

    mentalAction uses mental action verbs, being more polite and tentative, that are a common face-saving technique and that mark openness to feedback.

    state indicates personal characteristics and corresponds to actions without definite limits and strong differentiations.

distancing uses second person pronouns and shows how an author establishes distance from the matter.

3   Feature Engineering

To validate our hypothesis on actions, we looked at various types of information provided by verbs. We considered a general information provided by the use of verb categories, including verb past and continuous forms which reflect uncertainty of speakers [13], specific information resulting from the use of individual verbs, and information enhanced by words collocated with the pattern terminals.

We constructed three feature sets based on the pattern terminals (Figure 1):[1]

I The first feature set generalizes the use of word categories, separating their use in present, past and continuous forms. We are interested in density and diversity of the words in each category. For a text T, for each category C_j, the number of word tokens $N_j(T) = \sum_{t_i \in C_j} n(t_i)(T)$ and the number of word types $V_j(T) = \sum_{t_i \in C_j} I(t_i)(T)$ estimate these two parameters respectively; $n(x)$ denotes the number of occurrences of x; t_i is a terminal token; $I(x)$ equals 1 if x appears in T and 0 otherwise.

As a result, for each non-modal verb category we built six features. To represent modal verbs, we built four features: two – for primary modals, two – for secondary modals [2]. Altogether, there are 40 features with numerical attributes.

II The next set has individual terminals as its features. Each terminal is represented by its occurrences in the text: $N_i(T) = \sum_{t_i \in t} n(t_i)(T)$. There are 301 features.

III The third feature set expands the pattern terminals with words appearing with a high probability after or before a terminal. We estimate this probability by computing:

$$P(w|t) = \frac{\sum_{t_i \in t} n(w, t_i)}{\sum_{j=1}^{m} n(w_j)} \tag{1}$$

t is the set of all terminals; w, t_i is the event where the word w appears immediately after or before t_i; m is the size of the data vocabulary. In practice, we find collocated words with the following extraction procedure:

Step 1: we build the bigram model of data $w_{k-1} w_k$; bigrams are used because they avoid multiple extraction of the same word with respect to the same terminal;

Step 2: we extract bigrams $t_i w_k$ where the pattern terminals appear on the left side; this captures modified and intensified words appearing on the bigram's right side;

---

[1] Note that only negations preceding a terminal will appear in text representation.

[2] Modal verbs do not have past and continuous forms.

Step 3: we find $n(w_k|t_i)$ – occurrences of words appearing on the right side of terminals; the resulting $n(w_k|t_i)$ shows what words w_k were modified and intensified most (recall that rule terminals can be synonyms; in this case they may modify and intensify the same words);

Step 4: we keep w_k with $n(w_k|t_i) > 5$; the occurrence threshold 5 is chosen based on the language modeling characteristics.

Attributes are normalized to eliminate the bias introduced by the text length.

4   Data

We experimented with two types of data sets. One, consumer-written product reviews posted on the web, representing loosely-edited, free structured texts, presumably written by general population. The other, records of the US Congress debates, are structured, edited and professionally written. There are some commonalities between the data sets: each set covers several topics, i.e., several products reviewed by consumers and multiple legislations debated by congressmen; for each data set, its records come from hundreds of contributors. Both characteristics ensure that our empirical results will not be confined to a specific group of people or events.

We use consumer reviews data set introduced in [14]. Consumer reviews are posted on a web site dedicated to consumer goods evaluation. They are written by users of consumer goods. Although with some restrictions, reviews satisfy the following criteria of spoken language: they are spontaneous, loosely structured and socially interactive. The data set in our experiments consist of 314 reviews evaluating consumer electronics. The set size is 71,711 words (tokens) and 6,908 distinct words (types). Some text segments, but not all, have been manually tagged by Hu and Liu according to positive or negative opinions expressed by the reviewers. The following excerpt – from a positive review of a digital camera g3 – has a positive score 3:

> this is *my* first digital camera , and what a 'toy' *it* is! *i* am a software engineer and am very keen into technical details of everything *i* buy, *i* spend around 3 months before buying the digital camera; [3] and *i* must say, g3 worth every single cent . . . .

For the regression problem, three numerical labels are computed for each text for learning the strength of opinions:

- the number of positive tags; its range: 0 – 24;
- the number of negative tags; its range: −18 – 0;
- a signed sum of the two numbers; the range is −13 –24.

In the classification problem for learning the strength of opinions, we apply unsupervised equal-frequency discretization to each numerical label [15]. This makes fine distinctions between data entries that are close (e.g., with 4-6 positive opinion labels) and ignores big differences among data entries that are far apart (e.g., with 18-24 positive opinion labels).

We also used 1,117 Congress debate records [3]. Congress data are recorded speeches made by congressmen during legislation debates. Congress debates speeches are usually prepared in advance by congressmen and their assistants and read by congressmen during debate time. They are non-spontaneous, well-structured, and often close to immediate interaction. Each text is a recorded speech of the member of the US Congress, that either supports or opposes a proposed legislature. The debate record size is 1,139,470 words (tokens) and 21,750 distinct words (types). Thomas et al. labeled texts by numerical polarity scores, computed by SUPPORT VECTOR MACHINE. SVM builds a decision surface that separates positive and negative texts. The distance from a text to the surface defines the text's score value. The text's position with respect to the surface defines whether the score is positive or negative. We keep their scores as the data labels. The following excerpt has a positive score of 0.72:

> we have known that small businesses and working families need tax relief, and we have fought hard to make that happen so that we see the opportunity right there . . . .

For the data, the opinion labels range from −1.56 to 1.74. For classification purposes, we use the score signs as the data labels.

5   Language Pattern Distribution

In Figure 1 of Section 2, we outlined implications for the use of verb categories. To compare their use in consumer reviews and Congress debates, we computed the rule distribution reported in Table 2.

The upper part of Table 2 reports percentage held by the rules and the subrules for consumer reviews data. 100% is the total use of two pattern rules. To simplify the table, we combined results for pronouns I and we and for patterns with and without modifiers. In consumer reviews the use of mental verbs prevails over the use of physical action verbs. In fact, patterns with cognition verbs are the most frequent among all action patterns. Cognition verbs are common as a face-saving technique, thus their frequent use moderates the level of the author's involvement.

Since reviews tell about the experience of the authors with consumer goods, we could expect a frequent and diverse use of the *activity* verb categories. However, this is not the case: *closeness* patterns of the *physicalAction* verbs use more frequently *process* verbs, but not *activity* or *event* ones. Among distancing patterns, consumer reviews use straightforward *physicalAction* more often than any other sub-rule. The Congressional debate patterns are distributed differently than the ones in consumer reviews (the lower part of Table 2). Frequent use of physical action patterns demonstrates a stronger level of involvement. This also can be seen through a frequent use of activity verbs. In contrast with consumer reviews, congressmen do not use second-person pronoun often: only 4.37% of the rule patterns belongs to distancing while it is 40.90% in consumer reviews.

Comparison of extracted patterns supports the assumption that patterns vary across different communication environments. In Congressional debates a combined share of the most straightforward *primaryModal* and *activity* patterns

Table 2. Percentage held by the patterns in the consumer reviews and the US Congress debates data. 100% is the total number of the used rules in each data set. Results are combined for I and we and for patterns with and without modifiers. The largest percentage is given in **bold**, the second largest – in ***bold italic***, the smallest – in *italic*.

Consumer review data					
Rules	%	Subrules	%	Verb categories	%
closeness	**59.10**	*logic*	***17.77***	*primaryModal*	**14.51**
				secondaryModal	3.26
		mentalAction	***17.77***	*cognition*	9.27
				attitude	7.14
				perception	1.36
		physicalAction	13.04	*process*	8.42
				activity	3.46
				event	1.16
		state	10.52	*havingBeing*	***10.52***
distancing	*40.90*	*physicalAction*	**19.43**	*event*	7.72
				process	6.21
				activity	5.50
		logic	11.27	*primaryModal*	8.27
				secondaryModal	3.00
		mentalAction	9.58	*attitude*	5.32
				cognition	2.40
				perception	1.86
		state	*0.62*	*havingBeing*	*0.62*
Congress debates data					
Rules	%	Subrules	%	Verb categories	%
closeness	**95.63**	*logic*	**31.15**	*primaryModal*	**26.57**
				secondaryModal	4.58
		mentalAction	***29.16***	*cognition*	***17.76***
				attitude	10.43
				perception	0.97
		physicalAction	28.60	*process*	13.91
				activity	13.07
				event	1.62
		state	6.72	*havingBeing*	6.72
distancing	*4.37*	*logic*	3.81	*primaryModal*	3.29
				secondaryModal	0.52
		physicalAction	0.33	*event*	0.28
				process	*0.05*
		mentalAction	*0.23*	*perception*	0.23

is 39.64% of all the rules, whereas in consumer reviews their combined share is 17.97%. Patterns for *distancing* substantially vary across two data: they are frequently present in consumer reviews (40.90%) and rarely found in Congress debates (4.37%).

To illustrate the difference between the verb distributions we projected them with respect to *closeness* vs *distancing* axes. The plot on Figure 2 shows the

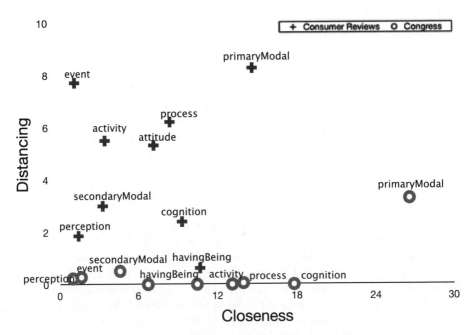

Fig. 2. Distribution of verb categories in Congress debates and Consumer data sets. The horizontal axis estimates *closeness* (in per cent), the vertical axis – *distancing* (in per cent). Crosses denote Consumer reviews categories, circles – those in Congress debates.

resulting two clusters, crosses indicate Consumer review and circles – Congress debates. Each cluster has only one outlier: *havingBeing* – for consumer reviews, *primaryModal* – for Congress debates. The clusters do not overlap, meaning that the category distribution differs across *closeness* and *distancing* dimensions.

The difference can be attributed to the impact of the social environment of the discourse. In consumer reviews the authors try to appeal to the audience, thus, using second person pronoun more often than congressmen who focus on presenting their own opinion during debates. On the other hand, congressmen emphasize their active involvement in the discussed matters more than consumer reviewers. We could partially attribute this to the fact that congressmen should show their involvement to the constituency whereas authors of consumer reviews remain anonymous to readers.

6   Learning Results

We solved four regression problems to learn how the expressed actions estimate the strength of opinions and four classification problems – for learning positive and negative opinions. For the Congress data set, we learned opinion scores and positive and negative opinion labels. For the consumer review data set, the number of positive evaluations in a review (# pos), the number of negative evaluations

Table 3. Smallest *RelativeAbsoluteError* and *RootRelativeSquaredError* obtained by the algorithms. Rows report results for each algorithm. Columns report results for each problem. For each problem, the smallest *RAE* is in *italic*.

Algorithms	Consumer reviews						Congress	
	positive		negative		overall		debates	
	RAE	*RRSE*	*RAE*	*RRSE*	*RAE*	*RRSE*	*RAE*	*RRSE*
KNN	91.19	87.97	90.77	88.70	93.56	96.50	78.74	86.60
SVM	80.98	84.15	89.33	96.71	91.38	94.38	90.89	94.80
BM5P	*80.26*	82.21	*87.21*	85.81	*89.82*	96.61	*73.73*	78.84

in a review (# neg), the overall score define three regression problems; their equal-frequency splits define three classification problems. We used ten-fold cross-validation to estimate the quality of learning. Ten-fold cross-validation is chosen because of its high generalization accuracy and reliability of results.

We ran algorithms available on Weka [16]. Our goal was to tackle regression (*quantitative*) problems. These are new problems for opinion learning. So far, machine learning experiments of opinion detection and prediction concentrated on classification (*qualitative*) tasks. Because of the novelty of this application, we wanted to try different types of learning paradigms. We chose KNN, a prototype-based algorithm, an optimization algorithm, SVM, and M5 TREES, a decision-based one. We applied BAGGING (bootstrap aggregating) to assess the influence of training data. BAGGING allows an algorithm to train its classifiers on randomly selected training subsets and then choose the best performing classifier. The more a bagged algorithm improves its performance, the more the choice of training data is important. In our experiments, BAGGING improved performance of M5 TREES, but not KNN nor SVM. An exhaustive parameter search was applied to every algorithm, separately on every problem. The search is necessary because of performance variance, especially high for NEAREST NEIGHBOR and SUPPORT VECTOR MACHINE.

Table 3 reports smallest relative absolute error *RAE* and corresponding root relative squared error *RRSQ* obtained by the algorithms. The best performance, with the smallest error, was obtained on the Congress data set. Positive consumer opinions were learned better than negative and overall opinions. An interesting phenomenon emerges when comparing algorithm performance – in terms of the learned correlation coefficients. The best performing algorithm in terms of accuracy is BAGGED M5 TREES. Since better accuracy implies that the algorithm learns dependencies between opinions and expressed actions better than other algorithms, we conclude that the output decision trees provide a reliable model of the data sets.

For Congressional debates, all output tree models agree that demand, has, have are the most important features, followed by should, would. We only report here the results of the best performing algorithms. Since this implies that the algorithms model dependencies better than other algorithms, we conclude that the strong language verbs have a positive correlation with attitude toward proposed legislations. On the consumer review data set, bagged trees placed can, are, find as the most important features for learning the overall opinions.

Table 4. *Accuracy* (per cent) and corresponding *Recall* (per cent) obtained by SVM. Rows report results for each feature set; B means *binarized*. Columns report results for each problem. For each problem, the largest accuracy is reported in **bold**. Baselines are the majority class accuracy: for the consumer data set – 52.22, for Congress – 59.76.

| Features | Consumer reviews | | | | | | Congress | |
| | positive | | negative | | overall | | debates | |
	Acc	*Recall*	*Acc*	*Recall*	*Acc*	*Recall*	*Acc*	*Recall*
Categories	74.52	74.50	63.64	61.50	66.24	67.30	65.70	67.90
Terminals	76.12	75.80	66.56	67.20	70.06	74.50	69.63	72.00
Terminals-B	76.43	75.70	67.83	73.20	73.60	75.20	70.61	73.40
Collocations	77.75	79.00	68.33	69.50	73.82	78.90	75.18	77.60
Collocations-B	**78.87**	80.10	70.95	71.40	75.21	79.70	**78.14**	81.10

Somehow expectedly, like was among most decisive features for learning positive opinions. Learning negative opinions relied on be, am, would, should more than on other verbs.

To better display abilities of our approach, we performed a more traditional task of opinion classification (Table 4). We chose SUPPORT VECTOR MACHINE for solving classification problems. SVM is well-known for a high accuracy of text classification. Also, its use enabled us to directly compare our results with those of [3], obtained on the Congress debate data set.

Their reported test accuracy for positive/negative classification starts from 66.05, obtained on the data set that we used for the current work. To increase accuracy to 76.16, Thomas et al. linked each data entry with previous speeches of the same speaker. Our Congress results have a better accuracy, although we did not use previous records of speakers or other data reinforcements; the results are reported in the right part of Table 4. The obtained results show that the expressed actions do speak loud. Under certain conditions, they reveal more than the previous history of the same speaker. For consumer reviews, learning positive opinions was easier than learning negative and overall opinions.

7   Related Work

Opinion and sentiment analysis that focuses on whether a text, or a term is subjective, bears positive or negative opinion or expresses the strength of opinion has received a vast amount of attention in recent years. Application of learning algorithms - through classification - has been pioneered by Lee et all [1] and successfully used in works of many others. The authors of this much-cited, pioneering work used machine learning algorithms on reviews written by only four professional critics. This means that the algorithms were trained and tested on overly specific, undiversified data. It is not surprising, perhaps, that to achieve a comparable accuracy on the Congress data, the same team had to enhance the data set by using previous speeches of speakers. Our goal, instead, is to work with a large diverse group of data contributors and seek general enough features that reliably represent the resulting diversity of data.

Consumer review data set in our experiments has been used in summarization and feature extraction studies [17]. Some of the listed publications relied on a list of characteristics of reviewed products [14]. Popescu [18] extracted these characteristics from noun phrases and matched them with known product features. We opted for a domain-independent method that does not involve the use of domain's content words.

For automating recognition and evaluation of the expressed opinion, texts are represented through N-grams or patterns and then classified as opinion/non-opinion, positive/negative, etc. [19]. Syntactic and semantic features that express the intensity of terms are used to classify opinion intensity [2]. The listed works do not consider hierarchy of opinion disclosure. We, however, built the pragmatic-lexical hierarchy of the use of semantic categories. The hierarchy allows machine learning models, which are formulated in the lexical terms, to be interpreted in terms of the text pragmatics.

8   Conclusion

This study has shown that, in opinion mining, the difference between structured well-edited and loosely composed texts can be important. To support our claim, we studied the relations between expressed actions and opinions on samples that exhibit different qualities. We built language patterns using modal, event, activity, process, cognition, perception, state verbs and personal pronouns. We extracted and analyzed the resulting patterns and applied machine learning methods to establish quantitative relations between the use of verb categories and opinions.

Defining and solving *regression* problems is a new type of problem for opinion, subjectivity and sentiment analysis. Previous studies stated their problems either as binary classification or multi-class classification problems. Unlike a regression problem, that predicts *quantitative* output, a classification output is *qualitative*. Our combination of quantitative and qualitative learning allows a more detailed opinion analysis.

Our empirical results were obtained on two data sets: consumer-written product reviews [14] and the US Congress debate records [3]. For consumer reviews, the most frequent and diverse action patterns coincided with the passive involvement from the authors. For Congressional records, the most frequent and diverse immediacy patterns coincided with an active involvement from the speakers. Regression problems were successfully learned by BAGGED M5 TREES. SVM obtained a reliable accuracy in classification problems.

Learning from verbs is then justified and desirable when the context dictates the avoidance of negative adjectives and adverbs, because empirical results showed that negative adjective and adverbs discriminate better between positive and negative opinions than those with a positive affect. In the future, we intend to analyze the use of different types of verb modifiers (always, never). We are also interested in studying the relations between opinions and the pragmatics of communication, e.g. intensity, immediacy.

Acknowledgments. This work has been supported by *Natural Sciences and Engineering Research Council* of Canada. The authors thank Fabrizio Gotti for technical support of experiments.

References

1. Pang, B., Lee, L., Vaithyanathan, S.: Thumbs up? sentiment classification using machine learning techniques. In: Proc Empirical Methods of Natural Language Processing EMNLP 2002, pp. 79–86 (2002)
2. Wilson, T., Wiebe, J., Hwa, R.: Recognizing strong and weak opinion clauses. Computational Intelligence 22(2), 73–99 (2006)
3. Thomas, M., Pang, B., Lee, L.: Get out the vote: Determining support or opposition from congressional floor-debate transcripts. In: Proceedings of the 2006 Conference on Empirical Methods in Natural Language Processing, pp. 327–335 (2006)
4. Kim, S.M., Hovy, E.: Determining the sentiment of opinions. In: Proceedings of the of the 20th international conference on Computational Linguistics (COLING 2004), pp. 1367–1373 (2004)
5. Sokolova, M., Lapalme, G.: Performance measures in classification of human communication. In: Orgun, M.A., Thornton, J. (eds.) AI 2007. LNCS (LNAI), vol. 4830, pp. 159–170. Springer, Heidelberg (2007)
6. Halliday, M., Matthiessen, C.: An Introduction to Functional Grammar, 3rd edn. Arnold (2004)
7. Leech, G.: Meaning and the English Verb. Longman (2004)
8. Leech, G., Svartvik, J.: A Communicative Grammar of English, 3rd edn. Longman (2002)
9. Sokolova, M., Szpakowicz, S.: Language patterns in the learning of strategies from negotiation texts. In: Sattar, A., Kang, B.-h. (eds.) AI 2006. LNCS (LNAI), vol. 4304, pp. 288–299. Springer, Heidelberg (2006)
10. Biber, D., Johansson, S., Leech, G., Conrad, S., Finegan, E.: Longman Grammar of Spoken and Written English. Longman (1999)
11. Roget's interactive thesaurus (2006), http://thesaurus.reference.com/
12. Perkins, M.: Modal Expressions in English. Ablex Publishing Corporation (1983)
13. Sherblom, J., Rheenen, D.V.: Spoken language indices of uncertainty. Human Communication Research 11, 221–230 (1984)
14. Hu, M., Liu, B.: Mining opinion features in customer reviews. In: Proceedings of Nineteeth National Conference on Artificial Intelligence (AAAI 2004), AAAI Press, Menlo Park (2004)
15. Boulle, M.: Optimal bin number for equal frequency discretizations in supervised learning. Intelligent Data Analysis 9(2), 175–188 (2005)
16. Witten, I., Frank, E.: Data Mining. Morgan Kaufmann, San Francisco (2005)
17. Feiguina, O., Lapalme, G.: Query-based summarization of customer reviews. In: Orgun, M.A., Thornton, J. (eds.) AI 2007. LNCS (LNAI), vol. 4830, pp. 452–463. Springer, Heidelberg (2007)
18. Popescu, A., Etzioni, O.: Extracting product features and opinions from reviews. In: Proceedings of HLTC/EMNLP 2005, pp. 339–346 (2005)
19. Kim, S.M., Hovy, E.: Crystal: Analyzing predictive opinions on the web. In: Proceedings of the 2007 Joint Conference on Empirical Methods in Natural Language Processing and Computational Natural Language Learning (EMNLP-CoNLL), pp. 1056–1064 (2007)

A Stochastic Point-Based Algorithm for POMDPs

François Laviolette and Ludovic Tobin

Laval University, Computer Science Department
Quebec, Canada
francois.laviolette@ift.ulaval.ca, ludovic.tobin@ift.ulaval.ca

Abstract. We introduce a new backup operator for point-based POMDP algorithms which performs a look-ahead search at depth greater than one. We apply this operator into a new algorithm, called Stochastic Search Value Iteration (SSVI). This new algorithm relies on stochastic exploration of the environment in order to update the value function. This is in opposition with existing POMDP point-based algorithms. The underlying ideas on which SSVI is based are very similar to temporal difference learning algorithms for MDPs. In particular, SSVI takes advantage of a soft-max action selection function and of the random character of the environment itself. Empirical results on usual benchmark problems show that our algorithm performs a bit better and a bit faster than HSVI2, the state of the art algorithm. This suggests that stochastic algorithms are an alternative for solving large POMDPs.

1 Introduction

Partially Observable Markov Decision Processes (POMDPs) constitute a sound model for sequential decision making problems in uncertain environments. However, solving a POMDP is highly untractable and this is the main drawback of the framework. For this reason, most of the efforts are currently concentrated toward finding good approximation algorithms that will allow POMDPs to be applied on larger problems. Many such algorithms use the concept of point-based value iteration [1,2,3] which consists of increasing the accuracy of a solution by considering only a limited set of belief states.

On the other hand, researchers have recently started to explore online algorithms as an efficient way to act in a partially observable environment [4,5,6]. Online algorithms, such as RTBSS [5], do not compute a policy prior to the execution but simply use a little bit of computation time before each action. They have been proved to be quite competitive with offline algorithms in addition to being able to scale larger problems.

Our idea is to take advantage of the strengths of both a point-based algorithm and an online algorithm. Notably, RTBSS is of interest because it performs a look-ahead search very locally. Therefore, there is no "waste" of time updating the policy at belief states that will never be visited. Also, it uses a look-ahead

S. Bergler (Ed.): Canadian AI 2008, LNAI 5032, pp. 332–343, 2008.
© Springer-Verlag Berlin Heidelberg 2008

search that explores at a farther horizon, thus improving the odds of returning a good action.

In this paper, we first introduce a new backup operator that performs a look-ahead search of depth greater than one. This leads us to the construction of a new stochastic algorithm that uses this operator in addition with a new exploration strategy in order to update its value function. Finally, we present convergence proofs and empirical results that show that our algorithm is sound and competitive.

2 POMDP

Formally, a POMDP is fully described by a tuple $\langle S, A, \Omega, T, O, R, \gamma \rangle$ where:

- S is the set of all the possible states of the environment. A state is a particular description of how the environment is at a given time.
- A is the set of all the possible actions.
- Ω is the set of all possible observations.
- $T(s, a, s')$ is the state transition function. It gives the probability of reaching state s' if action a is performed in state s.
- $O(s', a, o)$ is the observation function. It gives the probability of observing o if the state s' is reached by performing a.
- $R(s, a)$ is the reward function, which associates a reward for performing action a in state s.
- γ is the discount factor and satisfies $0 < \gamma \leq 1$. The discount factor expresses how the agent favors immediate rewards over future rewards.

Since the environment is partially observable, the agent does not know exactly in which state it is. In order to represent this uncertainty, the agent must maintain a belief state. Formally, a belief state b is a probability distribution over the state space; $b(s)$ denotes the probability of being in state s. We denote by $\tau(b, a, o)$ the belief state that results in performing action a in belief state b and receiving observation o, and it is defined so that:

$$\tau(b, a, o)(s') = \sum_{s \in S} T^{a,o}(s, s') b(s) \tag{1}$$

where $T^{a,o}(s, s') = P(s'|s, a, o)$ (i.e. the probability that the agent reaches state s' from state s when performing action a and perceiving observation o).

In a partially observable environment, the objective of an agent is to define a way of behaving (called *policy*) that maximizes a specific cumulative function of the rewards. A key aspect of such problems is that decisions cannot be viewed in isolation; one must typically balance the desirability of high immediate rewards with the threat of low future rewards. More precisely, a *policy* is a function from the set $\mathcal{B}$ of belief states to the set A of actions. Therefore, solving a POMDP requires finding the optimal policy π^* (i.e. the policy that specifies the "best" action to execute in any possible belief state). To achieve this, we need to compute the optimal value function V^* which is known to be the only fixed point of the Bellman Equation:

$$V^*(b) = \max_{a \in A} \left[R(b, a) + \gamma \sum_{o \in \Omega} P(o|b, a) V^*(\tau(b, a, o)) \right]$$

Finally, from the value function V^*, the agent can compute a policy:

$$\pi^*(b) = \operatorname*{argmax}_{a \in A} \left[R(b, a) + \gamma \sum_{o \in \Omega} P(o|b, a) V^*(\tau(b, a, o)) \right]$$

Unfortunately, the belief space $(\mathcal{B})$ is uncountable so computing $V^*(b)$ for each belief state might seem impossible. However, it has been shown that the value function is piecewise-linear and convex [7], and can be represented by a finite set Γ of $|S|$-dimensional hyperplanes of $\mathcal{B} \times \mathbb{R}$ (those hyperplanes are also called α-vectors). This means that the optimal value function V^* can be represented by a finite set Γ^* such that:

$$\max_{\alpha \in \Gamma^*} \alpha \cdot b = V^*(b) \qquad (\forall b \in \mathcal{B})$$

where $\alpha \cdot b$ is the dot product between the vector α and the belief state b considered as a vector.

Moreover, from any set Γ of α-vectors, we can associate a canonical value function on the belief states as follows:

$$\underline{V}^\Gamma(b) \stackrel{\text{def}}{=} \max_{\alpha \in \Gamma} \alpha \cdot b \tag{2}$$

A policy π can be extracted from any set Γ of α-vectors using Equation (3).

$$\pi(b) = \operatorname*{argmax}_{a \in A} \left[R(b, a) + \max_{\alpha \in \Gamma} \gamma \sum_{o \in \Omega} P(o|b, a) \alpha \cdot \tau(b, a, o) \right] \tag{3}$$

The value V^π of the policy π that is associated with a set of α-vectors Γ, is not related to $\underline{V}^\Gamma(b)$, in general. However, as we will see later on, under specific circumstances, $\underline{V}^\Gamma$ is a lower bound of the optimal value V^* (i.e., $\underline{V}^\Gamma(b) \leq V^*(b)$ for any belief state b). Later on, we will use the notation $\underline{V}^\Gamma \leq_\mathcal{B} V^*$ to represent that $\underline{V}^\Gamma$ is a lower bound of V^*.

Finally, note that the optimal solution for a finite horizon is always a finite set of α-vectors, but its size can be exponentially large. For this reason, actual exact algorithms cannot scale to large problems.

3   Existing Point-Based Algorithms

Many POMDP approximation algorithms rely on point-based value iteration, that was first introduced in [1]. They use a *backup* operator based on a Bellman equation which, given a set Γ of α-vectors and a belief state b, returns a single α-vector, $\alpha' = \text{backup}(\Gamma, b)$. The operator is defined in three steps as follows:

$$\Gamma_{b'} \stackrel{\text{def}}{=} \underset{\alpha \in \Gamma}{\text{argmax}} \; \alpha \cdot b' \quad (= \underset{\alpha \in \Gamma}{\text{argmax}} \; \underline{V}^{\{\alpha\}}(b'))$$

$$\alpha'_a(s) \stackrel{\text{def}}{=} R(s,a) + \gamma \sum_{(o,s') \in \Omega \times S} P(o|b,a) T^{a,o}(s,s') \; \Gamma_{\tau(b,a,o)}(s')$$

$$\alpha' \stackrel{\text{def}}{=} \underset{\{\alpha'_a | a \in A\}}{\text{argmax}} \; \alpha'_a \cdot b \tag{4}$$

This backup operator has three important properties[1].

(1) – The α-vector α' is maximal at b (i.e., $\alpha' \cdot b \geq \underline{V}^\Gamma(b)$).
(2) – If $\underline{V}^\Gamma$ is a lower bound of V^* for any belief state, then so is $\underline{V}^{\Gamma \cup \{\alpha'\}}$.
(3) – Because the backup operator is based on a Bellman equation, any algorithm that starts with a set Γ_0 for which $\underline{V}^{\Gamma_0}$ is a lower bound of V^*, and that is designed to eventually backup every reachable belief state an unbounded number of times, will converge to the optimal policy. More precisely, if $b_1, b_2, \ldots$ is the sequence of belief states on which the algorithm performs a backup, and if $\Gamma_{i+1} \stackrel{\text{def}}{=} \Gamma_i \cup \{\text{backup}(\Gamma_i, b)\}$, then $\underline{V}^{\Gamma_i}(b) \stackrel{i \to \infty}{\longrightarrow} V^*(b)$ for each belief state b.

The backup operation approach is very similar to temporal difference learning methods in reinforcement learning. Basically, the backup operation will expand belief state b up to a depth of one. For each child, it will backtrack the best α-vector at b. Then for each action a, it combines them, via a Bellman equation, in order to form one single hyperplane α'_a. Finally, the best among all the constructed α'_a-hyperplanes is added to Γ.

All point-based algorithms rely on the backup operator we just presented. The distinction among them is only on the choice of the belief states to be backuped. Indeed, the selection of the right belief states is a crucial aspect of such algorithms. Selecting a large number of belief states will lead to good results but at the expense of more computation time. In [8], the authors showed that it is more important to update belief states that are easily reachable from the initial belief state because they have more impact on the value of the policy. Intuitively, it is even more crucial to update belief states that are likely to be visited by the optimal policy.

The algorithm PBVI [1] uses a sampling set of belief states to perform backups. Thus, in PBVI, there is a direct link between the number of belief states to use and the quality of the solution.

In the case of HSVI2 [8], the algorithm relies on an upper bound value function (initially Q_{MDP}) in order to select which action to explore. Similarly, it also uses an heuristic function in order to choose an observation. Both heuristic functions allow HSVI2 selecting which belief states to update. When it performs a backup,

---

[1] They can be viewed as special cases of Theorems 1, 2 and 3 of Section 6.

it also updates the upper bound value function so that it slowly decreases. HSVI2 always selects the action with the highest upper bound. By doing so, it ensures convergence because if the action with the highest upper bound is sub-optimal, the algorithm will eventually find it out (this is true only because it updates the upper bound). This algorithm performs exceptionally well in comparison with other point-based algorithms.

4   Modified Backup Operator

The standard backup operator updates the value function based on a look-ahead search of depth one (only one use of the Bellman equation). In this section, we extend this operator in order to search deeper. In addition, our backup operator uses an action selection function (or a pruning function) in order not to explore all the possible sequences of actions.

Intuitively, if we "look-ahead further", we should be able to find a better policy and therefore backup a better hyperplane. This is similar to what has been done in totally observable reinforcement learning: temporal difference algorithms can look a few moves ahead before backing up the value. Of course, there exists an important tradeoff here: looking deeper should require fewer updates, but each update requires more time. In order to reduce the computation time required to perform the look-ahead search, we propose to explore fewer actions. This pruning idea is sound because, if one performs a backup at b, the α'_a-hyperplane that will be added to Γ is the hyperplane associated with the best action to perform at the belief state b. For this reason, if one believes that a certain action a is not likely to be the best action at b, he can then choose not to compute α'_a in the process, and still have a high confidence to nevertheless obtain the same backup.

Given a depth parameter d, a set of α-vectors Γ and a belief state b, we introduce an action selection function $\varphi(\Gamma, b, d)$ that returns only a limited subset of actions A' to explore at belief state b ($A' \subseteq A$). As we will explain later, this function will have to be stochastic and have a non-zero probability of choosing any possible action.

Let us now define our generalized backup operator. Given an action selection function φ, a depth parameter d, a set of α-vectors Γ and a belief state b, the backup operator constructs an α-vector $\alpha' = \text{backup}(\Gamma, b; d, \varphi)$, and is recursively defined as follows:

$$\text{backup}(\Gamma, b; 1, \varphi) \stackrel{\text{def}}{=} \underset{\{\alpha'_a \mid a \in \varphi(\Gamma, b, d)\}}{\text{argmax}} \ \alpha'_a \cdot b$$

$$\text{backup}(\Gamma, b; d, \varphi) \stackrel{\text{def}}{=} \text{backup}(\Gamma', b; d - 1, \varphi)$$

where α'_a is as defined in the three steps definition of the original backup operator (Equation (4)), and where

$$\Gamma' = \left\{ \text{backup}(\Gamma, \tau(b, a, o); d-1, \varphi) \right\}_{\substack{o \in \Omega \\ a \in \varphi(\Gamma, \tau(b, a, o), d-1)}}$$

When we perform a traditional backup of depth 1 at b (Equation (4)), we use Γ in order to evaluate each child b' of b. However, if we perform a backup of depth d

(with $d > 1$) at b, then it does not make sense to evaluate the children b' with Γ, because if so, a backup of depth d will output exactly the same hyperplane as a backup at depth 1. In our actual definition, a backup of depth d on a set of α-vectors Γ corresponds to a backup of depth d on a set of α-vectors $\Gamma' \supseteq \Gamma$. Moreover, it follows from Property (2) of the original backup operator that each α-vector of $\Gamma' \backslash \Gamma$ is maximal for at least one of the b's children, grand-children, grand-grand-children,... This in turn implies that, when we perform a backup at b, we only need to consider the α'_a-hyperplanes of its first level children instead of all the α-vectors in Γ'. For this reason, performing a backup of depth d does not require much more time than a simple look-ahead search of depth d. The following algorithm illustrates how we implemented the backup operator:

Procedure backupAlgo(b, d)
Static variables :Γ, φ

if (d $= 0$) **then**
    return $\max_{\alpha \in \Gamma}(\alpha \cdot b)$
end if
$max \leftarrow -\infty$
for all $a \in \varphi(\Gamma, b, d)$ **do**
    for all $o \in \Omega$ **do**
        $b' \leftarrow \tau(b, a, o)$
        $\alpha_{a,o} \leftarrow$ backupAlgo($b', d-1$)
    end for
    for all $s \in S$ **do**
        $\alpha_a(s) \leftarrow R(s, a) + \gamma \sum_{s'} \sum_o P(o|b, a) \cdot T^{a,o}(s, s')\alpha_{a,o}(s')$
    end for
    if $\alpha_a(b) > max$ **then**
        $max \leftarrow \alpha_a(b)$
        $\alpha \leftarrow \alpha_a$
    end if
end for
$\Gamma \leftarrow \Gamma \cup \{\alpha\}$
return α

We notice that this backup operator may add more than a single hyperplane to Γ (i.e., not only $\alpha' = $ backup$(\Gamma, b; d, \varphi)$). The reason is that we also backup every belief state that are visited in the look-ahead search. Actually, a single execution of this backup may add up to $((|A||\Omega|)^t - 1)/(|A||\Omega| - 1)$ new hyperplanes to Γ. Note also that, in order to speed up the backup operation, we implemented an idea similar to the masked α-vectors introduced in [8].

5   Stochastic Point-Based Algorithm

One potential weakness of HSVI is that the upper bound (Q_{MDP}), on which the choice of the belief states to be backup is based, is usually not as good as the lower bound value function. While this heuristic action selection is a good idea because it ensures convergence, it does not necessarily explore the best actions. Therefore, it potentially spends a lot of time updating belief states that might never be visited again when the agent finally "realizes" that visiting them does not lead to a maximum amount of rewards. In addition, the upper bound value function decreases very slowly. Hence, it may require many visits through the same belief state b before realizing that action a is sub-optimal at b.

Intuitively, we believe that selecting greedily the best action based on the lower bound should lead to better results since the agent will visit the most promising belief states more quickly. Unfortunately, with this approach, we do not have any convergence guarantees to the optimal policy, because the algorithm might get trapped in a local optimum. It is nevertheless possible to overcome this problem by replacing a small percentage ϵ of all the greedy choices of the algorithm by random choices. So our approach is based on the intuition that updating the belief states that are reached when acting ϵ-greedily according to $\underline{V}^\Gamma$ may require fewer backup operations in order to reach the optimal policy.

We now present our stochastic algorithm SSVI that uses the backup operator introduced in the previous section. While running, SSVI simulates episodes in the environment[2]. Each time a belief state b is visited, our algorithm performs a backup of depth d at b. Then, the action selection function selects which action the agent should execute in the environment. We repeat this process until a final belief state is reached, and then we restart another simulation until we run out of time[3].

As for all point-based algorithms, SSVI is initialized with a value function $\underline{V}^\Gamma$ that has the property of being a lower bound of the value function V^* (i.e., $\underline{V}^\Gamma \leq_B V^*$).

Procedure SSVI(Γ, d, φ, t)
$t_0 \leftarrow$ CURRENTTIME()
while CURRENTTIME() $- t_0 < t$ **do**
    $b \leftarrow b_0$
    while $notterminal(b)$ **do**
        BACKUP(b, d)
        $a \leftarrow$ EXPLORE(Γ, b, d)
        $z \leftarrow$ EXECUTE(b, a)
        $b \leftarrow \tau(b, a, z)$
    end while
end while
return Γ

---

[2] Notice that the knowledge of the model is needed here.
[3] We could adapt the algorithm to other stop criteria. For example, when the value function is not improved for a certain number of simulations.

5.1   The Function   EXPLORE(Γ, b, d)

In reinforcement learning problems, one important aspect in order to guarantee convergence is the tradeoff between exploration and exploitation. It is important to act randomly enough to make sure that all the states will be visited sufficiently enough. On the other hand, one should not behave too randomly because, to ensure efficiency, it is important to visit the best states as quickly as possible. To ensure convergence, the exploration should guarantee Infinite Exploration. In other words, if the algorithm was to be executed infinitely many times, then for each reachable belief state, every action should be considered for backup infinitely often[4]. Purely random functions allow just that, but they converge very slowly. GLIE (Greedy in the Limit with Infinite Exploration) exploration functions also ensure convergence. Such functions are acting randomly at the beginning and, as the solution improves, execute the greedy action more often.

No particular exploration function is better than the others. For our algorithm, we used a softmax function, which is a stochastic function that returns an action with a certain probability, depending on how good the action is in relation with the greedy action. Instead of returning action a with probability $1/|A|$, it gives more weight to the most promising actions. Equations (5) shows how we compute the probability of selecting action a in belief state b. The equation includes a parameter δ which is called the temperature. This parameter must be tuned manually depending on the problem. When the temperature is high, it favors a uniform exploration of the environment. On the opposite, when the temperature tends to zero, the greedy action will be returned with probability 1. We define $P(a|b)$ as the probability of executing action a in belief state b:

$$P(a|b) = \frac{e^{\frac{\underline{V}^{\Gamma}(b,a)}{\delta}}}{\sum_{a' \in A} e^{\underline{V}^{\Gamma}(b,a')\delta}} \tag{5}$$

where $\underline{V}^{\Gamma}(b, a)$ is the one step look-ahead value of performing action a in belief state b. So basically, the EXPLORE(Γ, b, d) function of SSVI will return an action to perform at b according to the distribution probability defined in (5).

5.2   Action Selection

As we mentioned earlier, action selection seems like a logical choice in order to improve the backup operation. However, one must be very careful on how to select actions. It is crucial that every action has a non-zero probability of being selected. For this reason, we once again incorporate some randomness into our function. The idea is to explore the most promising actions most of the time,

---

[4] Note that in a POMDP, the number of belief states is uncountable. So no algorithm, even if executed infinitely many times, can explore each belief state infinitely often. Fortunately, there is only countably many belief states that are reachable from a *fixed* initial belief state (a finite number for each possible horizon). Since there is no need to have a policy defined on unreachable belief states, to ensure convergence, we only have to visit every reachable belief state "infinitely often".

while also exploring some actions at random. There is an infinite number of ways to perform action selection and this matter alone could justify extended researches. For now, we simply identify some concepts that can be useful when designing such a function. First of all, if the underlying value function is very bad (this generally occurs at the beginning of the algorithm's execution), pruning actions based on it should yield poor results. For this reason, the better the value function is, the more inclined to pruning we should be[5]. In addition, belief states that are easily reachable have a greater impact on the solution; pruning these beliefs is potentially more dangerous than pruning at a very deep level. Furthermore, some a-priori knowledge can be incorporated in the function.

The function φ that we use in this version of SSVI is pretty simple. For each belief state b, we return a subset of three actions: the two best actions according to $\underline{V}^\Gamma(b)$, and one action chosen based on a soft-max function. This simple function explores the most promising action, while making sure that every action has a non-zero probability of being explored.

6   Theoretical Guarantees

We now show that the three properties of the original backup operator that we stated in Section 3 are still valid for our generalized backup operator. We first introduce the following definition:

Definition 1. Let Γ^{i+1} be the value of the static variable Γ at the end of the procedure backupAlgo(b, d) assuming that the value at the beginning of the procedure is Γ^i.

Theorem 1. $\underline{V}^{\Gamma^i} \leq_\mathcal{B} \underline{V}^{\Gamma^{i+1}}$.

Proof. A direct consequence of $\Gamma^{i+1} \supseteq \Gamma^i$.

The following theorem shows that the current value function will always remain a lower bound.

Theorem 2. *If Γ^i is a set of α-vectors such that $\underline{V}^{\Gamma^i} \leq_\mathcal{B} V^*$, then $\underline{V}^{\Gamma^i} \leq_\mathcal{B} \underline{V}^{\Gamma^{i+1}} \leq_\mathcal{B} V^*$*

Proof. $\underline{V}^{\Gamma^i} \leq_\mathcal{B} \underline{V}^{\Gamma^{i+1}}$ is a direct consequence of $\Gamma^{i+1} \supseteq \Gamma^i$. For $\underline{V}^{\Gamma^{i+1}} \leq_\mathcal{B} V^*$, just note that, in the procedure *backupAlgo*, Γ^{i+1} is obtained from Γ^i by adding successively elements of the form α'_a that are calculated according to Equation (4) with sets Γ's such that $\Gamma^i \subseteq \Gamma \subset \Gamma^{i+1}$. Hence, one can recursively deduce the preceding theorem from the following lemma.

Lemma 1. *Let Γ be a set of α-vectors such that $\underline{V}^\Gamma \leq_\mathcal{B} V^*$. Then for any action a, we have*

$$\underline{V}^{\Gamma \cup \{\alpha'_a\}} \leq_\mathcal{B} V^*.$$

---

[5] There is no simple way to measure how good is a solution. We could use the difference between an upper bound Q_{MDP} and $V(b)$; the smaller the difference is, the more drastic the pruning should be.

Proof. By way of contradiction, choose $b \in \mathcal{B}$, α'_a and $b'' \in \mathcal{B}$ such that $\underline{V}^{\Gamma \cup \{\alpha'_a\}}(b'') >_{\mathcal{B}} V^*(b'')$. It follows from the definition of $\underline{V}^{\Gamma \cup \{\alpha'_a\}}$ that

$$\alpha'_a \cdot b'' > V^*(b''). \tag{6}$$

On the other hand,

$$
\begin{aligned}
\alpha'_a \cdot b'' &= \textstyle\sum_{s \in S} \alpha'_a(s) \cdot b''(s) \\
&= \textstyle\sum_{s \in S} b''(s) \cdot \left[R(s,a) + \gamma \sum_{o \in \Omega} \sum_{s' \in S} P(o|b,a) T^{a,o}(s,s') \Gamma_{\tau(b,a,o)}(s') \right] \\
&= \textstyle\sum_{s \in S} (b''(s) R(s,a) + \gamma \sum_{s \in S} \sum_{o \in \Omega} P(o|b,a) T^{a,o}(s,s') \Gamma_{\tau(b,a,o)}(s') b''(s)) \\
&= R(b'',a) + \gamma \sum_{o \in \Omega} P(o|b,a) \cdot \sum_{s' \in S} \Gamma_{\tau(b,a,o)}(s') \sum_{s \in S} T^{a,o}(s,s') b''(s) \\
&= R(b'',a) + \gamma \sum_{o \in \Omega} P(o|b,a) \cdot \sum_{s' \in S} \Gamma_{\tau(b,a,o)}(s') \tau(b'',a,o)(s') \\
&= R(b'',a) + \gamma \sum_{o \in \Omega} P(o|b,a) \Gamma_{\tau(b,a,o)} \cdot \tau(b'',a,o) \\
&= R(b'',a) + \gamma \sum_{o \in \Omega} P(o|b,a) \underline{V}^{\{\Gamma_{\tau(b,a,o)}\}}(\tau(b'',a,o)) \\
&\leq R(b'',a) + \gamma \sum_{o \in \Omega} P(o|b,a) \underline{V}^{\Gamma}(\tau(b'',a,o)) \\
&\leq R(b'',a) + \gamma \sum_{o \in \Omega} P(o|b,a) V^*(\tau(b,a,o)) \\
&\leq V^*(b'')
\end{aligned}
$$

The third to last line follows from the fact that, $\{\Gamma_{\tau(b,a,o)}\} \subseteq \Gamma$. The second to last line follows from the hypothesis. We therefore reach a contradiction.

As explained in Subsection 5.1, our algorithm is designed to eventually visit each reachable belief state infinitely often. Since a generalized backup at a belief state b improve the policy at least as much as the original backup does, the following theorem follows from Property (3).

Theorem 3. *For a finite horizon POMDP and given sufficient time, our algorithm will converge. More precisely, let $b_1, b_2, \ldots$ be the sequence of belief states on which the algorithm performs a backup, and let $\Gamma^0, \Gamma^1, \ldots$ be the sequence given by Definition 1. If $\underline{V}^{\Gamma^0} \leq_{\mathcal{B}} V^*$ then $\underline{V}^{\Gamma^i}(b) \overset{i \to \infty}{\longrightarrow} V^*(b)$ for each belief b.*

7   Empirical Results

In this section, we present the results we obtained on two well-known benchmark problems in the POMDP litterature: Tag [1] and RockSample [2]. Since SSVI is a non-deterministic algorithm, the reported results for SSVI are averages over 10 runs. While we only present the average performance of our algorithm, it is important to mention that we observed very little variability in our results. Indeed, our algorithm almost always converge to the same policy and in similar time from one try to another.

Figure 1 shows a comparison on four different problems. For each algorithm, we specify the source of the results we used. If nothing is specified, then the results are based on our own implementation of the algorithm.

Problem: ($|S|,|A|,|\Omega|$)	Tag (870, 5, 29)		R.S.[4,4] (257, 9, 2)		R.S.[5,5] (801, 10, 2)		R.S.[7,8] (12545,13,2)	
	R	sec	R	sec	R	sec	R	sec
QMDP	-16.75	0.9	8.6	0.2	13.9	0.625	n/a	n/a
PBVI [1]	-9.18	180880	17.9	17200	19.1	36000	n/a	n/a
HSVI1 [2]	-6.37	10113	18	577	19	10208	15.1	10266
HSVI2 [2]	-6.36	24	18	**0.75**	n/a	n/a	**20.6**	1003
SSVI	**-6.17**	**15.8**	18	1.6	**19.23**	29	20.1	**796**

Fig. 1. Empirical Results on Tag and RockSample problems

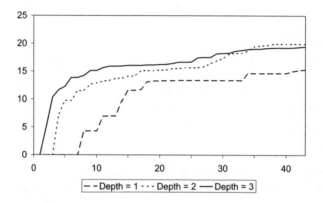

Fig. 2. Evolution of the value function on RockSample[7,8] for different search depths

We notice that we are very competitive on all benchmark problems. On the Tag problem we even obtain a better reward than HSVI2 almost twice as fast. Also, the performance of our algorithm on a large problem (RockSample[7,8]) is also very encouraging.

Finally, Figure 2 shows an example of how the lower bound value function progresses, in function of the depth used for the backup operator, as we run simulations on a large problem. Two things can be noticed: (1) The value function improves very quickly in the first few simulations and stabilizes after that and (2) The deeper we search, the fewer simulations it requires to achieve a good value function. Since the value function improves quickly, it seems that applying our algorithm on a large problem with a limited amount of time should still yield good results because the biggest improvements occur rapidly.

8   Conclusion

In this paper, we first proposed a new point-based backup operator that relies on a look-ahead search at a depth greater than one. This operator can be used in any point-based algorithm. Secondly, we presented a new stochastic algorithm (SSVI) that uses this backup operator in combination with an exploration function in order to compute a policy. Given enough time, our algorithm will converge to the optimal value function. In addition, empirical results on benchmark problems show that this approach find better solutions in less computation time than state of the art algorithms.

These initial results are very promising and we strongly believe that further researches will greatly improve the performance of our algorithm. Notably, we plan to explore the impact on the performance of the algorithm of other action selection and exploration functions than the ones proposed here. Another idea that we will explore is to allow variable depth search. Indeed, the deeper we search, the fewer backups is required. Therefore, if one action appears more promising than the others, we may want to explore it deeper than the others.

Acknowledgments. Work supported by NSERC Discovery grants 262067 and FQRNT master scholarship 108357. Ludovic Tobin was also supported by DRDC-Valcartier.

References

1. Pineau, J., Gordon, G., Thrun, S.: Point-based value iteration: An anytime algorithm for pomdps. In: Proceedings of the International Joint Conference on Artificial Intelligence (IJCAI 2003), Acapulco, Mexico, pp. 1025–1032 (2003)
2. Smith, T., Simmons, R.: Heuristic search value iteration for pomdps. In: Proceedings of the 20th Conference on Uncertainty in Artificial Intelligence (UAI 2004), Banff, Canada (2004)
3. Vlassis, N., Spaan, M.T.J.: A fast point-based algorithm for POMDPs. In: Benelearn 2004: Proceedings of the Annual Machine Learning Conference of Belgium and the Netherlands, Brussels, Belgium, January 2004, pp. 170–176 (2003); (Also presented at the NIPS-16 workshop 'Planning for the Real-World', Whistler, Canada, December 2003)
4. Paquet, S., Tobin, L., Chaib-draa, B.: An Online POMDP Algorithm for Complex Multiagent Environments. In: Proceedings of The fourth International Joint Conference on Autonomous Agents and Multi Agent Systems (AAMAS 2005), Utrecht, The Netherlands (2005)
5. Paquet, S., Chaib-draa, B., Ross, S.: Hybrid POMDP Algorithms. In: Proceedings of The Workshop on Multi-Agent Sequential Decision Making in Uncertain Domains (MSMD 2006), Hakodate, Hokkaido, Japan (2006)
6. Ross, S., Chaib-draa, B.: AEMS: An Anytime Online Search Algorithm for Approximate Policy Refinement in Large POMDPs. In: Proceedings of The 20th Joint Conference in Artificial Intelligence (IJCAI 2007), Hyderabad, India (2007)
7. Sondik, E.J.: The Optimal Control of Partially Observable Markov Processes. PhD thesis, Stanford University (1971)
8. Smith, T., Simmons, R.: Point-based POMDP Algorithms: Improved Analysis and Implementation. In: Proceedings of the 21th Conference on Uncertainty in Artificial Intelligence (UAI 2005), Edinburgh, Scotland (2005)

Semi-supervised Self-training for Sentence Subjectivity Classification

Bin Wang[1], Bruce Spencer[2], Charles X. Ling[3], and Harry Zhang[1]

[1] Faculty of Computer Science, University of New Brunswick
P.O. Box 4400, Fredericton, NB, Canada E3B 5A3
[2] National Research Council of Canada,
Fredericton, NB, Canada E3B 9W4
[3] Department of Computer Science, The University of Western Ontario
London, Ontario, Canada N6A 5B7
{bin.wang,hzhang}@unb.ca

Abstract. Recent natural language processing (NLP) research shows that identifying and extracting subjective information from texts can benefit many NLP applications. In this paper, we address a semi-supervised learning approach, self-training, for sentence subjectivity classification. In self-training, the confidence degree that depends on the ranking of class membership probabilities is commonly used as the selection metric that ranks and selects the unlabeled instances for next training of underlying classifier. Naive Bayes (NB) is often used as the underlying classifier because its class membership probability estimates have good ranking performance. The first contribution of this paper is to study the performance of self-training using decision tree models, such as C4.5, C4.4, and naive Bayes tree (NBTree), as the underlying classifiers. The second contribution is that we propose an adapted Value Difference Metric (VDM) as the selection metric in self-training, which does not depend on class membership probabilities. Based on the Multi-Perspective Question Answering (MPQA) corpus, a set of experiments have been designed to compare the performance of self-training with different underlying classifiers using different selection metrics under various conditions. The experimental results show that the performance of self-training is improved by using VDM instead of the confidence degree, and self-training with NBTree and VDM outperforms self-training with other combinations of underlying classifiers and selection metrics. The results also show that the self-training approach can achieve comparable performance to the supervised learning models.

1 Introduction

Many natural language processing (NLP) applications can benefit from identifying and extracting subjective information that expresses opinions and emotions from texts. For example, information extraction (IE) systems aim to extract facts related to a particular domain from natural language texts. Suppose we are looking for information about bombings and physical assaults in some news articles. From the sentence: *"The parliament exploded into fury against the government*

S. Bergler (Ed.): Canadian AI 2008, LNAI 5032, pp. 344–355, 2008.
© Springer-Verlag Berlin Heidelberg 2008

when word leak out...", the IE system may report that a bombing took place and "The parliament" was the target of the bombing. But it is not correct because the verb "exploded" is used metaphorically. If we first do the subjectivity analysis, IE systems are not easily misled by the language that contains metaphors or hyperboles. For instance, the above sentence that describes negative emotions will be considered as a subjective sentence which frequently contains metaphors and hyperboles. The observations in [11] show that many incorrect extractions can be prevented by identifying subjective information and filtering extractions from them.

Machine learning models have attracted much attention when applied to subjectivity analysis. However, the subjective language can be expressed by various words and phrases, and many subjective terms occur infrequently. Subjectivity learning systems using supervised machine learning models must be trained on extremely large corpora that contain a broad and comprehensive subjective vocabulary. It is very time-consuming and expensive to collect and manually annotate a great amount of texts in corpora. Semi-supervised learning is a useful approach for reducing the effort devoted to obtaining the expensive training data. It initially builds a model with a small number of fully labeled instances and utilizes a large number of unlabeled instances to improve the model. Previous contributions to subjectivity analysis mainly focus on supervised machine learning models at the document-level. It is worthwhile to penetrate subjectivity study at the sentence-level using semi-supervised learning.

In this paper, we use self-training, a semi-supervised learning approach, to classify sentences as subjective or objective. Initially, an underlying classifier is trained using a small number of labeled sentences with all the features. Then the classifier classifies unlabeled sentences, and a selection metric is used to rank these classified sentences and to select some sentences that have high rankings to update the labeled training set. The procedure iterates until all the unlabeled sentences have been included into the training set or the maximum number of iterations is reached. The selection metric is crucial to the performance of self-training. The confidence degree is a popular selection metric, which depends on class membership probability estimates. Traditionally, naive Bayes (NB) is often used as the underlying classifier because the class membership probabilities produced from NB have the good ranking performance. In this paper, we study the performance of self-training using decision tree models, such as C4.5, C4.4, and naive Bayes tree (NBTree), as underlying classifiers. However, the class membership probabilities produced by decision tree classifiers do not have good ranking performance [4]. Therefore, we propose an adapted Value Difference Metric (VDM) [21] as the selection metric that does not depend on class membership probabilities. Based on Multi-Perspective Question Answering (MPQA) [19] corpus, a set of experiments have been designed to evaluate the performance of self-training with different underlying classifiers using different selection metrics under various conditions. The experimental results show that the performance of self-training is improved by using VDM as the selection metric instead of the confidence degree, and self-training with NBTree and VDM outperforms self-training with other combinations of underlying classifiers and selection metrics. The results also show that self-training can achieve comparable performance to the supervised learning models for sentence subjectivity classification. Although the study of self-training in this paper concentrates on sentence subjectivity classification, the approach can also be used for other applications of machine learning.

The rest of the paper is organized as follows. In Section 2, we present the related works on subjectivity study and semi-supervised learning methods. In Section 3, we introduce the self-training algorithm, underlying classifiers, and selection metrics. In Section 4, the experiments and results of sentence subjectivity classification are presented and analyzed. We summarize and propose the future research in Section 5.

2   Related Works on Subjectivity Analysis

Much research has appeared recently in the areas of opinion extraction, sentiment analysis, polarity classification, and subjectivity recognition. The work of subjectivity recognition mainly focuses on document-level classification. Turney et al. [15] propose methods for classifying reviews as positive or negative. Some research in genre classification has included recognition of subjective genres, for example, editorials and objective genres of business or news [18]. Subjectivity classification at sentence-level is more useful than at document-level. Most documents consist of a mixture of subjective and objective sentences. For example, newspaper articles are generally considered as relatively objective documents, but 44% of sentences in a news collection are found to be subjective [18]. Moreover, subjectivity classification at the sentence-level assists when identifying and extracting more complex subjectivity information, for example, the opinion expression, holder extraction, and opinion relationship.

Most previous methods of sentence-level subjectivity classification are developed by supervised learning approaches [12] [1]. One of the main obstacles for supervised learning methods is the lack of fully labeled training data. It is much more difficult to obtain collections of individual sentences that can be easily identified as subjective or objective. Previous work on sentence-level subjectivity classification [16] uses training corpora that had been manually annotated for subjectivity. Manually annotations are expensive and time-consuming so that only a relatively small amount of annotated sentences are available. This situation gives researchers motivation to explore the semi-supervised learning way to solve the task.

Ellen Riloff et al. have developed a boostrapping method to learn patterns for extracting subjective sentences [10]. They build two separated high-precision subjective and objective rule-based classifiers that utilize subjectivity clues to assign subjective or objective labels to sentences. The labeled sentences from two classifiers are represented by extraction patterns. The extraction patterns are learned by a fully automatic process similar to AutoSlog [8]. The subjective patterns generated by the pattern learner further label more unannoatated texts.

In a recent paper, Wiebe et al. extend the above work by replacing two rule-based classifiers with one NB classifier [17]. The procedure is similar to our method. But their work was restricted by using the confidence degree and applying NB model as the underlying classifier. Because the confidence degree is based on the differences among class membership probability estimates, other classifiers whose produced class membership probabilities have poor ranking performance are not suitable for this setting.

3 Self-training with Various Underlying Classifiers and Selection Metrics

3.1 General Algorithm of Self-training

Self-training, as a single-view semi-supervised learning method, has been widely used in NLP research [7] [13]. In self-training, an underlying classifier is first trained with a small number of labeled data which is also called the initial training set. The underlying classifier is used to classify the unlabeled data. The most confident unlabeled instances with their predicted labels are added to the training set. The underlying classifier is then re-trained and the procedure repeats. The following is the general procedure of self-training algorithm.

Algorithm Self-training

Input: L is labeled instance set, U is unlabeled instance set, C is underlying classifier, t is the number of times of iteration, θ is the number of selected unlabeled instances for next iteration, M is the selection metric, $S(U_t, \theta, C, M)$ is the selection function, and $maxIteration$ is the maximum number of iterations

Initial: $t = 0$, $L_t = L$, $U_t = U$, where L_t and U_t are the labeled and unlabeled instance set at the tth iteration

Repeat:
 train C on L_t;
 $S_t = S(U_t, \theta, C, M)$, where S_t is the selected unlabeled instance set;
 $U_{t+1} = U_t - S_t$; $L_{t+1} = L_t + S_t$;
 $t = t + 1$;

Until: (U_t is empty) $\vee$ ($maxIterations$ reached)

Note that the selection function is used to rank the unlabeled instances and select a certain number of unlabeled instances to update the training instance set for the next iteration. The function is not only influenced by the underlying classifier that should have good ranking performance, but also affected by the selection metric.

3.2 NB vs. Decision Tree as Underlying Classifiers

NB and decision tree classifiers have been commonly used in many machine learning applications. NB classifier is very fast for induction, and robust to irrelevant attributes. However, the strong conditional independence assumption often influences the performance of NB classifier. Decision tree classifiers are comprehensible and fast. The trees grow by choosing a split attribute recursively using some criterion from the root to leaves. In decision tree algorithms, C4.5 [5] executes a pruning step to reduce the tree size after a full tree is built. C4.4 [4] turns off the pruning and uses Laplace correction when producing the class membership probabilities. But as the underlying classifiers of self-training, decision tree classifiers face two obstacles to producing good ranking of instances: one is that the sample size on a leaf is small, and the other is that the instances falling into the same leaf are assigned to the same class membership probability.

Kohavi proposed the hybrid approach, NBTree [3]. NBTree is similar to the classical decision tree algorithms except that a NB classifier is deployed on the leaf nodes. NBTree combines the advantages of both NB and decision tree classifiers. Moreover, it deals with the above obstacles of decision tree classifiers. In the NBTree algorithm, a threshold is chosen that prevents the sample size on a leaf from being too small. A NB classifier is deployed on a leaf, which assigns the different class membership probabilities. Among the decision tree algorithms, NBTree is suitable to be used as the underlying classifier in self-training.

3.3   Confidence Degree vs. VDM as Selection Metrics

The selection metric used to rank and select classified unlabeled instances for the next iteration is crucial to the performance of self-training. Traditionally, the confidence degree is often used as the selection metric in self-training. The confidence degree ranks a classified unlabeled instance by the differences among its class membership probability estimates. Most previous works on self-training choose NB as the underlying classifier because the class membership probabilities produced from NB classifier have good ranking performance [2]. However, it has constrained the capability of self-training to apply other machine learning models whose class membership probabilities do not have good ranking performance.

In order to overcome the constraint, we propose adapting Value Difference Metric (VDM) [21] as the selection metric in self-training. The original idea of VDM is to evaluate the distance between instances from the differences among feature conditional probability estimates. Given two instances x and y, the VDM distance between them is defined as

$$VDM(x,y) = \sum_{i=1}^{C} \sum_{j=1}^{N} |P(c_i|a_j(x)) - P(c_i|a_j(y))|, \tag{1}$$

where C is the number of class labels, N is the number of features in instances, and $P(c_i|a_j(x))$ is the feature conditional probability of class i given the feature a_j's value in instance x.

Since self-training is an iterative procedure, it is very time-consuming to compute the VDM distance between a classified unlabeled instance and each labeled instance in the training set. We adapt VDM to compute the average VDM distance between an unlabeled instance and the training set. Given a feature value of an instance, the feature's conditional probability is compared with the probabilities of the corresponding feature for all possible values in the training set. The adapted distance function of VDM for a classified unlabeled instance x is defined as

$$VDM(x) = \sum_{i=1}^{C} \sum_{j=1}^{N} \sum_{k=1}^{M} |P(c_i|a_j(x)) - w_j^k P(c_i|a_j^k)|. \qquad (2)$$

where M is the number of possible values of feature a_j in the training set, $P(c_i|a_j^k)$ is the feature conditional probability of class i given the kth value of feature a_j, and w_j^k is the proportion of the kth value in all the possible values of feature a_j within the training set. We rank an unlabeled instance higher if it has a smaller VDM distance.

Using VDM as the selection metric relaxes the constraint of the underlying classifier to depend on class membership probabilities, and provides the opportunity to apply decision tree classifiers in self-training. For example, C4.5 algorithm assigns the same class membership probabilities for the instances that fall into the same leaf node, which makes it difficult to rank and select such instances using the confidence degree. VDM is based on feature conditional probabilities that are different for instances even in the same leaf node. NBTree deploys NB models in leaf nodes and produces the different class membership probabilities. However, using VDM makes NBTree not restrict to the leaf nodes any more because the feature conditional probabilities are estimated in the whole training set.

4   Sentence Subjectivity Classification

4.1   Data

The benchmark data set for sentence subjectivity classification is hard to achieve because the sentences should be manually annotated and the annotation process is time-consuming and expensive. Recent research on subjectivity analysis for the English language uses the Multi-Perspective Question Answering (MPQA) corpus [1] as the benchmark [14] [17] [11]. The MPQA corpus consists of 535 news articles. These articles that are collected from a variety of countries and publications have been manually annotated. The sentences used in the following experiments also come from the MPQA corpus, where there are 11,112 sentences.

Private state is a concept that generally covers the components of subjectivity, such as opinions, beliefs, thoughts, feelings, emotions, goals, evaluations, and judgments [6]. Analysis of sentence subjectivity recognizes and characterizes expressions of private states in a sentence. Wiebe et al. put forward an annotation scheme for evaluating private state expressions [19]. Two kinds of private state frames have been proposed: one is the expressive subjective element frame, and the other one is the direct subjective frame. Both frames consist of several attributes. For example, the attribute *Intensity* indicates the intensity of

---

[1] http://www.cs.pitt.edu/mpqa/

the private state expressed in sentences, and the attribute *Insubstantial* denotes whether the private state is not real or not significant.

The gold-standard classes that are used to label the sentences as subjective or objective in this paper are the same as in other subjectivity research [17] [10] [12]. The gold-standard classes are defined as follows: a sentence is considered as subjective if (1) the sentence contains a direct subjective frame with the value of attribute *Intensity* NOT low or neutral, and NOT with an attribute *Insubstantial*; or (2) the sentence contains an expressive subjectivity frame with the value of attribute *Intensity* NOT low. Otherwise, the sentence is an objective sentence.

4.2   Structure of Sentence Subjectivity Classification

In the procedure of self-training for sentence subjectivity classification, the entire set of sentences are first put into the part of pre-processing, where OpenNLP [2] is used to tokenize sentences into a set of words, and assign part-of-speech (POS) tags to each word. In this part, the Abney stemmer of SCOL [3] is also used to stem words.

After pre-processing, sentences go through the part called feature maker where the features of sentences are built in terms of subjectivity clues and subjectivity patterns. The subjectivity clues are those which have been published with OpinionFinder [20]. They are divided into strongly subjective clues and weakly subjective clues. A strongly subjective clue is one that is always used with a subjective meaning, whereas a weakly subjective clue is one that commonly has both subjective and objective meanings. The subjectivity clues are matched with sentences according to the stemmed words and their POS tags. The subjectivity patterns consist of subjective patterns and objective patterns that are extracted by the Sundance information extraction system [9]. Using the extraction patterns defined in [10], Sundance searches and extracts the subjective patterns and objective patterns from sentences.

Next, we build the instances of sentences with features made from feature maker. Each instance representing a sentence includes several features: the strong subjective clues, the weak subjective clues, the subjective patterns, and the objective patterns. The following POS tags are also added into the feature set: pronouns, modal verbs (excluding "will"), adjectives, cardinal numbers, and adverbs (excluding "not"). In addition, the above features in the previous and next sentences are taken into account in the current sentence's feature set in order to incorporate the contextual information. All the features have three possible values (0, 1, ≥ 2) which are based on the presence of features in the corresponding sentence. Finally, the gold-standard classes are assigned to corresponding sentence instances as class labels (subjective or objective).

In the part of sentence set separation, all the sentence instances are separated into the train set and test set. The test set is held for evaluation. In the train

---

[2] http://opennlp.sourceforge.net/
[3] http://www.ivnartus.net/spa/

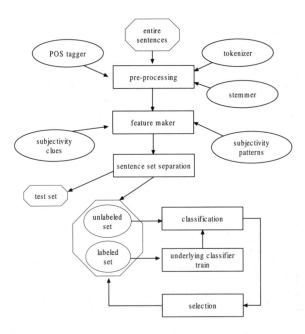

Fig. 1. Self-training process for sentence subjectivity classification

set, we hide the labels of most sentence instances to make the unlabeled instance set, and keep the remaining portion as the labeled instance set which is initially used to train the underlying classifier.

The underlying classifier is trained by the labeled instance set, and classifies sentences in the unlabeled instance set. Then, the unlabeled instances with predicted labels are ranked and a user-defined number of instances with top rankings are selected. The underlying classifier is trained again by the selected instances together with the original labeled instances. This iterative procedure is repeated until it runs out of all the unlabeled sentence instances or the maximum number of iterations is reached. The overall process is depicted in Figure 1.

4.3 Experiments

The experiments conducted on WEKA [22] machine learning environment compare the performance of self-training using different underlying classifiers and different selection metrics under various conditions. We implement the self-training structure and selection metric methods in WEKA, and utilize the implementations of NB, C4.5, C4.4 and NBTree in WEKA as the underlying classifiers. The experiments are evaluated by three kinds of measures: accuracy, the area under the ROC curve (AUC), and F-measure (F-M) which combines precision and recall. All the results of the evaluation measures are averages of 100 runs (10 runs of ten-fold cross validation) for the focused algorithm. Runs with the various algorithms are carried out on the same train sets and evaluated on the same test sets.

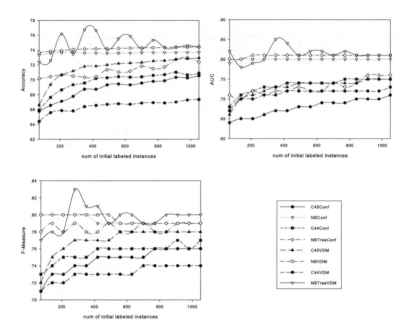

Fig. 2. The experimental results of self-training with different sizes of initial labeled instance sets

There are two factors which may influence the performance of self-training: one is the size of the initial labeled instance set, and the other one is the number of classified unlabeled instances selected for the next iteration. First, a set of experiments is developed for self-training with different sizes of initial labeled instance sets. Then, we design the experiments of self-training with different numbers of selected unlabeled instances for the next iteration. The experimental results are plotted in Figure 2 and Figure 3. Each curve in the two figures represents self-training with a kind of combination. For example, "C4.5Conf" represents self-training using C4.5 as the underlying classifier and the confidence degree as the selection metric. From Figure 2 and Figure 3, we can see that using VDM as the selection metric improves the performance of self-training with various underlying classifiers except C4.4. Self-training with NBTree and VDM outperforms self-training with other combinations of underlying classifiers and selection metrics, especially when the size of the initial labeled instance set is small.

Instead of assigning the same probability to the same leaf node, C4.5 with VDM needs only to consider the feature conditional probabilities that are different even within the same leaf node, which makes ranking on unlabeled instances perform better. NBTree is no longer required to generate class membership probabilities on leaf nodes. The larger instance space can be used to improve the ranking using VDM as the selection metric. However, the performance of C4.4 with VDM is not better than the one using the confidence degree. The original

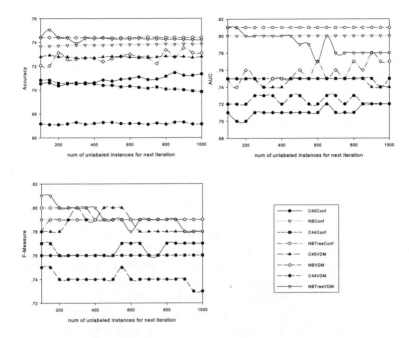

Fig. 3. The experimental results of self-training with different numbers of unlabeled instances for next iteration

Table 1. The results of baseline, self-training, and supervised learning classifiers

%	C4.5			NB			C4.4			NBTree		
	Acc	AUC	F-M	Acc	AUC	F-M	Acc	AUC	F-M	Acc	AUC	F-M
Base	63.88	62.65	69.10	69.47	75.00	74.86	61.32	64.24	68.26	66.97	70.81	72.91
Conf	68.74	67.87	74.56	73.59	80.00	78.10	67.64	73.26	74.69	70.34	72.93	78.46
VDM	71.79	73.00	77.05	74.13	80.96	78.68	66.38	71.24	73.09	74.74	81.42	78.79
Super	74.13	78.52	79.19	75.05	82.00	79.00	68.29	74.19	75.63	75.05	82.26	79.13

purpose of C4.4 is to improve the ranking performance of C4.5 by turning off pruning and using Laplace correction. But turning off pruning results in a large tree so that unlabeled instances with the same class label in the same leaf node share more identical feature values along the path from root to leaf. As a result, the large tree hurts the ranking performance of VDM that is based on feature conditional probability estimates. We also observe that, self-training with NB as the underlying classifier achieves better performance when using VDM as the selection metric.

In Table 1, the results of various evaluation measures on self-training are compared with the results from baseline and supervised learning classifiers. The results from baseline are obtained from the corresponding supervised classifiers that are trained by initial labeled set whose size is 350. The results from self-training show averages of 100 runs when the number of selected unlabeled instances for next iteration is 100 and the size of the initial labeled instance set is 350. From the results, we can see that the performance of self-training is better than the baseline and comparable with the performances of corresponding supervised learning classifiers for sentence subjectivity classification, especially when VDM is used as the selection metric.

5   Conclusion and Future Work

In this paper, we introduce a semi-supervised learning method, self-training, to solve the task of sentence subjectivity classification. Instead of focusing only on NB classifier, we bring decision tree classifiers into self-training as the underlying classifiers. However, the class membership probabilities produced by decision tree classifiers do not have good ranking performance. The traditional selection metric, the confidence degree, is not suitable when using decision tree classifiers as underlying classifiers. We adapt VDM as the selection metric in self-training, which does not depend on class membership probabilities. Based on MPQA corpus, a set of experiments have been designed to compare the performance of self-training with different underlying classifiers using different selection metrics under various conditions. The experimental results show that self-training with NBTree and VDM outperforms self-training with other combinations of underlying classifiers and selection metrics, and VDM improves the performance of self-training that uses NB, C4.5 and NBTree as underlying classifiers. The results also show that self-training can achieve comparable performance to the supervised learning models for sentence subjective classification.

In future work, we will extend our study of self-training to other applications of machine learning. The experiments on other benchmark data sets of machine learning will be done to see whether self-training with NBTree and VDM is better than other combinations of underlying classifiers and selection metrics.

References

1. Dave, K., Lawrence, S., Pennock, D.M.: Mining the Peanut Gallery: Opinion Extraction and Semantic Classification of Produce Reviews. In: Proceedings of the 12th International World Wide Web Conference (WWW 2003) (2003)
2. Huang, J., Lu, J., Ling, C.X.: Comparing Naive Bayes, Decision Trees, and SVM using Accuracy and AUC. In: Proceedings of The Third IEEE International Conference on Data Mining (ICDM 2003) (2003)
3. Kohavi, R.: Scaling Up the Accuracy of Naive-bayes Classifiers: a decision-tree Hybrid. In: Proceedings of the Second International Conference on Knowledge Discovery and Data Mining (1996)
4. Provost, F., Domingos, P.: Tree Induction for Probability-based Ranking. Machine Learning 52, 199–216 (2003)
5. Quinlan, J.R.: C4.5: Programs for Machine Learning. Morgan Kaufmann Publishers, Inc., Los Altos, California (1993)
6. Quirk, R., Greenbaum, S., Leech, G., Svartvik, J.: A comprehensive Grammar of the Enligsh Language. Longman, New York (1985)

7. Reichart, R., Rappoport, A.: Self-Training for Enhancement and Domain Adaptation of Statistical Parsers Trained on Small Datasets. In: Proceedings of the 45th Annual Meeting of the Association of Computational Linguistics (ACL 2007) (2007)
8. Riloff, E.: Automatically Generating Extraction Patterns from Untagged Text. In: Proceedings of the AAAI 1996 (1996)
9. Riloff, E., Phillops, W.: An Introduction to the Sundance and AutoSlog Systems. Technical Report (2004)
10. Riloff, E., Wiebe, J.: Learning Extraction Patterns for Subjective Expressions. In: Proceedings of the Conference on Empirical Methods in Natural Language Processing (2003)
11. Riloff, E., Wiebe, J., Phillips, W.: Exploiting Subjectivity Classification to Improve Information Extraction. In: Proceedings of the 20th National Conference on Artificial Intelligence, AAAI Press, Menlo Park (2005)
12. Riloff, E., Wiebe, J., Wilson, T.: Learning Subjective Nouns Using Extraction Pattern Bootstrapping. In: Proceedings of the 7th conference on Natural Language Learning (CoNLL 2003), pp. 25–32 (2003)
13. Steedman, M., Osborne, M., Sarkar, A., Clark, S., Hwa, R., Hockenmaier, J., Ruhlen, P., Baker, S., Crim, J.: Bootstrapping statistical parsers from small datasets. In: Proceedings of the 11th conference of the European Association for Computational Linguistics (EACL 2003) (2003)
14. Seki, Y., Evans, D.K., Ku, K., Chen, H., Kando, N., Lin, C.: Overview of Opinion Analysis Pilot Task at NTCIR-6. In: Proceedings of NTCIR-6 Workshop Meeting (2007)
15. Turney, P.: Thumbs Up or Thumbs Down? Semantic Orientation Applied to Unsupervised Classification of Reviews. In: Proceedings of the ACL 2002 (2002)
16. Wiebe, J., Bruce, R., O'Hara, T.: Development and Use of a Gold Standard Data Set for Subjectivity Classifications. In: Proceedings of the ACL 1999 (1999)
17. Wiebe, J., Riloff, E.: Creating Subjective and Objective Sentence Classifiers from Unannotated Texts. In: Gelbukh, A. (ed.) CICLing 2005. LNCS, vol. 3406, Springer, Heidelberg (2005)
18. Wiebe, J., Wilson, T., Bell, M.: Identifying Collocations for Recognizing Opinions. In: Proceedings of the ACL 2001 Workshop on Collocation: Computational Extraction, Analysis, and Exploitation, pp. 24–31 (2001)
19. Wiebe, J., Wilson, T., Cardie, C.: Annotating Expressions of Opinions and Emotions in Language. Language Resources and Evaluation 39, 165–210 (2005)
20. Wilson, T., Hoffmann, P., Somasundaran, S., Kessler, J., Wiebe, J., Choi, Y., Cardie, C., Riloff, E., Patwardhan, S.: OpinionFinder: Asystem for subjectivity analysis. In: Proceedings of HLT/EMNLP Interactive Demonstrations (2005)
21. Wilson, R.D., Martinez, T.R.: Improved Heterogeneous Distance Functions. Journal of Artificial Intelligence Research 6, 1–34 (1997)
22. Witten, I.H., Frank, E.: Data Mining-practical Machine Learning Tools and Techniques with Java Implementation. Morgan Kaufmann, San Mateo (2000)

A Novel Approach for Social Behavior Analysis of the Blogosphere

Reza Zafarani, Mohammad-Amin Jashki, Hamidreza Baghi,
and Ali A. Ghorbani

Faculty of Computer Science, University of New Brunswick
Fredericton, NB, Canada
{r.zafarani,a.jashki,hamid.baghi,ghorbani}@unb.ca

Abstract. The web, as a real mass medium, has become an invaluable data source for Information Extraction and Retrieval systems. Digital authoring is a relatively new style of communication, usually facilitated by computer networks and the Internet. We believe that the behavior of the people in cyberspace can be a representative of the real social behaviors and that this data can be employed to analyze the behavior of a society. In this paper we have used blogs as the main representative of this digital data. A system of blog analyzing, named *Blogizer*, has been designed to analyze these blogs. The system employs two specific measurements to determine the level of citizen engagement. The detailed analysis and the proof of concept case study provides promising results. Based on the obtained results, more than 70.52% of the topic assignments and 58.10% of the significance assignments were ascribed successfully.[1]

1 Introduction

Investigating social behavior has shown that sometimes some sensitive topics emerge as issues that can result in unexpected social consequences. For example, in an election, the results of the election might become unexpected in comparison to pre-election polls. The issues related to the election rise in pitch very quickly and within a short period of time become the key issues that result in a changing of the government. These issues might come onto the political/social stage only in the last few weeks of the election. However, there might be a way to mine the information in cyber discussion forums, the governments sources, local blogs, network payloads and other collaborative vehicles for evidence that these issues are emerging. Technology might also be used to detect the point of deflection when simple discussion becomes a burning political issue. The research in this paper is dedicated to provide the possible means to automate the process of this detection and data analysis.

To facilitate the discovery of socio-political issues, we need to first identify the possible topics (categories) of discussion. Then we need to employ some measuring techniques to determine the level of citizen engagement for each topic.

---

[1] The authors have had the same amount of contribution.

S. Bergler (Ed.): Canadian AI 2008, LNAI 5032, pp. 356–367, 2008.
© Springer-Verlag Berlin Heidelberg 2008

This will give us a list of the possible topics and an indication of how strongly the citizenry feels on each of these topics.

In this paper we have used blogs as the main source of data. A blog analyzing system, named *Blogizer*[2], has been also designed to analyze these blogs. The system conducts two specific measurements to determine the level of citizen engagement which will be described in the following sections.

In the next section, we review the structure of the Blogizer system and how it is used to analyze the social behavior of blogs. In Sections 3-6, a detailed overview of different components of Blogizer system along with the methods used in each is given. Finally, the last two sections conclude with the attained simulation results, a final system analysis, and a detailed case study of our system.

2 The Blogizer System

The proposed model for the social behavior analysis of blogs has five components: namely, *corpus construction, preprocessing and vectorization, topic discovery, measurements,* and the *final analysis* component. These components along with the dataflow between them are depicted in Figure 1.

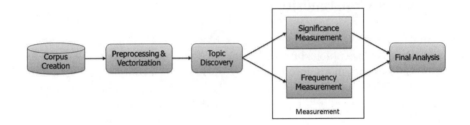

Fig. 1. The Blogizer Big Picture

In order to analyze topics for the emergence of political issues, a corpus of blog data is required. This corpus must be created using the available blog posts on the web and should be regularly updated. The *corpus creation* component takes care of this task in the Blogizer system. The created textual corpus is processed and its words are extracted, stemmed, and the stop words are eliminated. Finally, the posts are vectorized based on the remaining stemmed wordlist. The mentioned keyword extraction, stemming, and stopword removal takes place in the *preprocessing and vectorization* component.

In order to discover the possible topics, a mechanism for dynamic categorization of these vectorized posts is employed by the *topic discovery* subsystem. These extracted topics are the popular subjects discussed in the blog posts.

Following this phase, a set of measurements are conducted for two different metrics: *frequency* and *significance*. Frequency of a topic is the volume of discussion on that topic compared to the total volume of discussion. The temporal

---

[2] Blogizer stands for Blog Analyzer.

frequency of a specific topic is determined as a part of frequency measurement process.

Significance, also known as quality, is the measure of textual data worthiness and trustablitiy. It can be utilized in detecting worthwhile discussions in Information Retrieval systems. Eliciting Significance value in textual data is therefore to some extent a linguistic problem. Algorithms are required to determine the Significance of a text. Let us consider the following two sample sentences in order to assist in clarifying the significance factor:

> A message containing "*I don't trust you mister politician*" should be rated higher in significance if the message said "*I don't trust you mister politician because you promised to eliminate poverty and you didn't deliver.*"

Finally, the system provides a detailed analysis of the Blogs. This analysis can be extensively used to detect *issues*. Issues are the items of debate that require socio-political attention, and without that attention, citizens (or customers) will be unsatisfied and create difficulty for the government and the society.

3   Corpus Construction

The first stage in corpus construction is blog list gathering. As already mentioned, Blogizer uses blog data as its input. There exists lots of blogging websites on the Internet in numerous languages. However, a complete social/political repository of the blog and blogpost URLs is not currently available on the web[3]. Therefore, we designed a bot to extract blog links. The bot used a dictionary of around 1500 common words and constructed a 30-word random query from this dictionary in each execution time. This query was sent to Google Blog Search[4] and the retrieved blogs, which were identified by their URL, were saved. Only the top 20 related links to the search query were fetched. For the initial corpus creation we gathered a total number of 15326 blog links using this technique.

Furthermore, for the purpose of Social Network Analysis (SNA) and considering the relationship between different blogs, all friends of a given blog were extracted. A friend of a blog is a blog which is listed on the friends panel of that blog. The friend panel of a blog shows the blogs that are of interest to the authors of that blog. To extract this information, BlogRolling.com was used. This website provides a friend-list for each given blog. A bot was designed to automate this process to the retrieve this blog relationships. After this phase, the total number of blogs in our initial corpus was increased to 17548.

A crawler was designed to retrieve all posts in each given blog for later use. Around 280000 posts shared between 17548 blogs was retrieved in the initial executions of this crawler. Blogizer is dedicated to the analysis of English blogs; therefore, non-English blogs were filtered out after this stage. Language detection

---

[3] TREC BLOG06[1] Web corpus can be used for general purposes.
[4] http://blogsearch.google.com/

is performed using the statistical properties of the languages [2]. Non-English blogs can introduce noise in these systems due to the excessive impact they would have on the TF-IDF based phrase extraction phase, which will be explained in the following sections.

4   Preprocessing and Vectorization

Like any other text mining system, a conversion from unstructured text to structured data is required. For each post, the plain text is extracted and HTML tags are removed. The extracted text is tokenized; then, the stopwords are removed. The resulting tokens are stemmed. WordNet [3] and Porter [4] stemmers were used and Porter stemmer was finally selected because of its high performance. The documents are vectorized using TF-IDF and the wordlist of stemmed words. During vectorization, two filtering tasks are also performed. These tasks are described below.

Word List Creation and Pruning. A wordlist is generated from all given posts right after the stemming phase. This wordlist is pruned based on the frequency of the words to remove words with excessive usage (e.g. articles) or rarely used words (words with low occurence frequency).

Keyword Extraction. In order to extract representative keywords for each given post, the top 7 frequent words in each post based on the TF-IDF measure is selected as representative keywords of that document in the Topic Discovery phase.

5   Topic Discovery

Measurements are performed on posts in each topic; therefore, topics should be discovered in the given posts before this stage. There exists a variety of solutions to the topic discovery. Clustering of vectorized documents, is our provided solution to topic discovery. The measurement variations over time for each cluster will be analyzed by the system at the end.

For the clustering algorithm, different clustering methods were tested and evaluated. Among these, we concentrated more on K-Means, X-Means[5], and Bisecting K-Means [6]. The best results, as empirically proved by Steinbach et. al[6], were obtained by utilizing Bisecting K-Means.

Cluster Representatives. The clustering algorithm prototypes (centroids in here) are used to build cluster representatives. The centroid is typically not presented among the cluster documents; therefore, top 7 words from the closest document to the cluster centroid, based on the TF-IDF measure, are selected as the cluster representative. Table 1 contains cluster representatives for a number of clusters.

Table 1. Cluster Representatives for a Sample of 5 Clusters

john father church christian bishop pope doctrin
pound weight diet loss exercis lose calori
onlin internet medic engin search pharmaci medicin
congress democrat iraq troop bush presid petraeu
mississippi hurt happen nick bridg collaps sadden

6   Measurements

6.1   Frequency Measurement in Textual Data

Frequency measurement is one of the parts of the Blogizer measuring component. It provides the system with the necessary means to track the occurrences of events in a specific topic. Within each topic, the fraction of posts sent daily within that topic over the total number of daily posts in all the tracked topics represents the daily frequency of the topic. This value is saved for different topics and its variations are analyzed by the system through out the time.

6.2   Significance Measurement in Textual Data

Significance measurement is the other measurement part of the Blogizer measuring component. The process of significance measurement is shown in Figure 2. Significance measurement in Blogizer is performed based on two criteria: namely, *Significance measurement based on social network analysis* and *Content-based significance Measurement*.

Significance measurement based on Social Network Analysis. The impact of bloggers on each other plays an important role in measuring significance

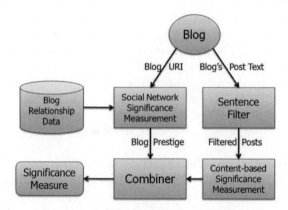

Fig. 2. The Significance Measurement Model

in measuring significance. The general assumption that those blogs which contain more significant posts are more attractive to other bloggers is made. This leads to the basic idea of employing Social Network Analysis algorithms, such as PageRank [7], to assign a value to each blog. This value, which we call the *blog prestige*, is one of the two final features used to measure the posts significance.

In order to detect the significance of the posts, the PageRank value of all blogs are calculated. Based on the friend-URL list gathered, which is the list of friends of a particular blog, a link graph is constructed. This graph is used by the PageRank algorithm to compute the PageRank values of the blogs. These computed values are later combined with the Content-based significance in the final signifance calculation.

Content-Based Significance Extraction. Significance can also be analyzed based on the textual content of the blog posts. The relevance between post data and the summaries created for blogs has been used as a measure in the system to quantify what we call content-based significance. Hence, a blog post related to a certain topic is more significant if its summary is closer to the summaries created for that specific topic. Let us consider the example of a news blog. The more this blog is containing the daily headlines the higher significance value should be ascribed to it. Therefore, to achieve this goal the following procedure of significance measurement is defined:

1. *Sentence Filter*: All the sentences in a given post are first fed into a significant sentence filtering which filters out sentences with low significance values or sentences which are unlikely to be significant.
2. *Post Summarization*: For each post a summary is created using the methods which will be discussed later in this section. This summary is in fact a good representation of what the post is talking about.
3. *Topic Summarization*: For each cluster of documents (posts on the same topic), a summary of all the posts is created. This summary is in fact a representative of the topic.
4. *Significance Measurement*: For a given post in a topic, a value is assigned to that post based on the closeness of its summary to the summary of the topic.

We have used an LSI based summarization [8] to create summaries for both posts and topics. The significant sentence filtering is inspired by the work done in [9]. This filter consists of five main components, which are demonstrated in Figure 3. These components are the pre-processor, POS-tagger, frequent pattern extractor, significance-signs and length extractor, and the classifier. Besides the normal pre-processing and POS-tagging, three different feature values are measured for each sentence: sentence length, number of occurrences of significance-demonstrative words, and the number of occurrences of a set of frequent grammatical patterns. Significance-demonstrative keywords are mostly English conjunctions which result in high significance sentences if present. Frequent patterns are grammatical patterns that are common in sentences with high

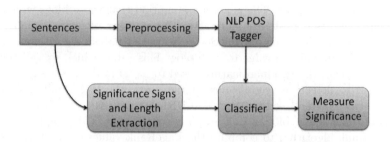

Fig. 3. The Architecture of the Proposed Model

Table 2. Frequent POS Tag patterns in sentences with high significance

IN PRP$	IN DT NN	DT NN VBZ TO VB	VBZ DT IN
DT NN IN DT JJ NN	PRP VBP	JJ NN IN IN IN JJ	
PRP VBD NN VBZ VBN NN IN DT	MD VB	VBZ DT JJ	

significance. These calculated feature values for different sentences are given to a SVM classifier which filters out the insignificant sentences.

A bag of 105 words is used as the set of significance demonstrative words. For example, the existence of a word such as *because* represents a sentence with a probable high degree of significance (see examples in introduction). A subset of used words is shown in Table 3.

Moreover, a set of frequent patterns is considered as a feature in our system. Apriori [10] frequent pattern mining algorithm is used to extract frequent patterns in hand-labeled POS-tagged sentences of high significance. In addition, a set of frequent patterns in a dataset of low significance sentences were extracted. Any frequent pattern in the high significance sentences which was also frequent in the low significance sentences was removed. This is to make sure that the set of patterns represent significant sentences. The number of existing patterns in a sentence is considered an important feature for the significance. A subset of patterns used is shown in Table 2.

From table 2 it can be seen that the frequent patterns are a set of consecutive grammatical roles represented by POS-tags which are to be matched with the POS-tagged input sentences in order to recognize high significance sentences. Different sentences may result in similar POS-tags as long as they obey a similar grammatical pattern; therefore, extracting frequent patterns from POS-tagged sentences reveals the underlying structure of significant sentences.

These features are calculated for each given sentence and the attribute values are provided to our binary classifier, which filters out improbable significant sentences.

The classifier was trained using sentences from three different datasets. The first dataset (generated by the authors) is gathered from conclusion sentences in scientific papers, which probably have high significance factor. The other sentences

Table 3. A Subset of the Bag of Words Used

for	and	nor	since	though	before
or	yet	so	unless	now that	when
because	although	if	while	as	whereas
in order that	until	in case	but	after	thus

were randomly selected from MPQA [11] and Subjectivity [12] datasets. All these sentences were hand-labeled. A total of 1000 sentences were hand-labeled and used in our simulation.

Significance Combiner. Currently, a combination of content-based significance value and the blog prestige value is used to calculate the final significance measure. This simplified version of significance measure is calculated by employing a polynomial utility function.

7   Results and Discussions

7.1   Topic Discovery Simulation Results

In order to evaluate the topic discovery algorithm, we selected a number of posts randomly and checked whether they were placed in a topic which was representative of the post. Two hundred random posts were selected from the post collection. For each post, human subjects determined if the topic, which is a set of seven representative words, corresponds to the subject of that post. Each document was shown to each human subject along with the seven keywords of the topic. Topic assignments were considered valid if a majority of human subjects approved the topic assignment.

The results showed that among these 200 posts, 122 were assigned correctly; this means that 61% of the posts were assigned to correct topics. Further analysis showed that among the topics, two containing noisy data existed. These two topics contain the posts which either are unrelated to the other topics or contain only pictures and videos. By removing these two topics and their related posts the accuracy is increased to 70.52%.

7.2   Significance Simulation Results

In the beginning, we conducted some evaluations for different components of the proposed *significance* measuring system. One the most important components taken into consideration in this phase was the *significance sentence filter*. The sentence filtering system was tested under two different situations: offline evaluation and live evaluation. For the offline evaluation, the system was tested using 10-fold cross validation. More than 88% of the instances were classified correctly with RMSE of 0.3464. The system was able to classify nearly perfect

Table 4. Classification Results Over Train Data (different features removed)

Parameter assessed	L	S	Fr
Correctly Classified Instances	81%	75%	82%
Incorrectly Classified Instances	19%	25%	18%
Mean absolute error	0.19	0.25	0.18
Root mean squared error	0.4359	0.5	0.4243

over its training data. This is not a complete proof of concept since our data was limited; therefore, the system was also tested under a live evaluation mode in order to determine its generalization capabilities. To test the system, 100 random sentences were selected from the web to test the system's generalization performance. These sentences were hand-labeled and over 72% of the sentences were classified correctly. It can be seen that the results obtained in the live evaluation mode is not as accurate as those of the offline evaluation mode.

Moreover, it is also important to prove that the existence of each feature is important in the results obtained. In other words, features should have positive effects toward the results obtained, and redundant features should be removed. In order to analyze this, each feature was removed once and the system was tested once again over its training data. The results are available in Table 4. In this table L, S, and FR represent the length, signs-of-significance, and frequent patterns, respectively. The removal of signs-of-significance had the most effect whereas the frequent patterns had the minimum effect on our results.

Finally, we evaluated the overall significance measurement of our system. The overall significance measurement is evaluated using a similar method used in topic discovery evaluation. A total number of 665 pairs of posts were used in this evaluation. For each post in the pair, the system gives a significance value which can be used to distinguish which post is of higher significance. The human subjects also chose the post that they believe is of higher significance in each pair. The results showed that the system significance measurement was correct in 58.10% of the pairs. Although this value is not very high, it is considerably above the baseline.

8   Final System Analysis

In this section an overview of the final analysis of the proposed system is provided. The system demonstrates the temporal variation in frequency and significance of different topics. In order to perform this task better, a detailed case study of a social issue and its effect on our system is provided. We have also shown a comparison of the results provided by our system with another famous system in this area, BlogPulse [13].

As described previously, in order to detect the topic of discussion in the blogs, the set of blog posts are clustered and for each cluster a set of keywords are chosen. The chosen keywords represent the topic of each cluster.

Fig. 4. Frequency Diagram for Topic: *iran, iranian, ...*

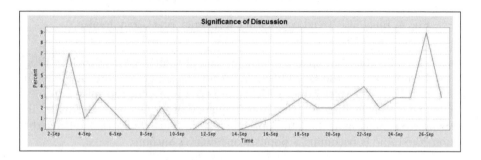

Fig. 5. Significance Diagram for Topic: *iran, iranian, ...*

For each topic the frequency of posts are calculated over time. The frequency percentage of a topic is visualized by a diagram, which shows relative amount of discussion on that topic compared to all other discussions in the blogs over time. The frequency diagram for topic (*"iran, iranian, ahmadinejad, jewish, columbia, holocaust, israel"*) is shown in Figure 4.

In addition, for each topic the average significance value is calculated for all posts in that topic and a diagram of its variation is shown to the user. The temporal variations of significance for the same topic is shown in Figure 5.

8.1   Case Study

In order to conduct this case study, we have selected one of the popular social topics found by our system among the blogs under analysis. This topic is identified by these seven keywords: *"israel, iran, iranian, ahmadinejad, jewish, columbia, holocaust"*. The significance and frequency diagrams for this topic are taken into consideration and sudden spikes in these diagrams are analyzed. The frequency and significance diagrams of this topic is shown in Figures 4 and 5, respectively. It can be observed in these figures that on the September 24th, 2007, there is a noticeable spike in both textual frequency and significance diagrams of this topic. This spike is due to the Iranian president speech at Columbia

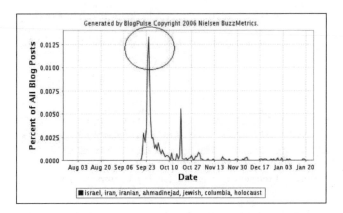

Fig. 6. BlogPulse Trend Analysis for Keywords: israel, iran, iranian,...

University [14]. The same spike can also be seen in similar systems such as Blog-Pulse. Figure 6 shows the BlogPulse output for the set of keywords available in this topic. The red circles in both Figures 4 and 6 represent the spike date.

It can be seen in Figure 4 that the frequency of discussion is gradually increasing from September 2nd to September 25th. This shows that during this period, the topic is becoming a popular one among authors.

9   Conclusions

In this paper, a novel approach of behavior analysis in blogs has been presented. This approach harnesses the power of significance and frequency measures. Besides these factors, social network analysis has been employed to improve the results inferred from our system. Our detailed analysis and our proof of concept case study provides some promising results. Based on the obtained results, more than 70.52% of our topic assignments and 58.10% of our significance assignments were ascribed successfully.

For the future, we plan to measure the significance and frequency of textual data more accurately and by employing more related features. We also plan to automate the complete process of socio-political issue discovery by means of these features and other possible factors.

Acknowledgments

This work was funded by the Atlantic Canada Opportunity Agency (ACOA) through the Atlantic Innovation Fund (AIF) and through grant RGPIN 227441-00 from the National Science and Engineering Research Council of Canada (NSERC) to Dr. Ali A. Ghorbani.

References

1. Macdonald, C., Ounis, I.: The trec blogs06 collection: Creating and analysing a blog test collection. Department of Computer Science, University of Glasgow Tech Report TR-2006-224 (2006)
2. Dunning, T.: Statistical Identification of Language. Computing Research Laboratory, New Mexico State University (1994)
3. Fellbaum, C.: Wordnet: An Electronic Lexical Database. MIT Press, Cambridge (1998)
4. Porter, M.F.: An algorithm for suffix stripping. Readings in information retrieval, 313–316 (1997)
5. Pelleg, D., Moore, A.: X-means: Extending K-means with efficient estimation of the number of clusters. In: Proceedings of the 17th International Conf. on Machine Learning, pp. 727–734 (2000)
6. Steinbach, M., Karypis, G., Kumar, V.: A comparison of document clustering techniques. In: KDD Workshop on Text Mining, vol. 34, pp. 35–36 (2000)
7. Brin, S., Page, L.: The anatomy of a large-scale hypertextual Web search engine. Computer Networks and ISDN Systems 30(1-7), 107–117 (1998)
8. Gong, Y., Liu, X.: Generic text summarization using relevance measure and latent semantic analysis. In: Proceedings of the 24th annual international ACM SIGIR conference on Research and development in information retrieval, pp. 19–25 (2001)
9. Jindal, N., Liu, B.: Mining comparative sentences and relations. In: AAAI 2006 (2006)
10. Agrawal, R., Imieliński, T., Swami, A.: Mining association rules between sets of items in large databases. ACM SIGMOD Record 22(2), 207–216 (1993)
11. Wiebe, J., Breck, E., Buckley, C., Cardie, C., Davis, P., Fraser, B., Litman, D., Pierce, D., Riloff, E., Wilson, T., Day, D., Maybury, M.: Recognizing and organizing opinions expressed in the world press. In: Working Notes-New Directions in Question Answering (AAAI Spring Symposium Series) (2003)
12. Pang, B., Lee, L.: A sentimental education: Sentiment analysis using subjectivity summarization based on minimum cuts. In: Proceedings of the ACL, pp. 271–278 (2004)
13. Glance, N., Hurst, M., Tomokiyo, T.: BlogPulse: Automated Trend Discovery for Weblogs. In: WWW 2004 Workshop on the Weblogging Ecosystem: Aggregation, Analysis and Dynamics (2004)
14. Wire, C.T.: President Ahmadinejad Delivers Remarks at Columbia University, Washington Post, September 24 (2007)

Seller Bidding in a Trust-Based Incentive Mechanism for Dynamic E-Marketplaces

Jie Zhang and Robin Cohen

David R. Cheriton School of Computer Science
University of Waterloo
Waterloo, ON, Canada
{j44zhang,rcohen}@uwaterloo.ca

Abstract. In this paper, we develop a detailed bidding strategy for selling agents in electronic marketplaces, in a setting where buyers and sellers have incentives to be honest, due to a particular framework for trust modeling. In our mechanism, buyers model other buyers and select the most trustworthy ones as their neighbours to form a social network which can be used to ask advice about sellers. In addition, however, sellers model the reputation of buyers based on the social network. Reputable buyers provide fair ratings for sellers, and are likely to be neighbours of many other buyers. Sellers will provide more attractive products to reputable buyers, in order to build their own reputation. We include simulations of a dynamic marketplace operating using our mechanism, where buyers and sellers may come and go, and show that greater profit can be realized both for buyers that are honest and sellers that are honest.

1 Introduction

People across the world today have embraced the Internet as part of their everyday life. While buyers and sellers can now find suitable business partners online, the promise of e-commerce will not be enjoyed unless electronic marketplaces are designed that provide users with some level of comfort that their partners can be trusted. Artificial intelligence provides that promise, by offering techniques from the traditional fields of user modeling and machine learning, in order for buyers and sellers to reason about each other.

In previous work [1], we promoted the use of a trust-based incentive mechanism to promote honesty in e-marketplaces populated by buying and selling agents. In particular, we observed that there are scenarios where buying agents in e-marketplaces would benefit from advice provided by other buying agents, when selecting the appropriate seller with which to do business. This may arise, for instance, when buyers may have limited experience with the population of sellers or in a scenario where buyers are migrating to different e-commerce environments in order to purchase goods, therefore failing to build up a longstanding history with sellers in any one environment. One major challenge, however, is the fact that these advisors may not always be truthful when providing ratings of sellers, offering unfairly high or unfairly low ratings (issues discussed in [2]).

S. Bergler (Ed.): Canadian AI 2008, LNAI 5032, pp. 368–379, 2008.
© Springer-Verlag Berlin Heidelberg 2008

In the incentive mechanism that we propose, buyers are encouraged to be truthful in order to gain more profitable transactions. This idea is supported by Gintis et al. [3]. They argue that altruism in one context signals "quality" that is rewarded by increased opportunities in other contexts. In our mechanism, the reputation of buyers is modeled by sellers. A buyer is considered reputable if it is well respected in the community - i.e. it is a neighbour of many other buyers. This is also supported by Gintis et al. [3]. They argue that agents reporting honestly will be preferred by others as allies and will be able to attract a larger audience to witness their feedback. Sellers increase quality and decrease prices of products to satisfy reputable buyers, in order to build their own reputation. Our mechanism, therefore, creates incentives for buyers to provide fair ratings of sellers.

In this paper, we examine the seller strategy more clearly, specifying how sellers should bid, in order to make best use of our mechanism to enhance their reputability and therefore increase their profit. We also emphasize the importance for buyers to adopt a strategy to limit the number of sellers that are considered for each good to be purchased.

We then present a series of experimental results in a simulated environment where buyers and sellers may be deceptive and they may be arriving and departing. This provides a stronger defense of the mechanism as one that is robust to important conditions in the marketplace. In addition, we validate the benefit of our specific proposal for the seller bidding strategy and for the buyer strategy of limiting the sellers being considered, clearly showing the gains in profit enjoyed by both sellers and buyers when our mechanism is introduced and our proposed strategies are followed.

2   System Overview

The electronic marketplace environment we are modeling is populated with self-interested buying and selling agents. Our incentive mechanism is generally applicable to any marketplace where sellers may alter quality and price of their products to satisfy buyers. For the remainder of this paper, we discuss the scenario where the buyers and sellers are brought together by a procurement (reverse) auction, where the auctioneer is a buyer and bidders are sellers. There is a central server that runs the auction.

In our system, a buyer that wants to purchase a product sends a request to the central server. This request indicates not only the product that the buyer is interested in but also the buyer's evaluation criteria for the product (discussed in more detail in the following section). Sellers interested in selling the product to the buyer will register to participate in the auction.

Each buyer maintains a neighbourhood of trusted other buyers, which will be asked to provide ratings of the sellers. As we will demonstrate in Section 4, it becomes very valuable to limit the number of sellers the buyer will consider for each auction, based on ratings it receives. The buyer will then convey to the central server which sellers it is willing to consider, and the pool of possible sellers is thus reduced. Sellers that are allowed to participate in the auction will submit their bids and the buyer will select the winner of the auction as the seller whose product (described in its bid) gives the buyer the largest profit, based on the buyer's evaluation criteria. In order to formulate their bids, sellers model the reputation of buyers and make more attractive offers to more reputable buyers. A buyer's reputation is based on the number of other buyers considering this buyer as their neighbour. Information about the neighbourhoods to which the buyer belongs is maintained by the central server and released to the sellers. Note that it is challenging for sellers to determine which bids to offer to buyers. We focus on this problem in the next section.

Once a buyer has selected the winning seller, it pays that seller the amount indicated in the bid. The winning seller is supposed to deliver the product to the buyer. However, it may decide to alter the quality of the product or to not deliver the product at all. The buyer will report the result of conducting business with the seller to the central server, registering a rating for the seller. It is precisely these ratings of the seller that can then be shared with those buyers that consider this buyer as their neighbour.

In summary: the central server runs the auction and maintains information that is shared with sellers and buyers; buyers announce their intention to purchase products, consult with neighbours, choose a winning seller and report a final rating for the seller; sellers bid to win the sale to the buyer, consider buyer reputation in formulating their bids and then decide what product to deliver to the buyer (if at all).

3   Proposed Seller and Buyer Strategies

3.1   Seller Strategy

We discuss the seller strategy in the context of the Request For Quote (RFQ) system [4]. We consider a scenario where a buyer b wants to buy a product p. The buyer specifies its evaluation criteria for a set of non-price features $\{f_1, f_2, ..., f_n\}$, as well as a set of weights $\{w_1, w_2, ..., w_n\}$ that correspond to each non-price feature. Each weight represents how much its corresponding non-price feature is worth. A higher weight for a non-price feature implies that the buyer cares more about the feature. The buyer also provides information in its evaluation criteria about the conversion from descriptive non-price feature values to numeric values (for example, a 3-year warranty is converted to the numeric value of 10 on a scale of 1 to 10).[1] We define the function $\tau()$ to denote such a conversion. Sellers $\{s_1, s_2, ..., s_m\}$ $(m \geq 1)$ allowed to join the auction are able to know the buyer's values of their products, which can be formalized as follows:

$$V_b = \sum_{j=1}^{n} w_j \tau(f_j) \tag{1}$$

---

[1] In this paper, we focus on non-price features that are still objective - e.g. delivery time. Handling subjective features is left for future work.

A seller s_i ($1 \leq i \leq m$) sets the price and values for the non-price features of the product p, depending on how much instant profit it can earn from selling p to the buyer b. The instant profit is the profit earned by the seller from the current transaction if it wins the auction. We define the seller's instant profit as follows:

$$U_{s_i} = P_{s_i} - C_{s_i} \qquad (2)$$

where P_{s_i} is the price of the product set by the seller s_i and C_{s_i} is the cost for the seller to produce the product p with certain values for the non-price features in its bid.

The profit gained by the buyer if it chooses to do business with the seller s_i can be formalized as follows:

$$U_b = V_b - P_{s_i} \qquad (3)$$

The buyer's profit is also called the seller's "surplus offer", denoted as O_{s_i}. The seller s_i will try to gain profit from the transaction. It is reasonable to assume that $P_{s_i} \geq C_{s_i}$. Therefore, the best potential gain of the buyer from the transaction is when the price of the product is the same as the cost for the seller to produce the product, which can be formalized as follows:

$$S_{s_i} = V_b - C_{s_i} \qquad (4)$$

S_{s_i} is so called "realized surplus", the best possible surplus for the buyer that the seller can offer. We also define the cumulative distribution function for S_{s_i} as $F()$ and the support of $F()$ is $[S_L, S_H]$. We assume $S_L \geq 0$ to ensure that the value of a seller's product always exceeds its cost.

The seller whose surplus offer is the highest will win the auction. The RFQ auction then becomes a first-price sealed auction. As argued by Shachat and Swarthout [4], a symmetric Bayes-Nash equilibrium surplus offer function can be derived as follows:

$$O_{s_i}^* = S_{s_i} - \frac{\int_{S_L}^{S_{s_i}} [F(x)]^{m-1} dx}{[F(S_{s_i})]^{m-1}} \qquad (5)$$

where m is the number of bidders. Recall that O_{s_i} is the same as U_b. From Equations 3, 4 and 5, the equilibrium bidding function for the seller can then be derived as follows:

$$P_{s_i}^* = C_{s_i} + \frac{\int_{S_L}^{S_{s_i}} [F(x)]^{m-1} dx}{[F(S_{s_i})]^{m-1}} \qquad (6)$$

The seller in our mechanism also reasons about the expected future gain from winning the current auction. It takes into account the reputation of the buyer b. In our mechanism, each buyer in the marketplace has a fixed number of neighbours that the buyer trusts the most and from which it can ask advice about sellers. This forms a social network of buyers. A buyer is reputable if it is the neighbour of many other buyers. Cooperating with reputable buyers will allow the seller to build its reputation and to be known as a trustworthy seller by many buyers in the marketplace. It will then be able to obtain more opportunities of doing business with buyers and to gain more profit in the future. We use R_b (reputation of b) to denote the number of other buyers considering b as their neighbor and $E_{s_i}(R_b)$ to denote the amount of the expected future gain. We then have the following inequality:

$$\frac{\partial[E_{s_i}(R_b)]}{\partial R_b} \geq 0 \qquad (7)$$

Let us consider a scenario where sellers $\{s_1, s_2, ..., s_m\}$ have the same productivity. They have the same cost for producing the products that are valued equally by the buyer. Let us also assume that the seller's lowest realized surplus S_L for a transaction is 0. Equation 6 then can be simplified as follows:

$$
\begin{aligned}
P_{s_i}^* &= C_{s_i} + \frac{\int_{S_L}^{S_{s_i}} [F(x)]^{m-1} dx}{[F(S_{s_i})]^{m-1}} \\
&= C_{s_i} + \frac{\int_0^{S_{s_i}} (\frac{x}{S_H})^{m-1} dx}{(\frac{S_{s_i}}{S_H})^{m-1}} \\
&= C_{s_i} + \frac{S_{s_i}}{m} \qquad (8)
\end{aligned}
$$

From Equations 2, 3 and 4, we can see that the seller's realized surplus is in fact equal to the sum of the buyer and the seller's profit. Since the seller has expected future gain from winning the current auction, the seller's realized surplus S_{s_i} can then be changed as follows:

$$
\begin{aligned}
S_{s_i}' &= U_b + U_{s_i} + \lambda E_{s_i}(R_b) \\
&= V_b - C_{s_i} + \lambda E_{s_i}(R_b) \\
&= S_{s_i} + \lambda E_{s_i}(R_b) \qquad (9)
\end{aligned}
$$

where $\lambda \in [0, 1]$ is a discounting factor.[2] The lowest S_{s_i}' becomes $\lambda E_{s_i}(R_b)$ instead of zero and the upper bound of S_{s_i}' becomes $S_H + \lambda E_{s_i}(R_b)$. Accordingly, the symmetric Bayes-Nash equilibrium surplus offer function formalized in Equation 5 should be changed as follows:

$$O_{s_i}^* = S_{s_i} + \lambda E_{s_i} - \frac{\int_{\lambda E_{s_i}}^{S_{s_i}'} [F(x)]^{m-1} dx}{[F(S_{s_i}')]^{m-1}} \qquad (10)$$

From Equations 3, 4 and 10, we then can derive the modified equilibrium bidding function for the seller as follows:

---

[2] The discounting factor is used to allow sellers to learn over time the likelihood of receiving their expected future gain.

$$P_{s_i}^* = C_{s_i} - \lambda E_{s_i} + \frac{\int_{\lambda E_{s_i}}^{S'_{s_i}} [F(x)]^{m-1} dx}{[F(S'_{s_i})]^{m-1}}$$

$$= C_{s_i} - \lambda E_{s_i} + \frac{\int_{\lambda E_{s_i}}^{S_{s_i} + \lambda E_{s_i}} (\frac{x}{S_H})^{m-1} dx}{(\frac{S_{s_i} + \lambda E_{s_i}}{S_H})^{m-1}}$$

$$= C_{s_i} + \frac{S_{s_i}}{m} - \frac{1}{m} [\frac{(\lambda E_{s_i})^m}{(S_{s_i} + \lambda E_{s_i})^{m-1}} + (m-1)\lambda E_{s_i}] \qquad (11)$$

We have already shown that sellers will gain better future profit when successful with more reputable buyers (Equation 7); this therefore suggests that the seller should offer better rewards to more reputable buyers as well. The bidding function outlined in Equation 11 provides for this, as the final term in the equation becomes a positive term times the change in E_{s_i}. Note that since the value of $P_{s_i}^*$ in Equation 11 is smaller than that of Equation 8 the reward for buyers can either be lower price or higher cost (i.e. greater product quality). The seller sacrifices its current profit in both cases.

3.2   Buyer Strategy

To avoid doing business with possibly dishonest sellers, the buyer b in our mechanism first models the trustworthiness of sellers. Different existing approaches for modeling sellers' trustworthiness can be used here, for example the approach advocated by Zhang and Cohen [5] and the TRAVOS model proposed by Teacy et al. [6]. Both approaches propose to take into account the buyer's personal experience with the sellers as well as ratings of the sellers provided by other buyers. A seller is considered trustworthy if its trust value is greater than a threshold γ. It will be considered untrustworthy if the trust value is less than δ.

However, buyers may provide untruthful ratings of sellers. Our mechanism allows the central server to maintain a fixed number of neighbours for each buyer: a list of the most trustworthy other buyers to this buyer, used to provide advice about sellers, in order to form a social network of buyers.[3] The trustworthiness of these other buyers then also needs to be modeled. In the experiments presented in Section 4, the approach of Zhang and Cohen [5], combining personal experience and public knowledge, is used for this purpose.

A final element of importance in the buyer's strategy is limiting the number of sellers being considered with each good that is being purchased. More specifically, the buyer will allow only a limited number of the most trustworthy sellers to join the auction. If there are no trustworthy sellers, the sellers with trust values between γ and δ may also be allowed to join the auction. Motivated by research from economics such as [7], this added restriction promotes honesty among sellers because honest sellers are offered sufficient future gain.

---

[3] Note for a new buyer, the central server randomly assigns to it some other buyers as its neighbours.

4   Experimental Results

We simulate a dynamic marketplace operating with buyer and seller strategies for a period of 30 days. The marketplace involves 90 buyers. These buyers are grouped into three groups. They have different numbers of requests. Every 10 of the buyers in each group has a different number (10, 20 and 30) of requests. In our experiments, we assume that there is only one product in each request, that each buyer has a maximum of one request each day, and that the products requested by buyers have the same non-price features. After they finish business with sellers, buyers rate sellers. Some buyers will provide unfair ratings. Each group of buyers provides different percentages (0%, 20% and 40%) of unfair ratings. We allow 2 buyers from each group to leave the marketplace at the end of each day. Accordingly, we also allow 6 buyers to join the marketplace at the end of each day. These buyers will also provide different percentage (0%, 20% and 40%) of unfair ratings, to keep the number of buyers in each group the same. Initially, we randomly assign 5 buyers to each buyer as its neighbours.

There are also 9 sellers in total in the marketplace. Every 3 sellers acts dishonestly in different percentages (0%, 25% and 75%) of their business with buyers. We assume that all sellers have the same cost for producing the products because all products have the same non-price features. The sellers all follow our proposed bidding strategy.

4.1   Promoting Honesty

Here, we provide some general results to show that our proposed strategies promote buyer and seller honesty. We first measure the reputation of buyers that provide different percentages of unfair ratings. In our experiments, a buyer's reputation is represented by the number of other buyers considering this buyer as their neighbour. The results[4] are shown in Figure 1(a). From this figure, we

(a)   (b)

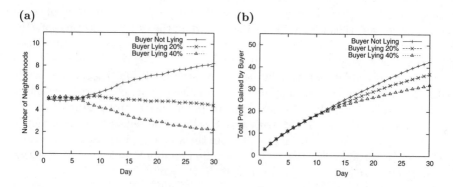

Fig. 1. Buyers' Reputation and Total Profit

---

[4] All experimental results in Section 4 are averaged over 500 rounds of the simulation.

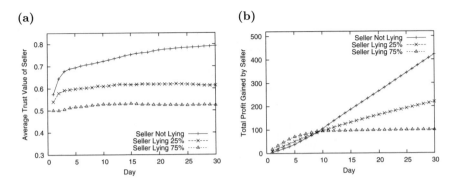

Fig. 2. Sellers' Average Trust and Total Profit

can see that the buyers providing the smaller percentages of unfair ratings will
have the larger reputation values. Due to the randomness of the initial setting for
our experiments, buyers' reputation values change stochastically at the beginning. After approximately 6 days when our marketplace converges, the changes
of buyers' reputation will clearly follow a trend. After each day, we measure total
profit gained by buyers that provide different percentages of unfair ratings. The
profit gained by a buyer from buying a product is formalized in Equation 3. From
Figure 1(b), we can see that buyers providing fewer unfair ratings will gain more
total profit. Note that the profit difference of different types of buyers is fairly
small. This is because buyers have at most 30 requests in total. In summary, it
is better off for buyers to provide truthful ratings of sellers.

We compare the average trust values of different sellers. The average trust
value of a seller is calculated as the sum of the trust value each buyer has
of the seller divided by the total number of buyers in the marketplace (90 in
our experiments). As shown in Figure 2(a), results indicate that sellers being
dishonest more often will have smaller average trust values. From this figure,
we can see that the average trust values of the sellers being dishonest in 75% of
their business are nearly 0.5. This is because they do not have much chance to
do business with buyers and will not have many ratings. A seller without any
ratings will have a default trust value of 0.5. We also compare total profit gained
by different sellers. Results are shown in Figure 2(b). From this figure, we can
see that sellers being honest more often will gain more profit. Therefore, it is
better off for sellers to be honest. We can also see that sellers lying more often
may gain more profit in the first few days. When our marketplace converges,
they will gain much less profit.

4.2   Seller Strategy

The purpose of this experiment is to examine the average trustworthiness of and
the total profit gained by sellers using different strategies. We have two groups
of sellers. One group of sellers will model reputation of buyers and offer better
rewards to reputable buyers. Another group of sellers will not model reputation

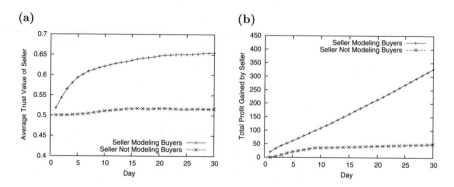

Fig. 3. Sellers' Average Trust and Total Profit

of buyers and ask for the same price from different buyers. Sellers in each group will lie in different percentages (0%, 25% and 75%) of their business with buyers.

We measure the average trust values of sellers from each group. Results shown in Figure 3(a) indicate that sellers modeling the reputation of buyers will have higher average trust values. We also measure the total profit gained by different buyers. Results in Figure 3(b) indicate that sellers are better off to model reputation of buyers and adjust prices of products according to buyers' reputation, in order to gain more profit. Our proposed bidding strategy for sellers is shown to be effective.

4.3   Buyer Strategy

Limiting Number of Bidders. In the experiments in this section, we have 90 sellers. Similarly, every 30 sellers acts dishonestly in different percentages (0%, 25% and 75%) of their business with buyers. In the first experiment, we allow 30 sellers to join each buyer's auctions. Figure 4(a) shows the amount of

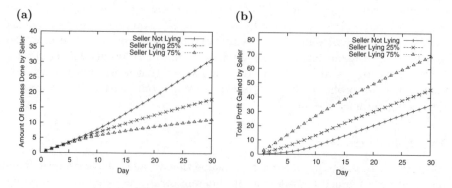

Fig. 4. Sellers' Amount of Business and Total Profit

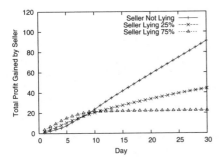
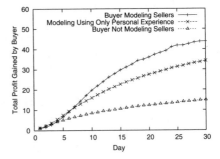

Fig. 5. Total Profit Gained by Sellers   **Fig. 6.** Profit Gained by Different Buyers

business (number of transactions) done by different sellers. Sellers being honest more often are still able to gain more opportunities to do business with buyers. We also compare total profit gained by different sellers in this setting. However, from the results shown in Figure 4(b), we can see that sellers being dishonest more often will gain more total profit. In this case, because more sellers are allowed to join buyers' auctions, each seller's equilibrium bidding price should be lower in order to win the auctions. Sellers being honest gain very little profit from each business with a buyer; therefore, dishonesty will be promoted.

In the second experiment, we limit the number of bidders allowed in each of the buyers' auctions to be 6. As shown in Figure 5, sellers being honest more often are able to gain more total profit. Honest sellers in this case are more likely to win the future auctions of buyers. They are offered sufficient future gain because limiting the number of bidders increases each seller's equilibrium bidding price. Therefore, limiting the number of bidders will promote seller honesty.

Buyer Modeling Sellers. In this experiment, one third of the buyers models the trustworthiness of sellers based on their personal experience with the sellers and advice about the sellers provided by their neighbours. Another third of the buyers uses only personal experience to model the trustworthiness of sellers. These buyers allow only a number of the most trustworthy sellers to join their auctions. The rest of the buyers do not model sellers. They randomly select some sellers to be allowed to submit bids.

We compare the total profit gained by these three types of buyers. Results are shown in Figure 6. From this figure, we can see that buyers modeling the trustworthiness of sellers and limiting their participation will be able to gain more total profit. It is also clear that buyers modeling sellers by taking into account as well the advice provided by other buyers will be able to gain more profit. In summary, it is better off for buyers to selectively choose sellers to participate in their auctions and to take into account the advice provided by other buyers when buyers lack personal experience with sellers.

5   Related Work

The framework outlined in this paper has buyers modeling sellers, using ratings provided by advisors but also has sellers modeling buyers, in order to make effective bids in the marketplace. This is in contrast to the majority of approaches for modeling the trustworthiness of agents in e-marketplaces (e.g. the probabilistic reasoning model of TRAVOS [6]), that focus on methods for buyers to determine the reliability of advisors and hence of sellers. Tran and Cohen [8] do introduce seller modeling of buyers, but this framework focuses on direct experience alone and has sellers learning how to adjust quality and price of goods to satisfy buyer preferences. In contrast, our approach has sellers reasoning about how their reputation will be spread in the marketplace, leading to future gain, and models the reputability of the buyers.

We have also discussed the incentive for honesty among agents that results from our proposed buyer and seller strategies. A competing approach for creating incentives for honesty in e-marketplaces is the side-payment mechanism [9,10] that offers payment to buyers that fairly rate results of business with sellers. One facet of the side payment mechanisms in these papers is the requirement of a center to control monetary payments, so that budget balance is a concern. In contrast, in our mechanism the central server does not handle payments; rewards are directed from sellers to buyers.

6   Conclusions and Future Work

In this paper, we proposed detailed bidding strategies for sellers and limits on sellers being considered by buyers, when using our trust-based incentive mechanism in e-marketplaces. Buyers acting as advisors learn that they are better off providing truthful feedback when reporting ratings of sellers, thus becoming neighbours of as many other buyers as possible. Sellers are also kept honest, because buyers are modeling the sellers' trustworthiness, based on ratings provided by their trustworthy neighbours. With buyers limiting the number of sellers being considered when doing business, sellers are even more inclined to be honest, in order to maintain a profit. Our mechanism and our strategies are validated through experiments in a dynamic marketplace of significant size.

For future work, we will explore in greater detail how selling agents should formulate bidding strategies, when reasoning about competing agents in the marketplace. One promising approach is to estimate future gain using evolutionary game theory, as proposed in [11]. We should consider less uniform behaviour amongst the sellers as well. Another topic of future work is to determine the number of sellers allowed to join each buyer's auction, which ensures that dishonest sellers' instant profit does not exceed honest sellers' long-term profit. Kim [7] provides some insights into how to derive an optimal number of bidders.

We will also carry out more extensive experimentation in large-scale or real-world environments and continue to validate our model by comparing directly to models such as [9]. In our future experiments, we will also examine the situation where agents may vary their behaviour widely to exploit the marketplace, which has been well studied by Sen and Banerjee [12]. In addition, we are particularly interested in empirically demonstrating how our framework is able to handle marketplaces where strategic agents collude with each other.

References

1. Zhang, J., Cohen, R.: Design of a mechanism for promoting honesty in e-marketplaces. In: Proceedings of the Twenty-Second Conference on Artificial Intelligence (AAAI 2007) (2007)
2. Dellarocas, C.: Immunizing online reputation reporting systems against unfair ratings and discriminatory behavior. In: Proceedings of the 2nd ACM Conference on Electronic Commerce (EC), Minneapolis, MN (2000)
3. Gintis, H., Smith, E.A., Bowles, S.: Costly signaling and cooperation. Journal of Theoretical Biology 213, 103–119 (2001)
4. Shachat, J., Swarthout, J.T.: Procurement auctions for differentiated goods. Working Paper, IBM Research Labs (2003)
5. Zhang, J., Cohen, R.: A personalized approach to address unfair ratings in multi-agent reputation systems. In: Proceedings of AAMAS 2006 Workshop on Trust in Agent Societies (2006)
6. Teacy, W.T.L., Patel, J., Jennings, N.R., Luck, M.: Coping with inaccurate reputation sources: Experimental analysis of a probabilistic trust model. In: Proceedings of AAMAS 2005 (2005)
7. Kim, I.G.: A model of selective tendering: Does bidding competition deter opportunism by contractors? The Quarterly Review of Economics and Finance 38(4), 907–925 (1998)
8. Tran, T., Cohen, R.: Improving user satisfaction in agent-based electronic market-places by reputation modeling and adjustable product quality. In: Proceedings of the Third International Joint Conference on Autonomous Agents and Multiagent Systems (AAMAS 2004) (2004)
9. Jurca, R., Faltings, B.: An incentive compatible reputation mechanism. In: Proceedings of the IEEE Conference on E-Commerce, Newport Beach, CA, USA (2003)
10. Miller, N., Resnick, P., Zeckhauser, R.: Eliciting informative feedback: The peer-prediction method. Management Science 51(9), 1359–1373 (2005)
11. Vytelingum, P., Cliff, D., Jennings, N.R.: Analysing buyers' and sellers' strategic interactions in marketplaces: An evolutionary game theoretic approach. In: Proceedings of the Sixth International Joint Conference on Autonomous Agents and Multiagent Systems (AAMAS) Workshop on Agent-Mediated Electronic Commerce (2007)
12. Sen, S., Banerjee, D.: Monopolizing markets by exploiting trust. In: Proceedings of the Fifth International Joint Conference on Autonomous Agents and Multiagent Systems (AAMAS) (2006)

Author Index

Printing: Mercedes-Druck, Berlin
Binding: Stein+Lehmann, Berlin